K 3165 GLE

OXFORD CONSTITUTIONAL THEORY

Series Editors:
Martin Loughlin, John P. McCormick, and Neil Walker

The Cosmopolitan State

OXFORD CONSTITUTIONAL THEORY

Series Editors:
Martin Loughlin, John P. McCormick, and Neil Walker

Oxford Constitutional Theory has rapidly established itself as the primary point of reference for theoretical reflections on the growing interest in constitutions and constitutional law in domestic, regional and global contexts. The majority of the works published in the series are monographs that advance new understandings of their subject. But the series aims to provide a forum for further innovation in the field by also including well-conceived edited collections that bring a variety of perspectives and disciplinary approaches to bear on specific themes in constitutional thought and by publishing English translations of leading monographs in constitutional theory that have originally been written in languages other than English.

ALSO AVAILABLE IN THE SERIES

The Twilight of Constitutionalism?
Edited by Petra Dobner and Martin Loughlin

Beyond Constitutionalism
The Pluralist Structure of Postnational Law
Nico Krisch

The Constitutional State
N. W. Barber

Sovereignty's Promise
The State as Fiduciary
Evan Fox-Decent

Constitutional Fragments
Societal Constitutionalism and
Globalization
Gunther Teubner

Constitutional Referendums
The Theory and Practice of Republican Deliberation
Stephen Tierney

Constituting Economic and Social Rights
Katharine G. Young

The Global Model of Constitutional Rights
Kai Möller

The Three Branches
A Comparative Model of Separation of Powers
Christoph Möllers

After Public Law
Edited by Cormac Mac Amhlaigh, Claudio Michelon, and Neil Walker

The Cosmopolitan State

H. Patrick Glenn

OXFORD

UNIVERSITY PRESS

Great Clarendon Street, Oxford, OX2 6DP,
United Kingdom

Oxford University Press is a department of the University of Oxford.
It furthers the University's objective of excellence in research, scholarship,
and education by publishing worldwide. Oxford is a registered trade mark of
Oxford University Press in the UK and in certain other countries

British Library Cataloguing in Publication Data

Data available

ISBN 978-0-19-968242-3

Printed in Great Britain by
CPI Group (UK) Ltd, Croydon, CR0 4YY

For Shannon, Jeremy, Martin, Carey, Louis, and Heidi

Preface

Law may be thought of in terms of different legal traditions, or common laws, but in all cases such masses of normative information must alight somewhere on the earth, to function as law. The territory of the earth is now divided into states, however, so states inevitably become places of meeting—of people, legal traditions, and common laws[1]—and the first and most important function of the state is reconciliation of the ensuing diversity. Some states have been more successful at this than others. Some have failed and are now known as failed states. The means of reconciliation, successful and unsuccessful, have been as diverse as the states themselves, and no state is the same as any other. This is a book about the means of such reconciliation, about how states are cosmopolitan in their origins, structures, populations, sources and thought.[2] It follows two other books that have dealt with transnational legal traditions and common laws; it complements them in looking at the state as a product of those legal traditions and common laws, and as a structure of conciliation.[3]

A brief word of explanation is perhaps useful, before plunging into the argument. The argument is not that states should declare themselves to be cosmopolitan, or multi-cultural, or federal, or consociational, or any other such expression. Some states choose to do so; others prefer not to. There is great debate about whether this should be done, or not, and how to do it if it is to be done. The argument presented here is meant to be both broader and, perhaps paradoxically, more detailed. It is broader because it affirms that *all* states are cosmopolitan, whether they identify themselves as such or not. It is more detailed because it attempts to show how states are cosmopolitan even if they do not so declare themselves. Some states are very successful as states while denying their cosmopolitan character, though they are profoundly cosmopolitan in operation. France and the United States of America are probably the best examples. Other states have failed while affirming, unsuccessfully, their cosmopolitan character. Success is not brought about by declarations or dogma.

The conclusion that all states are cosmopolitan is not a simple declaration. It is based on the empirical reality that there never has been and, it may safely be

---

[1] These now include the tradition of each particular state, as to which see Glenn (2007b), 'National Legal Tradition'.

[2] On the (usual) understanding of the word 'cosmopolitan' used here and throughout, corresponding to that of the *Oxford English Dictionary* ('having the characteristics which arise from, or are suited to, a range over many different countries'), see Ch. 9, 'Globalization, Cosmopolitan Theory, and the State'.

[3] Glenn (2010b), *Legal Traditions*; Glenn (2007c), *On Common Laws*.

added, there never will be, a nation-state. All states are therefore cosmopolitan. This may come as a surprise to all those who regularly use the expression 'nation-state' (and it has become a commonplace), but the coincidence or overlapping of a nation or homogeneous group of people with the legal and political structure of a state has never occurred, anywhere. The fundamentally romantic nature of the idea is now coming to be recognized, and a major study of world history recently concluded that 'nation-states could never exclude, expel, and assimilate enough to produce uniform populations or erase crosscutting loyalties'.[4] The minority question is a global one.[5]

The law of states, moreover, is as cosmopolitan as their populations. The main instruments of legal cosmopolitanism have been those of common laws, constitutionalism, and what I describe as institutional cosmopolitanism. Their relative importance has changed over time, as the book attempts to show, but all three have been constantly operative even in times of attempted national closure. All three remain present in the contemporary cosmopolitan state and the final part of the book attempts to demonstrate this in examining notions of cosmopolitan citizens, cosmopolitan sources, and cosmopolitan thought.

While the idea of a cosmopolitan state corresponds with social reality, its assertion is not a descriptive exercise. There are those who believe it should not and cannot be so. If it is so, there are normative consequences, notably as to whether populations should continue to be inculcated with ideas of social uniformity as the underlying norm, and whether measures of social 'uniformization' (to be neutral in choice of language) have some institutional justification. States have brought about much good in the world and can continue to bring about much good; they are not, however, unqualified goods in themselves.

This book builds on many others and research into them was splendidly carried on by David Jenkins, Katherine Gibson, Meaghan Enright, Matthew Jackson, Graciela Jasa Silveira, Nafay Choudhury, and Scott Horne. Research was also facilitated by funding from the McGill Law Faculty John Dobson Fellowship Fund, and by funding and support from the McGill research group 'Private Justice and the Rule of Law' directed by my colleague Fabien Gélinas. The writing was made possible through the Henry G. Schermers Fellowship granted to me by The Hague Institute for the Internationalisation of Law (HiiL) and the Netherlands Institute for Advanced Study (NIAS) in 2010–11. Writing was facilitated by perceptive comments made at presentations at the Faculties of Law of the Universities of Nijmegen and Rotterdam and at the Department of Legal Philosophy of the University of Tilburg, as well as by anonymous reviewers of Oxford University Press. My Deans Nicholas Kasirer and Daniel Jutras provided both moral support and precious leave. I am very grateful to all.

Wassenaar, The Netherlands
and Sutton, Quebec,
November, 2012

---

[4] Burbank and Cooper (2010), *Empires*, at 458. Even this statement uses the expression nation-state while denying its possibility.

[5] See Ch. 5, 'A Nation-State?'

Contents

List of Abbreviations

AJCL	American Journal of Comparative Law
ANCL	African Network of Constitutional Jurists
AOSIS	Alliance of Small Island States
ASEAN	Association of South-East Asian Nations
BGB	(German) Bürgerliches Gesetzbuch
BVerfG	Bundesverfassungsgerichthof
ECJ	European Court of Justice
ECtHR	European Court of Human Rights
EU	European Union
FRA	(EU) Fundamental Rights Agency
GATT	General Agreement on Tariffs and Trade
GONGO	(China) government-organized NGO
IACHR	Inter-American Court of Human Rights
ICLQ	International and Comparative Law Quarterly
INGO	international non-governmental organization
IOSCO	International Organization of Securities Commissions
LICUS	low-income countries under stress
MERCOSUR	Mercado Comun del Cono Sur (South American Common Market)
NAFTA	North Atlantic Free Trade Agreement
NGO	non-governmental organization
OIC	Organization of Islamic Conference
PofP	priority of practice (over theory)
PofT	priority of theory (over practice)
RTA	Regional Trade Agreement
SIDS	small-island developing states
TANGOs	Transnational Advocacy NGOs
TEU	Treaty of the European Union
TFEU	Treaty on the Functioning of the European Union
TPR	transnational private regulation
WTO	World Trade Organization

1

Introduction: Thinking the State

How does one think about an institution or concept as large and as widespread as the state? Some would prefer not to. Others have 'succumbed to analysis'. If today the 'question of the state is posed everywhere in the world' it may be difficult not to think about it.[1] Yet, in thinking about it, should one be empirical or normative, theoretical or descriptive? Are we concerned with an essence of the state, or with legitimate or possible functions?[2] There is no agreement on the answers to these questions, yet it has been said that 'it does appear foolish to deny a state tradition'.[3] So the simplest and most basic answer to the question of the state is probably that it exists as a tradition, a body of normative and often inconsistent information that is inevitably instantiated or institutionalized in various and particular forms. This is the case for law in general,[4] and states are legal constructions.

There remains much to be said, however, about different readings of the tradition, about their influence through time, and about the potential variety of instantiations of the state as tradition.

READINGS OF THE STATE TRADITION

The word 'state' has a totalitarian ring to it. It is often presented with a capital initial letter, thus State, and with the capital letter 'Leviathan and Behemoth are already casting their enormous and oppressive shadows'.[5] So, in reaction, there are very visible readings of the state tradition that would essentially read the state out of it, leaving only some important constituent elements. One of these readings was widespread in academic circles in the anglo-american world in

---

[1] Picq (1995a), *Il faut aimer l'État*, at 15 ('Partout dans le monde, la question de l'État est posée'). Unless otherwise indicated, all translations are by the author.

[2] Against 'methodological essentialism', rejecting the essentialist question 'what is the state, what is its true nature, its real meaning' yet concluding that the 'fundamental purpose' of the state is the protection of freedom which does not harm others, Popper (1963), *Open Society*, vol. I, at 109–10.

[3] Vincent (1987), *Theories of the State*, at 8, contrasting critical enquiry with historical purity or accuracy, concluding at 9 that the state has 'no innate essence'; and see Nelson (2006), *Making of Modern State*, at 5 ('To understand the state is to understand it historically . . . the product of historical contingency . . . the result of centuries of structural and ideological developments, none of which were predictable'). For support of indefinability, Dyson (1980), *The State Tradition* at 205, though himself providing (at 206) a ten-line definition.

[4] Glenn (2010b), *Legal Traditions*; Glenn (2008), 'Concept of Legal Tradition'.

[5] Avineri (1972), *Hegel's Theory of State*, at ix (selective capitalization of state 'as arbitrary and intellectually scandalous as any other wilful misrepresentation').

the mid-twentieth century when the state was 'dropped from American social science', partly in reaction against various forms of totalitarianism, partly to concentrate on the workings of government processes, political parties, pressure groups, and other features of contemporary states.[6] Some concluded even that the state did not exist, or was only an imaginary community.[7] This particular 'rival tradition' of pluralist political thought, itself challenging a 'tradition embodying the total experience of statehood',[8] has declined in influence, as traditions do. The state would have been brought 'back in' in the later twentieth century, a necessary consequence of its persistence at the international level and the impossibility of treating it as a regress-stopper or pre-social fact.[9]

The academic movements of the twentieth century, however, can be seen as rooted in broader intellectual and institutional perspectives. England and Commonwealth jurisdictions have their Crown, but this has remained a 'theoretically undeveloped and lifeless abstraction',[10] a tolerable and useful feudal remnant. The absence of development of a concept of the state would itself be a matter of philosophical choice, an underlying predominance of empiricist and pragmatic attitudes, happy with specific instances and discrete parts, mistrustful of juristic or other theory.[11] It has recently been described as 'a particular state tradition rather than its absence'.[12] The chaos of the common law would follow from this, or perhaps contribute to it. Groups do not threaten a society but constitute it; the trust is an acceptable, non-state form of legal ordering.[13] In the United States of America the underlying pragmatics would be reinforced by deliberate marginalization of the state, both in politics and in language, with reference usually to 'the

---

[6] For the state receding to the background 'during periods of stability', today the object of 'critical attention and conceptualization', Ghani and Lockhart (2008), *Fixing Failed States*, at 26; and for reading out, Terrill (2003), *New Chinese Empire*, at 30.

[7] Friedrich (1939), 'Deification of State', at 29 ('pseudo-theological claptrap'); Anderson (1983), *Imagined Communities*, at 15 (imagined since most members of a state will never know or hear of their fellow members, yet 'in the minds of each lives the image of their communion').

[8] Bartelson (2001), *Critique of State*, at 81, 83 (critics impliedly accepting existence of the larger tradition).

[9] Evans, Rueschemeyer, and Skocpol (1985), *Bringing State Back In*; Bartelson (2001), *Critique of State*, at 28, 76 (on 'futility' of efforts to exclude); Rae (2002), *State Identities*, at 16 (once 'back in' state seen as 'normative order'); Migdal (2001), *State in Society*, at 49–50 (for model of 'state in society').

[10] Dyson (1980), *The State Tradition*, at 42 (no identification of corporate and collectivist capacity); though for resurrection of the 'honour of the Crown' to impose a fiduciary obligation in regard to aboriginal peoples, see Ch. 12, 'Reconciliation'.

[11] Oakeshott (2006), *Lectures*, at 31 (events, actions, beliefs not understood as example of general laws but only in relation to other events, actions, and beliefs); Dyson (1980), *The State Tradition*, at 4, 52 (even contrasting 'state' and 'stateless' societies, latter tend to diffusion of power); Vincent (1987), *Theories of the State*, at 2 (on mistrust of 'metaphysical or juristic theories', corresponding importance of linguistic and analytical philosophy).

[12] McLean (2012), *Searching for the State*, at 1, and see at 6 (for writing which rejects 'superhuman overtones').

[13] On the importance of the trust as a non-corporate structure, prohibited in many continental jurisdictions, and the influence of von Gierke (from Germany) on the underlying confidence in non-state structures, Vincent (1987), *Theories of the State*, at 204–5.

administration' or 'the government'.[14] Federalism would also be more centrifugal in emphasis.

In contrast to these minimalist readings of the state tradition, the German readings are unquestionably the most developed and conceptually rich in the world. It remains necessary to speak of readings in the plural, however, since there are traditions within what has now become a national tradition, and which even antedate the national tradition. Germany had many states prior to its unification in 1871 (the present pejorative expression is Kleinstaaterei) and some conceptual sense had to be made of their characteristics and relations. Thus, entire legal disciplines have existed that have no real counterpart in much of the rest of the world, notably those of Staatslehre (teaching or doctrine of the state) and even Allgemeine Staatslehre (general teaching or doctrine of the state). Staatslehre tells us that it is not only appropriate to think of the state, but that we should think of it in the broadest possible terms, and on a world-wide basis. Constitutions, and constitutional law (Verfassungsrecht), exist only within this broader cadre so one must first understand that which is prior, more general, and foundational.[15] This appears today to be an entirely justifiable proposition, and this book can even been seen as an example of it, but Staatslehre too has had its ups and downs. There have been three, related, problems. The first is the breadth of the project and, in a world of specialized disciplines, Staatslehre was taxed with being methodologically ambiguous, or even with having no 'method' whatsoever, being incapable of situation within political philosophy, legal theory, sociology, constitutional history, or political science.[16] This was explicitly recognized by some of the major writers on Staatslehre: Jellinek, for example, described his work as descriptive though at the same time theoretical ('zugleich Erklarung').[17] It was just law, and interdisciplinary before the hour. The second problem was that Staatslehre was pan-national in a time of rising nationalism, with national constitutions seen as the appropriate object of attention. So constitutional law (Verfassungsrecht) came to be seen as the central activity in a field increasingly seen as national. Third and finally, Staatslehre became driven in large part by Hegelian ideas of the state, which reified it even prior to articulation of its formal sources. While Carl Schmitt wrote on constitutional law, he saw it as a 'systematic unity' of norms deriving its validity from a superior 'Will' and wrote

---

[14] Nelson (2006), *Making of Modern State*, at 3, 104 (on fears of absolutist state); Eppler (2005), *Auslaufmodell Staat*, at 48–9 (though both inadequate to capture continuity of state).

[15] Thus constitutional law is the narrower discipline, taking only an 'inner view' (Innensicht) of the state; Doehring (2000), *Allgemeine Staatslehre*, at 7; and for general state doctrine enabling a view of the general as well as the particular, and teaching that present state structures were not simply found independently by different groups in the world, Starck (2005), 'Allgemeine Staatslehre', at 718. For the conditions of origin ('Entstehungsbedingungen') of Staatslehre in the pre-national legal and political diversity of what is now Germany, Friedrich (1997), *Geschichte deutschen Staatsrechtswissenschaft*, at 24.

[16] Vosskuhle (2004), 'Renaissance der "Allgemeinen Staatslehre"', at 2.

[17] Jellinek (1922), *Allgemeine Staatslehre*, at 9; and for the need for and impossibility of dealing with all literature, of all provenances, Krüger (1966), *Allgemeine Staatslehre*, at viii.

of Allgemeine Staatslehre as 'Politik'.[18] Kelsen, in contrast, defended a notion of pure law, and left Germany for Switzerland in 1933.[19]

In spite of such twentieth-century clouds over Staatslehre, it remains entirely appropriate to speak today of two 'constitutional traditions' in Germany,[20] which concentrate respectively on general teaching of the state (on one hand), and on the national constitution (on the other). Some continue to criticize Staatslehre for a view of the state as sovereign and impermeable, and prefer what would be a more open idea of a national constitution.[21] Others, in the contemporary context of Europe and the world, speak of a return of Staatslehre as a means of overcoming 'nationally introverted norm and case-law exegesis' and as favouring a 'problem-oriented, trans-border exchange of legal arguments, solutions and experience'.[22]

So there are different readings of the state tradition, which have waxed and waned. If we are of strong conviction, we can take up the torch for any of these, and any of them may wax again at a particular time. Caution is suggested, however, by the fact that no one of them has obviously prevailed, even within a particular state. Since no one of them has prevailed, no one of them has been able to shut out the others, which continue to float within relatively easy reach. Some readings are more obviously cosmopolitan in their reach; others are potentially so but may have been subject to non-cosmopolitan interpretation. So our present or current thinking of the state may have some effect on its cosmopolitan character but does not appear capable of precluding it. It has also been said, in relation to an apparently non-cosmopolitan theory of national sovereignty, that 'the fact preceded the theory',[23] so this too is a reason for conceptual caution.

There is not only the complication of multiple readings of the state tradition. There is also the problem of thinking the state through time.

THE STATE TRADITION THROUGH TIME

Staatslehre has taught, consistently with its own objectives, that there is no spatial or temporal limit in thinking the state.[24] Our readings of the state tradition can therefore extend, as it is said, backwards in time. Is there, however, a temporal

---

[18] Schmitt (1928), *Verfassungslehre*, at viii, and 9 (for constitution based on a power ('Gewalt') acting through its will ('Wille'), constitution as purely positive norm a 'contradictory confusion'); and for Hegelian and other notions of the state, see Ch. 5, 'Nation'.

[19] Kelsen (1989), *Pure Theory*. One of Kelsen's first books was on Allgemeine Staatslehre and his Pure Theory of Law demonstrates great knowledge of the public law of the world.

[20] Murkens (2007), 'Future of Staatsrecht', at 732.

[21] For the debate, Murkens (2007), 'Future of Staatsrecht'; though for national constitutions as scarcely immune from phenomena of closure, see Ch. 11, 'The Cosmopolitan Turn in Constitutional Sources'.

[22] Vosskuhle (2004), 'Renaissance der "Allgemeinen Staatslehre"', at 4, and also at 6 for return of Allgemeine Staatslehre as coinciding with an 'open constitutional state'; Starck (2005), 'Allgemeine Staatslehre', at 712 (on a 'new' discipline dealing with the state).

[23] Post (1964), *Studies Medieval Legal Thought*, at 449; though for the question whether there has ever been a 'fact' of sovereignty, see Ch. 7, 'Sources'; and on the wider phenomenon of the relations of 'theory' to 'practice', see Ch. 9, 'Cosmopolitan Theory'.

[24] Starck (2005), 'Allgemeine Staatslehre', at 712.

limit to the state, one which limits or expands our conception of it, and of its cosmopolitanism?

Contemporary historians and others, impressed with notions of periodization and the nation-state, as it has been perceived, have spoken of the state as existing essentially from the time of the Italian renaissance. Machiavelli would have played a large role in this, and is often credited with effecting a tilt to the Italian word stato from a status or condition to the institution we know today as the state.[25] The emergence of the word, and its contemporary meaning, would therefore correspond to the emergence of the institution. The state would be a 'recent phenomenon', a 'construction politique nouvelle', a 'comparatively recent invention', an intellectual product of 'modern Europe'.[26] It would even be an anachronism to speak of the state prior to its linguistic emergence, and the proposition is advanced that the modern idea of the state was born with the word.[27]

Historical work is insidious and diverse, however, and if the emergence of the word and concept 'the state' can be traced to the mid-sixteenth century, it also appears possible to trace the historic roots and development of the state to earlier times. States as we know them appear to have emerged from national monarchies (as opposed to cities, empires, and fiefdoms) and monarchies reach far back.[28] With such an 'open-textured' word as state, moreover, there might not have been a single, charismatic moment of emergence, but parallel, staggered shifts in meaning, in what remained a largely oral society. Dyson speaks of the first step towards the modern state in the Ständesstaat (literally the state based on status or classes) which emerged as early as the late twelfth century in many places in Europe, and of use of the word state to indicate a polity in the Netherlands in the fifteenth century and by particular authors in Italy in the fourteenth. The Germans would have taken it from the Dutch in the fifteenth century.[29]

If practice does indeed precede theory, then practice may precede precise language as well. Harding thus chose to write on a 'pre-theoretical understanding' of the state, finding it in various applications of the word (and its cousins

---

[25] See notably Skinner (1989), 'The State', at 101 (most important linguistic innovation of renaissance Italy), 102 (Machiavelli 'most consistent willingness to distinguish the institutions of *lo stato* from those who have charge of them').

[26] See respectively Vincent (1987), *Theories of the State*, at 10 (Greek or medieval states 'misnomers'); Chevallier (1999), *L'Etat*, at 9; van Creveld (1999), *Rise and Decline of State*, at 1 (distinguishing governments from states); Krüger (1966), *Allgemeine Staatslehre*, at 5. Add Spellman (1998), *European Political Thought: 1600–1700*, at 1 ('emergence' of sovereign state in seventeenth century); Böckenförde (1991), *Recht, Staat, Freiheit*, at 92 (no longer possible to speak of hellenic state, state of middle ages, etc.); Morris (1998), *Essay on Modern State*, at 17 (pleonastic to speak of 'modern state').

[27] Jellinek (1922), *Allgemeine Staatslehre*, at 131; Hont, (1995), 'Permanent Crisis of Divided Mankind', at 184 ('new model'); Dowdall (1923), 'The Word "State"', at 114–15 (by explicitly naming it, Machiavelli 'founded' the modern science of the state); and for anachronism, Bartelson (1995), *Genealogy of Sovereignty*, at 99.

[28] See Ch. 2, 'Affirmative Crowns'.

[29] Dyson (1980), *The State Tradition*, at 25–7, 56 (for the Ständesstaat); and for Henry III's affirmation of the 'prosperity of our state' as early as the thirteenth century, Harding (2002b), *Medieval Law and Foundations of State*, at 145.

status, estate, etc.) in the judicial and administrative practices of the middle ages, criticizing a teleology only interested in a 'modern' idea.[30] Bartelson finds states by 1300, in the continuity by then of bodies politic in time and space.[31] Limitation of the state to 'modern' times, therefore, may be simply an extension of the thinking of 'modernity', with its insistence on periodization and discontinuity. The 'modern' could not exist without these underlying attitudes, while the notion of an anachronism is tied to the notion of linear time and would itself be a nineteenth-century, pre-Raphaelite creation.[32] That nothing can be situate outside its distinct period is thus a 'modern' idea. There appears to be no fundamental reason why one cannot think of degrees in the emergence of what we know as states, just as it appears possible, and even necessary, to think today of degrees of their disintegration. If the term 'nation-state' came into being only in the early twentieth century, as appears to have been the case,[33] must it follow that there could have been no nation-states in the nineteenth century?

It may therefore be necessary to think of the state without any limit in time, though there will be variations in the types of state we then encounter. This would also flow from the strikingly large array of informed opinion, across disciplines, that rejects any temporal limit to the notion of the state. Experts differ, and differ greatly. Anthropologists appear particularly unimpressed with temporal boundaries to the state. Bruce Trigger has thus written extensively on 'States: City and Territorial' and demonstrates more interest in the possible difference between them than in the notion of a state. The 'city-state' is situated in ancient Greece, renaissance Italy, parts of the ancient Middle East, and in classic Mayan society.[34] Robert Bellah speaks without apparent hesitation of the 'early state' of pre-monarchical Israel.[35] Claessen, in *The Early State*, sees the state as a social phenomenon that first appeared 'only' several thousand years ago.[36] Broadly speaking, the anthropological and sociological literature would be interested in the 'rise of formal political organization as compared to tribal or kinship associations'.[37]

Even amongst historians, the modernist, periodized view is far from dominant. The great German historian of antiquity, Eduard Meyer, argued for the universality of the state in human history and for its being historically the 'primary form

---

[30] Harding (2002b), *Medieval Law and Foundations of State*, at v, 1, though, at 5, even 'theoretical' use began with Aquinas in thirteenth century.

[31] Bartelson (1995), *Genealogy of Sovereignty*, at 99; and see Ch. 2, 'Affirmative Crowns'.

[32] Manguel (2006), *Library at Night*, at 317 (notion of a 'cosmopolitan past' with us for many centuries, till then).

[33] See Ch. 5, 'Nation'.

[34] Trigger (2003), *Understanding Early Civilizations*, at 92 (for 'States: City and Territorial'), 93, 266 (on debated dichotomy between them).

[35] Bellah (2011), *Religion in Human Evolution*, at 289 (stimulated by military pressure from Philistines).

[36] Claessen and Skalnik (1978), *The Early State*, at 3.

[37] Spruyt (1994), *The Sovereign State*, at 195, pointing out discipline-specific concepts of the origin of the state; Morris (1998), *Essay on Modern State*, at 26 (state 'in broad anthropological sense' found in non-'primitive' social organization, first appearing in ancient Egypt, Mesopotamia, 'and elsewhere').

of human community'.[38] Contemporary historians may adopt the anthropological view, explicitly,[39] or for their own reasons extend the concept of the state to the various institutions they examine.[40] The 'empire-state' has also existed, in both pre- and post-renaissance times,[41] as has the 'company-state' of some empires.[42] Some, moreover, prefer nuance, applying a 'presumption' of independent communities, or allowing for how 'rigorous one wishes to be'.[43]

Specialists in explicitly normative views of the world are understandably less inclined to periodization. Charles Taylor has criticized the media, literature, and the social sciences for having us think of society in terms of 'vertical time-slices, holding together myriad happenings, related and unrelated',[44] apparently lacking any normative connection to that which has preceded, and Paul Ricoeur stoutly affirms his preference to 'summon this or that author according to the requirements of the argument, without concerning myself with the epoch'.[45] Without discussion, lawyers and legal historians have often identified early versions of their concept of the state. Jennings saw England already existing as a state by the middle of the fourteenth century;[46] going further back in time, Professor van Caenegem speaks of the 'rebirth' (even) of the state in the twelfth century.[47] Jellinek, Ellul, and Herzog wrote of different versions of states in antiquity,[48] while leading historians of Roman law also speak explicitly of the Roman state, in early and later forms.[49] Mitteis wrote of the 'state' of the high middle ages and,[50] more recently, Noah Feldman extended the notion of an Islamic state to the

---

[38] Meyer (1907), *Geschichte des Altertumes*, at 11.

[39] Wickham (2005), *Framing Early Middle Ages*, at 57.

[40] For example, Canning (1988a), 'Introduction: politics, institutions and ideas' at 350–52 (England a state from reign of Henry II, though given 'minimum requirements . . . for the existence of a state, it is arguably misleading' to apply term earlier than mid-twelfth century); and for further examples, Barber (2010), *Constitutional State*, at 4.

[41] Burbank and Cooper (2010), *Empires*, at 8; Benton (2010), *Search for Sovereignty*, at 36.

[42] Stern (2011), *The Company-State* (English East India Company and its problems of governance).

[43] Respectively Post (1964), *Studies Medieval Legal Thought*, at 247 (for as early as 1100), and at iii ('no distortion to use our own term "State" instead of the medieval term'); Canning (1988a), 'Introduction: politics, institutions and ideas', at 350.

[44] Taylor (2007), *A Secular Age*, at 195.

[45] Ricoeur (2004), *Memory, History, Forgetting*, at xvii.

[46] Jennings (1959), *Law and Constitution*, at 2 (a general and common law, main functions of government with 'central authorities').

[47] Van Caenegem (1988), 'Government, law and society', at 185; and for a still earlier 're-appearance' with Charlemagne, Lepointe (1965), *Histoire droit public français*, at 22.

[48] Jellinek (1922), *Allgemeine Staatslehre*, at 53 ('antike Staatslehre'); Ellul (1955), *Histoire des institutions*, at 48 (Spartan state, Etruscan city-state); Herzog (1988), *Staaten der Frühzeit*, notably at 9 (given imprecision of word, better to be inclusive in seeking understanding), 10–11 (state understood in terms of degrees of organization of society), 15 (state over 4,000 years); and see Jowett's translation of Aristotle's *Politics* (Aristotle (2008b) at I.1 ('[e]very state is a community of some kind'); Johnson (1990), *Aristotle's Theory of State*, at xxii (using both state and constitution to render Greek *politeia*).

[49] Notably Kunkel (1973), *Roman Legal and Constitutional History*, at 3, 9 (though not thought of in abstract way as today); Kaser (1967), *Römische Rechtsgeschichte*, at 19, 92 (original 'Bauernstaat' developing into 'Territorialstaat').

[50] Mitteis (1975), *State of the Middle Ages* ('Der Staat des hohen Mittelalters'); and the use of 'state' in Alan Gewirth's translation of Marsilius of Padua's *Defensor pacis* of 1324: Marsilius (1980), *Defensor pacis*.

time of Muhammad.[51] A specialist in the history of political theory recently and splendidly concluded that historical differences and fears of anachronism are 'no warrant to wallow in historical immediacy'.[52]

Why does all of this matter for the cosmopolitan character of the state? If the state is a modern, post-renaissance structure, we will see in Chapter 4 that some attempted form of territorial or other closure will have accompanied it throughout its history. The state will appear intrinsically less cosmopolitan; the argument for cosmopolitanism will be more difficult to make. If the state has existed throughout organized society, recent efforts at closure appear more as a blip in a much longer narrative. National closure has vastly more to overcome. Since the 'longue durée' of the state cannot be excluded, however, Chapter 2 will have to examine some antecedents of the contemporary state, and Chapter 3 the possibility of persistence of some of their fundamental concepts. These may constitute the cosmopolitan origins of the state as tradition, and later chapters trace the playing-out of the tradition.

THE STATE AS TRADITION

Since the state is today being questioned, both internally and externally, there is a normal reaction to no longer take it for granted but to seek its justification, historical or otherwise. Its possible disintegration is a factor for renewed interest in it;[53] in legal philosophy there would now be a 'burgeoning' group of 'normative' positivists, those who justify the state and its law as opposed to attempting to describe it.[54] Legal philosophy that is not purely descriptive, however, has obvious ties to normative philosophy that has preceded it, so normative arguments from both past and present come together; both are more visibly affirmations of a tradition. A rational justification of the state is provided, it is said, when people 'have reasons' to respect its laws,[55] and the best reasons may well be those that have attracted the widest adherence.[56]

---

[51] Feldman (2008), *Fall and Rise of Islamic State*, at 1 (Islamic states ranging from 'fortified towns to transcontinental empires').

[52] Nederman (1995), *Community and Consent*, at 147, while warning at 2 of 'undesirable byproducts' of the 'new historicist school'; and see Koselleck (2002), *Practice of Conceptual History*, at 8 (for warning against the 'mythical schema' of the triad of antiquity, the middle ages, and modernity). Douglass North and his colleagues are aware that specialists will argue that they have 'lifted . . . examples out of context, and we have. However, our intention is to put these examples in a new context, to provide a new framework for . . . human history . . . and to open new ways of thinking . . .'; North, Wallis, and Weingast (2009), *Violence and Social Orders*, at xii–xiii, and see also at 2, 13 (for 'natural state' having origins five to ten millennia ago).

[53] Nelson, (2006), *Making of Modern State*, at 128; and see, for pressure of globalization driving return to original sources, Goldman (2007), *Globalisation and Western Legal Tradition*, passim; Picq (1995a), *Il faut aimer l'État*, at 52 (on nation dying without its own memory).

[54] Coleman (2007), 'Beyond the Separability Thesis', at 600.

[55] Morris (1998), *Essay on Modern State*, at 122; and see Bagehot (1958), *English Constitution*, at 185 (on free government as government by persuasion, necessarily implying reasons for persuasion, as opposed to its simple fact).

[56] Condorcet famously sought to prove this through probability calculations and it is the case that an increase in participation can increase the probability of a correct solution, so long as precise conditions

Traditions are the objects of handing down, of *traditio*, but it is normative information that is the substance of tradition.[57] To the extent that states exist in institutional form, they so exist because there is normative information that favours institutionalization. Western institutions did not simply spring up on their own; there were underlying ideas of human control over human destiny, and of how that control was best brought about. They were ideas developed and refined over centuries, and handed down. This has consequences for our thinking about the state, consequences that are becoming clearer in present circumstances.

In the first place, the recognition of the state as a product of tradition requires greater reliance on historical data, an awareness of 'historical contingency'.[58] How is this material from the past developed and appreciated? There is (first of all) more of it, and Brian Tierney has commented on the importance of new research in making it possible to see continuity in the growth of constitutional thought from the twelfth to the seventeenth centuries.[59] In its turn, the ability to perceive continuities strikes at the periodization of legal history, so that the broad view of the state over time that is taken by some historians, as well as normative thinkers, is reinforced by historical work itself.[60] The more we learn of the disparate and early origins of the state the more plausible becomes its extension through time and the stronger is the case for its cosmopolitan character. We are, of course, interested in focused historical work, on the 'history of the present' as Foucault put it,[61] on lines of thought that took off, though in doing so we must stand within and without the tradition, both situating it so as to understand it and looking at temporal connections that could not be appreciated at an earlier time.[62]

In a second place, recognition of the state as a product of tradition, of diverse elements of normative information over time, situates the state squarely within

are met. If each of three persons has a 2/3 or 67 per cent chance of reaching a correct solution, together they have a 74 per cent chance, since they have 8/27 probability of a correct, unanimous solution (2/3x2/3x2/3 = 8/27) and a 12/27 probability of a correct, split decision (2/3x2/3x1/3 = 4/27, multiplied by 3 for the three possible combinations = 12/27, yielding 20/27 or 74 per cent). The calculation presumes, however, no mutual influence amongst the deciders and precise calculation of probability. For the original text (which apparently lacks a full English translation), Condorcet (1785), 'Essai sur l'application de l'analyse'. Condorcet, however, being 'subtle mathematically, but not philosophically . . . a Platonic realist, believing in objective moral truths' viewed the 'failure of humans to agree . . . [as] a failure of perception': McLean and Hewitt (1994), *Condorcet*, at 32. The idea was present in Proverbs 11:14 ('. . . in the multitude of counsellors there is safety').

[57] Glenn (2010b), *Legal Traditions*, at 13–14.

[58] Nelson, (2006), *Making of Modern State*, at 127 (problematical character of general and universal theories, empiricism reflective of historical given); Stolleis (1987), *Staatsdenker*, at 11, 12 (distance from nineteenth century permitting clearer view of its ideology, questions of end of state raising questions as to its beginnings).

[59] Tierney (1982), *Religion, law and constitutional thought*, at 7.

[60] Oakley (2005), *Natural Law, Laws of Nature*, at 23 (traditional periodization into ancient, medieval, and modern 'as much a hindrance as a help'); Nicholas (2003), *Urban Europe, 1100–1700*, at viii (on distinction between 'medieval' and 'early modern', 'essentially irrelevant' in study of urban history).

[61] Foucault, however, sought not a history of the past, but a 'history of the present' as an instrument of radical reform; Foucault (1979), *Discipline and Punish*, at 31.

[62] Tierney (1982), *Religion, law and constitutional thought*, at viii.

contemporary information theory. The state even emerges as the most significant of contemporary 'informational societies', 'virtual communities', or 'epistemic communities'.[63] It is true that it is usually thought of today as a combination of institutions and territory, but these are simply manifestations of the underlying informational base and are themselves variable over the history of the state, particularly when a non-periodized view of that history is taken. It is true that contemporary information theory sees a technological revolution in the application of knowledge and information to the processes of generating and communicating information, but this is precisely how the state achieved its pre-eminence in the places of its origin, through the application of second-order theories of sources of law to the actual production and use of it. Before there could be codes there had to be authorization of codes, and before codes became accepted as law there had to be normative information justifying their acceptance.[64] State officers were masters of information theory in bringing about a view that the state could be a source of law, despite massive resistance and attachment to prior sources. If, today, the state is losing some of its pre-eminence this is because it is losing some of its control over information. If there are competing sources of information there are inevitably competing sources of normativity, some of which will be recognized as law. The current debate about law and globalization is part of the ongoing tradition of the state.

In a third place, the nature of the state as tradition means that it is inherently open or cosmopolitan in character. Tradition as information is impossibly difficult to control or shut down. Efforts to reify states (or civilizations), by depicting them as 'entities' inevitably clashing or in conflict, are challenged by the ongoing, uncontrollable, flow of information that both constitutes them and questions them. They are not entities themselves, however many monuments, institutions, or gunboats they may bring about, and however massive may have been the doctrinal effort to constitute the state as an entity beyond the information that is its base.[65] Closure in the flow of information was key to some measure of closure of state structures and institutions in single territories, but closure in the flow of information is impossible to maintain over time. The collapse of the Soviet Union has been correctly identified as a failure in information control.[66] In the rise and relative decline of the state tradition we thus see that '[c]losures are realised in the context of an environment that is open, and are themselves open', in the sense that the completion of closure is impossible.[67]

---

[63] Castells (2000), *The Information Age*, vol. I, at 22; Haas (1992), 'Epistemic Communities'.

[64] Carbonnier (1982), '*Usus hodiernus pandectarum*', at 109–10 (cassation for violation of Roman law remaining possible for years after enactment of French Civil Code); and see Glenn (2004) 'La codification à la française'.

[65] For corporatist accounts, see Ch. 4, '*The state as body, crown, or corporate person*'.

[66] Castells (2000), *The Information Age*, vol. III, at 368.

[67] Lawson (2001), *Closure*, at 1, and 119 (closure always subject to failure because texture offers new closure which in turn potentially undermines current closure); and for the historical processes of flow from closures of tribe, city, manors, states, Clough and Cole (1952), *Economic History Europe*, notably at 20 (for decline of manor caused in part by rise of state).

Thinking the state as tradition, or information, means that states may vary, in degree and type, according to the information they rely upon.

In the twentieth century there was widespread resistance amongst legal thinkers to the idea of states existing in degrees or even in a variety of types. The state would be based on the idea of a legal system, with its territorial boundaries, and whatever the contents of the legal system it would above all *exist*. It would exist, moreover, as a dichotomous fixed idea ('dichotomischer Fixbegriff')[68] and, though there might be degrees of presence of various constitutive elements (such as levels of obedience), there could be no law without it. Either there is law and a legal system, or there is not.[69] In this insistence on the constancy and uniformity of the state in modern legal thought there is a curious parallel with Marxist and some sociological literature, in the sense that all states are simply the result of evolutionary stages of different economic or other systems, and there would be no need or even possibility of distinguishing amongst them.[70] Some have seen, in this overlooking of the legal (or its detail), an implicitly totalitarian character of the state.[71]

Conceiving the state as tradition is not incompatible with this view of a uniform and constant state (which is one instantiation of the tradition) but the state tradition is a larger one. We have already seen that it can be seen as extending far back in time and as including a multiplicity of predecessors or antecedents of the contemporary state. The contemporary state is thus the product of a process of emergence, and previous states would represent various degrees of present concepts of statehood. Many states in the world would also have failed or be failing, and there is no clearly recognizable boundary between

---

[68] Möllers (2000), *Staat als Argument*, at 424.

[69] On the tendency of legal philosophers of many persuasions to 'cling dogmatically to classificatory ideas', rejecting analysis of legal systems as matters of degree, Füsser, 'Farewell to "Legal Positivism"', at 124, 155, with references (Dworkin opposing Fuller's non-classificatory proposals); Coyle (2002), 'Hart, Raz and Concept of Legal System', at 282 (albeit in the complete absence of an uncontroversial theoretical characterization of a legal system). For John Finnis's acceptance that 'the central case of law and legal system is the law and legal system of a complete community', though warning that 'we must not take the pretensions of the modern state at face value', Finnis (1980), *Natural Law*, at 148, 149. Cf. van Creveld (1999), *Rise and Decline of State*, at 314 (for construction of Latin American states having succeeded 'only up to a point').

[70] Kriegel (1995), *State and Rule of Law*, at 5 (German romantic doctrine given canonical form by Marx), 66 (blind to juridico-institutional forms); Tilly and Blockmans (1994), *Cities and Rise of States*, at 3 (on sociological view of state of Poggi).

[71] Picq (2005), *Histoire et droit des États*, at 12, 19 (on totemic character of state in some societies, citing Russian philosopher Berdiaev that totalitarian state not accidental but implicit in concept of state). For impatience with the detail of the law in the theoretical conceptualization of national legal systems, and corresponding abandonment of treatises of civil law after the first volume, Gambaro (2002), 'Structure of Legal Systems', at 56 (authors not considering it fruitful 'to strain themselves in writing the remaining part').

these categories.[72] It therefore cannot be a question of states existing or not, but only of the degree to which the concept of a state is currently persuasive for the people said to be subject to it. This notion of degrees of statehood (degrees of sovereignty if you prefer) appears also to be the only way of appreciating what is happening to states in current world circumstances. Traditions are not on–off in their realization. They are phenomena of influence, even when instantiated as a national legal system or modern state. It is accurate, therefore, to speak of a possible decline in the influence of states in a time of globalization, since this may be what is actually going on. Moreover, since today many things are quantified (levels of corruption, quality of life), it would also be possible to quantify the extent to which individual states function as such, or have achieved statehood. In French it is possible to speak of degrees of 'étatisation' and this is a useful expression, difficult to duplicate in English.[73] Quantifying levels of state existence does not yet appear to have been done, but it would provide a more useful form of appreciation than that of international diplomatic recognition. Even the latter, however, is beginning to recognize degrees in the process.[74]

States vary, however, not only in the degrees of their acceptance by populations, but also in their type and structure, and these differences are primarily legal. The great variety of contemporary states is an indication of the cosmopolitan character of the state tradition, and its internal variety. The state tradition, like any tradition, 'tolerates and unites an internal variety and displays an ability to change without losing its identity'.[75] If there is some control over the degree of 'statehood' through the process of diplomatic recognition, there is no control over the type or structure that may be adopted, and in developing their own instantiation of the state tradition states have been inventive in the extreme.[76] There is widespread agreement on the singularity of individual states, their 'utter particularity' in the language of Phillip Allott.[77] This is important both for the

---

[72] See Ch. 5, 'Fragmentation, failure, and violence'; and for historical examples (Litva, Borussia, Etruria, Tsernagora), Davies (2011), Vanished Kingdoms, notably at 729ff. ('How States Die').

[73] Chevallier (1999), L'État, at 11; and in German, with a touch of Gallic elegance, 'Etatisierung', though once accomplished the result is a more solid 'Staatlichkeit'; for different levels of 'statishness' (in English) during the nineteenth century, Bayly (2004), Birth of Modern World, at 253.

[74] See, e.g., The Economist, 10 April 2010 at 62 on the difficulty of qualifying as a state (citing South Yemen, South Ossetia, Taipei, Kosovo, others), degrees of diplomatic recognition (ranging from full diplomatic ties to denying a state's existence) as a 'calibrated set of tools' to reward and penalize; recognition of a state may be distinguished from recognition of its government for diplomatic purposes, but here degrees are also possible (de jure, de facto, belligerent status, etc.); and for a rare recognition of 'degrees of legitimacy', Morris (1998), Essay on Modern State, at 110 (no such thing as legitimacy simpliciter). For the complexity of the process, Crawford (2007), Creation of States, though recognizing at 37 that 'there has long been no generally accepted and satisfactory legal definition of statehood'. For failed states, see Ch. 5, 'Fragmentation, failure, and violence'.

[75] Dyson (1980), The State Tradition, at 5.

[76] This is not to suggest a clear boundary between degrees of 'statehood' and its type or structure. Micro-states have been said to represent a 'category problem': Saladin (1995), Wozu noch Staaten?, at 226.

[77] Allott (2002), Health of Nations, at 117 and 118 ('of the nature of a nation to be uniquely itself'). The World Bank agrees: see World Bank (1997), The State in a Changing World, at 1 ('differences in size, ethnic makeup, culture and political systems make every state unique'); as do Saladin (1995), Wozu noch Staaten?, at 225; Picq (2005), Histoire et droit des États, at 11; Chevallier (2004a), L'État post-moderne, at 9; and Opello and Rosow (2004), Nation-State and Global Order, at 245.

idea of law (since recognition of difference implies recognition of law's role) and for any idea of exceptionalism on the part of a particular state. All are exceptional, out of the necessity of adapting to local circumstance, whether historical or social. Here is to be found the detail of the cosmopolitanism of each.

Yet at the same time there is language of commonality in discussion of states. Henke even speaks of the 'relative uniformity' of present states, the product of European expansion,[78] and Jellinek, while insisting on individuality, nevertheless acknowledged common elements, better appreciated if the state or legal elements can be isolated from all else.[79] It remains a state tradition, in spite of all of the differences. How this is brought about is the subject of this book.

---

[78] Henke (1988), *Recht und Staat*, at 294; and for sharing by some states of particular traditions of democracy, the rule of law, human rights, open government, Koopmans (2003), *Courts and Political Institutions*, at 7.

[79] Jellinek (1922), *Allgemeine Staatslehre*, at 33.

PART I

COSMOPOLITAN ORIGINS

Antecedents

Much expert opinion favours the view that different forms of states existed prior to the emergence of the modern state.[1] The idea of a modern state, therefore, is not a pleonasm, and the modern state would be a particular variant of a larger tradition of the state. Examining states antecedent to the modern or contemporary state therefore presents a double interest: i) to the extent that these antecedents are cosmopolitan in character this will mark the state as cosmopolitan from its early, and distant, origins; ii) to the extent that there may be persistence in the concepts, ideas, or even norms of earlier states, this persistence is an indication of the cosmopolitan origins of the contemporary state. This chapter and the next therefore examine antecedents of the contemporary state, and persistence of their teaching.

EARLY COSMOPOLITANISM

Peoples have never lived in complete isolation from one another. There have been great difficulties of communication, but even in the total absence of communication at a given time, some residue of previous contact and knowledge has always persisted, however dimly recalled. Palaeontologists and geneticists are now tracking the movement of early peoples (the early movement out of Africa would have occurred some 60,000 years ago, or 2,400 generations past) so that entirely autonomous, parallel development is excluded.[2] This tiny, initial grain of cosmopolitanism could only grow as contacts developed over space, and in the absence of any formal, institutional mechanisms for excluding it. Unwritten law is local, but there is contact and exchange at its periphery, even if some forms of (largely ecological) boundary cannot be excluded.[3]

Earlier communities were mobile ones until the development of farming some 10,000 years ago. With the shift to farming some concept of settlement or particular territory began to exist, but notions of private property and fixed

---

[1] See Ch. 1, under 'The State Tradition through Time'.

[2] Glenn (2012), 'Origins of Peoples and of Laws'; and for slow growth in interconnections over millennia, Chanda (2007), *Bound Together*, notably at xiii (differences between current and early globalization ones of velocity and visibility). For largely autonomous development, however (as local knowledge grows beyond initial knowledge), and parallels, in seven early civilizations across Africa, Asia, the Middle East, and Latin America, Trigger (2003), *Understanding Early Civilizations*.

[3] For the notion of boundaries as a persisting element of potential closure, see Ch. 3, under 'Persistence of Elements of Closure'.

boundaries, on the ground, had yet to appear.[4] Human groupings were those of kinship or tribe, though their names on occasion came to reflect places of origin. Kings did emerge in times of unwritten law, however, so it is very difficult to associate the institution of monarchy with either European history or historical time.[5] The essential feature of human groupings was that of human relations, conceived either in terms of kinship or in terms of loyalty, or some combination of both. This idea of peoples defined simply in terms of their relations to one another is an essential feature of early cosmopolitanism. The criteria for recognition of groups provide no means of separating them from one another in space, and life is necessarily, in some measure, cosmopolitan. It is true that peoples who see themselves as common will often live together, but the absence of strict territorial delimitation means that those who do not cannot live entirely apart. At points of contact, either of individuals or groups, adjustments are necessarily made.

Groupings defined in terms of personal relations persisted well into historical times. Monotheistic religious groupings could see themselves as chosen peoples, united by kinship in some measure but also by common belief. The Jewish concept of a chosen people could thus be taken over by Charlemagne for his Christian empire.[6] Islamic teaching recognized and recognizes an Islamic community or umma, but the territories of Islamic populations were not closed to non-Islamic people, and such dhimmi were even entitled to application of their own laws.[7] Confucius taught that 'a gentleman cherishes benign rule, but a small man cherishes his native land' and Chinese history was one of 'frontier zones' of merging and shifting identities.[8] Hindu teaching has focused on political or personal allegiance and still today it is said that 'territory cannot be seen as a primary constituent of the Indian state'.[9]

In these historical and even institutionalized societies, the absence of any strict principle of territoriality of laws continued to preclude any definitive form of normative closure. Laws were of course applied to those subject to them, and not to others, but there was a constant necessity to deal with interpersonal relations (which persist over different laws), to respond to the intellectual challenge of

---

[4] For transition to agriculture in the ninth and eighth millennia BCE, Barker (2006), *Agricultural Revolution in Prehistory*, notably at 38, 59 (for shift in 'cognitive world', however, from being part of world to controlling and appropriating it).

[5] For extra-European monarchs, see later in this chapter, under 'Affirmative Crowns'. Historical time is thought to be that which is evidenced by writing, though there is debate over what constitutes writing. Phonetic writing, as opposed to markings or symbols, appears to date from the fourth millennium BCE.

[6] Ullmann (1969), *Carolingian Rennaissance*, at 23. For the text as the historic and metaphorical Jewish homeland, Steiner (2001), *Grammars of Creation*, at 281; and for Jewish people as a continuity through time as opposed to a contiguity in space, Boyarin (1992), *Politics of Jewish Memory*, at xvii.

[7] See Ch. 13, under '*State and religious legal sources*'.

[8] Bell (2003), 'Making and Unmaking of Boundaries', at 75, and 58 (classical Confucianism ruling out possibility that rulers could justifiably exercise authority over a particular territory and establish boundaries between that territory and the rest of the world); Perdue (2005), *China Marches West*, passim (on 'borderlands').

[9] Wink (1986), *Land and Sovereignty in India*, at 161, and see also 48 (concept of dharma no connection with a geographical territory), 386 (Indian state today a form of 'institutionalized dissidence', with many forms of non-state law).

other, allegedly better, laws, and to deal with countless problems of the diversity of populations in a given territory. If we can see a form of closure, or a type of distinction between peoples, in a principle of the personality of laws, this closure can at best be partial. It is, in the language of modern logic, non-monotonic, in that it is always conditional or contingent, yielding to better argument or circumstance, making no claim to effect any form of radical separation. These historically recognizable legal traditions were also internally diverse; they were necessarily cosmopolitan towards their own internal diversity, as well as towards other communities.[10]

In the absence of any developed concept of closure, and given ongoing degrees of openness, there is no need to detail the extent or nature of the cosmopolitan character of these proto-historical and historical societies. They were cosmopolitan by necessity and there is no real challenge to this basic reality. The challenge to cosmopolitanism comes from later times, and from Europe, but Europe too had its cosmopolitanism.

EARLY EUROPEAN COSMOPOLITANISM

The greatest legacy in European thought is clearly cosmopolitan in character. The Greeks were cosmopolitan, moreover, not only in the universalistic dimensions of their thought, but in their legal practice, and the law of other city-states was simply used, wherever it seemed appropriate, and without much concern for its source.[11] They also designated foreigners to draft their written constitutions.[12] Herodotus thus thought it worthy of remark that there was a people of central Asia, the Scythians, who 'avoid foreign customs at all costs, especially those of the Hellenes'.[13] Cosmopolitanism existed as a way of thought, amongst relatively small city-states, but it became a necessity of life with the growth of empires, notably that of Rome. The Romans had a notion of natural law that was applicable to the entire world, including animals, though they made relatively little use of it. There were three operative kinds of law within the Roman empire: the law of the Romans themselves, the *ius civile*; the law used in Roman tribunals in cases involving foreigners, the *ius gentium*; and the law of those others, not yet entitled to Roman law, whose law was not only tolerated by the Romans but which appears to have had some influence on the content of Roman law itself.[14]

---

[10] For the nature of the internal diversity, represented often by 'schools' of law, Glenn (2010b), *Legal Traditions*, Chs 3–9.

[11] Assimakopoulou (1986), 'Comparative Law in History of Greek Law', at 325.

[12] Lanni and Vermeule (2012), 'Constitutional Design in Ancient World', at 910 (noting an advantage of impartiality).

[13] Strassler (2007), *The Landmark Herodotus*, at 4.76, p. 311.

[14] Glenn (2007c), *Common Laws* at 4–6, with references; Meyer (2004), *Legitimacy and Law in the Roman World*, notably at 205–7 (Romans in eastern provinces not overwhelmed by 'tsunami of foreign practice, instead fished happily and comfortably from the ocean'); and, for specific changes to Roman law in Egypt, Watson (1974), *Legal Transplants*, at 31–5, notably at 34 (where 'Roman traditions of law were not so strong').

The Romans were not very interested in law other than their own, but some knowledge of it was one of the burdens of empire. Fixed geographic boundaries could not do the work of separation. Maps were those of itineraries, not space; boundaries existed only on the ground as defensive fortifications, if at all; trade with partners as far away as India was extensive.[15]

Historically, medieval Europe was also a very cosmopolitan place, with many different types of law operating on the same territory. Some of these laws purported to be common; others were recognized as particular; and commonality did not preclude particularity.[16] There had to be many laws since there was no authority to exclude any of them. Kingdoms, fiefdoms, cities, empires, and the church all had their own law; legal boundaries were substantive and interpretive rather than spatial. Spatial boundaries, moreover, took centuries to fix on the ground. All of this diversity had to be reconciled, furthermore, with Christian notions of unity, and Ullmann concluded that Christian 'wholeness' is the best explanation for the 'openness' of medieval law: 'in order to accommodate a great many divergent social systems the law had to manifest a corresponding flexibility so that it was, if necessary, capable of absorbing alien matter'.[17]

Since the contemporary state is widely and correctly seen as a European construction it becomes necessary to look in some detail at European cosmopolitanism, both because no clear boundary exists between earlier states and the contemporary state in Europe, and because earlier European states may have contributed directly to any cosmopolitan origins of the contemporary states. This historic European cosmopolitanism is best appreciated by looking at the principal actors involved and the dynamic of their relations.

THE CHURCH AS STATE

Today, the Catholic church is seen as one of many, attending to religious needs within contemporary states. Earlier, however, (and still often today), it was referred to as 'the' church, a reflection of its universal ambitions and in spite of the existence of other major religions within Europe. It was also, however, an official church, designated as such in the fourth century CE, in the late Roman empire, and this official designation may be the explanation for the assumption by this church of major functions and obligations. It thereby became an organized church, the better presumably to serve, and organized in a way that sharply distinguishes Christianity from other monotheistic religions such as Judaism

---

[15] Whittaker (2004), *Rome and its Frontiers*, at 6 (for defensive lines), 63 (for maps), 147 (for trade); Kratochwil (1986), 'Systems, Boundaries, and Territoriality', at 35–6 (for Roman *limes* (pl. *limites*) not as boundary but as 'temporary stopping place' of 'potentially unlimited' empire, where the 'Pax Romana had come to a halt').

[16] For the variety of common laws (English, Roman, French, German, Spanish, Dutch) and their relations with particular laws, such as those of cities, regions, kingdoms, and eventually contemporary states, Glenn (2010c), *Common Laws*.

[17] Ullmann (1976), *Law and Politics in Middle Ages*, at 49.

or Islam.[18] We can see in the early, hierarchical organization of the Christian church, with a pope at its head, a clear antecedent to the structures of contemporary states. All currently recognized powers here come into view—legislative, judicial, and administrative—and they are all exercised in a given territory, Europe, for the presumed benefit of its population.[19]

There is therefore widespread historical opinion that the Christian church is not simply a significant antecedent to the contemporary state but is itself its first manifestation. Figgis concluded textually that 'the Church was not a State, it was the State' and that it had no recognizable civil counterpart.[20] Others concur but differ in the timing. Berman situated the assumption by the church of 'the distinctive characteristics of the modern state' only after the Cluniac reforms of the eleventh century,[21] though Strayer took the position that by then the church 'already' had many of the 'attributes of a state' including enduring institutions and a developing theory of papal sovereignty.[22] Others have seen in the medieval Christian church a 'quasi-state' or the 'first form' of the modern state.[23] Ullmann did not use the language of state in describing the church but spoke of 'one body public', the product no longer of 'natural forces' but of 'the mind of the spirit'.[24]

The medieval Christian church would therefore confirm the thesis that the institution of the state could exist before the name, and before its theoretical articulation.[25] This initial version of the contemporary state was faced, however, with very large problems of governance, pan-European in dimensions. The Latin

[18] Neither Judaism nor Islam is vertically structured. The scriptural authority for the pope's authority, as Bishop of Rome and successor to Peter, the first Bishop of Rome, is found in Matthew 16:17–19 (giving the 'keys of the kingdom' to Peter) and John 21:15–17 (telling Peter to 'feed my sheep'). The scriptural authority has of course been contested, historically, notably by Protestant theology, but its limits have also been the object of intense debate within the Catholic church. On persistence of conciliarist doctrine setting limits to papal authority, see Ch. 3, under '*Constitutionalism*'.

[19] Efforts to render the population uniform were undertaken by the church through proselytism and the ensuing Inquisition (to prevent backsliding after conversions), and by individual political units (such as England and Spain) through expulsion.

[20] Figgis (1931), *Political Thought*, at 4.

[21] Berman (1983), *Law and Revolution*, at 113 ('an independent, hierarchical, public authority', impossible to frame any acceptable definition of the state that would not include the medieval church, citing Maitland) and 115 ('an overarching ecclesiastical state'). On the reforms see later in this chapter.

[22] Strayer (1970), *Medieval Origins of Modern State*, at 15 (also that no secular ruler could function without the advice of churchmen).

[23] Van Caenegem (2002), *European Law in Past and Future*, at 15 ('vast, self-sufficient, self-contained and efficient organization' though 'not really' a state since no army, no citizenship, no territory); Picq (2005), *Histoire et droit des États*, at 135 (with strong central government, jurisdictional and legislative authority, bureaucracy, and first public law in the form of canon law); and see also van Creveld (1999), *Rise and Decline of State*, at 60 (for assets of church 'scattered all over Europe', strong financial, judicial and administrative apparatus capable of overcoming distance and time, far in advance of that of secular rulers).

[24] Ullmann (1969), *Carolingian Renaissance*, at 8, 9 (corresponding to 'new creature' of baptized Christian).

[25] For these notions of institutions preceding their designation, and of practice preceding theory, see Ch. 1, under 'Readings of the State Tradition' and 'The State Tradition through Time', and see Ch. 9, under 'Cosmopolitan Theory'.

language helped, and was indeed essential in providing a paravernacular means of communication, both within the church and beyond it. The differences in Europe went far beyond those of language, however, extending notably to law in its many forms, and successful church administration had to find means of ensuring church unity in the face of major differences. Arguably the most important and enduring church document was Gratian's *Decretum*, also known as the *Concordance of Discordant Canons*, written around 1140 as a means of reconciling a millennium of conflicting and confusing papal and other forms of church legislation.[26] Reconciliation began at home. Yet this effort at closure faced still greater challenges in the church's second millennium.

The church within

There were three recognizably distinct challenges to be faced in the church's second millennium, all dictating cosmopolitan and conciliatory responses, and all originating from within the church itself. The first challenge was that of schism, representing deep theological differences. The millennium began with the great schism of the eleventh century separating the Roman Catholic church in the west from the Greek Orthodox church in the east (the division was on linguistic as well as religious lines) and this major disaster provided a model to avoid for the future. The temporary schism of the fourteenth century, when several popes were elected at the same time (resident respectively in Rome and Avignon, both still known as cities of popes), was thus the object of conciliation, and an entire conciliarist tradition grew from the process.[27] It preserved the unity of the church until the great shattering known as the reformation, when multiple Protestant churches broke away in a schism closely related to the emergence of the contemporary state.[28]

The second challenge was that of enforcement, over the entire European territory, even where no threat of schism existed. Could the legislation of Rome bind, and need it? The answers apparently were yes, and not necessarily. This was the object of the great controversy in England between the historians Maitland and Stubbs, Maitland taking the part of Rome and Stubbs that of the autonomy of English ecclesiastical courts, this of course before the reformation. Charles Donahue has referred to these as still 'unresolved issues' and they may well remain so.[29] He concludes that there was 'great deference but not blind adherence' so some measure of local autonomy existed within the church. Canon law, even in legislative form, thus functioned in some measure as a common,

---

[26] Gratian (1993), *Treatise of Laws*. For the need to overcome previous 'incoherencies', Padovani (2007), 'Metaphysical Thought of Late Medieval Jurisprudence', at 95; and for Gratian's *Decretum* as embodying a 'pyramid of Church authority culminating in the pope', MacCulloch (2009), *Christianity*, at 377 (also Catholic church as 'essentially an unequal society', with pastors and flock).

[27] For the persistence of the tradition, see Ch. 3, under *'Constitutionalism'*.

[28] See Ch. 5, under 'Religion'.

[29] Donahue (1974), 'Roman Canon Law' at 653.

subsidiary law, yielding to local forms of imperativity.[30] It also recognized that local custom might prevail, and distinguished between what are known today as civil and criminal law, the latter having a higher level of institutional enforcement.[31]

The third challenge was perhaps the greatest one, and stemmed from basic teachings of the Christian religion, textually based in affirmations by Jesus that one should 'give to Caesar what is Caesar's, and to God what is God's', and that 'My kingdom is not of this world'.[32] Jesus thus reasoned as Plato had done, in terms of a binary division (or *diairesis* or dichotomy) and this has prompted centuries of effort to find a middle ground or included middle between worlds perceived as secular *or* religious.[33] The discovery of the writings of Aristotle in the twelfth and thirteenth centuries exacerbated the dichotomy and Aristotle's teaching of a 'natural', i.e. non-ecclesiastical, world was first prohibited and then only became widespread once Aquinas had brought about a certain synthesis in the thirteenth century. Aquinas accepted much of Aristotle's teaching about the physical and natural world, yet retained God as an unmoved mover.[34] The natural world could thus coexist with the theocratic one, though its 'corroding' influence would be felt for centuries to come.[35] 'Politics' was to become a category of thought, and Aristotle taught that the state was a 'plurality' characterized by unity 'in some respects only'.[36] This too the church learned to live with.

Toleration by the Catholic church of internal diversity was necessarily matched by toleration (however reluctant) of external challenge. As an affirmatively secular world became more and more visible the church's original universalism became more and more evidently cosmopolitan in character, in its

---

[30] Donahue (1974), 'Roman Canon Law' at 701. For this character of canon law becoming more evident on its alliance with revived Roman law, from the twelfth century, as a *ius commune*, Glenn (2007c), *Common Laws* at 108ff.

[31] Donahue (1974), 'Roman Canon Law' at 701, and 653 (for custom) and 703 (for 'instance' (civil) and 'office' (criminal) cases). For similar 'gallicanisme', tending to the autonomy of the church in France, Sueur (2007), *Histoire du droit public français*, vol. II, at 435.

[32] Respectively Matthew 22:21 and John 18:36. For a further binary, John 3:6 ('[t]hat which is born of the flesh is flesh, and that which is born of the Spirit is spirit').

[33] For Plato, see Ch. 14, '*The cosmopolitan limits of binary logic*'; and for the absence of any moment of separation of church and state in Christianity since separation would have existed from the origins, Brague, (2005), *Loi de Dieu*, at 15, 16; Prodi (2003), *Geschichte der Gerechtigkeit* at 111–12 (western or Christian concept of justice, constitutionalism, found in duality of religious and secular jurisdictions, refusal of unification), 283 (even 'Theologisierung' of law); Ahdar and Leigh (2005), *Religious Freedom*, at 13 (for 'jurisdictional demarcation of dualism' which 'runs right through Christian thought'), 14 (Augustine's two cities). For conversion of the Christian 'secular' world to that of 'modernity', Gillespie (2008), *Theological Origins of Modernity*, notably at 11 (for 'borrowing' by founders of 'new age').

[34] For Aquinas's characteristic gift of 'distinguishing without dividing, subordinating without suppressing, identifying without merging', Gilby (1953), *Philosophy and Theology of the State*, at 66.

[35] For corrosion, Ullmann (1988), *Law and Jurisdiction*, at VI–19; and for Aquinas's regime as fundamentally 'unstable', Nelson (2006), *Making of Modern State*, at 43. God thus could become only an indirect cause of secular authority, nature being seen as primary, and a legitimate world of secular or human law could also emerge, freed from Augustiniana notions of corruption and sin, described by Gilby as a 'vale of tears': Gilby (1953), *Philosophy and Theology of the State*, at 61.

[36] Aristotle (2008b), *Politics*, II.2 and II.5.

relations with emperors and kings but also in some measure with cities and lords. Then and now the church had no divisions, so the last resort, force, was unavailable. It was the word which had to prevail.

The church without

The emergence of secular authorities within Europe in the second millennium CE can thus be seen as compatible with, or even authorized by, Christian teaching. In a sense Christianity could not make up its mind, and it has even been described as a 'religion for leaving religion'.[37] The ambiguity or tension of the second millennium only paralleled, moreover, that of the first, during which various forms of 'Christian halakhah' testified to the ongoing normative force of Jewish law and the Jewish bible (retained as the 'old testament').[38] Closures always fail, the argument (once again) is, since there is no way to protect against new forms of closure provided by external texture.[39] Nor, in spite of its universal ambitions, could Christianity preclude the emergence of Islam.

In the secularizing context of Europe, the relations between the church and secular authorities are often depicted as struggles for power. In a sense they were, but power in itself was of little or no interest for the participants. They had larger themes in mind, and what is referred to as 'power' was simply a means to larger and nobler ends. The mission of the church was to realize God's word; the mission of others was to supplement it, if not replace it. The dualism of the scriptures inevitably found theological expression, notably in Pope Gelasius's fifth-century doctrine of the two powers or two swords, the heavenly and earthly weapons to be put to use in the Christianizing mission. The two swords were thus collaborative and not opposing ones, in the oneness or wholeness of the church, and the metaphor is best seen as one designed to maintain them both and avoid binary choice between them.[40] In this ongoing and deliberate ambiguity questions of bias or tilt inevitably were raised. Which sword was winning? In the eastern empire there had been no downfall of emperor, and the ensuing relations lent themselves to imperial dominance, a doctrine cumbersomely known as caesaropapism. In the fragmented west the tendency was for earthly authority to seek ecclesiastical support, and Charlemagne was fervently Christian in perspective, seeing in himself the successor of Jewish kings.[41] The oneness of

---

[37] Gauchet (1985), *Désenchantement*, at 133 ('[u]ne religion de la sortie de la religion').

[38] Hite and Ward (1990), *Canon Law*, at 48 (as Christian teaching moved away from the Talmudic).

[39] See Ch. 1, 'The State as Tradition'.

[40] Robinson (1988), 'Church and papacy', at 289 ('a duality, divinely ordained to govern the world side by side'). Recall Ullmann's view, cited earlier in this chapter under 'Early European Cosmopolitanism', that such 'wholeness' was the primary reason for the openness of medieval law. The view was inevitably expressed, however, that the earthly sword was derived directly from God and need not therefore be the gift of the church: Gierke (1951), *Political Theories of the Middle Age*, at 16. The biblical source is Luke 22:38 ('Lord, behold, here are two swords').

[41] Fichtenau (1964), *The Carolingian Empire*, at 57 (comparisons to David and Solomon); Luscombe (1988), 'Formation of political thought', at 167 (entire Carolingian image of kingship shaped by Old Testament models of holy kings); Ganshof (1968), *Frankish Institutions*, at 12 (Charlemagne according great importance to religious aspect of his authority).

the church was here meant to prevail but, according to reports, imperial authority often had the controlling hand, owning property used by the church and providing necessary material support to local bishops and monks.[42] Church leaders were concerned about this; there were protests against lay influence generally and particularly against lay influence in the sale of church offices and privileges (simony).[43] If one loved the church, corruption within it had to be rooted out. By the eleventh century, therefore, there was real friction between the two powers or swords, which came to open dispute during the papacy of Gregory VII (1073–85). Gregory was a reforming pope with apodictic views who, it has been said, 'knew no gray areas; all issues were black or white, one or the other' and who therefore saw the duality of Christianity as requiring choice rather than ambiguity.[44] In the ensuing struggle, which has come to be known generally as the investiture controversy (over who had the power to name bishops and church officials to office), he purported to depose the emperor Henry IV, was subject to reciprocal deposing himself, and undertook a series of measures designed to ensure church autonomy. Gratian's *Decretum* was a part of these efforts, a major intellectual bringing-together. Many have seen in this controversy a revolutionary event, a separation of church and state, but there is doubt as to whether the investiture issue was even the cause of the controversy,[45] and greater doubt as to its consequences.[46] There was certainly some unsettling of the earlier equilibrium or balance, which had become too comfortable for many, but Ullmann, for example, saw only 'the first glimmerings of the modern idea of the State'[47] and Stein sees the eventual Concordat that resolved the issue (for the time and place) as restoring 'a sense of Europe as a Christian unity, ruled by pope and emperor', though with two legal regimes.[48] Canning has concluded

---

[42] Nelson (1996), *The Frankish World*, at 105 (on 'very real dependence' of the clergy on rulers' protection and material support); Canning (1988a), 'Politics, institutions and ideas', at 345 ('practical control' of rulers over churches in own territory); Robinson (1988), 'Church and papacy', at 296 (no pope able to find emperor willing to accept subordinate role, once crowned by church); Berman (1983), *Law and Revolution*, at 88 (west even approaching caesaropapism of east).

[43] So called after Simon Magnus, who would have offered payment to Peter and John in return for the power to lay on hands. Simony was closely related to lay designation of church officials since church offices came with property, and payment could be required.

[44] Blumenthal, (1988), *The Investiture Controversy*, at 116 (also as a 'holy Satan').

[45] Blumenthal, (1988), *The Investiture Controversy*, at 120 (on investiture as product of existing dispute, Gregory's prohibition of lay investiture even coming after Henry's deposing).

[46] For revolution, Berman (1983), *Law and Revolution*, passim, notably at 113, 115; and for church 'independence at the highest level' which 'almost demanded the invention of the concept of the State', Strayer (1970), *Medieval Origins of Modern State*, at 21, 22; Böckenförde (1991), *Recht, Staat, Freiheit*, at 95 (for controversy as end of a politically and religiously unified world or 'Einheitswelt').

[47] Ullmann (1988), *Law and Jurisdiction*, at VI–16.

[48] Stein (1999), *Roman Law in European History*, at 42 (controversy 'rumbled on' for a half century, formally concluded by Concordat of Worms of 1122, which called for vesting with possessions and prerogatives by emperor and receipt of symbols of spiritual authority from ecclesiastical superior); for the 'somewhat ambiguous' resolution of the conflict, Beauthier (2007), *Droit et genèse de L'État*, at 118; MacCulloch (2009), *Christianity*, at 375 (controversy 'itself ended inconclusively' in twelfth century but 'similar issues flared up repeatedly later'), 552 ('indecisive results' of eleventh century); and for controversy not one of separation of church and state but of jurisdictional question within the *respublica Christiana*, Loughlin (2010), *Foundations of Public Law*, at 32.

that the issues were never resolved and that the dispute itself simply 'withered away as times changed'. There were later disputes and later concordats.[49] The church had to accommodate earthly concerns and institutions and had no way of closing them out; it had to act as a bridging institution.

The bridging church

If as a result of the investiture controversy the church had freed itself from lay influence in some measure (though in some measure only), the fundamental duality of medieval institutions continued to require delineation between them, and this still within the ongoing idea of Christian unity. The process of delineation was on occasion confrontational, but Prodi has written that it is both abstract and false to see the reciprocal relations as those of opposition between distinct normative blocks.[50] The process was rather one of osmosis,[51] or reconciliation and compromise,[52] since there could be no abstract and definitive solution. The idea of sovereignty was in the air but it was vaguer and less ambitious than it was later to become; a sovereignty that could easily be shared.[53] The osmosis took place notably at the level of institutional collaboration, though we will see that it also occurred at the level of substantive law, which persisted.[54]

There was institutional collaboration, both in terms of the learning of the canonical world being placed at the disposition of lay rulers, and in terms of collaboration between lay and ecclesiastical institutions, and notably the courts. A king's 'clerks' were often 'clerics', holders of ecclesiastical benefices,[55] and arguably no ruler could function without their advice.[56] Ecclesiastical and lay tribunals shared the range of judicial competence, with ecclesiastical competence in fields of family law, the law of successions, spiritual crimes, matters of contract when faith was pledged, and more. Ecclesiastical lawyers appeared in secular courts as witnesses on points of spiritual law and there was a high level of civility

---

[49] For that of Bologna of 1516, still attempting resolution of investiture questions but now between the pope and the king of France, Ellul (1956), *Histoire des institutions*, at 125, 303; for 'perpetual struggle' of later middle ages, Loughlin (2010), *Foundations of Public Law*, at 32. For the current debate between the government of the People's Republic of China and the Catholic church over the power of naming Catholic bishops in China, *Le Monde hebdomadaire*, 7 July 2007 at 5; S. Meichtry, 'Vatican Lashes Out at China over Bishop's Appointment', *Wall Street Journal*, 24 November 2010; 'Your billion or ours?', *The Economist*, 20 August 2011.

[50] Prodi (2003), *Eine Geschichte der Gerechtigkeit,* at 283.

[51] Prodi (2003), *Eine Geschichte der Gerechtigkeit,* at 112.

[52] Berman (1983), *Law and Revolution*, at 111.

[53] Gilby (1958), *Principality and Polity*, at 131 ('not even the Pope was generally regarded as omnipotent by himself within the Church').

[54] See Ch. 3, 'Institutional cosmopolitanism'.

[55] Tierney (1982), *Religion, law and constitutional thought*, at 10.

[56] Strayer (1970), *Medieval Origins of Modern State*, at 15.

and mutual respect.[57] Church lawyers collaborated with those of secular courts in equal measure, moreover, both on the continent and in common law England. Only in the nineteenth century did ecclesiastical courts lose their broad jurisdiction in England.

The cosmopolitan character of the church, as an early European state, was necessarily matched by its principal interlocutor, the empire.

THE DIVERSITY OF EMPIRE

In the medieval European context the empire in question was that initiated by Charlemagne, which came to be designated as the Holy Roman Empire. It was holy because Charlemagne had been crowned by Pope Leo III in December, 800, in Rome (adding divine to temporal authority) and it was an empire because it was seen as a successor to the Roman one. In a sense the church created the empire, since Charlemagne's original authority was that of king of the Franks and this has been described as the 'only solid foundation of his authority'.[58] Papal coronation of the emperor, repeated regularly thereafter as a constitutive act, was intended to create an earthly papal defender and in some measure it did this,[59] while at the same time creating a rival authority within the world of Christendom. The ongoing rivalry has been discussed above, from the perspective of the church, as has been the bridging function of the church.

The emperor thus participated with the church in the process of Christian bridge-building but, as a temporal authority, also needed bridges to other temporal authorities, notably the kings, princes, and lords of the entire imperial territory, which eventually extended well beyond that of the Franks. Here is seen the essential character of empires, that they are deliberately and supportively multi-national in character, 'self-consciously maintaining the diversity of people they conquered and incorporated';[60] they imposed no single law, while the longest-lived amongst them were those most successful in recruiting local allies and least efficient in extracting tribute.[61] The cosmopolitanism of the Roman empire was thus an antecedent to later imperial cosmopolitanism. In medieval

[57] Jones (1970), 'Relations of the Two Jurisdictions', 77; Bassett (1978), 'Canon Law and Common Law', at 1407ff.; and for 'compromise' in difficult situations, such as clerical common law judges having to participate in condemnations to death, Helmholz (1991), 'Conflicts between Religious and Secular Law', notably at 718 (clerics simply withdrew since judges can always recuse themselves) and 723 (for clerical witnesses).

[58] Ganshof (1968), *Frankish Institutions*, at 10 (imperial power intensification of royal power, but little more).

[59] Robinson (1988), 'Church and papacy', at 295.

[60] Burbank and Cooper (2010), *Empires*, at 2, and 8 (contrasting the nation-state's proclaiming of the commonality of its people, 'even if the reality is more complicated'). For 'crossing and mixing' as well as 'separation and division', Jasanoff (2006), *Edge of Empire*, at 7 (as opposed to a contemporary situation where 'theoretical and ideological discussion of empire is prevalent but the willingness to engage and understand other cultures is not').

[61] Parsons (2010), *Rule of Empires*, at 448; and for partial explanation in terms of deficiency of imperial administrative systems, faced with already-organized communities, van Creveld (1999), *Rise and Decline of State*, at 49.

times the most obviously cosmopolitan of empires was the Ottoman empire, extending well into Europe by the fourteenth century and eventually approaching Vienna. The Ottoman empire was composed of a millet or nationality-based structure, a particular instance of Islamic recognition of non-Islamic laws on Islamic territories. It has been returned to recently by western writers discussing minority questions.[62]

In discussing empires as antecedents of contemporary states it should be recalled that empires would have existed not only as sources of persistent concepts and norms, taken over in contemporary states, but as states themselves.[63] They were 'composite' or cosmopolitan states,[64] the only kind of temporal governance available beyond chiefdoms or city-states.[65] Their state-like character is more evident if they are compared to some contemporary, recognized states such as India or Indonesia, with their diverse populations and laws, largely natural (or contested) boundaries, and federal or regionally autonomous structures. The boundaries of empires were not fixed everywhere on the ground, as is the case for at least some contemporary states, but there were markers, geographic boundaries, and local loyalties. Historical map-makers appear to have no difficulty in tracking their contours over time.[66]

Today the medieval empires have all failed, though the Holy Roman Empire came to an official close only in the nineteenth century. Their cosmopolitanism remains of interest, however, since it was replicated by the later empires within which contemporary states developed, some of these later empires lasting until well into the twentieth century. These will be returned to below,[67] after necessarily examining the remaining antecedents of the contemporary state, the city-state and the monarchy.

COLLABORATIVE CITIES

In their origins, cities were not municipalities subordinated to a single territorial authority, as they have become today. They had room to manoeuvre, and the designation 'city-state' captures both their importance and the relative autonomy

---

[62] Kymlicka (1995), *Multicultural Citizenship*, at 156–8 ('an important precedent and model for minority rights', 'legal traditions and practices of each religious group . . . respected and *enforced* through the Empire'); and for the general principle of autonomy of legal regimes in Islamic territories, see Ch. 13, under '*State and religious legal sources*'.

[63] For the 'state' designation, Burbank and Cooper (2010), at 8 ('Empire as a Type of State', implicitly recognizing a range of state forms); Muldoon (1999), *Empire and Order*, at 7; Horowitz (2004), 'International Law and State Transformation', at 447 (on Chinese, Siamese, and Ottoman empires as 'three old Eurasian states').

[64] For 'composite', Muldoon (1999), *Empire and Order*, at 7.

[65] Van Creveld (1999), *Rise and Decline of State*, at 58 (in the absence of any developed concept of a territorial nation-state); Muldoon (1999), *Empire and Order*, at 63 (virtually all attempts at large-scale government in medieval Europe imperial in nature).

[66] Google any empire you prefer, bearing in mind that the mapping of space, conceived as essentially empty or carte blanche, inviting control, is a western development following Mercator, crucial for the development of territorial states.

[67] See Ch. 6, 'Common Laws beyond Europe'; Ch. 8, 'Internationality and Empire'.

that accompanied it. In Europe, there were first the Greek city-states, a form of state perhaps dictated by the mountainous Greek terrain and the difficulty of wider forms of governance. Their cosmopolitanism amongst themselves has already been noted, notably in things legal.[68] While it existed elsewhere as well,[69] the city-state was reborn in Europe towards the end of the first millennium CE and survives today in places such as Monaco, Singapore, and the Vatican.[70] Some also see near-city-states in the 'global cities' that in some cases overshadow their own national territories.[71] Close to city-states, moreover, are some forty-five small-island developing states (SIDS), such as the state of Tuvalu (population around 10,000) that have formed an alliance for purposes of international relations (Alliance of Small Island States, AOSIS), notably in regard to climate change.

The medieval city-state was a privileged one, in the original sense of benefiting from a private law (*privatae leges*) exempting it from application of the general law.[72] The privilege was a concession from higher authority, either emperor or king, and the concession was not simply benevolent, but a recognition of the realities of the situation. Higher authority (in the absence of any state bureaucracy) did not have the means to regulate towns. With their privileges, cities could create their own law, becoming islands of particular law (*iura propria*) in the wider seas of imperial, royal, and common law, which retained only suppletive roles.[73] The other laws did not bind there, and we see in the law of cities a first and striking antecedent of the territoriality of state laws. In Germanic territories they were 'little empires within the empire', legally acceptable even in the absence of formal privilege because parties could by agreement or *pactum* derogate in some measure from Roman law.[74]

Cities understandably legislated in the interests of their inhabitants and from this activity came the freedom of the city. 'Stadt Luft macht frei' (City air brings freedom) was the popular expression of the legal principle that personal, feudal bondage disappeared within city walls.[75] What then followed has been described as the 'urban revolution' of the eleventh and twelfth centuries, a flourishing of

---

[68] Earlier in this chapter, under 'Early European Cosmopolitanism'.

[69] See Ch. 1, 'The State Tradition through Time'.

[70] For their development south and north of the Alps, in an 'urban belt' extending from Italy through Switzerland to Germany and The Netherlands, Scott (2012), *The City-State in Europe*.

[71] Sasken (2001), *Global City*.

[72] On origins, Nicholas (1997), *Growth of the Medieval City*, notably at 4 (for 'ferocity' of debates over causal theories, though since 'diverse city scape' theories not incompatible with one another); Rörig (1967), *The Medieval Town*; Friedrichs (1995), *Early Modern City*, notably at 44 (cities in return providing important political and economic services to higher order); Lepointe (1965), *Histoire du droit public*, at 58 (privilege by way of derogation from the common law).

[73] Glenn (2007c), *Common Laws*, at 16–17.

[74] Calasso (1970), *Introduzione al diritto commune*, at 67, 69; Picq (2005), *Histoire et droit des États*, at 104 (on recognition by Bartolus of primacy of fact of urban regulation).

[75] For origination of the principle and maxim in settlement recruitment efforts of towns in northern Spain in tenth and eleventh centuries, Nicholas (1997), *Growth of the Medieval City*, at 157 (then spreading in twelfth century to France, Flanders, Germany, England, often linked with residence requirement of a year and a day); Poggi (1978), *Development of the Modern State*, at 40 (prohibition not only of feudal law but of feudal jurisdiction; prohibition of duels).

horizontal, cooperative activities amongst equals within a small and defined space, which contributed greatly to the general renaissance of the time and to European reaction to Islamic science and law.[76] Aquinas was now writing, providing firmer ground for the earthly city.

In what respects were cities cosmopolitan? They were cosmopolitan both vertically and horizontally. They had first to work with multiple authorities recognized as superior, whether imperial, royal, feudal, or ecclesiastical.[77] Given commercial interests and peer city-states, they also worked with trading and legal partners, often at long distance and over differences of laws and language. It was the multiplicity of potential superiors that gave the cities room to manoeuvre in their vertical relations. The tension between empire and church has been noted above; outside the empire there were similar tensions between crown and church, neither excluding the jurisdiction of the other. In all cases emperor or king exercised some measure of authority over the feudal princes within whose territory the cities were situate. There was also ecclesiastical jurisdiction. Urban authority in a sense grew up in the gaps between these superior authorities, none having full jurisdiction or the wherewithal to come to grips with urban reality. As a counterweight to local feudal overlords, cities could look to an emerging national monarchy to provide a framework for trade, both locally and abroad,[78] and some measure of executive authority. In return, they even collected royal taxes,[79] so there was a real alliance of crown and town to the detriment of the feudal lords.[80] The latter were stronger in the territory of empire, given its decline, but here as well there was room to 'play off' the emperor against the princes.[81]

In horizontal relations there were extensive activities with other peer cities and city-states. These were predominantly commercial relations, sometimes intense, developing into entire networks of trade, and the major trading cities would have

---

[76] For 'urban revolution', Cipolla (1976), *Before the Industrial Revolution*, at 144 (also noting urban guilds, universities); and for the stimulus provided, Roberts (1997), *History of Europe* at 142, also at 105–7 (for Islam as the 'great threat of the age'); Landes (1999), *Wealth and Poverty of Nations,* notably at 240 (cities making 'all the difference', Russia, in contrast, tying people to land, 'a large prison'). Yet for freedom of cities as commercial monopolies, with close regulation of foreign traders, Kim (2000), *Aliens in Medieval Law* at 32–3.

[77] See notably Scott (2012), *The City-State in Europe*, Ch. 3, 'Cities and their Adversaries, 1150–1300'.

[78] Poggi (1978), *Development of the Modern State*, at 63.

[79] Harding (2002b), *Medieval Law and Foundations of State*, at 116 (towns 'central to the king's fiscal arrangements'); Spruyt (1994), *The Sovereign State*, at 105–6 ('royal and bourgeois interests converged on the issues of taxation and administration').

[80] For alliance, Rörig (1967), *The Medieval Town*, at 48 (strong monarchy surest protection against excessive demands by lord) and 63 (sacrifices demanded of the town used to overcome 'the hated feudal system'); Lewis (1971), 'Introduction', in *The Recovery of France*, at 19 (kings of France creating 'stable and oligarchical regimes' in towns, suppressing popular disorder, securing sources of revenue in cash and kind).

[81] For the language of playing off, van Creveld (1999), *Rise and Decline of State*, at 107, and 100, for greater influence of local nobility in the weakening empire (local nobility cooperating with great cities of Augsburg, Nuremberg, Strasbourg; merchant bankers not able to resist).

acted on 'world economic' presuppositions.[82] The Italian city-states of Genoa and Venice even developed their own Mediterranean colonies, in Palestine, Antioch, and Cyprus, and this as early as the eleventh century, preceding colonization by modern states by some four to five centuries.[83] The intense commercial activity generated various forms of law, the persistence of which will be seen in Chapter 3.

As with the earlier Greek city-states,[84] the European city-states and cities also exchanged law between themselves. The written, constitutive, and other laws of some individual cities, such as Magdeburg and Lübeck, became models for other cities (giving rise to designations as 'mother city' and 'daughter cities'), constituting ongoing relationships as opposed to one-time receptions.[85] We are even speaking here of territorial states having constitutions: written models of structured forms of government emerged here well before the state version in the eighteenth century.[86] There was much commonality of urban government structures from city to city, characterized mostly by the institution of an elected council, described as the 'constitutional form' that prevailed over earlier supremacy of the nobility.[87] The means of election varied greatly, however, and Friedrichs concludes that 'each city's constitution was unique' in spite of fundamental commonalities.[88]

The autonomy and partial closure of European cities was not to last, however, and the most challenging element of the surrounding texture was that of the European monarchy, with its rapidly increasing administrative capacity. Cites may have shaped the destinies of states through their financial control, but they were eventually to lose their political independence to those same states.[89] The cities would even have lost their place as fast as monarchies

---

[82] Rörig (1967), *The Medieval Town*, at 181; and for networks, van Creveld (1999), *Rise and Decline of State*, at 56.

[83] Verlinden (1954), *Précédents médiévaux de la colonie*, at 21–2 (also for Italians, such as Sebastian Cabot, subsequently playing major role in later colonial explorations).

[84] See earlier in this section.

[85] The mother cities would provide not only the initial model of urban law, but also ongoing advice in its implementation: Lück (1999), *Über den Sachsenspiegel*, at 56–8; Hattenhauer (1994), *Europäisches Rechtsgeschichte*, at 264. For mapping of influence of German mother cities, Nicholas (2003), *Urban Europe*, at 56 (law of Magdeburg spreading as far as western Russia). The process was not limited to Germany, however. For the municipal laws of Edinburgh, Aberdeen, and London as models for other towns in Scotland and England, Guth (2004), 'Law' at 91.

[86] Lanni and Vermeule (2012), 'Constitutional Design in Ancient World', at 912 (enactments not complete, comprehensive statements but 'first systematic attempt to set forth in writing the community's norms and institutional structure', later viewed as 'founding'); van Caenegem (1995), *Historical Introduction Western Constitutional Law*, at 74 (Italian 'municipal Constitutions' from eleventh century), with references.

[87] Rörig (1967), *The Medieval Town*, at 26.

[88] Friedrichs (2000), *Urban Politics Early Modern Europe*, at 11, 46 (and commonalities 'common to the constitutional structures of cities all across early modern Europe').

[89] Tilly and Blockmans (1994), *Cities and Rise of State*, at 8 (cities as 'containers and distribution points for capital', states as 'containers and deployers of coercive means').

developed.[90] The monarchies, however, were necessarily as cosmopolitan as the other medieval actors.

AFFIRMATIVE CROWNS

Kings and queens are well-known phenomena. About a fifth of the world's present states are monarchical in form (absolute, semi-constitutional, constitutional, sub-national) so we already know of the persistence of the tradition. We have been warned that they are not, and were not, 'the natural order of things' though much of the 'known world' was ruled by monarchs in the first millennium CE.[91] Given the events of the second millennium, there is now widespread agreement that of all the medieval European actors it is monarchy that was the immediate predecessor of the contemporary state.[92] It was a predecessor but not the state itself, since medieval monarchs encountered 'fierce resistance' and the unitary ideal was overshadowed by different forms of political plurality.[93] Crowns were affirmative, but there was much to be affirmative against, and absolutism turned out to be more theoretical than real.

European kings were cosmopolitan even in their own origins. To Germanic traditions of 'inherited charisma and election by acclamation' were added Christian anointment and Roman notions of authority.[94] Charlemagne was most visible in accumulating sources of legitimacy by seeking anointment by the

---

[90] Chevalier (1971), 'The Policy of Louis XI', at 293 (city leaders reconciling themselves to fact that king alone could ensure order). In France Colbert is seen as establishing royal tutorship ('tutelle royale') over the cities, this in the late seventeenth century: Lepointe (1965), *Histoire du droit public*, at 99.

[91] Wormald (2005), 'Kings and Kingship', at 571. Monarchy was also known in the rest of the world, as in South America and Africa; see, for the Aztecs, Margadant (1994), *Historia derecho mexicano*, at 27 (kings functioning with *curia regis*); Cruz Barney (1999), *Historia del derecho*, at 9, 10; for African forms, Sacco *et al* (1995) *Diritto africano*, at 97–102 (divine character based on Egyptian model).

[92] Van Caenegem (1988), 'Government, law and society', at 188 ('national monarchies were the bases of the new states'); Sueur (2007), *Histoire du droit public français*, vol. I, at 23 (state contained in seed form—'contenu en germe'—in monarchy progressively more unitary); Mayer (1963), 'Vorwort', in *Das Königtum*, at 6 (monarchy as crystallizing kernel—'kristallisationskerrn'—of the developing state).

[93] Vincent (1987), *Theories of the State*, at 85 (crown no standing army, necessary reliance on nobility and church, vast 'sub-life' of semi-independent towns, colleges, guilds); Given (1990), *State and Society in Medieval Europe*, at 258; King (1988), 'The barbarian kingdoms', at 123; and for even 'absolute' monarchy as an association, imposed largely by force, of 'differentiated, sometimes totally disparate communities which only a slow process of coexistence would forge, in the most favourable cases, into a common sentiment', Vives (1972), 'The Administrative Structure of the State', at 64 (warning against confusion between absolute monarchy and nation-state, even in France).

[94] Wormald (1999), *The Making of English Law*, at 444 (first kings of English relying on Roman model, but 'pervasive effect' of Carolingian example); Bendix (1978), *Kings or People*, at 23, 26 (election amongst descendants of military leadership) though cautioning, at 21, that '[w]e do not know how the belief in kingship originated' and suggesting, at 25, emergence from clan authority and word kindred. Lupoi contests the frequency of elections but accepts designation by consensus following nomination by a present king, or seizure by force: Lupoi (2000), *Origins of European Legal Order*, at 245. For fluctuation between 'genuine election' and 'mere acceptance of king already designated', Kern (1985), *Kingship and Law*, at 12. For the exceptional character of hereditary succession, Wood (1977), 'Kings, Kingdoms and Consent', at 15 ('marital practices' of Merovingians did not help to clarify royal lineage, speaking of 'dynastic confusion'). The Roman kings themselves traced their origins to Etruscan models: Kunkel (1973), *Roman Legal and Constitutional History*, at 5 (Etruscans also as mediators with Greeks), 13.

church as emperor, but kings had begun to 'move into an ecclesiastical atmosphere' by the seventh century under the Merovingians.[95] Charlemagne's father Pepin had been anointed as king of the Franks; the two swords were coordinating. The church then developed notions of kingship as sacral office, using Roman and Jewish models,[96] later to blossom into notions of divine right. We have already seen the 'infinite cross-relations'[97] between church and temporal authority from the perspective of the church, but crowns were no less cosmopolitan in their appreciation of religious and secular necessities. The church filled a bridging function, but bridges are necessarily built from both sides of the river. The bridging, and ambiguity, went on for most of what we know as the middle ages.

Crowns had many relations, moreover, beyond those with ecclesiastical authority. There was complexity everywhere. If the French crown was the leading example of royal authority on the continent, there were ongoing entanglements with the emperor to the east, of the germanic territories, which led to near-armed conflict between Louis VI of France and Emperor Henry V in the twelfth century. The retreat of the imperial forces has been seen as the origin of national sovereignty in France, after which relations with the empire became more formally diplomatic.[98] The king of France (soon followed by others) saw himself as 'emperor within his own kingdom' (*rex in regno suo est imperator*) and the idea of imperial authority thus came to be used against it. Both *de facto* and *de jure* justification for the maxim came to be articulated,[99] and some form of sovereignty over other temporal authority would thus have come to be exercised well before its later theoretical development by Bodin in the sixteenth century.[100]

If 'external' relations of the crown were coming to be recognized there was a remaining problem of internal authority. This presented itself both in terms of institutions and in terms of governing law. Institutionally the crown had to deal with territorially based princes; in the empire these even shut out the emergence of a single monarch. With the abdication of the Emperor Charles V in 1555 the princes would even have swept through the territory 'like raging boars',

---

[95] Wallace-Hadrill (1971), *Early Germanic Kingship*, at 47–8; Kaiser (1993), *Das Römische Erbe*, at 87 ('gradual' transition from Merovingians of religious foundation); and even for the sixth century, Kern (1985), *Kingship and Law*, at 35 (though precise introduction 'remains almost entirely obscure').

[96] Nelson (2006), *Making of Modern State*, at 32.

[97] Kantorowicz (1957), *King's Two Bodies*, at 193 (pope even adorning tiara with gold crown, emperor wearing mitre under crown); and earlier in this chapter, under 'The Church as State'.

[98] Van Caenegem (1995), *Historical Introduction Western Constitutional* Law, at 15. The diplomacy was not able to prevent further outbreaks of hostility.

[99] For *de facto*, Canning (1988b), 'Law, sovereignty and corporation theory', at 465, 468, with references; for *de jure*, relying on king's prescriptive acquisition of territory, Ullman (1988), *Law and Jurisdiction*, at VII–5, 14. For origins of the maxim as early as Azo in the twelfth century, Ullmann (1988), *Law and Jurisdiction*, at I–52, note 46, though for dispute over authorship, Bossuat (1971), 'The Maxim "The King is Emperor in his Kingdom"', at 185.

[100] Ullmann (1988), *Law and Jurisdiction*, at VII–14 ('modern concept of sovereignty had its birthplace in France'); Post (1964), *Studies in Medieval Legal Thought*, at 482 ('independence' from the empire had arisen); Strayer (1970), *Medieval Origins of Modern State*, at 53 ('sovereignty' of French king 'clearly established' by thirteenth century).

launching individual territories to near-statehood.[101] In France and England the single monarchs were more visible, but were constantly engaged in internal contests, themselves challenging the reality of sovereignty. The French king was originally one of many great nobles, required to collect his estate 'piecemeal' until a monarchy became recognizable, in a territory still far from that of contemporary France.[102] If internal authority increased from the fourteenth century this was often due to 'prior approval' by barons, a form of 'contractual sharing' of sovereign prerogatives.[103] Privileges of the nobility decentralized authority, even though acceptance of privileges carried an eventual price of loss of independence.[104] In England the Norman kings achieved a military triumph, but ongoing rule required maintenance of the old laws, while royal legislation, to the extent it occurred, fell to be implemented in local courts and, even in the royal courts, by local juries. There was no question of laying down a comprehensive royal law in the face of noble opposition.[105] Magna Carta was part of the process.

Nowhere therefore was the law governing the lives of the population a royal law. It was principally unwritten law or 'custom', as it is usually designated, that prevailed in variable form across royal territories. Royal legislation often purported to be a simple restatement of the substance of custom.[106] It gained thereby in legitimacy. The crown and its servants had to be knowledgeable about such local law, and respect it, but they could and did offer alternatives, more amenable to royal or imperial rule. There was of course much resistance to such modernization.[107] In the empire it was the reworked Roman law that became the

[101] Van Creveld (1999), *Rise and Decline of State*, at 100, 103 (principalities large enough to be considered more than private property of ruler); though for princes as less than absolute in seventeenth century, Krieger (1957), *German Idea of Freedom*, at 12 (divisive power of notion of sovereignty 'so graduated' as to be 'blunted').

[102] Van Creveld (1999), *Rise and Decline of State*, at 118; and see Lepointe (1965), *Histoire du droit public*, at 44 (for seigneur as 'cellule politique' in tenth century); van Caenegem (1988), 'Government, law and society', at 179, 181 (in late eleventh century, only discipline that of lords over peasants, continent living 'without legislation'); Picq (2005), *Histoire et droit des États*, at 93–4 (France in thirteenth century only federation of seigneuries, fragmentation of judicial power).

[103] Lepointe (1965), *Histoire du droit public*, at 7; Ellul (1956), *Histoire des institutions*, at 223 ('partage contractual des prerogatives de la souveraineté'); and for general need to *attract* adherence by granting of franchises, freedom, privileges, Landes (1999), *Wealth and Poverty*, at 37.

[104] Major (1960), *Representative Institutions in Renaissance France*, at 4 (even separate 'sovereign courts' for 'semi-autonomous' regions); van Creveld (1999), *Rise and Decline of State*, at 103 (from being crown's competitor, nobility turned into its associates; privileges more and more difficult to justify).

[105] For the old law, Glenn (2007c), *Common Laws* at 13, with references; and for dominance in England of feudal concepts, as opposed to theocratic ones in France, with corresponding fragmentation of authority and loyalties in England, Dyson (1980), *State Tradition*, at 52. For 'centralization' by Normans, however, Luscombe (1988), 'Formation of political thought', at 157. The Normans would have been faced with a 'tribal legacy' of Anglo-Saxon decentralized rule; Bendix (1978), *Kings or People*, at 178.

[106] Kern (1985), *Kingship and Law*, at 70, (purpose of the 'State' in Germanic territories to 'fix and maintain . . . the good old law'); though for custom operative only for matters fixed in the past, inciting crown to legislate for the future, Sueur (2007), *Histoire du droit public français*, vol. II, at 61.

[107] Strauss (1986), *Law, Resistance and the State*; Whitman (2003), 'Long Live Hatred of Roman Law!', (narrowly defined, materialist Roman law as inadequately reflecting Roman ritual, loyalties, morality); and for resistance even in Italy, city by city, Wickham (2003), *Courts and Conflict*, at 4, 11, 55 (Lucca 'firmly in a tradition of Lombard [feudal] law').

common law though, as a common or relational law, it yielded to particular laws, of cities and regions. In France the French 'droit commun' escaped royal control entirely and remained a doctrinal construction based on customs until the Napoleonic codification of 1804. Kings could only create specific ordonnances, and hopefully command their registration and adoption by local parlements. If this was refused the king or chancellor had to appear personally to require adherence, a potentially tense occasion (the so-called 'lit de justice' or bed of justice).[108] The common law of England was not the king's law but the judges' law, and the judges saw royal law or legislation as deviation from the common law, to be strictly interpreted.[109] Floating over these fields of 'internal' law was the attraction of various common laws across what are today recognized as national boundaries. There was probably at least some knowledge of Roman law in every jurisdiction in Europe, though its intellectual seduction was countered in France by explicit prohibition of its teaching in Paris in 1219, an early example of attempted legal information control, such as was later to lead to the Zitiergesetze (or citation laws) used to attempt to protect national codifications against citation of foreign law in the nineteenth century.[110] Ferocious doctrinal opposition also developed; affirmative crowns were supported by affirmative (though more knowledgeable) jurists, most notably Hotman as late as the sixteenth century.[111] In England relations with the Empire never approached open conflict, and the common law was notoriously resistant to substantive continental models. There was mutual influence, however, and civilian institutional presence in recognizably English courts. Legal information floated over boundaries, and could be used openly where it was felt useful to do this.[112]

Royal authority thus had to deal with many institutions and laws that were not its own—those of the church, of other crowns (including the emperor's), of the judges, of the people, of the scholars. There were also the cities, flourishing sources of wealth, technology, and law, which also had to be brought on board, through negotiation and alliance. This is a complicated picture, with no clear, vertical lines of authority. It was a world of multiple, interlocking unities, yet it generated normative content that was to last for centuries, and over vast amounts of territory.

---

[108] For opposition of French parlements to the crown, notably in refusing registration of royal ordonnances, Lepointe (1965), *Histoire du droit public*, at 111, in addition to legislative and judicial functions; and for their 'political role', Brissaud (1915), *History of French Public Law*, at 445; for royal resort to the lit de justice to overcome opposition, Ellul (1956), *Histoire des institutions*, vol. 2 at 310–11; Church (1969), *Constitutional Thought in Sixteenth-Century France*, at 150.

[109] For such particular laws or *iura propria*, Glenn (2007c), *Common Laws*, at 11 (distinction by fitzNigel, in 1177), 29.

[110] See Ch. 4, 'Codes'. For prohibition in Paris, though authorization for Orléans by 1235, Gaudemet (1997), *Les naissances du droit*, at 302. The prohibition was not that of the French crown but of a 'royally inspired papal decree': Ullmann (1976), *Law and Politics in Middle Ages*, at 103. The prohibition was lifted only in 1679; see Ch. 3, 'Institutional Cosmopolitanism'.

[111] For relations of the imperial *ius commune* and French droit commun, Glenn, *Common Laws* (2007c) at 20–5, 36 (Hotman as the most militant of anti-Romanists).

[112] For examples, and the debate, Glenn (2007c), *Common Laws*, Ch. 3 (influence of *ius commune* on the common law felt to be greater than the reverse, though citations of *ius commune* often seen as only 'ornamental make-weights').

3

Persistence

There have thus been antecedents to the contemporary state, all exemplifications of a broadly conceived state tradition and all irresistibly cosmopolitan in character. They were irresistibly cosmopolitan because there were no effective instruments of closure that could be put to use. Church, empire, city, and kingdom could not be separated from one another; they necessarily lived together. To the extent that we see historical struggle amongst them today, this too is evidence of their cosmopolitanism. There was necessary engagement; to say nothing of violence, which did erupt. It is not unknown today. Cosmopolitan coexistence did not preclude identity, however, and today we can still perceive differences of constitutive structure and belief. A church was not a kingdom, even where both prevailed in a given territory.

To the extent that more rigorous forms of closure were to develop that facilitated the contemporary state, these new forms of closure necessarily developed from existing structures and texture, in response to new, external forms of stimulus. Yet new forms of closure are 'constrained . . . by the historical legacy of previous closures', even if these are only partial.[1] In the language of tradition, it is always a case of decline of influence and never of radical elimination or *tabula rasa*. There is thus persistence, and the persistence here appears initially to be of two forms. There is persistence of the antecedents themselves, the institutions of church, empire, city, and kingdom, and we still know the reality or concept of each of these. Empires are no longer with us, but their disappearance dates back only half a century, and some have said new empires are emerging. The teaching of each of the antecedent states also persists, in the form of the normative justifications for, and the methods of, the activity they undertook. The argument of this book, however, recognizes no sharp distinction between institutions and their normative justifications and methods. The institutions live or die on the strength of such normativity. So in examining the persistence of the ideas underlying the contemporary state both previous institutions and previous teaching must be included. They are both normative, and normative debate is continuing, for example, between monarchists and republicans in various parts of the world.[2]

There is, moreover, a selectivity to the phenomenon of persistence. The French monarchy is gone, but the idea of sovereignty that supported it has had

---

[1] Lawson (2001), *Closure*, at 6.

[2] And for the need of earlier royalist and papalist writers to establish the 'instrinsic legitimacy for the systems of government they defended', Tierney (1982), *Religion, law and constitutional thought*, at 38.

a longer life. That which survives is that which is seen as most worthy of survival in particular, subsequent, settings. Choices will vary, so the variety of sources is one of the explanations for the variety of later institutions, and the variety of contemporary states. The emergence of the contemporary state has been described as a 'ramshackle affair', neither identical nor simultaneous from country to country.[3] It was 'never designed by anybody'.[4]

The antecedents that have been examined thus far have been those of 'early European cosmopolitanism' ending with the close of what are known as the middle ages. Since there is no obvious limit in time to the notion of the state, however,[5] there is no limit in time to the teachings that may have contributed to the contemporary state. Some would have the contemporary state originating in the Italian renaissance, some in the renaissance of the twelfth century and the investiture controversy, but the only test for sources of the contemporary state is that of persistence over time, and present vitality. Periodization fails if recognizable institutions and norms persist through periods, destroying radical notions of discontinuity. Halliday thus writes, on the writ of *habeas corpus*, that '[b]y writing across many centuries, I am looking past traditional chronological barriers... that block our analytic vision' and this is justifiable in the face of obvious persistence.[6] In looking for persistence we are thus bound neither by linear concepts of time that would distance or periodize past events, nor by the territorial, ethnic, and nationalist constraints of the nineteenth and twentieth centuries. It goes without saying, but should be said again, that the longer the regard the more sensitive we must be to distortion of meaning over time.[7]

What then has persisted since the so-called middle ages and what has been its effect? In very general terms we can look for persistence of ideas that sustained and supported the cosmopolitanism of antecedent states. If we still recognize them today we will know of their persistence, or at least of their significant revival. We must also be on the watch, however, for teaching that has contributed to closure, notably in the formation of the contemporary state. There has unquestionably been friction between the two.

PERSISTENCE OF COSMOPOLITAN WAYS

Cosmopolitan ways exist at different levels of human relations. At a very general level they may exist as a response to claims of unity or hegemony, and it is

---

[3] Dyson (1980), *State Tradition*, at 29.

[4] Oakeshott (2006), *Lectures in History of Political Thought*, at 3 (dependent on temporary and contingent enterprises, failures as well as successes); and for states understandable only in terms of their particular history, see Ch. 1, 'Degrees and Varieties of States'.

[5] See Ch. 1, 'The State Tradition through Time'.

[6] Halliday (2010), *Habeas Corpus*, at 3; cf. Berman (1983), *Law and Revolution*, at 4 (modern state having origin 'in the period 1050–1150 *and not before*' (emphasis in the original). For continuity through revolutions, however, see Ch. 4, '*Constitutions*'; and for the investiture controversy relied on by Berman as continuing through time, see Ch. 2, '*The church without*'.

[7] For the ways in which political theorists of the late middle ages 'adapt and modify to their own uses distinctions taken from an authoritative and traditional source', Gilmore (1941), *Argument from Roman Law 1200–1600*, at 3, given that, at 37, 'no sense of history intervened'.

possible to see much of western history as such a response, in reaction to an underlying view of the world perceived as unified.[8]

At the same level of generality they may exist as a response to a world seen as fragmented and diverse, as a means of constructing some measure of unity, or some measure of collaboration, amidst the diversity. At this level of generality, and difference in world views, the cosmopolitan ways are likely to be seen in the relations between and amongst what we see as institutions. Cosmopolitan ways may also exist, however, at more precise levels of human relations, for example in the choice of sources in particular areas of law, given existing institutional relations. We need to look therefore at the persistence of early cosmopolitan ways at multiple levels.

Institutional cosmopolitanism

Discussion of the antecedents of the contemporary state in the preceding chapter has shown that there were many of them, and that they coexisted at the same time in Europe. There was a basic, underlying idea, therefore, of institutional cosmopolitanism and this fundamental idea was undeniable whatever world view was adopted. The empire and the church are associated with notions of unity, and papal teaching on leadership came together with the teaching of Carolingian jurists in the idea of a *corpus Christianum*, of European dimensions.[9] Here, cosmopolitanism takes the form of reaction to this underlying idea of unity, and neither empire nor church was able to translate that underlying idea into an operative idea of legal uniformity. From the perspective of those resisting, unity did not exist, and cosmopolitanism was therefore a necessary feature of life amidst the diversity. Harold Berman thus concluded (and we therefore need not solve the problem of competing world views) that '[p]lural jurisdictions and plural legal systems became a hallmark' of law in Europe.[10] This underlying cosmopolitanism persisted, not only through what we know as the middle ages, but beyond, and Krieger has written of the 'undifferentiated cosmopolitanism' of even the eighteenth century.[11]

The institutional dimension of the unity debate is evident in the claim that European institutions themselves were subject to a single law, that of the empire, and that this single law was Roman in its origins. Even the concept of a public law is thus said to be Roman, and its spread throughout Europe would be a natural

---

[8] Puett (2006), 'Innovation as Ritualization', at 26 (for Chinese view of world as 'discontinuous and fragmented' with innovative goal of building continuity, as opposed to twentieth-century western view of innovation as 'the transcendental will breaking out of a confining continuity').

[9] Ewig (1963), 'Zum christlichen Königsgedanken', at 69 (for teaching of legal unity by Agobard in ninth century), 73 (for *corpus Christianum*); Halphen (1949), *Charlemagne et l'empire carolingien*, at 239–40 (for 'unité chrétienne', Agobard criticizing 'discordances choquantes' of multiple laws); van Caenegem (1988), 'Government, law and society', at 188 ('old' notion of Christian monarchy 'real source of inspiration' for 'revival of the state' in twelfth century); Ullman (1976), *Law and Politics in the Middle Ages*, at 90 (Roman law to be 'general and basic norm applicable to all mankind') and 78–9 for importance of teaching of Roman law in new universities to achieve this end, though 'tallied badly with reality').

[10] Berman (1983), *Law and Revolution*, at 268.

[11] Krieger (1957), *German Idea of Freedom*, at 4.

consequence of this.[12] It is unquestionably true that Roman law exercised influence at the institutional level, yet influence is always a matter of degree. Frequently statements of the importance of Roman law do not differentiate in terms of place and time, talking (for example) of the influence of Roman notions of public law on 'medieval institutions' or for 'the jurists' of the twelfth and thirteenth centuries.[13] Place is important, however, and geography and distance played an obvious role in controlling the level of influence. Roman law would thus have had much less influence in Scandinavian countries, where the Vulgate Bible became known later than elsewhere, and was therefore unable to do 'the spadework'.[14] John of Salisbury was a 'cosmopolitan Englishman' who relied on Roman public law in his writings,[15] and Bracton's writing in England in the thirteenth century shows familiarity with the language and concepts of Roman law, but the English monarchy would have acquired its distinctive characteristics well before the revival of Roman law, and there was ongoing resistance to the 'naturalization' of the Roman texts.[16]

The cosmopolitan reaction to claims of unity was most evident in the region we now know as France, which had been part of the Carolingian empire but which had assumed a more and more distinctive character with the shrinking of that empire. Roman law was widely known and widely influential in France,[17] but stoutly resisted, and the historical resistance has today reached polemical levels in French academic writing. For Blandine Kriegel the formal prohibition of the teaching of Roman law in Paris was but an indication of a much wider phenomenon of the rejection or 'relegation' of Roman law in general, a rejection that would be fundamental in understanding the genesis of the contemporary state.[18] For Kriegel, the rejection of Roman public law would have been justified

---

[12] For the origins of public law in Ulpian's notion of a *ius publicum*, eventually anchored in D. I.1.2, Stein (1999), *Roman Law in European History*, at 21 (indicating shift from that which could not be departed from by agreement to a notion of public authority); Friedrich (1997), *Geschichte der deutschen Staatsrechtswissenschaft*, at 11; Vincent (1987), *Theories of the State*, at 84; Ullmann (1988), *Law and Jurisdiction*, at 1–37 (public peace presupposed a united body); and for emergence of a 'theory of public law' by the twelfth and thirteenth centuries, Post (1964), *Studies in Medieval Legal Thought*, at 17, 19, 22 (also theory of 'the State'). For nuanced appreciation of 'general influence', Johnston (1997), 'General Influence of Roman Institutions', at 87.

[13] Post (1964), *Studies in Medieval Legal Thought*, at x, and 12 ('kings and popes' frequently appealing to Roman law); Pennington (1988), 'Law, legislative authority and theories of government', at 430 (for 'the jurists'); Kaser (1967), *Römische Rechtsgeschichte*, at 273 (Roman law deeply affected 'early middle ages').

[14] Ullmann (1976), *Law and Politics in the Middle Ages*, at 45.

[15] Van Caenegem (1988), 'Government, law and society', at 208.

[16] For pre-Norman roots, Wormald (1999), *The Making of English Law*; and for resistance to naturalization, Zeefeld (1969), *Foundations of Tudor Policy*, at 130 (this more evident by Tudor times).

[17] Vincent (1987), *Theories of the State*, at 84 (on notion of *merum imperium* or undiluted authority), Lepointe (1965), *Histoire du droit public*, at 20 (public law sources both Germanic custom and Roman law); Gilmore (1941), *Argument from Roman Law 1200–1600*, at 5 (for citations by DuMoulin, Charondas, Bodin, Loyseau to both Roman authors and later glossators).

[18] For the fundamental character of the rejection, Kriegel (1998), *Philosophie de la République*, at 70 (not simply 'maniacal obsession of scholars'); and for Kriegel's use of it, Kriegel (1995), *The State and the Rule of Law*, at 22 (against powers of church, empire, and seignories, which threatened 'fragile inroads' made by state). For the prohibition, and its lifting only in 1679, see Ch. 2, 'Affirmative Crowns'; and for the wider

both by its failure to have developed any notion of the state and for its failure to recognize the individual as a subject of law.[19] This justified innovation in France and the foundation of the French state on entirely different foundations.[20] The French developments would be similar to those of other western monarchies, however—notably those of England—and both France and England would have succeeded in rooting their versions of the contemporary state in their own historical and legal traditions.[21]

The vigour of French resistance to imperial claims and Roman law has overshadowed, however, an equally interesting form of resistance to Roman law, which is that which existed within the imperial territory itself. Roman law was contrasted with the 'good old law' and,[22] while the view has prevailed that a Romanist form of *ius commune* was received in German territory, this reception has been resisted more vigorously in matters of public law than in those of private law. The superficial use of Romanist concepts would not have undermined the substantive validity of underlying Germanic concepts. Perhaps the most famous defender of this view was Gierke, who saw Germanic notions of community as untouched by the law of 'unassociative' Romans.[23] Ulmann also saw in the Germanic Mund the underlying concept of German public law.[24]

This debate about finding the legal origins of the state in Roman or other law is striking for the range and provenance of normative information that was used. German authors divided over the relative influence of Roman and Germanic sources, both operative in some measure on imperial territory. French authors resisted Roman law in the name of a law increasingly recognized as French, and in the name of a French crown and French sovereignty, but it was Roman law that provided much of the theoretical justification for the French crown being autonomous from the empire and free to develop its own law.[25] The French king, it may be recalled, claimed to be 'emperor within his own kingdom' and it

---

sense of the prohibition, Saint Louis declaring that 'Roman law does not bind': Sueur (2007), *Histoire du droit public français,* vol. II, at 129.

[19] Kriegel (1998), *Philosophie de la République,* at 40 (citing also Augustine's rejection because of iniquity of slavery). For Kriegel's writing, in many volumes, Jennings (1996), 'From "Imperial State" to "L'Etat de Droit" '.

[20] Kriegel (1998), *Philosophie de la République,* at 70, 71 (justifiying later developments of Grotius, Hobbes, Spinoza, Locke, Rousseau) and in France, at 39 (of Bodin, Hotman, Dumoulin, Coquille, all denouncing Roman law with a 'male energy').

[21] Kriegel (1998), *Philosophie de la République,* at 63, 66, though speaking at 67 of England as 'state of justice' and of France as 'administrative state'.

[22] Kern (1985), *Kingship and Law,* at 149, 151 ('new law is a contradiction in terms').

[23] The word 'unassociative' would be that of Maitland; Barker (1957), 'Introduction', in Gierke (1957), *Natural Law,* at lix; and see Post (1964), *Studies in Medieval Thought,* at 10–12 (on different emphases on reception of Roman public law); Strauss (1986), *Law, Resistance and the State,* at 72–3 ('most jurists' rejecting Roman absolutist notions, favouring 'traditional constitutional role for their prince').

[24] Ullmann (1961), *Principles of Government,* at 133 (for *mundeburdium* or 'supreme protection' of the people 'inherent in theocratic king').

[25] Stein (1999), *Roman Law in European History,* at 66 (on Beaumanoir choosing to write in French rather than Latin in thirteenth century, and his reliance on Roman maxim that 'what pleases the prince has the force of law').

was a Roman imperial concept, known and used by French royalist jurists, that thus was one of the main instruments used to resist imperial authority. Blandine Kriegel thus opposes any single theory of state development in Europe, objecting to the idea of 'a single law, a single politics, and a single theology',[26] and Ertman has reflected on the difficulty of any single theory capable of explaining the variations in political, administrative, and financial structures within existing territorial states.[27] He rejects as a false dichotomy any distinction between absolutist and constitutionalist regimes, and proposes instead a multi-factor, causal explanation that includes the role and influence of local governments, geopolitical competition, and representative institutions, each of these, however, being highly variable in influence itself.[28]

States would thus exist as a result of particular interweavings of multiple strands of law and the differences between states would flow from the persistence of these multiple strands of normative information. Today we have some confidence in identifying the particular strands that have been significant in the formation of particular contemporary states, but throughout the middle ages there was no way of predicting ultimate influence. The jurists of then-existing institutions worked at a cosmopolitan interface between variable and sometimes contradictory norms, with no means of definitive inclusion or exclusion. That which persisted most significantly, over centuries, was this underlying institutional cosmopolitanism in the sense of multiple institutions. In the result, however, there was a form of institutional cosmopolitanism in another sense, which was that of the legal conciliation of the different institutions. There were wars, but they were wars largely between competing, similar institutions, between rival kings or adherents to rival religions. There were, however, no conflicts of laws as we know them today (with the exception of some cases between Italian cities, and there is doubt even of that), since boundaries were not sharply drawn on the ground, but existed only substantively between different domains of law subject to different institutional sources. Family law was thus governed largely by ecclesiastical law, across Europe, commercial law by the *lex mercatoria*, likewise, so that differences between laws were resolved by the interpretive methods still used today to establish subject-matter jurisdiction. Lawyers in a given territory were conversant with multiple laws, of different provenances. The multiplicity of jurisdictions prevails today, in the sense that the substantively defined jurisdictions of the middle ages have become the territorially defined jurisdictions of the present day. There has been no avoidance of multiplicity.

Given existing institutions and the diverse laws that supported them, there were also cosmopolitan ways within the laws that each of them produced or generated. This was most visible in the relations between the church and either emperor or crown, throughout the time of the Christian monarchs and the

---

[26] Kriegel (1998), *Philosophie de la République*, at 65; Kriegel (2002), 'Rule of the State and Natural Law', at 13.

[27] Ertman (1997), *Birth of the Leviathan*, at 4 (rejecting notably the idea that war has been the dominant force, as incapable of explaining different kinds of representative institution).

[28] Ertman (1997), *Birth of the Leviathan*, at 5, 6.

cooperating two swords. The osmosis between the two was not just a result of seconding learned jurists, but occurred at the level of the law that was developed and applied. Lay tribunals could borrow ecclesiastical law where their own was deficient in particular cases,[29] but this was only one example of the porous frontier between what came to be known on the continent as the *utrumque ius*, often translated as 'the two laws', working together, but more accurately seen as 'the one and the other law', suggesting both aggregation and ongoing distinct identities. Canonists drew on Roman law while secular law was in some measure 'theologized',[30] both in England and on the continent and to the mutual benefit of heavenly and earthly cities.[31] The church was said to live according to law,[32] but itself contributed greatly to secular forms of law.[33] This interaction persisted well beyond the middle ages, and church law has been seen as essential in the development not only of public law but of major areas of private law, notably contract, trusts, and property.[34]

The multiplicity of sources of law in a given field is also evident in matters of commercial law where the *lex mercatoria* emerged from proto-national commercial practice, developed and administered largely by commercial people themselves.[35] The *lex mercatoria* drew on Roman law,[36] commercial practice, local codifications emulated elsewhere, and from as far afield as Islamic law (notably for partnership and investment agreements for overseas ventures)[37] and Jewish law.[38] Where civil courts were seized with commercial cases they could and did draw on this known *corpus* of commercial norms. English commercial law is seen

---

[29] Lupoi (2000), *Origins of European Legal Order*, at 274 (citing charitable donations, wills, sworn relationships), 279 (conflation of sacred and secular).

[30] For the reciprocal processes, Tierney (1982), *Religion, law and constitutional thought*, at 14; Prodi (2003), *Eine Geschichte der Gerechtigkeit*, at 290 ('theologizing' of secular law as means of legitimation); Ullman (1976), *Law and Politics in the Middle Ages*, at 42, 44 (on Bible as 'inexhaustible source' of governmental thought after translation into Latin in fourth century, Bible itself infused with notions and language of Roman law).

[31] For detail and references, Glenn (2010b), *Legal Traditions* at 141–2, 239, 246, 270; and for mutual benefit, Loughlin (2010), *Foundations of Public Law*, at 23 (emperor treated as both king and priest, papal monarchy entrenched in Christian empire).

[32] '*Ecclesia vivit iure Romano*'; Ullman (1976), *Law and Politics in the Middle Ages*, at 41 ('large-scale borrowings'), 45 (Vulgate Bible as transmitter of Roman law), 54 (immeasurably 'in advance' of anything the 'illiterate West' had experienced, and advantage of being written in Latin).

[33] Nelson (1986), *Politics and Ritual in Early Medieval Europe*, at 67 (on lawyers using ideas of rebirth and renewal originating in the church) and 104 (for seeds of constitutionalism in ecclesiastical theory); and for rotation of concepts from Roman to church law and back, Tierney (1982), *Religion, law and constitutional thought*, at 25 (all parties drawing on a 'common pool of legal doctrines that they found both persuasive and useful').

[34] Glenn (1997b), 'Historical Origins of the Trust'.

[35] Trakman (1983), *The Law Merchant*; for commercial custom, Gouron (1993), *Droit et coutume en France*, at 185 (*mos mercatorum*).

[36] Stein (1999), *Roman Law in European History*, at 39–40.

[37] The Islamic partnership of mudaraba would thus have been the model for the Italian commenda or collegantia, used for financing the trip of a merchant and said to be at the origin of the western 'financial revolution': Hobson (2004), *Eastern Origins of Western Civilisation*, at 119–20.

[38] Glenn (2010b), *Legal Traditions*, at 127, 246–7, with references.

as benefiting from refusal to create separate institutions for foreign traders, in contrast to Ottoman experience.[39]

In the result the most general and persistent feature of the law of the middle ages is its openness. 'Legal unity was still not a goal', concludes Hattenhauer, given masses of law overlapping and interacting with one another and the absence of any general idea of a bounded legal system.[40] Authorities could thus be used and re-used with 'blithe unconsciousness of anachronism'.[41] Both periodization and closure were still centuries away. The cosmopolitan character of the law of the middle ages was evident in more crystallized fashion, however, in the two, mutually supporting concepts of constitutionalism and common law.

Constitutionalism

The institutional cosmopolitanism that prevailed throughout European legal history displayed the persistence it did because of the means that were deployed for mutual survival. In the collaboration of the two swords there is an underlying idea of mutual constraint and control. In the delineation of royal authority in relation to custom there is an underlying idea of limited jurisdiction. There was not only a 'dual pattern of authority' (secular and religious)[42] but multiple patterns of authority. Each somehow found a place in what was recognized as the world of law. Division of authority was fundamental to the middle ages; its instruments inevitably would be looked to as models within subsequent contemporary states. Absolutism is difficult in the face of competing and sustained visions of truth.[43]

The sources of what today we know as constitutionalism and public law were, however, multiple and varied.[44] Given imperial claims of unity, Roman law was inevitably looked to but, as has been noted above, its strength was variable throughout Europe and Savigny famously declared that Roman public law was not even received in the empire.[45] Roman law, moreover, was internally ambiguous. If some of its well-known maxims came down in favour of the unlimited power of the prince, an imperial legacy ('what pleases the prince has

---

[39] Klerman (2009), 'Emergence of English Commercial Law' (English courts using 'mixed juries' composed of both domestic and foreign traders).

[40] Hattenhauer (1994), *Europäisches Rechtsgeschichte*, at 326 (and for Carolingian law as 'not a system at all' since lacking any defence against, or even concept of, a 'foreign' rule).

[41] Nelson, J. (1988), 'Kingship and empire', at 213.

[42] Spellman (1998), *European Political Thought: 1600–1700*, at 72.

[43] For interaction as essential to constitutional theories, Tierney (1982), *Religion, law and constitutional thought*, at 10; for later assimilation of ideas and procedures generated by the debate between church and state from the tenth century, Graves (2001), *Parliaments of Early Modern Europe*, at 11; and see Prodi (2003), *Eine Geschichte der Gerechtigkeit*, at 284 (for absence of ultimate truth as essential to 'freedom and democracy'). Berman finds mutual limitation as the 'idea and reality' of a 'law State' (Rechtsstaat); Berman (1983), *Law and Revolution*, at 292.

[44] Loughlin (2010), *Foundations of Public Law*, passim.

[45] Von Savigny (1840), *System des heutigen römischen Rechts*, vol. I, Bk. 1, Ch. 1.3, p. 2; and for influence elsewhere, see this chapter, '*Institutional cosmopolitanism*'.

the force of law', 'the prince is not bound by the law'),[46] Roman lawyers had also looked to Greek justifications of authority and the idea of a 'mixed' constitution,[47] based on the ultimate consent of the ruled, was discernible in Roman juristic writing, often associated with an early *Lex Regia* that would have bestowed original royal authority.[48] This general Greek/Roman idea of the consent of the ruled would flourish in the middle ages, eventually yielding the notion of a presumed social contract,[49] but it was combined with use of more technical notions of Roman law such as the concept of *imperium* or authority and its rightful exercise. This even gave rise to a famous legal pun, in Latin of course, when the two jurists Azo and Luthair wagered on whether *imperium* could be exercised by lower magistrates. Azo said yes (implying division of authority); Lothair said no, and Azo bet a horse that he was wrong. The emperor awarded the horse to Lothair, unsurprisingly, but the community of scholars agreed with Azo, who therefore was right (*aequum tulerat*) though Lothair went off with a horse (*equum tulerat*).[50] The humour may have leavened the debate, though perhaps you had to be there.

　　There was therefore persistence of Roman ideas, but they inevitably came to be woven into the much larger tapestry of medieval constitutionalism, reflecting the variety of laws underlying the institutional cosmopolitanism. The church and its canon law contributed in the most general way with the notion of divine or natural law that necessarily constrained earthly authority, in some world. If the prince is not bound by the law, the law in question is only that of the prince; there

---

[46] Respectively *'quod principi placuit legis habet vigorem'*, D. 1, 4.1; and *'princeps legibus solutus est'*, D. 1.3.31; and see Kantorowicz (1957), *King's Two Bodies*, at 104 (on Roman law experts ruling out legislative power of the people in favour of the prince); Lintott (1999), *Constitution of the Roman Republic*, at 18 (on prince's authority as *merum imperium* (undiluted authority), though noting uncertainty); and for 'façade' of republican institutions during time of empire, Stein (1999), *Roman Law in European History*, at 14; Kunkel (1973), *Roman Legal and Constitutional History*, at 51 (republican constitution slowly deprived of breathing space).

[47] For the Greek sources, including both Plato and Aristotle, Spellman (1998), *European Political Thought: 1600–1700*, at 70 (on importance of Aristotelian revival); Johnson (1990), *Aristotle's Theory of the State*, at 155 (Aristotle 'deeply ambivalent'); Tierney (1982), *Religion, law and constitutional thought*, at 87 (Polybius, Cicero); Vincent (1987), *Theories of the State*, at 99 (even Plato arguing corrupting influence of single holder of power). The 'mixed' constitution would represent various combinations of aristocracy, monarchy, and democracy.

[48] Kunkel (1973), *Roman Legal and Constitutional History*, at 51 (jurists of imperial period, in second and third centuries); Ullman (1976), *Law and Politics in the Middle Ages*, at 56 (Ulpian); Nelson (2006), *Making of Modern State*, at 38 ('incipient doctrine of popular sovereignty'); Vincent (1987), *Theories of the State* at 84 (*potestas* and *ius* ultimately derived from the people); and for acknowledgment in the Digest, D. 1.4.1 ('by a *lex regia* the people transfer to [the Emperor] and confer upon him the whole of their own sovereignty').

[49] Post (1964), *Studies in Medieval Thought*, at 12 (Roman influence on Bracton's notion of consent of governed); Skinner (1978), *Foundations of modern political thought*, at 130 (consent as mere delegation and not grant or original sovereignty); Ullmann (1976), *Law and Politics in the Middle Ages*, at 56 (becoming major instrument for restriction of monarchic powers); Prodi (2003), *Eine Geschichte der Gerechtigkeit*, at 111 (tension between power and contract/representation theory); Gierke (1939), *Development of Political Theory*, at 100 (by sixteenth century social contract 'partially matured'); and see Ch. 7, 'France and the world'.

[50] For the pun Skinner (1978), *Foundations of modern political thought*, 127; and for *merum imperium* or full authority, Stein (1999), *Roman Law in European History*, at 59 (as absolute power to legislate); Berman (1983), *Law and Revolution*, at 289 (*imperium* and jurisdiction developing into notion of sovereignty); Vincent (1987), *Theories of the State*, at 84 (on sharing Azo's view).

remains a higher authority.[51] Put slightly differently, the law resides within the prince, who is prince only by virtue of it and who is therefore bound by it.[52] The church teaching was enhanced by church experience, and notably that of the conciliar movement, which grew out of the phenomenon of multiple, competing popes in the fourteenth and fifteenth centuries and the need for the church council to choose amongst competing authority, ultimate authority therefore resting below the papal level. The council would have acted rather like a 'feudal representative assembly'.[53]

Feudal notions of accommodation of authority also had a necessary place in the slow development of cosmopolitan constitutionalism. If unwritten law or custom filled the entire space of private law, or most of it, there was an implicit but very important limit on legislative authority. The good old law was not to be tampered with, let alone improved, made more rational, or more responsive. There was also a 'tradition de consultation'[54] and an ensuing 'right of resistance', feudal in origin and founded not on a notion of contract but on that of mutual fealty, anchored in objective law.[55] The unwritten law could even be taken as an expression of natural law, constituting fundamental norms that joined with canon and natural law to limit the sovereignty of the prince.[56] The controlling place of custom even achieved written expression, and the Sachsenspiegel of the early thirteenth century provided explicitly for rejection of unlawful acts by those in authority, and was widely emulated elsewhere.[57] There also came to be more specific charters, by which affirmative crowns were driven to acknowledge the need to treat subjects according to existing law. The practice would have begun

---

[51] Canning (1988b), 'Law, sovereignty and corporation theory', at 454–5 and 460 (no possible 'truly positivist theory of law'); Gierke (1951), *Political Theories of Middle Age*, at 93 ('unanimous agreement' that prince limited by natural law, reviving notion of mixed constitution); Church (1969), *Constitutional Thought in Sixteenth-Century France*, at 334–5 (preclusion of notion that might is right, though often neutralized by 'raison d'état'); Kern (1985), *Kingship and Law*, at 82 ('absolutism in practice never developed into absolutism in theory'), 115 (church's 'tireless opposition to royal irresponsibility'); Kantorowicz (1957), *King's Two Bodies*, at 105–6 (on emperor binding himself to law and reason, influence of Aquinas, with danger of 'reason of state').

[52] Congar (1963), *Tradition and Traditions*, at 190 (absolutism 'completely alien to the spirit of the age'); and for the scriptural authority, Kern (1985), *Kingship and Law*, at 97 (Acts 5:29 ('we ought to obey God rather than men')).

[53] Vincent (1987), *Theories of the State* at 86; Nelson (2006), *Making of Modern State*, at 46 ('implied...democratic model', Aristotle great ally); Tierney (1982), *Religion, law and constitutional thought*, at 2 (in conciliar movement proposing council to choose, implicitly proposing some form of constitution); Loughlin (2010), *Foundations of Public Law*, at 35 (papal authority not exceeding that of corporate whole; conciliarists challenging hierocratic power with sophisticated notions of representation); Picq (2005), *Histoire et droit des États*, at 125 (conciliarists nourished by nominalist ideas); and generally Oakley (2003), *The Conciliarist Tradition*.

[54] Beauthier (2007), *Droit et genèse de L'État*, at 287 (royal authority limited to what recognizable as public law).

[55] Kern (1985), *Kingship and Law*, at 129, 196; and for Coquille's notion of an implied division of sovereignty, Lloyd (1991), 'Constitutionalism', at 286 (customs 'true civil and common law', 'bedrock').

[56] Canning (1988b), 'Law, sovereignty and corporation theory', at 461 (on Baldus on the *Libri feudorum* statement of feudal law).

[57] Kern (1985), *Kingship and Law*, at 83–4 (though variety of expression and debate on application beyond kings to emperor); and for geographic expansion and emulation, Glenn (2007c), *Common Laws*, 37–8.

in Spain in the late twelfth century; Magna Carta followed in 1215. Here, we are now dealing not only with constitutionalism, but with written forms of constitutional restraint, and this is itself a 'legal tradition'.[58]

The combination of sources of medieval constitutionalism is perhaps best illustrated in examining a final, essential element of this constitutionalism, the idea of the inalienability of the royal domain. The idea probably received its fullest articulation in the writings of Roman and canon lawyers, thus in the one and the other law, and it would have constituted an essential part of the definition of *imperium*. That which was full or undiluted authority could be nothing other than itself, so alienation of a part was incompatible with the notion itself.[59] This rational construction was complemented, moreover, by feudal notions of the inalienability of land and holdings, evident in Carolingian texts and the basic structures of feudal organization.[60] The feudal dimension arguably diminished as land became generally alienable (e.g. with the Statute *Quia Emptores* in England in 1290, substituting sale for subinfeudation), but the underlying notion of inalienability of authority would have remained applicable throughout Europe.[61] It would have been common, which brings us to the related cosmopolitan notion of common law.

Common laws

There are different possible meanings of the expression 'common law'.[62] The Romans saw it as law of a single source that was uniformly applied in a territory, subject only to its own exceptions. The expression can also refer to law that flows from different sources but that contains common elements or produces similar results, as where the law of France and England reach similar results in cases of tortious or delictual liability through application of similar principles of fault of

---

[58] Van Caenegem (1995), *Historical Introduction to Western Constitutional Law*, at 70, 80 ('direct continuity' between such fundamental laws and contemporary constitutions and bills of rights); though for breadth and vagueness of restrictions, resulting 'legal maze', Kern (1985), *Kingship and Law*, at 123. The imprecision allowed subsequent creative construction, notably with *habeas corpus* being found within its broad language: Halliday (2010), *Habeas Corpus*, at 15, 16 (now joined to Charter in 'popular imagination').

[59] Riesenberg (1970), *Inalienability of Sovereignty*, at 3 (for Roman and canonical sources, king in position of trust), 5 (less than the sum of authority could not be passed on), 53 (for admitted exceptions), 79 (on importance here of Aristotelian idea of essence of things), and 81 (as essential element in construction of national monarchies).

[60] Riesenberg (1970), *Inalienability of Sovereignty*, at 10 (basic feudal antagonism between central and local power); and for Roman, canon and feudal sources, Pennington (1988), 'Law, legislative authority and theories of government', at 438 ('blending together to create constitutional doctrines').

[61] Riesenberg (1970), *Inalienability of Sovereignty*, at 5, 87 (for canonist carrying doctrine across frontiers, availability of articulating texts in monastic and Episcopal libraries throughout Europe), 127 (though 'slowness' of admitting in France given need to deal with feudal concepts); Kantorowicz (1957), *King's Two Bodies*, at 353 (clause of inalienability initially applied in England to tenants in chief, then transferred to coronation oath), 345 (Henry II in twelfth century, however, having to embark on revocation of alienations of Stephen, notions of inalienability still in 'formative stage', 'legal terminology limping behind the administrative practice'), 358 (non-alienation clause of coronation oath finally going 'on record' in England by early fifteenth century).

[62] On the following see generally Glenn (2007c), *Common Laws*.

negligence. Neither of these meanings conveys, however, the principal use that was made of the expression throughout Europe, which was to capture the nature of a law treated as common in order to distinguish it from a coexisting law treated as local or particular. The common law of England was that law of England that was not a particular custom, or the law of a particular city or fair, or the law of the crown. The *ius commune* derived from Roman law was a *ius commune* in relation to all of the *iura propria* of the imperial territories, again in the form of customary or unwritten law, the laws of cities and fairs, the laws (even) of particular princes and kings. This historical sense of common law treats it not as binding but rather as suppletive law. Put slightly differently, it is relational law, in the sense that it exists always in relation to another law and its application depends on the application of the other law. This application depended always on the claim to application or imperativity of the particular law, since common laws were not binding. Again, in the language of the new logics, common laws are non-monotonic in character, not constant and invariable in application but rather default or contingent. Germanic jurisdictions knew this principle most pithily, with the maxim that 'Stadtrecht bricht Landrecht; Landrecht bricht gemein Recht' (city law has priority over regional law; regional law has priority over common law). This notion of common law was one of the most important European legal concepts, and was an essential element in the reconciliation of laws, notably as populations spread into new territories and adjustments between old and new laws were constantly necessary.[63] It was also the case that a law was common not only in terms of its relations but in terms of its sources, so its existence required more than commonality of single texts or of results.

Common laws in this historical sense were therefore profoundly cosmopolitan; they had no autonomous existence of their own. Lawyers working with them were always, at least potentially, working at the interface with a particular law. Moreover, since common laws were not binding, their relations with other common laws were porous, and such relations existed, however insular particular individuals or professions may have been.[64] The concept of common law would eventually assume even greater importance when European laws expanded across the world from the fifteenth century and it is through the process of extra-European expansion that the multiplicity of the common laws of the world became more evident. The French too had a droit commun, and it became the suppletive law not only of France but of French territories 'outre mer'; the Spanish had a 'derecho commún' that floated over Spain, Latin America, and the Philippines; the Dutch had a common law that is now known as Roman Dutch law in South Africa and that is still taught in Indonesia. These common laws are known as such, however, in the field of what is known today as

---

[63] Hattenhauer (1994), *Europäisches Rechtsgeschichte*, at 326 (notably on local law prevailing); for population spreading, Luscombe (1988), 'Formation of political thought', at 158; Vives (1972), 'The Administrative Structure of the State', at 65 ('internal colonization'); and see Ch. 6, 'Common Laws beyond Europe', on reasons for mobility.

[64] On insularity in Rome, see Ch. 2, 'Early European Cosmopolitanism'; and in England Pocock (1987), *Ancient Constitution*, notably at 264 (on the 'common law mind (I shall not readily be persuaded that there was no such thing)'); cf. Glenn (2007c), *Common Laws* at 98 with references.

private law and, while private law is an essential part of the law of states, their experience does not translate directly into what we know as public law. Savigny, it was noted earlier, rejected the notion of an operative *ius commune* in public law matters,[65] so if the notion of common law has had persistent cosmopolitan importance in matters of private law, how can it be translated into public law?

The range and variety of contemporary states warns us against any notion of a single common public law or *ius publicum universale*. There is such a notion in German legal history, but it was essentially the law of the late empire, running from the sixteenth to the nineteenth centuries, and accordingly it was both too late for our present discussion and too territorially centred, in spite of its name.[66] The notion of common law might still be relevant for public law purposes, however, if its multiple instantiations are brought into play. Law may be common even though not universal. What is the relevance of the multiple common laws of Europe for public law, for ongoing institutional cosmopolitanism, and for the eventual emergence of the contemporary state?

If we take the common law of England as an example, its source was found in the decisions of judges and it existed in relation to, and in a manner suppletive to, both the regional and urban customs as well as legislation (all seen as particular laws). Moreover, even within itself, it developed no doctrine of *stare decisis* until the nineteenth century.[67] The common law was also, and remains, both public and private, and the two are inextricably bound together, perhaps most notably today in the submission of crown liability to the common law of torts (and not a separate administrative regime of liability as in many continental jurisdictions).[68] In the result, the public law origins of the state are conditioned largely by the common law, which has both private and public law dimensions. The common law recognized a law-making authority vested in the monarchy, but the law of the monarchy was largely that which was established by the common law.[69] There was thus an ancient constitution, and it exemplified the ancient notion

---

[65] See this chapter, '*Constitutionalism*'; and see Glenn (2007b), 'National Legal Tradition', at 2 (citing Brandsma that 'private law is the only field of law with a common tradition on the continent of Europe . . . that goes back beyond a couple of centuries').

[66] Stolleis (1990), *Staat und Staatsräson in der frühen Neuzeit*, at 16 (nevertheless with 'mountains of literature', known as Reichspublizistik, or today's Allgemeine Staatslehre). For at least one echo in the anglophone world, however, Bowyer (1854), *Universal Public Law*.

[67] Glenn (2010b), *Legal Traditions*, at 252, with references.

[68] Allison (1996), *A Continental Distinction*, notably at 169 (public/private law distinction 'has traditionally been unimportant and is now proving unsatisfactory'). For application of the law of torts, *Home Office v. Dorset Yacht Co* [1970] AC 1004; and for debate, Cornford (2008), *Public Law of Tort*. The question re-emerges in the basis of liability for governmental breaches of fundamental rights: see *Vancouver (City) v. Ward*, 2010 SCC 27, [2010] 2 SCR 28 (Supreme Court of Canada award of 'constitutional damages').

[69] Lieberman (2006), 'The Mixed Constitution and the Common Law', at 341 (citing John Cartwright in 1776 that '[t]he constitution is a frame of government coeval with, erected upon, and regulated by the spirit of the common law of England'), 342 (symbiosis between common law and mixed constitution), 345 (central institutions conceived as particular cluster of rights of persons, e.g. *habeas corpus*); Weston (1991), 'England', at 375–6; Vincent (1987), *Theories of the State*, at 85 (king as part of 'community of the realm'); Jennings (1959), *Law and Constitution*, at 109 (even today, '[i]t is . . . *common law* that Parliament can do as it pleases').

of a 'mixed', as opposed to absolutist, constitution.[70] If the English model holds elsewhere, the origins of the contemporary state, and the variety of them, can thus be explained by the operation of multiple common laws from which state structures were derived and legitimated. Thus the existence of states, as a common institution, would not be explicable as the result of a single common law, but from the interaction of different common laws with the particular laws, including crown law, of their territories of operation. Common institutions, or results, may derive from different laws.

This conclusion appears supported by the general manner in which royal authority was seen as subject to the 'objective' law of the community, on the continent not the law of judges but residual, underlying law, though there were differences in its definition. These underlying laws governed, notably, all private relations, but by necessary inference (since private rights could not be violated by public authority) that which we today call public law, so that as a concept public law emerged very slowly.[71] In France the 'droit commun' was in the form of a doctrinal appreciation of the multiple customs of France, a product both of informal society and learned synthesis.[72] Custom contained, however, an implicit principle of its respect by royal authority and the customs of France incorporated and gave authority to the 'lois fondamentales' that regulated the origin, exercise, succession, and inalienability of royal authority.[73] The crown

---

[70] Pocock (1987), *Ancient Constitution*, notably at 36 (on 'doctrine or myth' of ancient constitution), 38 (resting on assumptions 'fundamental to the practice of the common law'); Spellman (1998), *European Political Thought 1600–1700*, at 86 ('well before the emergence of the dynastic state'); Vincent (1987), *Theories of the State*, at 84 (power 'neither absolute nor constrained but diffused'), 92 (fundamental laws and custom treated as coeval); Lieberman (2006), 'The Mixed Constitution and the Common Law', at 318 (king, lords, and commons, as representing Aristotle's monarchy, aristocracy, and democracy), 319 (though competition with more absolutist accounts).

[71] For the absence or much later development of a concept of public law, Kern (1985), *Kingship and Law*, at 182 ('no special public law, no differentiation of public from private right'); and for various points of origin, van Caenegem (1995), *Historical Introduction to Western Constitutional Law*, at 2, 4 (seventeenth century, though no teaching in French universities until later eighteenth century); Asch (1997), *Thirty Years War*, at 20 (early seventeenth century); Stolleis (2001), *Public Law in Germany 1800–1914*, at 10–11 (late eighteenth century, early nineteenth century, 'finally triumphant binary division').

[72] Petot (1961), 'Le droit commun en France'; and for further references, Glenn (2007c), *Common Laws*, at 35ff.

[73] For inalienability, as a common element of monarchy, now visible as an element in various common laws, see this chapter, 'Constitutionalism'; and for custom giving their authority to the 'lois fondamentales' (having their source in pre-sixth-century unwritten law, codified in the Salic Laws), Ellul (1956), *Histoire des institutions*, at 232 ('[c]'est la coutume qui leur donne autorité'); Keohane (1980), *Philosophy and State in France*, at 27 ('virtually unassailable'); Kriegel (1995), *The State and the Rule of Law*, at 80 (legitimizing the monarchy); Lloyd (1991), 'Constitutionalism', at 270 (each law springing from 'established and ancient custom'); Sueur (2007), *Histoire du droit public français*, vol. I, at 76 (laws of crown 'revealed by custom'). Parts of the fundamental laws would have been drawn directly from private law, e.g. the idea of instantaneous succession from the private law of succession ('la mort saisit le vif'); Sueur (2007), *Histoire du droit public français*, vol. I, at 105–6. The ensemble of fundamental laws and customs are seen (at least now) as constituting a 'veritable constitution': Sueur (2007), *Histoire du droit public français*, vol. I, at 115, or as a 'customary constitution': Kriegel (1995), *The State and the Rule of Law*, at 80. French high courts, or parlements, could remonstrate, moreover, with royal authority through delaying registration of royal ordonnances, though never explicitly challenging royal authority: Lemaire (1907), *Lois fondamentales*, at 213 ('interminable remontrances', moderator of sovereignty through means of *free* registration (*libre* enregistrement)

here, as in England, could be the source only of a particular law. In Germany the thirteenth-century Sachsenspiegel, the written compendium of Saxon unwritten law, was part of 'German common law' (gemeindeutsches Recht), a pan-German common law just below the level of the *ius commune*, and it clearly extended to the exercise of feudal authority (Lehnrecht) as well as private legal relations.[74] Here too feudal custom presented itself as fundamentally normative, an implicit but important limit on princely authority.[75] In Spain the Castillian Siete Partidas, containing both public and private law, became a common law throughout both Spain and what was to become Latin America.[76] As elsewhere it both structured and legitimated subsequent forms of public authority, both authorizing the local fueros and drawing support from them, as a residual source.[77]

Understanding the importance of cosmopolitan common laws in the development of national legal traditions allows us to situate commonalities and differences within a larger framework. There have been and are many commonalities, but they exist within the unique combinations of common and particular laws that have given rise to particular states. Commonalities are of great interest and should perhaps be applauded wherever they are found, like diamonds in the rough, but they represent only a very small part of what a uniform law might be. The crowns were common throughout Europe and they both made crown law and were surrounded by other laws, supporting and limiting them. Lupoi has therefore argued for a 'European common law in relation to the institution of kingship' and defines such a common law in terms of the 'shared *principia* and *regulae*' that can be seen as defining the institution.[78] That there was considerable substantive commonality amongst the laws of the crowns of Europe seems unquestionable, and much of the existing literature on kingship is unmindful of today's national boundaries and even of many local particularities. It is pan-European in character and comparative in the sense of identifying commonality.[79] Yet, as European legal history has been understood for centuries, there was

<hr />

(emphasis in original)); Moote (1971), *The Revolt of the Judges*, at 11; Hardy (1967), *Judicial Politics in the Old Regime*, at 17; and for use of 'fundamental laws' in English constitutional history, particularly in the seventeenth century, Gough (1955), *Fundamental Laws in English Constitutional History*.

[74] Glenn (2007c), *Common Laws*, at 38, with references.

[75] *The Saxon Mirror*; Kern (1985), *Kingship and Law*, at 91 (on difficulty of destroying a custom that prince had promised to observe), 190 (on royalty subject to 'pre-existent objective law which is the sum of every freeman's subjective rights'); Canning (1988b), 'Law, Sovereignty and Corporation Theory', at 461 (custom perceived as revelation of natural law; and for law understood as a 'framework' as opposed to an instrument of power, Poggi (1978), *Development of the Modern State*, at 72.

[76] For the text, in a new edition, Burns (2000), *Siete Partidas*.

[77] Grandon (2000), *Historia derecho indiano*, at 203; Lalinde Abadia (1983), *Derecho histórico español*, at 129–30; Gibert (1968), *Historia derecho español* at 53.

[78] Lupoi (2000), *Origins of European Legal Order*, at 4, 237, though see 241 for the 'variety of forms' of succession to kingship.

[79] Lupoi (2000), *Origins of European Legal Order*, notably at 237 (for reception in kingships of institutions of late-medieval Rome, though acknowledging differences applying to the Anglo-Saxon, Saxon, Thuringian, Frisian, and Aleman peoples, and the Celtic monarchies of Ireland and Wales), 240 (for 'single frame of reference' only after several centuries; Kern (1985), *Kingship and Law*; Wood (1977), 'Kings, Kingdoms and Consent'; Wallace-Hadrill (1971), *Early Germanic Kingship*, at 35 (early influence of Visigothic law,

no common law of kingship since there was no common source of such a law and the law of kings constituted a particular law within the respective common laws. Each kingship has thus been a unique institution, the combination of its local law, its common law, and (perhaps in some measure) other common laws.[80]

There are other common features of the constitutional traditions of Europe. Picq provides a list of such common elements including a concept of church–state relations, separation of powers, law indigenous to each state, and parliamentary assemblies.[81] Each of these, however, differs from how it is understood elsewhere, since there has been no common source of any of them. Parliaments grew out of informal processes of consultation between crown and subjects. The participants differed greatly and the differences grew as the more and more nationally distinct institutions developed. Some were organized, as often on the continent, according to a principle of representation of estates; others were not.[82] Some were consulted frequently; others not.[83] Some judged, some advised, some legislated.[84] If they became visible between the twelfth and the fifteenth centuries, their roots can be traced to centuries earlier, to a time of unwritten law and prior to the 'rediscovery' of Roman law.[85] There can thus be 'parallels' in the development of the French and English parliaments, but the resulting diverse institutions have different and varied roots.

Institutional cosmopolitanism, its accompanying constitutionalism, and multiple common laws thus persisted through the middle ages. The antecedents to the contemporary state were deeply cosmopolitan in nature. In these antecedents and their relations, however, there were elements of closure that eventually contributed greatly to the emergence of the contemporary state. What we know

close parallels with Kentish law), 38 (on widespread borrowing of 'barbarian' laws), 98 ('fairly sophisticated thinking' from later eighth century, such opening marked by incursion of Arabs into southern France), 109 (common political situations leading to comparable ideas); Ewig (1963), 'Zum christlichen Königsgedanken', again pan-European in character; Brunner (1963), 'Vom Gottesgnadentum', at 286 (comparing European with African kings).

[80] For criticism that 'far too much political narrative of the early middles ages homogenizes political structures, making all kings pretty much the same', Wickham (2005), *Framing the Early Middle Ages*, at 56.

[81] Picq (2005), *Histoire et droit des États*, at 20.

[82] For the estate principle in France, Castile, and Aragon, Nicholas (1999), *Transformation of Europe 1300–1600*, at 66; yet for there being no estate model from which England deviated, Graves (2001), *Parliaments of Early Modern Europe*, at 27 ('many variations in the structure, organisation and composition of medieval European representative assemblies' during development from thirteenth to fifteenth centuries').

[83] For Edward I summoning Parliament more than forty times in the twenty years from 1274 to 1294, Graves (2001), *Parliaments of Early Modern Europe*, at 18; and generally for the effect of distance on frequency of meeting, Stasavage (2010), 'When Distance Mattered', notably at 642 (assembly may have assisted in raising taxes, but itself depended on ongoing transaction costs, those of 'collecting, processing, and acting on information').

[84] For opposition of French parlements to the crown, and for royal resort to the lit de justice to overcome opposition, see Ch. 2, 'Affirmative Crowns'.

[85] Graves (2001), *Parliaments of Early Modern Europe*, at 7 (as products of 'established socio-political system'), 30 ('kaleidoscope' rather than 'pattern'), though at 8 for later influence, through the ecclesiastic channel, of Roman maxim *quod omnes tangit, ab omnibus approbatur* ('what touches all shall be approved by all'); and for origins of English parliament well before thirteenth century origins of the word (from the original French), Maddicott (2010), *Origins of the English Parliament*, at 3, 4 (origins in tenth century witan or assembly of wise, emerging with the then 'newly unified English state').

as the state drew heavily on these elements of closure, which came in some instances to dominate state structures. At the same time, as we will eventually see, the cosmopolitan ways could not be radically eliminated. Closures are always partial and limited in time, given surrounding texture.

PERSISTENCE OF ELEMENTS OF CLOSURE

Which elements persistent through the middle ages, and beyond, were most significant in the closure inherent in contemporary states? Some explanations are causal in character, suggesting a role for material factors, or for preparation for war.[86] There may be some truth in these explanations, but the normative tradition of the state is one that was guided by a number of fundamental ideas, not necessarily those of high theory but ideas that provided normative justification or legitimation for the emergence of contemporary state structures. These may be tentatively identified as writing, hierarchy, and boundaries. By necessary implication they all suggest some form of closure.

Writing

Writing was by now widespread across legal traditions, and is even found in some instances in contemporary customary law, as with the written version of the Iroquois Longhouse People.[87] Yet through the middle ages the oral or written form of laws was perhaps the most controversial question of all, since change from the former to the latter implied a dramatic shift in the source of legal authority, from the people however defined to the holders of the pen. Lupoi states that medieval Europe was a place of 'primary orality' until the fifth century CE, while Rome before it had known 'absolute predominance' of orality until the second century BCE.[88] In both instances there was therefore a major task of displacement before law could come to be recognized in written form. We have already observed the resistance to Roman law in France and Germany and much of the resistance was inevitably due to its written form.[89] It was not the 'good old law'.

Arguably, in itself writing is not a form of closure, since anything can be written and, in principle at least, anything can be read. Yet writing has played a significant role in the closure that has been brought about in contemporary states because of its combination with the other elements of closure discussed in this section. Writing is open, but writing as an instrument of hierarchy within fixed boundaries becomes an instrument of closure. The law comes to be seen as that which is found in the writing, and in certain particular kinds of writing only.

---

[86] See Ch. 4, *'Organizational success'*.

[87] *Great Law of Peace* (1977) (this in spite of ongoing opposition to redaction of unwritten law); and for dating to twelfth century, Mann (2005), *1491/Ancient Americans*, at 333.

[88] Lupoi (2000), *Origins European Legal Order* at 24–5 (Europe of 'primary orality' until fourth and fifth centuries).

[89] Earlier in this chapter, *'Institutional cosmopolitanism'*.

As early as the twelfth century the claim was made by Azo that no texts outside of the *Corpus Juris* could be cited as authority, and the fixation on this particular text has been said to have contributed more than anything else to creating an autonomous discipline of law during the twelfth century.[90] Important as the written form of Roman law has been, however, it is Greece that provided the first European model of the written, and even constitutional, text. We see in the city-states of ancient Greece the first states with written constitutions, and if the texts were multi-purpose they clearly dealt with structures of government.[91] Roman lawyers owed both their notion of rationality in law, and its written form, to the Greeks, though by the fall of the Roman empire it was the Roman model that was most widely known. Written law was then produced by the 'barbarian' leaders, arguably first by Visigothic rulers in the fifth century CE, and Buchner has referred to the 'foundational importance' of Merovingian kings adopting writing as the technical means of 'state direction' ('Staatsfuhrung').[92] Clovis produced the *Lex Salica*, a 'wholly pagan code' though largely in Latin, the language of written learning.[93] Under Charlemagne the laws or charters grew to such lengths they had to be divided into chapters (hence capitularies) and the ancient idea of simply stating existing law began to be departed from openly.[94] Here would be the origin of a major tradition to 'refashion society'.[95] After Charlemagne the royal charter prevailed as the 'principal instrument of government' and Ullmann wrote of the 'rule *of* law *by* kings' (emphasis added).[96] In the British Isles the notion of simply restating the good old law may have held longer sway. Aethelbert's laws in the ninth century could still be said to have 'recorded customs that were old and new, and sometimes contradictory' though the king, by 'causing them to be written, makes them his own'.[97] His successor Albert, however, acknowledged that he was 'renovating and amending existing law'.[98]

With the Greek/Roman example, followed with varying intensity by early medieval royalty, a full flowering of legal writing was perhaps inevitable in the

---

[90] Ryan (2010), 'Succession to Fiefs', at 143, citing E. Landsberg, *Die Quaestiones des Azo* (1888) at 74.

[91] See Ch. 2, 'Collaborative Cities'.

[92] Büttner (1963), 'Anfängen des abendländischen Staatsgedankens', at 149 (a 'meaningful step towards a higher form of state organization'); and for codex of Visigoth king Euric in late fifth century, Wallace-Hadrill (1971), *Early Germanic Kingship*, at 33.

[93] Wallace-Hadrill (1971), *Early Germanic Kingship*, at 36 ('*Lex Salica* was as active as yeast').

[94] Ullmann (1969), *The Carolingian Renaissance*, at 30 ('first-class transformative agents'), and 46 (*Capitulare* of 790 itself stating that enacted law may do away with customary law, a first legislative bootstrap operation).

[95] Ullmann (1969), *The Carolingian Renaissance*, at 7 (though actual doctrines to do so 'differ radically').

[96] Ullmann (1976), *Law and Politics in the Middle Ages*, at 209 (charter re-emerging after disorder of break-up of Carolingian regime).

[97] Wallace-Hadrill (1971), *Early Germanic Kingship*, at 37, 44 (lawbooks as 'modest political manifesto . . . binds together . . . the mixed peoples of Kent'); and for royal pronouncements in Francia in the eighth and ninth centuries some ten times more frequent than in England in the tenth and eleventh, Wormald (1999), *The Making of English Law*, at 480.

[98] Wormald (1977), '*Lex Scripta* and *Verbum Regis*', at 110 (paraphrasing Justinian); though for recorded law in middle ages always being deemed to be merely 'a fragment' of existing customary law, Kern (1985), *Kingship and Law*, at 167 (capitularies pointing to unwritten law as criterion to be followed).

European renaissance (and reaction to Islamic science and law) of the twelfth and thirteenth centuries. The fullness of Roman legal writing was re-appreciated, if not precisely rediscovered,[99] and vast literatures began to be accumulated, both in the form of glosses on the Roman texts and as statements of local law (Glanville in England, the Sachsenspiegel in Germany, Beaumanoir's *Coutumes de Beauvaisis*, the Welsh Hywel Dda).[100] Gratian undertook his *Concordance of Discordant Canons*.[101] The proliferation of writing was the external sign of a discovery, or rediscovery, of the real-world importance of human learning and rationality. The clerics were its instrument, responsible for the greater part of the new literature and, in England, for much of the early work of the common law courts. They were able to put to use both the abstraction and precision of the Latin language and the binary and syllogistic forms of logic that the recovery of Aristotle's writing made available once more.[102] The writing produced, and its content, was able to provide structure to the hierarchy that needed it.

Hierarchy

Kings were to produce the contemporary state, but kingship did not in itself imply a vertical structure or hierarchy of authority. In their origins kings were much dependent on others, both for election and for ongoing support.[103] Their territories were relatively limited. The emergence of a 'descending theme' of government and law has been located by Ullmann with Charlemagne, and what Charlemagne accomplished was the union of royal authority with ecclesiastical anointment.[104] The king became emperor, and shared divine authority with the pope at the head of what had been recognized for centuries as an organized church, with its own law.[105] The king could not be less hierarchical than the pope. It appears to be the pope that made the difference, since other monotheistic

---

[99] For the extent of discontinuity, Glenn (2010b), *Legal Traditions*, at 134 with references.

[100] Harding (2002b), *Medieval Law and Foundations of State*, at 191.

[101] See Ch. 2, 'The Church as State'.

[102] For the clerics, Ullmann (1969), *The Carolingian Renaissance*, at 11, 28 (supplying 'legal instruments'); for importance of scholastic, abstract Latin in the development of western science, Ong (1982), *Orality and Literacy*, at 113, 114; and for the logic, Errera (2007), 'The Role of Logic', at 81–4 ('the Dichotomous Technique'). The monks of Ireland would have done much to preserve the writing during the early ages, when literacy became near-extinct elsewhere in Europe: Lupoi (2000), *Origins European Legal Order*, at 131 ('[t]he Irish did not merely conserve the classical heritage, they enriched it'); and for mythical character of Irish contribution, though acknowledging 'the true originality and creativity of Irish Christian culture at that time', which 'created something new', Brown (2003), *Rise of Christendom*, at 240.

[103] For election and ongoing resistance, see Ch. 2, 'Affirmative Crowns'.

[104] Ullmann (1969), *The Carolingian Renaissance*, at 10 ('descending theme' as 'conceptual component of the Renaissance of Frankish society'); and see Ewig (1963), 'Zum christlichen Königsgedanken', at 21 (for Christian accent on role of leader from seventh century). For the hierarchical apparatus of church which 'tended to become the perfect prototype of an absolute and rational monarchy', Kantorowicz (1957), *King's Two Bodies*, at 194; and for the use of Roman imperial notions to explain 'plenitude' of papal authority, Tierney (1982), *Religion, law and constitutional thought*, at 14.

[105] For the scriptural authority of the pope's position, see Ch. 2, 'The Church as State'.

religions such as Judaism and Islam developed no such hierarchical structures, and exist today with no central authority.[106]

Vertical structures, however, need coherence, or buttresses, or some form of shoring up. In the case of both church and monarchy, and eventually the state, this coherence or support was provided by a type of abstraction, and hence continuity, of the institution. There were, however, differences in the form of the abstraction, and differences in the timing of its emergence. This is consistent, of course, with the notion of a tradition of the state, the notion of a tradition being tolerant of internal contradiction and not dependent on consistency. In the diversity of types and forms of abstraction of the state we see the influence of the diverse common laws that have contributed to its formation, and differences in theoretical appreciation. Practice, moreover, may here again have preceded theory.[107] Kantorowicz states that 'in general' it was the case that 'theory followed existing practice' in ensuring continuity of authority, and that an early manifestation of the practice was found in the kings of France and England assuming authority on the day their predecessor was buried and not on the day of coronation, this in the thirteenth century.[108] Already in the seventh century, however, Lupoi finds in Visigothic law a notion of perpetual kingship, separate from the person of the king, though whether this was simply a practice of necessity or some form of theoretical construction is unclear.[109] Roman law was available for possible use, and Roman law had a collective notion known as a *universitas*, used mostly for purposes of succession to property but available in some measure to describe a group. It was not defined, but could prove useful in terms of allowing groups to be represented in court, or to allow one of the group to bind the others. It has been described as 'a piece of grammar, not a social entity',[110] but it was at least a vocabulary that could be put to subsequent use. The question then became what a *universitas* or corporate person actually was, since there were 'hundreds of variations' possible and the debate about them goes on to this day.[111]

---

[106] See Ch. 2, 'The Church as State'. Cf., for what would be inappropriate Christian reliance on 'monotheism', Ullmann (1976), *Law and Politics in the Middle Ages*, at 34 (monotheism 'powerful agent in the promotion of monarchic ideas'); Kern (1985), *Kingship and Law*, at 8 ('monotheism and monarchy supported each other'). Kantorowicz more precisely pointed to the hierarchical apparatus of the 'Roman Church' as the prototype of an 'absolute and rational monarchy': Kantorowicz (1957), *King's Two Bodies*, at 194.

[107] For a 'fact' of sovereignty preceding its theory, see Ch. 1, 'Readings of the State Tradition', and more generally for the relations of theory and practice, see Ch. 9, 'Cosmopolitan Theory'.

[108] Kantorowicz (1957), *King's Two Bodies*, at 9, 301 (thus abolishing the 'little interregnum'). By the sixteenth century this had become the popular cry 'le roi est mort, vive le roi!'), as to which see Ch. 4, '*The state as body, crown, or corporate person*'.

[109] Lupoi (2000), *Origins of European Legal Order*, at 246 (citing the Eighth Council of Toledo).

[110] Gilby (1953), *Philosophy and Theology of the State*, at 246 (equating medieval acceptance as 'mere collective name for . . . partners'); and for failure of Greek and Roman law to develop 'abstract' notion of state distinct from citizens, van Creveld (1999), *Rise and Decline of State*, at 57.

[111] For the variation, Tierney (1982), *Religion, law and constitutional thought*, at 26 (Roman law relying more on principle of delegation, later canon law more complex, relying more on notions of inherent jurisdiction of internal offices); and for ongoing contemporary debate on the 'endless' problem, see Ch. 4, '*The state as body, crown, or corporate person*'.

An apparently common point of departure would have been recognition of a group as a spontaneous social product, requiring no intervention of authority or formal grant. The analogy is with a family or partnership; ownership is seen as joint and the rights of the whole are bound up with the rights of the individual members.[112] The original Roman notion of the *universitas* is not incompatible with this underlying view. Probably the simplest expression of it was to recognize the group as a 'body', known as such and demonstrable by its existence and activity. The word 'corporation' is even derived from this basic proposition, from the Roman *corpus* or body. Linguistically, this variation appears most prominent in English and in the common law notion of the king's two bodies, the physical and the mystical, the personal and corporate.[113] The language of the body politic is drawn from this, a process of being 'bodified'.[114] Maitland criticized even this as 'metaphysical nonsense',[115] but the language was constant over centuries. The English and the French also used the language of the crown, another attempt to seize the metaphysical through metaphor, and which in the case of England and the Commonwealth has lasted through centuries.[116] The crown is invisible, but not less useful for that.

On the continent the Roman notion of an (unstructured) *universitas* drew theoretical attention, particularly that of the canonists, who were charged with providing coherence to a hierarchical structure that had emerged over centuries. By the thirteenth century groups were being treated as distinct from their members and in mid-century Pope Innocent IV used the language of a *persona ficta*, though still without a developed justification.[117] The language of a fiction is important, since fictions are distinct from underlying group reality and can be seen as requiring creation or authorization. Unity would be imposed from

---

[112] Gilby (1958), *Principality and Polity*, at 251 (no accreditation by political and legal theory with 'a soul of its own'): Kantorowicz (1957), *King's Two Bodies*, at 270 (on 'state' in 1300 not as a 'fictitious person' but as an 'organic or organological whole', not existing apart from its members); Ullmann (1988), *Law and Jurisdiction*, at IX–397 (on Marsilius in the early fourteenth century thinking of sovereign corporation essentially as 'an association or a community of persons . . . a Personenverband', thinking rooted in 'old-Germanic ideas of corporate bodies').

[113] Kantorowicz (1957), *King's Two Bodies*, notably at 270 (distinguishing language of *corpus* from that of *persona*, and state as simply 'bodified'). The process also occurred on the continent; for emperors and kings as soul and brain, others as simple limbs of the body, in King Alfonso's Siete Partidas of the thirteenth century, Bertelli (2001), *The King's Body*, at 10.

[114] Kantorowicz (1957), *King's Two Bodies*, at 270–1.

[115] Kantorowicz (1957), *King's Two Bodies*, at 3, 449 (Maitland joking that English king being 'parsonified', by analogy to representative status of village parsons) and 43 (on medieval notion of 'dual capacity' and 'extreme cases' of French bishop claiming to be celibate as bishop while duly married as baron).

[116] Van Caenegem (1988), 'Government, law and society', at 207 (first used as abstract concept in France in 1147); though for 'pleas of the Crown' in England around 1130, Kantorowicz (1957), *King's Two* Bodies, at 342 and 346 (in *Leges Anglorum* in late twelfth century).

[117] Gilby (1953), *Philosophy and Theology of the State*, at 119, 120 ('the logic should not be pressed too far', members still personally responsible for acts of group); Canning (1988b), 'Law, Sovereignty and Corporation Theory', at 473–4 (glossators developing corporate theory from Innocent IV's formulation, both as plurality of human beings and as abstract unitary entity).

outside and above, a notion fundamental for later state control of corporate identity.[118] There were problems in knowing who could grant such identity to the church itself, but this was apparently overcome by the process of simply recognizing the underlying social reality, in language that would later suggest the need for a formal grant. It was a 'conceptual leap' that was accomplished by the canonists.[119]

Once the 'fiction' of corporate identity was established within canonical thought, it could be transferred to groups beyond the church, initially most clearly to cities granted by royal charter, then to that which a physical monarch represented.[120] Once it was possible to see church and monarchy as distinct, if fictitious, persons, the collaboration between them becomes more formal and less obvious. The single body of a religious commonwealth, cohabited by king and pope, could become a bifurcated structure, with an inherent tendency towards divided responsibilities. We are still talking, however, of tendencies, of a long 'Vorgeschichte' prior to any notions of definitive separation.[121] And while the elements of a contemporary state are visible in these persisting notions, there remained remarkable diversity in their formulations. Kantorowicz acknowledges the existence of kindred ideas in England and on the continent but insists on there being no exact equivalent to the king's two bodies on the continent.[122] Moreover, there remained ongoing dissent from the personification process, both in terms of loyalty to a Germanic, non-fictional view of the human group defended vigorously by Gierke in the nineteenth century,[123] and in the persistent view that the state, even as an abstraction, remained an element of the royal patrimony. Historians of 'modernity' are said to have treated this as an aberration, but it would have represented the 'ordinary practice of the time' and this even in the nineteenth century.[124]

---

[118] Gilby (1958), *Principality and Polity*, at 254.

[119] Picq (2005), *Histoire et droit des États*, at 105; Nelson (2006), *Making of Modern State*, at 39 ('almost as revolutionary' as recovery of Aristotle); Pennington (1988), 'Law, legislative authority and theories of government', at 447 ('no other canonistic doctrine was as important for constitutional thought'); and for reliance by Baldus in the thirteenth century on fiction theory, Gierke (1951), *Political Theories of Middle Age*, at 69. For debts of a corporation no longer owed by members as individuals, Tierney (1982), *Religion, law and constitutional thought*, at 19.

[120] For transfer to 'political entities', Kantorowicz (1957), *King's Two Bodies*, at 267, 237 ('secular state' was 'almost forced to follow the lead', making 'the polity co-eternal with the Church'); Tierney (1982), *Religion, law and constitutional thought*, at 20 (placing the assimilation into 'secular' thought, however, in the fifteenth century); and for benefit by cities, Canning (1988a), 'Politics, institutions and ideas', at 363; van Creveld (1999), *Rise and Decline of the State*, at 104 (towns 'corporate bodies' 'from the beginning').

[121] Brunner (1963), 'Vom Gottesgnadentum' at 288 (notions of separation only emerging by beginning of sixteenth century); Ullmann (1976), *Law and Politics in the Middle Ages*, at 85 (political institutions 'began' to be released from 'religious encumbrances').

[122] Kantorowicz (1957), *King's Two Bodies*, at 20 (continent 'no exact parallel'), 447 ('practically absent from the continent', 'hopeless task' of effort to 'explain' a historical phenomenon since 'too many layers of life effective at the same time', yet suggesting importance in England of parliament as living 'body politic' and never a fictitious person).

[123] See Ch. 4, *'The state as body, crown, or corporate person'*.

[124] Rowen (1980), *The King's State*, at 159 (state owned either by king or by people), 169 (as 'ordinary practice'); Shennan (1974), *Origins of Modern European State*, at 25 ('patrimonial, dynastic outlook' which was 'fundamental' to sixteenth century).

The hierarchy of contemporary state structures eventually came to be founded in many instances on this general idea of a perpetual, ongoing state, distinct from individual rulers or governments. The fundamental idea was supported and justified in many ways, sometimes (as they say in France) 'du bout des lèvres',[125] yet in the theory and practice of continuity there were elements of closure that could be taken up in the construction of the contemporary state. Some notion of the corporate person, however defined, solved both the problem of structure and that of its duration over time.[126]

Boundaries

The hierarchical structure of early state forms in Europe was therefore buttressed by efforts to cast them as abstract, distinct, and ongoing entities. As persons or bodies, they could be presumed to have outlines. The other persisting element of closure was not one of personal identity but of territorial identity, in the form of geographical boundaries. These represent the real challenge to cosmopolitanism since, as noted above,[127] they not only allow people to live together but require at least some people to live apart.

Historically, the notion of a boundary was imprecise, though not entirely absent from early state forms. It was simply not used as a fixed, geo-political demarcation of competing sovereignties.[128] The Greek city-states used walls for defensive purposes, and often had 'natural' limits such as mountains or rivers. Towns did fade into countryside, however, so early on there is a notion of a zone of uncertain geographic status. The Romans knew the limits of their territory but these were 'dynamic... ill-defined zones of power' and there is debate about whether they ever became fixed for purpose of defence.[129] Any notion of boundaries within the empire became entirely irrelevant with the extension of Roman citizenship. There were boundary markers, however, at least for fields, and even a god, Terminus, to watch over them.

An imprecise or nebulous notion of boundaries continued into the middle ages, with ideas of the limits of the *Imperium Christianum* and the necessity of effecting some kind of spatial delineation for the partition of Charlemagne's

---

[125] Literally at the edge of one's lips, or unenthusiastically. Recall the various forms of disenchantment seen in Ch. 1, 'Readings of the State Tradition'.

[126] Kantorowicz (1957), *King's Two Bodies*, at 273 (king's two bodies 'camouflaged a problem of continuity').

[127] See Ch. 2, 'Early Cosmopolitanism'.

[128] Guichonnet and Raffestin (1974), *Géographie des frontières*, at 83, 84; Trigger (2003), *Early Civilizations*, at 94, 104 (disputing claim that boundaries only associated with modern state: also identifiable in city-states); and for boundaries of tribal communities, Kratochwil (1986), 'Of Systems, Boundaries, and Territoriality', at 29 (as title to a cycle of migration).

[129] Whittaker (2004), *Rome and its Frontiers*, at 6, 8 ('simply incorrect' that Rhine or Danube 'definitive frontiers'), 28–30 (on 'frenzied scientific debate' over whether 'old strategy of open, expansive and zonal frontiers' gave way under Augustus to 'static lines of defence').

empire.[130] Territorial demarcation became less significant, however, in an era of personal and feudal loyalties. One was loyal to one's king, not to a territory, though by the beginning of the thirteenth century kings were becoming known no longer as kings of peoples but as kings of territory, however ill-defined.[131] As in Greece, moreover, the vital city-states had walls and territory and within them the freedom of the territory overcame personal bondage.[132] We will see that they gave birth to what are known today as 'conflicts of laws', derived from a notion of territorial exclusivity. These too would persist.

The imprecision of medieval boundaries is most clearly indicated, however, by the notion of marches or *limes*. Where a boundary was known it did not separate 'two distinct, foreign worlds' but rather constituted the 'backbone of a broader zone' of mutual influence, spreading out on either side of that backbone.[133] They were 'soft' border zones,[134] recognized and administered as such, and Charlemagne appointed governors for them, known as *marchiones* or marquises, a word of ancient nobility still (dimly) recalled today.[135] So, while the notion of a border in a very general sense was known, it neither played the same role that borders play today nor had a precise vocabulary to signal it. A vocabulary of boundaries had to be developed, and this would have occurred first in French in the thirteenth century with the word 'frontier' being developed from the original 'front' or forehead, then later the German 'Grenz' and even, much later (approaching the Treaty of Westphalia in the seventeenth century), the word 'boundary' in English.[136]

The imprecision of the concept and vocabulary was reflected at the institutional level. There could be many kings for the same territory with no felt necessity to proceed to territorial division,[137] while boundaries could not capture the disjunction between royal claims and 'real disunity' that prevailed on the

---

[130] Fichtenau (1964), *The Carolingian Empire*, at 65 (at least in the language of Alcuin); and for partition, Nelson (1988), 'Kingship and empire', at 225 (to deny the ninth century any idea of the state is to 'throw out the baby with the bathwater').

[131] For the 'king of the Franks' becoming the 'king of France', van Caenegem (1995), *Historical Introduction to Western Constitutional Law*, at 76; and for 'sovereign power' being exercised through personal vassalage rather than through territorial claims, Whittaker (2004), *Rome and its Frontiers*, at 183 (also on use of 'natural' boundaries, Petrarch in fourteenth century using rivers as natural frontiers in Italy, Boccaccio also in fourteenth century exalting the Alps). For enlightenment development of the 'natural' boundary, see Ch. 4, 'Boundaries'.

[132] Rörig (1967), *The Medieval Town*, at 27; and see Ch. 2, 'Collaborative Cities'.

[133] Guenée (2001), 'From Feudal Boundaries', at 85 (border zone with its own life and own problems); Boggs (1940), *Boundaries*, at 7 (control of A beginning to yield to control of B).

[134] Zielonka (2006), *Europe as Empire*, at 11 (even these in flux).

[135] Riché (1993), *The Carolingians*, at 133.

[136] Guichonnet and Raffestin (1974), *Géographie des frontières*, at 11, 12. The earliest example of 'boundary' in the *Oxford English Dictionary* is dated 1626 and it is said to originate from the Old French bodne, bone, bune, bonne, bunne, and the Anglo-French bounde, hence the 'metes and bounds' description of land.

[137] Wood (1977), 'Kings, Kingdoms and Consent', at 17 (where kingship divided, Gaul aside, 'power was shared; there is nothing to suggest it was divided territorially').

ground.[138] Marsilius of Padua, writing an important tract in the fourteenth century in which he defended the emperor against the pope, saw no need for a territorially-centred secular authority.[139] The concept of a boundary thus both existed and would persist into later times, but required a major reworking to achieve the type of closure that contemporary states were meant to bring about. It is therefore time to turn to such new and major efforts of closure.

---

[138] Lewis (1968), *Later Medieval France*, 32 (for France); Given (1990), *State and Society in Medieval Europe*, notably at 244 (for inability of French and English monarchs to integrate new territories); van Caenegem (1995), *Historical Introduction Western Constitutional Law*, at 73 (on 'emerging states' centred on monarchies, in Spain 'not one single embryo' of national monarchy).

[139] Ullmann (1988), *Law and Jurisdiction*, at IX–401 ('reification of sovereignty' not part of Marsilius's thought processes, though territorialized concepts of law not unknown at time), IX–409 (Marsilius's writing 'not a theory of the State').

PART II

CLOSURE?

4

A Territorial State?

Throughout the middle ages various institutions in Europe had attracted adherence. There were partial closures around these poles of interest and loyalty. The church developed early, state-like structures, the cities promoted freedom on their (limited) territories, the empire struggled for survival over many centuries, and the affirmative crowns considered themselves emperors on territory increasingly seen as their own. No one of them, however, could exclude or pre-empt the others. The ensuing institutional cosmopolitanism developed many cosmopolitan ways, yet the cosmopolitan ways could function only because no elements of closure were, or were allowed to become, entirely dominant. With the benefit of hindsight we know that in the periods of European history triumphantly known as the renaissance and the enlightenment there were major efforts to complete the process of closure, most successfully around the affirmative crowns. We are therefore able to identify a slow but important shift in the relative importance of the cosmopolitan ways and the elements of closure seen in Chapter 3. The elements of closure, which we now come to re-examine, increase in importance; the cosmopolitan ways decline, at least for a time. The flow of normative information becomes more focused, centred around the emerging continental states, now designated as such. Powerful means of control of information are asserted.

This picture of the emergence of the European state is complicated in a major way, however, by the realities of colonialism, empire, and the development of contemporary state structures beyond Europe. It is striking, moreover, that what is usually described as the period of emergence of the contemporary state in Europe from, say, the sixteenth century, coincides exactly with the expansion of European authority across the seas. This may not have been accidental. It has clear consequences, however, for our understanding of the cosmopolitan state, since the state beyond Europe was and remains a very different institution from the state within Europe. They are all, however, states, with their particularities.

The elements of closure that were ratcheted up in importance in Europe are the medieval ones of writing, hierarchy, and boundaries, each inextricably linked to the others.

WRITING

As an instrument of closure writing moved from customs, to codes, to constitutions, in Europe and beyond, with highly varying levels of intensity.

Customs

Royal legislation was historically intermittent, and often purported only to restate the good old law. Charlemagne's ambition to refashion society was never achieved. Writing was simply unable to do the job, in spite of its choice as the technical means of direction.[1] In the fifteenth century the French crowns began to move things along, however, by convincing people to accept the writing down, or 'redaction', of their local customs. They did this by promising faithful reproduction, according to local testimony as to content. The Custom of Paris was written down first in 1510, then in an 'improved' version in 1580.[2] It thus became a vector of expansion and could serve essentially as a civil code when transported by royal decree to overseas territories, notably in that swath of North America known as New France. Throughout the sixteenth century other customs were also captured (Burgundy, 1575; Brittany, 1580; Normandy, 1585). Once captured in positive, written form they were subject to potential revision by the holder of the pen; in the redaction of the customs we see a necessary pre-condition of eventual codification. Custom had to be brought under control.[3]

The effect of the redaction of customs was not simply to prepare the way for codification centuries later. In the initial royal ordinance authorizing the redaction process it was courageously stated what the effect of the redaction would be. The Ordinance of Montil-les-Tours of 1454, which started the process, stated that judges would have to conform to the new versions of the customs, and even that lawyers would be permitted to cite no customs other than those that had been agreed to.[4] The law retains its customary content, but now it would be law because a written law so declared it.

The capture of custom not only took place in writing; it also took place in French. This too came about by royal, written decree, in the Ordinance of Villers-Cotterets of 1539, which required all acts of justice to be written in French, thus excluding not only cosmopolitan Latin but also the local patois. There was linguistic centralization, of vital importance for national communication since only a small percentage of the population of what is now France actually spoke a correct and recognizable French.[5] A national language was an essential element

---

[1] See Ch. 3, 'Writing'.

[2] The latter more a product of doctrinally inclined practitioners than popular recall: Church (1969), *Constitutional Thought in Sixteenth-Century France*, at 109 ('practitioners' law') and 110 (for doctrine that redacted custom draws its authority not from popular consent but from act of king permitting redaction); and for the ordonnances as 'general reform', Sueur (2007), *Histoire du droit public français*, vol. II, at 94–5.

[3] Glenn (1997a), 'Capture of "Custom"'.

[4] Filhol (1972), 'The Codification of Customary Law', at 267–8.

[5] For 'domestic colonization' with regions 'linguistically subdued', Scott (1998), *Seeing Like a State*, at 72. For the Ordinance directled mostly against Latin, Fenet and Soulier (1989), *Les minorités et leurs droits*, at 125: Ostler (2005), *Empires of the World*, at 326 ('Latin yielded'); though for elimination of patois van Creveld (1999), *Rise and Decline of State*, at 197; and for language use even centuries later, see Ch. 5, 'Language'.

of what was to be a national law.[6] This was a remarkable development, since now it is not only the true law that is made subject to written language, but also language itself. No explanation was given as to how this could be done. It involved a conceptual leap, or bootstrap operation, comparable to corporate identity being conferred on the church.[7] In some measure, however, it worked. Doctrinal authority contributed to the process, and in 1576 Bodin explicitly noted that he wrote in the 'langue populaire', to better be understood by all 'natural French'.[8]

Codes

A path to codification having been opened by the redaction of customs in the sixteenth century, some distance down that path was travelled in the seventeenth, with the major ordinances promulgated under Colbert. Civil procedure (1667), crime (1670), commerce (1673), maritime affairs (1681), and the colonies (1685) all became subject to 'les Grandes Ordonnances'. These were large and important, though subtle, legislative instruments. They were codes, though they did not call themselves codes; they regulated much private law, though they purported to be public law, since private law was governed by the redacted customs.[9] This progression of central, written instruments in France is remarkable in comparison with other parts of Europe. Legislative authority was far more fragmented in what we now know as Germany and Spain; England's judges filled most of the space occupied by both public and private law, and in variable combinations of language, until some way into the eighteenth century.[10]

It is symptomatic of the importance of empire for our understanding of the state that the world's first successful, national civil code was produced by an emperor and not by a king, president, or prime minister. Napoleon's imperial reign was relatively short, from 1804 to 1814, but important for the model of a comprehensive, written statement of all of private law, exportable through the empire. It was the first 'natural law code', characterized by supreme legislative

---

[6] For the parallel rise of local languages and laws, Jacob (1994), 'Doctrine et culture nationale'; and for the decline of Latin as an indication of nationalization of legal doctrine, Halperin (2000), 'L'approche historique' at 725.

[7] On the question who could confer corporate identity on the church, see Ch. 3, *'Hierarchy'*. The assumption that written language could control law, and through law language itself, was of course a test of loyalty to the French crown. It was also part of a major shift in the understanding of language as a means of representation and of bestowing order on the world, 'no longer woven into the world by an original and divine gesture': Bartelson (1995), *A genealogy of sovereignty*, at 146.

[8] Bodin (1986), *Six livres*, at 10.

[9] Ellul (1956), *Histoire des institutions*, at 425 (public law of 'justice', economy, finance): Filhol (1972), 'The Codification of Customary Law', at 276. By the eighteenth century there were ordinances on gifts (1731) and wills (1735), presented to remedy diversities of interpretation.

[10] For the use of Latin and of Law French over seven centuries, Baker (1998), 'Three Languages of the Common Law'; and for contemporary English legal language still 'medieval French of a particular type', Woodbine (1943), 'Language of English Law', at 395.

confidence in spite of the modesty and elegance of its prose style.[11] It bound France together (the empire was less successful) in private law matters, and its binding character throughout French territory was thought to be demonstrable by its first article, declaring its coming into force in 1804 on successive days in a series of concentric circles radiating out from Paris, each a day's ride further than the last. Unity was its primary objective, as opposed to any particular view of private law, though of course it had one: necessarily, as they say, bourgeois.[12]

A written code of private law proved to be an irresistible model of state construction, and closure. The nineteenth century was one of codification in Europe and while Savigny in Germany resisted, his resistance was based on an alternative model of closure, that of the nation or Volk, which should be allowed to produce spontaneously its own form of law.[13] Savigny lost that battle and the German Civil Code or Bürgerliches Gesetzbuch (BGB) of 1900 came to rival that of France for the world's favour. Even places having very different legal traditions were tempted, and civil codes came to exist in common law jurisdictions such as California in the USA, in Islamic countries, and in Asia.[14] Yet civil codes outside Europe, and in some measure even derivative civil codes within Europe, did not bring about closure to the same extent as the original models. This is a complex subject, rooted not only in colonial relations but in more ephemeral notions of legal influence and prestige. To the extent that extra-European jurisdictions enacted codes based on a European model (and almost all were based on a European model), they came within the orbit of the original models. The lawyers of those places looked back to those original models and the jurisprudence developed under them, either to consolidate reciprocal relations or to sever them more effectively. They were cosmopolitan in outlook, in thinking law in a trans-state manner. The colonial or imperial mind was inherently cosmopolitan, constantly juggling the metropolitan with the local or particular, constantly

---

[11] Wieacker (1995), *Private Law in Europe*, at 257ff. (the 'Natural Law Codes'); for comprehensiveness, Vanderlinden (1967), *Le concept de code*. Contrast the more pragmatic and local concerns of contemporary codifications in Glenn (1998), 'Grounding of Codification'; and for even the 'natural law codes' as specific historical phenomena originating in late seventeenth- and eighteenth-century legal science, Zimmermann (1995), 'Codification: history and present', at 98. The Prussian Code of 1794, vast in length, is generally seen as a failure.

[12] See notably van den Berg (2007), *Politics of European Codification*, at 19 (criticism of legal practitioners infrequent, code brought new uncertainties in purporting to eliminate supplementary sources of law, change stimulated not by legal practice but by politicians) and 273 (continental codifications in general introduced to establish monopoly of state on making of law, with interest of state in mind); Jansen (2010), *Making of Legal Authority*, at 9 for sovereign's 'full public control of private law' as characteristic of modern state; and for 'juridical absolutism' as 'unnatural' and 'rigid monism' ('monismo rigidissimo'), Grossi (1998), *Assolutismo giuridico e diritto privato*, at 3, 5.

[13] Von Savigny (1831), *Vocation of Our Age*, though Savigny's argument paradoxically led to the conclusion that contemporary Roman law was the law of the German people. For the debate and consequences in the USA, Reimann (1989), 'The Historical School'; and for the purported closure of the 'nation', see Ch. 5.

[14] For the common law world, Fairgrieve (2007), *Influence of French Civil Code*. Jeremy Bentham was notably committed to the codification process. In the Islamic world the most significant codification was the Ottoman Medjelle in the late nineteenth century; the Egyptian civil code, based largely on the French, was to be highly influential throughout the Middle East. The codes of Japan, China, and Vietnam have borrowed extensively from French and German models, though more from the German.

working at the interface of a law seen as common, metropolitan in origin, and a law seen as particular. Codes seen as radically exclusive and territorial in the countries of their European origin thus became simple, ongoing sources of normative information or common law abroad.[15] Some of this was a clear result of efforts at colonial imposition, as with the imposition of the Dutch Civil Code in Indonesia. More frequently it was the result of local and independent codification that was deliberately derivative in character, as was the case for the Latin American, Middle Eastern, or Asian codes, as well as those of Quebec and Louisiana. In some cases this followed a colonial history or pattern. It also occurred outside colonial experience, as with the adoption of BGB models in places that have never been subject to German imperial or colonial authority, simply as a result of professional respect and admiration.[16]

In most cases, therefore, codes were capable of bringing about only partial forms of closure. They would usually have been a major source of ongoing openness and alliance. In the biological language of nineteenth- and twentieth-century comparative law, there were 'legal families' of codes within which relations extended over state borders. Even in the European codes of origin, however, doubts have been raised about the extent of closure that any codification can bring about. Reinhard Zimmermann has written that 'no codification can ever hope to be comprehensive'[17] and some codes are quite explicit in acknowledging the need for suppletive sources, the best-known being Article 1 of the Swiss Civil Code of 1907, which expressly refers to sources beyond the code, in customary law, legal doctrine, and case law.[18] Doubts about comprehensiveness and closure are also inspired by the reality that codes rarely mark a sharp departure from the past and are evidently rooted in ongoing sources from which they are derived. Jean Carbonnier referred to the French Civil Code as a 'lieu de mémoire', a 'repository of earlier texts from the near and distant past'.[19] New forms of closure are 'constrained . . . by the historical legacy of previous closures', even if these are only partial.[20] Since the sources continue it remains within the realm of the possible that they might be resorted to again, and this even occurred with some regularity in the early years of the French and Belgian civil codes, before they became accepted in practice.[21] Laws or rules that attempt to shore them up by stipulating or prohibiting citation practices (Zitiergesetze), notably references to academic writing or foreign law, have been conspicuous

---

[15] Glenn (2007c), *Common Laws*, Ch. 2, notably at 72–5 (for French Civil Code abroad).

[16] The German model thus prevails in Japan and in the Mexican state of Quintana Roo: Glenn (2007c), *Common Laws*, at 83.

[17] Zimmermann (1995), 'Codification: history and present', at 95 and 107 ('no code has ever been "comprehensive"').

[18] For further examples, Weiss (2000), 'The Enchantment of Codification', at 456 (Prussian Code leaving local laws untouched, practice of exclusivity abandoned in Austria and France).

[19] Carbonnier (2001), 'French Civil Code', at 337.

[20] See Ch. 3, introductory section, with references.

[21] See Ch. 1, 'The State as Tradition'.

failures.[22] Important doctrinal writing has suggested that the importance of codes lies in the questions they ask, rather than in the answers they provide.[23]

In some places in the world, however, codes and other high forms of western legal writing have been quite incapable of surmounting or displacing other forms of good old law. They have not brought about closure around themselves. This is most evident in two situations. The first is where western law, though intended to be 'general' in application, has been held by courts to be inapplicable to peoples never having renounced their adherence to unwritten forms of law. For such peoples, referred to as 'aboriginal', 'indigenous', or (harking back to a millennia-old, pre-colonial tradition) 'chthonic', the notion of 'customary' law is a western notion based on the non-normative phenomenon of repeated behaviour. Unwritten law, however, is profoundly normative, even sacred, and may be impossible to renounce. Cosmopolitan judges have recognized this in many instances and preserved within western states a type of personal law in unwritten form, applicable in matters of what are described as 'aboriginal rights' or even, in matters of land, 'aboriginal title'. In some cases there has even been state constitutional recognition of this, a form of inclusive closure brought about by high-level and written recognition of the non-exclusivity of writing.[24] Indigenous people have become equally cosmopolitan (if not more so) in perspective, by working within the cadre of western, written law to advance their case for unwritten law, most successfully recently at the level of international diplomacy in bringing about adoption of the UN General Assembly Declaration on the Rights of Indigenous Peoples.[25] We are here forced to recognize the 'simultaneity of the nonsimultaneous', the coexistence at the same time of what were seen in the nineteenth century as multiple stages in human development.[26]

The second situation in which western forms of legal writing have been unable to bring about closure around themselves is where various other forms of written, though less formal, law are deeply embedded in a state population, often for religious grounds. This is a more widespread phenomenon than is generally recognized. In some cases state law nests in an unacknowledged but powerful normative background such as Confucianism or Buddhism, and one is unable to appreciate the operation of the state norms without an appreciation of the deeper normative background.[27] In other cases state law simply acknowledges the operation of non-state law, often in specific areas of law, as in Israel for Jewish law applicable in family law matters, or in Saudi Arabia for Islamic law,

---

[22] Glenn (2007c), *Common Laws*, Ch. 2, at 46–7 (Prussian, French, Spanish, Dutch examples); Jansen (2013), 'Legal Pluralism in Europe', at 119 (citing prohibition on any commentary on Prussian Land Law).

[23] Rémy (1982), 'Éloge de l'exégèse', notably at 121 ('from the rule to the questions', 'de la règle aux questions').

[24] See Ch. 7, 'Relations and guarantees', and Ch. 12, 'Reconciliation'.

[25] See Ch. 12, 'Reconciliation'.

[26] Koselleck (2002), *Practice of Conceptual History*, at 8 (on contemporaries who have rejected not only modernity but also its immediate religious and rational predecessors).

[27] For East Asian and notably Confucian resistance to state law, Glenn (2010b), *Legal Traditions*, at 328 ('limiting Fa'), 330 ('limiting religion').

traditionally defined and applied more broadly.[28] In other cases state law undertakes the task of restating a religious law in legislative or codified form, as in India for Hindu law or in Morocco for Islamic law. This is a contentious matter since there are those who maintain that religious law cannot be based on secular instruments but, once again, at least in some measure and over the last few centuries, the idea has worked.[29] In all of these cases the lawyers and parties involved are necessarily familiar with multiple normative frameworks, some defined as law (formally or informally), others not. Each requires recognition and familiarity with its operation.

Constitutions

Constitutions are now recognized as the most hierarchically superior form of western legal writing. We begin to see the interrelationships of the elements of closure that are writing, hierarchy, and boundaries. Hierarchy requires writing, is supported by it, and contributes to its elevation. Prior to the contemporary state, however, the hierarchies that existed were able to function with less exalted forms of writing than (some) present constitutions. More modest forms of written constitution began with the Greek city-states;[30] on occasion these surfaced elsewhere, perhaps most notably in Cromwell's short-lived Instrument of Government of 1653.[31] In North America from the seventeenth century onwards there were many instances of written company charters, a form of limited government; on arrival in North America the Pilgrims drew up codes of law that extended to basic liberties; there were written constitutions for individual colonies and for the US Confederation of 1781.[32] The notion of a written constitution was therefore available and within relatively easy reach, and the political circumstances of empire rendered it more likely to be adopted outside Europe than within Europe. There were no religious problems with the idea of an earthly polity; no real difficulty with a notion of human law; no (non-indigenous) opposition to law in writing; and no sacred sources that precluded a 'founding' document. There could be, moreover, a foundation in the sense of something

---

[28] See Ch. 8, 'Churches and Religions' (for 'statuts personnels') and Ch. 13, *'State and religious legal sources'*.

[29] For the debate, see Ch. 13, *'State and religious legal sources'*.

[30] See Ch. 2, 'Collaborative Cities'.

[31] Even this was preceded by three 'Agreements of the People' of 1647, 1648, and 1649: Vincent (1987), *Theories of the State*, at 97; Wood (1969), *Creation of American Republic*, at 260 (notion of written instrument of government 'decidedly obsolete' after fall of Cromwell); Jennings (1959), *Law and Constitution*, at 7 (Cromwell's document exception to unwritten form of English constitution).

[32] For corporate charters, Loughlin (2010), *Foundations of Public Law*, at 279–80 (on improbability of written constitution without this 'extensive experience'); Bilder (2009), 'Colonial Constitutionalism and Constitutional Law', at 31–6 (on shift from 'patent' to 'charter' to 'constitution'); for the Pilgrims, Bailyn (1967), *Ideological Origins of American Revolution*, at 194 (with other efforts to extract 'essentials' of liberty); for colonial constitutions (Pennyslvania, Virginia), Vincent (1987), *Theories of the State*, at 97; for Articles of Confederation, van Creveld (1999), *Rise and Decline of State*, at 284 ('first constitution' of 'extremely loose entity').

actually 'brought about' by collective action.[33] The idea of a political 'revolution', moreover, called for a written document and both the US and the French experience confirmed this.

A written constitution is essential for a successful revolution, since it is a marker of a 'revolutionary zero hour',[34] a rupture with an ancient regime. As an element of closure, the written constitution also nationalizes the constitutional order, at least for a time and in some measure, and depending on its success. Some revolutions, like that of the USA, are successful; others, like that of Cromwell, are not, in spite of his written constitution. The success of a revolution appears to depend on two underlying circumstances. There must first be a world view open to the idea of discontinuity, and this would imply the breaking away from a world seen in principle as continuous or organic or unitary. Something must no longer continue.[35] Empire played this role well, but there were and are wider notions of western or religious unity. The French were not resisting empire. If this basic condition exists it is possible for revolutionary acts to be seen as such, and not as simply the usual banging-around. Innovation is always defined *ex post*, something that is later deemed to be exemplary,[36] and if later judgement can come to this conclusion the revolution may turn out to be successful. John Searle speaks of the creation of institutional facts through acting as if they already exist, and concludes that the drafters of the US Constitution 'got away with this'.[37] In short there must be a kind of conceptual leap, similar to that of conferring corporate identity on the church, or accepting that written law

---

[33] Taylor (2007), *A Secular Age*, at 197 (notion of foundation 'taken out of the mythical early time', seen as 'something that people can do today', this happening at some time in eighteenth century).

[34] The phrase is that of Stolleis (2001), *Public Law in Germany*, at 59. For the constitution as necessarily written when 'la nation' is seen as becoming sovereign, Lepointe (1965), *Histoire du droit public*, at 124, as to which see Ch. 5, 'Nation and State'.

[35] As noted see Ch. 3, 'Persistence of Cosmopolitan Ways'; and see Nora (2001), 'General Introduction' to *Rethinking France*, at xiii ('Historical time of the revolutionary type is informed by the desire for rupture'); and, again, Puett (2006), 'Innovation as Ritualization', at 26 (on 'western theory' accepting a notion of an 'otherwise continuous world', innovation as breaking out of it, contrasting with Chinese 'fractured cosmology' in which the world is one of 'things ... banging against each other' with a consequent goal of building continuity).

[36] Puett (2006), 'Innovation as Ritualization', at 30 (on innovation constantly occurring in a fractured, non-western cosmology since all acts are different, once a given action defined subsequently as one to be followed becomes a founding, innovative act).

[37] Searle (1995), *Construction of Social Reality*, at 118 (acting as though 'by performing a certain declarative speech act X they created an institutional fact of independence Y. They got away with this'); and see Wood (1969), *Creation of American Republic*, at 291 (final meaning of constitution not its fundamentality or creation by people but rather subsequent implementation by courts); Gardner (2011), 'Can There Be a Written Constitution', at 170 (essential question how constitution 'is received by its official users'; '[c]onstitutions cannot be, or be contained in, documents'). For the apparently very real risks of failure of the US founding, Ferling (2003), *A Leap in the Dark*, notably at 167 ('[n]one who favoured independence was blind to the uncertainty of the future'): Slauter (2009), *State as a Work of Art*, at 20 (on bare ratifications by state conventions): Hulsebosch (2005), *Constituting Empire*, at 210, on why *The Federalist* remembered as a success ('[b]ecause the constitution succeeded'): Armitage (2007), *Declaration of Independence*, at 26 (Declaration 'entirely ignored' by many).

supersedes customary law.[38] There must be a kind of Münchhausen moment, and only the passage of time will allow us to conclude that this has occurred.[39]

The second basic circumstance is that the revolution and its written constitution must have content that will survive the test of subsequent appreciation. The French revolutionary constitution of 1791, creating a type of constitutional monarchy, failed almost immediately and abjectly. It in no way contributed to closure; the unity of France owes more to its civil code than to any of its many constitutions. The content of the US Constitution was vastly more successful. It brought about just the right amount of rupture, while retaining elements of stability. In part this was due to the cosmopolitanism of its authors and sources (more on this below)[40] but it was also due to a kind of inner tension between the idea of fundamental rights inherent in an unwritten constitution, and the positive instantiation of those rights in a written document. The rights and language were well known, so the content could be seen as a realignment with respected sources (as opposed to their imperially corrupt practices) while the document itself was the necessary sign of rupture and nationhood.[41] In Rosenfeld's language it succeeded in 're-integrating traditions' while distancing itself from their original sources.[42] It carried forward an appropriate level of former closures.

The success of the US written constitution, and the closure it effected, brought about an astonishing level of world-wide emulation, which continues today. Unwritten constitutions would today be the exception rather than the rule, whereas the very idea of 'constitutional law' would have been largely unknown prior to 1789.[43] There have been global waves both of declarations of independence and of written, 'comprehensive' constitutions.[44] Has the European model of written law, boosted to the constitutional level by the US example, brought about a constant level of national closure around the chosen instruments? Two grounds of caution or reserve appear necessary. The first is that the written

---

[38] See Ch. 3, '*Hierarchy*' (for the church) and '*Writing*'. For the latter giving priority to western law as 'revolutionary', Lupoi (2000), *Origins European Legal Order*, at 285.

[39] Baron Münchhausen famously told of having pulled himself out of a swamp by his own hair.

[40] See Ch. 7, 'Constitutionalism'.

[41] For 'confusion' about the nature of law operative in the constitution, Wood (1969), *Creation of American Republic*, at 293; and for its 'ideological contradictions', Horwitz (2009), 'Constitutional Transplants' at 540 (looking both forwards and backwards, making or declaring of law).

[42] Rosenfeld (2010), *Identity Constitutional Subject* at 32; and see, for the necessary stability of successful revolutions, Glenn (1990a), 'Law, Revolution and Rights'.

[43] Horowitz (2009), '*The Federalist* Abroad', at 503 (UK, New Zealand, and Israel leading though 'fragile' examples of unwritten constitutions); and for 'constitutional law', Hulsebosch (2005), *Constituting Empire*, at 40.

[44] For declarations of indpendence, of some 100 jurisdictions, Armitage (2007), *Declaration of Independence*, notably at 3 (over half the countries of the world, though, at 143, aboriginal peoples now preferring other instruments); for constitutions, Grewe and Ruiz Fabri (1995), *Droits constitutionnels européens*, at 36 (waves of nineteenth century (Norway, Belgium, Switzerland), first half of twentieth century (Finland, Austria, Ireland, Italy, Germany), late twentieth century (Sweden, Greece, Portugal, Spain, Holland)); and for post-Soviet constitutions, Tomkins (2005), *Our Republican Constitution*, at 9 (US and German models); and for written constitutions in Commonwealth countries in spite of the unwritten UK model, Borda (2009), 'Constitutional Law in the Commonwealth', at 37 (enacting into law previously unwritten conventions or understandings).

constitutions have been remarkably diverse, and demonstrate an observable pattern of adherence to 'colonial institutions'. Thus francophone countries often have semi-presidential systems and run-off elections; anglophone countries often have parliamentary or presidential systems and plurality elections.[45] Put slightly differently, the written constitutions that have emerged have followed the patterns and concepts of the diverse common laws that have so much influenced, in different ways, legal developments in the world, in both public and private law. If the 'state tradition' is a purely formal one, in calling only for the existence of a state, it is the common laws and their local reception that have provided the basic building blocks of national laws. If the common laws were tolerant of local, particular law, notably in aboriginal form, the constitution may well continue this tradition, as has been noted above.[46] There is thus cosmopolitanism in the drafting of written constitutions, and this includes assessing common law models against the general influence of the US Constitution.

The second ground of caution regarding the extent of national closure brought about by written constitutions lies in their capacity for comprehensiveness. Here for the moment it is necessary to refer only to recent books by Lawrence Tribe and Akhil Amar as indications of how tenuous the notion of a comprehensive, written constitution remains. Tribe is categorical in concluding that the US Constitution *'at every moment* depends on extratextual sources of meaning' and that it 'floats in a vast and deep—and, crucially, invisible—ocean of ideas, propositions, recovered memories, and imagined experiences that the Constitution as a whole puts us in a position to glimpse'.[47] Akhil Amar writes of the 'unwritten' or 'implicit' constitution, to which resort must necessarily be made even for purposes of identifying which version of the written constitution *is* the constitution, to say nothing of 'unenumerated rights'.[48] He finds that '[s]eemingly firm textual ground at times simply dissolves underfoot'.[49] If national constitutions reflect the content of the common laws within which they are nested, they remain open, in some measure, to those (often distant) common laws for purposes of ongoing interpretation. The demonstration of this

[45] Horowitz (2009), *'The Federalist Abroad'*, at 521 (even 'disproportionately influenced' by colonial models; world filled with 'idiosyncratic hybrids' as opposed to a few clear-cut models), 522 (a 'mix-and-match world' given international diffusion of institutions heavily modified by constitutional processes).

[46] See *'Codes'* in this chapter.

[47] Tribe (2008), *The Invisible Constitution*, at 6 (emphasis in original) (also that text declaring its own supremacy cannot in itself establish that text as legitimate) and 7; and for ongoing constitutional effect of law outside the constitution, Young (2007), 'The Constitution Outside the Constitution', notably at 410 ('*most*' of constitutional work done by norms outside 'The Constitution'); Palmer (2006), 'Using Constitutional Realism to Identify the Complete Constitution' (applying New Zealand understanding of unwritten constitution to US constitution); A. Greene (2012), *Against Obligation* (sovereignty only 'permeable' or partial, constitution requiring ongoing justification against external sources of normativity).

[48] Amar (2012), *America's Unwritten Constitution*, at 1 (for 'implicit'), 63ff. (for signed and unsigned versions, various printings, of Constitution), 109 (unenumerated rights emerging after founding).

[49] Amar (2012), *America's Unwritten Constitution*, at 5.

will be found in discussion of cosmopolitan sources of contemporary constitutional law.[50]

In itself written law might not bring about national closure. Its effect is more powerful, however, when combined with hierarchy and a notion of geographical boundaries.

HIERARCHY

Through the middle ages affirmative crowns developed some of the intellectual means to ensure their institutional cohesion, as well as their duration over time and across individual office-holders. Various forms of 'bodification' or personification of the state began to emerge, following that of the church, and in the various royal alliances particular crowns were able to exercise increasing levels of political and legal influence. John Searle has written that power does not grow out of the barrel of a gun, but 'grows out of organizations'.[51] Organizations, or institutions if you prefer, are themselves dependent on the normative information or tradition that supports them, and the adherence to this information by significant numbers of people.[52] Crowns were able to obtain this adherence, to the detriment of other medieval institutions, notably imperial and religious ones. They did so by developing hierarchical forms of organization that in turn induced greater measures of adherence. The hierarchy built around the crowns was facilitated by ongoing and more refined notions of bodily or corporate existence, by organizational success on the ground, and through emerging theory of the state and its sovereignty. Their combination was highly effective, and produced what we know as the contemporary state. It should be observed, however, that the contemporary state emerged not only in a time of European colonial expansion, but during and after a time of severe religious and social crisis in Europe. From the mid-sixteenth to the mid-seventeenth centuries Europe was in a state of almost constant war, related in part to religious schism. The way was open for construction of a powerful means of social ordering.

The state as body, crown, or corporate person
Roman practice, canonical theory, and practical necessity had produced a largely undefined type of abstraction that could be seen as a state, particularly once the word had achieved some general acceptance by the sixteenth century.[53] There was great variation, however, in acceptance of the idea of an abstract state. Louis

---

[50] See Ch. 11, 'The Cosmopolitan Turn in Constitutional Sources'.

[51] Searle (1995), *Construction of Social Reality*, at 117; and similarly North, Wallis, and Weingast (2009), *Violence and Social Orders*, at 270 ('[i]nstead of a monopoly on violence we suggest that the governance structures of societies can be described in terms of organizational sophistication').

[52] Searle (1995), *Construction of Social Reality*, at 90 ('[w]e cannot assume that Leviathan will come to our aid in a genuine crisis: we are in a state of nature all the time, but the state of nature is precisely one in which people do in fact accept systems of constitutive rules, at least nearly all the time') and 92 (though no single motivation for adherence).

[53] See Ch. 3, 'Hierarchy'.

XIV is most famously reported to have rejected it in the seventeenth century, with his famous 'l'état, c'est moi',[54] and in the eighteenth century Friedrich II of Prussia is said to have been the first to distinguish between monarch and state, referring to himself as the first servant of the Prussian state.[55] The *practice* of permanence of the *res publica* was clearly evident, however, in the French maxim 'le roi ne meurt jamais' and the more widely known 'le roi est mort, vive le roi', both known at least from the early sixteenth century.[56] There was also the model of the cities, even though the royal grant of their charters reduced the conceptual difficulty in their case.[57]

Hobbes's claim to have invented the abstraction of the commonwealth in mid-seventeenth century has thus been described as 'extraordinary'[58] but from approximately that time the notion of the state 'matured', as 'an entity, less the object of divine intention and more the abstract harvest of human need'.[59] There remained the 'awkward problem'[60] of its actual origin since, though the personality of the state became 'dogma' by the nineteenth century,[61] its explanation was

---

[54] There is doubt, however, about whether he actually said this, though Voltaire reported it (without having heard it himself) in the eighteenth century.

[55] Cipolla (1976), *Before the Industrial Revolution*, at 44 (in general no distinction between royal private and public patrimonies prior to eighteenth century); for 'endeavours' to distinguish royal private and public property, Gierke (1951), *Political Theories of Middle Age*, at 63 (church again as model): Gilmore (1941), *Argument from Roman Law 1200–1600*, at 108, 111 (Bodin distinguishing person from office, though ongoing problem of venality of offices).

[56] For the immortality of the crown, Kantorowicz (1957), *King's Two Bodies*, at 409 (as descended from the canonical *dignitas non moritur* and therefore 'merely another twist of the well-worn corporational doctrines of mediaeval canonists and civilians'; yet legalistic in character and not dynastic, as with 'le roi est mort . . . '). Yet for the cry 'le roi est mort . . . ' as representing depersonalization of power, Picq (2005), *Histoire et droit des États*, at 116; and to 'close the hiatus' between death and coronation, van Creveld (1999), *Rise and Decline of State*, at 177. For still earlier practice of immediate succession, see Ch. 3 'Hierarchy'.

[57] See Ch. 3, 'Hierarchy'; for cities as 'laboratories' for the state, Picq (2005), *Histoire et droit des États*, at 25; and for their influence in Germany as 'sovereign' entities, Strauss (1986), *Law, Resistance and the State*, at 141.

[58] Springborg (1976), 'Leviathan, the Christian Commonwealth Incorporated', at 171 (given in particular the notion in England of king's two bodies) and 173 (for corporation argument traced through Hobbes's writing, notably for reliance on notion of *persona*); though for 'credit' to Hobbes for 'inventing the state', van Creveld (1999), *Rise and Decline of State*, at 179 and 183 (between Hobbes and Locke, 'the theoretical structure of the modern state was substantially complete'). Church concluded that Bodin, writing on sovereignty in the sixteenth century, would have emphasized the 'abstract concept of power', 'absolute, undivided, perpetual': Church (1969), *Constitutional Thought in Sixteenth-Century France*, at 226; yet ultimately Shennan was of the view that Bodin would have generated only a 'half-way concept, between renaissance monarchy and abstract entity': Shennan (1974), *Origins of Modern European State*, at 76; and for the problem of duration over time as implicit in Bodin but not resolved by him, van Creveld (1999), *Rise and Decline of State*, at 177 ('he did not really provide an answer').

[59] Spellman (1998), *European Political Thought: 1600–1700*, at 169 and 135 ('final and absolute judicial entity' even by 1700); though for 'abstraction' without content and in diverse forms, as early as sixteenth century, Ellul (1956), *Histoire des institutions*, at 286.

[60] Dyson (1980), *The State Tradition*, at 14.

[61] Häfelin (1959), *Die Rechtspersönlichkeit des Staates*, at 1 (on dogma of 'Rechtssubjektivität' of state) and 398 (on history of debate showing inner structural change, historical differences, and contradictions), 404 (on 'Vieldeutigkeit des Begriffs' or multiple meanings of concept of state). The debate became a staple feature of the general theory of the state or Allgemeine Staatslehre in Germany in the nineteenth and

never adequately brought about and became part of the ongoing swirl of debate about the nature of corporate identity, an 'endless problem'.[62] If the state as corporate person was a fiction, who brought it about? If it was not a fiction, was there really the 'group personality' ('Gesammtpersonlichkeit') dear to Gierke and potentially absolutist in character?[63] Answers to these questions have become embroiled in the still larger questions of the theory of and justification for the state in general, questions closely tied to its functions and its relation to the governed. Some have said that the state exists if it is recognized in international law, by other states, but what exactly then are these other states that would be doing the recognizing?[64] We appear to be looking at yet another conceptual leap, or Münchhausen moment, something for which no adequate explanation is available, or even possible.[65]

Theoretical anguish of this kind was largely avoided in common law jurisdictions, through reliance in the Commonwealth on the simple metaphor of 'the Crown', already noted as a 'lifeless abstraction',[66] and in the USA through recognition of 'the administration', equally lifeless. Both can (now) sue and be sued so each has acquired recognition as a legal person, again without real explanation of how this could be possible. In many colony-derived states the problem was seen as resolved through enactment of metropolitan legislation creating a constitutive constitutional document. If the law is accepted its author must necessarily also be accepted. It must be said as well that in a considerable number of extra-European states the question did not exercise many minds. Whether the state was personified was a largely invisible question behind the larger question of the existence of the state in any particular form. Nor was the state seen as a necessary form of social ordering, as it had been in seventeenth-century Europe. There were other forms of social ordering, and often resistance against the foreign form of social ordering that the state represented.

The contentious character of the corporate personality of the state should not obscure, however, its importance as an element of closure. Lacking such identity the state really does wither away, conceptually inapt for many precise functions. Personified, however, the state becomes a possible object of further reification,

---

early twentieth centuries, received in some measure in France. See Hallis (1930), *Corporate Personality*, at 190; and for reception in France Chevallier (1999), *L'Etat*, at 35 ('acclimatized'); Carré de Malberg (1920), *Théorie générale de l'État*, Ch. 1 (on 'Théorie de la personnalité de l'État').

[62] Radin (1932), 'The Endless Problem'; and for the ongoing, contemporary debate amongst theorists and between theorists and anti-theorists, the symposium in (2006) 63 *Washington & Lee Law Review* 1273–1598.

[63] Gierke (1951), *Political Theories of Middle Age*, at 68; and for the earlier origins of the debate, see Ch. 3 'Hierarchy'.

[64] For that state as 'authorized' solely by 'others of its own kind', van Creveld (1999), *Rise and Decline of State*, at 1; yet international lawyers debate on whether recognition, when it takes place, is of a constitutive or purely declaratory character, rarely taking up the question of how either could be possible; see Crawford (2007), *Creation of States*, notably at 19 for the 'great debate' and 45 for the criteria including, at 72, 'real and actual independence'. On the emergence of international law at the same time, and subject to the same conceptual weaknesses, as the contemporary state, see this chapter, 'Boundaries'.

[65] For other such moments, see this chapter, 'Constitutions'.

[66] See Ch. 1, 'Readings of the State Tradition'; and for action against 'the crown' though not against the Queen, Jennings (1959), *Law and Constitution*, at 221.

not simply a procedural device for facilitating public law litigation. It exists as a totality, a 'Ganz',[67] and once its existence is established it is perfectly capable of effecting further forms of closure, whether through controlling boundaries or in more subtle forms: control of information and law. Acceptance of the inexplicable dogma of state personality was facilitated greatly, moreover, by its success on the ground.

Organizational success

Closure around a hierarchy is made easier by visibility and success of the hierarchy. With hindsight we have no difficulty in seeing the success of the affirmative crowns in establishing the foundations of contemporary state hierarchies. The crowns, and the personified states they came to represent, undertook many functions and developed many (bureaucratic) instruments to carry them out. There is a vast literature describing the growth of the functional state, variously known as the trading state, the tax state, the predator state, the neopatrimonial state, the welfare state, the regulatory state, the market state, the enterprise state, the competition state, and many other designations. The functional explanations are important, however, since they flesh out the organizational success of the state as an important means of closure around national functions and national bureaucracies.

There is thus little doubt that the state fulfilled important though questionable functions in raising funds by taxation and waging war. Van Creveld in particular sees much of the development of the contemporary state as based on 'the need to wage war'[68] and others have insisted on the importance of a tax base as a means of supporting a standing army and the 'dramatic augmentation' of seventeenth-century military capacity.[69] The development of the contemporary state system in Europe was thus 'extremely bloody' over a period of 'at least five hundred

---

[67] Von Busse (1928), *Staat als Organismus*, at 5 (and as 'Totalität'); and for state as organism and hence system, and as alternative to revolution, Friedrich (1997), *Geschichte der deutschen Staatsrechtswissenschaft*, at 155.

[68] Van Creveld (1999), *Rise and Decline of State*, at 336–7 (war also as emotionally unifying, few citizens having read Rousseau, Herder, Fichte, Hegel).

[69] Spellman (1998), *European Political Thought: 1600–1700* at 14, 18 (nobility not disarmed but converted into officer and diplomatic classes), 28–9 (half of early modern state expenditures on military, this also allowing maintenance of hegemony within defined borders); Ertman (1997), *Birth of the Leviathan*, at 4 (superior fighting ability based on access to urban capital and coercive authority over peasant taxpayers); Elton (1953), *Tudor Revolution in Government*, at 421 (Tudor development of military bureaucracy within state); Cipolla (1976), *Before the Industrial Revolution*, at 51–2 (on military expenditures running over half of state budgets, contemporary parallels); Vives (1972), 'The Administrative Structure of the State', at 67 (triumph of monarchy based on external aggression, internal violent partisanship); Tilly (1994a), 'Entanglements of European Cities and States', at 11 (causal effect of type of war, fiscal strategy, character of economy); Bobbitt (2002), *Shield of Achilles*, at 80 (origins pinpointed even in French king Charles VIII invading Italian peninsula in 1494 with forty horse-drawn artillery pieces). For the tax base, Cipolla (1976), *Before the Industrial Revolution*, at 45; Nicholas (1999), *Transformation of Europe 1300–1600*, at 217 ('insatiable demand for money'); van Creveld (1999), *Rise and Decline of State*, at 336–7 (Bank of England, legal tender, income tax all products of war).

years'.[70] Beyond the belligerence, however, the monarchical state brought organization, and some benefits, over as wide a territory as it was able to. It began to 'see like a state', abstracting, mapping, and quantifying both 'natural' and 'human' resources.[71] This information base was obviously closely tied to an expanding tax base, so successful state vision led to more successful state action. All of these activities required larger and more sophisticated forms of hierarchical organization, and the word 'bureaucracy' emerged in the eighteenth century to describe these, a combination of the French 'bureau' (for office) and the Greek *kratio* (for rule or power). The word is just right, since it is the resources of the hierarchy that enable it to undertake a widening range of functions.[72] In the sixteenth century in France there was 1 official for every 1,250 inhabitants; by 1934 the ratio was 1 to 70.[73]

Some have therefore spoken of the state 'caging' or 'officializing' civil society[74] and the growth of the state hierarchy does appear to have displaced the power of many of the historic intermediaries between crowns and people.[75] The language and theory of royal 'absolutism' also appears in early modern times, as we will shortly see. Yet the early modern state was not, and could scarcely be, a totalitarian or closed state. Its population remained diverse, both within Europe and beyond; its own agents and officials (at local levels) were often themselves the source of resistance;[76] the transport and communication technology it engendered was Janus-faced, transcending the borders that it sought to consolidate.[77]

---

[70] Morris (1998), *Essay on Modern State*, at 54, and 15 (for preparation for war as 'the great state-building activity').

[71] For the 'seeing', Scott (1998), *Seeing Like a State*, notably at 13 (not seeing the forest for the (commercial) trees), 31 (need for uniform weights and measures, 'one king, one law, one weight, one measure'), 35 (imposition of cadastral map essential to taxation of property), 87 (purposive character of mapping), 71 (imposition of standardized last names for all members of population, as late as 1808 in France, on arrival of no-name immigrants to USA); and for general 'dirigisme', Clough and Cole (1952), *Economic History of Europe*, at 195 (goal of economic 'unity'), 203 (mercantilism fostering distrust of foreigners), 316 (role of tariffs and duties in creating national economies), 321 (great 'codes' of Colbert (see this chapter, 'Codes') as part of mercantilist policies); and for dirigisme as compatible with a western view of a world 'out there', identifiable from its coordinates and manipulable by individual or state, Boyarin (1994b), 'Space, Time and the Politics of Memory', at 5 ('problem-oriented').

[72] Bureaucratic development was preceded or at least facilitated by creation of central state archives. On these and standardization of bureaucratic structures and entry qualifications, development of a national police force and conseil d'état (the model of the latter to spread through the world), van Creveld (1999), *Rise and Decline of State*, at 136, 139–40, 167; and more generally for bureaucratic growth, Elton (1953), *Tudor Revolution in Government*, at 3 (national administration as opposed to administration of king's estate), 422 (growth of national 'departments' of government): Strayer (1970), *Medieval Origins of Modern State*, at 28 (origins in estate-keeping centuries previously), 34 (gaining legitimacy by enduring through generations).

[73] Major (1960), *Representative Institutions in Renaissance France*, at 5.

[74] Mann (1986), *Sources of social power*, at 504–5: Kriegel (1995), *The State and the Rule of Law*, at 30.

[75] Tilly (1994b), 'Afterword: Political Memories in Space and Time', at 250 (for creation of 'direct relations' between state agents and majority of heads of household, supplanting of old regime of 'indirect rule'); and generally for France, Sueur (2007), *Histoire droit public français*, vol. 2.

[76] Mettam (1977), *Government and Society in Louis XIV's France*, at ix (ministers at centre lacking effective executive arm).

[77] Van Creveld (1999), *Rise and Decline of State*, at 377.

We are therefore properly warned both of the dangers of reductionism, in judging the state narrowly in terms of only one or a few of its functions,[78] and of a 'modernization' paradigm that would see the state developing according to an 'inbuilt logic' so as to develop its 'true form'.[79] Within Europe there were 'profound differences' in structures and their intensification[80] and much more would have depended on popular support than on military authority.[81] Beyond Europe metropolitan authority was often simply ignored, or received a laconic response such as that known in Spanish imperial history in Latin America, 'I obey but do not carry out'.[82] Where the writing of the colonial state was not acknowledged as a source of law, the hierarchy it sought to generate was profoundly compromised. An emerging theory of the state could seek to overcome these difficulties, with no possibility of overcoming them entirely.

An emerging theory of the state

There is debate on the relation of theory to practice, and the notion of practice preceding theory has already been encountered.[83] If there is much truth in the statement, it should not be taken, however, as an absolute, or as implying a rigid distinction between practice and theory. Theory may often be inspired by events on the ground, or seek to provide a remedy for them, yet it may also provide an impetus for subsequent conduct. Much useful thinking occurs at the interface between what we know as theory and practice. An identifiable theory of the contemporary state emerged in a visible manner from the sixteenth century and, though it had been preceded by many developments on the ground, nevertheless contributed greatly to the growth of state structures thereafter. We do not know whether that growth would have occurred in the absence of the theory, but it did occur in its presence. Whether theory actually justifies practice will depend on how good it is, and how much need for justification remains. Riesenberg has written that 'incipient fact forms theory which in turn acts back upon original reality to strengthen it',[84] and this is entirely consistent with the cyclical, reflexive

---

[78] Kriegel (1995), *The State and the Rule of Law*, at 90 (on economic analysis of state skirting around principal objective—juridification—of state actors).

[79] Given (1990), *State and Society in Medieval Europe*, at 255–6 (overlooking 'dialectical interaction', and more, criticizing Weberian notions of 'rationalization').

[80] Strayer (1970), *Medieval Origins of Modern State*, at 106–7 (notably, Russia 'barely able to survive'): Spellman (1998), *European Political Thought: 1600–1700* at 44 (in terms of bureaucratic centralism, seventeenth-century Spain 'clearly does not qualify').

[81] Major (1960), *Representative Institutions in Renaissance France*, at 14 (strongest rulers most popular ones); Harding (2002b), *Medieval Law and Foundations of State*, at 252 (monarchical state itself that which made taxing and military adventures possible).

[82] 'Acato pero no cumplo': Mirow (2004), *Latin American Law* at 235; Elliott (2006), *Empires*, at 132.

[83] See Ch. 1, 'Readings of the State Tradition', and for further debate, see Ch. 9, 'Cosmopolitan Theory'.

[84] Riesenberg (1970), *Inalienability of Sovereignty*, at 82 (on twelfth-century integration of 'political reality' into debates of canonists); and for 'political theory' that both accompanies and justifies, van Creveld (1999), *Rise and Decline of State*, at 126ff.

notion of tradition as information, captured and transmitted at different levels of abstraction.[85]

The theory that functioned to reinforce hierarchy as an element of closure was initiated largely by Jean Bodin in France. Bodin of course had predecessors, perhaps most notably Marsilius of Padua (defending empire against church) and Machiavelli (darkly defending the autonomy of Italian city states), but neither provided the impetus that Bodin did.[86] They now appear as too early, even as part of the prehistory of the contemporary state, though some would give more importance to Machiavelli. Bodin wrote, however, at the right time, at the confluence of some major streams of thought and reality. His *Six livres de la république* was published in 1576, in the midst of the French wars of religion and during a general time of ferocious, pan-European conflict. He is said to have 'witnessed' the St Bartholomew's Day massacre of thousands of Huguenots in 1572, and he warned of the possible 'shipwreck' ('naufrage') of the French state.[87] What Bodin did was to articulate or 'magnify' a notion of 'sovereignty' that has been with us ever since.[88] It was a highly abstract concept, not based on any explicit notion of legitimacy (conspicuously absent from the discussion) while concentrating exclusively on sovereign ability to make and enforce law. It was a 'puissance absolue' or absolute power,[89] and this would have 'inaugurated the modern supremacy of the political nation'[90] since (logically at least) indivisible, concentrated sovereignty eliminated other sources of authority in the state. There could be no more institutional cosmopolitanism, no 'mixed' constitution. There was therefore an implicit normative base to Bodin's argument since, while it did not rely explicitly on religious or monarchic justification, its abstract notion of sovereignty exercised in the general interest was close to Aristotelian naturalist notions of human community. The essential was sovereignty—one, indivisible and perpetual.[91] With it, the state would have become an 'entity'.[92] The entity

---

[85] Glenn (2010b), *Legal Traditions*, at 13ff.

[86] For Marsilius, see Ch. 5, 'Religion'; and for Machiavelli as advocate of brute force, Shennan (1974), *Origins of Modern European State*, at 74 (though as largely 'subterranean aspect'); Skinner (2002), *Visions of Politics*, at 144 (as 'absolutely indispensable feature of good princely government').

[87] Bodin (1986), *Six livres*, I, Préface, at 10; for 'witnessing', Skinner (1978), *Foundations of modern political thought*, at 284–5 (though the 'ideological task' of *Six Livres* that of repudiating Huguenot theory of resistance); and for similar impetus to royal absolutism, given 'anarchy' in England during the Wars of the Roses of the previous century, van Caenegem (1995), *Historical Introduction Western Constitutional Law*, at 97.

[88] For magnification, Gierke (1939), *Development of Political Theory*, at 157; and for 'popularization', Spellman (1998), *European Political Thought: 1600–1700*, at 54.

[89] Bodin (1986), *Six livres*, I, Ch. 8, at 179, and Ch. 10, at 306 for law-making 'en général'.

[90] Spellman (1998), *European Political Thought: 1600–1700*, at 55 (stripping allegiance of any ethical dimension, allegiance of all subjects obligatory).

[91] Van Creveld (1999), *Rise and Decline of State*, at 177 (essential character of sovereign's ability to create order out of chaos). Bodin distinguished 'perpetual' sovereignty from time-limited grants of authority, even from the people: Bodin (1986), *Six livres*, I, Ch. 8, at 179–80.

[92] Lloyd (1983), *The State, France and the Sixteenth Century*, at 159 (as 'epoch-making idea'), with location of sovereignty (in monarch, aristocracy, or people) defining nature of the state; and for combination of people, sovereignty, and state as a 'Denkkontinuum' or closed system, di Fabio (1998), *Das Recht offener Staaten*, at 17.

was a hierarchical one, already developing on the ground. The idea of sovereignty topped off the hierarchy very nicely. The word even derives from the Latin *super*, or above, so necessarily entails hierarchy.[93]

Bodin's thought was surreptitiously Aristotelian in other ways. Like Aristotle, he was, paradoxical though it may appear, cosmopolitan and comparative in his methods of contemplating human society. Aristotle, who examined many constitutions in his *Politics*, may even have been the inspiration.[94] Bodin is thus known both as the originator of national sovereignty *and* as the first theoretical exponent of comparative law. He proceeded not on the basis of Roman law (concurring in its French rejection), nor on the basis of ecclesiastical teaching, but on a naturalist examination of the juridical experience of a wide number of states, even on the basis of a notion of 'universal history'.[95] His proposals, moreover, were clearly meant to be pan-European or general in application. Bodin's manner of appreciating his different models was also Aristotelian, or even Platonic, in character, since he proceeded by a strict process of 'separation and juxtaposition', according to which 'nothing can be understood except in contradistinction to what it is not, by setting it over against what is opposed to it'.[96] By this process of separation Bodin was able to subdivide notions of the state, and their constituent parts, with a view to generating a logical system for law in its entirety.[97] We see here an early version of constructivist comparative law, the mining of diverse sources for constructive purposes of legal reform and unification. Cosmopolitanism is put to use for largely non-cosmopolitan ends. Bodin would ultimately have been motivated by a 'logic of indivisibility',[98] the state once again as 'entity'.

Bodin's teaching was widely received throughout Europe, and its effect was magnified by its compatibility with religious justifications of royal authority. Kings had long been religiously anointed and the abstract notion of sovereignty

---

[93] Forey (2007), *État et institutions religieuses*, at 117–18 (word first appearing in French in thirteenth century, derived from Latin, originally as comparative or relational to indicate a superior, then in superlative manner); and for theories of sovereignty as 'theories of unity', Vincent (1987), *Theories of the State*, at 199.

[94] Aristotle is frequently cited in Bodin (1986), *Six livres*, and Bks II and IV–VI are largely comparative in character in examining 'toutes sortes de Républiques en general' (Bk. II, title of Ch. 1).

[95] See, e.g. Bodin (1986), *Six livres*, V, Ch. 1, at 23 ('[l]a courtoisie et humanité venue d'Asie'); Franklin (1963), *Jean Bodin*, at 2, 70 (for 'comparison and synthesis'); Skinner (1978), *Foundations of modern political thought*, at 291 (for 'vastly ambitious enterprise'); Franklin (1991), 'Sovereignty and the mixed constitution', at 301 (inadequacy of Roman law, need for 'universal, comparative legal science'); Friedrich (1997), *Geschichte der deutschen Staatsrechtswissenschaft*, at 32 (with Bodin, Roman law 'untergegangen', ties with past broken).

[96] Keohane (1980), *Philosophy and State in France*, at 68 (thus regime of virtue distinguished from one of vice and disorder); for the origins of such a logic of *divisio* or separation, see Ch. 14, 'The cosmopolitan limits of binary logic'.

[97] For categories, Bodin (1986), *Six livres*, II, Ch. 1, at 7, and 10 ('contrary' republics requiring 'contrary' laws). For subdivision and classification, Skinner (1978), *Foundations of modern political thought*, at 291; Church (1969), *Constitutional Thought in Sixteenth-Century France*, at 227 (classification based on *locus* of sovereignty in various states); Franklin (1963), *Jean Bodin*, at 3 (for 'general theory of law'), 63 ('logical arrangement for law in its entirety'), and 67 (for codification).

[98] Franklin (1991), 'Sovereignty and the mixed constitution', at 307.

now contributed to a notion of the character of their rule as divine and absolute.[99] Bodin had not relied on religious justification but was quickly taken up by supporters of the 'great light that never sets', the divine monarch.[100] It may well have been Bodin who gave rise to the sixteenth-century notion of royal absolutism, since prior to Bodin royalty had been more evidently encumbered by the cosmopolitan ways examined earlier in this chapter.

Bodin's cosmopolitan reflections on the need for sovereign authority were eventually overshadowed by the giant form of Hobbes' Leviathan, a distinctly uncosmopolitan figure, both in terms of its origins and theoretical conception. Hobbes founded his reflections largely on his own, imagined state of nature, one of 'continual fear and danger of violent death' in which human life would famously be 'solitary, poor, nasty, brutish and short'.[101] Today it appears that Hobbes was describing more his own violent seventeenth century, one of emerging contemporary states, than that of earlier state or non-state human orders, but he drew remarkably broad legal consequences from his non-empirical point of departure.[102] It was notably the case that 'notions of right and wrong, justice and injustice, have there no place' and that in a pre-Leviathan world 'nothing can be unjust'.[103] Hobbes displayed a 'bullish irreverence' for the common law, itself an ongoing challenge to his argument.[104] Yet from his initial scene of physical and moral desolation, a strong Leviathan had to emerge, and compared to that of Bodin or anyone else Hobbes's sovereign has been described

[99] From the Latin *ab solver*, as disengaged or freed from restriction. The description 'absolutist' may have been an eighteenth-century revolutionary epithet, though it might have been used in a non-pejorative manner during the sixteenth century in the sense of 'independent'. For revolutionary neologism, Spellman (1998), *European Political Thought: 1600–1700*, at 34, and for earlier, non-pejorative use, Sueur (2007), *Histoire du droit public français*, vol. I, at 123.

[100] Keohane (1980), *Philosophy and State in France*, at 241 (citing de Priezac); and for absolutism as sixteenth-century concept, Ellul (1956), *Histoire des institutions*, at 293; Spellman (1998), *European Political Thought: 1600–1700* at 36 (to avoid 'localist bedlam'); Brissaud (1915), *History of French Public Law*, at 334 (absoluteness of God and king as vicar of God); Church (1969), *Constitutional Thought in Sixteenth-Century France*, at 45 (humanist writing of time in 'complete unanimity in glorification of the monarch'), 179 (population reduced to great body of subjects); Sueur (2007), *Histoire du droit public français*, vol. II, at 61 (end of autonomy of both cities and nobility). For Bodin's 'immediate' taking-over by royalist absolutists, Church (1969), *Constitutional Thought in Sixteenth-Century France*, at 244 (with ensuing distortion).

[101] Hobbes (1958), *Leviathan*, at 107.

[102] For Hobbes and Rousseau both 'talking through their hats', Pinker (2011), *Better Angels*, at 36; and for his state of nature as 'not a historical fact but a logical postulate', Spellman (1998), *European Political Thought: 1600–1700*, at 159; and as 'presupposing' a sort of moral vacuum, Malcolm (2000), *Aspects of Hobbes*, at 34. For both Bodin and Hobbes as reflections of their violent renaissance surroundings, Vincent (1987), *Theories of the State*, at 201; and for contemporary, empirical research on collaborative structures of informal society, Ostrom (1990), *Governing the Commons*; Mann (2005), *1491/Ancient Americans*, notably at 201, 264–5, 314, 321 (chthonic North American peoples managing large tracts of land, appropriate herds); and for 'few theorists today' subscribing to Hobbes' (draconian) views, Morris (1998), *Essay on Modern State*, at 217. Pinker, however, presents evidence from a number of archaeological sites as supporting higher levels of violence in hunter-gatherer societies than in contemporary states: Pinker (2011), *Better Angels*, at 49 (though no tabulation of cost of colonialism and acknowledgement at 193 and 297 of difficulties in establishing death rates). For present-day violence, see Ch. 5 '*Fragmentation, failure, and violence*'.

[103] Hobbes (1958), *Leviathan*, at 108.

[104] Goldie (1991), 'The Reception of Hobbes', at 596.

as 'much more powerful',[105] though here we may somehow be contemplating degrees of theoretical absoluteness.

Hobbes was enormously influential, and controversial, in England and abroad. He brought about a cosmopolitan movement towards political and legal unity of the state.[106] Yet after a few centuries of reflection and debate, it is not only the empirical foundations of his teaching that have been challenged, but also the theoretical. Hobbes sought theoretical justification for his Leviathan neither from on high nor from simple force but from a notion of representation, by which the represented mandate the representor to act on their behalf. Thus the multitude is 'so united' in one commonwealth or Leviathan.[107] Hobbes provided little information, however, on how this actually came about, or on how to evaluate claims of valid representation. Even assuming valid representation as a legitimation of Leviathan's authority, there is the underlying problem of necessary limits to any mandate, so Hobbes's Leviathan has been said to be both a product of and limited by the natural law that Hobbes did rely upon, even though it was incapable of creating detailed notions of right and wrong in the state of nature. Hobbes accepted necessary limits.[108]

Hobbes's logical foundations are also questioned. Hobbes sought to anchor his political thought in still larger scientific and rational constructions. He planned a major work on 'Logike' and the totality of his work evidences an 'urge to systematize' located 'deep in his intellectual character'.[109] He avoided the clutter of human diversity that preoccupied Bodin and he has been described as a 'notorious dichotomiser'.[110] We face a choice between amoral anarchy or Leviathan, between dissolution of the state or affirmation of its total decisional authority. Leibniz concluded that Hobbes was setting up a 'false alternative' in

---

[105] Van Creveld (1999), *Rise and Decline of State*, at 179.

[106] For trans-societal influence, Malcolm (1991), 'Hobbes and Spinoza', at 545 (notably in The Netherlands where 'greatest influence') and 546 (for compatibility with teaching of Descartes); Goyard-Fabre (1975), *Droit et loi dans la philosophie de Hobbes* (for contemporary France).

[107] Hobbes (1958), *Leviathan*, at 142, and 144–5 (for permanence of delegation, making unlawful any new covenant).

[108] For Hobbes himself, Hobbes (1958), *Leviathan*, at 109–10, 119, 211 (for subjection to laws of nature), and 179 for termination of representation in the face of its inadequacy). For inherent normative limits, Stankiewicz (1976), 'Sovereignty as Political Theory', at 143–4 (sovereign 'cannot violate the logic of the contract', system 'must have room for the norms it is designed to protect', sovereignty not a statement about 'power' but about government and the state). A binary distinction between law and morality had not emerged by the time of Hobbes, so admission of natural law was a legal and not simply a moral conclusion. Natural law could be law, though lacking immediate temporal sanction. For Hobbes as a natural lawyer and not as a positivist (in spite of positivist acceptance of much of his teaching), Boyle (1987), 'Thomas Hobbes and the Invented Tradition of Positivism', at 383, 397: Malcolm (2000), *Aspects of Hobbes*, at 438 (if law of nature, cannot be true that state of nature one of 'simple amorality').

[109] Malcolm (2000), *Aspects of Hobbes*, at 12; and 15, 23 (on Hobbes's basic assumptions about a mechanistic physical universe), 146 (disputed relations between Hobbes's natural and civil science), 152 (model for civil science in geometry); Goyard-Fabre (1975), *Droit et loi dans la philosophie de Hobbes*, at 26 (for Hobbes's 'mécanique politique'); Friedrich (1997), *Geschichte der deutschen Staatsrechtswissenschaft*, at 91 (for 'analytical-deductive' method in social theory).

[110] Condren (2002), '*Natura Naturans*: Natural Law and the Sovereign', at 61 (also for dichotomous nature of debate *on* Hobbes).

civil science, denied notably by the constitutional theory of the Holy Roman Empire.[111] The Dutch, much influenced by Hobbes on sovereignty, decided to 'leave the question open' in their 1815 constitution.[112] Outside Europe, in the European empires of the world, the notion largely washed out, or became a 'discursive practice'.[113] Sovereignty was neither something to be obtained, within the empire, nor an instrument of total authority. States beyond Europe, within empires, remained largely untouched by notions of sovereign closure. There was scepticism even towards the notion of boundaries, the third and vital element of a territorial state.

BOUNDARIES

Boundaries of states existed before the eighteenth century, but since the states were not territorial ones the boundaries were often incomplete or ill-defined. They did not rigorously separate people, and communities would inevitably 'interact and overlap', trading, quarrelling, and intermarrying. Sometimes they would even 'incorporate elements of other traditions into theirs'.[114] Greek city-states had walls but those walls may not have been complete, and natural geo-physical features were often pressed into use. Chthonic or indigenous people knew the (rough) boundaries of their collective land. In medieval Europe there were marches in place of boundaries.[115] A major change in the appreciation of space occurred, however, in the seventeenth and eighteenth centuries. It became susceptible to mapping, and a discernible boundary came to be taken, if not as an element of the state itself, at least as a condition of its existence.[116] Major efforts were made both to fix boundaries on the ground and to draw legal conclusions from their existence. Somewhat surprisingly, there was little theoretical justification of them. They simply became part of the landscape. Geographical and legal developments, however, went hand in hand.

---

[111] Malcolm (2000), *Aspects of Hobbes*, at 529 with references; and for the impossibility of a 'state within the state' in Hobbes's writing, Gierke (1939), *Development of Political Theory*, at 270.

[112] Herringa and Kiiver (2007), *Constitutions Compared*, at 7 ('[w]ho is the Dutch sovereign is truly anybody's guess').

[113] Wachspress (2009), 'Rethinking sovereignty', at 318 (an experience, practice, or performance, rather than a capacity or status).

[114] Buchanan and Moore (2003), Introduction, in *States, Nations, and Borders*, at 3.

[115] For medieval and earlier ambiguity on spatial delimitation, see Ch. 3, *'Boundaries'*; and for the general absence of delimitation of territorial sovereignty, Guichonnet and Raffestin (1974), *Géographie des frontières* at 83, 84.

[116] The condition of boundaries is usually expressed in terms of a territory, though the territory must be precisely determined. See in contemporary international law, e.g. Brierly (1963), *Law of Nations*, at 137 ('defined territory'); Dupuy (1995), *Droit international public*, at 30, 31 ('détermination exacte' of spatial field of sovereignty); cf. Shaw (2008), *International Law*, at 199 (need for 'defined territory' but 'no necessity . . . for defined and settled boundaries' so long as 'consistent band of territory' . . . 'undeniably controlled'). The proliferation of boundary disputes is the best indication, however, of the felt need for delineated boundaries. For ongoing boundary disputes see the website of the International Boundary Research Unit at Durham University, at <http://www.dur.ac.uk/ibru>.

Van Creveld treats borders as 'information', an 'exact definition as to which territories belonged to which ruler', and the process of developing such precise definitions, recognizable on the ground, has lasted from the fifteenth century to the twenty-first, and is still going on.[117] Modern mapping has been essential to the process.[118] Yet modern mapping could not avoid the countless decisions as to where precisely a line *should* be drawn. If it went on one side of a village, what about a neighbouring, dependent hamlet? What about an isolated house, a wood long used by a village? We are told that personal loyalties often controlled the delimitation of space, and not the reverse,[119] and the reality of political map-making of the time was a reflection of the difficulty of translating personal loyalties into spatial ones. In the mid-eighteenth century lawyers were still speaking of a state as a group of people, not as a territorial domain.[120] While space for enlightenment cartographers had become 'pure quantity, abstracted from the qualities of meaning and experience' (and hence carte blanche),[121] populations had yet to make the shift. Often, therefore, nature was invoked in support of the mapping process and the idea of a 'natural' legal and political boundary became widespread, though nature never divided in this way. The idea was particular and European, originating in the renaissance. Nature had to be compliant with the frontier as 'vouloir'.[122]

Kruger concluded that '[t]he border thus establishes itself as the unique and single cause of modern time', with the decisive moment the drawing of a line.[123] The line once drawn, 'sovereignty', the complete and effective control of an organizational hierarchy, becomes possible. In the absence of a boundary such a concept is unrealistic or even unthinkable, since no one can be sovereign in an

---

[117] Van Creveld (1999), *Rise and Fall of State*, at 143 (first European boundary stone between Sweden and Brandenburg on completion of Treaty of Westphalia, 1648; USA–Canada border still unmarked in nineteenth century, as much of Asia, Africa; Bauban in 1692 misestimating surface of France by as much as a third); and see Kratochwil (1986), 'Of Systems, Boundaries, and Territoriality', at 33 (for Spain–France boundary first official 'modern' boundary, inaugurated 1659).

[118] Van Creveld (1999), *Rise and Fall of State*, at 143–4 (also for seventeenth-century innovation of different colours for territories of different monarchs, itself becoming one of 'important symbols of statehood'); and for instrumentalism of contemporary mapping, Scott (1998), *Seeing Like a State*, at 87 ('high modernism'); Bayly (2004), *Birth of Modern World*, at 274 (links between warfare and mapping); Black (1997), *Maps and Politics*, notably at 136 (49th parallel in North America as example of use of European science to subject territory to European notion of space).

[119] Biggs (1999), 'Putting the State on the Map', at 386 ('rule was exercised over subjects rather than land'); and for the slow process of territorial logic superseding both imperial and feudal logic, Badie (2000), *The Imported State*, at 58–9.

[120] Horowitz (2004), 'International Law and State Transformation', at 476 (on Vattel).

[121] Biggs (1999), 'Putting the State on the Map', at 377.

[122] Nordman (1982), 'Problématique historique des frontières', at 19; and for renaissance origins of the 'natural boundary', see Ch. 3, '*Boundaries*' (Petrarch, Boccaccio in fourteenth century); Guichonnet and Raffestin (1974), *Géographie des frontières*, at 19; Jones (1973), 'Boundary Concepts' at 167. Pagden concludes that 'such claims could never stand any close examination': Pagden (2003), 'The Christian Tradition', at 108.

[123] Krüger (1966), *Allgemeine Staatslehre*, at 21.

unlimited manner *everywhere*.[124] The elements of a territorial state are thus brought together: writing as the technique of control; hierarchy as a means of structure and enforcement; and boundaries as the necessary encadrement of both.

Given the necessary relation of boundaries to everything else that was going on in Europe from the sixteenth century, their existence was largely presumed and not justified. It was an 'assumption' that discernible and populated territories existed; at most they were *de facto*.[125] Hobbes did not include territory in his definition of sovereignty; it would have been 'implied' as the outer limits of authority.[126] In expansive, crowded Europe there was arguably not much point in theorizing about borders. The lawyers concerned about such things said simply, in a spirit of exhaustion, '*uti possidetis*' (since you have it), and left the detail to the surveyors.

The legal consequences of map making and territorial thinking were not long in being drawn. Most consequentially, the notion of legal territoriality was first (apparently) expressed by Ulrich Huber, a Dutch law professor also writing in the turbulent seventeenth century and concerned with effecting Dutch independence from a range of European powers. Huber unfortunately coined the expression 'the conflict of laws' to describe the relations of the laws of different states. The most important principle of Huber's discipline of the conflicts of laws was that the laws of a state apply within its territory and bind all persons within its limits.[127] Today this may seem banal but it has been rightly described as a 'complete change in theory' since in principle it eliminated all but the laws of the state on a given territory.[128] The writing of the state would be exclusive, and 'binding', since '[l]'autorité de l'Etat ne souffre point le vide'.[129] Closure would be total.

If the notion of a territorial state thus came to be, there remained the sticky problem of the loyalty of its people. The state would have to be a nation-state.

---

[124] Krüger (1966), *Allgemeine Staatslehre*, at 22 (border-making 'Herrschaft' possible and defining its limits); Morris (1998), *Essay on Modern State*, at 175 (sovereignty pertaining to authority within a realm). Cf., for Bodin as working with a 'spatially elastic' notion of sovereignty (in relation to persons), though the territoriality of the French state may have been simply assumed by him, Benton (2010), *Search for Sovereignty*, at 288; and for the notion of territorial sovereignty as acquired by mid-sixteenth century, Thorne (1985), 'Sovereignty and the Conflict of Laws', at 174–5, 181.

[125] Hont (1995), 'Permanent Crisis of Divided Mankind', at 187 (though 'new theory said virtually nothing about the legitimacy of the spatial borders themselves'). The maritime limits came to be accepted as the length of an eighteenth-century cannon shot, now set at three miles, a *de facto* proposition of Bynkershoek in 1702; Brierly (1963), *Law of Nations*, at 202.

[126] Ivison (2002), 'Property, Territory and Sovereignty', at 222.

[127] For Huber's text in English translation, Lorenzen (1947), 'Huber's *De Conflictu Legum*'. A Dutch translation of Hobbes's *Leviathan* appeared in 1667, five years before Huber's volume on the conflict of laws: Malcolm (1991), 'Hobbes and Spinoza', at 545.

[128] Thorne (1985), 'Sovereignty and the Conflict of Laws', at 181.

[129] Nordman (1982), 'Problématique historique des frontières,' at 19 ('the authority of the state cannot tolerate a vacuum'). For the combined process of growth in the ambit of state law, its declining association with morality, and its increasing politicization (philosophical attention turning away from concepts of justice towards abstract definitions of law), Wesel (2006), *Geschichte des Rechts*, at 47–9.

5

A Nation-State?

The primary instruments of closure of the territorial state have been those of writing, hierarchy, and boundaries. Each became more intensely used than in previous state forms. In a sense, they constituted the framework, structure, or outline of the contemporary state, with varying degrees of success. There remained the people, the basic stuff, and people too had to be rendered compatible with the contemporary form of the state. This did not follow inevitably from the development of written law, hierarchy, and boundaries. Personal loyalty did not follow from a structure of territoriality. So it became necessary to bring about, in some measure at least, a second form of closure of the people of the contemporary state. They had to recognize themselves as such and, while writing, hierarchy, and boundaries imply significant measures of separation and coercion, loyalty is difficult to coerce. People can be brought together; the question is whether, over time, they will choose to stay together.

We know this second form of closure, of the people of the contemporary state, as the nation-state, in which a people, or nation, coincides with a state. The notion of the nation-state is of very recent vintage. Prior to an operative notion of a nation, however, there were other and important efforts towards human closure in the development of the contemporary state. The most important were the strivings for a common language and a common religion; both were eventually to constitute important elements of any possible nation. Citizenship then could become the final cement between the individual and the nation-state.

LANGUAGE

The capture of language, as an element of the nation, began with writing, and the requirement of the Ordinance of Villers-Cotterets of 1539 that juridical acts be written in French had the necessary, and intended, effect of reducing the significance of both Latin and local languages.[1] A national language was to replace both the universal language and the previous vernaculars. Language was essential to the later notion of the nation, and in Germany Herder spoke

---

[1] See Ch. 4, 'Writing'. There may even have been skulduggery at work; prefects in France wrote of the necessity of corrupting local languages, or at least that of Brittany, so as to make them incomprehensible from village to village: Plasseraud (1989), 'Les revendications des minorités', at 219 (language differences 'exploitées' by Paris in its policy of 'eradication' of local forms of expression).

of language as going to the 'heart and soul' of a people or nation.[2] If the sixteenth century saw the beginning of national languages, however, the process of their development was very slow. By the time of post-revolutionary France, when it was declared by the Constitution of 1791 that France was 'one and indivisible' ('une et indivisible'), only some 12 per cent of the population would have spoken French correctly, and only 50 per cent would have spoken it at all. In Italy, by the time of unification in 1860, only 2.5 per cent of the population used Italian on a daily basis.[3] The situation is said to have been little different in other western European states such as Great Britain and Spain, where dialects and even entirely different languages persisted.[4] Today there are functional national languages in most European states though in some instances, notably that of France, the situation would date only from the twentieth century.[5]

Today there is a widespread practice of legislating on national languages, evidence of an ongoing faith in the power of written, formal language to control language itself.[6] In French it would be said that 'un langage' is being used to control 'la langue'. This was earlier referred to as a conceptual leap that in some measure worked, and there seems little doubt that some degree of national linguistic unity has been achieved through legislative measures.[7] Legislation even contributed to the revival of Hebrew in Israel and Welsh in Wales.[8] The longer the experience with the idea, however, the more evident become the challenges to it. There are ongoing guerrilla tactics against national languages, whether individually on the ground or through formal litigation.[9] The 'audible minorities' make themselves heard. More generally, there appears to be a growing

---

[2] Herder (1991), *Briefe*, at 65 (entire wealth of ideas of tradition, history, religion, and principles of life residing in language, most loved element of people); and see Schulze (1996), *States, Nations and Nationalism*, at 157 (in stories and songs 'nation bared its soul'). For Herder's biting critique of French-style enlightenment and the priority of the French language, Leersen (2006), *National Thought*, at 100 ('improvement through assimilation').

[3] Van Caenegem (1995), *Historical Introduction Western Constitutional Law*, at 187, on 'indivisibilité'. For both France and Italy, Hobsbawm (1990), *Nations and Nationalism*, at 60, for France relying notably on Brunot (1927–43), *Histoire de la langue française*, vol. IX. For French spoken in only fifteen of eighty-three départements in 1790, Schulze (1996), *States, Nations and Nationalism*, at 159.

[4] For dialects, Welsh, and Gaelic in Great Britain and dialects, Catalan, Basque, and Galician in Spain, Schulze (1996), *States, Nations and Nationalism*, at 160 (spread of literacy, however, accelerating standardization of language).

[5] Schulze (1996), *States, Nations and Nationalism*, at 159; Laitin (2007) *Nations, States, and Violence*, at 32 (nineteenth-century 'language zones' even 'incommensurable' with national boundaries; Britain, France, Spain originally 'multilingual empires' though over 'prolonged nation-building experiences' a 'hegemonic language regime emerged').

[6] For Quebec, states of the USA, France, and Venezuela, Jayme (1999), *Langue et Droit*, at 65, 181, 154, and 364.

[7] See Ch. 4, 'Writing'.

[8] For Israel, though it was said by Herzl in 1896 that no Jew was familiar enough with Hebrew to buy a train ticket in it, Navot (1999), 'Language Rights in Israel', at 199.

[9] For examples, Molfessis (1999), 'La Langue et le Droit', at 184 (person writing cheque in Breton to pay for railway ticket, using cheque itself as ticket when cheque refused at ticket counter), 196 (bills in Chinese issued in France); Schroth (1999), 'Language and Law' at 167 (on litigation in USA over employer prohibition of Spanish speaking during working hours).

phenomenon of multilingualism within state borders (as well as reaction to it), either an outgrowth of population movement or a revival of previously quiescent linguistic practices. States have had to acknowledge the existence of multiple languages, at times grudgingly, as where an Italian municipality posts public prohibitions of theft in Albanian, Arab, Romanian, and Serbo-Croatian,[10] at times more obviously to protect the languages of politically significant minorities. This has been undertaken, for example, in Belgium, Canada, Italy, The Netherlands (now recognizing Frisian, Lower-Saxon, Yiddish, Roma, and Limburgian), New Zealand (Maori), and South Africa (where there are now eleven official languages, though only English and Afrikaans are used in legislation).[11] The European Union, which some compare to a state, is linguistically very cosmopolitan, with twenty-three official languages and a policy of encouraging multilingualism on the part of its citizens.

The shift to legal multilingualism has consequences for methods of legal interpretation, as law must be sought in multiple versions. This is said by some to improve, not weaken, legal understanding.[12] There is also a phenomenon of simultaneous drafting in two or more languages, avoiding translation from an 'original' language, in the effort to articulate law in a way that is linguistically sound in more than one language.[13] People, or peoples, who are functionally bilingual or multilingual frequently engage in 'code switching', changing from language to language even within a single sentence, a practice very visible in countries such as India or The Philippines. Code switching is the most obvious sign of the fundamental openness of languages, and of the difficulty of controlling them through legislation. English, and notably legal English, is filled with words of French origin, an absorptive capacity that has contributed greatly to the role of English in the world today.[14] Given open languages, and informal linguistic

---

[10]   Sacco (1999), 'Langue et Droit', at 241.

[11]   See Vanderlinden (1999), 'Langue et Droit', at 82–8 (Belgium and Canada); Sacco (1999), 'Langue et Droit', at 247 (Italy); de Groot, (1999), 'Language and Law', at 342 (The Netherlands); Angelo (1999), 'Culture Protection, Language and Law', at 286–7 (New Zealand); and du Plessis (1999), 'Report on Language and Law', at 55 (South Africa).

[12]   Jutras (2000), 'Énoncer l'indicible' (norms only partially rendered by different linguistic efforts to express them); Viau (1999), 'Considérations sur la langue', at 141 (noting Bible in multiple versions); du Plessis (1999), 'Report on Language and Law', at 56 (on impossibility of literal interpretation in face of multiple versions of text).

[13]   Gémar and Kasirer (2005), *Jurilinguistique/tics*, notably at xiii, citing Ricoeur ('il est toujours possible de dire la même chose autrement'); Beaupré (1986), *Interprétation de la législation bilingue*, at 209 (translation in drafting as 'error of the past'); Šarčević (1997), *New Approach to Legal Translation*, at 181 (now 'room for stylistic diversity in parallel texts').

[14]   E.g. 'trespass'; 'tort'; 'mortgage'; the residual bilingualism of twinned expressions, such as 'will and testament', 'give and grant', 'goods and chattels', 'devise and bequeath'; the double 'ee' of employee, mortgagee; the trailing adjective of court martial, accounts payable, fee simple; and for this as example of phenomenon of the 'language beyond' contributing to a target language, Kasirer (2006), 'L'outre-langue du droit'; and see Cormack (2007), *Power to do Justice*, at 180 (linguistic paradox that language as marker of legal autonomy inevitably one of accommodation, assimilation, and even previous hybridity); and for borrowing in English beyond French, Bragg (2003), *Adventure of English*, at 118–19 (from Spanish, Dutch (e.g. smuggle, yacht, cruise, reef, knapsack, landscape), Persian, Turkish, Tamil, Welsh, Hindi, Arabic, Hebrew) and 124–6 (on explicit and unsuccessful efforts (inkhorn controversy of sixteenth century) to exclude foreign words from language).

practices, closure may be attempted around national languages, and may be effected in some measure, but there is always linguistic texture beyond the closure, which threatens its maintenance. Language is a fragile base for a nation.

RELIGION

Bodin and Hobbes were theoreticians of hierarchy and did not much concern themselves with legitimacy, religion, or the nature of the people subject to hierarchy.[15] Hierarchy simply had to exist, given the absence of alternatives. There is another stream of thought in European legal and political theory, however, which proceeded in a more contextual manner, more concerned with all three questions of legitimacy, religion, and people. This stream of thought may be seen as more closely connected to the nation part of the nation-state, or at least as insisting on the need for something more than a simple hierarchical structure for the state. Perhaps the earliest exponents of this way of thinking were Marsilius of Padua and Martin Luther.

Marsilius wrote his *Defensor Pacis* or *Defender of Peace* in 1324, was condemned by the pope in 1326, and fled to Bavaria to die there in 1342 in his early fifties. He thus wrote in the ongoing aftermath of the investiture controversy, with the two swords of church and empire less and less inclined to collaboration.[16] Marsilius did not side with the pope, and his book was one 'at which solid men of the age shuddered'.[17] The age was not one of uncontrolled violence, however, (at least not yet in the manner of the sixteenth century), and Marsilius wrote and thought in a time of institutional cosmopolitanism, with emperor and king committed to ultimate Christian objectives and working each in their way towards the accomplishment of those objectives.[18] There were underlying claims of legitimacy and no simple assertions of brute authority. There was a Christian community, a grouping of people whose beliefs were fundamental. Marsilius would have initiated an 'ascending' theme of government and law, and people were therefore at the base of his notions of government, not as a one-time source of ongoing and absolute power but as an ongoing source of Christian legitimacy.[19] Marsilius was concerned with 'excessive claims' by the papacy,[20] and the underlying notion therefore is not one of radical, binary choice between either secular or religious authority but one of control or correction of 'a history of gradual, papally-inspired perversion' based on greed for temporal possessions.[21] This was, of

---

[15] See Ch. 4, '*An emerging theory of the state*'.

[16] See Ch. 2, '*The church without*'; Ch. 3, '*Institutional cosmopolitanism*', '*Constitutionalism*'.

[17] Gewirth (1980), 'Introduction', in Marsilius (1980), *Defensor Pacis*, at xix.

[18] For the 'ambiguity' of the two swords doctrine as preventing formulation of a theory of sovereignty, Nelson (2006), *Making of Modern State*, at 37.

[19] Ullmann (1988), *Law and Jurisdiction*, at IX–398 ('the totality of the citizens'); and see Gewirth (1980), 'Introduction', in Marsilius (1980), *Defensor Pacis*, at xxiii ('the whole body of citizens').

[20] Marsilius (1980), *Defensor Pacis*, at 312 ('without the consent of any group or individual, of whatever dignity or authority').

[21] Garnett (2006), *Marsilius of Pauda*, at 146 and 151 (advocating 'resurrection of a pristine priesthood').

course, strong language and Marsilius has been seen as an early proponent of the all-absorbing modern state, but context is important. Marsilius contributed to 'emancipation' but did not himself write in such language. He wrote of the importance of people, but from a perspective of both imperial and papal authority. The taking of sides does not imply radical rejection of the side not taken, even where there is a shift of emphasis in the terms of the debate.[22]

Martin Luther was also strongly influenced by what he saw as corruption within the church, notably in the sale of indulgences (remission of penance on confession of sin, for cash). He too used strong language ('[t]he canonists are lawyers for asses')[23] but like Marsilius his aim was one of religious cleansing. It was, again, a question of sorting out appropriate jurisdictions, and their exercise. Luther's effect on the state in bringing about the reformation, however, was much greater than that of Marsilius, in a double sense. Luther's reformation was one in which the church had to be brought to its true spiritual mission, which could not be confounded with temporal functions. Once limited to its proper sphere of activity, it could rid itself of the earthly temptations, with Scripture as the only infallible authority (*sola Scriptura*). This left much room for state development and state law and it has been said that without Luther there would have been no Louis XIV.[24] The two swords became that of the prince. These ideas had 'enormous impact', not only in the many jurisdictions in the north of Europe that adhered to them, but as reinforcement of absolutist monarchical authority generally.[25]

The second sense of Luther's reformation is more closely connected to the closure of people and eventually of the nation. Luther's faith in princes did not mean they were free of religious obligation, and the most important of their religious obligations was that of maintaining the true religion of the people. 'It was the duty of the state to support the church.'[26] If the reformation had brought about division of the Christian religion there was to be no division within the kingdom of a Protestant king, and by the end of the sixteenth century Protestant lawyers had formulated the principle *cuius regio, eius religio*: the prince who controls a territory is entitled to dictate its religion.[27] Luther had himself embraced the principle,[28] with an inevitable ensuing process of 'confessionalization' of

---

[22] For diverse views on Marsilius, and differences amongst historians (medievalists emphasizing context, renaissance scholars defending republican interpretation), Garnett (2006), *Marsilius of Padua*, at 11 and warning, at 5, against imposing on Marsilius's text 'the categories and pre-occupations of a political philosopher writing at the University of Chicago in the mid-twentieth century'.

[23] Luther, M. (1989), 'On the Councils' at 555; and for 'I shit on the law of the pope and of the emperor', Witte (2002), *Law and Protestantism*, at 2.

[24] Vincent (1987), *Theories of the State*, 48.

[25] For 'impact', Berman (2003), *Law and Revolution, II*, at 373; and for Catholic absolutism, Skinner (1978), *Foundations of modern political thought*, at 113.

[26] Spellman (1998), *European Political Thought: 1600–1700*, at 25.

[27] Asch (1997), *Thirty Years' War*, at 10 (the maxim summing up what was taken to be the core of the agreement at the Peace of Augsburg in 1555).

[28] Hoffmann (1985), *Martin Luther and the Modern Mind*, at 105.

populations.[29] In the result, the emerging contemporary states of Europe in the sixteenth and seventeenth centuries were not secular but confessional.[30] Church attendance became obligatory in England, as a matter of state law.[31] In France the toleration of the Edict of Nantes (1598) following the French wars of religion was abrogated in 1685 and the notion 'une foi, une loi, un roi' prevailed until the Revolution.[32] In Italy from the late sixteenth century ghettos were created for Jews, a physical separation of religions within the polity, now understood as clearly related to the process of early modern state-building and confessional formation.[33] Jews were also expelled from many places in Europe, from the thirteenth century and for many centuries thereafter.[34]

The seventeenth century, however, marked the high point of the idea that emerging states could be founded on a religiously uniform population. In some measure the unification of crown and religion had accelerated the integration of the state. The Treaty of Westphalia of 1648, often seen as the foundation of contemporary states and an international legal order, consecrated both the priority of individual states over empire and the crown's authority over the religion of the kingdom.[35] Yet even Westphalia could not paper over the tensions of the reformation, which persisted within jurisdictions. The Treaty therefore provided that a king who changed his religion could not require his subjects to do the same, and excluded any power of expulsion.[36] Religious diversity could not be eliminated by spatial delimitation, nor by royal command. Yet the religious civil wars of the sixteenth and seventeenth centuries could not simply be perpetuated. A binary choice—either imposed uniformity or institutional destruction—

---

[29] Asch (1997), *Thirty Years War*, at 17 ('conflicts in all spheres of life'); Gierke (1939), *Development of Political Theory*, at 70 (notion of religious liberty 'completely foreign' to Calvinist writers).

[30] Burns (1991), 'Introduction', in Burns (1991), *Cambridge History of Political Thought 1450–1700*, at 2.

[31] Field (2008), 'A Shilling for Queen Elizabeth', notably at 214 (first enacted 1552, repealed 1553 as prejudicial to Catholics, re-enacted 1558–9 with fine of twelve pence for non-attendance, falling into disuse by 1601), 246 (still convictions in 1840s) and 250 (finally abolished 1969, after 418 years). For 'Catholic Christianity' as a 'compulsory religion' under Charlemagne, Luscombe (1988), 'Formation of political thought' at 166 (with obligations of emperor within the church); and for continuance of the principle under the 1812 Spanish Constitution of Cádiz, Mirow (2013), 'Spanish Colonial Law', at 3 (SSRN version).

[32] Sueur (2007), *Histoire du droit public français*, vol. II, at 476 (progressive seventeenth-century loss of Protestant privileges, long strategy of 'reunification').

[33] Siegmund (2006),*The Medici State*, at xvii (policy of tolerating Jews by simply ignoring them 'became insupportable'), 2 (feature of Italian confessionalization and state-building 'so intimately linked to it'), 30 (Catholicism used as 'powerful unifying category').

[34] For examples, Picq (2005), *Histoire et droit des États*, at 169 (also expulsion of Muslims from France in 1526).

[35] Nelson (2006), *Making of the Modern State*, at 60 ('[t]he theory of the modern state finally emerges in clear form'); though for differing views, see Ch. 8, 'Churches and Religions'.

[36] See notably the Treaty of Osnabrück, s. VII, para. 1; and Beaulac (2000), 'Westphalian Legal Orthodoxy', at 164; Picq (2005), *Histoire et droit des États*, at 156; Toulmin (1990), *Cosmopolis*, at 92 ('few people still considered the price of imposing religious conformity worth paying'), Christenson (2012), 'Liberty in the Exercise of Religion' (for limited freedoms in Westphalia, influence in USA).

could not be accepted, and some other form of human bonding appeared urgently required.[37] It was to be found in the idea of the nation.

NATION

The expression 'nation-state' was first used in 1918, according to the *Oxford English Dictionary*,[38] and while the expression is now widely used (it has a more comfortable and contextual ring than 'state') it remains highly contested. If the state has become a 'social reality' there is much more doubt about the status of any alleged 'nation', and corresponding doubt about what a 'nation-state' could be. The imprecision of the concept is compounded, as will be seen, by difficulties in identifying obvious or even any examples. The concept of the nation has played, however, an important role in contemporary state-building even though, unlike the case of language and religion, law has played almost no role in its understanding, regulation, or development. It is a creation principally of romantics, historians, philosophers, and patriots. It will inevitably suffer in treatment by a lawyer.

A nation has been variously described as a 'soul', a 'spiritual principle', a '*locus* of a common history', the 'social milieu in which the state is produced,' and as a 'superorganic representative of all the individual consciousnesses that it comprises'.[39] If these descriptions appear too pithy, then it may be seen as a 'named and self-defining human population whose members cultivate shared symbols, memories, myths and values, inhabit an historic homeland, disseminate a distinctive public culture, and observe common laws and customs'.[40] It has a subjective element,[41] yet can be analysed in terms of material criteria such as an agrarian or industrial base, or in terms of place and territory.[42] To the extent that it has a theoretical base, and that this has been denied,[43] it is largely found in German romanticism and the writings of Herder, the Brothers Grimm, Fichte, and Savigny. Fichte addressed the 'German nation' in 1807 and became a 'rabble-rousing orator'.[44] The French tended towards enlightenment universalism, but

---

[37] For the binary option, Schulze (1996), *States, Nations and Nationalism*, at 119 (though civil war only, though 'always', a threat).

[38] *The Oxford English Dictionary*, 2nd edn, under 'nation', at §9, attributing to J. R. Marriott.

[39] Respectively Renan (1991), *Qu'est-ce qu'une nation?* at 40, (for soul and spiritual principle); Ghéhenno (1995), *End of the Nation-State*, at 19; Duguit (1923), *Traité de droit constitutionnel*, at 2; Boyarin (1994b), 'Space, Time and the Politics of Memory', at 24.

[40] Smith (2007), 'Nation and Covenant', at 214.

[41] Moore (2001), *Ethics of Nationalism*, at 7, with references; White (2004), *Nation, State and Territory*, at 6 ('self perception').

[42] For materiality, Gellner (1983), *Nations and Nationalism*, passim; White (2004), *Nation, State and Territory*, at 7.

[43] Anderson (1983), *Imagined Communities*, at 14 (nationalism producing no great thinker, citing Gertrude Stein on Oakland that 'there is no there there').

[44] Van Creveld (1999), *Rise and Decline of State*, at 192–3 (elevating anti-French sentiment 'almost to the rank of religious sentiment'); and see Leersen (2006), *National Thought*, generally, with Fichte's lectures described at 113 as 'the first blueprint for European civil nationalism'. Hobsbawm concludes that,

France too had its proponents of national character and organic growth, most notably Montesquieu in the mid-eighteenth century, while Diderot's *Encyclopédie* actually wrote of national character in terms of an individual being 'airy as a Frenchman...jealous as an Italian...wicked as an Englishman'.[45] In Germany Gierke and Hegel had little need for the concept 'nation', since their notion of an organic collectivity, needing no formal identification or creation, was a nation without the name and could simply assume the designation 'state'.[46]

The German romantics saw the reconciliation of the state and nation as the fulfilment of a natural historical process;[47] much of the heavy lifting was then undertaken by historians who, from nineteenth to at least mid-twentieth century, made national history the dominant form of historical writing.[48] Berman observed that 'we still suffer from the nationalist historiography that originated in the nineteenth century' and that, it may be recalled, gave us not only national history but periodized national history.[49]

This rallying together of citizens in the name of their underlying common identity was reinforced by patriotic wars, so that by the late nineteenth century nationalism had become a 'mass political force',[50] and so it continues today,

during the classic period of nineteenth-century liberalism, very little other than 'nationalist and racist rhetoric was being written': Hobsbawm (1990), *Nations and Nationalism*, at 2, and 103 (for 'folkloric' discovery of 'the people').

[45] Leersen (2006), *National Thought*, at 68 (as 'habitual disposition of the soul').

[46] Gierke (1957), *Natural Law*, passim and notably at 50 (state as 'an organic whole'); and see Barker (1957), 'Introduction', in Gierke (1957), *Natural Law*, at lxxxiv ('if we once accept the theory of the real personality of groups, we are bound to see behind the State the figure of the greatest and the most real of all groups—the figure of the nation and Folk itself'); Hegel (2008), *Philosophy of Right*, para. 257 ('the realized ethical idea or ethical spirit'), para. 258 ('the realized substantive will'); Avineri (1972), *Hegel's Theory of State*, at 178 (the 'unity of subjective consciousness and the objective order'), 45 (for Hegel's lack of interest in specific notions of language, religion, nation); Taylor (1979), *Hegel and Modern Society*, at 116 (social and political differentiation as 'expressive of cosmic order...the final and complete fulfilment of the modern aspiration to autonomy'); and for Gierke committing the 'same errors' as Hegel in supporting 'state-absolutism', Hallis (1930), *Corporate Personality*, at 157–8.

[47] Laitin (2007), *Nations, States, and Violence*, at 81.

[48] For the process, Berger and Lorenz (2010), *Nationalizing the Past*, and the volumes of the European Science Foundation project on nationalist historiography, available at <http://www.uni-leipzig.de/zhsesf/index.php>; though for the need for return to world history, O'Brien (2006), 'Historiographical traditions and modern imperatives', notably at 7 (for 'cosmopolitan concerns' of Herodotus); and see Himmelfarb (2004), *The New History and the Old*, asking at 139 'Is National History Obsolete?'; Bayly (2004), *Birth of Modern World*, at 2 ('no longer really possible' to write even European or American legal history in a narrow sense); Bender (2006b), 'No Borders: Beyond the Nation-State', at B6 (national history now 'has exhausted itself'); Wilf (2011), 'Law/Text/Past', at 553 ('straitjacket of national jurisdictions...has made legal historians seem fixed upon rigid national boundaries'); and for state archives prefiguring a state history, Jordan (2001), 'Introduction', in Nora (2001), *Rethinking France*, at xxviii.

[49] Berman (1983), *Law and Revolution*, at 17, notably on 'insularity' of English and American legal historians; and see Girard and Phillips (2011), 'Rethinking "the Nation" in National Legal History', at 608 (for 'comforting boundedness', assuming 'exceptionalism of their own nation'). For periodization, see Ch. 1, 'The State Tradition through Time'.

[50] Hobsbawm (1990), *Nations and nationalism*, at 79; Schulze (1996), *States, Nations and Nationalism*, at 137 ('most compelling proof of political legitimacy'); and for the 'virulent nationalist ideologies' of the time, extending to ethnic cleansing, Rosenberg (ed.) (2012), 'Introduction', *A World Connecting 1870–1945*, at 11.

though with arguably less force than in the nineteenth century. There is notably a more detached academic perspective, and we are now told that the nation is simply 'myth',[51] or 'emotive artifice',[52] or 'fiction',[53] expressing a 'more or less imaginary unity'.[54] The nation itself would be a 'matter of more-or-less rather than either-or'.[55] It may therefore be best understood in terms of its use and effects.

NATION AND STATE

Böckenförde usefully refers to the idea of a nation as a 'new binding element' of the state, while Geary refers to it as a 'reinforcing device'.[56] The idea of the nation-state thus would describe a confluence or coincidence of a nation and a state, a people defined in non-state terms (principally language, religion, some measure of ancestry) that is at the same time the people of a territorial state.[57] While the nation would exist over time, with an image of a shared heritage, the people of a state would exist over space, never ageing or dying (in a kind of eternal present), while the nation-state would, miraculously, bring the two together.[58] With the idea of the nation building on 'source traditions'[59] of language, religion, and the still more recent notion 'culture', its increased prominence in the nineteenth century is clearly linked to this role as a reinforcing

[51] Geary (2002), *The Myth of Nations*, notably at 1 (myth of distant historical formation of stable European ethnicities), 62 (initial alliances based more on 'willingness to identify' than biology, culture, language, or geographic origin), 156 (underlying static notion of history, rather than continuous process).

[52] Vincent (1987), *Theories of the State*, at 29 ('theoretically incoherent . . . a crude amalgam of birth, bloodline, culture, tradition. . . . simplistic and inchoate').

[53] Schulze (1996), *States, Nations and Nationalism*, at 323 (of an 'objective and ineluctable identity of people, nation, history, language and state').

[54] Habermas (1998), *The Inclusion of the Other*, at 105 (the product of 'writers and historians, and scholars and intellectuals in general').

[55] Pogge (1994), 'An Egalitarian Law of Peoples', at 197 (also not coinciding with official borders 'in many parts of the globe').

[56] Böckenförde (1991), *Recht, Staat, Freiheit*, at 112 ('neue einheitsbildende Kraft', as idea rather than enduring reality); Geary (2002), *The Myth of Nations*, at 1 (construction at same time both of state and nation).

[57] Gellner (1983), *Nations and Nationalism*, at 1 ('the political and the national unit should be congruent'); Rae (2002), *State Identities*, at 51 (approving Gellner); Wokler (2006), 'Ideology and origins of social science', at 689 ('unity of all subjects going hand in hand with the political unity of the state'); Rosenfeld (2010), *Identity of Constitutional Subject*, at 227 (in traditional nation-state 'there is only one nation', comparing to 'multinational state').

[58] For space and time Yack (2003), 'Nationalism, Popular Sovereignty', at 36 (*all* individuals within state as members of a community) (emphasis added); Boyarin (1994b) 'Space, Time and the Politics of Memory' at 15 (states 'map history onto territory').

[59] The expression is that of Leersen (2006), *National Thought*, at 15, 20. The word 'nation' derives from the Latin *natio*, birth or descent, and for application to clans, fellow-inhabitants, and linguistically defined law students in medieval Italy, Woolfson (1998), *Padua and the Tudors*, Ch. 2 ('students of law'); Schulze (1996), *States, Nations and Nationalism*, at 99 (Germans taking long time to realize they *were* Germans).

device, as 'tribal ancestry myths' began to be used for a 'fresh political function': anchoring the post-Westphalian territorial states.[60]

The nation came to be most explicitly invoked as the constituent element of the state by the French at the time of the French revolution in 1789, and thereafter. The name most commonly associated with the idea is that of the Abbé Sieyès, who declared in a pamphlet in 1789 that only the nation could grant a mandate to the state and its government, and who implanted the same idea in Article 3 of the Declaration of the Rights of Man and Citizen.[61] The texts gave no definition of the nation but it has been consistently invoked thereafter as the foundation of the state and its ongoing legitimacy.[62] This has worked, in some measure, and France has been given as an example of a 'relatively homogeneous' community of language and religion giving rise to a nation, this in spite of both linguistic and religious diversity in France at the time of the revolution.[63] Where the French level of national consistency is absent, resort to the nation as a founding element has been less specific and less constant. In the United States the language of the nation never took hold, but it would have been a previous (and conceptually prior) 'people' who established the US constitution, acting through representatives who adopted it at the Constitutional Convention of 1787, again in spite of major social differences amongst the population, notably exemplified by blacks, loyalists to the English crown, and people of diverse religions and languages.[64] A nation was difficult to perceive, but it was only a slight shift in

---

[60] Leersen (2006), *National Thought*, at 50–1 (to show state a 'moral collective', 'organically linked by traditions, institutions, virtues and values').

[61] Art. 3: 'The principle of all sovereignty resides essentially in the nation. No body nor individual may exercise any authority which does not proceed directly from the nation.'

[62] For the absence of definition, Halpérin (2004), *Histoire des droits en Europe*, at 39; and for the nation as constituting element, Carré de Malberg (1920), *Théorie générale de l'État*, at 2 ('l'élément constitutif'); Ellul (1956), *Histoire des institutions*, at 560 (state as simple 'expression' of nation, itself subject to no legal limits); Chevallier (1999), *L'État*, at 20 ('prenant appui sur la nation', even conceived as 'une entité indivisible'); though for simple 'social milieu', Duguit (1923), *Traité de droit constitutionnel*, at 14. For diversity, see this chapter, 'Language' and 'Religion'.

[63] Bayly (2004), *Birth of Modern World*, at 20 (itself 'fortified' by centralized state). For diversity, see this chapter, 'Language' and 'Religion'; and see Connor (1994), *Ethnonationalism*, at 95 (for eighteenth-century Alsatians, Basques, Bretons, Catalans, Corsicans, Flemings, and Occitanians, 'as well as Frenchmen').

[64] Adams spoke specifically of a constitution 'established by the people', cited in Wood (1969), *Creation of American Republic*, at 290. For the 'Sovereignty of the People' see also Wood (1969), *Creation of American Republic*, at Ch. IX (notably for the utility of the idea in combating advocates of the ongoing rights of individual states), and at 283 (for the supplementary, Lockean idea of a 'social agreement among the people', as to which see Ch. 7 of this book, '*France and the world*'). For diversity, Rosenfeld (2010), *Identity of Constitutional Subject*, at 35 ('the 1787 "We the People" is in most respects not yet a people'); Clark (2011), 'Comparative Law in Colonial British North America', at 653ff., notably at 655 (religious diversity within single colonies); Walt Whitman (1881) in his Preface to the 1855 edition of *Leaves of Grass*, at 4 ('[h]ere is not merely a nation but a teeming nation of nations'); Wood (2009), *Empire of Liberty*, at 39 (in 1790 only 60 per cent of white population English in ancestry), though see also at 49 ('dream' of being single people 'tended to trump all reality'); Tomlins (2010), *Freedom Bound*, at 215–17, 297 (diversity even amongst arrivals from England, reflected in diverse received 'folkways', no template of 'English law'), 576 (Germans and Irish largest immigrant groups 1709–79, though both outnumbered by English, Scots, and Welsh combined). For the number of those leaving the USA after the fall of New York in 1783 (still in British hands until then)—estimated at 75,000 (including 15,000 slaves)—Jasanoff (2011), *Liberty's Exiles*, at 6 ('other, less cheerful faces', representing 1/40th of entire population); Marshall (2012), *Remaking British*

language to move from people to 'the' people. The national or Federal govern-ment could thus have its own source of legitimacy, as opposed to being simply a union of previous states.[65] As has already been noted, the Founding Fathers 'got away with this'.[66]

The United States of America and France would thus have provided a late-eighteenth-century model of how to construct a state around a founding people or nation. They each did so, however, by providing some, even considerable, state structuring of the people or nation, and the academic opinion has now become commonplace that, to the extent that it exists, the nation is the construc-tion of the constitution, and not the reverse. Thus Britain, Italy, and France would have seen their existing state hierarchy work on, promote, and construct some form of national identity, a project still not finished today. Britain would have been 'forged' during the long wars with France;[67] Italy saw 'Italians' only after it saw itself;[68] France's nation was a 'constructed identity derived from the action of a power'.[69] Nietzsche put it brutally, with his '[t]he state is the coldest of all cold monsters . . . and this lie creeps from its mouth: "I, the state, am the people"'.[70] Others have been less flamboyant in reaching the same conclusion.[71] Even if one could convince oneself of the preceding nation, however, the process of hearing its voice might not inspire confidence. The US Constitutional Con-vention would have worked, in spite of a lack of popular participation or ratification, but there has been great difficulty in replicating the experiment. The authors of a recent study of some 800 constitutions promulgated over more than 200 years since 1789 concluded that 'actual constitutional design processes employ scattered and usually rather anaemic forms of popular participation and

---

Atlantic, at 243–4 (those leaving could be seen both as 'loyalist refugees' and 'Americans on the move', 30,000 to Nova Scotia, 6,000 to Quebec).

[65] For Madison 'inventing a sovereign people to overcome the sovereign states', Morgan (1988), *Inventing the People*, at 26.

[66] See Ch. 4, 'Constitutions'; and see Morgan (1988), *Inventing the People*, at 198 ('the sovereignty of the people, however, fictional, has worked').

[67] Bayly (2004), *Birth of Modern World*, at 207; and see Jennings (1956), *Approach to Self-Government*, at 56 ('. . . the people cannot decide until somebody decides who are the people'); Colley (1992), *Britons*, notably at xi (even after 1707, British nation 'remained divided in all kinds of ways', but 'sufficient cohesiveness for a series of domestic insurrections to fail').

[68] Bell (2001), *Cult of the Nation*, at 198, citing D'Azeglio ('[w]e have made Italy. Now we have to make Italians'), and recalling Sicilians, Piedmontese, Tuscans, Calabrians, Venetians, and others. The Italian nineteenth-century Risorgimento or unification was accompanied by much violence, and for contemporary interrogation on the Italian 'nation', Saviano (2011), 'Ist Italien überhaupt eine Nation?', at 12.

[69] Chevallier (1999), *L'État*, at 24 (nation not a 'donnée' imposing itself on a state); and see Weber (1976), *Peasants into Frenchmen*; Bell (2001), *Cult of the Nation*, at 14 (paradox of political leaders at time of French revolution making demands on behalf of nation while simultaneously acknowledging nation did not exist).

[70] Nietzsche (1969), *Thus Spoke Zarathustra*, at 75.

[71] Morgan (1988), *Inventing the People*, at 13–4 ('world of make-believe'); Habermas (1998), *Inclusion of the Other*, at 109 ('states existed long before there were "nations" in the modern sense'); Hobsbawm (1990), *Nations and Nationalism*, at 10 ('nations do not make states and nationalism but the other way round').

oversight to substitute for actual consent'.[72] This is not the language of the nation of the eighteenth century, nor that of popular sovereignty.

Given these weaknesses of the founding nation hypothesis, there has been intensification and radicalization of the process of building a founding nation. This has taken two recognizable forms. The first has been referred to as 'pathological homogenization', the expression referring to a range of measures designed to secure a unified population. The measures have included exclusion of minority groups from citizenship rights, forced conversion or assimilation, expulsion, and extermination.[73] These are all pathological, in the sense of constituting an abnormal or morbid condition, yet all are capable of being seen as an 'integral part of the state system'.[74] The second form of intensification of the process of building a nation has been the negative one of persistently denying the existence of minorities. This occurs at the level of states themselves and at the international level. Historically France has taken the position that there are no minorities in France,[75] and the United Nations Charter makes no mention of minorities or their protection. In the case of the United Nations this would have derived from the failure of the League of Nations regime for the protection of minorities, which was massively abused by Hitler and was ineffective in any event.[76] In

[72] Ginsburg, Elkins, and Blount (2007), 'Does Constitution-Making Matter?', at 206 (though there would be an upward trend); and for the Constitutional Convention of 1787 being preceded in the USA by a period of 'groping' for institutional representation of the people, though agreement in 1780s on Convention, Wood (1969), *Creation of the American Republic*, at 330.

[73] Rae (2002), *State Identities*, at 5; Bart (2008), *Equality of Nations and the Minority Legal Tradition*, at 45 ('mandatory migration movements' from 1912–25), 46 (7 to 16 million victims of genocide since 1945); and see Bloxham (2009), *The Final Solution*, at 38 (for early life of European states in nineteenth, twentieth centuries characterized by intergroup violence perpetrated in quest for ethnic dominance), 39 (ethnic dominance requiring suppression of competing nationalities, 'complete ethnic exclusivity').

[74] Rae (2002), *State Identities*, at 14 (measures 'have, in part, *constituted* the state system' though such measures not inevitable, rather simply possible in system based on sharp distinction between insiders and outsiders); Doumais (2013), *Before the Nation*, at xiv ('unmixing'), contrasting prior 'intercommunality'. For 'mass expulsion or extermination of minorities' as a 'logical implication' of division into territorial states of homogeneous populations, Hobsbawm (1990), *Nations and Nationalism*, at 133.

[75] Fenet and Soulier (1989), *Les minorités et leurs droits*, at 9 (on French representations to the United Nations; absence of any mention in Declaration of Rights of Man and Citizen, though see passim for alternative French terminology for its minorities), 52 (for Great Britain, Italy, Belgium also denying internal minorities); and for denials generally Bart (2008), *Equality of Nations and the Minority Legal Tradition*, at 38 (A. W. B. Simpson describing as 'perverse'). For Middle East states that 'claim to be homogeneous' and fail to identify minority groups, Castellino and Domíngo Redondo (2006), *Minority Rights in Asia*, at 43.

[76] Kymlicka (1989), *Liberalism, Community and Culture*, at 210–15, with references ('Nazi manipulation' to justify intervention, e.g. in Sudetenland); Bart (2008), *Equality of Nations and the Minority Legal Tradition*, at 67–70 (fifth column assisting Nazi military offensive operations). For the history of the League of Nations regime, itself dating from the 1919 Versailles Peace Conference, Preece (1998), *National Minorities*, at 14ff. The regime was necessary in spite of massive 'remodelling' of states designed to stop movement of nationalities, as to which Fenet and Soulier (1989), *Les minorités et leurs droits*, at 49 (population movement of some 2 million); Simpson (2001), *Human Rights and End of Empire*, at 123 (mass movement of populations, 'in theory by voluntary choice, in practice by coercion'). On its failure, Thornberry (1991), *International Law and Rights of Minorities*, at 41 (also detailing minorities of Poland, Austria, 'Serb-Croat-Slovene State', Czechoslovakia (as it then was), Bulgaria, Romania, Hungary, Greece, Free City of Danzig, Åaland Islands, Albania, Lithuania, Latvia, Estonia, Iraq, Upper Silesia, Turkey, and others); Bart (2008), *Equality of Nations and the Minority Legal Tradition*, at 67–70.

mid-twentieth century a 'different psychology' therefore prevailed, founded on twin principles of non-intervention and universal human rights.[77] The international order thus came to replicate state mistrust of mediating orders or communities, leaving individuals and their rights to face the structure of the state.[78] The position would be consistent with liberalism's efforts to be 'colour blind' on the question of minorities.[79]

In spite of all such efforts, however, states today are not coincident with nations. In the language of the 2004 UN *Human Development Report*, '[i]f the history of the twentieth century showed anything, it is that the attempt either to exterminate cultural groups or to wish them away elicits a stubborn resistance'.[80]

THE UNREMITTING DIVERSITY OF STATES

The diversity of states antedates the contemporary state. McNeil traces 'polyethnicity' through Indo-European expansion into Europe and India, and then subsequently in population movements driven by the slave trade, other trade, and warfare.[81] It is of course possible to see a level of ethnic homogeneity in 'remote and barbarous lands' but, as has been noted, this is a factor of relative coherence and not a factor of separation.[82] Contact inevitably occurs, and must be dealt with. Deliberate geographical separation and closure are features of the contemporary state.

The contemporary state is marked, however, by the unremitting diversity of its human populations. The size of political units shrank with the decline of empire in the twentieth century, and the size of states declined following the remodelling of the period after the First World War, but no state has ever shrunk to the size of a homogeneous population. Put slightly differently, every state has one or more minorities or 'hidden nations' and Pinker speaks of the demographic landscape as a 'fractal, with minorities inside minorities inside minorities'.[83] Studies of 'ethnic' and 'cultural' diversity warn both of the difficulties in defining

---

[77] Thornberry (1991), *Rights of Minorities*, at 118, for human rights (noting that 'universal' human rights can become merely vacuous, benefiting everyone in general and no one in particular); and see Wheatley (2005), *Democracy, Minorities*, at 10; Bart (2008), *Equality of Nations and the Minority Legal Tradition*, at 76 (for US opposition to minority regime); Simpson (2001), *Human Rights and End of Empire*, at 325 (some 2 million deaths in population transfers after Second World War 'hardly augured well for the new age of human rights'). For non-intervention, Mazower (2009), *No Enchanted Palace*, at 195.

[78] For rights as the 'sole *approved* discourse of resistance', Rajagopal (2003), *International Law from Below*, at 9.

[79] Kymlicka (1989), *Liberalism, Community and Culture*, at 215 (contrasting position of consociationalists) and 210 (sign of defeat of liberalism if any recognition of ethnicity or group membership).

[80] UN Development Program (2004), *Human Development Report 2004*, at 3.

[81] McNeill (1986), *Polyethnicity and National Unity*, at 10. Language and religion could be added to ethnicity as factors of diversity, though religion is seen by McNeill (at 16) as providing simply a 'cultural carapace for trade' without explanation as to how this would have been so, given trade itself.

[82] McNeill (1986), *Polyethnicity and National Unity*, at 15; and see Ch. 2, 'Early Cosmopolitanism'.

[83] Pinker (2011), *Better Angels*, at 241 (government claiming to embody a 'nation' will 'in fact' fail to embody the interests of many individuals living within the territory, while taking 'proprietary interest' in others living in other territories).

groups, given the extent of 'fractionalization', and of the preponderance of 'ethnic groups' over states. In the early 1990s Fearon found 822 ethnic groups in 160 countries, looking only at minorities representing at least 1 per cent of the population; Kymlicka and Norman expand the estimate to between 5,000 and 8,000 'ethnocultural' groups.[84] The smallest state in the world appears to be Tuvalu in the South Pacific, with a population of some 10,000 people.[85] Of the population, 96 per cent would be Polynesian in origin, but 4 per cent Micronesian; 97 per cent would adhere to the church of Tuvalu (Congregational) but there are also Seventh Day Adventists, Bahá'i, and others. There are two official languages, Tuvalu and English, but also spoken unofficial languages (Samoan and Kiribati). Iceland has its people of Celtic or Irish origins and its 'foreign population'; 80 per cent (only) of its population is Lutheran. Japan has its Koreans, its Chinese, its Ainu.[86] Its population would largely be *both* Buddhist and Shinto, but 10 per cent of the population is Christian or other. South Korea is 26 per cent Christian. North Korea has a 'small Chinese community'; its population is both Buddhist and Confucian, and there are 'some Christian and Syncretic Chondogyo'. In South Asia, 'Bhutan appears most homogeneous' but has at least three ethnic groups and two religions.[87] There are Christian populations representing from 1 to 5 per cent of the population of many Middle Eastern countries.[88] The 'most ethnically diverse state in the world' is Papua New Guinea, with some 840 distinct living languages, while the state with the highest number of languages per capita in the world is Vanuatu, with approximately 109 languages.[89] Foreign-born populations are rising steadily in many jurisdictions that have been seen, by some at least, as nation-states.[90] In some cases, it is true, the minority population is relatively small in number, at least in percentage terms. The difficulty is that, however small, a recognizable minority remains a minority, and presents the same problem of legal and political treatment as does a larger minority. The Roma population of France probably represents less than 1 per cent of the population of France. It has given rise to a major debate on the treatment of minority populations, at the European level.[91]

---

[84] Fearon (2003), 'Ethnic and Cultural Diversity', at 195 and 197 (for 'all manner of borderline-arbitrary decisions' in coding ethnic groups); Kymlicka and Norman (2000b), 'Citizenship in Culturally Diverse Societies', at 1; and see Kymlicka (1995), *Rights of Minority Cultures*, at 4 (5,000 ethnic groups), with references; White (2004), *Nation, State and Territory*, at 4 (5,000 nations); Opello and Rosow (2004), *Nation-State and Global Order*, at 257 ('number of ethnically pure states could be as high as eight thousand', referring to 'deglobalization'). The University of Maryland Minorities at Risk project tracks 283 minority groups in states having more than 500,000 inhabitants: see <http://www.cidcm.umd.edu/mar/>.

[85] For the following data, CIA, *The World Factbook*, accessible at <https://www.cia.gov/library/publications/the-world-factbook>.

[86] Though for governmental efforts of assimilation, and ensuing litigation, Webster (2011), 'Insular Minorities', notably at 109 for Japan at centre of 'multiethnic empire' 1895–1945.

[87] Castellino and Domíngo Redondo (2006), *Minority Rights in Asia*, at 43.

[88] *Le Monde*, 4 November 2010 (80,000 Christians in Turkey, 135,000 in Iran, 5 to 8 million in Egypt).

[89] Castellino and Keane (2009), *Minority Rights in Pacific*, at 5.

[90] See Ch. 10, 'Citizenship and Mobility'.

[91] S. Castle, 'EU lays out plans to fight bias against Roma people', *Int. Herald Trib.*, April, 2011, at 4; 'L'Union appelle les Etats membres à agir en faveur des Rom', *Le Monde*, 6 April 2011, at 10; and see generally Council of Europe (2012), *Human Rights of Roma*; Liégeois (2012), *The Council of Europe and*

For whatever reason, there has been little direct acknowledgement of the pervasiveness of the internal diversity of states. In other words, the language and concept of the nation-state continue to exercise their attraction, to the point where even the words nation and state are used interchangeably.[92] McNeill speaks of the idea 'so deliberately inculcated . . . half a century ago, to the effect that it is right and proper and normal for a single people to inhabit a particular piece of territory' and the rightness of the idea continues to prevail, with all its consequences.[93] There has been an enlightening debate in political theory on the normative consequences to be drawn from diversity, but the debate has centred on obvious instances of diversity, on recognizably 'plurinational' states such as Canada, Scotland, and Spain, or on the position of aboriginal peoples.[94] Thus, Tierney writes of the influence of classic accounts of liberalism that are supportive of notions of equality within states and that fail to recognize even the *possible* existence of a plurality of populations within a state.[95] Connor concludes that amongst analysts there is a 'predisposition' in favour of the nation-state and ensuing downplaying or ignoring of ethnic diversity.[96] In the present writer's trawling through the immense literature on the state only three instances have been found of the existence of a nation state being denied. Oakeshott wrote in mid-twentieth century that 'every modern European state is, and always has been, "plural" in respect of its population'.[97] McNeill wrote in 1986 that '[t]he ethnically unitary European nation-state never existed except as an ideal'.[98] Dahrendorf wrote in 1994 of '[d]er heterogene Nationalstaat' (thus nevertheless using the expression) and concluded that 'there is no fully homogeneous polity'.[99] These rare statements have been tucked away in writing on wider subjects and have not received the attention they deserve. Yet many commentators have now begun to acknowledge that 'most' states are not nation-states,[100]

Roma; and the website of the EU Fundamental Rights Agency (FRA) at <http://fra.europa.eu/en/theme/roma>.

[92] Connor (1994), *Ethnonationalism*, at 95 (both words seen as 'alternative abbreviations' for the term 'nation-state') and 96 ('unfortunately' term 'nation-state' applied indiscriminately to all states).

[93] McNeill (1986), *Polyethnicity and National Unity*, at 6 (whereas reality one of a 'laminated polyethnic structure'), and 7 ('unquestionably begun to weaken in western Europe').

[94] E.g. Kymlicka (1989), *Liberalism, Community and Culture*; Taylor (1994), *Multiculturalism*; Tully (1995), *Strange multiplicity*; Carens (2000), *Culture, Citizenship and Community*; Tierney (2004), *Constitutional Law and National Pluralism*.

[95] Tierney (2004), *Constitutional Law and National Pluralism*, at 9, himself treating, at 4, the 'plurinational state' as a 'discrete category' defying standard classifications.

[96] Connor (1994), *Ethnonationalism*, at 57.

[97] Oakeshott (2006), *Lectures*, at 380 ('[e]ach, in some respect or other, is a barely stable balance of diversities').

[98] McNeill (1986), *Polyethnicity and National Unity*, at 84 (and since the world wars 'has plainly become obsolete in the place of its birth . . . can scarcely be taken as a viable model any longer').

[99] Dahrendorf (1994), 'Zukunft des Nationalstaates', at 751 ('keine völlig homogenen Gemeinwesen', citing Greece, Sweden, Japan as only purported nation-states).

[100] Morris (1998), *Essay on Modern State*, at 254; Kymlicka (1995), *Cultural Rights of Minorities* at 1; Guibernau (2003–4), 'Nations Without States', at 1255; Shapiro and Brilmayer (1999), *Global Justice*, at 69 (though populations 'are everywhere mixed up, mottled, and interspersed').

or that 'almost' all states have diverse populations,[101] or that 'nearly all' states are not ethnically homogeneous,[102] or that nations and state 'rarely' or 'seldom' coincide.[103] The 'vast majority' of states would thus be multi-cultural[104] and pluralism would be therefore be the 'norm rather than the exception in contemporary societies'.[105] For Rosenfeld, contemporary constitutional democracies are 'typically' both communally and individually pluralistic (different concepts of self-realization).[106] These affirmations, of at least the infrequency of nation-states, appear to be driven by the visibility of internal state diversity having heightened.

MANIFEST DIVERSITY

The internal diversity of states has been obscured for decades by liberal philosophy, by the teaching of the nation-state, and by the concentration of both theorists and historians on a relatively small number of European or anglo-american states that have themselves been heavily committed to a nation-state analysis. This situation has been changing slowly and a clearer vision of the composition of states has been emerging, largely as a result of three circumstances: the decline of empire, the fragmentation and failure of states, and the recognition of minorities.

The decline of empire

Until the mid-twentieth century many if not most contemporary states were subservient units of empire and their composition was not obviously relevant to discussion of the state. Many peoples and states were also beyond the pale of analysis since European international law of the nineteenth century excluded those that were not 'civilized' or Christian.[107] More will have to be said about empire, but it contributed greatly to awareness of social difference.[108] When the empires then declined the number of states in the world increased greatly,

---

[101] Thornberry (1991), *Rights of Minorities* at 3; Tilly and Blockmans (1994), *Cities and Rise of States*, at 4: UN Development Program (2004), *Human Development Report 2004*, at 2, also concluding at 2 that '[o]ne way or another every country is a multi-cultural society today'.

[102] Raič (2002), *Statehood and Self-Determination*, at 248.

[103] Preece (1998), *National Minorities*, at 30 ('rarely'); Connor (1994), *Ethnonationalism*, at 4 ('seldom').

[104] Theissen and Napel (2009), 'Taking Pluralism Seriously', at 365; and for data as of 1993, concentrating on large states and 'politically active' minorities, Gurr (1993), *Minorities at Risk*.

[105] Tully (1995), *Strange Multiplicity*, at 164.

[106] Rosenfeld (2010), *Identity of Constitutional Subject*, at 21; and for 'problems' in distinguishing mono-national and multi-national states, Stojanovic (2011), 'When is a Country Multinational?', notably at 268–70 (Germany 'often cited' as mono-national, in spite of Turkish-speaking population, officially recognized minorities of Danes, Sorbes, and Frisians), 271 (Austria six 'national minorities').

[107] Bowden (2005), 'Colonial Origins of International Law'; Anaya (2004), *Indigenous Peoples*, at 27–31.

[108] See Ch. 6, 'Common Laws beyond Europe'; van Creveld (1999), *Rise and Decline of State*, at 321 (colonists found themselves 'ruling over people who were most emphatically *not* their members'); Herbst (2000), *States and Power in Africa*, at 129 (lack of any shared historical mythology and memory on which nation could be built); Belaïd (1994), 'Constitutions dans le Tiers-Monde', at 102 (African state faced with 'pre-existing cultural heritage' that could not be ignored).

leading to better appreciation of their internal diversity or heterogeneous character. The colonizers had created only 'minimum ruling arrangements', with few
resources expended on state creation. There was inevitable fragmentation into
indigenous nationalist movements.[109] The diversity was compounded by state
boundaries, drawn by colonial authorities, that were largely insensitive to societal
differences and that were driven by European deals over the allocation of
resources.[110] Boundaries bore no relation to purported nations; there was also
deep-seated opposition to the idea of societal homogeneity, notably in India.[111]
Diversity tended to prevail, within and across borders, and continues to do so
today.

Fragmentation, failure, and violence

By the late nineteenth century the concept of the nation-state had been clearly
revealed to be double-edged, justification both for the creation of states and for
their destruction. Thus, J. S. Mill debated vigorously with Lord Acton (he of
'absolute power corrupts absolutely') on whether state boundaries should coincide with those of nationality. Mill defended the by-then familiar notion of the
coincidence of nation and state; for him '[f]ree institutions are next to impossible
in a country made up of different nationalities'.[112] Where the nationalities are
unreconciled, there was even a 'necessity for breaking the connection
altogether'.[113] Acton preferred multi-national states as 'the necessary vehicle of
civilization' and objected to the 'servility which flourishes under the shadow of a
single authority'.[114] On the ground, given ongoing diversity of populations, the

---

[109] Kohli (2004), *State-Directed Development*, at 396 (ensuing absence of normative and organizational
underpinnings of modern state); Bryde (2001), 'Der Verfassungsstaat in Afrika', at 207 (introduction of
nationalist ideology into multi-cultural Africa prepared way for 'catastrophes'); Migdal (1988), *Strong
Societies and Weak States*, at 37 (third world societies lacking 'centralized, pyramidal structure' found in
many European countries, rather 'web-like' societies; 'areas of accommodation' rather than sources of
major change).

[110] For the 'scramble for Africa' culminating in the Berlin Conference of 1885, Herbst (2000), *States and
Power in Africa*, at 66. Fixed boundaries were also incompatible with deeply held beliefs, about mobility
(particularly in the Arab world), shared resources, and intergenerational equity. On the conceptual and
normative problems of boundaries and their implementation, Glenn (2003a), 'Nationalist Heritage'
(notably on contrast between abstract, Mercatorian conception of space as carte blanche to be occupied
and Asian conception of space as place of human richness); Horowitz (2004), 'International Law and State
Transformation', at 478 ('rigid delineations' of British and French contrast with 'flexibility and ambiguity'
of Asian interstate relations).

[111] Kaviraj (1995), 'Crisis of Nation-state in India', at 119 (Gandhi and Nehru seeking to accommodate
great diversity).

[112] Mill (1862), *Representative Government*, at 310.

[113] Mill (1862), *Representative Government*, at 319.

[114] Acton (1948), *Essays*, at 185; for the debate, Connor (1994), *Ethnonationalism*, at 7 (and for later
nineteenth-century views that only autocratic states could be multi-national; democratic state necessarily
dissolving into as many states as nations). Contemporary comment distinguishes between 'state-led
nationalism' and 'state-seeking nationalism': Tilly and Blockmans (1994), *Cities and Rise of States*, at 24;
Bayly (2004), *Birth of Modern World*, at 208 (on leaders 'not really sure' whether to foster or suppress
national movements; Yack (2003), 'Nationalism, Popular Sovereignty', at 38 (on difficulty of reconciling
nation as both pre- and post-political community, given absence of boundaries in pre-political stage and
their defining character in post-political stage); and for social unity linked to totalitarianism, Picq (2005),
Histoire et droit des États, at 330 ('fiction' of a united people).

notion of the nation-state 'convulsed' the international politics of Europe in generating new states, particularly at the end of the First World War.[115] The process of fragmentation has continued steadily, often accompanied by violence. There is also a recognizable and new phenomenon of simple failure.

At the end of the Second World War there were approximately seventy recognized states in the world.[116] Some fifty joined the United Nations. The total number of states then doubled in three decades, and there are now 194 (though there are borderline cases). Therefore the number of states has nearly tripled in just over half a century. This is a remarkable statistic, since for decades new states have emerged at the expense, not of empires, but of old states. Fragmentation of states is a widespread phenomenon. The Sudan is the latest, but recent memory also provides the names of ex-states of the USSR, Czechoslovakia, and Yugoslavia, as well as those of fractured states such as Ethiopia and Indonesia. There is also a recognizable phenomenon of cascading fracture, as states derived from former states themselves divide. The present tensions of Kosovo are those of a state derived from Serbia, itself derived from Yugoslavia. We are thus in an age of reconstitution of states, though geographers remind us that borders have shifted constantly over time, notably on the same European continent that gave rise to the idea of the nation-state.[117] It has been pointed out that the process of fragmentation could go on indefinitely, since there are now (only) some 200 states but, as observed above, approximately 600 language groups and between 5,000 and 8,000 ethnic groups.[118] During this century the number of states 'could well top 300'.[119] The requirements for statehood, it has been cynically suggested, would then consist of a television station, an airline (though this is already beyond the reach of most), a police force, and a budget sufficient to support a UN representative.[120]

---

[115] Hobsbawm (1990), *Nations and Nationalism*, at 101 and 132–3 (on 'utter impracticability' of Wilsonian principle of making state frontiers coincide with the frontiers of nationality and language).

[116] Cranston (2004), *The Sovereignty Revolution*, at 50.

[117] White (2004), *Nation, State and Territory*, notably at 112 (for shifting of European boundaries over last 400 years; most boundaries fixed only in last half-century, only borders of Switzerland, Portugal fixed for more than 400 years); and for only eight countries whose borders or governments have not been changed by violence since 1914, Cranston (2004), *The Sovereignty Revolution*, at 50 (Australia, Canada, New Zealand, South Africa, Sweden, Switzerland, the UK, and the USA); de Senarclens (2009), *Frontières dans tous leurs états*, at 1 (still a very contemporary phenomenon, citing Soviet Union, to which can be added Indonesia, Czechoslovakia, The Sudan, Yugoslavia, etc.). For a 3.5-minute European History Time Lapse Map of boundary changes in the last millennium, with musical score, see <http://www.huffingtonpost.com/2012/05/16/europe-history-time-lapse_n_1520724.html>. Prior to the nineteenth century, in contrast, state formation led to consolidation rather than fragmentation, notably of many smaller kingdoms and polities: Armitage (2007), *Declaration of Independence*, at 106 (circa 1,000 polities in Europe in fourteenth century, some 350 by French revolution).

[118] See this chapter, 'The Unremitting Diversity of States'.

[119] Schmitter (1996), 'If Nation-State were to Wither Away', at 217.

[120] Havel and Sanchez (2011), 'Restoring Global Aviation's "Cosmopolitan Mentality"', at 19, citing W. Laqueur.

Beyond the phenomenon of violent fragmentation, there is also a process of slow decline or failure, resulting in quasi-states, fragile states, failing states, and failed states (many expressions are used).[121] These would not (yet) have fractured, but they are incapable of providing essential state functions, notably that of ensuring security within their territory. Travel warnings are a good indication of their existence. Such states are a source of insecurity elsewhere as well, since they may be used as staging grounds by non-state groups for sorties elsewhere. Estimates of the number of failed or failing states in the world vary from twenty-five to sixty.[122] They are characterized by high levels of corruption and have been described as 'neo-patrimonial', since they would represent a reversion to, or reproduction of, patrimonial notions of kingship and rule.[123] The range of such states, each unique in itself, illustrates the necessity to think in terms of degrees of 'statehood'.[124] States do not exist as matters of social fact such that attention can be directed solely to their inner workings. They exist according to the normative force and acceptance of the state tradition, and this can be very weak or even non-existent.[125]

The processes of fragmentation and failure are more often than not accompanied by violence. While the incidence of inter-state war has been reduced since the Second World War, the level of 'societal warfare' has been much higher, and is now accompanied by a sharp increase in terrorist violence.[126] The prospects for the immediate future are not heartening. The International Crisis Group now

---

[121] For 'quasi'-states, Jackson (1990), *Quasi-States*, notably at 20–1 ('juridical statehood', lacking institutional strength or effective hierarchy); Jackson (1987), 'Quasi-states, dual regimes', (independence not empirically based but derived from sudden change of mind about legitimacy of colonialism); Morris (1998), *Essay on Modern State*, at 52 (states in name only though recognized by international order of states); Kaplan (2008), *Fixing Fragile States*, at 6 (for LICUS, low-income countries under stress); and for 'withering away' at the local level, Ranger and Vaughan (1993), *Legitimacy and the State*, at 259 (Rossiter and Palmer on Mozambique, Zambia). For tables of 'state fragility', Marshall and Cole (2009), *Global Report* at 25ff. (Sudan, Somalia of highest fragility, quantified at 25, 23 respectively; 21 states have 0 fragility).

[122] Kaplan (2008), *Fixing Fragile States*, at 6; Ghani and Lockhart (2008), *Fixing Failed States*, at 3 ('home to nearly two billion people'); James (2006), *Roman Predicament*, at 111 (state failure as 'contagious'). The World Bank has referred to sixty-nine states that 'are performing their core functions poorly': World Bank (1997), *World Development Report 1997*, at 5.

[123] For 'neo-patrimonial', Fukuyama (2004), *State Building*, at 16 (predatory behaviour and rent-seeking by elites); Kohli (2004), *State-Directed Development*, at 405 ('grafted onto existing organized societies'); and for local leaders as 'brokers', Migdal (2001), *State in Society*, at 93. Ghana has been described as a 'vampire state': Ranger and Vaughan (1993), *Legitimacy and the State*, at 259.

[124] For degrees, explicitly, van Creveld (1999), *Rise and Decline of State*, at 314 (on states in Latin America) and 332 (treating as sovereign 'travesty of reality').

[125] See Ch. 1, 'Degrees and Varieties of States'.

[126] Marshall and Cole (2009), *Global Report* at 3, 4 (though both declining since 1980s). For 170 'wars', however, since Second World War, killing 35 million people, Cranston (2004), *The Sovereignty Revolution*, at 50 (90 per cent of victims civilians, compared to only 15 per cent civilian death rate a century ago). For waning of 'major interstate war' that would have been brought about 'primarily' by introduction of nuclear weapons, van Creveld (1999), *Rise and Decline of State*, at 337; and for widespread character of 'ethnic conflict', Horowitz (1985), *Ethnic Groups*, notably at 443ff. on 'militarization'. Pinker argues for a generalized decline in violence but acknowledges that the case for decline in intra-state wars and conflict is 'tenuous' and 'tentative', particularly difficult with respect to 'indirect' deaths and 'non-state conflicts' ('no one kept track'): Pinker (2011), *Better Angels*, at xxiv, 297, 300, 316.

lists a total of eighty crisis jurisdictions (not all are states) in which there is 'current or potential conflict' and provides alerts only in cases of 'particular risk of new or significantly escalated conflict'.[127] The World Bank's *Development Report* for 2011 concludes that violence is now becoming a major cause of poverty for 1.5 billion people in the world.[128] A number of commentators have linked this level of actual or potential violence with national sentiment. Bobbitt is perhaps most explicit in affirming that insecurity is 'a consequence of the *national* character of nation states which alienates substantial minorities of citizens'.[129] Hallaq has written on the principal cause of 'Muslim rage' being the imposition of a national and uniform law.[130] Yack argues that nationalism is linked to notions of popular sovereignty, producing an image that tends to 'nationalize political loyalties'.[131] In spite of the noble motivations behind the construction of the European Union, joint or shared institutions therefore do not provide any guarantee of peace if societal homogeneity is the object of those institutions.[132] It is the nation state that has most obviously failed in these cases. Instead of closure there has been collapse.

Minorities

Minorities, it has been said, are groups that 'do not belong to the dominant tradition in a given country or culture'.[133] They may appear physically distinct, or believe in different things, or do things differently, or communicate differently; but in all cases there is normative information that tells at least some people that the differences are important and a cause of exclusion. Some minorities are said to be indelible, in the sense that there is nothing the individual can do about their status, but this only indicates that at present the normative information does not allow for autonomy of choice, or integration, or simple overlooking of difference. The identity is imperatively ascriptive, according to the information seen as governing. In other cases the minority status is subject to abandonment by individual choice. The variety of types of minority, and their variable status, explain why no definition of a minority has been accepted at the international

---

[127] See <http://www.crisisgroup.org>; and for increasing frequency of civil war in Africa through the 1990s, Bates (2008), *When Things Fell Apart*, at 3, 4 (fifteen in 1990s; only eight in 1970s).

[128] World Bank (2011), *World Development Report 2011*, at 60 (for poverty rates 21 per cent higher in violence-afflicted countries).

[129] Bobbitt (2002), *Shield of Achilles*, at 219 (crime defined in 'ethnic ways', asking why marijuana criminalized but not martinis, polygamy but not divorce).

[130] Hallaq (2003), 'Muslim Rage', notably at 1714–15.

[131] Yack (2006), 'Popular Sovereignty and Nationalism', at 211; and see Gellner (1983), *Nations and Nationalism*, at 134 (for nationalist sentiment 'deeply offended' by violations of principle of congruence of state and nation); Kymlicka (1996), 'Social Unity in a Liberal State', at 123 (refusing demands for self-government 'will simply aggravate alienation' and increase the desire for secession).

[132] Cooper (2005), *Breaking of Nations*, at 33 ('[j]oint institutions do not lead automatically to peace. Nor are they even necessary', citing Yugoslavia).

[133] Fresco and van Tongeren (1991), *Perspectives on Minorities*, at 1; and see Bart (2008), *Equality of Nations and the Minority Legal Tradition*, at 3 (for concept of 'minority legal tradition').

level, or even at the level of domestic legislation.[134] Whatever the form of the minority, however, its recognition is incompatible with the existence of the nation-state.[135] Historically, however, minorities have been recognized for a long time, though the examples usually given are those associated with the rise of the territorial state from the sixteenth and seventeenth centuries. Following the reformation in Europe, religious minorities became a widespread phenomenon, no longer to be ignored. The Treaty of Westphalia of 1648, and many others thereafter, sought to provide some measure of protection for minorities in the new territorial states.[136] A significant shift in attitude occurred in the nineteenth and twentieth centuries, when the notion of the nation-state emerged and previous forms of minority protection were judged ineffective and abusive. We have seen how the United Nations chooses to place its faith in non-intervention and (individual) human rights.[137] Since the mid-twentieth century, however, the persistence of societal differences within states has inevitably brought minority protection back to national and international agendas. The Soviet Union had created many 'hidden nations' and its collapse necessitated their recognition. The result has been new recognition and new efforts at protection for minority groups within states. In 1992 the United Nations issued a Declaration on Minorities, recognizing an obligation on the part of states to ensure non-discriminatory treatment of 'all persons belonging to minorities'.[138] In the enlarging Europe, a Framework Convention for the Protection of National Minorities was concluded in 1995, 'considering that the upheavals of European history have shown that the protection of national minorities is essential to stability, democratic security and

---

[134] Raič (2002), *Statehood and Self-Determination*, at 265 (ensuing difficulty of classifying in homogeneous manner). There is ongoing debate, for example, on whether indigenous peoples can properly be described as minorities. The definition would be important for determination of the 'peoples' or 'nations' (not minorities) entitled to 'self-determination' under international law. For the debate, Raič (2002), *Statehood and Self-Determination*, at 266 (minorities acquire only 'minority rights'); Wheatley (2005), *Democracy, Minorities*, notably at 64–5 ('ethno-cultural groups' describing themselves as 'peoples'); Preece (1998), *National Minorities*, notably at 19 for UN efforts to deal with the question; Thornberry (1991), *Rights of Minorities*, passim; and for an attempted definition, Caportorti (1977), 'Study on Rights of Minorities', Addendum 5 at 7 ('[a] group numerically inferior to the rest of the population of a State, in a non-dominant position, whose members—being nationals of the State—possess ethnic, religious or linguistic characteristics differing from those of the rest of the population and show, if only implicitly, a sense of solidarity, directed towards preserving their culture, traditions, religion or language').

[135] Preece (1998), *National Minorities*, at 166 ('living proof' that practice of state sovereignty in nation-state system does not conform to the principle that legitimizes it).

[136] See generally Thornberry (1991), *Rights of Minorities*, passim, though noting at 27 treaty in which Louis of France undertook protection of Maronites in France; Preece (1998), *National Minorities*, at 55ff. (minority question 'from the 1640s onward', and listing treaties; Fenet and Soulier (1989), *Les minorités et leurs droits*; Wheatley (2005), *Democracy, Minorities*, at 8 ('throughout the history of international law', the latter usually taken to be of seventeenth century origin); Krasner (1999), *Sovereignty*, at 77 ('every major peace treaty' from Westphalia to Vienna (1864) containing provisions for treatment of religious minorities, this in spite of notions of sovereignty).

[137] See this chapter, 'Nation and State'.

[138] On the Declaration, itself not a binding instrument, Wheatley (2005), *Democracy, Minorities*, at 43.

peace'.[139] Europe has also had, since 1992, a High Commissioner on National Minorities.[140] The work of the European Court of Human Rights is increasingly devoted to the protection of minorities and 'marginalized individuals', though this was not in the contemplation of its founders.[141] Minorities are increasingly recognized elsewhere in the world;[142] the concept of the nation-state is weakened by the process. Nowhere is there, of course, any true nation-state. Cosmopolitanism has been sustained throughout the period of purported national closure.

---

[139] Preamble to the Convention; and see Wheatley (2005), *Democracy, Minorities*, at 47 (adopted rather than additional protocol to European Convention on Human Rights); Topidi (2010), *EU Law, Minorities*, passim (though at 12 EU 'timidly commenced participating in this effort'). The Convention is described in the Council of Europe's *Explanatory Report* to the Convention, para. 10, as 'the first ever legally binding multilateral instrument devoted to the protection of national minorities in general'. The Convention came into force in 1998 and has now been signed and ratified by thirty-nine states. France, Monaco, and Turkey have not signed.

[140] See <http://www.osce.org/hcnm/43199>. One of the Commissioner's concerns is that of 'kin protection', measures taken by one state to protect kin of its citizens who are resident and citizens of a neighbouring state, as to which see Palermo and Sabanadze (2011), *National Minorities* (on the Commissioner's 2008 Bolzano/Bozen Recommendations).

[141] Anagnostou and Psychogiopoulou (2010), *The European Court of Human Rights and the rights of marginalised individuals*, notably at 3 ('neither intended nor anticipated by the original architects of the Convention system').

[142] Castellino and Domíngo Redondo (2006), *Minority Rights in Asia*; Kymlicka (2007), *Multicultural Odysseys*, notably Ch. 2 ('The Shifting International Context: From Post-War Universal Human Rights to Post-Cold War Minority Rights').

PART III

COSMOPOLITANISM SUSTAINED

∞ 6 ∞

Common Laws

The closures around a territory and around a nation were never complete since they could not be. Boundaries in themselves do not prevent relations across them; if a nation exists it cannot be tied down to geography. In the result both types of closure have exercised considerable influence, but this influence was never entirely controlling anywhere in the world and today it is declining, everywhere in the world. The ways of cosmopolitanism that persisted through the middle ages were therefore capable of being sustained, with admittedly more difficulty, through the period in which contemporary states were formed, along with the closures that they in some measure represented. The sustaining of cosmopolitan ways was clearly evident beyond Europe, in an initial context of empire, but it was also evident within Europe. There were, however, shifts in emphasis. In the middle ages it was institutional cosmopolitanism that was most visible, supported by notions of constitutionalism and by diverse common laws. Today it has become the state that is most visible, while institutional cosmopolitanism (though still present) is less in evidence, at least on any given national territory. The states of the world, however, have been dependent on common laws for their formation and continue to exist (or not) because of their underlying constitutionalism. It is therefore appropriate to return in Chapters 6, 7, and 8 to the cosmopolitan ways examined in Chapter 3, in an appropriately different order, to determine the extent to which they have been sustained through periods of national closure. Given unremitting human diversity, no state could avoid some measure of cosmopolitanism in its operation.

To recall, the common laws of European history were not binding laws. They were relational laws, non-monotonic in character, existing always in relation to a particular law to which they yielded whenever the particular law claimed application.[1] The common law of England yielded, and yields, to local custom and local or national legislation, all seen as particular. The *ius commune* of the empire yielded to both Stadtrecht and Gemeinrecht. The droit commun français yielded to both particular custom and royal ordonnance. The castillian derecho commún yielded to local fueros and royal ordenamiento. These common laws have not been lost sight of, though national codifications and nationalist historiography have obscured them in some measure.[2] In spite of national codifications, the common laws have been most visible in matters of private law, where the law is dense, detailed, and of long standing. They have been less visible in matters of

---

[1] See Ch. 3, '*Common laws*'.

[2] For nationalist historiography, see Ch. 5, 'Nation'; and for codifications, see Ch.4, '*Codes*'.

public law, where the law is less dense, historically less detailed, and usually of much more recent origin. That the common laws contain public law appears, however, incontrovertible, and in medieval times it received expression in notions of fundamental laws, inalienability of crown domain, and laws of royal succession.[3] Each European polity organized itself according to its priorities and traditions and its own combination of these and other such rules and principles. Each had its common public law and, as in private law, there were multiple common laws. With the attempted closures around territorial states, nation-states, and national sovereigns, the question then became one of the ongoing importance of these common laws, and their relation to the instruments of closure. The question of the importance of the common laws has to be asked both within Europe and beyond Europe, in the context of empires.

COMMON LAWS WITHIN EUROPE

Common laws existed prior to the emergence of the contemporary state from the seventeenth century. The Treaty of Westphalia of 1648 is often seen as the beginning of the contemporary state system, but the Treaty neither brought the empire to an end nor replaced existing monarchies and their authority.[4] The Treaty's principal effect may have been on what is now known as the 'inter-national' order,[5] in clarifying the nature of the players in such an order. The players themselves continued to exist because of local support and legitimacy. This has consequences for our understanding of the cosmopolitan origins of the contemporary state and of the (ongoing) cosmopolitan sources of its legitimacy.

Contemporary states evolved out of prior monarchies. In many cases the monarchies continue to exist, though in such cases there has been a non-violent shift towards a notion of constitutional monarchy. Where the monarchies are gone other hierarchical institutions have taken their place, making use of many of the monarchical structures and bureaucratic instruments of government. The common laws that underlay monarchies did not suddenly disappear, there-fore, with the arrival of the contemporary state. Given that, according to the prevailing view, the contemporary state is simply a continuation of previous state forms, such a disappearance would be highly unlikely.[6] Even in cases of revolution most existing law is carried forward.[7] Put slightly differently, a political

---

[3] See Ch. 3, *'Constitutionalism'*, *'Common laws'*. These laws were often followed though they could scarcely be described as 'binding' in contemporary language, lacking means of enforcement and, as will be seen, eventually yielding to state constructions, as *iura propria*.

[4] Burbank and Cooper (2010), *Empires*, at 182–3 (empire surviving another 158 years, signatories 'neither very national nor neatly bounded', 'Westphalian sovereignty' more to do with 1948 than 1648); Beaulac (2000), 'Westphalian Legal Orthodoxy', at 151 ('independence . . . only achieved long after the Peace'). The Treaty did nothing to prevent the rise of new empires, moreover, some of which survived well into the twentieth century, as to which see this chapter, 'Common Laws beyond Europe'.

[5] For invention of the word 'international' only in the late eighteenth century, however, see Ch. 8, 'Internationality and Empire'.

[6] See Ch. 1, 'The State Tradition through Time'.

[7] See Ch. 4, 'Constitutions'; and later, this section.

revolution can be successful without changing *everything*. It cannot do the impossible. New forms of closure are inevitably constrained by the historical legacy of prior closures.[8]

The important conclusion that follows from this is that there was law before the contemporary state, which both justified it and provided means for it to function. There was 'droit avant le droit', as it has been nicely put, law before the law of the state.[9] Given the contemporary primacy of the idea that the state is the only source of law, it needs to be said that this idea of pre-state law is not idiosyncratic but one that is widely held amongst those who have immersed themselves in the history of the state. Gierke has been probably the most explicit in affirming that the state is founded upon pre-existing law, as law was understood at the critical time. 'All were agreed,' wrote Gierke, that 'before the State existed the *Lex Naturalis* already prevailed as an obligatory statute, and that immediately or mediately from this flowed those rules of right to which the State owed even the possibility of its rightful origin.'[10] The question, thus, is not how law is presently conceived, but how law was then conceived. C. K. Allen wrote of the dangers of 'incuriousness about the ascertainable facts of the past institutions of law and politics' and of the difficulty we have today in realizing how powerfully notions of natural law had 'taken possession of men's imagination'.[11] Curiously, there may even have been elements of such 'incuriousness' driving the natural lawyers of times past, since in much of the natural law writing justifying the state, the old, true law, the common law respectful of custom, plays a very reduced role if any role at all. Both natural law and common law were, however, major sources of law justifying contemporary states. They were complemented by ancient thinking. The resulting eclectism is why Krieger spoke of the 'undifferentiated cosmopolitanism' of the eighteenth century.[12] Law was found in many sources, but unquestionably functioned as law. More will have to be said about how this was possible.

In the seventeenth and eighteenth centuries natural law was seen as a modern phenomenon.[13] It became institutionalized and was formally taught in universities with its own disciplinary status and university chairs. Samuel Pufendorf held such a chair in Heidelberg as early as the 1660s. Natural law thinking even became the 'dominant form of moral and political thought in the Enlightenment in general'; it was useful to governments in their task of state-building.[14] Natural

---

[8] See Ch. 1, 'The State as Tradition'.

[9] Vrellis, S. (2007), *Conflit ou coordination*, at 425.

[10] Gierke (1951), *Political Theories of Middle Age*, at 75 (natural law radiating from a principle 'transcending earthly power' yet 'true and perfectly binding Law') and see Gierke (1939), *Development of Political Theory*, at 306 ('no one doubted' that maxims of natural law 'were actual rules of Law').

[11] Allen (1861), 'Introduction', in Maine (1861), *Ancient Law*, at xi.

[12] Krieger (1957), *German Idea of Freedom*, at 4, and see Ch. 3, '*Institutional cosmopolitanism*'.

[13] Haakonssen (2006), 'German natural law', at 251 (a new role, beyond classical thought, given the schism of Christianity and the emergence of modern statehood).

[14] Haakonssen (2006), 'German natural law', at 258.

law was not, however, a uniform *corpus* of thought and it developed in many streams. There was Catholic natural law and secular natural law, German natural law and French natural law. There was a Pufendorf stream (on the need to restrain an ungovernable human nature) and a Leibniz stream (on the perfectibility of human nature).[15] Once Grotius (b. 1583) had 'broken the ice' the new 'science of morality' became an object of various efforts at formulation and the great names of European legal thought became known as such for their contribution to this effort.[16] Since natural law thinking was eclectic it could and did draw on many sources. It was very cosmopolitan in its sweep, in spite of its direction towards national closure. The writing of the great jurists swept over political and linguistic borders. Bodin's teaching was inspired more by realities on the ground than by pure reflection, but it had assumed a natural law dimension by the time of Hobbes. It had a 'trailblazing' ('bahnbrechend') effect in Germany,[17] and was widely influential elsewhere. There was then a 'cross-fertilization' between natural law traditions, with French thinkers riding on the then 'universal' character of the French language, and German refinements being translated back into French.[18] Both were translated into English and Hobbes and Locke did not come to the continent 'as alien imports'.[19]

Yet in spite of natural law's modernity its proponents did not hesitate to draw on ancient sources. Their cosmopolitanism was temporal as well as spatial. For some, the *ius gentium* of Roman private law became part of the law of nature,[20] and in the troubled seventeenth century in England 'neo-Roman' sources (notably Cicero) were used by opposing parties.[21] A 'republican constitution' drifted inevitably towards Roman sources, while behind them lay the naturalism of Aristotle.[22] Machiavelli had turned to Roman sources in preference to canonical

---

[15] Haakonssen (2006), 'German natural law', at 259 (on 'lack of unity' though common features in elaborate systematics).

[16] For the scientific and even mathematical basis of much of the reasoning, Tuck (1991), 'Grotius and Selden', at 505 (Grotius with nine fundamental rules, thirteen associated laws); Dufour (1991), 'Pufendorf', at 563 (Pufendorf's attachment to physical and mathematical science).

[17] Friedrich (1997), *Geschichte der deutschen Staatsrechtswissenschaft*, at 34 (Bodin had included German law in his discussion); though for the incompatibility of Bodin's teaching with the actual circumstances of the empire, Franklin (1991), 'Sovereignty and the mixed constitution', at 310 (emperor less power than other kings).

[18] Dyson (1980), *The State Tradition*, at 160 (French late nineteenth- and twentieth-century reliance on Staatslehre); and for French reception of German concepts of personality of state, Chevallier (1999), *L'État*, at 36.

[19] Keohane (1980), *Philosophy and State in France*, at 11 (on translations of Barbeyrac, Burlamaqui, resonance with French Huguenot teachings). For French Huguenot influence in the Netherlands, van Gelderen (1992), *Political Thought of the Dutch Revolt*, at 269; and for French revolutionary influence in general, Halpérin (2004), *Histoire des droits en Europe*, at 39.

[20] Gierke (1939), *Development of Political Theory*, at 304 (even implanted by God); and for reliance of both Pufendorf and Leibniz on Roman legal tradition, Haakonssen (2006), 'German natural law', at 259.

[21] Skinner (2002), *Visions of Politics*, at 318 (for 'explicitly anti-monarchical perspective') and 326 (for Cicero on Twelve Tables and safety of the people).

[22] Tomkins (2005), *Our Republican Constitution*, passim; for Aristotle, see Ch. 2, 'The church within'.

and religious ones as a means to 'mantenere lo stato',[23] while the French 'revolution' was known as such because it involved a re-volving to ancient sources, the better to critique the ancien régime.[24] Ancient Israel was not neglected, and the sentiments of the time were even 'in great part' inspired by 'Old Testament ideals of covenantal election'.[25]

Stephen Toulmin has described much natural law and enlightenment thinking as based on a 'myth of the clean slate'.[26] Rationally validated methods could replace much if not most of all that preceded. Natural law reflections on the contemporary state do appear to have proceeded on this basis, and Krieger concluded that the theorizing did have a 'genuine operative function'.[27] It is important to attempt to understand the extent of this operative function. There is now a state tradition, which this book is attempting to explain, and today there is often said to be a 'European tradition' or even a 'Western tradition' in law, of which the state would be a major part.[28] Traditions, however, are of widely varying types and accommodate diverse and even conflicting elements. It does appear possible to speak of a state tradition, but Chevallier concludes that it is a 'formal envelope', the content of which can be highly diverse.[29] Some therefore

---

[23] Skinner (2000), *Machiavelli*, at 33 (and totally ignoring Christian injunction to avoid worldly temptations of glory and wealth); though for rejection of Machiavelli's teaching in the Netherlands as 'sheer viciousness', van Gelderen (1992), *Political Thought of the Dutch Revolt*, at 277.

[24] The political sense was derived from the scientific one of Galileo, who announced the revolution of the earth around the sun. For political 'revolution' preserving much existing law, Glenn (1990a), 'Law, Revolution and Rights'; and for French revolutionaries posturing as Romans, Athenians, Spartans, yet discrediting classical authors by following them 'too closely, too blindly, and too much', Sellers (2009b), 'Revolution, French', at 826; Keohane (1980), *Philosophy and State in France*, at 11 (French dependence on 'philosophers of the *polis*'). Revolutionary political fervour, at an abstract political level, overcame French mistrust of Roman law in some measure, as to which see Ch. 2, 'Affirmative Crowns'. Montesquieu rejected even the Roman political model, as belligerent: Tomaselli (2006), 'Spirit of Nations', at 17 ('an embarrassment and a burden on the nation'); Lintott (1999), *Constitution of the Roman Republic*, at 251 (Rome an 'empire of war'). Not all use of classical authority was revolutionary; for Aristotle in vindication of royal authority, Lloyd (1983), *The State, France and the Sixteenth Century*, at 147; and for Roman law supporting tax authority, Sueur (2007), *Histoire du droit public français*, vol. II, at 295.

[25] Smith (2007), 'Nation and Covenant', at 238 and 244 (covenantal nationalism possibly first type of nationalism).

[26] Toulmin (1990), *Cosmopolis*, at 176ff., notably 177 (for 'clean slate and fresh start').

[27] Krieger (1957), *German Idea of Freedom*, at 46 ('sometimes anticipating and sometimes ruminating').

[28] For the state as tradition, see Ch. 1, 'The State as Tradition'. For 'European tradition', Brunner (1963), 'Vom Gottesgnadentum', at 301 (tradition of European constitutional history); Carey Miller (1997), 'Scottish Celebration of European Legal Tradition', at 19; Grewe and Ruiz Fabri (1995), *Droits constitutionnels européens*, at 140 (though drawn from 'sources multiples'); and for 'Western tradition', Berman (1983), *Law and Revolution*, passim; Guterman (1972), *From Personal to Territorial Law*, at 7 ('Western Legal-Constitutional Tradition'). Henke speaks of the 'states of our tradition' ('die Staaten unserer Tradition'): Henke (1988), *Recht und Staat*, at 300; and Loughlin of a 'common European discourse': Loughlin (2010), *Foundations of Public Law*, at 2. Yet for doubt as to an overarching single European legal tradition, see Ch. 12, 'Reciprocity'.

[29] Chevallier (1999), *L'État*, at 81; and see Ch. 4, '*Constitutionalism*' (state tradition as 'purely formal one' calling only for existence of a state). For tradition as phenomenon that 'tolerates and unites an internal variety', Dyson (1980), *The State Tradition*, at 5. Henke perceives two streams of state tradition, the idealistic (Plato, Augustine, Hobbes, Rousseau, Kant, Hegel) and the realist (Romans, Machiavelli, Montesquieu): Henke (1988), *Recht und Staat*, at 278ff.

prefer to speak of traditions in the plural,[30] but if we are to speak of a single state tradition we must be alive to its great internal diversity, certainly beyond Europe but also within Europe. This large and expansive concept of the tradition of the contemporary state would recognize it as constituted largely by written sources, hierarchy, and boundaries, the elements of closure already examined,[31] but the content of all of these would be entirely open.

Why is the state tradition so remarkably diverse in its content? The diversity of natural law thinkers, at an abstract level, did not extend to the full range of diversity found on the ground, at the level of particular state institutions and concepts of public law. This diversity comes from elsewhere, and most notably in the 'droit avant le droit', the law that legitimated the institutions that grew into contemporary states and that continued to prevail even through revolutions. However 'operative' it actually was, natural law thinking in the universities and political theory could not displace the largely unwritten law of people and existing institutions. Even with the apparent increase in coherence of states from the seventeenth century, their constitutions thus 'continued very largely to be governed by the law and custom of the past'.[32] Bodin was highly influential, but his theory of sovereignty was 'hopelessly at odds' with the reality of empire and of other monarchies, and total victory was simply impossible.[33] The historic common laws of Europe were thus as different from one another in matters of public law as in private law; they each had different relations with the *iura propria* that were the proto-state monarchies; the differences continued to exist with the acceleration of state construction from the seventeenth century. Chevallier informs us that in France the common law could be derogated from, in favour of the state, more easily than in England, with the latter country's particular

---

[30] Dyson thus speaks of French and German 'intellectual traditions' of the state, though with common elements: Dyson (1980), *The State Tradition*, at 157. Picq speaks of the 'traditions étatiques' of European partners: Picq (2005), *Histoire et droit des États*, at 8; while Art. 6 of the Treaty on European Union (TEU) speaks intriguingly of the 'constitutional traditions common to the Member States'. Shennan warns that only through comparing and contrasting European states can any 'common pattern' be discerned. One must contemplate a 'spectrum' of states from Russia to Spain: Shennan (1974), *Origins of Modern European State*, at 9.

[31] See Chs 3 and 4.

[32] MacCormick (1999), *Questioning Sovereignty*, at 25 ('customary normative order is a condition for the grounding of the constitutional order that a state requires'); Elton (1963), *Reformation Europe*, at 298 and 301 (law 'one secure thing in an uncertain world, the known framework of society', kings as 'protectors of the law'); Lewis (1968), *Later Medieval France*, at 85 ('generally agreed' that king should conserve the laws); Brissaud (1915), *History of French Public Law*, at 330 (France no written constitution but 'all were in agreement' in recognizing existence of fundamental laws); Gilby (1953), *Philosophy and Theology of the State*, at 251 (while modern state said to be 'both the child and the parent of the law' (citing R. McIver, *The Modern State*, at 1), medieval state 'certainly subject to law, both to Natural Law and to inherited customs older than itself'); Picq (2005), *Histoire et droit des États*, at 51 (for 'subordination' of positive forms of law); Haakonssen (2006), 'German natural law', at 259 (contrasting 'tradition-based political and legal ideas' with 'the new natural law'); and most recently Feldman (2007), 'Cosmopolitan Law?', at 1028 ('there was law before there were modern states—law that claimed to derive its binding authority not from political association but from other sources . . . '). For the content of the laws and constitutions, see Ch. 3, '*Common laws*'.

[33] Franklin (1991), 'Sovereignty and the mixed constitution', at 298, and 309 (also inconsistent with 'constitutional realities' of Spain or England).

notion of the rule of law;[34] Dyson cites Francis Bacon that 'the justices of the peace were an institution that made England unique';[35] Doehring writes of the *degrees* of judicial independence in European states.[36] The differences may even have become greater as state structures assumed more specific and positive forms. This does not exclude convergence, which may be occurring today, but the influence of the historic common laws becomes still more evident when the state is examined beyond Europe.

COMMON LAWS BEYOND EUROPE

The common laws of Europe emerged as a response to the phenomenon of expansion of European populations *within* Europe. The English moved into Wales, then Ireland; the Dutch and Germans moved east; the Spanish Christians moved back into the previously Islamic lands; the French moved into the regions. The expansion was not driven by centrally organized, contemporary states. The process began too early for that. It was rather religious proselytism and the need for land and markets that drove people from feudal villages and free cities to seek better lives.[37] They brought their laws with them, as 'vectors of expansion',[38] and these mobile laws became known, to the movers at least, as common. They were at least intended to be common since new settlement was intended to replicate previous ways of life in the area of origin. The mobile law had to be designated, however, as common, to distinguish it from the generally unwritten laws found amongst the locals. The classic distinction between common law and particular laws (*iura propria*) thus emerged everywhere in Europe from the thirteenth century, and everywhere the common laws yielded, necessarily, to the local.[39] Lawyers everywhere had to work with multiple laws.

Today European expansion overseas is thought of as the work of centralized European states, but it is more accurate to view it as a simple expansion of the mobility that was already taking place within Europe. It too was driven by

---

[34] Chevallier (1999), *L'État*, at 18. France thus has an 'administrative law' and administrative law institutions, which are located outside the courts of general jurisdiction. It is even difficult to speak of courts of general jurisdiction in France.

[35] Dyson (1980), *The State Tradition*, at 45 (presumably for rendering a large, bureaucratized judiciary unnecessary).

[36] Doehring (2000), *Allgemeine Staatslehre*, at 136–7 (from socialist to western continental to common law, referring also to USA at federal and state levels).

[37] For the process generally, Bartlett (1993), *Making of Europe*, notably at 5–7 for religious expansion and 47–51 on the territorial requirements of feudalism ('the demand of vassals for fiefs and the desire of lords for fighting men'). For the process by which Christianity came to 'hold the centre', Brown (2003), *Rise of Western Christendom*, passim; and for the attraction of new settlements as opposed to life in feudal German villages, Wesel (2006), *Geschichte des Rechts*, at 307. Vigorous recruitment of settlers was undertaken, notably of Flemish for their skills in drainage: Hattenhauer (1994), *Europäisches Rechtsgeschichte*, at 261.

[38] Bartlett (1993), *Making of Europe*, at 310.

[39] See Ch. 3, '*Common laws*'; and for emergence of the language of 'common law' in different languages and different regions, over approximately the same era, Glenn (2007c), *Common Laws*, at 10–11.

religion, the need for markets, and the need for land.[40] When Columbus and Cartier arrived in North America, in 1492 and 1534 respectively, neither Spain nor France could qualify as a contemporary state. Westphalia was more than a century away and there were no national borders to prevent movement, either within Europe or beyond it. Overseas expansion thus occurred at the same time as contemporary European states were being constructed, and these states grew up not as isolated structures but within expanding empires under their own eventual control (at least in some measure). The contemporary European state has thus been cosmopolitan from its inception, in the sense that the closures of territory and nation have had to accommodate the diversity of empire, with its attendant movement of people, goods, and laws, in both the metropolitan and colonial areas. Imperialism was 'not a one-way street' and imperial relations have been seen as essential in forming metropolitan culture even as late as the nineteenth and twentieth centuries.[41] This extended even to colonial contribution to metropolitan constitution-making.[42] Burbank and Cooper conclude that in the seventeenth and eighteenth centuries states became more powerful as a consequence of empire and not the reverse.[43] Armitage puts it simply: 'Empire gave birth to states, and states stood at the heart of empires'.[44] Nor was it the case that empires simply gave a quick jump-start to contemporary states. The two lived together for centuries, with the nineteenth century known as one of a 'new imperialism' (into Asia and Africa) and many empires winding down (though not entirely) only in the middle to late twentieth century.[45] By 1914 some 84 per cent of the world's surface was controlled by Europeans.[46] Thus empires were constantly cosmopolitan over centuries and cosmopolitan

[40] For state formation within Europe paralleling the formation of overseas empires, Muldoon (1999), *Empire and Order*, at 8 (state and empire, moreover, 'in tension'); and for overseas colonization as extension of intra-European colonization, Verlinden (1954), *Précédents médiévaux*, at 9 ('continuité dans le temps'), 11 (on need to prefer a 'supranational' concept of colonial history, as opposed to traditional and nationalist one) and 28–9 (on transfer of feudal models to Americas).

[41] Kaplan (2002), *Anarchy of Empire*, notably at 1 (challenging idea of 'one-way imposition of power', calling attention to 'ambiguities and contradictions of imperial relations'); and generally for rejection of 'one-way street', Jasanoff (2006), *Edge of Empire*, notably at 7 ('crossing and mixing' as well as 'separation and division').

[42] Paquette (2011), 'Brazilian origins of 1826 Portuguese Constitution', notably at 457 (for Brazilian contribution also influenced by English institutions), 463 (Latin American ideas 'creating unexpected havoc' for those accustomed to 'operating in a closed system'); Mirow (2013), 'Spanish Colonial Law', notably at 3 (SSRN version) ('first truly transatlantic or bicontinental constitution', drafters of Spanish constitution including overseas representatives).

[43] Burbank and Cooper (2010), *Empires*, at 8 (empires channelling resources into state institutions, concentrating revenue and military strength) and 219 (as stage rather than victim of revolutions).

[44] Armitage (2002), *Ideological origins of British Empire*, at 15.

[45] For the new imperialism, with its profiteering and vicious impulses, Parsons (2010), *Rule of Empires*, at 7; and see Burbank and Cooper (2010), *Empires*, at 416 (for dates of independence of states of declining empires—India 1947, Singapore 1965, Papua New Guinea 1975, Malaysia 1963, Cambodia 1954, Qatar 1971). There are still some twenty-five to thirty imperial dependencies today (Martinique, Guadeloupe, Montserrat, New Caledonia, Bermuda, Guam, St Pierre and Miquelon, French Polynesia, the Falkland Islands, Saint Maarten, and others).

[46] Fieldhouse (1973), *Economics and Empire*, at 3 (35 per cent in 1800).

throughout their territories, though the accommodation of diversity was more evident and developed beyond the metropolitan territory.

Empire was cosmopolitan in its own justification, but it may not have been the cosmopolitan justification that brought it about. It may have been something that was simply going to happen, given Christianity and underlying pressures on land and markets or, to put it slightly differently, given the expansionist effect of everything else that was going on in European society from the fifteenth century. That included proselytism, technology, mapping, industrialization, mercantilism, and capitalism. The legal justification of empire was a part of all of that but it is right to question how much of a part, given its obvious weaknesses. Boyarin has seen a 'legal apparatus that determined in advance the property to be acquired', making colonial endeavours conceivable,[47] yet colonial acquisitions were precarious in the extreme. The justifications were challenged on all fronts. A series of papal bulls of the late fifteenth century would have originally justified conquest of infidels but by the mid-sixteenth century, under the influence of Vitoria and de las Casas, canonical doctrine had shifted to notions of universal human identity and even indigenous sovereignty.[48] Religious justification was also used by Locke, relying on the natural law concept that God had commanded humanity 'to subdue the earth',[49] yet the Lockean notion that property could be acquired by European settlers through forms of appropriation and use unknown to indigenous populations was challenged both empirically and theoretically, the latter by none other than Kant. North American indigenous peoples were intense users of land, engaging in farming from the end of the first millennium, and both Locke and English colonists were aware of this.[50] They also had highly developed political and legal structures, which Locke simply dismissed.[51] The non-existence of indigenous peoples was inconsistent with Kant's views of human agency.[52]

---

[47] Boyarin (1994b), 'Space, Time and the Politics of Memory', at 14 (citing Gonzalez-Echevarria that America existed 'as a legal document before it was physically discovered').

[48] Tuck (2003), 'Making and Unmaking of Boundaries', at 152 (preferring world of 'independent and equal political communities'); Headley (2008), *Europeanization of the World*, at 76 (on shift in emphasis to protection in papal bull *Sublimis Deus* of 1537, announcing 'a unique, astounding effort at an open-ended inclusion').

[49] Locke (1933), *Two Treatises*, at 130.

[50] Banner (2005), *How Indians Lost Their Land*, at 46–8 (for farming, Lockean knowledge); and for widespread Mesoamerican, North American farming from the end of the first millennium, Mann (2005), *1491/Ancient Americans*, at 39, 177 (maize, peppers, tomato, squash, beans), 201. For Locke's view as 'scurrilous interpretation' of known circumstances, Buchanan (2003), 'The Making and Unmaking of Boundaries', at 238–9; and for Vattel's echoing of Locke, Tully (1995), *Strange Multiplicity*, at 79 ('savages . . . making no present and continuous use').

[51] For a present-day, indigenous Saami view of Locke's arguments, Oskal (1999), 'Moral foundation for disqualification of aboriginal people's rights', at 106 (Locke also apologizing that European use of land 'would not be very large'), 109 (denying sovereign status since unwritten law not 'established law').

[52] Kant (1996), *Metaphysics of Morals*, at 122, §62 ('settlement may not take place by force but only by contract, and indeed by a contract that does not take advantage of the ignorance of those inhabitants with respect to ceding their lands'); for amplification, Benhabib (2004), *Rights of Others*, at 31 (*res nullius* as 'thinly disguised formula for expropriating'); and see Muthu (2003), *Enlightenment against Empire*, notably Ch. 5 (for 'Kant's Anti-Imperialism', rejection of Locke's property ideas). For Kant's views on settlement as part of his larger notion of a *ius cosmopoliticum*, see Ch. 9 of this book, 'Cosmopolitan Theory'.

Roman law notions of property were also invoked, notably the famous doctrine of the *res nullius*, the unowned property capable of acquisition, yet overseas lands were clearly occupied in all cases, and private law notions of property were not obviously relevant to claims of territorial expansion.[53] Vitoria had even used the notion of *res nullius* as a means to *protect* indigenous property, since it was inapplicable to existing indigenous property rights.[54]

Ultimately there may be no justification for what was done by European colonizers, in spite of these cosmopolitan efforts. Most of the common laws, however, played little role in the process of justification. They came into operation on the ground, given established relations between metropolitan and colonial societies. It is true that Roman law was part of the *ius commune*, and it was used for justificatory purposes, but Roman law was not one of the common laws (English, French, Spanish, and Dutch) that were vectors of expansion across the seas as part of the colonization process. There were no Roman colonizers from the fifteenth century, and neither Italy nor Germany developed empires similar to those of the eventual states of westernmost Europe.

The common laws that were transported abroad had already begun at home the process of allocating legal authority and legitimacy. They recognized and yielded to particular laws that satisfied their conditions of legitimacy, and this process simply continued abroad. There was no reason for distinguishing that which occurred beyond the seas from that which occurred at home. There were no sharp distinctions between the national and the international, the foreign and the local. It is often said that the reception of European laws abroad occurred by the operation of common law (in the absence of express legislation) but it was more a case of the common law simply continuing to do what it did in its jurisdiction of origin. So English, French, Spanish, and Dutch common laws recognized the validity of royal legislation, and where appropriate the royal prerogative, and through this recognition and legitimation the monarchies, with their royal laws, came to be the states we know today. The same process occurred abroad. French royal edicts were thus recognized in New France as they were in France, and the proclamations of the English crown were recognized in North America as they were in England. They were recognized because they were informed by and compatible with the role assigned to them by the common laws. The common laws yielded, moreover, not only to them but to other legitimate sources of law, historically unwritten sources of law in the metropolitan jurisdictions and so, in similar manner, to unwritten sources of law in the colonies beyond the seas. In 1870 a Malayan decision thus stated that the general English law in Malaya 'would no more supersede the custom in question than

---

[53] Benton and Straumann (2010), 'Acquiring Empire by Law', at 3 (on 'inclusive, not to say scattershot approach to legal rationales', though Roman law used to make actions understood by European rivals); and for the influence generally of Roman notions of empire, Pagden (1995), *Lords of All the World*, Ch. 1 ('The Legacy of Rome'). For the 'absurd' argument that greater productivity justifies entitlement to territory, Buchanan (2003), 'The Making and Unmaking of Boundaries', at 238–9 (would justify annexation of territory when resources could be used more productively).

[54] Benton and Straumann (2010), 'Acquiring Empire by Law', at 23 (barring Spaniards from claims of sovereignty).

it supersedes local customs in England'.[55] In the colonies unwritten forms of law could thus preclude the operation of the common laws, as *iura propria,* and in English colonies the traditional law of indigenous peoples came (sooner or later) to be recognized, and even a notion of indigenous 'sovereignty'.[56] A similar process occurred in Dutch, French, and Spanish colonies in spite of the visibility of imported legislation.[57] Where the local people were adherents to written forms of law, as in Islamic or Asian lands, the accommodation with local law was still more evidently necessary. In Mughal India English company agents had no choice but to 'learn and abide by, however imperfectly, its workings, rituals, and language'.[58] Late eighteenth-century India would have been characterized by its 'sheer cosmopolitanism'.[59]

Law was thus thought of in a similar manner throughout empires but this in no way precluded diversity from empire to empire, since the common laws differed in their appreciation of different sources of law, and the *iura propria* differed in the imperative claims they made. In Europe, legislation in the common law world differed from legislation in the civil law world, and similar differences were replicated abroad. Spanish metropolitan legislation was omnipresent in Latin America and Spanish colonies therefore differed considerably from English ones, though in both empires a local margin of appreciation informed legislation's application.[60] As in Europe, lawyers worked at the interface between multiple laws, local and distant.

[55] *Sahrip* v. *Mitchell* (1870) Leic. 466, discussed in Matson (1993), 'Common Law Abroad', at 763; and for the process of reception, Glenn (2007c), *Common Laws*, Ch. 2; Glenn (1987a), 'Persuasive Authority'; McPherson (2007), *Reception of English Law Abroad*, notably at 368 (for reception of English common law not as of a given date but in an ongoing manner) and 370 (for test of whether English law 'suitable' for application in colonial circumstance).

[56] For the 'distinct pattern' of recognizing the juridical capacity of tribes, McHugh (2005), *Aboriginal Societies and Common Law*, at 66; and for recognition by officials in the field as 'one of the most enlightened acts of the eighteenth century', in refusing to follow concepts of 'armchair European theorists', Tully (1995), *Strange Multiplicity*, at 119, 127. This has been said to involve a process, however, of 'aboriginal interests and customary laws' being 'absorbed into the common law as right'; see *Minister of National Revenue* v. *Mitchell* [2001] 1 SCR 911 at para. 10. In Australia indigenous law as such ('traditional law') is now recognized by legislation, following *Mabo and Others* v. *State of Queensland (No. 2)* (1992) 107 ALR 1, 175 CLR 1, though may not survive historical discontinuities; see Glenn (2007a), 'Continuity and Discontinuity'. For tribal sovereignty in the USA, see Ch. 7, '*Relations and guarantees*'; and Ch. 12, 'Reconciliation'.

[57] For Hispanic territories, Pihlajamäki (2003), 'La heterogeneidad del *Ius Commune*', at 69 (on need to accept solutions other than those of mother country); and generally Glenn (2007c), *Common Laws*, at 70–9.

[58] Jasanoff (2006), *Edge of Empire*, at 51 and see at 9 (for Britain and France, deriving imperial legitimacy from 'older, non-European reservoirs of power'). For Europeans having 'duplicated the precolonial system', ruling 'indirectly' in Africa, Herbst (2000), *States and Power in Africa*, at 81–3, and 86–7 (for colonial failure to provide infrastructure, notably roads, outweighing any differences in 'colonial practice'). The rule of reception is usually expressed in terms of previous law being retained in cases of 'cession or conquest', as to which Keith (2005), 'The Unity of the Common Law', at 197.

[59] Jasanoff (2006), *Edge of Empire*, at 12.

[60] Elliott (2006), *Empires*, notably at 131 ('contractualist doctrines' of Spanish theory of state allowing for different levels of resistance); Ross (2008), 'Legal Communications and Imperial Governance', at 111 (English 'unwittingly' encouraging local diversity), 133 (on 'metropolitan legal understandings' spreading to colonial networks); Verlinden (1954), *Précédents mediévaux*, at 39 (on increasing control by Spain from sixteenth century); Owensby (2008), *Empire of Law*, at 11 (on Spanish efforts to control local authorities, 'cosmopolitan' resort by Indians to Spanish law as means of control).

Everywhere in the world colonial powers sought to instal the contemporary state via the colonization process. They had some success in this but there has also been great resistance. Different people in different places oppose one or more elements of the contemporary state. There are people opposed to writing, to hierarchy, and to boundaries. Writing is opposed by indigenous or chthonic peoples; hierarchy is opposed by many if not most Jews and Muslims; boundaries are opposed by nomadic peoples.[61] The result has been different degrees of 'statishness', since the global construction of the contemporary state could not have been a linear process.[62] It is often regarded with 'sullen indifference, even hostility'[63] and has been treated recently as a 'poisoned gift', a tool for personal aggrandizement of those having seized its controls.[64] In some cases, such as Afghanistan, a deliberately fragmented state was created, if only as a territorial buffer.[65] The *type* of state sought to be created has been largely that suggested by the common law of the colonizing power, subject as always to local deviation. Some 75 per cent of former colonies adopted legal systems similar to that of their colonizer, a general phenomenon that has been identified as 'constitutional iso-morphism',[66] resulting in a clean slate that is somehow déjà vu. In the world of

---

[61] For opposition notably to fixed boundaries, widespread dispute over their tracing, and simple neglect in the tracing process on the ground, Glenn (2003a), 'Nationalist Heritage', at 89–90; more particularly for Arab nomad resistance to fixed boundaries, Wilkinson (1991), *Arabia's Frontiers*, notably at xiii ('territorial definition' as feature of 'institutions of empire'); and for the tendentious nature of the territorial boundary, see Ch. 4, 'Boundaries'.

[62] Bayly (2004), *Birth of Modern World*, at 253 (though whole range of authorities 'increasingly speaking the language of the state').

[63] Van Creveld (1999), *Rise and Decline of the State*, at 335 ('moment of the state's greatest triumph may yet prove to be the beginning of its decline. What everybody has may turn out to be worth very little'), 332 (implanting of state most successful in North America and Australasia where continents 'practically uninhabited'); Chevallier (1999), *L'État*, 1999 at 94 on state as 'empty shell' ('coquille vide'), and 98–9 on 'soft state' ('état mou') at both domestic and international levels; Kohli (2004), *State-Directed Development*, at 396 (roots of neopatrimonial states in encounter of societies devoid of state traditions with powerful, colonizing Europeans). Eberhard feels compelled to give a 'constat d'échec' or judgement of failure, to the institutional transfer of the state: Eberhard (2006), *Le droit au miroir des cultures*, at 141.

[64] Hardt and Negri, (2000), *Empire*, and generally for failed, failing, and 'neopatrimonial' states, see Ch. 5, 'Fragmentation, failure, and violence'.

[65] Gulzad (1994), *External Influences and Development of Afghan State*, at 235 (British having decided in nineteenth century that conquering Afghanistan impossible, best alternative was a weak and divided state).

[66] Schmidhauser (1997), 'European Origins of Legal Imperialism', at 345; Horwitz (2009), 'Constitutional Transplants' (for British, French, German, US models and their influence); for 'isomorphism', Ginsburg, Elkins, and Blount (2007), 'Does Constitution-Making Matter?', at 208; and for state formation having moved from internal to a strongly 'external' process, Horowitz (2004), 'International Law and State Transformation', at 484. Balaguer-Callejon explains that institutions 'cannot be derived from nothing' in the Latin American case ('aus dem Nichts entstehen'); Balaguer-Callejon (2001), 'Verfassungsstaat in ibero-amerikanischen Kontext', at 191 and 192–3 (for influence of US presidential model); and for use of the model of the Fifth French Republic in Africa, Bryde (2001), 'Verfassungsstaat in Afrika', at 205. For 'eclectic' choices, however, of Ottoman, Qing, and Siamese authorities (French, Prussian, British, Belgian), Horowitz (2004), 'International Law and State Transformation', at 456; and for variance amongst Asian states owing to experimentation, Bracken (1995), 'Military Crisis of the Nation State', at 103.

the (English-derived) common law, it is explicitly recognized that constitutions 'take their character largely from the context of common law principle and doctrine which provides the context and the foundation against which a constitution is to be read and understood'.[67]

Perhaps the most successful state emerging from empire has been the United States of America and there was much originality in the creation of this state. Recent US historical writing has been at pains, however, to recall the profoundly imperial context in which the US written constitution was formulated. The empire in question was that of the English, and the common law that circulated within this empire was that known as the common law, more precisely the common law of English judicial origin. It was received in colonies where English settlers arrived, by virtue of its own norms, and went on to structure in large measure the relationships between province and metropolis. Sarah Bilder has thus written of a 'transatlantic constitution' prior to US independence, which was both written and unwritten as an 'overarching arrangement of authority'.[68] As a common law, it allowed that 'particular localities with different circumstances should be allowed to follow particular customs'[69] and we therefore see in the particular circumstances of colonial North America, replicated north of the St Lawrence river in what was to become British North America,[70] the same cosmopolitan forms of adjustment to the local as had been occurring in Europe. While there may have been a belief in a binary distinction between colony and crown, the reality of the transatlantic world was 'not so binary'.[71] There were unresolved arguments about what the common law actually said, whether local circumstance justified departure, and where the *locus* of decision actually lay.[72] Invoking English law, moreover, was a means of winning a case and not a 'theoretical goal'.[73] In Daniel Hulsebosch's language, it was English legal culture that 'structured relationships' between province and metropolis, and there was even 'no sense of *an* American law'.[74] Here as elsewhere there was law before the

---

[67] Mason (2004) 'The Common Law', at 183.

[68] Bilder (2004), *Transatlantic Constitution*, at 2, and 4 (as 'transatlantic legal conversation' of statutes, appeals, replies, reversals, affirmances, and dismissals; Rhode Island courts themselves disagreeing on whether English or colonial law applicable).

[69] Bilder (2004), *Transatlantic Constitution*, at 35.

[70] Glenn (1987a), 'Persuasive Authority', notably on notion of law as enquiry as opposed to definitive response.

[71] Bilder (2004), *Transatlantic Constitution*, at 89.

[72] Bilder (2004), *Transatlantic Constitution*, at 7, and 73ff. (for dispute over appellate authority).

[73] Bilder (2004), *Transatlantic Constitution*, at 110 (English and colony law therefore 'not often forced to clash').

[74] Hulsebosch (2005), *Constituting Empire*, at 3, 277 (though change by early nineteenth century); and see Witt (2007), 'Anglo-American Empire and Crisis of Legal Frame', at 765 (for American constitutionalism as 'inescapably the outgrowth and continuation of the British imperial project'); Wood (2006), 'American Revolution', at 602 (for American colonists in early 1760s thinking of themselves 'not as Americans but as Britons . . . living on the edges of a great pan-British world' and sharing fully 'the enlightened eighteenth-century's enthusiasm for the English constitution'); Scheppele (2003), 'Aspirational and aversive constitutionalism', at 308 (influence on framers of 'English constitutional structure'); Ginsburg (2005), ' "A Decent Respect to the Opinions of [Human]kind" ', at 578 (US framers 'inspired by jurists and philosophers from other lands').

state, though there was no law-maker recognized as exclusive and corresponding accommodation of different sources of law.

The colonial empires came to their deserved end by the late twentieth century, victims both of their own exploitative character and the rise of the notion of a nation-state.[75] The territorial and national closures of the contemporary state had consequences for the notion of common law. The purportedly totalitarian character of national law-making involved a re-conceptualization of law, now meant to be derived from a single formal source, and this has been an enormously powerful idea over the last two centuries. It involved not only a narrow and formal definition of law, the product of state authorities, but also the conclusion that there could be no law outside this formal version of it. There was here a real dilemma for the contemporary state and the full extent of it is only now coming to be recognized. There clearly had been law before the state, and the different states of the world assumed their different shapes because of the foundational and ongoing influence of these different, and common, laws. Yet if the state decides that the only recognizable law is that which it creates, has it not removed its own foundations? The conclusion was formulated very clearly by the Jellineks, who wrote that the creation of the state occurs 'outside the law'.[76] This conclusion is implicit in the writing of those who found the state on extra-legal sources, whether this is the power (or Macht) of Schmitt, the culture of Haberle, or the pre-supposed basic norm, recognized as fictional, of Kelsen.[77] We are here faced with an anachronism of some consequence. It involves the extension of a state-centric concept of law backwards in time, to eliminate prior concepts of law and to create the *tabula rasa* from which the contemporary state would arise. If the creation of a contemporary state cannot be justified by existing and applicable law, its justification requires invention of other foundations, less

[75] Parsons (2010), *Rule of Empires*, at 7 (for nationalism making recruitment of local allies more difficult, given populations imagined as homogeneous), and 447 (for empire 'never humane').

[76] Jellinek (1922), *Allgemeine Staatslehre*, at 284, and see Ch. 7 'Justifying the Contemporary State', on different, non-legal justifications (religious-theological, power, theory, etc.). Richard Kay has written perhaps most recently that '[c]onstituent authority cannot be legal authority': Kay (2011), 'Constituent Authority', at 716.

[77] Schmitt (1928), *Verfassungslehre*, at 9 (for constitution based on power ('Gewalt', 'Macht', or 'Autorität')); Schmitt (1976), *Concept of the Political*, at 43 ('the political entity is by its very nature the decisive entity'); and see Grewe and Ruiz Fabri (1995), *Droits constitutionnels européens*, at 51 (for similar views of Sièyes and Carré de Malberg in France); Häberle (1992), *Kraftfeld der Verfassungsstaates*, at 656 (constitutional culture as 'non-juridical constituting of a constitution of a political community'); and Kelsen (1989), *Pure Theory*, at 201 ('The Basic Norm as Transcendental-logical Presupposition'); and for Kelsen's late recognition of its fictional character, Duxbury (2008), 'Kelsen's Endgame', notably at 54 (Finnis describing as 'spectacular debacle') and 60 (basic norm as 'imaginary act of will'). For further materialist, institutionalist, power-based, or rational choice explanations, Rae (2002), *State Identities*, at 24ff. The underlying foundational notion of culture can extend well beyond traditional legal and political writings; see, e.g. Slauter (2009), *The State as a Work of Art*, on how the switch to culture becomes necessary in the absence of formal justification of a constitution in the USA, though acknowledging at 11 that no notion of 'culture' in use at time of US founding. Also, Hegelian or organic justifications of the state (see Ch. 5, 'Nation') are not obviously recognizable as legal, situating it as part of a more comprehensive totality. Gierke concluded that there was 'no lack' of writing on the development of political ideas but 'a dearth of literature on the history of the legal formulation of ideas of the State': Gierke (1939), *Development of Political Theory*, at 10.

rooted socially but arguably more appropriate for the contemporary state. We therefore need to look at the constitutionalism that underlies contemporary states to determine whether it provides justification and structuring for the contemporary state, on the basis of something other than earlier, ongoing law. If not, the contemporary state will retain its cosmopolitan origins and, inevitably, its ongoing cosmopolitan character. Its common law, or laws, will still be visible.

7

Constitutionalism

Contemporary constitutionalism has set itself the dual and related tasks, within the assumed territorial boundaries of the contemporary state, of justifying the state and providing limits on the exercise of authority within it. In examining the constitutional history of particular states, however, it does not appear that any has been able to escape an ancient heritage of extra-territorial origin, or effect contemporary closure. Neither territory nor nation provided effective means for doing so, as has been seen.[1] Doctrinal constructions are yet weaker instruments of closure, and ancient ideas of constitutionalism may thus be sustained, largely conditioned by the common laws from which they emerged.

JUSTIFYING THE CONTEMPORARY STATE

Constitutional thinkers have in general been dissatisfied with extra-legal justifications of the contemporary state, such as power, culture, or legal pre-suppositions. They have been ambitious in their enquiry and a truly vast literature has emerged. Why has all of this been necessary? It is not an easy question to answer and the answer must be sought in particular cases. In general it may be said that the contemporary state, at least in Europe, has needed no justification, since the theory of the corporate identity of the state, with us since at least the middle ages if not since Roman law, means the state simply continues as an entity regardless of any simple change of government. Many states have carried on in this manner, in some cases adding a written constitution, in some cases not, as is the case for the United Kingdom.[2] Theoretical justification has not been a major concern here and the old law continues to apply. This conclusion is important, since non-legal explanations do not adequately cover the detail and diversity of states that have simply continued over centuries. In other cases, which have also produced little theoretical debate, a contemporary state has been created by colonial powers or their immediate successors and the justification for the new state is found in the structures of colonial authority. Conceptual difficulties are overcome by established consensus on the process and ongoing acceptance of old law.[3] A more

---

[1] See Chs 4 and 5.

[2] For an 'already startlingly powerful and active' state in England at the time of Henry II's twelfth-century reforms, Wormald (2006), *Lawyers and the State*, at 9.

[3] Oliver (2005), *Constitution of Independence*, at 1 on 'well-behaved Dominions' (Australia, Canada, New Zealand), and at 7 (on notion of 'disguised revolution'); Dale (1993), 'Making and Remaking of Commonwealth Constitutions', notably at 67 (Whitehall drafting at least thirty-three final independence constitutions, most reproducing British-style parliamentary government) and 69 (twenty-nine are now republics).

controversial situation is that of revolution within an existing state, as occurred in France. Here was a major form of political rupture, and major theoretical efforts were undertaken to justify it. France, however, remained the France that it had been, so that the theoretical writing was directed more towards the change from ancien to nouveau régime than towards the existence of the state itself, though often the distinction has not been drawn. Finally, political revolution may occur within an imperial structure so that a new contemporary state emerges. This, as in the case of the USA, would most clearly require theoretical justification. There was no recognizable predecessor state that could simply continue (though this too can be debated). There is therefore reason to look to the creation of the United States of America, as the principal case in which a new state may have been created that was free of prior normative constraint or support.

The United States of America

The most important feature in the creation of the United States of America is the existence of a single, written document that would contain the 'complete organization' of civil government.[4] This written document would have the effect, as an instrument of closure, both of nationalizing law (if you are of the view that any law existed before the constitution) and providing a national and exclusive base for the creation of further, national law. It might have been a brilliant, original idea, since until this time the notion of a constitution had been (first, in the Roman era) an enactment by imperial authority and later (by the eighteenth century) a 'composite' entity or 'repository' of unwritten customs, rules, and enactments.[5] Blackstone drew no distinction between the constitution and the system of laws as a whole.[6] The notion of *a* constitution was thus an important one, and would eventually yield the notion of a national constitutional law (Verfassungsrecht as opposed to Staatslehre). Yet there is great debate, within the contemporary USA, as to the extent of originality in or self-sufficiency of the Constitution. The debate has concentrated both on the general idea of a comprehensive constitution and on the actual content of the document.

   Differences amongst colonial historians on whether a sharp break occurred in North American history in the late eighteenth century have been described as 'radical'.[7] On one hand there is insistence on the 'distinctive' character of US

---

[4] Wood (1969), *Creation of American Republic*, at 600 (citing Thomas Paine); and for the general phenomenon of written constitutions as an instrument of territorial closure, see Ch. 4, '*Constitutions*'.

[5] For the Roman idea, Vincent (1987), *Theories of the State*, at 84; for 'composite', Spellman (1998), *European Political Thought*, at 68 ('made up of historic and customary patterns' together with 'a host of written laws'); for 'repository', Hulsebosch (2005), *Constituting Empire*, at 40 (also 'not a thing', a 'cultural commons'); and see generally Ch. 3, '*Constitutionalism*'.

[6] Wood (2006), 'The American Revolution', at 612 ('all were of a piece').

[7] Horwitz (2009), 'Constitutional Transplants', at 541 (those favouring 'sharp break' contrasted with those insisting on ongoing significance of seventeenth-century codes and charters).

government, a view widespread in popular sentiment;[8] on the other hand there is vigorous denial of any US exceptionalism.[9] Outside the USA the position has even been advanced that in its early history the country was not a state but a commercial undertaking, taking on state-like qualities ('Verstaatung') only once a frontier had been eliminated.[10] A potential middle ground has been advanced by some leading historians, to the effect that the achievement of the founding fathers was not to create a new set of ideas but to bring diffuse ideas into a 'comprehensive whole'.[11] This was feasible, tapping into the known idea of a written charter of authority and liberties, which had a genealogy extending back through the charters of then-existing colonies, Cromwell's Instrument of Government in seventeenth-century England, and the written constitutions of the Greek city-states.[12] The authority of the written constitution, as well as its content, could therefore have been found in existing, cosmopolitan forms of legitimation.

When one turns to the actual arguments used to justify a new constitution their cosmopolitan character is immediately recognizable and is clearly their most striking feature. The founding fathers searched far and wide for sound ideas recognized as such, and went to extraordinary lengths to obtain documentation to support them. Jefferson shipped trunks of books to Madison from Paris, the shipment taking months, and Madison immersed himself in them at home in Virginia, eventually producing long briefs on different political entities, from Greece to the United Netherlands.[13] They pursued a 'wealth of legal learning' across time and space, and from an evident sense of necessity.[14] The 'animating

---

[8] Kammen (1988), *Sovereignty and Liberty*, at 5 (though similarities, 'continual sense of difference'); Hulsebosch (2005), *Constituting Empire*, at 4 ('most Americans' equating founding with writing of Constitution and view event as 'exceptional break' with past, though American colonies 'much like' others protective of their autonomy); and for some 800 law review articles from 1900 to 2006 arguing for US 'exceptionalism', Safrin (2008), 'Un-Exceptionalism of US Exceptionalism', at 1309.

[9] Bender (2006a), *A Nation Among Nations*, arguing generally, at ix, for the 'transnational nature of national histories' and seeking a 'more cosmopolitan sense of being an American'; Gardbaum (2008–9), 'Myth and Reality of American Constitutional Exceptionalism', at 397 (USA 'actually well within the contemporary global constitutional mainstream').

[10] Krüger (1966), *Allgemeine Staatslehre*, at 7, citing Pogodin (process not even completed until New Deal of 1930s).

[11] Wood (1969), *Creation of American Republic*, at 564; Wood (2006), 'The American Revolution', at 601 ('creative' era but no great theorists of stature of Hobbes, Locke, Montesquieu, Rousseau, 'not even' a Burlamaqui or Pufendorf); Bailyn (1967), *Ideological Origins of American Revolution*, at 22 ('hitherto inconclusive' ideas 'fused into a comprehensive view').

[12] For colonial charters, see Ch. 4, '*Constitutions*'; and for the written constitutions of Greek city-states, see Ch. 2, '*Collaborative Cities*' and Ch. 3, '*Writing*'. Mention may also be made of the Magna Carta and the Salic Law of the seventh century (which was public law or Lehnrecht in considerable measure).

[13] Riker (1957), 'Dutch and American Federalism', at 498 (192 volumes, shipped September 1785, arriving February 1786); LaCroix (2010), *Ideological Origins of American Federalism*, at 136 (Madison returned to Virginia where he 'immersed himself' from April to June, 1786, producing forty-one pages of handwritten notes); and for their eventual publication in *The Federalist*, Nos 18, 19, 20, Wood (1969), *Creation of American Republic*, at 472.

[14] Bailyn (1967), *Ideological Origins of American Revolution*, at 224 (and 'careful logic'); for John Adams's significant reliance on Roman, civil, and natural law authority, and his corresponding library, Clark (2011), 'Comparative Law in Colonial British North America', at 673 (library larger than that of Harvard Law School at time).

purpose' of the new constitution would even have been to ensure acceptance and diplomatic recognition in a Eurocentric world of emergent states, an 'anxious and cosmopolitan context' largely lost sight of today.[15]

The primary source, given questions of language, knowledge, and availability, appears to have been the English common law. This may appear paradoxical, given a revolution, yet we are reminded that the revolution was not directed against English ideas and common law, but rather against their corruption and distortion in circumstances of empire.[16] Certain currents of English thought were more influential than others, but the entire repository of the common law was available and largely relied upon.[17] Like the French using Roman law against the Holy Roman Empire,[18] the colonists used English law against the English. The common law's actual content could thus be taken up in positive and national form, and the common law itself seen as a primary source of the legitimacy of such an undertaking. It had recognized the Magna Carta. This provided the stabilizing element that a successful revolution required, so that the founding fathers 'got away with' the new constitution.[19] It would not have been the paper and the writing but the underlying ideas that were the essential elements in the founding process, that which Lawrence Tribe describes as the 'invisible constitution'.[20] The common law, cosmopolitan character of US public and private law

---

[15] Golove and Hulsebosch (2010), 'A Civilized Nation', at 932 (necessity of adhering to recognized law of nations, qualifying in range of 'civilized states').

[16] See notably Wren (2006), 'Common Law of England in Virginia', at 152 (Virginians believed their revolution 'was not a revolution at all but merely a last, desperate attempt to recover the traditional English liberties . . . lost at the hands of a "corrupt" English government'); Unger (2004), 'Exceptional Myths and Myths of Exceptionalism', at 85 (perspective of 'an expatriate English gentry, striving for freedom from infringements on what they considered their own business'); Wood (2006), 'The American Revolution', at 603–4 ('no intention of repudiating the classical ideal and assumptions behind the constitution', 'revolting not against the English constitution but on behalf of it'); Wood (1969), *Creation of American Republic*, at 262 (ascertaining 'sacred Laws of Justice' of English constitution); MacCulloch (2009), *Christianity*, at 720 (majority of settlers 'not separatists but Puritans'); Marshall (2012), *Remaking British Atlantic*, at 282 (common law ideals to which even the 'most radical' American subscribed), 285 (common law 'indelibly identified' with liberty and security).

[17] For understandably different perceptions of the multi-sourced English constitution, and reliance in the USA on 'country' and 'coffeehouse radicals' in England, Bailyn (1967), *Ideological Origins of American Revolution*, at 35 ('seventeenth-century heroes of liberty . . . little known today'), 45 (themselves 'not original', borrowing 'commonplaces of time'); Goldie (2006), 'The English system of liberty', at 64 (on 'country platform'), 69–70 (for classical learning amongst 'country' politicians); Wood (2006), 'The American Revolution', at 604–5 (colonists concentrating on particular strains of thought, 'radically critical' perspective on English life; US state constitutions meant as what 'English constitution should have been'); and for Bagehot's view that Americans thought they were copying the English constitution but actually 'contriving a contrast to it', Bagehot (1958), *The English Constitution*, at 201.

[18] See Ch. 3, '*Institutional cosmopolitanism*'.

[19] See Ch. 4, '*Constitutions*'.

[20] See Ch. 4, '*Constitutions*'; and see Strauss (2010), *The Living Constitution*, at 3 ('our constitutional system, without our fully realizing it, has tapped into an ancient sources of law . . . the common law'); Strauss (1996), 'Common Law Constitutional Interpretation', at 890 (for important distinction not that of written or unwritten constitution but whether 'well-established' or 'insecure' constitutional traditions, contrasting USA and UK with new east European states); Jenkins (2003), 'From Unwritten to Written', at 908 (written constitution not an originating source of parliamentary limits or judicial review but rather 'means of expressing those principles'), 929 (written constitution simply expression of 'already existing principles'); Böckenförde (1991), *Recht, Staat, Freiheit*, at 112 ('[t]he liberal, secularized State is dependent on

sources continued after the founding, with positive state adoptions of the English common law and ongoing citation of English case-law precedents in everyday judicial practice.[21]

Beyond the common law the authorities relied upon were as diverse as those used to justify colonial empires, and often the same. The Declaration of Independence of 1776 had been 'jurisprudentially eclectic', formulated in the 'discourse of the *ius gentium*', and the Constitution followed this model.[22] The classical authors were the 'most conspicuous', even if often seen as only 'window dressing'.[23] The founding fathers had been schooled intensively in classical writing; they now found a splendid occasion to use it. There would be a Republic, a Senate, a Capitol Hill; some even adopted Roman pen names ('Publius') for their writing.[24] As with questions of empire, and in Europe, the Roman sources were taken as indicative of a universal, natural law, and complemented by political and legal writing of what is known as the enlightenment. The great European names were echoed; what may be seen as a revitalized and non-colonial *ius commune* (of Roman origin) appears to have also had a certain 'operative' function in the new world, in spite of its lack of territorial attachment.[25] The Roman model was of course an ambiguous one, and there was much difference within the body of then contemporary natural law: there would have been a 'Lockean' stream (more insistent on individual liberties) and a 'republican' stream (more insistent on the common good), but both these and other tendencies were sweeping in their use of literature seen as supportive.[26]

---

conditions which it cannot itself guarantee') (italics in original); Hamburger (2008), *Law and Judicial Duty*, notably at xiii (continuity of inherited 'ideals of law and judicial duty'), 16–17 (continuing common law judicial duty to decide according to law of land, including constitution in broad sense).

[21] Wood (1969), *Creation of American Republic*, at 299 (on 'most state constitutions' affirmatively adopting, though as 'suitable' in the circumstances); Wren (2006), 'Common Law of England in Virginia', at 152 ('immediately embraced the English system'); though for occasional state prohibition of citing English decisions, McPherson (2007), *Reception of English Law*, at 26; Brown (1964), *British Statutes*, at 41 (New Jersey, Kentucky, Pennsylvania in early nineteenth century).

[22] Armitage (2007), *Declaration of Independence*, at 65, and 89 (neither 'wholly naturalist nor exclusively positivist'); Lobban (2007), *History of Philosophy of Law in Common Law World*, at 130 (reliance on both Blackstone and natural law).

[23] Bailyn (1967), *Ideological Origins of American Revolution*, at 23–4 (and knowledge limited to Roman political history from first century BCE to second CE).

[24] Lintott (1999), *Constitution of the Roman Republic*, at 253–3 (pen name chosen by both Madison and Hamilton, 'steeped in classical authors'); Bederman (2008b), 'Classical Constitution', notably at 407ff. (for classical education of founders, recent, major studies on classical tradition and American mind); Sellers (2009a), 'Influence of Marcus Tullius Cicero', at 35 (for earlier English practice of Roman pen-names (Cato)), 36 ('conscious imitation of Cicero'), 48 ('successful revolutions usually begin as appeals to the past'); Bederman (2008a), *Classical Foundations of American Constitution*, at 4 (even grammar schools provided 'rigorously classical education'), 50 (classical influence 'can hardly be overestimated'); Bonventre (2006), 'Aristotle, Cicero and Cardozo', at 647 (extending also to Greek philosophy); Sirico (2006), 'The Federalist and Lessons of Rome', at 434 ('centrality' of classical history).

[25] For the 'operative function' in Europe, see Ch. 6, 'Common Laws within Europe'.

[26] For Lockean and republican views, Tomkins (2005), *Our Republican Constitution*, notably at 42–3; though for rejection of a dichotomy and of a view that 'split' focus of attention, Huyler (1995), *Locke in America*, at 251. The republican view has been traced by Pocock to Machiavelli, rejecting the notion of an eighteenth-century republican rupture: Pocock (2003), *The Machiavellian Moment*, notably at 462

Continental writing was perhaps as visible and present in the founding process as that of England, and there was even a process by which continental writing on English authors became influential.[27]

Nor were sources beyond England and the continent excluded. The Jewish Bible and Jewish law had been influential in the founding of the colonies with their constitutions, and these were relied upon in the eventual formulation of the Bill of Rights.[28] The Scottish enlightenment was not ignored, and is now said to be vital in understanding notably Article III of the US Constitution.[29] Many sources thus contributed to original understanding. As was the case with English common law sources, moreover, use of continental sources continued after the adoption of the Constitution.[30] Chancellor Kent's writing in the first third of the nineteenth century is said to represent a 'Cosmopolitan Law for America', relying extensively on both continental and common law material.[31] Nationalism had not yet fully arrived in the world but, as has generally been seen above, it was unable to effect the closure its proponents would have preferred, given existing flows of information.[32]

The model of the United States of America is important because it appears to have represented the sharpest break with previous authority and the most intensely national process of state creation. It was inevitably seen as a model in the great age of nationalism that followed, through the late nineteenth and twentieth centuries.[33] The end of the empires generated great interest in the generation of new states in many parts of the world. The underlying US cosmopolitanism was not what was looked to in this process. What attracted

(US revolution 'last act of the civil Renaissance'), 506 ('complex relation both with English and renaissance history'), 522 (US checks and balances linked to sense of decline of virtue), though at 577 acknowledging 'dialectic' between notions of 'modern liberty' and 'classical republicanism').

[27] For influence of Burlamaqui, a French, seventeenth-century 'popularizer' of Locke, Unger (2004), 'Exceptional Myths and Myths of Exceptionalism', at 85 (notably for 'pursuit of happiness'); and for that of Molyneux, providing 'prototype' use of Locke, Goldie (2006), 'English system of liberty', at 56.

[28] Maoz (1998), 'Values of a Jewish and Democratic State', at 149 (Puritan settlers having chosen laws of Hebrews, Jewish law sailing to America 'aboard the *Mayflower*').

[29] Pfander and Birk (2011), 'Article III and the Scottish Judiciary', notably at 1615 (scholars and jurists 'should not end' with Blackstone's England), 1625 (general importance of Scots law 'on structural matters' in the USA), and 1628 (emphasis on English law 'fails to capture the breadth of ideas' that influenced framers' legal thought).

[30] For continued use of English and continental sources, participation 'in a cosmopolitan Atlantic world', Hulsebosch (2005), *Constituting Empire*, at 205–6 (for Federalists' centre 'not a physical place but an ideal').

[31] Hulsebosch (2005), *Constituting Empire*, at 277, and see 278 (Kent's law appearing 'Anglo-European' in form), 282 (continental sources cited alongside English ones 'whenever possible'); Lobban (2007), *History of Philosophy of Law in Common Law World*, at 148 (Kent 'went out of his way' to incorporate continental material). For Roman law being held in esteem, 'almost to the point of veneration', Helmholz (1992), 'Use of the Civil Law', at 1649; and generally for influence of continental law throughout making-over of US law in nineteenth century, Glenn (2010b), *Legal Traditions*, at 263 with references.

[32] See Ch. 5, 'Manifest diversity'; and see Marshall (2012), *Remaking British Atlantic*, at 280 ('communications across the Atlantic . . . quickly revived').

[33] Billias (2009), *American Constitutionalism Heard Round the World, 1776–1989* (for seven 'echoes' of US constitutional influence—eighteenth-century Europe, nineteenth-century Latin America, etc.), though cautioning at xiv that influence has 'always been limited despite its impressive spread' and xv that 'frequently indirect, resulting in hybrid constitutions'.

attention was the existence of a written constitution, as a kind of blueprint of a successful contemporary state. This generated widespread though less successful emulation, as well as intense and cosmopolitan efforts at justification.

France and the world

The vastness of the phenomenon of written constitutions has already been noted,[34] but the first failure of the US model of a written constitution occurred only five years after that of the USA, when the French Constitution of 1791 collapsed in the chaos of 1792. Paper is only paper, unless there is an invisible constitution that supports it, and this was obviously lacking in post-revolutionary France. There have been many subsequent constitutions in France, some more successful, but the entire process shows the difficulty of saying all that is necessary in a single document. Length is not the answer, since this inevitably brings a document meant to be fundamental closer to ordinary forms of legislation. This explains why states can exist with no written constitution; if the invisible constitution exists there is no need for a written one. Most, however, have decided that writing is necessary, and so we see a great range of written constitutions in the world, and great variance in their levels of success. Rightly, current French doctrine thus concludes that all constitutions are characterized by 'precariousness and contingency' and where a constitution is successful this will depend very largely on circumstances beyond it, legal and extra-legal.[35] France is a successful state but this has historically been due to the success of its droit commun and its laws, codes, and institutions rather than its written constitutional instruments. Foundations can be other than constitutional.

Given unremitting human diversity within states, and the absence of any actual nation-states in the world, the conciliatory function of a written constitution is a very difficult one. Most written constitutions therefore fail.[36] A major study of approximately half of the near eight hundred constitutions written over the last two centuries found that most 'die young', only a few lasted more than fifty years, and the average life expectancy was nineteen years.[37] Writing is too easy to change. Where states have been successful this has occurred when long-standing common laws have legitimated specific types of public and private law-making, specific *iura propria*. In the absence of such deeply rooted common law states fail, or are at least unsuccessful in varying degrees, and theoretical or extra-legal forms of justification simply cannot carry the weight. Power is not an

---

[34] See Ch. 5, 'Nation and State' (some 800 written state constitutions in last 200 years).

[35] Chevallier (1999), *L'État*, at 48 ('de précarité et de contingence').

[36] Scheppele (2008), 'A Constitution Between Past and Future', at 1406 (since success is not dependent on initial design).

[37] Ginsburg, Melton, and Elkins (2009), *Endurance of National Constitutions*, at 1–2. Cranston arrives at an average constitution's life of twenty-two years: Cranston (2004), *The Sovereignty Revolution*, at 50 (only eight states—Australia, Canada, New Zealand, South Africa, Sweden, Switzerland, the UK, and the USA—have not had their governments, and in many cases their borders, changed by violence since 1914. Tarr speaks of the need to consider 'how successful' a particular constitution is. There would be no binary phenomenon of existence or non-existence: Tarr (2005), 'Constitutional Origins' at 10.

explanation, neither for particular, detailed forms of state nor for ongoing constitutionalism; culture was relied upon by no one since it was a twentieth-century invention with no inherent content; fictions are simply what they are. The principal theoretical justification that has had some purchase in constitutional thinking was that of a social contract of some form or another, and this has had profound development amongst social and political thinkers, in a line of thought extending from John Rawls back through Rousseau, the Jesuits and Dominicans, the middle ages, and Greek and Roman notions of the consent of the governed.[38] Its main difficulty has been its presumptive or idealistic character. Kant regarded it as an 'idea of reason' (as understood by him in eighteenth-century Europe) as opposed to historical fact,[39] and Gierke saw it as having 'succumbed' to the historical school of law ('invincible opponents').[40] 'The people' who would have entered into it are thus as undefined, variable, and disaggregated as any corresponding, later notion of a 'nation'.[41] The US Constitution has been described as the product of a 'runaway convention, acting far beyond its original mandate'.[42] It has been said that the idea of a social contract does signify a shift in justification of authority, from external or transnational authority to internal authority,[43] but this too assumes the existence of a defined community. It is also challenged by adherents to older, religious forms of law, who see any pre-state contract as necessarily rooted in existing law, including their own, so that it is possible to remain Jewish and also *participate* in a liberal

---

[38] See Ch. 3, 'Constitutionalism'; Rawls (1971), *A Theory of Justice*; Rousseau (2003), *On the Social Contract* (1762); for the Jesuits' contribution to 'resistance theory', Spellman (1998), *European Political Thought*, at 84; and for that of both Jesuits and Dominicans, Vincent (1987), *Theories of the State*, at 89 (notably de Vitoria), Skinner (1978), *Foundations of modern political thought*, at 175 (influence on Locke). For Pufendorf's notion of separate contracts of association and subjection, Dufour (1991), 'Pufendorf', at 574; and for Althusius's opposition to Bodin on grounds of the sovereign rights of the people, Gierke (1939), *Development of Political Theory*, at 16, 102 (even as 'creator of genuine theory of social contract'). For such a 'voluntaristic' tradition in the writings of Marsilius of Padua in the fourteenth century, Gewirth (1980), 'Introduction', in Marsilius (1980), *Defensor Pacis*, at xxxi, Canning (1988a), 'Politics, institutions and ideas', at 364 (popular theories becoming 'full-blown' from 1250), and see Ch. 5, 'Religion'. For adoption by glossators, notably Bartolus, Baldus, and by conciliar movement, Canning (1988a), 'Politics, institutions and ideas', at 365.

[39] Kant (1974), *On the Old Saw*, at 65 ('rather a *mere idea* of reason') (emphasis in original); and for Kant as marking beginning of its downfall by divesting it of 'all historical reality', Gierke (1939), *Development of Political Theory*, at 111.

[40] Gierke (1939), *Development of Political Theory*, at 111 and 112 (yet 'we of this day enjoy the fruits which . . . it won').

[41] See Ch. 5, 'Nation and State'. For social contract as the 'foundation myth' of the modern state, Nelson (2006), *Making of Modern State*, at 67; as long decried as 'illusion' though given some credibility by US and French revolutions, Wokler (2006), 'Ideology and origins of social science', at 688. For the earlier, Hobbesian notion of simple 'representation' as equally a 'fiction' since 'the represented does not create the representative', Chevallier (1999), *L'État*, at 53, citing Troper, and generally Post (1964), *Studies in Medieval Legal Thought*, Chs 2, 3, and 4.

[42] Tribe (2008), *The Invisible Constitution*, at 150 (originally to revise Articles of Confederation); and for the view of Joseph Story that the American revolution 'was brought about against the wishes and resistance of a formidable minority of the people', Story (1994), *Commentaries on the Constitution*, at 298, cited and discussed in Parker (2011), 'Law "In" and "As" History', at 599.

[43] Spellman (1998), *European Political Thought*, at 135.

state, as opposed to simply becoming part of a whole.[44] Hans Lindahl therefore writes of the 'irreducible' ambiguity of collective self-constitution both *by* and *of* a collective self, and of the impossibility of a founding 'we' otherwise than as an 'ambiguous and provisional achievement'.[45]

The presumptive notion of a social contract of a unanimous people has had some 'operative effect', however, perhaps most notably in those jurisdictions least in need of it and where underlying common laws provided ongoing continuity of state structures. Its most operational feature, however, would be by way of limiting authority, to be examined in the next section, as opposed to serving as a free-standing justification of the state. This becomes most evident when the state is examined across its many manifestations in the world, where the notion of a social contract of a unanimous people becomes more and more implausible the greater the number of actual states examined. It is an obviously otiose construction if the particular state is based originally on imperial enactment (as was the case with Australia, Canada, New Zealand, and India)[46] and still more implausible when the existing state expressly consecrates plural structures and laws into its identity, as in the cases of Canada, Israel, India, and many other states, notably in Africa, Latin America, and the middle east.[47] Here the state is obviously cosmopolitan, and obviously dependent on its cosmopolitanism. No fiction can support a more encompassing role for state structures. African doctrine is instructive. Djoli asserts that the theoretical and formal models of the USA and France that have been adopted in Africa have degenerated into personal power, lacking a 'real base' in African society.[48] The adoption of a purely written model of a constitution, if no means exist to capture and integrate the common law upon which the model is based, results in a phenomenon of rejection. Van Creveld thus writes that there has been no development of the notion of an 'abstract' state in Africa or Asia, an entirely understandable phenomenon since the concept is rooted in largely unwritten sources extending back over

---

[44] Novak (2005), *The Jewish Social Contract*, at xvii (social contract as blueprint for multi-cultural society rather than one of assimilation), 7 (parties retaining 'original rights'), 18 (primacy of community 'can be really located in history').

[45] Lindahl (2007), 'Constituent Power', at 9–10; and see MacCormick (2007), *Institutions of Law*, at 45 ('in the republic, however, neither citizens nor nation exist until the constitution brings them into being as such . . . '); Hahm and Kim (2010), 'To Make "We the People"', notably at 806–7 ('the people are given a definition, an identity in the act of attribution itself . . . status comes about only as a result of constitution-making').

[46] See Oliver (2005), *Constitution of Independence*, at 8 (on Hartian 'self-embracing' constitution of UK, able to bind itself in 'patriating' constitution to Canada) and 7 (thus 'possible to have the constitutional cake and eat it too', maintaining constitutional continuity while obtaining independence).

[47] See the discussions in Ch. 8, 'Churches and Religions'; and Ch. 13, 'States and Religious Authority'.

[48] Djoli (2005), 'Le constitutionalisme africain', at 182 (modern state translates Judeo-Christian vision, articulated in pyramidal manner, as opposed to (African) symbol of circle). For autonomous forces in Senegal shaping the state more than they were shaped by it, Migdal (2001), *State in Society*, at 107; and for African states not being 'effectively organized', Jackson (1987), 'Quasi-states, dual regimes', at 526 and 528 (medieval and modern at same time). Fombad speaks not of an absence of constitutions but of an absence of 'constitutionalism': Fombad (2007), 'Challenges to Constitutionalism', at 3.

centuries in different forms in different European common laws.[49] There is also a failure to distinguish private interests from public affairs, a patrimonial view of public office struggled against for centuries in Europe.[50] Written constitutions rely on underlying ideas, but do not state them. The ideas must be understood, and there are different levels of understanding.

All states of the world can therefore be thought of as practising a form of cosmopolitan constitutionalism. Where the population is irreducibly cosmopolitan, as in India, this is simply irresistible,[51] as it is in states with recognizable indigenous populations.[52] Where the population has a relatively high level of homogeneity, as in Japan, the cosmopolitanism more evidently results from importing a western constitutional model.[53] In western states that have been most successful in implementing a notion of state structures and law, constitutional cosmopolitanism finds itself notably in age-old sources of constitutional law, in constitutional structures tailored for diversity, and in the forms of institutional cosmopolitanism resulting from constitutional guarantees of religious liberty.[54] These latter forms of cosmopolitan constitutionalism constitute limits on state authority.

LIMITS OF AUTHORITY

As contemporary states emerged out of monarchies, or continued them, there was inevitable continuation of the common laws that justified and limited authority. Van Caenegem situates the 'historic starting point' of European constitutionalism in the late twelfth century, with the first charters limiting the

---

[49] Van Creveld (1999), *Rise and Decline of the State*, at 315 (government does not 'in itself a state make').

[50] Van Creveld (1999), *Rise and Decline of the State*, at 404 (citing nineteenth-century Chilean example of wife of one president also being daughter of a second president, sister of a third, and mother of a fourth). For the 'nominal' character of many Latin American constitutions until at least the 1980s, Balaguer-Callejon (2001), 'Verfassungsstaat in ibero-amerikanischen Kontext', at 189; and for their failure to become 'entrenched', Schor (2006), 'Constitutionalism Through the Looking Glass', notably at 3 (no institutionalization of 'fundamental rules of the game'); Karst and Rosenn (1975), *Law and Development*, at 60 (citing Spanish and Portuguese maxim 'for our friends, everything; for strangers, nothing; and for enemies, the law!').

[51] See Eisenstadt (2003), *Comparative Civilizations*, at 330 (for India's concept of sovereignty emphasizing 'the multiple right of different groups and sectors of society and not the existence—real or ideal—of a unitary, almost ontological concept of the state') and 333 (political arena not commanding 'high degree of transcendental commitment'); and for 'hybrid Eurasian state forms' contrasted with 'classic types of European states', Bayly (2004), *Birth of the Modern World*, at 258. For contemporary functioning of such states, see Chs 11–14.

[52] For the place of indigenous law in contemporary states, see Ch. 4, 'Codes', 'Constitutions' and Ch. 12, 'Reconciliation'. The phenomenon is present on all continents.

[53] Higuchi (2006), *Constitution*, at 87 (generalization of europeo-continental form of constitutional justice), 119 (too simplistic to see US-style constitution simply 'imposed' by USA following Second World War); and for nineteenth-century reception of German constitutional model, Kuriki (2001), 'Der Verfassungsstaat in den ostasiatischen Traditionen', at 181 (model of Kaiser or emperor). There is of course cosmopolitanism in Japan that is less visible, notably in the reduction of conflict in the relations between Buddhist and Shinto religions, and in relations with minority populations.

[54] See Ch. 8, 'Institutional Cosmopolitanism'.

increased impact of royal power.[55] At that time there was no clear differentiation between public and private law, no imposed dichotomy, but there was content, and the objective law that prevailed was seen as 'the sum or combination of all the subjective rights of the people'.[56] This notion of subjective rights may be anachronistic here, but the result of the common laws' protection of unwritten custom was unquestionably to secure existing entitlements, however designated. Moreover, there would have been less need for a clearly recognizable public law given existing diffusion of authority. Whether a distinctive public law has now emerged is the object of debate, and the answer may well depend on the jurisdiction, but in any case the continuity of content, often in varied form, is unquestionable.[57] Cosmopolitanism is evident both in the sources and structures of constitutionalism and in terms of the diverse relations with which it must inevitably deal.

Sources

The idea that there are limits on the exercise of authority in a community is as old as human communities themselves. Those who lived by unwritten law did not, *pace* Hobbes, live in an unregulated world.[58] Their states did not have written constitutions but they did not want or need them. Prior to the contemporary state, one characterized by written forms of law, hierarchy, and fixed spatial boundaries, European states had also developed limits on the exercise of authority and even written records of those limits. It was one of the primary duties of the prince or king to protect and apply the law, said many common laws.[59] Prior to Bodin and Hobbes there was no recognized theory of sovereignty that could be used to dispute the old law. Roman law had a maxim that the prince was not bound by the law, but this was disputed even within Roman law itself.[60] The old, limiting law was supported by informal, cosmopolitan, non-state sources

---

[55] Van Caenegem (1995), *Historical Introduction Western Constitutional Law*, at 80 (eliminating 'specifically named abuses' and calling for treatment according to to law); and see Loughlin (2010), *Foundations of Public Law*, at 17 for 'modern idea' of state evolving out of 'thought and practice between the twelfth and seventeenth centuries'). Both of these statements assume rather than reject ongoing influence of Roman law, in varying degree, in canonical and civilian writings from the twelfth century.

[56] Kern (1985), *Kingship and Law*, at 182 ('the indivisibility of subjective and objective law, as well as of private and public law').

[57] Van Caenegem (1995), *Historical Introduction Western Constitutional Law*, at 2 concludes that the 'theoretical elaboration' of the public law/private law dichotomy has had 'no immediate impact on legal practice and has even left some countries completely untouched', and finds it unsurprising that public law was not even taught in France until the late eighteenth century. Loughlin sees an 'autonomous field' of public law emerging from the sixteenth to seventeenth centuries, altering the character of 'fundamental law' though with a 'powerful set of theological borrowings'. It would, however, have been 'suppressed' in Britain for much of the last 250 years. Loughlin (2010), *Foundations of Public Law*, at 2, 3, 45, 50. For 'elements of constitutionality' that would 'lie scattered' among academic works' to the sixteenth century, Lloyd (1991), 'Constitutionalism', at 257.

[58] See Ch. 3, 'Writing'; and for earlier forms of the state, Ch. 1, 'The State Tradition through Time'.

[59] Scheuner (1956), 'Begriff und Entwicklung des Rechtsstaats', at 81, and see Ch. 3, '*Constitutionalism*' and '*Common laws*'.

[60] See Ch. 3, '*Common laws*'; Ch. 6, 'Common Laws within Europe'.

(including Roman and canonical ones), and was applied for the benefit of non-state populations and institutions (including the church). The real challenge to this underlying constitutionalism (and the institutional cosmopolitanism that it supported) came briefly in the sixteenth and seventeenth centuries with the theory of Bodin and the then-absolutist notions of royal authority (the 'Sun King' who was Louis XIV). Two remarks appear appropriate.

The first is that there is great doubt about the efficacy on the ground of the theories of sovereignty and absolute royal authority, even in France. Some do acknowledge the 'absoluteness' of royal authority, or at least the contemporary acknowledgement of it.[61] More frequently there are suggestions of ultimate limits, however illogical these might appear within a concept of 'indivisible sovereignty'. In late-sixteenth-century France Guy Coquille spoke openly of 'degrees' of sovereignty,[62] and there was ongoing affirmation of 'fundamental laws' (those of the droit commun) applicable to the monarch.[63] Since custom remained valid there had to be a notion that this was through the 'tacit' approval of the crown.[64] Bodin himself retained 'the judicial check' in verifying royal enactments, a necessary acknowledgement of obstreperous provincial parlements and their occasional refusal to register royal ordonnances.[65] Law should not even have been changed without the advice of these high courts or parlements.[66] There is also serious doubt as to the reality of absolutist rule. French kings were beset by material difficulties, those of communication, transport, and the weakness of police and bureaucracy.[67] Outside France the notion of an absolute monarchy never achieved the status it did in France. In the Holy Roman

---

[61] See, e.g., Keohane (1980), *Philosophy and State in France*, at ix ('outright' rejection in sixteenth- to eighteenth-century France of limits of authority); Church (1969), *Constitutional Thought in Sixteenth-Century France*, at 179 (break with 'older constitutionalism' to 'substitute in its stead a theory of absolutism') and 335 (only 'ruler and ruled' in sixteenth-century French constitutional thought, though crown only free to act 'short of violating the general principles of universal justice').

[62] Lloyd (1991), 'Constitutionalism', at 285; and for such ideas, as well as those of limitations, not clarifying the concept but having an effect 'to explain the concept away', Stankiewicz (1976), 'Sovereignty as Political Theory', at 143 (also 'constitutional conventions' and 'practical limitations'); Vincent (1987), *Theories of the State*, at 37 (notions of shared sovereignty 'defy the logic of sovereignty'). The notion of degrees of sovereignty has today become inescapable: see *The Economist*, 15 September 2012, p. 51 ('Kosovo gains more sovereignty').

[63] Church (1969), *Constitutional Thought in Sixteenth-Century France*, at 325 (as 'exception' to absolutism).

[64] Church (1969), *Constitutional Thought in Sixteenth-Century France*, at 324 (contrasting with 'pure monarchy' where only crown can make laws).

[65] Church (1969), *Constitutional Thought in Sixteenth-Century France*, at 221 ('remonstrance' though no control over 'public policy'), 234 (Bodin's insistence on monarch's subordination to natural law, contracts, and consent to taxation), 238; and Sueur (2007), *Histoire du droit public français*, vol. II, at 81 (for parlements even developing 'legislative memory'—'mémoire du droit législatif'), and see Ch. 2, 'Affirmative Crowns'. For Bodin as 'imperfect Hobbes', Keohane (1980), *Philosophy and State in* France, at 71.

[66] Franklin (1991), 'Sovereignty and the mixed constitution', at 306 (this as 'the main tradition').

[67] Ellul (1956), *Histoire des institutions*, at 339 (and ongoing 'feudal structures'); Spellman (1998), *European Political Thought*, at 67 (on 'simple reality'); Moote (1971), *Revolt of the Judges*, (on recalcitrance of royal officials, and fronde, making 'mockery' of absolute monarchy); Major (1960), *Representative Institutions in Renaissance France*, at 14 (no coincidence that most popular rulers the strongest); and for an overview of recent historical writing to this effect Breen (2011), 'Law, Society and State', notably at 353 ('wave of revisionist studies', Bourbons 'cooperating and colluding' rather than commanding).

Empire, authority was even officially acknowledged as limited and absolutism has been characterized as simple 'myth'.[68] In the seventeenth century England settled on a notion of sovereignty in the king and parliament, described from a continental perspective as abandonment of the sovereignty concept and 'either–or' reasoning, in favour of a 'compromise' or 'both–and' solution.[69] There was need of ongoing (constitutional) control of its operation. The medieval world was therefore not 'congenial soil' for Sun Kings; it gave little scope for 'fanatical Caesarism'.[70] New forms of closure are inevitably constrained by the heritage of previous ones.

The second necessary remark about the emergence of an absolute form of monarchy and a decline in limitations is that this is in no way incompatible with the notion of a common law. Common laws do not purport to be binding law. They are relational and yield to local law claiming imperative application.[71] It should not therefore be surprising that in France 'the constitutionalist tradition of a complex and pluralistic polity gradually receded' before arguments of absolutism.[72] Yet common laws, like the Cheshire Cat, may reappear whenever memory permits and invocation occurs. So today the absolutist crown (assuming it existed) appears as a mere blip on the historical horizon,[73] and constitutionalism in its diverse forms is today more vibrant than ever as a concept (with varying effect in the jurisdictions of the world). From a cosmopolitan perspective, moreover, the precise location of any sovereignty within an entity defined already as hierarchical and bounded is of relatively little interest. What matters is closure, and it is only writing, hierarchy, and boundaries that can effectively bring this about.

That there are limits on authority in states today is beyond question. It is more a question of their respect. Where do the limitations come from and what limits do they impose? All may be seen as descending from an ancient notion of a

---

[68] Franklin (1991), 'Sovereignty and the mixed constitution', at 308 (for limits); Wilson (2004), *From Reich to Revolution*, at 208 (for myth); and for general 'revisionist' challenge to notions of absolutism, Black (2004), *Kings, Nobles and Commoners*, at 2–3 ('composite state' surviving till twentieth century).

[69] Brunner (1963), 'Vom Gottesgnadentum', at 281 (for logic) and 281 (as separation of powers—'Teilung der Gewalten'); and for 'Crown-in-Parliament' as 'general idea capable of supporting different theories of representation', an ideal of 'practice of civility', Dyson (1980), *The State Tradition*, at 40; and as 'new order which lacked precision', Shennan (1974), *Origins of Modern European State*, at 99.

[70] Kern (1985), *Kingship and Law*, at 68 (on 'general legal convictions of the time' combined with 'actual weakness' of most monarchies); Shennan (1974), *Origins of Modern European State*, at 76 ('restrictive traditions of the monarchy'); and see Keohane (1980), *Philosophy and State in France*, at 3 (differences between 'absolutist' French state and 'traditional' monarchy not so great as sometimes supposed); Major (1971), 'French Renaissance Monarchy', at 44 ('despotic' nature of French crown 'not well grounded in fact').

[71] See Ch. 3, 'Common laws'.

[72] Keohane (1980), *Philosophy and State in France*, at 128 (though 'echoes of that tradition' still found in speeches at meeting of Estates-General in 1614).

[73] Van Caenegem (1995), *Historical Introduction Western Constitutional Law*, at 108 ('no lasting model'). Despots, of course, are still with us, but they would represent a corruption of the notion of an absolute monarch, as opposed to an exemplification of it.

'mixed' constitution.[74] In the anglo-american world the vocabulary is often that of an 'ancient' or a 'balanced constitution' but this is a refinement of language and not content. The ancient or balanced constitution was unquestionably a mixed one.[75] The idea probably originated with Aristotle who in his *Politics* distinguished between democracy, aristocracy, oligarchy, and monarchy and, almost in passing, acknowledged that they could be combined or mixed.[76] The debate over whether and how to mix them has continued ever since. In the heady times of the sixteenth century Althusius appears as the next most significant defender of the idea. Althusius's monarch was one limited by law and bound to cooperation with others, so no successful monarchy was lacking in democratic and aristocratic elements.[77] Canonical lawyers supported the idea as God-given, citing the Old Testament and Israel.[78] Bodin had to fight against this widespread, cosmopolitan idea and was eventually unsuccessful, though he succeeded at least in launching an idea of political sovereignty that became almost equally cosmopolitan in its diffusion, though more narrowly directed than that of the mixed constitution.

Structures

The idea of checks and balances has thus been with us for a very long time, while the idea of a mixed constitution was given new life with the emergence of the strong governments of contemporary states, suggesting some form of restraint on the *type* of power being exercised within whatever mixture was functional. Another Frenchman, Montesquieu, is usually seen as the source of this doctrine of limiting types of power through their separation, though he relied extensively on Locke and on English practice.[79] The doctrine of the separation of powers is now widely known in the world as a constitutional doctrine, but it should be recalled that it emerged most clearly in the writings of Montesquieu and that Montesquieu was committed to notions of legal diversity and protection of religious minorities, that he was struggling against the idea of a single, all-encompassing authority within a unitary state. He had a 'dread of uniformity'

---

[74] See Ch. 3, 'Constitutionalism'.

[75] Jennings (1959), *Law and Constitution*, at 18 (constitution after Act of Settlement in 1701 could be described as 'mixed' or 'balanced').

[76] Aristotle (2008b), *Politics*, Bk. IV, Ch. vii, s. 4 (Spartan constitution combining goodness and numbers and hence a mixture of democratic and aristocratic).

[77] Gierke (1939), *Development of Political Theory*, at 47 (so unmixed constitution 'scarcely to be found in history').

[78] Tierney (1982), *Religion, law and constitutional thought*, at 88 (and hence USA and England seeing themselves as 'new Israel').

[79] Montesquieu (1989), *Spirit of Laws*, Part II, Bk. 11, Ch. 6 ('Of the Constitution of England'); and for his use of the English model, Tomaselli (2006), 'The spirit of nations', at 18 ('the government of England is wiser'), 74 (guest of Bolingbroke in England in 1729, 1731); and for his debt even to antiquity, Keohane (1980), *Philosophy and State in France*, at 393 ('though he is regarded largely as original'). For the shift to a notion of a *qualitative* division of powers, Vincent (1987), *Theories of the State*, at 99 (separate 'functions' of government); Gierke (1957), *Natural Law*, at 157 (distinctions by virtue of 'essential character', a character sought subsequently in thousands of judicial decisions distinguishing judicial and executive functions in matters of administrative law); Wood (2006), 'The American Revolution', at 624 (founders of USA undertook to 'collapse' balanced or mixed constitution into separation of powers).

and his work has been seen as a 'celebration of the diversity between and complexity within legal systems'.[80] Enunciation of the doctrine of separation of powers must be placed within this cosmopolitan doctrinal context. Diversity does not thrive under a single, sovereign authority; support of diversity requires diffusion and collaboration of authorities. The separation of powers is itself a cosmopolitan concept, since protection of particularity can always be sought from another power, or in the play amongst powers. Appreciation of Montesquieu in the USA was also a cosmopolitan phenomenon. He was referred to by the Continental Congress as 'the immortal Montesquieu' for crystallizing such an essential element in the operation of popular, delegated sovereignty.[81] Madison referred to him as an 'oracle who is always consulted and cited on this subject'.[82] As a cosmopolitan idea, then, the separation of powers has been implemented in different constitutions in different ways. No state follows exactly the practice of any other state, though there are patterns. In Africa there would be degrees of separation, some jurisdictions having 'more of it', some having 'less of it'.[83] Nor is separation anywhere complete. In the USA impeachment of executive authority is in legislative hands, legislation is reviewed by judges, and there is a Presidential veto over Congress. Life is always more complicated than apparently simple principles. Each jurisdiction varies in its pursuit of a cosmopolitan ideal, often subject to influence but invariably finding a unique path.

In the contemporary state a separate, distinct, and independent judiciary has come to play an important role in limiting the authority of legislative and executive powers and therefore in limiting their treatment of minorities. This did not flow simply from Montesquieu's articulation of a principle of separation of powers. The notion of separation of powers made possible, however, a more explicit recognition and guarantee of a judicial function that had previously been recognized as fundamental.[84] Put differently, the judicial function has been an

---

[80] Tomaselli (2006), 'The spirit of nations', at 30–1 (especially praising guarantees of free exercise of Jews in Christian or Muslim countries); and see notably Montesquieu (1989), *Spirit of Laws*, Part 5, Bk. 25, Ch. 13 ('A most humble Remonstrance to the Inquisitors of Spain and Portugal'), at 491 ('if you do not give up your old prejudices . . . it must be admitted that you are incorrigible, incapable of all enlightenment').

[81] Wood (1969), *Creation of American Republic*, at 152, 548 (for linking of separation of powers with popular sovereignty, to detriment of anti-Federalists), and 449 (for judiciary as primary beneficiary). There is some irony in Montesquieu being thus linked to the Federalist cause, yet over time it has been the judiciary that has had to determine the rights of individual states and the sovereignty of native Americans (see later, this section).

[82] Bederman (2008b), 'Classical Constitution', at 411.

[83] Fombad (2007), 'Challenges to Constitutionalism', at 15 though, at 13, all constitutions of southern African countries providing for it.

[84] In the common law world the high court judges enjoyed independence from the late seventeenth century, notably following the Bill of Rights of 1688 and the Act of Settlement of 1701. For Lieberman, a 'far more generalized version of judicial independence and institutional autonomy' became common once Montesquieu's theory gained currency, this in England and elsewhere: Lieberman (2006), 'The mixed constitution and the common law', at 335. An initial two-fold distinction between legislative and executive functions would have become apparent by the seventeenth century, though executive functions were still seen as including judicial ones: Vincent (1987), *Theories of the State*, at 101 (even Montesquieu not committed to three-fold distinction, 'hovers' between two- and three-fold classification).

essential element of western common laws, and is therefore an essential element in the contemporary cosmopolitan state. In other laws it has not enjoyed the same status. The history of the function of judging in the civil and common laws has been described as the history of a transfer from a monotheistic God to officials.[85] It has thus been pan-jurisdictional in its origins. Bribes to judges, the principle of 'reciprocity' of treatment, were eliminated only once the model of the perfect justice of this particular God had been accepted.[86] The elimination of bribes is found elsewhere, yet Christianity would have been unique in attempting to capture the transcendent character of God's justice and in attempting to implement it on earth in the judicial process and in the contemporary state.[87] The device for so doing was initially the ordeal, as indicative of God's will. Today in German the word for judgment remains 'Urteil', from the original germanic 'ordal'. The ordeal gave way, in the civil and common laws, to the oath of judicial office and, in the common law, to the sworn jury, but all are evidence of a function or mission profoundly impressed by a particular religious belief. It was ripe to become a 'power' or at least an 'authority' and to play a role in ensuring ongoing respect for limitations of authority and respect for diverse constituents. The origins of this power are cosmopolitan, as is its function. There are of course differences across traditions in its implementation,[88] now most notably with respect to the extent of judicial review of legislation. The US model of judicial review has had great influence in the world and some four-fifths of all states now have adopted some form of it.[89] This is a subject that will have to be returned to, but for the moment it must be pointed out that heightened standards of judicial review have been closely linked to the protection of 'discrete and insular minorities' in the US model.[90] Given that all states are cosmopolitan in terms

---

[85] Jacob (1995), 'Le jugement de Dieu', at 90.

[86] Noonan (1993), 'God Does Not Take Bribes' at 3ff., citing notably Isaiah 1:12–13 ('No more shall you trample my courts. The offer of your gifts is useless').

[87] Jacob (1995), 'Le jugement de Dieu', at 89 (judgment of God distinct in western Christianity) and 95 (judicial history of western Europe therefore 'entirely original', with its 'judicial miracle' allowing the presence of God in the judicial decision-making process). For Charlemagne's insistence on biblical authority for royal justice, Munz (1960), *Origin of Carolingian Empire*, at 2 (reliance on Matthew 7:2, 'You will be judged as you have judged').

[88] For historical French hesitation in recognizing a judicial power, linked to abuses under the ancien régime, Brissaud (1915), *History of French Public Law*, at 547 (Constitution of Year VIII making judiciary a dependency of executive). The present French constitution treats the judiciary as an 'authority' but there are major guarantees of independence, though less complete than in the common law world. For the older French tradition of judicial collegiality of decision and secrecy in deliberations, yielding a pre-revolutionary practice of an absence of written reasons for decisions of high courts, Jacob (1996), *Le juge et le jugement*, at 161.

[89] Ginsburg (2008), 'Global Spread of Judicial Review', at 81; Horowitz (2009), '*The Federalist* Abroad', at 515 (though many with undemocratic regimes, and with a strong trend to distinct constitutional courts as opposed to courts of general jurisdiction); yet for what would be a current decline in influence, a consequence of ageing, Law and Versteeg (2012), 'Declining Influence of United States Constitution', notably at 781–4 (similarity to US model reached apex in 1980s, notable evolution away from US model in Latin America). For current debates on judicial review and democracy as closure, see Ch. 11, 'Constitutional Structures and Sources of Law'.

[90] *United States* v. *Carolene Products Co*, 304 US 144 (1938) at 152–3, in footnote four; as to which see Cover (1982), 'Origins of Judicial Activism', notably at 1294 ('[m]inorities . . . became a special object of

of their population, the case has been irresistible that at least national judicial review is necessary for the protection of minorities.[91]

A final constitutional structure tailored for diversity is that of a federation. Like the separation of powers, federalism is a constitutional structure of cosmopolitan origins and cosmopolitan function. Though now largely accepted as a constitutional structure amongst others, its cosmopolitan character is evident when considered against prevailing views of sovereignty in the seventeenth and eighteenth centuries, which would have rigorously precluded any division of sovereignty. There could be leagues of states, but a state within a state was unacceptable, and any 'mixed' state could at best be considered 'irregular'.[92] Pufendorf viewed the empire as a monstrosity.[93] Gierke saw acceptance of the separation of powers, however, as clearing a path for the 'revival and advancement' of the notion of a federal state, and the moribund Holy Roman Empire then began to be viewed in such terms.[94] There were, moreover, both theoretical and institutionalist streams of thought that could be tapped into. Althusius's defence of a mixed constitution contained a 'federalistic idea'[95] and Leibniz challenged even the existence of unitary states in Europe, noting that a good part of France consisted of 'les pays des Etats'.[96] The Dutch United Provinces had been created by the Treaty of Utrecht of 1579 as an 'indissoluble union' and as a 'federal body', so possessing more coherence than the Swiss 'old confederation' dating from the thirteenth century.[97] There were also 'traces of federalism' within the Catholic church, given two levels of government (pope and bishop).[98]

protection only with footnote four') and 1298 (for international recognition that the twentieth-century 'nation-state was characteristically built upon the consolidation of a particular racial or ethnic group's political hegemony over a territory that included a mixed population').

[91] And for the international, Follesdahl (2007), 'Why International Human Rights'.

[92] Dufour (1991), 'Pufendorf', at 580 (Pufendorf's view of irregularity); and for impossibility of state within a state, Gierke (1939), *Development of Political Theory*, at 263 (dichotomy of 'single articulated state' or league, confederations of Switzerland, the United Netherlands classified as 'mere Leagues').

[93] Pufendorf (2007), *Present State of Germany*, at 176 ('like some mis-shapen Monster'—'monstre simile'); and see Gierke (1951), *Political Theories of Middle Age*, at 268 (standing between binary options of a 'System of States' and a unitary state); Dufour (1991), 'Pufendorf', at 583 (something 'between the two').

[94] Gierke (1939), *Development of Political Theory*, at 268–9 (citing Nettelbladt's general theory of Federal State, first edn, 1762).

[95] Gierke (1939), *Development of Political Theory*, at 269 (as part of 'gradual and historically continuous outgrowth' of the federal state); Tierney (1982), *Religion, law and constitutional thought*, at 74–5 (local units prior to sovereign state 'as cause precedes effect', distinguishing 'partial' from 'complete' confederations); Spellman (1998), *European Political Thought*, at 76 (society as series of 'ascending communities') and 78 (taking medieval society in general, empire and Dutch Republic as models); Forsyth (1981), *Unions of States*, at 78 (Althusius's constitutionalism 'genuine federal element').

[96] Tomaselli (2006), 'The spirit of nations', at 24 ('nor was it the case that they were in constant political turmoil as a result').

[97] Shennan (1974), *Origins of Modern European State*, at 81 (with federation having 'ultimate sovereignty' in matters of war, peace and taxation affecting entire union) and 84 (Dutch 'adding significantly to the complexity' of concept of sovereignty); and for contrast between Netherlands and Switzerland, Forsyth (1981), *Unions of States*, Ch. 2 (the 'main historical examples').

[98] Tierney (1982), *Religion, law and constitutional thought*, at 65 (citing Godfrey of Fontaines in 1280s that power of bishop 'not derived from the higher').

The institutional model of federation that has been most significant in the world, however, has been that of the USA, and the framers of the US Constitution were knowledgeable of much of the federalist debate that preceded them. They relied on it extensively, though there is debate on the extent of their knowledge and its accuracy.[99] As with the separation of powers, the federalism debate was successfully linked by Federalists to the idea of 'the people', whose protection required division of authority not only functionally but geographically. Federalism thus emerged as a middle ground between the continental unitary state and the decentralization of the anti-Federalists.[100] It has been so perceived elsewhere and valued as such.

There are now some twenty-five federal states in the world, some of them very large (the USA, India, Brazil, Russia, Nigeria) some less so (Belgium, Switzerland).[101] There are also cases of 'devolution' within unitary states, as has recently occurred in the United Kingdom in relation to Wales and Scotland, where the division of authority derives from central legislation as opposed to a constitution. Spain is 'semi-federal', with autonomous regions and even cities. China has its 'special administrative regions', and some fifty-five officially recognized 'nationalities'. The European Union might, or might not, be working towards federalism. The federal structure has thus become part of the legal and political landscape, though Tierney has recently and happily warned that the 'classical and formalistic' distinction between unitary and federal state offers no account of the 'sociological distinctiveness' of the 'plurinational' model, nor of the nuanced constitutional practice that accompanies it.[102] In short, federation implies a cosmopolitan perspective and Donald Horowitz points out that virtually all federal systems were created because strong regional minorities had the leverage to insist on retention of some local or domestic authority, this including 'slaveholding interests' in the USA.[103] Federalism turns out not to be a single model but a remarkably flexible conciliatory instrument, allowing minority

[99] See most recently LaCroix (2010), *Ideological Origins of American Federalism*, passim and notably at 3, 12 (for influence of empire, 'long metropolitan shadow'), 6 (for that of Pufendorf's 'political league', this in spite of his attachment to sovereignty), 20 (New England confederation of 1643, i.e. pre-Pufendorf), 25 (influence of union of crowns of England, Scotland in 1603), 79 (on 'Continental strand . . . funnelled into the North American debates of the 1770s', 'striking' reliance on it); though for US debate not relying on German thought, perhaps because of 'moribund state' of contemporary German empire, Tierney (1982), *Religion, law and constitutional thought*, at 78 (for Madison, German empire a 'nerveless body incapable of regulating its own members'); and for misunderstanding of Dutch model, though vigorous debate over it, Riker (1957), 'Dutch and American Federalism', at 513–4 ('awful example' though vigour of dispute indicating an important argument; experience 'only slightly Dutch and mostly American').

[100] Wood (1969), *Creation of American Republic*, at 499 (for anti-Federalist position that country of such 'climates, production, interests' could never be a republican state), 532ff. ('primal power of the people', constitution, unlike confederation, to be 'scheme of the people'); Wood (2006), 'The American Revolution', at 622 (both state and national legislatures 'equally and simultaneously representative of the people').

[101] Griffiths (2002), *Handbook Federal Countries*.

[102] Tierney (2004), *Constitutional Law and National Pluralism*, at 13; and for US theory concentrated on 'compartmentalization' and 'sovereignty divided', Kammen (1988), *Sovereignty and Liberty*, at 3, though at 18 this seen as natural for 'pluralistic people'.

[103] Horwitz (2009), 'Constitutional Transplants', at 538.

control of a region, quarantining conflict within sub-state boundaries, allowing asymmetric arrangement for regions, and more.[104] It is not simply a question of giving a 'nation' a sub-state territory but of variable ways of thinking diversity, in the context of each existing state. The 'nation-state' is challenged, yet again, by the recognized combination of ethnic diversity and federalism.[105] Federations deal with more than political and geographic differences.

Relations and guarantees

If the sources and structures of constitutionalism are irresistibly cosmopolitan there is also a residual cosmopolitanism in the relations that are the object of constitutional control, and the constitutional guarantees that accompany them. In the thinking of the contemporary state a sovereign legal and political authority would exercise its power over an undifferentiated mass of rights-bearing citizens, with no intermediate agencies or communities having an inherent legal authority of its own.[106] Over the range of states, however, everything is much more complicated. The relations between a state and individual human beings can be very complex and, as will be seen in Chapter 8, there is also an ongoing institutional cosmopolitanism, within and beyond contemporary states.

In the ancient constitutions the notion of individual (or 'subjective') rights had not been articulated. The entire notion of the rights of an individual was one of very slow construction, and arguably did not come to fruition until the nineteenth or twentieth centuries. Its sources too were vast and cosmopolitan.[107] Individual entitlements were protected, however, and notably in private law through the necessity of the crown's respect of custom.[108] The notion of a social contract entered into by an entire 'people' was also important for its emphasis on individuals. Ongoing individual rights thus became a necessary consequence of the role of individuals in coming together to found a state. They could be articulated in a founding document. Yet if 'the people' as justification for the state is a questionable assumption, the notion of individual rights has become an unquestionably 'operative' concept of contemporary constitutionalism, at least in many places. They are a limit on governmental authority, of constitutional import. The question is as to

---

[104] Horwitz (2007), 'Many Uses of Federalism', at 958–62 (also stimulus for 'interethnic alignments and coalitions'); and for multiple variations of federalism, consociationism in complex societies, Choudhry (2008), *Constitutional Design.*

[105] Fessha (2010), *Ethnic Diversity*, notably Ch. 3 ('Federalism as Institutional Design to Recognize and Accommodate Ethnic Diversity').

[106] Tully (1995), *Strange Multiplicity*, at 83 ('culturally indifferent members of one society', as 'fiction of the early modern theorists'); Hont (1995), 'Permanent Crisis of Divided Mankind', at 192 ('the logic underlying the case for undivided sovereignty (i.e., an undivided and all-inclusive community)'); Gierke (1951), *Political Theories of Middle Age*, at 87 ('at the cost of all intermediate groups', 'the Sovereignty of the State and the Sovereignty of the Individual' as two central axioms).

[107] For a largely unsympathetic history of the development, Villey (1983), *Droit et droits de l'homme*; cf. Tierney (1988), 'Villey, Ockham'; Tierney (1997), *Idea of Natural Rights* (identifying notions of subjective right in twelfth-century commentaries on Gratian); and for further references Glenn (2010b), *Legal Traditions*, at 149–50.

[108] See Ch. 3, 'Constitutionalism'; see also this chapter, 'Sources'.

their undifferentiated character. This is evident both with respect to the right to religious liberty and with respect to the rights of non-state peoples.

The origins of the contemporary state system are often seen in the Treaty of Westphalia of 1648 and its formulation of the principle of *cuius regio, eius religio*: the prince who controls a territory is entitled to dictate its religion, though there were qualifications.[109] Given religious diversity, even within states, this proved to be an impossible principle. The idea of a nation then provided some glue for the contemporary state but the nation too was unable to overcome profound differences in religious belief. In the emerging rights consciousness of European states, religious diversity had to be recognized at least at the level of the individual human being, and inevitably in the form of a right to religious liberty. A right to religious liberty is by now found in the 'overwhelming majority of the world's constitutions, including virtually every European constitution and the constitution of every independent country in the Western Hemisphere'.[110] In contrast to the Westphalian regime, this is a remarkably cosmopolitan principle, which explains why there is so much resistance to its actual implementation, particularly in jurisdictions described as 'theocratic' (this not in itself excluding an articulated right to religious liberty). Some one-third of the jurisdictions of the world have implemented high levels of restriction and 70 per cent of the world's population lives in such jurisdictions.[111] Some of these restrictions, however, are simply a reflection of a general lack of freedom in certain countries, despotic more than theocratic. In the European jurisdictions that have given rise to the purported closure of the nation-state, religious cosmopolitanism is now a matter of positive law.[112] Montesquieu, it has been noted, was a powerful voice in its favour.[113] Some common laws may even place it beyond constitutional or legislative infringement.[114]

If all citizens enjoy the same right to religious liberty it is possible to maintain an idea of equality amongst citizens, or an undifferentiated notion of rights.

---

[109] See Ch. 5, 'Religion'.

[110] Martinez-Torrón and Durham (2010b), 'Religion and Secular State', at 6; Law and Versteeg (2012), 'Declining Influence of US Constitution' at 773 (97 per cent of constitutions in 2006); and for a 'common law freedom of religion', supported by international law, Boreham (2008), 'International Law as an Influence', at 271. For the history of religious toleration (though the word toleration indicates 'grudging acceptance of unpleasant necessity') dating to Tertullian in third century, with variations in subsequent persecution of 'heretics', Wallace, (2009–10), 'Justifying Religious Freedom', at 499 (for 'toleration'), 502 (for Tertullian and subsequent persecution), 527 (eventual Gelasian 'dualism' of fifth century), 531 (ongoing persecution); Ahdar and Leigh (2005), *Religious Freedom in Liberal State*, at 12–15, though at 17 citing Murray averring 'intolerance whenever possible . . . tolerance whenever necessary'. For isolated instances of religious liberty from the late sixteenth century, MacCulloch (2009), *Christianity*, at 640 (Diet of Transylvania in 1569, 'extraordinarily by the standards of the time', 1647 in Rhode Island of Roger Williams, contrasting Massachusetts). On subsequent church–state relations, see Ch. 8, 'Churches and Religions', and Ch. 13, 'States and Religious Authority'; and for the change from 'toleration' to 'religious liberty' in late-eighteenth-century USA, Beneke (2006), *Beyond Toleration*.

[111] Martinez-Torrón and Durham (2010b), 'Religion and Secular State', at 5, citing Pew Forum on Religion and Public Life (2009), 'Global Restrictions on Religion'.

[112] See generally Evans (2001), *Freedom of Religion under European Convention*, notably at 23–31 (on instrumental, historical, religious, and personal autonomy justifications for religious liberty).

[113] See this chapter, '*Structures*'.

[114] Jennings (1959), *Law and Constitution*, at 148 (Dicey and Laski pointing out things an otherwise sovereign parliament cannot do, notably disenfranchising Roman Catholics).

It is much more difficult to maintain such a position, however, with respect to state recognition of non-state peoples or, to put it from a state perspective, state citizens who have successfully resisted application of state law to themselves. This is a very widespread phenomenon in the world, much more frequent outside Europe than within it, but the phenomenon has been well-known in European legal history and still manifests itself today, notably with respect to the Saami people of northern Europe.[115] Beyond Europe the phenomenon is most evident with respect to the so-called personal law or 'statut personnel' of religious minorities within many states, to which it will be necessary to return.[116] It is also found in the increasing number of jurisdictions that have moved through judicial decision or constitutional change towards formal recognition of the collective rights or 'traditional law' of indigenous or chthonic peoples.[117] In the early nineteenth century the United States Supreme Court even used the language of sovereignty to describe the position of native tribes in the USA, and the notion of 'tribal sovereignty' remains operative in that country today, though some maintain in diminished form.[118] A notion of tribal sovereignty and tribal law, functioning alongside that of civil authority within a civil jurisdiction, is of course entirely incompatible with seventeenth-century notions of indivisible sovereignty. The existence within contemporary states of groups that are entitled to application of their own unwritten or religious law is a contemporary replication of the medieval respect owed by crowns to unwritten custom, as a matter of common law. It is a reaffirmation of an 'ancient constitution' respectful of multiple sources of authority and it is not surprising that contemporary doctrinal writing has referred to the existence of 'hidden' constitutions of modern states.[119] A link has been drawn between the 'common law constitution' and cosmopolitanism.[120] Given the diversity of contemporary states it is surprising that such a situation is not more widespread, but many states have been successful in centring legal authority around themselves in some measure and it is only such long-standing *iura propria* that have come to widespread recognition. To the extent that such forms of legal recognition go beyond the notion of individual rights, they may also be seen as instances of institutional cosmopolitanism.

[115] Svensson (1999), *On Customary Law and Saami Rights*.

[116] See Ch. 8, 'Churches and Religions'.

[117] See notably for Latin America, Assies, van der Haar, and Hoekema (2000), *Challenge of Diversity*, at 3 (listing twelve South American countries), 197ff. (for Andean countries); and for further countries and references, Glenn (2010b), *Legal Traditions*, at 90.

[118] The early cases were those of *Johnson* v. *McIntosh*, 21 US (8 Wheat.) 240 (1823) and *Worcester* v. *Georgia*, 31 US (6 Pet.) 350 (1832), preserving indigenous entitlement though subject to right given by 'discovery'; and for the current state of the doctrine in the USA, see Ch. 12, 'Reconciliation'.

[119] Tully (1995), *Strange Multiplicity*, at 100 (and casuistry of decision making in application, recalling diversity of 'ancient constitutions' of pre-modern Europe, which 'did not disappear' with the rise of modern constitutionalism), and 66 (for ancient constitution as 'assemblage of laws, customs and institutions', contrasted with 'monist' view of post-Westphalian state theory).

[120] Walters (2004), 'Common Law Constitution and Legal Cosmopolitanism', in Dyzenhaus (2004), *Unity of Public Law*, notably at 444 (*ius gentium* as part of common law, not supportive of domestic–international dualism), 450 ('universal' law of reason capable of addressing concerns of 'non-state beings').

8

Institutional Cosmopolitanism

With various levels of territorial and national closure, European states became more autonomous than they had been in the middle ages. They no longer had to contend with a Holy Roman Empire; their hierarchies had achieved some priority over those of the European churches. The level of autonomy that they enjoyed, however, did not absolve them of ongoing institutional relations, notably those with the churches and with other (emerging) contemporary states. There were also institutional questions lurking within their own empires.

CHURCHES AND RELIGIONS

Notions of royal absolutism, together with Lutheran belief in the immunity of the church from lay influence, had contributed to a decline in active collaboration between the church and the emerging contemporary state.[1] These developments from the seventeenth century exacerbated underlying tendencies of Christianity, the 'religion for leaving religion'.[2] Church and state were beginning to be seen as occupying distinct spheres of activity, the state that of the *res publica*, the church that of the spirit. Since, however, the church had been a 'keystone in the system of political power throughout Europe' this could not be a sharp demarcation and there were inevitably major differences in appreciation from state to state.[3] The state, even though secure in its domain, had necessary ongoing relations with a church that was transnational in character.[4] Given the decline of the *cuius regio, eius religio* principle, it even had to establish and maintain relations with more than one transnational church. The major church religions may be conceptualized as private associations within a particular state but they are clearly more than that, and the seat of the Roman Catholic church is itself a state. Each state has therefore had to acknowledge not only individual guarantees of religious liberty, as discussed in the last chapter,[5] but also to define its institutional relations with an increasingly wide range of religious beliefs (that might or might not assume

---

[1] See Ch. 4, '*Organizational success*'; and Ch. 5, 'Religion'.

[2] See Ch. 2, '*The church within*' and '*The church without*'.

[3] Gilby (1953), *Philosophy and Theology of the State*, at 56; and for 'old and new building elements long lying beside one another', Böckenförde (1991), *Recht, Staat, Freiheit*, at 107.

[4] This was acknowledged even by the high theorists of state sovereignty. For Hobbes, Malcolm (1991), 'Hobbes and Spinoza', at 543 ('allowed for a great deal of religious toleration'); and for Pufendorf, Miller (2008), 'Dawn of Age of Toleration', at 265 ('circumstances where a ruler may safely tolerate dissenters').

[5] See Ch. 7, '*Relations and guarantees*'.

institutional form). The result has been one of great diversity. No state is the same as any other.

Javier Martinez-Torrón and Cole Durham have recently documented, at a world-wide level, the extent of this institutional diversity in church–state relations.[6] The diversity exists not only across states but within them, since abstract constitutional provisions are the object of diverse interpretations across time, space, and even judicial districts within a state.[7] Martinez-Torrón and Durham establish a wide continuum of relations, from those of theocratic states (Iran) to those that would abolish religion entirely on the state territory, if that were possible (North Korea).[8] Religious freedom is excluded or severely limited at either end of the continuum but blossoms in the middle ground. Between these ideas (only one religion or no religion whatsoever) there is a wide range of options, characterized by a more or less neutral state and with attendant degrees of religious freedom.

The most theocratic present regime would appear to be that of Iran, in which an official religion of the state is established and religious leaders play a major role in state direction. The state is not protected from religious authority. Even Iran, however, provides constitutional protection for 'protected' religious minorities, so the discussion focuses on abuse or violation, and not on principle.[9] The coexistence of a hierarchical state with a non-hierarchical religion thus implies a non-negligible level of cosmopolitanism (though not a high one), and that amongst both state and religious authorities there is awareness of the objectives and restraints of each. A step removed from theocracy would be captured in the notion of 'theocratic constitutionalism' or, if you prefer, 'constitutional theocracy', in which political authority is exercised by lay political officers but there is an official religion of the state and its norms have considerable, ongoing, influence on state law. Many jurisdictions fall within this category, often with Islam as the (or a) principal source of law (Saudi Arabia, Egypt, Iraq, Syria).[10] There is need for constant consideration of both state and religious norms. A still more developed form of institutional cosmopolitanism is found in states where multiple 'personal laws' or 'statuts personnels' are recognized for those belonging to different religions or groups, usually in family law matters and important not only for the effort towards institutional equilibrium but also, as has been seen, as

---

[6] Martinez-Torrón and Durham (2010b), 'Religion and Secular State', stating themselves at 55–6 that even the notion of a 'secular' state yields 'practice that tends to be the result of historical circumstances that are different in different countries'. See also, for the notion of a 'spectrum' of relations, from 'establishment' to 'active secularism', Evans (2001), *Freedom of Religion under European Convention*, at 19; and for relations from 'fruitful' ('fécondes') to 'hostile', with 'peaceful coexistence' between the two, Caparros (2000), 'Le droit religieux', at 4, with caution at 64 that relations are in 'constant movement'.

[7] Martinez-Torrón and Durham (2010b), 'Religion and Secular State', at 14 (difficulty of assessing 'actual' nature of religion–state relations on basis of 'constitutional provisions alone').

[8] Martinez-Torrón and Durham (2010b), 'Religion and Secular State', at 8–9; and for the spectrum within Europe, Evans (2001), *Freedom of Religion under European Convention*, at 19.

[9] US Department of State (2010), *International Religious Freedom* ('severely restricted religious liberty').

[10] For the debate on the notion of an Islamic state or democracy, see Ch. 13, '*State and religious legal sources*'.

a guarantee of individual religious liberty. Such distinct personal laws are found in a strikingly large number of countries, including Afghanistan, Bahrain, Bangladesh, Brunei, Egypt, Ethiopia, France (in its overseas territories), Gambia, Ghana, Greece (for Muslims of western Thrace), India, Indonesia, Iran, Iraq, Israel, Jordan, Kenya, Kuwait, Lebanon, Malaysia, Morocco, Nigeria, Pakistan, The Philippines, Qatar, Saudi Arabia (for Shi'ite civil matters), Singapore, South Africa, Sri Lanka, Sudan, Syria, Tanzania, and others.[11] The yielding of state law in such cases has been described as flowing from social structures being 'inextricably entwined' with religion.[12] The state tradition may have been sufficiently persuasive here, however, for its courts to replace those of religious authority, as in India, though this may also not be the case, as in Israel.[13]

States that cannot truly be considered theocratic may still prefer an established church, as in the UK, Greece, and Norway. This may still allow a considerable range of religious liberty and choice, though state law is generally applicable. Italy's constitution provides that the 'State and the Catholic Church are, each within its own order, independent and sovereign'.[14] There are also regimes of officially recognized religions (in the plural), in which the state remains neutral towards particular religions but recognizes and even supports a number of them, this also not excluding religious liberty. This is the case for a large number of European states, such as Germany, Italy, Luxemburg, Spain, Belgium, and Austria.[15] The most common model in the world, for Martinez-Torrón and Durham, would be one of 'cooperation' between religion and a neutral state, involving church freedom from state interference but positive rights to state action, including even state funding or taxation benefits for particular activities.[16]

[11] Aoun (2009), *Les statuts personnels*, notably at 25, 57 (for French overseas territories), 163 (Lebanon) and 279 (Muslims of Greece, derived from Ottoman empire); Mahmood (1995), *Statutes of Personal Law*; Amin (1985), *Middle East Legal Systems*. The precise number is difficult if not impossible to determine, given increasing constitutional protection of unwritten laws of aboriginal peoples, and the extent of protection accorded by constitutional guarantees of religious liberty. For the former, see Ch. 12, 'Reconciliation'; and the latter, see Ch. 13, '*Religious liberty*'.

[12] Jacobsohn (2003), *The Wheel of Law*, at 8 (hence the 'elusive goal of Indian secularism'), 50 (religion 'deeply etched') and 92 ('consequent need to provide space for cultural and religious diversity').

[13] See, for the debate in Israel, Hofri-Winogradow (2010), 'A Plurality of Discontent', notably at 85 (criticising Israeli Jewish tribunals as conservative and 'actively seek[ing] to draw litigants' from state courts).

[14] Art. 7; and see Forey (2007), *État et institutions religieuses*, at 28, suggesting compromise inspired by the writings of Santo Romano, coexistence of two legal orders 'called to cooperate in the service of their subjects', a distinct echo of the cooperating 'two swords', discussed in Ch. 2, '*The church without*'. Art. 8 then provides that '[a]ll religious denominations are equally free before the law'.

[15] Forey (2007), *État et institutions religieuses*, at 76 (also for particular regime of Concordat for Alsace in France); Rouland (2000), 'Le droit français devient-il multiculturel?', at 531 (notion of 'demi-laïcité' or quasi-secularism); Malaurie (2005), 'L'État et la religion', at 575 (recognition on basis of equality of religions).

[16] Martinez-Torrón and Durham (2010b), 'Religion and Secular State', at 12; and for a similar conclusion for Europe, Doe (2011), *Law and Religion*, at 35 ('the most prevalent model in Europe is the so-called hybrid or cooperation model', with matters of 'common concern' addressed 'usually in the form of agreements'), and see at 29 (for 'multitude of common tasks which link State and religious activity').

All of the states that officially acknowledge a religion or religions are obviously cosmopolitan in character in relation to religion, since even the theocratic state must define its relations with the exclusive religion. In other cases of state acknowledgement there are multiple relations. The religiously cosmopolitan character of the state would decline, however, the more one moved towards the abolitionist end of the continuum. If there were a truly abolitionist state it could not properly be designated as religiously cosmopolitan. There may, however, be no such state in the present world, since even North Korea has guaranteed religious freedom in its constitutions and would officially sponsor some religious activity as proof of its existence. The most significant form of closure that could threaten religious cosmopolitanism is therefore derived from state regimes often qualified as those of 'separation' or 'secularity'. These would be non-cosmopolitan in their efforts to avoid 'entanglement' though they would be non-threatening towards ongoing religious forms of activity. Perhaps the most visible forms of 'separation' and 'secularity' in the world today are those of the United States of America and France. In both cases, however, entanglement is difficult to avoid; separation becomes an objective rather than a reality. Abstract constitutional norms cannot bring about consistent interpretation, even within a single institution.

US efforts towards separation of church and state are older than those of France. The First Amendment of the US Constitution was adopted in 1791, only 143 years after the adoption of the radically contrary principle of *cuius regio, eius religio* by the Treaty of Westphalia of 1648. It did not use the language of separation but provided in deceptively simple language that 'Congress shall make no law respecting an establishment of religion'. The Amendment would have represented a break with earlier American church–state relations, more 'Pufendorfian' in character, with colonial civil magistrates enforcing ecclesiastical rules.[17] It was clearly influenced by enlightenment thinking in general and by Locke in particular, Locke finding it necessary 'to distinguish exactly the Business of Civil Government from that of Religion'.[18] More generally it would fall within the broad Christian, and particularly Protestant, insistence on distinguishing heavenly from earthly cities.[19] Paul had used the metaphor of a wall of separation, and this was taken up by Jefferson in a letter of 1802, making it the 'single most influential metaphor in American constitutional law'.[20] It appears also to

---

[17] Miller (2008), 'Dawn of Age of Toleration', at 257.

[18] Locke (1983), *Letter Concerning Toleration*, at 26 ('and to settle the just bounds that lie between the one and the other'); and see Ward (2008), 'Locke on Toleration and Inclusion', notably at 531 (Locke favouring a 'considerable' degree of separation, though 'potentially salutary counterweight to the overweening claims of political sovereignty').

[19] See Ch. 2, '*The church within*'.

[20] Feldman (2005), *Divided by God*, at 23 (on Jefferson's 'personal religious scepticism ... faith in unfettered reason'). For Paul, Ephesians 2:14 (Jesus breaking down the 'wall of partition'). For further predecessors to Jefferson (Luther, Calvin, Hooker, Williams, Burgh), Dreisbach (2002), *Thomas Jefferson and Wall of Separation*, at 72–81; and see Hamburger (2002), *Separation of Church and State*, at 1 (on Jefferson's words even displacing the Constitution in the 'minds of many').

have been influenced by Jewish notions drawn from the Hebrew Bible, favourable generally to republicanism and toleration.[21]

More than two centuries of litigation on the precise significance of these words of the First Amendment have followed, an indication of the importance of the text in a state whose population remains profoundly religious in spite of the non-establishment clause. Historically there has been debate over whether the Constitution was intended to be 'Godless', or simply one that prevented Federal preference for one religion over another. Separation would thus be a broader and more radical concept (one of absence of contact) than that of simple non-establishment.[22] Justice Black introduced Jefferson's 'wall' into the case law of the US Supreme Court in 1947;[23] only twenty-four years later Justice Burger concluded that any line of separation, 'far from being a "wall", is a blurred, indistinct and variable barrier depending on all the circumstances of a particular relationship'.[24] Accommodation has thus become an ongoing necessity with many religions. In some circumstances state aid may be permissible for religious institutions; in others it may not be.[25] The Ten Commandments may be displayed by state authority on grounds outside state buildings, but not inside.[26] It has been observed elsewhere that the notion of separation of church and state is 'naturally not false . . . only a little too simple—undercomplex one would say today'.[27]

---

[21] Nelson (2010), *The Hebrew Republic*, at 2, 3 (for God's 'constitutional preferences', monarchy as idolatry, seventeenth century as 'Biblical century'), 19 (Grotius's advocacy of 'Hebrew republic'), 21 (Selden's support, his influence on Hobbes's call for 'Christian Commonwealth'), 115 (Selden's view that Jewish Noachid laws demonstrate God's embrace of broad toleration, allowing non-Jews to reside amongst the Israelites without observing full array of commandments).

[22] Hamburger (2002), *Separation of Church and State*, at 2 ('more dramatic . . . segregation, or absence of contact'), 303 (for a narrow Protestant concept of separation as instrument against Catholicism, growing into liberal version attempting to limit all religions equally); Feldman (2005), *Divided by God*, at 21 ('that history is under dispute today as never before', citing Kramnick and Moore (1997), *The Godless Constitution*); Witte (2006), 'Facts and Fictions About Separation', at 28–30 (on whether church intended to be protected from the state or vice versa).

[23] *Everson v. Board of Education*, 330 US 1 (1947) at 16 (applying establishment clause to state though allowing a state subsidy to religious schools).

[24] *Lemon v. Kurtzman* 403 US 602 (1971) at 614; and for the view that 'separation' not the objective of religious dissenters whose demands 'shaped' the First Amendment, Hamburger (2002), *Separation of Church and State*, at 9 (refusing to conform to religions then established by law and whose ministers received civic salaries, but not sharing 'anticlerical' conception), 10, 15, 192 (notion of separation becoming known only in mid-nineteenth century, inspired in part by anti-Catholicism and 'secularists' seeking to obtain a separation 'not fully assured' by the Constitution); cf. Greenawalt (2009), *Religion and the Constitution*, at 43–4 (Hamburger overstating distinction between disestablishment and separation though differences exist and disestablishment a 'fuzzy, general' concept).

[25] Contrast *Walz v. Tax Commission*, 397 US 664 (1970), 669 (tax exemptions for religious edifices acceptable, that 'constitutional neutrality in this area cannot be an absolutely straight line . . . there is room for play in the joints productive of benevolent neutrality') with *Lemon v. Kurtzman*, 403 US 602 (1971) (subsidy not acceptable for salaries of teachers in religious schools teaching secular subjects).

[26] For outside acceptability *Van Orden v. Perry*, 545 US 677 (2005); for inside prohibition *McCreary County v. ACLU Kentucky*, 545 US 844 (2005).

[27] Hofmann (1999), 'Von Der Staatssoziologie', at 1073.

Others are more categorical, maintaining that 'it defies common sense to claim that we have a full-scale separation of religion from government'.[28]

In France the notion of 'une foi, une loi, un roi' was more resistant to revolutionary reform. Protestants were granted citizenship during the French revolution and Jews were emancipated in the early nineteenth century,[29] but the Catholic church retained a uniquely privileged position until the Law of 9 December 2005, which spoke explicitly of the 'separation' of church and state in its title.[30] Since then the notion of 'laïcité' has achieved constitutional status, in the constitutions of the Fourth (1946) and Fifth (1958) Republics, both of which spoke of France as a secular republic ('république laïque'). In spite of the language of the Law of 1905, however, which prohibits state aid to religion ('ne subventionne aucun culte'), French law is remarkable for the level of state aid to religious buildings and even to religious education, though it cannot bind itself to provide such aid on a permanent basis.[31] There is currently debate on the level of state funding for the building of mosques, some maintaining that French state funding is preferable to that of a 'country of origin'. Relations between religions and the state in France are therefore rightly described as 'complex'.[32]

Neither France nor the USA has therefore achieved a real separation or dissociation of religions and the state. Nor have any of the (few) other states that proclaim their secularity. Russia subsidizes the Russian Orthodox Church.[33] Turkey actually has a Department of Religious Affairs, so relations are institutionalized, though to the detriment of some measure of religious autonomy.[34] Martinez-Torrón and Durham conclude that 'virtually all States analyzed . . . grant some type of financial support to religion . . . either directly or

---

[28] Whitman (2011), 'Separating Church and State', at 234.

[29] Sueur (2007), *Histoire du droit public français*, vol. II, at 488, 499 (Jewish revolutionary emancipation only definitive after Napoleon, in 1818).

[30] The Law identifies itself as a law 'concerning the separation of church and state' ('concernant la séparation des Eglises et de l'État'). See generally Malaurie (2005), 'L'État et la religion' (previous concordat regime ensuring civic payment of salaries of Catholic priests, etc.); Lepointe (1965), *Histoire du droit public français*, 126 (religion seen as 'public service'; separation only obtained with Law of 1905).

[31] Tawil (2009), *Du gallicanisme administratif*, at 102 (on state ownership of churches), 105 (non-permanence, use of fine distinctions, e.g. between 'petit' seminaire et 'grand' seminaire), 145 (interpretation of non-financing rule by Conseil d'État has favoured public financing, benefiting Catholics in particular but also other religions); Zoller (2006), 'Laïcité in the United States', at 579 (hostility towards state aid to religious schools neutralized by Debré law of 1959 allowing private confessional schools to contract with state).

[32] Forey (2007), *État et institutions religieuses*, at 23, 368 (French authorities seeking 'equilibrium', this requiring 'cooperation' with representatives of religions, some forms of institutionalization); and see Bouchard and Taylor (2008), *Building for the Future*, at 66 (France less secular than Quebec, given greater French funding of private religious education, financial support of churches, notably for maintenance of churches and cathedrals, chaplain services).

[33] Martinez-Torrón and Durham (2010b), 'Religion and Secular State', at 13.

[34] Yildiz (2007), 'Minority Rights in Turkey', at 794 (constitution also prohibits discrimination on grounds of religion) and 812 (on 'interesting challenges' of Turkey's 'unique situation as a secular democracy with an Islamic majority').

indirectly.... whatever their constitutional principles'.[35] In funding different religions, at various levels and in different ways, while in the vast majority of cases respecting the internal autonomy of institutional churches,[36] contemporary states act in a remarkably cosmopolitan way, radically different from European practices three to four centuries ago. Their cosmopolitanism will become more evident when their different attitudes towards religious liberty are examined below.[37]

INTERNATIONALITY AND EMPIRE

The institutional cosmopolitanism of the middle ages and the early modern period was that which prevailed, as a type of informal equilibrium, amongst church, monarchy, empire, and what we refer to as custom, conditioned in some measure by the various common laws.[38] The contemporary state purported to effect various types of closure, while its ongoing relations with multiple churches could be conceptualized as those with private associations. They were therefore arguably consistent with notions of closure and autonomy. Relations with the secular outside world were still more problematical. There were two fundamental conceptual problems. The first was that of sovereignty, or more accurately the relations of different state hierarchies with one another. If the contemporary state was one of territorial and national closure, what was the extent of this closure and to what extent did it preclude relations with other states? The second problem was a related one. If states were sovereign and some solution could be found for their relations, how did this solution relate to the existence of empires that from the sixteenth to the mid-twentieth century extended to most of the surface of the earth? Today the concept of 'international law' is very visible and is taken as governing the relations between states. It is cosmopolitan in some measure, as we will see. For most of the last three hundred years of its existence, however, international law has had very little to do. It was empire that resolved most of the problems today seen as international, and it did so without recourse to any notion of international law.

We have already seen the cosmopolitan nature of empires and how they combined metropolitan common law and local particular law in their operation.[39] As well as combining multiple laws they also represented a form of institutional cosmopolitanism, since local authority was always in some measure

---

[35] Martinez-Torrón and Durham (2010b), 'Religion and Secular State', at 28; and similarly Doe (2011), *Law and Religion*, at 175 ('one way or another, all the States of Europe fund religion directly or indirectly').

[36] For the principle of autonomy of churches in Europe, Forey (2007), *État et institutions religieuses*, at 85 (though recognizing at 152, 172 possible state intervention to control public order or to prevent physical violence). The investiture controversy lives on in China, however, where in the course of negotiations to restore diplomatic relations between the Catholic church and the People's Republic, the papacy is currently resisting China's claim to name bishops: *Le Monde hebdomadaire*, 7 July 2007 at 5.

[37] See Ch. 13, '*Religious liberty*'.

[38] See Ch. 2 and Ch. 3, 'Persistence of Cosmopolitan Ways'.

[39] See Ch. 2, 'The Diversity of Empire', Ch. 3, '*Institutional cosmopolitanism*'.

of equilibrium with metropolitan authority. It was never in reality a relation of command and submission, as the occasional revolution demonstrated. For present purposes, however, what is important is how the metropolitan–colonial relations effectively displaced, in very large measure, any consideration of the relations between co-equal sovereign states. There was no need even for the word 'international', which appeared as a neologism only with the writings of Bentham.[40] Of course there could still be relations between the sovereign states at the centre of empires, so this problem did require an eventual solution of some kind, and there was a remaining problem of the relations of any such sovereign state with the world in general, or at least with those parts of it not subject to its own imperial control. The solution to the latter problem is difficult to qualify as cosmopolitan, though happily it no longer arises today.

Until the middle of the twentieth century non-western states were refused recognition as potential subjects of international law, initially on the basis of their non-Christian beliefs and then on the basis that they lacked the requisite character of 'civilization'.[41] This was clearly legal justification for imperial activity and must be added to the notion of *res nullius* as contributing to the 'legal apparatus' of imperialism.[42] It would have justified the 'unequal treaties, extraterritoriality and transgression of basic principles of international law in dealing with the non-Christian world'.[43] It made international law simply 'part of the colonist project'.[44] Put differently, imperialism was the 'most durable, visible, and significant violation of the Westphalian sovereignty of non-Western states'.[45] Moreover, the

---

[40] Bentham (1970), *Introduction Principles of Morals and Legislation* (1789) at 296. For application of 'international' law limited until late nineteenth century to Europe or 'Europe and America at most', Onuma (2000), 'When Law of International Society Born?', at 58; and for agreement that most parts of world then not members of international society but 'parts of members', Fisch (2004), 'Power or Weakness?', at 21. The ambiguity of non-European collectivities, capable of entering into treaties but lacking international personality, was 'never satisfactorily defined or resolved': Anghie (2004), *Imperialism, Sovereignty*, at 81.

[41] Onuma (2000), 'When Law of International Society Born?', at 24 (for simultaneity of colonialism and the development of international law, though exclusion of former from history of latter), 26, 38 (for exclusion on grounds of religion, then standard of 'civilization' until mid-twentieth century); Koskenniemi (2001), *Gentle Civilizer of Nations*, at 53 (though Ottoman empire accepted in 1856, then 'civilization' standard), 101 (relation to nineteenth-century anthropological and Darwinian ideas of social evolution), 127 ('logic of exclusion'); Bowden (2005), 'Colonial Origins of International Law', at 13 (hallmark of 'primitive' societies lack of formal machinery for enactment, enforcement, and administration of law), 16 (for Wheaton, international law founded on Christian morality); Onuma (2000), 'When Law of International Society Born?' (contrasting claims of universality with exclusionary view of 'European governments'); Anaya (2004), *Indigenous Peoples*, at 27–31.

[42] See Ch. 6, 'Common Laws beyond Europe'.

[43] Horowitz (2004), 'International Law and State Transformation', at 453, 462 (need for change to standard of 'civilization' since unequal treaties could not be justified under natural law); Bowden (2005), 'Colonial Origins of International Law', at 1 ('violent European civilizing missions that it helped give rise to'), 3 ('helped to serve the cause of European imperialism'); Onuma (2000), 'When Law of International Society Born?', at 64 ('critical role for creating this unequal international society'); Macklem (2008), 'Indigenous Recognition', at 183 (for validation by international law of imperial claims over indigenous people).

[44] Koskenniemi (2001), *Gentle Civilizer of Nations*, at 9 (according to much new scholarly work).

[45] Kayaoğlu (2010), *Legal Imperialism*, at 18 (imperialism moreover a 'non-issue' for those studying international relations and sovereignty).

Eurocentric perspective would continue to prevail today, to the extent that non-western states are seen as eventually having been 'admitted' to international society, such a society being taken to exist in the absence of non-European participants.[46]

International law did eventually overcome this exclusionary and discriminatory understanding of its field of application. It has become more cosmopolitan in character today.[47] The discussion must then revert to our first question, that of the nature of the relations of states taken to be sovereign. To what extent do these relations represent a form of institutional cosmopolitanism?

The territorial and national closures that were pursued from the sixteenth to the twentieth centuries inevitably had an effect on the relations between different legal orders. The primary effect was the emergence of a binary distinction between the national and the international. This had been impossible before the eighteenth century since much law ran across what were to become international borders. This was the case for common laws, church law, commercial and maritime law, customs that had not been severed by geographic boundaries, religious law in much of the world, imperial law, and European notions of natural law or the *ius gentium*. Governments did not have departments of foreign affairs.[48] The emergence of the national/international binary was inevitably slow, given the persistence of cosmopolitan ideas and institutions.[49] It is rightly contested today.[50] When Bentham first used the word 'international' in 1789 there had been many earlier, facilitating developments, all derived in some measure from the efforts of closure that have been examined above.[51] A normative tradition of internationality was emerging, eventually with a

---

[46] Onuma (2000), 'When Law of International Society Born?', at 63–4 (notion of 'international' law could come into existence only on their admission; until general admission, only 'European-centered regional international society') ; and for 'entry' of Ottoman empire, China, Japan, Siam, Gong (1984), *Standard of Civilization*, Part II, also at p. 82 for notion of 'civilised states' being abandoned in Oppenheim's *International Law* only in 8th edn in 1955.

[47] For the disappearance of the standard of 'civilization', Bowden (2005), 'Colonial Origins of International Law', at 22 (no such distinction in 'modern' international law), though its disappearance 'not due to European power but in consequence of European decline': Fisch (2004), 'Power or Weakness?', at 25.

[48] Van Creveld (1999), *Rise and Decline of State*, at 133 (until sixteenth century, 'comparatively late in the day', 'provincial governors' responsible for relations with neighbours); Strayer (1970), *Medieval Origins of Modern State*, at 83 (no concept of 'foreign affairs' if not certain which 'states' sovereign; Horowitz (2004), 'International Law and State Transformation', at 466 (Siamese department of foreign affairs created only 1885).

[49] For the conciliatory contribution of Leibniz (d. 1716) in avoiding 'extremes', Hertz (1962), *Development of German Public Mind*, 121; and for the necessity of a 'genealogical' understanding of the emergence of normativity, based on the impossibility of finding the origin or 'degree zero' of its object of study, Delacroix (2006), *Legal Norms and Normativity*, at 96, and 144 (need to understand 'fabric' from which it arises, 'other forms of normativity are always woven into it').

[50] Twining (2003), 'Province of Jurisprudence Re-examined', at 25 (perpetuating the 'myth that law is only concerned with two levels of ordering', citing Islamic law, *lex mercatoria*, European Union law, traditional African law).

[51] See Chs 4 and 5.

distinction between public international law and private international law.[52] If these forms of international law emerged in a time of closure, and as a result of it, they would represent nevertheless a certain 'spirit of internationality', the nature of which requires examination.[53]

Public international law

The Treaty of Westphalia of 1648 contributed in some measure to the 'state system', in the sense of loosening or eliminating much imperial authority. Its significance is disputed, but the debate is about the extent of its contribution to the existence of states, rather than about its contribution to their relations. It said nothing about international relations as they are known today.[54] Grotius, often seen today as the father of public international law, published intensively from 1601 to his death in 1645. Westphalia thus nested in an existing body of opinion on the relations of the future states. This has been seen as a 'theory-centred' path, at least on the European continent, and the theory of international law became very visible from Grotius onwards.[55] It should be recalled, however, that it followed centuries of parallel monarchical developments, based on writing, hierarchy, and boundaries, such that its 'operative' dimension is always a matter of speculation. There were, however, significant theoretical shifts. The new state hierarchies were conceptualized as persons, or at least as crowns, so that they could at least theoretically be subject to a law of persons.[56] The most visible sources of such a

[52] For the normative or ethical character of the tradition, Glenn (2011a), 'Ethic of International Law'. Story was the first to use the expression 'private international law' in 1834: Paul (2008), 'The Transformation of International Comity', at 25 (as a sub-category of international law more generally, expressing an underlying idea of the unity of public and private international law).

[53] Koskenniemi (2001), *Gentle Civilizer of Nations*, at 13; and for the idea of a European continental 'balance of states', Hunter and Saunders (2002), *Natural Law and Civil Sovereignty*, at 17 (no longer fighting 'with soldiers and muskets but with legal briefs and documents'); though for the paradox of international law emerging with the closed thinking of the statist theory of Hobbes, Friedrich (1997), *Geschichte der deutschen Staatsrechtswissenschaft*, at 91–5.

[54] For Westphalia as one element of many in the emergence of the contemporary state, Beaulac (2000), 'Westphalian Legal Orthodoxy', notably at 150 (does not close 'multilayered system of authority', state independence only achieved 'long after'), 166 (Swiss and Dutch independence already faits accomplis); Tierney (2005), 'Reframing Sovereignty?', at 164 (Westphalia as 'defining moment' 'simplistic and largely inaccurate' but continues as 'useful caricature'); Asch (1997), *Thirty Years War*, at 144 (on 'change in political balance'); Philpott (2000), 'Religious Roots of International Relations', at 206 (underlying importance of reformation), 209 (Westphalia 'consolidation, not the creation' of modern system), 240 (merely 'ratified' victory of state), though at 983 (Westphalia 'foundational', a new 'constitution of international relations'); Black (2004), *Kings, Nobles and Commoners*, at 64 ('circumspect shift'); though more positively Nelson (2006), *Making of Modern State*, at 60 ('theory of the modern state finally emerges in clear form').

[55] Toulmin (1990), *Cosmopolis*, at 76 (Grotius as representative of renaissance efforts to bring reason to law, 'increasingly formal and theoretical goals', notions of system, Euclidian axioms, dominant until Savigny's insistence on historical development).

[56] See Ch. 4, '*The state as body, crown, or corporate person*'; and for notion of sovereignty presupposing that state a civil person, Benyekhlef (2008), *Une possible histoire de la norme*, at 562 (state 'substituting itself' for individual).

law were the *ius publicum universale*,[57] which had attempted to control princely relations within the empire and which was largely dependent on natural law, and natural law itself, often expressed in the form of a *ius gentium* incorporating some measure of Roman legal ideas. Since Roman law was often ambiguous, there is ongoing dispute about the extent of its influence.[58] These sources of international law were non-formal and very cosmopolitan. They had influence even in England and France, where the particular common laws had not historically spoken to international relations as such. The *ius gentium* was not historically confined to what we now know as international relations. There was within it no sharp national/international binary. The same *ius gentium* was potentially applicable to inter-state relations and cross-border commercial transactions, though perhaps more so on the continent than in England. Huber's insistence in the late seventeenth century on the territoriality of state laws appears as the decisive doctrinal step.[59] The national was that which was confined to a territory; the international could be that beyond. Recognition of this possibility appears to be the work of Vattel, whose *Droit des gens* in 1759 limited the *ius gentium* to inter-state relations. His title was important.[60] The notion of a droit des gens or law of nations would be a translation of the expression *ius gentium*,[61] but with a new and radically distinct meaning, limited to public international law. It remained for Bentham to find a convincing, modern name for it.

Once conceptually founded, and named, public international law became subject to the same intellectual forces that were at work within the emergent national legal systems. If the only law is state law, consent to public international law must be given by states, and the need for state consent had even been urged by the early 'positivists' of the subject in the seventeenth century.[62] There has since been a vigorous positivist school of public international law, looking to

---

[57] Koskenniemi (2001), *Gentle Civilizer of Nations*, at 3; Haakonssen (2006), 'German natural law', at 256 ('the framework of confessional co-existence').

[58] Lessaffer (2011), 'Roman Law and Early Historiography of International Law', at 150 (for those seeing little Roman influence, others favouring 'continuity'), 152 (Lauterpacht's use of Roman law, positivist rejection of it); Kingsbury and Straumann (2011), *Roman Foundations*, notably at 1–2 (to a 'considerable extent', though 'much disagreement', 'much variation'). For Grotius's reliance on earlier canonical Decretists who accepted neither pope nor emperor as overlord, Tierney (1982), *Religion, law and constitutional thought*, at 22. The *ius gentium* was applied by Romans to relations with non-Romans, but it would not have been a synthesis of different laws but a slightly varied version of the *ius civile*; Kaser (1967), *Römische Rechtsgeschichte*, at 135 (simpler form of words, formless transactions, etc.). For Pufendorf's conflation of natural law and the *ius gentium*, states as moral persons having the same rights as physical persons, Dufour (1991), 'Pufendorf', at 585; Haakonssen (2006), 'German natural law', at 277 (also Grotius, Thomasius, Wolff).

[59] See Ch. 4, 'Boundaries'.

[60] Allott (2002), *Health of Nations*, at 410 (Vattel 'crucially' deciding to publish own book and not simply translate Wolff, view that international law beyond state control).

[61] Onuma (2000), 'When Law of International Society Born?', at 4, 5.

[62] See notably Rubin (1997), *Ethics and Authority in International Law*, notably at 54 ('the positivist practice'); and for early positivists Richard Zouche in England and Samuel Rachel in Germany, Nussbaum (1947), *Concise History Law of Nations*, at 118ff.; Gaurier (2005), *Histoire droit international*, at 177 (adding Weber, others). More clearly than later positivists, early positivists were making a normative argument.

'existing rules and their habitual obedience',[63] but paradoxically this has not been seen as positivist enough by the theoreticians of domestic legal systems, who require more formal mechanisms and sanctions. Public international law, in Austin's expression, would be 'law improperly so-called'.[64] It was caught in a logical conundrum: either states were sovereign, and there could be no binding international order, or there was such an order, and they were not sovereign.[65] So a 'spectre of natural law continued to haunt international law' and was never absent, since it could not be.[66]

The ambiguity of public international law has not prevented its growth and it achieved remarkable visibility during the last century, though it is now encountering many new challenges.[67] The ambiguity surrounding its doctrinal and theoretical foundations has been paralleled, however, by ambiguity surrounding its 'spirit of internationality'. It does deal with what is known as the international, and provides mechanisms for the peaceful relations of states, in the form of treaties, commissions, and even courts and tribunals. In its underlying acceptance of the 'state system', however, it can be remarkably uncosmopolitan and even bellicose. States became reified as the only subjects of public international law, and to the extent that public international law was seen as a simply positive (factual) phenomenon it was beyond normative engagement (notably with non-western laws and lawyers).[68] Foreign relations could only be undertaken by states themselves, and invariably only through the relatively new device of ministries of foreign relations. Contact with foreign states, and law, were proscribed for ordinary mortals. In the Hegelian conception, moreover, states reach their ultimate realization in these external relations, most adequately expressed in war.[69] Diplomacy would thus be regularly 'punctuated' by these 'medieval

---

[63] Sylvest (2004), 'International Law in Nineteenth Century Britain', at 39.

[64] Austin (1832), *Province of Jurisprudence*, at 147.

[65] Koskenniemi (2001), *Gentle Civilizer of Nations*, at 240 (Kelsen's monism as 'efficient critique' of idea that 'national and international could live harmoniously side by side as independent normative orders'). Institutional cosmopolitanism struggles in a binary world of sovereigns. For 'jurists' who require international law but have 'no clear way of defining it in the absence of a sovereign power', Stankiewicz (1976), 'Sovereignty as Political Theory', at 154.

[66] Sylvest (2004), 'International Law in Nineteenth Century Britain', at 41 (and on nineteenth-century thinking as 'neither uniform nor unequivocal').

[67] For the quasi-absence of its teaching in the nineteenth century, Koskenniemi (2001), *Gentle Civilizer of Nations*, at 31, 33 (in England 'virtually no' teaching of the subject in first half of nineteenth century), 274 (only one chair in France in late nineteenth century); and for contemporary adaptation, see Ch. 13, 'States and International Law', 'States and Regional Law', 'States and Transnational Law'.

[68] Koskenniemi (2001), *Gentle Civilizer of Nations*, at 280; and for the Bentham-inspired restriction to the 'international' as even less inclusive than what had formerly been regarded as the law of nations, suggesting more than a simple change in terminology, Sylvest (2004), 'International Law Nineteenth Century Britain', at 13, also citing, at 33, Montague Bernard, first Chichele Professor of International Law at Oxford, on state as 'divinely ordered instrument', this in 1860.

[69] Hegel (2008), *Philosophy of Right*, notably paras 322 (individuality as being 'exclusively' for oneself appears in relations with other states), 330 (international law dependent on distinct and sovereign will of state, state as 'embodiment of freedom'), 334 (conflicts resolved by war in absence of agreement); Taylor (1975), *Hegel*, at 448 ('as a reflection of an essential moment of the state, according to Hegel's ontological principles, war has necessarily to occur'); van Creveld (1999), *Rise and Decline of the State*, at 197 ('the one

entertainments' and Hobbes would be the only recognized social philosopher.[70] If war was and remains a fundamental preoccupation of public international law, being declared illegal only in the twentieth century,[71] the fundamentally conflictual character of international law becomes even more explicitly recognized in its private dimension.

Private international law

Huber is not only at the doctrinal origin of the principle of territoriality, he also originated the expression 'conflict of laws'.[72] It was not at all evident that different laws should be seen as conflicting, and for centuries the relations of various common laws and particular laws, and even the laws of different, territorially circumscribed cities, had been resolved by various interpretive methods with no underlying notion of conflict.[73] In the twelfth century in Bologna Aldricus had taught that in cases of legal difference the 'better' law should be chosen, and while this did represent a process of choice between legal orders it was also accompanied by still more supple methods of resolution, largely dictated by the circumstances of individual cases.[74] Huber was concerned, however, with Dutch independence from Spain; Hobbes was widely read and

way for states to play out their historical destiny was to pit themselves against other states by means of war . . . each state had to be made as strong as possible. . . . All this helped fuel the kind of interstate rivalry that was . . . a prominent feature of the period from 1848 to 1945'); Bartelson (1995), *Genealogy of Sovereignty*, at 215–6 ('dialectic of conflict', states in relation of 'mutual exclusion'); Nelson (2006), *Making of Modern State*, at 99 (interstate relations inherently conflictual); Cooper (2005), *Breaking of Nations*, at 12 (assumption of balance of power system that state 'fundamentally aggressive'); and for parallels with Hobbes, Malcolm (2000), *Aspects of Hobbes*, at 456 (only within the commonwealth can rights and duties be in harmony).

[70] Allott (2002), *Health of Nations*, at 409 (or in the 'miserable modern euphemism, *armed conflict*'), 410 (for Hobbes, as though external life of our societies 'still a reflection of the internal life of centuries ago').

[71] Brierly (1963), *Law of Nations*, at 398 ('international law had given up the attempt to regulate recourse to war'), 408 (Covenant of League of Nations), 413 (UN Charter, notably Art. 2, 'strictly framed').

[72] For the text of his 1689 *De conflictu legum* in English, Lorenzen (1947), 'Huber's *De Conflictu Legum*', at 136; and for his being a 'loner', breaking with traditional continental emphases on either personal or territorial laws, depending on the case, Watson (1992), *Joseph Story and Comity of Errors*, at 30; also Thorne (1985), 'Sovereignty and the Conflict of Laws', at 181 ('a complete change in theory'); Gutzwiller (1929), *Développement historique du droit international privé*, at 325 ('passion of independence', 'striking absolutism').

[73] For a magisterial treatment of such interpretive methods, in terms of the German / Italian *ius commune* and its *iura propria*, Vogenauer (2001), *Die Auslegung von Gesetzen*, notably vol. I at 448–9 (restrictive interpretation of 'odious' or excessivly burdensome laws). Similar interpretive techniques were employed in all the common laws, as to which see Glenn (2007c), *Common Laws*, notably at 68 (notion of 'suitability' in English common law); and Wijffels (2005), 'Qu'est-ce que le *ius commune*?', at 657 (*ius commune* fulfilling function of all common law, ensuring coherent and supple functioning of different particular laws, bringing about a 'minimum of system in the existing pluralism').

[74] For 'doing justice' in individual cases, Thorne (1985), 'Sovereignty and the Conflict of Laws', at 179 ('raising no issues of conflicts of laws'), 171 (idea of conflict of laws having origin only from sixteenth century with idea of sovereignty); Juenger (1993), *Choice of Law*, at 12 (though successors proceeding in 'conceptualist' fashion, theorizing about 'spatial reach' of laws in lieu of seeking substantive solutions); Yntema (1953), 'Historic Bases of Private International', at 301 ('genius' of Aldricus); Mills (2006), 'Private History of International Law', at 10 ('comparative nature' of test suggesting competitive improvement, not existence of diverse laws).

profoundly influential in The Netherlands, so a conflictual perspective came to prevail.[75] It was influential in England and the USA, notably on Story, and Story in turn influenced Savigny in Germany in the middle of the nineteenth century.[76] The rest of the story of private international law may be seen as a response to Huber, who allowed application of foreign law only on a basis of 'comity', but the type of response nevertheless remained profoundly impressed with an underlying notion of conflict.

Savigny is seen as the father of 'modern' private international law and even of the contemporary 'science' or discipline of private international law, and by this is meant the construction of a set of rules that allocate different legal relations to different states according to their geographic connections.[77] Thus tort liability is governed by the law of the place of tort, and rights in immoveable property are governed by the law of the *situs* of the property. This may appear banal and inoffensive but it effectively nationalizes and compartmentalizes the entire space of law and requires radical choice of one or the other competing or conflicting territorial state laws. The logic is classically binary. Since legal relations are complex, however, as are geographic ones, in practice the process has been strained and contentious, particularly since the rules in question have themselves been gradually nationalized, making private international law a national law dealing with private cases.[78] The result has been second-order conflicts, or conflicts of conflict-of-laws rules, where the conflicts rules differ from state to state. What do you do, as judge, when your rule refers a problem to the law of state X and the law of state X refers the problem to the law of state Y? There are many interesting possibilities. Conflict is here raised to a higher level; but there is conflict wherever you look. It is even presumed, as in the contemporary rule of some continental European jurisdictions, that a decision must be made on the law applicable to an international private law case even in the absence of any alleged difference between the laws in presence.[79] Here, 'conflicts justice', as it

---

[75] For Hobbes in The Netherlands, Malcolm (1991), 'Hobbes and Spinoza', at 545 (outside England, greatest influence Dutch translation of *Leviathan* in 1667). Huber's *De Conflictu Legum* was published two years later, inspired for Lorenzen by 'an intense jealousy of... local rights': Lorenzen (1947), 'Huber's *De Conflictu Legum*', at 138. For nineteenth-century views of conflicts of laws as conflicts of sovereignty, Mayer (2007), 'Phénomène de la coordination des ordres juridiques', at 101, and see at 103 (on need for resolution by superior order).

[76] For England, as territorialist by feudal nature, Lorenzen (1947), 'Huber's *De Conflictu Legum*', at 155, though England had remained cosmopolitan in its application of ecclesiastical law and transnational maritime law well into the nineteenth century; Watson (1992), *Joseph Story and Comity of Errors*, at 78 ('really no conflicts law' until mid-eighteenth century); Gutzwiller (1929), *Développement historique du droit international privé*, at 338 (no English writing on subject until nineteenth century). For Huber and Story, Yntema (1953), 'Historic Bases of Private International Law', at 307.

[77] The foundational private international law tract was vol. 8 of Savigny's nineteenth-century treatise on Roman law, published in an English translation in 1869: von Savigny (1869), *Treatise on Private International law*.

[78] For nationalization even in common law jurisdictions, in the absence of legislation or codification, through Dicey's method of black-letter choice-of-law rules, Mills (2006), 'The Private History of International Law', at 30; and for widespread national codification through the twentieth century, see Ch. 13, '*Private international law*'.

[79] Glenn (1993), 'Harmonization of law', at 58 ('a presumption of conflict'), with references.

has become known, is as far removed from justice between the parties ('material justice') as it can possibly be, and this in matters of private law. Even through the twentieth century there was considerable national codification of private international law, so a process of disunification of private international law logically followed from the process of unification or territorialization of national law.[80] In the most ambitious and radical forms of rule-based private international law, it would totally displace any non-state form of law, though we are now seeing re-emergence notably of transnational, substantive commercial law, a *lex mercatoria* once clearly identifiable as part of a larger *ius gentium*. Today there is also a general decline in the idea of rule-based private international law.[81]

The 'spirit of internationality' in international law over the last two centuries has therefore been a minimalist or grudging one. More precisely, it has been limited to internationality, refusing wider forms of cosmopolitanism. It has presupposed a monopoly of state law and conflict between multiple state laws, and precluded widespread use and knowledge of multiple laws, the latter either through the exclusive role of ministries of foreign affairs or through imperative application of conflict-of-laws rules even in the absence of legal difference. The nineteenth-century discipline of comparative law could do little in the face of these generalized perspectives, and even exacerbated them with its project of creating a generalized taxonomy of (static) national legal systems according to a broader, biological notion of 'legal families'.[82] Yntema referred to private international law as assuming 'a certain cosmopolitan respect, or at least tolerance, for foreign conceptions of justice' but the cosmopolitanism that was thus sustained was one sought to be made compliant with the notion of a 'state system'.[83] It could not preclude, and may even have contributed to, a phenomenon of closed states, those of Latin America for much of the twentieth century ('import substitution' economies), Soviet Russia, or today North Korea or Belarus. Closures always fail, however, and the remaining chapters will examine the primacy of 'texture' in the actual functioning of contemporary states.[84]

---

[80] Glenn (1993), 'Harmonization of law', at 50 ('zones of contrasting, formal unity . . . overall result is one of disunity').

[81] See Ch. 13, *'Private international law'*. For the views of nineteenth-century English positivist John Austin (reducing the *ius gentium* to nothing and the *ius inter gentes* to 'positive morality', a view 'so naive and simplistic' as to delay positivism for another century), Rubin (1997), *Ethics and Authority in International Law*, at 138 and 148 ('collapse' of *ius gentium* model), 150–1 (though *ius gentium* language persisting in maritime and prize cases, never abandoned by some jurists).

[82] Glenn (2006), 'Comparative Legal Families and Comparative Legal Traditions'.

[83] Yntema (1953), 'Historic Bases of Private International Law', at 297.

[84] For surrounding 'texture' always available as disruption to closure, see Ch. 1, 'The State as Tradition'.

PART IV

THE CONTEMPORARY
COSMOPOLITAN STATE

9

Globalization, Cosmopolitan Theory, and the State

The territorial and national closures of states were of some two or three centuries in duration. They were never complete and there was persistence, through the time of purported closure, of common laws, constitutionalism, and institutional cosmopolitanism, all in some measure transborder in operation. They were without prejudice to local laws, and are resurgent today. Like all closures, moreover, the closures of the contemporary state were limited in time, challenged by the ongoing texture that originally nourished them and that continues to nourish larger, smaller, or different forms of closure.[1] We know this challenge as 'globalization', and the globalization that we know today is part of the ongoing process of human grouping and regrouping, in response to circumstances that are never stable. Since each closure is burdened by the heritage of previous closures, however, the state will figure in any and all future legal and political ordering. Nevertheless, it appears already to be a different form of state from the 'modern' state that was constructed from the seventeenth century.[2] There is appropriate debate on the form and structure it will take. The debate on the future state is provoked by globalization; it is accompanied by what has become known as cosmopolitan theory. They are closely related to one another.

GLOBALIZATION

Globalization represents the inevitable challenge to the instruments of closure of the contemporary state.[3] Yet it would be inaccurate to think of globalization as a novel and purely contemporary phenomenon. The closure of the territorial state was not effected without conceptual and physical effort, often courageous. It had to be brought about in the face of the cosmopolitan structures of the time, behind which, as always, lay important vested interests. Put differently than in the

---

[1] On closure as a general concept, see Ch. 1 , 'The State as Tradition'.

[2] Michaels (2005), 'Welche Globalisierung?', at 532 ('globalization does not lead to the end of the state itself, but to the end of a unified concept of the state'); and for the state remaining as 'the most powerful political entity with which we interact', Barber (2010), *Constitutional State*, at xi.

[3] On its dimensions, Held *et al* (1999), *Global Transformations*; Baylis and Smith (2001), *Globalization of World Politics*; Gessner and Budak (1998), *Emerging Legal Certainty* (e.g. on banking relations). For the general inadequacy of contemporary legal theory in relation to it, Twining (2000), *Globalisation and Legal Theory*, notably at 51 ('black box' theories of national law, concentration only on state municipal law and public international law); Waldron (2012), *'Partly Laws Common to All Mankind'*, at 42 ('rather stale and rancid bread and butter—of jurisprudence since . . . Bentham'); though for globalization as yet to touch a 'large chunk' of the world economy (and half of the population of the developing world), World Bank (1997), *The State in a Changing World*, at 12; and for critique Singh (2005), *Questioning Globalization*.

previous chapters, the closure of the territorial state had to occur in the face of the globalization that then prevailed, and such earlier globalization did occur. It did not perhaps have the glamour of some of the current instruments of globalization, but it was globalization in and of its time. The oldest instrument of globalization may well have been the wheel, happily leaving room for further development, and the telegraph in the nineteenth century compressed the time for communication between London and New York by a factor of 4,000, from fourteen days to five minutes.[4] Nayan Chanda speaks of the 'initial globalization' of a 'tiny group of our ancestors' who 'walked out of Africa', eventually settling on all continents after some 50,000 years of wandering in coastal regions.[5] Osterhammel insists on various periods of intensification and decline of relations over distance and situates the 'turning point' for globalization in the early modern period of 'discovery', the slave trade, and 'ecological imperialism'. The late nineteenth and early twentieth centuries were those of a 'world connecting'.[6] Today, the degree of economic exchange in some areas has yet to return to that of 1913.[7] If today's globalization is marked by the 'velocity ... volume ... and visibility' of the process, we are reminded of various forms of 'archaic globalization' that have 'persisted strongly under the surface of the new international order'.[8] At the height of the nineteenth century the levels of closure proposed by both Marxism and the free trade philosophies of the time gave to the nation-state 'no more than a subordinate role as a political force'.[9] Moreover, in examining the state as a construction of various common laws, we have seen that it may itself be viewed as a product of earlier globalization, a world-wide expansion of certain ideas of group structure and identity.[10]

These identifiable forms of earlier globalization confirm the limited character of the closure of the territorial state. Today that closure is affected still more by the decline in importance of its main instruments of closure: writing, hierarchy,

---

[4] Joffe (2007), 'Schneller, besser, reicher . . .', at 3 (also on shipping costs falling by 40 per cent with steamships).

[5] Chanda (2007), *Bound Together*, at xiv, and at various places for contributions of 'traders, preachers, warriors and adventurers', thus looking methodologically at types of actor rather than the activities of a particular people or territory; and for the spread of people and laws in 'deep history', Glenn (2012), 'Origins of Peoples' (on 'genetic distances' of populations, including proto-humans; no human population completely isolated from others).

[6] Rosenberg (2012), 'Introduction', *A World Connecting 1870–1945*, and notably at 4 (for 'an ever-changing dyad of enclosure and permeability').

[7] Osterhammel and Petersson (2005), *Globalization*, at 146; and for levels of trade from 1870 to 1913 as comparable to those of today, Singh (2005), *Questioning Globalization*, at 166; Cranston (2004), *The Sovereignty Revolution*, at 37–8 ('first globalization' from mid-nineteenth century brought to end by 'protectionist backlash').

[8] Chanda (2007), *Bound Together*, at xiii (for velocity, etc.); Bayly (2004), *Birth of the Modern World*, at 234 ('the old, overlapping *ecumenes* and their circles of honorific exchange and trade diasporas').

[9] Osterhammel and Petersson (2005), *Globalization*, at 69; and for cosmopolitanism of Marx and Engels, Kleingeld and Brown (2006), 'Cosmopolitanism', s. 1.3 (on 'withering away' of state, at least in Marxist theory).

[10] See Ch. 6, 'Common Laws beyond Europe'.

and boundaries. We will see in Chapter 10 the challenge of globalization to the attempted societal closure that was the nation.

Writing

Today writing has become banal in most societies and this is a problem for the contemporary state. In the past writing itself was advanced by the state through its use as a means of government and, once established, it served very effectively to advance the role of state law.[11] The customs of France were redacted as a means to secure control over them. If the first redactions were unofficial the subsequent notion of an 'official' redaction was a clear indication of state control over both the process and the ensuing product.[12] Codification, a more exclusive form of writing, could then follow from the nineteenth century. From the mid-fifteenth century the Gutenberg press did much to spread the written word but for centuries its production was expensive and state-authorized forms of writing could occupy much of the field, at least in purported importance. There was also control of content by both church and crown prior to generalized rights to copy. Moreover, the formal, written sources of state law were supplemented by doctrinal forms of writing about them. Unwritten forms of law correspondingly declined in importance, relegated to an insignificant role by the written sources. If writing did eventually become open to all, when the state imposed compulsory education, writing remained the principal means of governing a hierarchical form of authority, within its fixed territorial boundaries. This is why it was an instrument of closure; it restructured consciousness and concepts of space and closure.[13] It was a vector for both territorial control and territorial expansion. This was true for both legislation and case law.[14]

In the twenty-first century, however, writing has lost much of its primacy as an instrument of government. This was foreseeable; even in the nineteenth century governmental authorities were expressing misgivings over the speed and potentially seditious use of the telegraph, open to all and any.[15] We also know now that constitutions do not necessarily succeed because of their written form.[16] With the advent of writing in electronic form the primacy of governmental writing has declined precipitously. The problem, in both a broad and a narrow sense, is one of legal sources. Global communication networks threaten not only national languages and cultures but also national law and legal authority. Law enforcement is rendered more difficult but so is the 'nation-building' function of the

---

[11] For the growth of writing in England from the eleventh century as a result of the needs of law and bureaucracy, as opposed to any general desire for education or literature, Clanchy (1993), *Memory to Written Record*, notably at 1, 3, 6 ('initially a product of distrust rather than social progress'), 19.

[12] See Ch. 4, 'Customs'.

[13] Ong (2002), *Orality and Literacy*, notably at 129 ('print encourages a sense of closure'); and for influence of writing, including codex form, on a fundamental transformation of 'western rationality', Stock (1990), *Listening for the Text* at 123–5.

[14] For case law in Ireland, Pawlish (1985), *Sir John Davies: A study in legal imperialism*.

[15] For French prohibition of its private use in 1837, Gleick (2011), *The Information*, at 135–6.

[16] See Ch. 7, 'France and the world'.

state, the generation of practices of adherence to state law.[17] Twitter is a still more potent menace for state authority than the telegraph of the nineteenth century and it is just writing in another, punchier form. The instances of popular resistance facilitated by electronic communication are multiplying. In a more narrow sense the shift to electronic forms of writing multiplies potential sources of law and the range of authority that can be made available. In the nineteenth century national law reporters deliberately restricted the number of cases they reported. With electronic reporting all may be made available, and there are major questions whether restrictions of access or citation are permissible.[18] The 'stable universe' of settled sources would thus be no more and the question is asked whether confidence can be given to a 'glitzy search engine' on the front end of electronic collections.[19] In the 'developing world' resort may be had to electronic sources of foreign law, where printed copies of local law are too expensive or rare for regular use. State law, in written form, is therefore more and more challenged as an exclusive source of legal authority. It is not a question so much of a decline in its quality (though this is often alleged) but of a multiplication of alternative sources, of local or distant provenance. Judgement in choice of sources becomes more necessary, and more evident in its operation.

Hierarchy

The hierarchy of the contemporary state explains much of its previous success. Over the centuries a theory of a corporate and lasting entity, beyond particular rulers, was combined with bureaucratic success on the ground to provide a base for monarchic and state authority that eventually overshadowed all others, at least in the western European states.[20] Abroad, both the notion of a corporate state identity and an effective bureaucracy were often lacking, or specifically rejected, with a consequent decline in the adequacy of the formal state. What we know as globalization does not directly attack the existing hierarchies of states; the bureaucracies of most states are larger than they have ever been, though subject to short-term fluctuations. Rather, what has occurred has been described as 'factual globalization', the emergence (or at least the recognition) of questions and problems that no state hierarchy is capable of solving unilaterally.[21] Many of

---

[17] Bobbitt (2002), *Shield of Achilles*, at 221 (political authorities unable to control international 'information standard', i.e. near-instant circulation of financial and other information), 224 (foreign broadcasts primary news source for 60 per cent of 'educated Chinese'), 227 (state inability to impose blackout rules on coverage of criminal trials in Canada, or prohibit receipt of pornography in Singapore); van Creveld (1999), *Rise and Decline of State*, at 392–3 (electronic information services 'another step in the retreat of the state', previous print circulation limited across international borders, information distributed on country-by-country basis, now states can only 'swim with the trend').

[18] For the debate in the USA over non-citation rules, Tusk (2003), 'No-Citation Rules' (selective and no-citation rules promulgated in 1960s, now trend to amending).

[19] Bering (2000), 'Legal Information', notably 1701–3 (freeing of case reports from central, paper source; citations to case law expanding in function of electronic availability).

[20] See Ch. 3, 'Hierarchy'.

[21] Sand (2007), 'From National Sovereignty', at 275 (increase in global 'social dynamics', presumption of national problem-solving capacities 'has been broken'); and for the breadth of fields affected by transnational normativity, Handl and Zekoll (2012), *Beyond Territoriality*.

these questions and problems are a direct result of state activity, or of activities that states have sponsored or promoted. National industrialization has created transborder pollution and global ozone depletion.[22] Liberal political economies have created transborder flows of capital.[23] Technology nationally promoted has opened transnational space to abuse, in the air and at the bottom of seas.[24] States necessarily depend on others for resources and products that they cannot themselves produce, and that their citizens require.[25] We are subject to an 'indefinite accretion of interdependent elements' and there is no one in control, or even possibly in control.[26]

It is remarkable that the language of sovereignty has persisted in these circumstances, in spite of its initial ambiguity and contemporary irrelevance. It is simply part of the heritage of previous attempted closures, but today has little or no purchase. There is today no empire, no church against which it must be asserted. It has become an 'an anachronism and an illusion' and, moreover, would never have existed.[27] Necessary cooperation and collaboration have become the order of the day; reconciliation of difference is becoming a primary objective for functional 'reasons of state'. It is a question of 'organizing compatibility, of preparing for convergence'.[28] The state thus has no effective option to act unilaterally in matters of 'factual globalization'. It may refuse to participate in

---

[22] For 'ineradicable interdependency' of biophysical systems and states, Kysar (2010), *Regulating from Nowhere*, at 147 ('even conventionally domestic environmental problems must be viewed as global in scope').

[23] For capital and migration flows removing vulnerability of 'isolated' peoples to empire, Parsons (2010), *Rule of Empires*, at 449; van Creveld (1999), *Rise and Decline of State*, at 391 (instantaneous currency transactions, both citizens and foreigners able to speculate against national currencies).

[24] Van Creveld (1999), *Rise and Decline of State*, at 380–1 (technology 'compelled attention' to problems it created).

[25] Rosecrance (1986), *Rise of Trading State*, at 15 (states no longer self-reliant, dependent on others for necessities), 140 (fragmentation of states after Second World War increasing interdependence as size of states decreased); Green (1988), *Authority of the State*, at 216 ('economic interdependency'); Munters (1975), 'Opening Up of Rural Social Systems', at 41 (agriculture forced to participate in world-wide economy; 'complete isolation . . . unimaginable'); Sørensen (2004), *Transformation of the State*, at 36 (the 'competition state').

[26] Ghéhenno (1995), *End of the Nation-State*, at 59 (world having become a gigantic information exchange); and for impossibility of globalization ever terminating, Chanda (2007), *Bound Together*, at 319 (calls to shut down globalization 'pointless, because nobody is in charge').

[27] Allott (2002), *Health of Nations*, at 179 (inappropriate as theoretical explanation); De Bonth (2002), 'Sovereignty Revisited', at 102 ('not a single country in the world can be fully sovereign'); Chevallier (2004b), 'L'État post-moderne', at 108 (state now existing in 'context' of interdependence, concept of sovereignty 'caduque' or expired); Badie (2000), *The Imported State*, at 9 (on states with only 'slimmest capacity' for even 'fictional sovereignty', mechanisms that 'obliterate sovereignty'); Horsman and Marshall (1994), *After the Nation-State*, at 178 (no longer any 'independent arsenal of policy tools'); Habermas (2000), *Après l'Etat-Nation*, at 83 (state 'obliged' by globalization to open towards new or foreign forms of life, consequent reduction of field of possible action). For historical inexistence, Maritain (1951), *Man and the State*, at 195 (need to abandon Hegelian concept of state as supra-human person, one of main obstacles to peace); Krasner (1999), *Sovereignty*, notably at 77 (every European peace treaty since Westphalia providing for external scrutiny of treatment of minority populations, violating Westphalian principle of autonomy).

[28] Ghéhenno (1995), *End of the Nation-State*, at 64 ('more than of building sovereignties').

international regimes, but the decision is not so much a simple reflection of sovereignty as it is a calculation of costs and benefits, and the costs of non-participation grow higher and higher. However, if sovereignty is today a conceptual (or, more exactly, rhetorical) impediment to state collaboration, the more fundamental notion of a state hierarchy provides no such impediment. Hierarchies can be more or less open, even when conceptualized in corporate terms. As physical persons, or subjects of rights, may contract, so may state hierarchies collaborate. Nothing is 'lost' in this process. So the immense process of states 'sharing' sovereignty with international organizations, or 'conceding' it to them, is in reality not a conceptual problem at all. States simply do it, and their essentially hierarchical structure is no obstacle, conceptual or otherwise, to their doing it.[29] Since 1865, when the International Telegraph Union became the first international organization with a legal persona of its own, capable of 'binding' its members, there has been a correspondingly great increase in international collaboration and a great increase in international organizations. There were 123 in 1951, 280 in 1972, and 395 in 1984.[30] There is both 'negative' integration (removing obstacles to circulation and collaboration) and 'positive' integration (more affirmative measures of collaboration).[31] It is an open field.

If these forms of collaboration are somehow external to the state, there is a corresponding cosmopolitanism in 'internal' affairs, brought about in large measure by a decline in the significance of physical or geographical boundaries.

Boundaries

'Factual globalization' not only surpasses the institutional capacities of state hierarchies, it also transcends the physical boundaries of states, so laboriously traced on the ground (at least in many places) over the last centuries. Boundaries are both barriers and places of interaction (controlled or less controlled) and the more interaction that occurs the less the boundary constitutes a barrier. Boundaries may be overrun, particularly by information; factual globalization is bringing this about in no inconsiderable measure. There is a process of 'de-bordering' ('Entgrenzung')[32] or 'despatialization',[33] as a result of which phenomena become 'trans-territorial'[34] or

---

[29] Sarooshie (2005), *International Organizations*, notably at 7 (for 'framework' of states doing so, distinguishing between agency, delegation, and transfer of powers); Allott (2002), *Health of Nations*, at 177 ('sharing' of sovereign power now major structural feature of international society, *the* major structural feature of European Union, with listed fields of sharing); Chevallier (2004a), *L'État post-moderne*, at 74 ('polycentric state'); Morris (1998), *Essay on Modern State*, at 221 (important part of constitutional order of Hobbes, Blackstone, Kelsen 'is mistaken—and . . . it doesn't matter').

[30] Van Creveld (1999), *Rise and Decline of State*, at 382. For their law-making, Alvarez (2005), *International Organizations as Law-Makers*.

[31] Eppler (2005), *Auslaufmodell Staat*, at 63.

[32] Beck and Lau (2004), *Entgrenzung*, passim.

[33] Auby (2003), *La globalisation*, at 14 (shift from purely national).

[34] Poggi (1990), *The State*, at 190 (state territory traversed or bypassed by vital processes, 'systemic interactions' that state cannot effectively survey and regulate); Rosecrance (1999), *Rise of Virtual State*, notably at xi–xii (on 'products of the mind' surpassing material forces), 31 ('virtualization').

'supraterritorial'.[35] If in the past borders changed with alarming frequency,[36] today they fade, and the process of fading affects the concept of the state and not simply the territories of particular states. There has been mention of 'aterritoriality'[37] and even of warfare becoming 'post-territorial'.[38] Land has become an 'old factor', no longer coveted by states, which have enough to do on the land they have.[39] Borders have to be 'smart' for transnational actors, providing security but not complication.

The increase in interaction across borders, assisted by 'space-time compression', itself contributes to a further decline in importance of borders. Flows become established, even institutionalized, and if a 'regime' becomes recognizable it will itself constitute a legal and normative conceptual space, applicable as a matter of interpretation whenever its components are found to be present. The triggering devices are functional rather than geographic, and geography thereby takes another hit. The regimes are highly variable and may relate to a field of activity such as international trade or standards, or a region or jointly administered border zone, recalling the marches of medieval times.[40] There is now a theory of international regimes, in its ensemble detracting from notions of strictly state control of territory.[41] The same may be said of the European Union, somewhere between the national and the international.

The decline of sharp geographical borders also indicates a decline in a strict and classical logic of separation. The logic is no longer 'either/or' ('entweder/oder') but rather 'both/and' ('Sowohl-als-Auch'), a reflection not of brutal dichotomies but of the true configuration of relations.[42] This requires more decisions to be made, in the intensification of exchange, and so'[t]he question is not whether to be cosmopolitan or not, but what kind of cosmopolis one

---

[35] Scholte (2001), 'The globalization of world politics', at 22 (events no longer at 'territorial locations'); Opello and Rosow (2004), *Nation-State and Global Order*, at 245 (lesser ability to 'represent' the state as territorially sovereign, questioning 'the possibilities of territorialized . . . power'); Kratochwil (1986), 'Of Systems, Boundaries, and Territoriality', at 42 (erosion of boundaries; this in 1986).

[36] See Ch. 5, *'Fragmentation, failure, and violence'*.

[37] Agamben (2000), *Means without End*, at 24 (aterritoriality or reciprocal extraterritoriality as solution for Jerusalem, two 'political' communities within the same region), demonstrating the modernity of the medieval, or renewed forms of institutional cosmopolitanism.

[38] Opello and Rosow (2004), *Nation-State and Global Order*, at 252 ('low intensity', non-state actors), and for decline in classic concepts of warfare, see Ch. 5, *'Fragmentation, failure, and violence'*.

[39] Cooper (2005), *Breaking of Nations*, at 17 ('governing people, especially potentially hostile people, is a burden') and 33 ('acquiring territory is no longer of interest'); Rosecrance (1999), *Rise of Virtual State*, at xi (now 'products of the mind take precedence'). Mineral and petroleum deposits in land should not, however, be overlooked.

[40] Boggs (1940), *Boundaries*, at 7; Kratochwil (1986), 'Of Systems, Boundaries, and Territoriality', at 43 (distinguishing spheres of responsibility, spheres of abstention, and functional regimes); and for the recent emergence of the idea of 'frontier' zones for purposes of regional maritime cooperation, Townsend-Gault (1997), 'Regional Maritime Cooperation', at 3.

[41] For borders being evaluated for their functionality and not just geopolitically, Adamson (2005), 'Law, Sovereignty, and Transnationalism', at 59 (redefined as tool for achieving certain social goods).

[42] Beck and Lau (2004), *Entgrenzung*, at 9 (citing Musil in 1922), 15–16 (breakdown of logic of 'High Modern', itself challenge of a new decisional logic).

should prefer . . . '.[43] The relation of globalization to cosmopolitan theory then becomes clearer.

COSMOPOLITAN THEORY

There has been a recent flowering of cosmopolitan theory, occurring at the same time as the process of globalization, such that the two are clearly related. It may be a case, as has been asserted before, of practice generating theory or, perhaps more likely, of theory generated by practice reflecting back on the practice in a reciprocal relationship.[44] At present it is not possible to say. The cosmopolitan theory has not produced easily identifiable results, but institutional change is slow to occur and initial change may be difficult to perceive. It does appear clear that national and territorial boundaries provide obstacles not only to the movement of material and immaterial things, but also to notions of obligation and loyalty, so that the decline of boundaries should be followed by an expansion of transborder obligation.[45] The existence of regimes is an indication that this has already happened, in some measure. It cannot always be traced, however, to cosmopolitan theory.

Cosmopolitan theory exists in multiple forms, and efforts at taxonomy are already being undertaken. Strong cosmopolitanism is thus contrasted with weak

---

[43] Koskenniemi (2001), *Gentle Civilizer of Nations*, at 515 (vision of a single space of 'the international' replaced by more fragmented and detailed understanding of world).

[44] For an earlier assertion of the priority of practice, see Ch. 1, 'Readings of the State Tradition'; and more generally on such priority, Strayer (1970), *Medieval Origins of Modern State*, at 9; Krawietz (1993), 'Recht ohne Staat?', at 105 (primacy of practice of law, all theory built on previous practice); Rynhold (2005), *Two Models* (Priority of Practice (PofP) over Priority of Theory (PofT) in Jewish thought and law); Tully (1995), *Strange Multiplicity*, at 106 (understanding general term nothing more than 'practical activity of being able to use it', citing Wittgenstein), 119 (crown negotiators with aboriginals did not redescribe them in terms of 'armchair European theorists' but listened to them); Monahan (1994), *From Personal Duties*, at 53 (conciliarist movement 'paradigm of the notion that political theory develops in response to political realities'); Kantorowicz (1957), *King's Two Bodies*, at 301 (theory following practice in notion of continuity of state); Peirce (1958), *Selected Writings*, at 336 ('[u]nfortunately practice generally precedes theory, and it is the usual fate of mankind to get things done in some boggling way first, and find out afterwards how they could have done them much more easily and perfectly'); Jackson (1987), 'Quasi-states, dual regimes', at 520 (a constitutional tradition, citing Grotius, Burke, and Oakeshott, that theory by and large the child and not parent of practice, contrasting Machiavelli, Kant, and Marx); Jennings (1959), *Law and Constitution*, at 20 ('theory, as usual, followed upon fact'); Brierly (1963), *Law of Nations*, at 11 (notion of sovereignty lies in history of modern state, while theory followed 'in the wake of the facts'); and for a recent trenchant critique of 'ideal' theoretical writing, insisting on the need to constantly situate it 'within the rest of human life', Geuss (2008), *Philosophy and Real Politics*, at 7, 9 ('the way social, economic, political, etc., institutions actually operate in some society at some given time, and what really does move human beings to act in given circumstances . . . There are no interesting "eternal questions" of political philosophy'), 79 (qualifying Rawls's philosophy as 'nonrealist', criteria for choice as 'an assumption'). For a reciprocal relationship, however, Riesenberg (1970), *Inalienability of Sovereignty*, at 83 ('incipient fact forms theory which in turn acts back upon original reality'); and for an 'operative function' of theory of natural law in state construction, see Ch. 6, 'Common Laws beyond Europe' (citing Krieger).

[45] Kratochwil (1986), 'Of Systems, Boundaries, and Territoriality', at 27 (closure to universal moral claims); Nussbaum (1994), 'Patriotism and Cosmopolitanism', at para. III.4 (acceptance of 'morally arbitrary' state boundary prejudicial to argument to citizens that they should 'join hands' across barriers).

cosmopolitanism;[46] moral cosmopolitanism with legal or institutional cosmopolitanism.[47] It is the strong version of cosmopolitanism that has become the most visible, presenting the greatest contrast with the nation-state as a single *locus* of legal and moral obligations. Strong cosmopolitanism starts with the assumption that all human beings belong to a single, world community and that entitlements are therefore to be determined independently of nation and state membership.[48] It has antecedents in Greek and Christian universalism (antedating the contemporary state), reflected in present-day notions of a 'global civil society'.[49] It is highly critical of ongoing defences of closed, national societies. The political philosophy of John Rawls, stated explicitly to be that of a 'closed system isolated from other societies'[50] and even as 'self-contained and . . . having no relations with other societies',[51] is faulted not only for the basic premise,[52] but also for the lack of an 'egalitarian distributive component'.[53]

[46] Ratner (2011), 'Between minimum and optimum world public order', at 201 (strong as 'equal regard for all persons', weak as implying both general duties to world and special duties to family, compatriots); and for similar 'strict' as opposed to 'moderate' cosmopolitanism, Kleingeld and Brown (2006), 'Cosmopolitanism' ('thick' or 'thin' cosmopolitanism); Held (2005), 'Principles Cosmopolitan Order', at 16. For further gradations, Hollinger (2003), 'New Cosmopolitans', at 228 (vernacular, rooted, critical, comparative, national, discrepant, situated, and even, as an apparent concession, 'actually existing cosmopolitanism'); and see generally Caney (2006), *Justice Beyond Borders*, at 3–5, with references.

[47] Hayden (2005), *Cosmopolitan Global Politics*, at 3.

[48] Hayden (2005), *Cosmopolitan Global Politics*, at 1 ('focus on interests or welfare of persons wherever they may reside rather than on the interest of states'); Tan (2004), *Justice without Borders*, at 1 (liberals correspondingly giving up their right to border restrictions, and 'greater international redistribution of resources'); van Hooft (2007), 'Cosmopolitanism as Virtue', at 303 ('national borders and national sovereignty are irrelevant to the scope of its concerns'); Feldman (2007), 'Cosmopolitan Law?', at 1069–70 (for cosmopolitans, 'legal duty does not ultimately derive from the state'); Brock (2009), *Global Justice*, at 3 ('every person has global stature . . . no matter what her citizenship'); Fine (2007), *Cosmopolitanism*, at x ('human species . . . understood only if it is treated as a single subject' though 'forms of difference respected'); Frost (2009), *Global Ethics*, passim.

[49] Keane (2003), *Global Civil Society*, though at 8 global civil society cannot be found in 'pure form', an 'unfinished product'. For the intellectual history, Kleingeld and Brown (2006), 'Cosmopolitanism', listing Augustine, Cicero, the Cynics, Dante, Erasmus, Grotius; for enlightenment philosophy, Kleingeld (1999), 'Six Varieties of Cosmopolitanism'; and for tracing even to early classic period in Greece, tenth century BCE (Homer), Harris (1927), 'Greek Origins of Idea of Cosmopolitanism', at 2.

[50] Rawls (1971), *Theory of Justice*, at 8 ('[t]he significance of this special case is obvious and needs no explanation').

[51] Rawls (1993), *Political Liberalism*, at 12 ('a considerable abstraction . . . free from distracting details'). His subsequent *Law of Peoples* (1999) is only marginally different from existing 'internationality' and, since it remains state-centric, remains subject to the same criticisms. See, e.g., Buchanan (2000), 'Rawls's Law of Peoples', at 698 (Rawls's 'peoples' simply groups with their own states, need for 'principles that track individuals across borders'), 701 (Rawls depicting 'vanished Westphalian world').

[52] O'Neill (2000), *Bounds of Justice*, at 4 ('strangely silent about the predicaments of outsiders . . . harsh realities of exclusion'); Sen (1999), *Reason before Identity*, at 29 ('interpersonal sympathies . . . practical interactions across borders'), 30 ('conflicting demands arising from different identities . . . This calls for reasoning—not for a mechanical formula'); Twining (2003), 'Province of Jurisprudence Re-examined', at 30 ('untenable position . . . when no such isolated units exist'); Vertovec and Cohen (2003), *Conceiving Cosmopolitanism*, at 93 (assumption of 'idealized nation-state as the natural form of society').

[53] Pogge (1994), 'Egalitarian Law of Peoples', at 195, 198 ('enormous distributional significance' of national borders, e.g. being born in USA or Mexico); Brock (2009), *Global Justice*, at 46 (unconvincing reasons for 'excluding principles of socio-economic equality'); Beitz (2000), 'Rawls's Law of Peoples', at

Legally or institutionally, strong cosmopolitanism translates easily into notions of world or global government, an ancient idea that remains attractive, to some.[54] It is also evident in much contemporary discussion amongst lawyers who are preoccupied with the 'global', though not yet perhaps convinced of the need for global government. There is a rich and flourishing literature on 'transnational', 'international', 'world', 'global', and even 'postnational' constitutionalism, which foresees the movement of constitutionalism from the level of states or common laws to a global level.[55] There are hierarchical implications though some would reject them.[56] Others speak of 'world law'[57] or the need for a 'general theory of society and law which is potentially universal'[58] or of a 'global public law'.[59] Jeremy Waldron sees in what would be a contemporary revival of the Roman *ius gentium* a 'body of world law'.[60]

There are understandably, however, many critics of strong cosmopolitanism. The criticism is directed even towards Diogenes, famous for the phrase 'I am a citizen of the world (*kosmopolites*)'.[61] Critics see this not as a heroic and ringing statement of human universality, as strong cosmopolitanism would have it, but as an artful dodge to avoid the obligations of citizens of his own city Sinope.

---

689 (no suggestion in Rawls that existing distribution of resources unfair), 694 (no effective rebutting of 'cosmopolitan principle of international distributive justice').

[54] For 'resurgence' of the idea, Tinnevelt (2012), 'Federal world government', at 221 (though even restraining devices tend to 'hierarchical centralization'); Yuker (2011), *Idea of World Government*; Cabrera (2004), *Political Theory of Global Justice*, at 2 ('a democratic global government' with 'democratic supranational bodies' as interim measure), and 90ff. (for review of earlier proposals for world government, many world federation proposals 1946–50); Keane (2003), *Global Civil Society*, at 94 (for advocates of world government or 'Weltbürgervereinigung'; Kleingeld and Brown (2006), 'Cosmopolitanism' (citing A. Cloots 1755–94, for single world state, la 'république du genre humain'); Cheneval (2005), *La cité des peuples*, at 17 (necessity of 'positive and global structure of law'); Hayden (2005), *Cosmopolitan Global Politics*, at 3 (global structure as consequence of legal cosmopolitanism, grounded on 'the equal legal rights and duties of all individuals'); for world federalism, the World Federalist Movement at <http://www.wfm.org/site/index.php>; and for notions of global democracy, Archibugi (2008), *Global Commonwealth*; Held (1995), *Democracy and Global Order*; Holden (2000), *Global Democracy*.

[55] Tsagourias (2007), *Transnational Constitutionalism*; Krisch (2010), *Beyond Constitutionalism*; Somek (2009), 'Transnational Constitutional Law', notably at 244 ('a final outlet left for utopian hope'); Ackerman (1997), 'Rise of World Constitutionalism'; Peters (2009), 'Merits of Global Constitutionalism'; Dunoff and Trachtman (2009), *Ruling the World*; Teubner (2004), 'Societal Constitutionalism' (criticizing existing efforts for not generalizing traditional concept of constitution sufficiently); and for 'constitutionalisation' of the World Trade Organization, Di Fabio (1998), *Das Recht offener Staaten*, at 99.

[56] Teubner (2004), 'Societal Constitutionalism' at 7 ('constitutionalism without the state').

[57] Berman (1995), 'World Law', though at 1617 new name required; Berman (2005), 'Conflicts of Laws Passé?' at 43 (for 'universal bodies of law', and 'emerging common law of mankind'); and see Domingo (2010), *New Global Law*.

[58] Allott (2001), *Eunomia*, at xlviii ('a universalizing capitalist economy requires a universalizing of legal systems') and xxv ('a legal system of all legal systems').

[59] Garcia (2005), 'Globalization and Theory International Law', at 10.

[60] Waldron (2012), '*Partly Laws Common to All Mankind*', at 32, though for the limited character of the original, Glenn (2007c), *Common Laws*, at 4–5 (*ius gentium* simply variation of Roman law in face of foreign litigants, in absence of knowledge of foreign law).

[61] Diogenes (2005), *Lives of Eminent Philosophers*, Book VI, para. 63 at 65.

He was, after all, a Cynic,[62] and historically the cosmopolitan individual has had to contend with ongoing suspicion of 'rootlessness'. In *Emile* Rousseau warned of 'those cosmopolitans who search out remote duties in their books and neglect those that lie nearest' and in 1762 the *Dictionary* of the French Academy declared peremptorily that 'a cosmopolitan is not a good citizen'.[63] The failings of strong cosmopolitanism at the level of the individual would be matched by dangers at the institutional level. These have been pointed out for centuries, some indication of the perennity of the idea. Marsilius of Padua joined forces with his contemporary Dante in defence of emperor (and not pope) but would not follow the 'playfulness' of Dante's suggestion that there should be a 'supreme *princeps*'. Divinity rather favoured a plurality of princes, though depressingly for the reason that this would help control population growth through war and disease.[64] The contemporary of Marsilius and Dante, John of Paris, preferred the complexity of the real world as a reason for avoiding a global secular ruler, though the same argument did not prevail with respect to spiritual authority. It was inherently better to have several kingdoms than one 'comprising the whole world'.[65] Grounds for suspicion of the 'supreme *princeps*' have since become more precise. There would be incompatibility with the self-determination of peoples, violation of national sovereignty, and widespread fear of hegemonic behaviour.[66] They are the reasons for state-like communities, though their assertion is made against an

---

[62] Kleingeld and Brown (2006), 'Cosmopolitanism', s. 1.1 (refusing to agree to special service to Sinope); Kleingeld (2012), *Kant and Cosmopolitanism*, at 2 (Diogenese and Cynics with 'negative' view of cosmopolitanism, contrasted with Kant's positive view); MacCulloch (2009), *Christianity*, at 29–30 (Cynics those deliberately living 'like dogs', committing basic and obscene acts in public, contempt for local and conventional values); and for the historical ambiguity of the remark, Jones (2006), 'Cosmopolitanism', at 567 (expression of positive duty or denial of obligations). For Diogenes's expression as 'exclusive, not complementary', Höffe (2006), *Kant's Cosmopolitan Theory*, at 24; though for Diogenes taking up the nobler sentiment of Socrates, Harris (1927), 'Greek Origins of Idea of Cosmopolitanism', at 8 ('tradition of cosmopolitanism', founder of Cynics Antisthenes a follower of Socrates).

[63] Rousseau (1948), *Émile*, at 7; *Dictionnaire* (1762), 4th edn, under 'cosmopolite' ('[c]elui qui n'adopte point de patrie. *Un Cosmopolite n'est pas un bon cityoyen*') (emphasis in original). By the 5th edn (*Dictionnaire*, 1798), however, the wind had turned and the entry had become '[c]itoyen du monde. Il se dit de celui qui n'adopte point de patrie. *Un Cosmopolite regarde l'univers comme sa patrie*'.

[64] Garnett (2006), *Marsilius of Padua*, at 161 (though Dante and Marsilius 'much closer' than has been recognized); and for Dante, after putting forth a theory of universal rule, eventually having 'returned' to modified Gelasian position, Muldoon (1999), *Empire and Order*, at 87, 92 (for 'playfulness').

[65] Ullmann (1988), *Law and Jurisdiction*, at VII–16 (advice followed three centuries later by Bodin).

[66] Generally Caney (2006), *Justice Beyond Borders*, at 13–15, 46–9; Tully (1995), *Strange multiplicity*, at 186 (on the spread of constitutionalism with its 'policies of discontinuity and assimilation', accompanying 'ecological imperialism and destruction'); Miller (1998), 'Limits Cosmopolitan Justice', notably at 171 ('comparative principles of justice operate only within national boundaries'), 175 (rather than international tax regime a 'more dynamic approach that sought to create incentives for population stability and economic development') and 179 (nothing unjust about international inequalities in which independent political communities pursue the aims and purposes of their members, though weak cosmopolitanism must occupy itself with failure to provide basic rights and care); and for vigorous defence of national (US) sovereignty, Rabkin (2005), *Law Without Nations?*, notably Ch. 7 (for highly critical perspectives on international human rights and 'world law'). For the frightful prospect of a 'Cosmopolis', Zolo (1997), *Cosmopolis*, at 9 ('prolonged agony' of UN), 53 ('blind alleys' of international ethics), 152 ('global civil society' lacking all foundation, world government 'a despotic and totalitarian Leviathan'), 154 (rather need for 'intercultural communication').

opponent more wraith-like than real. Perhaps more significantly there is the notion that a single hegemon would represent a distinctly European phenomenon, the European notion of hierarchy writ large, which would provoke more resistance in the world than even the notion of the contemporary state. Less dramatically, but more realistically, a world government simply would not be feasible in the present state of the world. We have been witnessing fragmentation, not aggregation, of polities, while populations have been taught the virtues of this for centuries. It is teaching that would take centuries again to overcome.[67]

The world of cosmopolitanism theory, however, is more subtle than strong cosmopolitanism would suggest. There are more conciliatory versions of it, more cognizant of the value of local as well as universal values. Most notably, Stephen Toulmin has recalled that our concept of the cosmopolitan is not necessarily rooted in the language of Diogenes but in a larger and more ancient notion of the coming together and necessary harmony of the *kosmos* and the *polis*, and while the *kosmos* is vast there is room for many types or variations of a *polis*.[68] The states of recent centuries, however, in their quest for stability, would have lost sight of the underlying interdependence of the state and the sciences, even opening the way to 'pathological nationalism', the genie let out of the bottle.[69] An 'ecological perspective' would thus be required, one that emphasizes 'differentiation and diversity, equity and adaptability'.[70] This is some distance from universal ethics and global institutions and may therefore be seen as a kind of non-global, 'complex',[71] 'rooted',[72] or 'bottom-up' cosmopolitanism.[73] It has many adherents and deserves more recognition than that of its 'strong' and more visible version. Both political philosophers and lawyers have seen the necessity of it in current circumstances. It implies the definition of the word 'cosmopolitanism' in its ordinary usage, as used throughout this text, and not the more rarefied and exceptional sense of implying universal obligations or institutions.[74]

---

[67] Krawietz (1993), 'Recht ohne Staat?', at 91 (for absence of all imaginable conditions for world state); Feldman (2007), 'Cosmopolitan Law?', at 1029 (decline of world state idea since century ago, today 'almost unheard of in serious circles' notwithstanding 'Michigan Militia and their paranoid brethren'); Currie (1959), 'Notes on Methods' at 173 ('not by establishing a single government; even if such a thing were remotely thinkable as a practical possibility ... The attainment of uniformity of laws among diverse states is, to put it mildly, a long-range undertaking').

[68] Toulmin (1990), *Cosmopolis*, at 67 (recalling renaissance notion of right conduct as 'natural', contrasting Augustinian emphasis on human failure as justification for order).

[69] Toulmin (1990), *Cosmopolis*, at 185 (national 'systems' now unfruitful and dysfunctional), 195 ('anachronistic forms of unqualified sovereignty').

[70] Toulmin (1990), *Cosmopolis*, at 194 (contrasting 'Newtonian' view encouraging hierarchy and rigidity) and 183 (need for 'elbow room' to ensure 'diversity and adaptability').

[71] Feldman (2007), 'Cosmopolitan Law?', at 1032 (which would 'steer away' from the universalist cosmopolitanism).

[72] Appiah (2005), *Ethics of Identity*, at 213.

[73] Perju (2010), 'Cosmopolitanism and constitutional self-government', at 327.

[74] R. J. Evans thus writes of *Cosmopolitan Islanders* (2009) (on showing greater interest in histories of countries other than their own, though this in itself would not be incompatible with nationalist historiography); and see Jasanoff (2006), *Edge of Empire*, at 101 (on 'cosmopolitan Lucknow' of the 1780s); Kumm (2010), 'How does European Law Fit?', at 125 (for 'cosmopolitan constitutionalism').

Kwame Appiah thus writes of the necessity to develop *practices* of coexistence, conversation in the older sense of living together.[75] In Spain it was known as *convivencia*. For Appiah this necessity is based on the inevitability of 'more than one reasonable account of the facts', so that conversation will not yield consensus but 'helps people get used to one another'.[76] A similar preoccupation with diversity of substance inspires Robert Brandom to conclude, with respect to questions such as 'Who are we?' or 'What sort of thing are we?', that 'the answers can vary without competing',[77] leaving cosmopolitan space. For David Held cosmopolitanism is not 'an exercise in seeking a general and universal understanding' and its principles are 'about the conditions of just difference',[78] while in his more recent writing Jürgen Habermas has moved from a notion of world government to one simply of world policy.[79] Amartya Sen criticizes the 'transcendental institutionalism' of Rawls and urges more focus on actual societies.[80] Seyla Benhabib concludes that cosmopolitanism is a 'philosophical project of mediations' that 'is not equivalent to a global ethic'.[81] These are not universalist proposals, nor would they support a global government. They do not deal with law but cannot be faulted for this, since there is no hierarchical structure proposed that would require explicit legal concepts and structures.

Many lawyers have indicated interest in 'rooted' or 'complex' cosmopolitanism as opposed to strong cosmopolitanism and the 'global'. They perhaps cannot conceive of the legal notions that would be required for strong forms of institutional cosmopolitanism, and have commitments, moreover, to existing forms of human ordering, of whatever type or variety. For William Twining it would therefore be a question of developing 'an increasingly cosmopolitan discipline of law' and the adjective here is consistent with the ordinary usage of the word, short of any notion of (somehow enforceable) universal obligations.[82] Jeremy Waldron has written of the need, in order to understand cosmopolitanism, to

---

[75] Appiah (2006), *Cosmopolitanism*, at xix, 163 (cosmopolitanism that 'prizes a variety of political arrangements', global state would imply too much power, unresponsiveness to local needs), and 77 (for 'practices and not principles are what enable us to live together in peace').

[76] Appiah (2006), *Cosmopolitanism*, at 40 (positivism overstating power of reason in justification of belief) and 36–8 (on difficulty of arguing against witchcraft other than by invoking authority, not recognized by Asante believers in witchcraft).

[77] Brandom (1994), *Making it Explicit*, at 4 ('each kind of "we"-saying defines a different community, and we find ourselves in many communities').

[78] Held (2005), 'Principles Cosmopolitan Order', at 16 (does not deny a 'world of diverse values and identities'); and Held (2010), *Cosmopolitanism*, at 16 (while volume 'aims at being universal, it tries to address cultural and political specificity', a 'layered cosmopolitan approach').

[79] Habermas (2001), *Postnational Constellation*, at 104 ('world domestic policy without a world government'—'Weltinnenpolitik ohne Weltregierung').

[80] Sen (2009), *Idea of Justice*, at 5 (contrasting 'perfect justice' of Rawls), 263 (wishing 'good luck' to 'builders of a transcendentally just set of institutions for the whole world'), and 401 (for 'immaculate' identification of just society).

[81] Benhabib (2006), *Another Cosmopolitanism*, at 20 ('norms that ought to govern the relations among individuals in a global civil society').

[82] Twining (2007), 'General Jurisprudence', at 3 (a 'General Jurisprudence' as to which see his *General Jurisprudence* (2009)).

'look at the ordinary as well as the extraordinary, the tedious as well as the exciting, the commercial as well as the ideological'.[83] Michel Rosenfeld warns that the actors of globalization do not seek to operate in a legal vacuum and that some legal regime 'or a plurality of them' is an ongoing necessity, not a future project.[84] For Hans Lindahl legal regimes are inevitably ones of borders, though the permeability of such borders means that anything that is excluded is also, in some normative sense, included, and we presently lack such an integrating concept of a legal order.[85]

Immanuel Kant's notion of a *ius cosmopoliticum* is often taken as the point of departure for the development of some type of world law and Kant was very precise in stating that his proposal was not an ethical one but a legal ('rechtliches') one.[86] It was also included in a section of his *Metaphysic of Morals* (1797) entitled 'Legal Doctrine' ('Rechtslehre'). Kant relied on 'Natur' and the spherical shape of the world as necessitating human interaction but himself described his notion of a 'world citizens' law' ('Weltbürgerrecht', to which he added in parentheses the Latin *ius cosmopoliticum*), as 'limited'. It was limited to a subjective or personal right attaching to every person to mobility on the face of the earth, free from immediate rejection or hostility. It was a law of 'universal hospitality', or 'right to visit', in no way authorizing colonization or exploitation, however.[87] This law of hospitality was placed by Kant as a third section in his 'Legal Doctrine' on 'Public Law' and followed initial sections on 'Staatsrecht' or constitutional law and 'Völkerrecht' (which we now call public international law and which Kant saw as dealing largely with war). The law of hospitality thus occupied a unique place but is perhaps best understood as a distinct place for the law of peace, to which he had dedicated his volume on *Perpetual Peace* (1795) two years earlier. This latter argued for a loose grouping of states, a league of nations (our concept of federation is too strong, as even would be the notion of a confederation) and the law of universal hospitality was therefore the most vital ingredient of this form of mutual state recognition.[88]

As a limited right of mobility, to be voluntarily accepted by states, Kant's cosmopolitan law is remarkably modest.[89] There is no endorsement of global

---

[83] Waldron (2006), 'Cosmopolitan Norms', in Benhabib (2006), *Another Cosmopolitanism*, at 97.

[84] Rosenfeld (2008), 'Rethinking constitutional ordering', at 423 (would 'actually abhor' a legal vacuum).

[85] Lindahl (2010), 'A-Legality', at 55 (permeability of border meaning 'amenable to transformation'), recalling the impossibility of closure to external texture suggesting different forms of closure, as to which see Ch. 1, 'The State as Tradition'.

[86] Kant (1996), *Metaphysics of Morals*, para. 62 (translated by Gregor as 'having to do with rights').

[87] Kant (1996), *Metaphysics of Morals*, para. 62; and see Kant (2005), *Perpetual Peace*, Section II, Third Definitive Article ('to be treated without hostility' host may 'send him away again if this can be done without causing his death'). As a 'droit de visite', Teló (2005), *L'État et l'Europe*, at 58.

[88] Kant (2005), *Perpetual Peace*, Section II, Second Definitive Article; Petermann (2001), 'Kant, précurseur de la mondialisation', at 171; for 'league of nations', Kleingeld and Brown (2006), 'Cosmopolitanism' ('much weaker form of international order'); and generally Bohman and Lutz-Bachman (1997), *Perpetual Peace*.

[89] Eleftheriadis (2003), 'Cosmopolitan Law', at 244, ('something quite limited'), 245 ('without abolishing the distinction between citizens and non-citizens').

coercive authority or a world state and Kant has been seen as inspired by apprehension before any notion of a world authority.[90] The proposal is even more modest when placed in the context of the times, with few obstacles to travel other than physical ones and precise national borders only in the process of demarcation. There was debate about passport control in post-revolutionary France, but not much was to come of it and a passport as a condition of border-crossing only became generalized after the First World War.[91] Kant's proposal was thus of little current consequence and has been seen as simply an effort to overcome 'the exclusion of foreigners from the fold of moral respect'.[92] Similar arguments had been made by Vitoria in the sixteenth century (a *ius communicationis*, or *ius peregrinandi*) and its main effect was to justify Spanish exploration (though not domination or harm).[93] Kant's thinking, moreover, was squarely within emerging 'internationality' in its respect for states, which he qualified unhesitatingly as moral (in the sense of non-physical) persons.[94] Vattel had converted the *ius gentium* into a 'law of nations' just a few decades before and,[95] while it is possible to see Kant's cosmopolitan law in terms of a subjective right attaching to individuals and therefore filling the 'black hole' between the emerging 'international' order and national law,[96] it is also quite capable of formulation as a (state) duty of non-refoulement, a narrower and now treaty-based feature of refugee protection in international (not cosmopolitan) law. As with many internationalist perspectives, Kant thus thought in terms of a process of superposition of norms on the entities that were states. He thought in terms of hierarchies. The cosmopolitanism was not one that was 'rooted' or 'complex' but one that was elevated and universalist in perspective, though stopping short of

---

[90] Höffe (2006), *Kant's Cosmopolitan Theory*, at 194 ('arrogation' by world authority violative of state's right to self-determination); Jones (2006), 'Cosmopolitanism', at 569 (Kant, Rawls, theorists, seeing world state as either 'global despotism or the backdrop for unending civil wars'); Haakonssen (2006), 'German natural law', at 290 (no world state given impossibility of enforcement; 'cosmopolitan right must be voluntary'); Hayden (2005), *Cosmopolitan Global Politics*, at 21; though for Kant's league as a prelude to a 'state of states', even in his own thinking, Kleingeld (2004), 'Approaching Perpetual Peace', notably at 306 (for voluntary league even as 'decidedly unKantian move'); Kleingeld (2012), *Kant and Cosmopolitanism*, Ch. 2, notably at 46–7 (Kant's earlier 1780s writing advocating world state), 50–1 (league as *initiating* departure from state of nature); and Lutz-Bachmann (1997), 'Kant's Idea of Peace' at 60 (league 'inconsistent with Kant's own assumptions and therefore proves to be untenable').

[91] See Ch. 10, 'Citizenship and Mobility'.

[92] Muthu (2006), 'Justice and Foreigners', at 450 (at same time securing a 'space for nations and groups to pursue distinct ways of life').

[93] O'Donovan (2003), 'Christianity and Territorial Right', at 135 (living in 'consciously insulated' community defiance of 'the horizon of universal humanity'); Ruston (2004), *Human Rights*, at 91 ('so long as no harm is done to the inhabitants').

[94] Kant (1996), *Metaphysics of Morals*, para. 53; and as 'unquestionable entities', Simons (2003), 'Emergence of Idea of Individualized State', at 319 (though not final end of humanity's moral progress). For the long, previous, development of the idea, see Ch. 4, 'The state as body, crown, or corporate person'.

[95] See Ch. 8, 'Public international law'.

[96] For this optimistic reading, Walters (2004), 'Common Law Constitution and Legal Cosmopolitanism', at 441 ('where old *ius gentium* once was'). Yet the old *ius gentium* had content of significance, and potential application, where it was heeded. The word 'international', of course was still a century away, a creation of Bentham, as noted in Ch. 8, 'Internationality and Empire'.

precise obligations of significance. Its ambiguity has been the object of much comment.[97] If one moves out from a position of rooted cosmopolitanism, however, and from the position of the contemporary state, it may be possible to be more precise in terms of obligations. There will at least be a *locus* for the making of decisions with cosmopolitan dimensions. We are approaching the notion of a contemporary, cosmopolitan state.

THE STATE AND GLOBALIZATION

Theoretical discussion of both globalization and cosmopolitanism often depicts the state as coming to an end or becoming a simple agent of execution for larger authority.[98] The reality appears otherwise, as states continue to multiply and shrink in average size.[99] The future, therefore, might not lie in larger and competing institutions, or a single behemoth, but rather in (attempted) preservation of the existing level of states and development of more intense forms of webbing and interaction. A recent proposal for 'global justice' thus left a space for the state, described as 'special'.[100] There is also more and more use of metaphors of networks and webs, and discussion of 'information societies' and 'infostructures'.[101] In 1995 a report to the President of France stressed the importance of 'circulating information', for reasons of state.[102] This is how rooted or complex

[97] For Kant's position as 'extraordinarily unsettled, sometimes leading to inconsistencies even within a single passage', Pogge (2006), 'Kant's Theory of Justice', at 62.

[98] Ohmae (1995), *End of the Nation State*, notably at 79 ('these political aggregations no longer make compelling sense as discrete, meaningful units on an up-to-date map of economic activity'); Ghéhenno (1995), *End of the Nation-State*; Bartelson (2001), *Critique of the State*, at 1 ('widespread conviction that the sovereign state is unlikely to remain the main source of political authority in the future.... will eventually enjoy a fate similar to that of the tribe, the city republic and the empire'); Tierney (2004), *Constitutional Law and National Pluralism*, at 84 ('theoretical deconstructions of established notions of statal authority'); yet for persistence of previous forms of closure (here the contemporary state), see Ch. 3, 'Persistence of Elements of Closure'; and see Schmitter (1996), 'If Nation-State were to Wither Away', at 212 (for 'law of conservation of political energy', postulating that 'nothing ever disappears... until its replacement has already been discovered and is functioning effectively'); Genschel (2005), 'Globalization and transformation of tax state', at 67 (that ten to fifteen years ago fashionable to question survival of state, now many doubting whether globalization of any consequence).

[99] See Ch. 5, '*Fragmentation, failure, and violence*'; and see Shapiro and Brilmayer (1999), *Global Justice*, at 1 ('centrifugal forces at work').

[100] Risse (2012), *On Global Justice*, at 2 (though enquiry into state only from a 'global' perspective).

[101] For networks or 'réseaux', Ost and Van de Kerchove (2002), *De la pyramide au réseau?*; Sørensen (2006), 'Transformation of State', at 235 (state as 'polymorphous entity, diffused into complex networks'); Hamann and Ruiz Fabri (2008), 'Transnational networks and constitutionalism'; and as a 'finely spun web', Baldus (1997), 'Zur Relevanz des Souveränitätsproblems', at 388 (on 'dependent relations'); and generally Castells (2000), *Information Age*, 2nd edn, vol. I, *Rise of Network Society*, notably at 500 (networks as 'new social morphology of our societies'). For 'information society', Chevallier (1999), *L'État*, at 103 (state traversed by *flows* ('*flux*') of all types; and for 'infostructures', Koopmans (2003), *Courts*, at 254 ('legal infrastructure of the flows of information'). Chevallier also writes of the state no longer as 'arborescent tree' but as 'rhizome' (or horizontal root system): Chevallier (2004a), *L'État post-moderne*, at 74.

[102] Picq (1995b), *L'État en France*, at 30 (on a 'nation open to the world', for the promotion of national interests).

cosmopolitanism would have it.[103] It corresponds, moreover, with the view of the state as an epistemic community, one whose institutions and structures correspond to its underlying, normative base of information, while the sources of information are never closed. Though, in some instances, the state has been remarkably successful in controlling normative information, this control can never be definitive and final. This is ultimately why the state is cosmopolitan and why it is entirely capable of development of, or return to, cosmopolitan structures and practices that it has known in the past. But just as information cannot be definitively closed off or shut down, neither can it be destroyed once large-scale diffusion has taken place, so the normative justification of the state continues to exercise its attraction, even in the face of strong cosmopolitan theory. Thus the state will survive, in some considerable measure, and this may be confirmed if we examine the actual role of the state in the process of globalization. The state appears far from withering away, and the logic is not one of either having a state, or not. The state must, however, justify itself and its laws, as it has always had to do in the world.[104]

The contemporary state appears related to the phenomenon of globalization in three discernible ways. It is an agent of globalization; it is a beneficiary of globalization; and it adapts to the necessities of globalization. In all cases this must be related to the flow of normative information.

The state as agent of globalization

Private actors are often seen as the principal engines of globalization, whether in the form of corporations, trade associations, TANGOs (Transnational Advocacy NGOs), international administrative agencies, or indirectly through allegedly determinist forces of technology. All of these understandings, however, overlook the more fundamental role of the state in providing support for these more visible agencies of globalization. It has been seen as a 'globalizing state'.[105]

The state thus continues to support the development of technology that easily runs across borders. It subsidizes international television channels, provides rights of way for railways, and coordinates the use of air space.[106] Its territorially

---

[103] See notably O'Neill (2000), *Bounds of Justice*, at 202 (moral cosmopolitanism not pointing 'to a stateless world, but to forms of institutional cosmopolitanism in which further boundaries become porous in further ways'); Kumm (2009), 'Cosmopolitan Turn in Constitutionalism', at 314 ('the cosmopolitan paradigm of constitutionalism does not denigrate patriotic commitments to the nation and national self-government'); Benyekhlef (2008), *Une possible histoire de la norme*, at 643 (in cosmopolitan context, state simply loses its political and normative monopoly).

[104] For negative reaction to states, see Ch. 4, '*Codes*', Ch. 7, '*France and the world*'; and for states no longer 'ontologically privileged', Held (2009), 'Restructuring Global Governance', at 535, and 541 (no longer as 'sole centres of legitimate power'); O'Neill (2000), *Bounds of Justice*, at 6 (states as institutions 'whose justice can, and often should, be queried'). For decades passing in France, moreover, before the French Civil Code was accepted as the exclusive source of civil law by the Court of cassation, Carbonnier (1982), '*Usus hodiernus pandectarum*' at 109–10.

[105] Aman (1998), 'Globalizing State', notably at 850 (for globalization exerting a 'downward pull', providing incentives for local forms of authority, or decentralization of power).

[106] See generally Clough and Cole (1952), *Economic History of Europe*, at 391 (subsidizing industry, development of multiple transport networks, provision of financial services, encouraging production of raw materials, ensuring supply of labour).

based intellectual property regimes allow ongoing private development of still more advanced information technology. While a private corporation is responsible for the allocation of domain names on the internet, it is a US state corporation, created by a state according to the fiction theory of corporations rooted in received notions of Roman law.[107] The informational character of the subject becomes clearer when particular states withdraw their explicit or implicit support of transnational technology and take active measures to limit or control it. This is happening today as jurisdictions such as China, Saudi Arabia, and others seek to restrict internet access, with some (limited) success.[108] Elsewhere states have seen themselves as having no choice but to accede to the unrestricted information flow that they have helped create. They have been described as the 'conveyor belts' between the local and the global.[109] It has even become difficult to enforce state-created rights to copy.

The visibility of the state as an agent of globalization becomes more obvious when the state is actively involved in international collaboration. This is most evident for 'state-generated legal orders', which range from the European Union, NAFTA, and MERCOSUR[110] through the hundreds of international organizations and their accompanying regimes.[111] These would constitute a form of 'revised statism' in establishing extra-national sources of authority,[112] but they remain dependent on national states for both material support and fundamental legitimacy.[113] There is even explicit borrowing of the language of state legitimacy ('positive sovereignty'). The international law that applies to them is a law of state construction, nourished by various forms of state consent, and their internal, 'global' administrative law can be seen as a form of state delegation.[114] The language of 'global governance' is an indication of their importance, subtly

---

[107] See Ch. 4, *'The state as body, crown, or corporate person'*. ICANN, the Internet Corporation for Assigned Names and Numbers, is a non-profit corporation under California state law.

[108] *The Economist*, 28 June 2008, at 67 (for attempts to control blogging in China, Saudi Arabia, Malaysia, Egypt, and Singapore, with protest by Global Voice Online). For China's blocking and filtering technology, Lee and Liu (2012), 'Forbidden City Enclosed by Great Firewall' (outlining control facilitated by a centralized hardware infrastructure and limited number of state-licensed access providers); Zheng (2008), *Technological Empowerment*, a 57–63 (for complex administrative structure).

[109] Eberhard (2006), *Le droit au miroir des cultures*, at 142 ('courroies de transmission').

[110] For regional and priority trade agreements now numbering in the hundreds, most created since 1990, Duina (2006), *Social Construction Free Trade*, at 3 (sixty-eight Regional Trade Agreements to 1994, a further one hundred from 1995 to 2001); Estevadeordal and Suominen (2009), *Sovereign Remedy*, at 4 (over 200 Priority Trade Agreements registered with WTO by 2007, many more unregistered). All of these represented institutionalization of Rosecrance's notion of the 'trading state', one necessarily dependent on others for products it is incapable of producing itself: see this chapter, *'Hierarchy'*. The 'import substitution' economy is no more.

[111] For their growth, see this chapter, *'Hierarchy'*.

[112] Caney (2007), 'Cosmopolitanism, Democracy', at 52–6 (on increased power of international organizations).

[113] Singh (2005), *Questioning Globalization*, at 170 (transnational capital requiring state support and structuring), 174 (World Bank and IMF controlled by handful of states); Gelber (1997), *Sovereignty Through Independence*, at 231 (transnational organizations having national structures as the 'only legitimate and politically defensible bases of their own authority').

[114] See generally Anthony *et al*, *Global Administrative Law* (2011).

distinguishing itself from any actual or contemplated 'global government'.[115] There is also international collaboration bereft of structure, such as where Scandinavian countries enact (nationally) joint legislation. Short of positive or at least visible measures of collaboration the state may also contribute significantly to globalization by voluntary retreat from particular functions or activities. Trade is liberalized through not imposing duties or foreign investment controls and while historically this has entailed active measures of suspension,[116] today the retreat of the state in some domains may come about by simple inactivity or abstention. Doing nothing is always a policy option.

The state as beneficiary of globalization

States may benefit involuntarily from globalization, for example where technology is developed elsewhere, imported by private parties, and contributes greatly to the local economy. Since today globalization has become so extensive, however, there is a wide range of activities for which states must decide on their level of collaboration and cooperation. This transborder calculus is necessarily a cosmopolitan one, that of assessing the risks and benefits of participation (with the probable partners), compared with those of non-participation. States must necessarily increase their cosmopolitan cognitive capacity, itself dependent on information. Where international collaboration is the result, the benefits may flow directly from that participation or from the possibilities it generates for domestic reform.[117] In all cases states will be engaged in an evaluative process and the results of those evaluative processes are evident in ongoing exclusivity of state functions. There will always be some room for manoeuvre or even 'backlash'.[118] Notably, states have retained national control in matters of taxation,[119] security,[120] criminal

---

[115] Commission on Global Governance (1995), *Global Neighbourhood*, at 4 (governance as 'sum of many ways individuals and institutions, public and private, manage their common affairs').

[116] This may occur for state-building purposes, through abolition of what have come to be seen as 'internal' customs duties; see, for France and the UK, Clough and Cole (1952), *Economic History of Europe*, at 391.

[117] For national innovation through international cooperation, Beck and Lau (2004), *Entgrenzung*, at 392; and intended domestic reform through the manner and form of implementing transnational norms, Di Fabio (1998), *Das Recht offener Staaten*, at 82 (even though action not autonomous); Gelber (1997), *Sovereignty Through Independence*, passim (for international industrial and technology policy pursued for national purposes).

[118] Beck and Lau (2004), *Entgrenzung*, at 388, for negotiating potential ('Handlungskapazitate') and 390, for adjustment space ('Anpassungsreserven'); Friedman (1996), 'Borders', at 89 (backlash in attempting to create new borders, impassable frontiers, legal fortresses).

[119] Genschel (2005), 'Globalization and transformation of tax state', at 53 (globalization not visibly undermining tax revenue, no perceptible drop in tax levels of OECD countries) and 68 (no substitute for the state as taxing unit, in EU Euro-tax a 'non-starter'); and see Osterhammel and Petersson (2005), *Globalization*, at 148 (no western country has succeeded in drastically reducing portion of national income administered and distributed by state); Singh (2005), *Questioning Globalization*, at 168 (for state spending not declining, even increasing, in 'most highly integrated countries').

[120] Sørensen (2004), *Transformation of the State*, at 109 (military and security issues); Zürn and Leibfried (2005), 'Reconfiguring national constellation', at 18 (though measures of international coordination, 'national sovereignty' not in question), 19 (territorial state 'relatively intact' with respect to use of force); Cooper (2005), *Breaking of Nations*, at 50 ('postmodern state' defining itself by security policy and risking 'transparency rather than armed force').

law,[121] and private, civil law,[122] to say nothing of democratic institutions.[123] Peter Saladin asks 'Why Still Have States?' and provides an even longer list.[124] The state would thus remain the 'unit of effective political organization' and would never have been 'so salient' in the organization of political life.[125]

Given residual state authority the argument is made that poverty results from bad choices, including the choice to prejudice human capabilities by failing to educate.[126] Thus globalization itself would not involve exploitation of particular countries of the world, but rather their abandonment by those making different choices.[127] If sufficiently cosmopolitan, however, state actors would be those most capable of acting beneficially, given the opportunities of globalization.

The adaptive state

The state that has been perceived as territorially and nationally closed, but that discovers both the necessity and benefits of globalization, and that it can be an active agent in the process, is necessarily an adaptive state. It will adapt its activities, which have been examined briefly in the discussion immediately above and which will be returned to in subsequent chapters below, but it will also adapt its self-conception and structures.

In Germany the expression an 'open state' has become current.[128] The doctrinal shift is largely a result of adherence to the European Union, but is symptomatic of a broader openness to the extra-national. Yet the notion of an 'open' state,

---

[121] Di Fabio (1998), *Das Recht offener Staaten*, at 91 ('a true Leviathan') and 92 (though 'defensive and bordered').

[122] Laporta (2005), 'Globalization and Rule of Law', at 127 ('*Meum* and *Tuum*').

[123] Cooper (2005), *Breaking of Nations*, at 32 ('firmly wedded to the territorial state', reason why 'traditional states' will remain fundamental unit of international relations).

[124] Saladin (1995), *Wozu noch Staaten?* (environment, currency, traffic and energy, space planning, health, technical development, social security, economic promotion, integration).

[125] Yeatman (2004), 'Idea of the constitutional state', at 84, 87 (as result of 'global society'); Ikenberry (2003), 'What States Can Do Now', at 351 ('no rival political formations' with 'full multidimensional capacities of state').

[126] Sen (2000), *Development as Freedom*.

[127] For this argument, Cohen (2006), *Globalization and Its Enemies*, notably at 2, 5, 35–6 (colonial powers all experiencing slower economic growth than non-colonial powers, though argument expressed in terms of exploitation of countries and not in terms of exploitation of individuals).

[128] Di Fabio (1998), *Das Recht offener Staaten*, at 2 (passage to a world of globalized economy and cosmopolitan elites removes from the territorial nation-state the base ('Boden') of its existence, territorial closure—'territoriale Abgeschlossenheit'), 5 (from territorially closed state to state that is only territorially 'located'—'radizierten'); Hobe (1998), *Der offene Verfassungsstaat*, notably Part I (for nineteenth- and twentieth-century 'Staatslehre' falling behind actual level of international cooperation, though at 58 exceptions of von Stein, Bluntschli), Part III on areas of international cooperation; Ladeur (2004b), 'Globalization and Public Governance', at 15 ('a political form in its own right'); Wahl, (2003), 'Der offene Staat', at 1147 (on openness rooted in Art. 24 of the German Constitution authorizing transfer of sovereignty to international and regional authorities), 1148–9 (comparable other texts in Europe, absence in USA, Russia, China). The language of openness is used in Germany as a specific contrast to notions of formal closure in the nineteenth century; see Krüger (1966), *Allgemeine Staatslehre*, at 87 ('*territorium clausum*'), though Hobe is explicit that there are different 'levels of intensity' of national opening: Hobe (1998), *Der offene Verfassungsstaat*, at 179.

though capturing a fundamental shift, appears to overstate what is happening. The open dike is one that provides no defences; the open door is open to all. So the idea of a cosmopolitan state allows for a more discriminating attitude at points of inevitable contact. The cosmopolitan state may *in principle* be open, or *in principle* be closed, and both formulations permit ongoing measures of collaboration, though inevitably in different measure. Cosmopolitan use of information must be adopted in deciding on that measure.[129]

There is also expert opinion on the 'transformation' that the state would now be undergoing, towards a greater degree of openness.[130] Here again some nuance appears appropriate, in two related ways. First, it is very unclear exactly how 'the state' is transforming, given its complexity and the multiplicity of its relations. There can thus be no simple overall view of the state 'winning' or 'losing' since different changes are taking place in different areas of state activity. The notion of transformation does not tell us a great deal about the exact type of change.[131] We are simply better informed in an institutional sense than when dealing with the abstract concept of strong cosmopolitanism and must be aware of precise forms of institutional variation. Washington would be a 'decentralized town'.[132]

It is also necessary to add nuance to the notion of 'transformation' by recalling that the state exists in a remarkable variety of forms, and that in some instances it has even become evanescent. 'The' state is not moving from one form to another. Many different states are adjusting in their own manner and form to current circumstances, and they are doing so in ways that are 'Traditionskonform'.[133] Some states have been and remain remarkably closed; others have been and remain remarkably porous. The middle range between them is very large; what is constant is the necessity to respond to the circumstances of globalization.

The need to adjust state activities, however, generates a need for adjustment of state structures. Here the major phenomenon appears to be that which Anne-Marie Slaughter describes as 'disaggregation' of the state or 'transgovernmentalism'.[134] Foreign relations are no longer the exclusive preserve of ministries or

---

[129] Compare Ghéhenno's emphasis on the number of points of opening or articulation: Ghéhenno (1995), *End of the Nation-State*, at 73. The notion of an 'open system' is also an overstatement, since a conceptual system can retain its integrity only if it engages in controlled measures of openness.

[130] Chevallier (2004a), *L'État post-moderne*, at 9 (using 'transformation'); Sørensen (2006), 'Transformation of State', at 191 (contrasting 'transformation' view with those of a retreat of the state or a 'state-centric' view); and see the 'sociological view of the state': Di Fabio (1998), *Das Recht offener Staaten*, at 112 (losing its unity, can no longer be understood simply as legal person, need for new juridical perspective); Poggi (1990), *The State*, at 183 (state becoming more complex, no longer strictly controlled by the centre).

[131] Sørensen (2004), *Transformation of the State*, at 6 ('state transformation' as 'open analytical position'), 191 (both retreat and strengthening according to the area); Zürn and Leibfried (2005), 'Reconfiguring the national constellation', at 17 (not a single transformation but 'a plurality of divergent changes . . . transformations in the plural'); Weiss (1998), *Myth of the Powerless State*, at 4 (difficult to speak of state capacity in general, must ask, capacity for what).

[132] Gotlieb (2006), *Washington Diaries*, at 132 ('in this decentralized town, no one seems to know where the authority really lies').

[133] Di Fabio (1998), *Das Recht offener Staaten*, at 35.

[134] Slaughter (2004), *New World Order*, at 12ff. (on 'the disaggregated state') and 41 (on 'transgovernmentalism'); and see in the last century Keohane and Nye (1989), *Power and Interdependence*, at 24 (for 'complex interdependence', multiple channels 'transgovernmental' and not simply interstate).

departments of foreign relations. Disaggregation means the taking up of foreign relations by essentially all levels of government, a process of 'reaching out' by both ministries and independent regulators to their foreign and international counterparts, developing networks of information, enforcement, and harmonization.[135] Even judges are talking to one another.[136] This would be a process taking place below the radar of international law, traditionally defined, but none the less real for that. It could undertake many of the functions of a world government, if adequately developed. It is, of course, not a new phenomenon, and we have already seen how ministries of foreign affairs were late-comers in state development, with cross-border relations traditionally left to those most concerned by them.[137] 'Internationality' put a stop to this, but the decline of 'internationality' is opening up old channels of communication. Government officials become generally more cosmopolitan in outlook. The 'foreign' is not an exclusive preserve; it inevitably becomes less foreign. While the notion of 'transgovernmentalism' has been most visible in US academic writing it is also well represented in French legal thought. Tourard speaks of 'internationalisation' that is accompanied by 'informalisme', to the benefit of executive authorities of government and resulting in an extension of the power to bind the state externally.[138] Chevallier finds the state losing its 'organic unity', its administrative authorities both diversifying and developing their autonomy. The USA and France appear even to be world leaders in the appreciation and development of this form of administrative cosmopolitanism.[139]

Globalization extends beyond trade and information, however. It extends also to people. The concept of citizenship is also in question.

---

[135] Slaughter (2004), *New World Order*, at 62, and see at 145 (for a corresponding process of international organizations aiming to 'harness' the coercive power of national officials) and 266 (for notion of 'disaggregated sovereignty').

[136] See Ch. 11, 'The Cosmopolitan Turn in Constitutional Sources'.

[137] See Ch. 8, 'Internationality and Empire'; and for Jean Monnet deliberately keeping foreign ministries ('with their natural interest in the sanctity of borders and the preservation of sovereignty') away from the creation of the European Communities, Cooper (2005), *Breaking of Nations*, at 142.

[138] Tourard (2000), *L'internationalisation*, at 100 (for 'diffusion horizontale'), 164 (power distributed amongst different authorities).

[139] For explicit recognition also in Germany, Di Fabio (1998), *Das Recht offener Staaten*, at 94 (loss of coherence of state), 105 (horizontal contacts of executive, decline of parliamentary importance).

10

Cosmopolitan Citizens

Throughout the nineteenth and twentieth centuries major efforts were made to bring about the closure of each contemporary state around a particular nation. Given the fluidity of the idea of a nation, however, they were accompanied by more formal and positive efforts to institutionalize the connection between people and the territorial state, through the notion of citizenship. This already tells us something about the inoperative or impossible notion of a nation, which would require this type of 'final cement' of national belonging. The closure around a single nation was unsuccessful, given the inexorable diversity of populations.[1] The notion of citizenship has survived, however, and many people of the world today define their identity, at least in some measure, in terms of their formal citizenship. Yet there are ongoing questions as to its nature, and these questions ultimately have their source in the underlying ambiguity of the idea of a nation. How is citizenship to be defined? Can it be unequivocal in character, over time, or will it be marked by the underlying cosmopolitanism of the population to which it applies?

CITIZENSHIP OVER TIME

In the circumstances of the eighteenth century it was impossible to define citizenship in terms of the main characteristics of alleged nations. Language boundaries did not coincide with those of the territorial state; religions were diversifying themselves within state territory; descent was a personal and not territorial connection. None of these criteria could provide by itself a unified population base in a given state territory. Some form of connection of people to state was essential, however, even if thinner than language, religion, or descent. The notion of citizenship therefore had to be invented, or perhaps reinvented, as an indication of loyalty to a territory. This modern notion of citizenship was appropriate for a state territorially defined but it presents two major deficiencies. The first is that it has no inherent, historically justified, content. Content had to be provided by legislation, so we see clearly in relation to citizenship the fundamental information base of all forms of human identity. The citizens of a state are perhaps most clearly of all an epistemic community. There is no *inherent* citizenship; it is stipulated by national legislators for each state.[2] Just as each state

---

[1] See Ch. 5.

[2] See Spiro (2008), *Citizenship*, at 7 (citizenship 'historically contingent institution', a modern phenomenon 'not inherent to social existence').

is different from every other state, moreover, so each national definition of citizenship differs from every other definition of citizenship. Bellamy tells us that 'different national traditions of citizenship emerge from the interactions between ... various factors', just as the structure of each state is dependent on the interaction of common laws and local circumstance.[3] Citizenship thus emerges, in general terms, as a 'mechanism for allocating persons to states',[4] a *status* that is formal and unsentimental, in German 'Staatsangehörigkeit' (belonging to the state).[5] Any *sentiment* of belonging has to be developed by other means.

The second deficiency of citizenship is that it could only function as an *additional* status or criterion of membership in a community. No national legislator could abolish linguistic or religious communities, for example, so the sense of belonging to a state had to be fashioned alongside, and not in place of, other senses of belonging. The logic of territoriality would even contradict the 'communal construction' of the social, so while citizenship would be egalitarian and liberal in character (at least within a state) it could not by simple enactment overcome the communally constructed.[6] Equality of citizens yes, but much remained to be said on the place, priority, and entitlements of citizenship, as opposed to other loyalties, and this most obviously in jurisdictions in which the contemporary state has not been an entirely indigenous production.

Contemporary states did look to historical precedent in fashioning their laws of citizenship, or even 'nationality'. Given a certain form of democracy in ancient Greece the Greek notion of citizenship (*politeia*) was an obvious model. Aristotle held an expansionist view of citizenship, moreover, identifying it in large measure with active participation in political life.[7] This was understandable, since the ancient Greeks had other forms of human grouping and the Greek model of democracy had to make its way amongst them. It *was* participation for civic purposes, beyond earlier groupings. 'Citizenship is civic' and the civic notion of the association was what distinguished the Greek city-states, in their view, from the 'barbarians'.[8] Aristotle's participation, however, was based on a prior status

---

[3] Bellamy (2004), 'Making of Modern Citizenship', at 3 (listing notably structure of state, its political regime, tensions between centre and periphery, available legal and political languages for expression of demands of different groups) and 15 (many of differences antedate era of mass politics and 'even the nation-state', reflecting church–state relations, arrival of industrialization, growth of monarchies).

[4] Brubaker (1992), *Citizenship and Nationhood*, at 31.

[5] Joppke (2010), *Citizenship and Immigration*, at 17 (this 'nothing new to the lawyer' though contrasting with participatory views of sociologists, notably those of T. H. Marshall (1950) in his *Citizenship and Social Class*).

[6] Badie (2000), *The Imported State*, at 58 (citizenship 'ambiguous or debateable' in the face of membership in tribe, clan, or extended family); and for citizenship as 'monocontextual citizen concept' (monokontexturalen Bürgerbegriff') opposed to 'polycontextual tradition' (polykontexturale Tradition), Di Fabio (1998), *Das Recht offener Staaten*, at 135.

[7] Aristotle (2008b), *Politics*, Bk. III, Ch. 1, s. 6 (person sharing in administration of justice and holding of office).

[8] Joppke (2010), *Citizenship and Immigration*, at 7 (also allowing aliens to become associates); and for the 'barbarians', Jones (1977), *Law of Greeks*, at 53.

and his insistence on democratic participation camouflaged to a considerable degree the limited or restrictive nature of this status. It passed by descent, but in Athens in the fourth century BCE there were 21,000 citizens, 10,000 *metics* (foreign residents), and 400,000 slaves.[9] Women who had Greek citizenship did not vote and there is debate as to their status as citizens.[10] Aristotle's definition of citizenship was meristic (from the Greek *meros*, or part), since a part of the phenomenon (here participation) was taken as the whole while the rest was abandoned or ignored.

The Aristotelian idea of citizenship as participation is one that remains alive today since it is essential to a functioning democracy. Citizenship is spoken of as a 'desirable *activity*' and distinctions are made between 'thick' and 'thin' or 'active' and 'passive' forms of citizenship.[11] This is all to the good, though the hortatory notion of active citizenship speaks to political participation rather than to the underlying legal notion of status. The latter came rather brutally to the fore with the Romans (whose *civitas* has given us the modern word), not themselves convinced of the virtues of democracy but very committed to the idea of membership in empire. By 212 CE citizenship was extended to all those living under Roman rule, eliminating earlier distinctions between *cives* and *peregrini* in the provinces.[12] Distinctions thereafter would be drawn only on the basis of class and wealth (and they remained plentiful).[13] This Roman notion of the status of citizenship, unencumbered by notions of democratic participation,[14] was that which would be taken over by the monarchies and then by the contemporary states of Europe. It was a very slow process, linked closely to the development of territorial states and to the slow articulation of how citizenship could possibly be defined.

---

[9] Sealey (1987), *Athenian Republic*, at 6; and for 'millennia-long practice' of forbidding many members of society from equal participation, Román (2010), *Citizenship and its exclusions*, at x (while seeming 'to extol the virtues of equality'), 8 ('gradations' of citizenship) and 11 ('vast majority' of literature on subject 'focusses on the more appealing, inclusive component of the construct').

[10] Sealey (1987), *Athenian Republic*, at 9, 22, 23, 30; MacDowell (1978), *Law in Classical Athens*, at 67 ('Athenian women'); Hunter and. Edmondson (2000), *Law & Status in Classical Athens*, at 66, note 45 and 14, note 6 ('[b]ecause women lacked direct political rights, scholars generally deny the title "citizen" to the female relatives of Athenian male citizens . . . The Athenians disagreed . . .' (with references)).

[11] Kymlicka and Norman (1995), 'Return of the Citizen', at 284–5 (for desirable activity (emphasis added), and notion of 'thick' and 'thin' citizenship); Pocock (1995), 'The Ideal of Citizenship', at 29 (for active and passive), though speaking at 29 of citizen as 'member' of *polis* and at 34 of citizens as 'persons acting on one another'. For citizenship as 'full participation' in or 'effective enjoyment' of a society, Woehrling (1999), 'Droits et libertés', at 271–2; and for the history of the idea, Magnette (2005), *Citizenship*, at 182 (for essential structure of citizenship found nevertheless in notions of exclusion and legality). Cf. Gardner (1997), *Citizenship*, at 9 ('active' citizen does not exist in English law).

[12] Whittaker (2004), *Rome and its Frontiers*, at 206 (Constitutio Antoniniana of 212 only formal recognition of long process of diminishing concept of citizen); Román (2010), *Citizenship and its exclusions*, at 23 (though only to 'free peregrine').

[13] Whittaker (2004), *Rome and its Frontiers*, at 207 (Roman Empire of fourth century 'reverse image' of nation-state of nineteenth century, though 'sharper distinctions' of class and wealth); Román (2010), *Citizenship and its exclusions*, at 23 (for those lacking property, different classes).

[14] For citizenship becoming a 'legal status' under the Romans, compared to the Greek 'political term', Pocock (1995), 'Ideal of citizenship', at 36.

The necessity of some modern form of citizenship became clearer with the slow emergence of the territorially bounded, hierarchically organized, contemporary state. In the sixteenth century Bodin wrote of the 'franc sujet', the free subject, and the expression is indicative both of the exclusionary nature of the status and its feudal and personal nature.[15] In 1608 in England *Calvin's Case* decided that a Scot born in Scotland after James VI of Scotland became James I of England in 1603 was a subject of the English crown and therefore entitled to succeed to real property in England.[16] The underlying notion was feudal: the crown subject was the person born in a territory subject to the crown's authority.[17] These narrow and personal links of allegiance had no wider spatial dimension; they clearly could not exclude other loyalties and other laws. Bodin did see clearly, however, the need for conceiving of the population as composed of individuals if the law of his sovereign was to be effective. His view of society was 'atomistic'.[18] A century later Hobbes too saw the necessity of placing the 'subject' under the sovereign's exclusive law, in the face of the anarchy otherwise perceived.[19] Pufendorf followed, citizenship for him including the prerogatives of the members of the commonwealth.[20] The necessity of a notion of citizenship was thus becoming evident in the circumstances of the contemporary state. The key conceptual development would then have been recognition that the *definition* of citizenship fell within the domain of political and legal authority; the emerging state was capable of bringing about the closure of its own population.[21] We have seen that this involved the sleight of hand that 'the people' could form the state,[22] and now it could provide an ongoing definition of who that people was. The challenge of definition then had to be met.

---

[15] Bodin (1986), *Six Livres*, Bk. I, at 112 ('holding from the sovereignty of another').

[16] (1609) 7 Co. Rep. 1a, 77 ER 377.

[17] McPherson (2007), *Reception of English Law Abroad*, at 181 ('nationality' as 'status of being a subject of the king', depending on birth in a place under king's dominion); Smith (1997), *Civic Ideals*, at 41 (re-emphasizing older feudal conceptions of status and obligation, rejecting sixteenth-century currents toward more territorially and ethnically defined sense of nationality); Hulsebosch (2005), *Constituting Empire*, at 22–5 (emphasizing personal nature of allegiance, to person of crown as opposed to head of political unit, though created naturally on birth in crown territory); Spiro (2008), *Citizenship*, at 11 ('subject, but not a citizen' since no rights against the crown); Bellamy (2004), 'Making of Modern Citizenship', at 14 (on 'subjecthood' short of full rights of citizenship).

[18] Magnette (2005), *Citizenship*, at 62, 65 (rejecting organistic conception of society, contributing to notion of individual rights).

[19] For this view of Hobbes and citizenship, Magnette (2005), *Citizenship*, at 75.

[20] Pufendorf (2005), *Law of Nature and Nations*, I.1.xx ('all Acts peculiar to the Members of that City'); Magnette (2005), *Citizenship*, at 77 (though women and slaves not citizens).

[21] Picq (2005), *Histoire et droit des États*, at 270 (from simple statement of being 'franc sujet' to generalized decision making on conditions of nationality).

[22] See Ch. 7, 'The United States of America' and 'France and the world'; and for US citizenship being created by necessary implication with the Declaration of Independence in 1776, Blackman (2010), 'Original Citizenship', at 98, 112 (though no definition of its content). For contemporary challenge to this possibility, however, Lindahl (2011), 'Recognition as Domination', notably at 208 ('reciprocity as deliberation between *citizens* presupposes a closure that by definition cannot itself be the outcome of reciprocal deliberation between citizens').

Of contemporary states France was the theoretical leader in attempting to define its citizens. Prior to the French revolution there was no legislative definition of citizenship and subjects were determined where it was necessary to do so, in a large and casuistic case law dealing mostly with succession to land in France, from which non-subjects were precluded by royal powers of escheat (the 'droit d'au-bain'). Having the 'qualité de Français' depended over time and cases on various combinations of birth in France, a parent or parents recognized as French subjects, and having residence on French soil. Residence in France was seen as paramount, often complemented by circumstances of birth given the absence of controls on entry onto the territory.[23] Being French meant largely not being subject to the disabilities attached to those determined to be foreign, requiring judicial determination in all cases.[24] There was naturalization, but this was dependent on previous determination of status and did not yield the full status of a 'natural' French person.[25] The most dramatic effect of the French revolution was to give effect to Bodin's idea of a sovereign commonwealth and its subjects, with no distinctions to be drawn amongst them. Jews became citizens like all others and for the first years after the Revolution everyone living in France was automatically taken to be a French citizen.[26] Then the inevitable doubt and complexity set in. French revolutionary thought was liberal in the classical sense and citizenship should therefore be largely a matter of individual autonomy and consent. Yet this was difficult to implement given the necessity of a citizenship ascribed from birth, and there were also strong national or communitarian concerns, emphasizing the need for a homogeneous citizenry.[27] Simple residence would not do. Was the criterion to be birth on the territory (the *ius soli*) or descent from existing citizens (*ius sanguinis*)? The French Civil Code of 1804 opted for the latter, nationality being attributed by fatherhood and accorded at birth.[28] By the end of the century, however, the wind had changed and the *ius soli* had increased in importance.[29] Neither of these principles was seen, however, as free-standing and autonomous; complementary and exceptional criteria were inevitable. Nationality became 'an object fraught with contradictory representations, beliefs and stereotypes'.[30]

---

[23] Weil (2008), *How to Be French*, at 11–12 (with shifting sixteenth-century case law); Wells (1995), *Law and Citizenship Early Modern France*, at 33 (and underlying notion of choice), 36 (though various reliance on both *ius soli* and *ius sanguinis*), 103 (even 'triumph' of *ius sanguinis* in mid-seventeenth century).

[24] Sahlins (2004), *Unnaturally French*, at 1 (neither ethnicity, nor language, nor national identity capable of providing justification for membership), 5 (status determined 'tacitly, in a singularly unmarked fashion' and principally 'by what they were capable of doing').

[25] Sahlins (2004), *Unnaturally French*, at ix (both foreigners and 'naturalized foreigners' standing opposed to 'naturals').

[26] Weil (2008), *How to Be French*, at 4, 13 (also for serfs, Protestants, slaves).

[27] Laborde (2004), 'Republican Citizenship', at 46 (for ensuing 'tension' in debate, 'theoretical impasse').

[28] Batiffol and Lagarde (1981–3), *Droit international privé*, vol. I, at 86 (eliminating *ius soli* 'almost completely'); Weil (2008), *How to Be French*, at 4, 21 (and nationality not lost on residence abroad).

[29] Batiffol and Lagarde (1981–3), *Droit international privé*, vol. I, at 87 (increasing number of French citizens, notably from families founded in France by foreigners).

[30] Weil (2008), *How to Be French*, at 1 (notably on political divisions, *ius soli* defended by 'left', *ius sanguinis* by 'right'); and see Laborde (2004), 'Republican Citizenship', at 52 (even advocates of *ius soli* not accepting it as sufficient, 'socialization' and residence also 'mattered').

In contrast to the French revolution, that of the USA did not bring about radical and egalitarian change in understanding of the new citizenry. Smith surmises that the great aim of a 'more perfect Union' compelled silence or ambiguity on crucial issues of definition, and the written Constitution scarcely mentioned citizenship or nationality.[31] Citizenship itself would not have escaped the clutches of earlier group understandings, those of race, ethnicity, gender, and religion.[32] It was not until the second half of the the nineteenth century that the Fourteenth Amendment to the US Constitution overcame US case law excluding blacks from citizenship, establishing the *ius soli* as an operative and even constitutional principle, for everyone.[33] It was not, however, an autonomous and exclusive principle and was complemented by birth citizenship based on parentage where birth occurred outside US territory, though subject to further exceptions and conditions.[34]

Most see the USA as adhering to a common law principle of the *ius soli*, though it is much tempered and very complex in operation. England too has historically been seen as adhering to what would be a territorial common law principle, though the feudal territoriality of *Calvin's Case* has been much affected by legislation, gradually becoming subject to many exceptions.[35] Notably, a move towards citizenship by parentage or descent has been identified as early as 1350.[36] There have been important contemporary developments.[37]

The visibility of a *ius soli* principle in France, the USA, England, and many Commonwealth countries is often contrasted with a more anchored *ius sanguinis* principle in continental countries such as Germany or Austria. Here again, however, nuances are essential. If Germany originally followed the nineteenth-century French *ius sanguinis* model it did so in continuation of a primacy of

---

[31] Smith (1997), *Civic Ideals*, at 115 (though mentioned as requirement for federal office, in defining congressional power over naturalization, and in fixing jurisdiction of federal courts), 139, 153 (for ongoing political controversy on definition).

[32] Smith (1997), *Civic Ideals*, at 1–2 ('a white nation, a Protestant nation . . . native born men with Anglo-Saxon ancestry'), 75 (yet an 'asylum nation'); Smith (2009), 'Beyond Sovereignty and Uniformity', at 912 (through nineteenth century no belief in identical bundle of rights for all citizens); Magnette (2005), *Citizenship*, at 86 (Locke, Spinoza also excluding women and 'servants' from citizenship).

[33] See notably *Dred Scott* v. *Sandford*, 60 US 393 (1857); and for the US Supreme Court's adoption of 'differentiated levels of membership' in the USA, Román (2010), *Citizenship and its exclusions*, at 94–5 (until 1922); Spiro (2008), *Citizenship*, at 9 (controversy not centred on citizenship but on race). The Fourteenth Amendment provides in its first sentence that '[a]ll persons born or naturalized in the United States, and subject to the jurisdiction thereof, are citizens of the United States and of the State wherein they reside'.

[34] Notably that one of the parents must have some period of previous residence (varied by legislation) in the USA: Spiro (2008), *Citizenship*, at 10 (where US citizen 'temporarily abroad').

[35] Harris (2004), 'Nationality, Rights and Virtue', at 76 (listing naturalization, private bills, children of British subjects born overseas, former British subjects owning property in Britain but in USA).

[36] McPherson (2007), *Reception of English Law Abroad*, at 182 (statute *De Natis*, making children born abroad of English mothers or fathers able to inherit in England); Kim (2000), *Aliens Medieval Law*, Ch. 5 (for fifteenth-century English courts protecting those born 'overseas' from proprietary disputes).

[37] See this chapter, 'Citizenship and Mobility'.

descent that prevailed prior to the emergence of the territorial German state, in the 'Kleinstaaterei' of the times. There were *ius soli*-type exceptions.[38] Germany became a state, moreover, in 1871, at the height of notions of nations and nationalities, so some preponderance of the idea was to be expected.[39] It would be inaccurate, however, to contrast French and German law in terms of *ius soli* and *ius sanguinis*. The opposition simply would not hold up as a matter of comparative history.[40]

Defining citizenship has therefore been difficult from the beginnings of the contemporary state. It would be a problem 'endemic in modern state-building'[41] and has only become more acute given the contemporary mobility of populations.

CITIZENSHIP AND MOBILITY

People have always moved: locally, nationally, even in an intercontinental manner.[42] Most people, however, do not move and migration remains therefore an exceptional phenomenon.[43] It is increasing in absolute numbers, however, and this has a more profound effect on what have been perceived as nation-states. The foreign-born population of contemporary states is now systematically increasing. It now represents one-third of the entire population of Luxemburg, one-quarter of the population of Switzerland, one-fifth of that of Canada.[44] In the OECD countries the populations of France and Italy contain the lowest foreign-born percentages, at 11 and 7 per cent respectively.[45] In both cases this involves

---

[38] Preuss (2004), 'Citizenship and German Nation', at 31–2 (toleration of those with residence or business for ten years, *ius soli* birthright for children of stateless and homeless parents).

[39] See Ch. 1, 'Readings of the State Tradition'; Joppke (2010), *Citizenship and Immigration*, at 44 (*ius sanguinis* 'epitome of modernity and progress' at dawn of nineteenth century); and see Schirmer (2004), 'Closing the Nation', at 48 ('closing' of German nation in citizenship law of 1913 that did not accept *ius soli*); though for ongoing strength of identities of being Bavarian, Prussian, or Saxon even in 1913, Herbert (2001), *Geschichte der Ausländerpolitik*, at 335 (German citizenship formulated only in reaction to immigration).

[40] Weil (2008), *How to Be French*, at 173; Bellamy (2004), 'Making of Modern Citizenship', at 15 (notions of *ius sanguinis* and *ius soli* both require added nuance, former because of exceptions, latter because of need for integration).

[41] Smith (1997), *Civic Ideals*, at 40 (that of 'asserting a measure of common governance over otherwise distinct societies').

[42] See Ch. 2, 'Early Cosmopolitanism' (for history of humanity as one of migration); and for the three large-scale migrations in the century from 1840 to 1940 (to Americas, to south-east Asia, the Indian Ocean rims, the south Pacific, and to northern Asia), Hoerder (2012), 'Migration and Belongings', at 435.

[43] See generally, for the 'highly selective' process of migration, with use of 'highly structured' routes, and corresponding need to escape from the imagery of 'mass invasion', Sassen (1999), *Guests and Aliens*, at 2, (though acknowledging at 7 mass movements of expulsion in European context—Huguenots from France, Lutherans from Salzburg, shifts following wars between Ottoman, Austrian, and Russian empires).

[44] Joppke (2010), *Citizenship and Immigration*, at 35.

[45] *The Economist*, 13 November 2010 at 35 (Netherlands 10.9 per cent, Germany 12 per cent, Spain and Sweden each 13.8 per cent).

millions of people. At present 214 million people in the world live outside their state of origin.[46] The figure is only that of first generation migrants. The number of international marriages is increasing significantly, on a global basis.[47] The predictions are for 'more and more ethnically heterogeneous political communities'.[48]

In the face of increasingly mobile populations, states in the last century developed highly sophisticated means to control their territorial borders. The passport was invented about the time of the French revolution and its use in traversing borders became generalized and mandatory in the early years of the twentieth century.[49] There have also been less sophisticated means such as walls. The twentieth century in general can therefore be seen as one of 'liberal nationalism' in which states sought to implement a principle of human equality internally but brutally abandoned it at territorial borders.[50] Human beings may become 'illegals' by their simple geographical presence, though there are immense problems of detection and sanction.[51] The movement has been well away from, and not towards, Kant's notion of a *ius cosmopoliticum*

---

[46] Pison (2010), 'The number and proportion of immigrants' (representing 3.1 per cent of world population, up from 2.9 per cent in 1990, 2.3 per cent in 1956). OECD countries are far surpassed by Qatar at 86 per cent, the UAE at 70 per cent, and Kuwait at 69 per cent, given the extent of foreign construction labour. China's foreign-born are only 0.1 per cent of the population (circa 1 million people).

[47] *The Economist*, 12 November 2011 at 67 (in France from 10 per cent of all marriages in 1996 to 16 per cent in 2009; in Germany from 11.3 per cent in 1990 to 13.7 per cent in 2010; in Switzerland 45 per cent of marriages are international; in Asia percentages are smaller but increases are larger: in Japan in 1980 1 per cent of marriages international, by 2009, 5 per cent; in South Korea 3.5 per cent in 2000, 10 per cent in 2010).

[48] Archibugi, Benhabib, and Croce (2010), 'Converging Cosmopolitan Project', in text of recorded conversation.

[49] Bayly (2004), *Birth of Modern World*, at 239 (France sought to exercise control over 'agitators'); Dauvergne (2004b), 'Sovereignty, Migration', at 589 (system of sovereign nation-states existing for three centuries without comprehensive migration regulation). For the particular history of the passport, Torpey (2000), *Invention of Passports*, notably at 32 (for French 1792 debate), 111–17 (for 'temporary' imposition of passport controls during the First World War, becoming permanent); Robertson (2010), *Passport in America*, notably at 251 (on new need for people to prove to official that 'they were the document'). Visas are a further means of control, constituting written permission to enter inscribed within the passport itself. Visa-free entry is thus a gauge of openness of states. For the continuum, *The Economist*, 11 February 2006 at 98 (USA then allowing nationals of 130 states visa-free entry, EU averaging 126, North Korea 18, Pakistan 17).

[50] Bosniak (2010), 'Persons and Citizens', at 10 ('hard-outside-soft-inside').

[51] Dauvergne (2008), *Making People Illegal*, notably at 9 (on the 'No one is illegal' movement), 12–13 (inevitable absence of data on 'illegal' immigration), 14 ('vast amount of population movement outside legal frameworks'); Ngai (2004), *Impossible Subjects*, notably at 2 (on 'illegal' immigrants working in every region of the USA, though best understood as a 'caste' situated outside boundaries of formal membership and social legitimacy), 5 (illegal alien as 'impossible subject', the 'person who cannot be and a problem that cannot be solved'); Bosniak (2010), 'Persons and Citizens', at 18ff. (on emptying of 'personhood' through notions of territoriality, 'the people' and emergency powers). For ensuing 'border cultures', e.g. between the USA and Mexico, Hicks (1991), *Border writing*, notably at xxiii (pollo as border crosser, mosca as US border helicopter, coyote as person bringing pollo).

of universal hospitality.[52] Global governance has yet to take such a first, fundamental step.[53]

The dimensions of international human mobility are such, however, that no state can exercise the control that its political authorities might prefer to exercise. Control of both citizenship and immigration is affected. Since citizenship has no fundamental core, it consists at present of the residue of nineteenth-century national attempts to provide a lasting definition, combined with current efforts to implement a national 'demographic policy'. The results in each case are highly complex, the complexity itself indicating ongoing perplexity and contest.[54] In some destination states, such as the UK, the *ius soli* has been sharply limited; in others, such as Germany, it has become more significant.[55] Each state responds to its particular place in the patterns of international mobility. Immigration can be channelled in some measure but many western states are dependent on it for economic growth, given declining birth rates and employment needs. There are intermittent but recurring outbursts of xenophobia amongst local populations, long immersed in notions of the nation-state, but some have concluded that it is currently 'impossible' for states to shape their populations and that current migration processes are irreversible.[56] Current efforts to test the 'cultural integration' of newcomers are highly problematic in terms of their content and are

[52] See Ch. 9, 'Cosmopolitan Theory'. It is true that Kant did not advocate a right of permanent installation, but border controls now extend to all visitors and there is no general right to entry. For a (legal) regime of 'porous borders' for immigrants, Benhabib (2004), *Rights of Others*, at 3 (alienage not to exclude fundamental rights), 19 ('irresolvable contradiction' between moral universalism and democratic closure); Carens (1995), 'Case for Open Borders' (especially for freedom of movement from developing to more developed world); though for 'regulated openness', Ghosh (2003b), 'Towards a New International Regime', at 25 ('politically achievable'); Miller (2003), 'Migration in Post-Cold War', at 42 (international regime should not call into question sovereign states, which must enforce policies).

[53] Dauvergne (2008), *Making People Illegal*, at 186 ('no serious attempts' to regulate migration globally though domestic regulation demonstrates repeated policy failure and lack of innovation).

[54] For complexity as a 'discernible trend' in last two decades, Joppke (2010), *Citizenship and Immigration*, at 70; and as result of a 'blend' of liberal, democratic republican and inegalitarian ascriptive elements in various combinations, Smith (1997), *Civic Ideals*, at 6 (a 'multiple traditions view of America'), 14 ('bewildering range of categories', citizenship as 'intellectually puzzling, legal confused ... and contested status'). For citizenship becoming simple 'instrument' of 'demographic policy', Weil (2008), *How to Be French*, at 4 (since the Second World War).

[55] For UK abandonment in 1981 of automatic UK citizenship on birth in Britain, Harris (2004), 'Nationality, Rights and Virtue', at 80 (now dependent on birth to parent settled in UK); Juss (2007), 'Slow Death of Citizenship Rights', at 95 (1981 legislation removing 'last remnants of territorial birthright'). The *ius soli* is also contested in the USA, given the phenomenon of 'anchor babies', children born of illegal immigrants. For German granting of birth citizenship to children of immigrants resident in Germany for eight years or longer, Spiro (2008), *Citizenship*, at 18; and for general European continental move to *ius soli*, given dangers of sizeable non-citizen populations, Joppke (2010), *Citizenship and Immigration*, at 31 (need for 'congruence between rulers and ruled').

[56] For impossibility, Kochenov (2011b), 'EU Citizenship, Naturalisations', at E114; and for irreversibility, Herbert (2001), *Geschichte der Ausländerpolitik*, at 9 (public debate breaking out every four or five years, as though solvable problem, this for more than a century; rather, question only of pragmatic and middle-term corrective measures), 341 (irreversibility).

subject to open ridicule.[57] Notions of citizenship are unhelpful in providing criteria for social integration.[58]

National control of migration is further hindered by international and even national efforts to impose rule-of-law constraints on the process of control. Executive decisions on claims to entry become part of the normal processes of administrative review and even broadly drawn privative clauses may be subject to judicial reading-down.[59] Today refugees are a particular category of migrants. They emerged with the population movement attendant on the idea of a nation-state,[60] and it is fitting that they are now broadly protected by treaty from immediate refoulement.[61] This leaves much room for expedited national proced-ures, particularly for return to 'safe' third countries through which a refugee may have passed, but the most exaggerated forms of refoulement are now largely excluded.[62] The refugee has even been seen, given the decline of the state, as the 'central figure of our political history'.[63] The challenge of human mobility to state resources is indicated by an emerging pattern of outsourcing control, territorial and extraterritorial, to private actors.[64] There is also a widespread practice of amnesties for those having gained entry illegally, so that residence and even eventual accession to citizenship do not depend on adherence to state norms.[65]

---

[57] For ridicule of Dutch efforts to test 'nation-specific' culture, Kochenov (2011b), 'EU Citizenship, Naturalisations', notably at E112 (for single correct answer to question what one should do on death of a neighbour, 'hypocritical bureaucratic exercise').

[58] Joppke (2010), *Citizenship and Immigration*, at 33 (citizenship identity, as such, consisting only of 'general rules and principles of liberal democracy, which are the same everywhere').

[59] See generally Dauvergne (2004), 'Sovereignty, Migration', notably at 605 (for Australian High Court case law), 614 (no longer exclusive executive control), and most recently *Plaintiff M70/2011 v. MIC* [2011] HCA 32 (Australia High Court striking down ministerial process of placing asylum claimants in third countries as not providing effective procedures for asylum determination); Sassen (1999), *Guests and Aliens*, for European states' necessary acceptance of human rights rulings in matters of migration, notably at xx ('and the world did not come to an end'); and for earlier Canadian, US, UK, German, and French decisional law, Glenn (1992), *Strangers at the Gate*, notably at 65ff. (executive or quasi-judicial primary adjudication, review by administrative tribunals or courts of general jurisdiction).

[60] Sassen (1999), *Guests and Aliens*, at xiii (millions displaced after each of World Wars, whole states eliminated, victors refusing citizens of eliminated states), 35 (no German word for refugee until after the Second World War), 87 (refugee crisis emerged as such only after closure of USA and Canada to much immigration in 1920s).

[61] Notably the 1951 UN Convention Relating to the Status of Refugees, 189 UNTS 137; as to which Hathaway (2005), *Rights of Refugees*.

[62] As to which Kneebone (2009), *Refugees, Asylum Seekers*, at 27 (notion of 'safe third country' dating from 1990 Dublin Convention, said to be necessary to prevent European asylum system from collapsing); and see Morris (2010), *Asylum, Welfare and Cosmopolitan Ideal*, at 19 ('how states go about managing the tensions involved in honouring obligations in principle but limiting access in practice').

[63] Agamben (2000), *Means without End*, at 16 ('unhinges the old trinity of state-nation-territory').

[64] Gammeltoft-Hansen (2011), *Access to Asylum*, at 169 (for effect on migrants and eventual state responsibility).

[65] Dauvergne (2008), *Making People Illegal*, at 139 (showing that 'the fiction of formal legal citizenship does not hold fast').

COSMOPOLITAN CITIZENS

Given mobility, millennia-long human loyalties, and the inherent thinness of citizenship, multiple and overlapping forms of human identity are inevitable on any national territory. Citizenship cannot pretend to hold the status of a 'unique categorization' of people and arguably does not do so. Even if it did, important objections have been raised to any such unique categorical device for human beings. For Amartya Sen, civilizational clashes would even be conceptually parasitic on efforts to implement such an exclusivist concept of identity.[66] Others insist on the primacy of non-state identities in most states of the world, where notions of territoriality and citizenship are only part of the 'imported state'.[67] This is not fatal to contemporary forms of state organization; they remain justifiable for many in the abstract, and justified in their implementation in many parts of the world.[68] It is only an exclusivist concept of citizenship and the state that appears both unjustifiable and impossible to realize. No 'stark dichotomy' between a political society's inside and outside would be either possible or desirable. The contested and historical variation of citizenship also precludes any exclusivity of its role.[69]

An exclusivist conception of citizenship is also increasingly incompatible with state practice in the world. This is reflected both in a decline in the actual use and importance of citizenship and in increasing flexibility and accommodation in its definition.

---

[66] See notably Sen (2007), *Identity and Violence*, at xii, xv, 10; and see UN Development Program (2004), *Human Development Report 2004*, at 2 (individuals have multiple identities, 'no inevitable need to choose between state unity and recognition of cultural differences'); Bosniak (2000), 'Citizenship Denationalized', at 505 (privileging by 'liberal nationalists' of national identities 'deeply problematical', may also 'simply be unrealistic'); Maskens (2005), 'Résilience des ideologies', at 17 (on 'idéologies mono-identitaires'); Sørensen (2004), *Transformation of the State*, at 90 (identity more a 'project for the individual'); Likhovski (2006), *Law and Identity*, at 4 (modern era saw rise of 'obsessive desire' for homogeneous sense of identity); Kymlicka and Norman (2000b), 'Citizenship in Culturally Diverse Societies', at 1 ('ethnocultural identities' matter to citizens, will endure over time, 'must be recognized and accommodated').

[67] Badie (2000), *The Imported State*, at 68 (for 'indistinct' idea of Hindu nationalism, territorial delimitation 'porous and mutable'); Sørensen (2004), *Transformation of the State*, at 98 (ethnic, religious, tribal identities 'dominate' national identity in 'weak states'); and for nomad, notably Arab, resistance, see Ch. 6, 'Common Laws beyond Europe'.

[68] See for defence of citizenship and notions of national identity, Miller (2000), *Citizenship and National Identity*, contrasting at 3 'republican citizenship' of active involvement with 'liberal' and 'libertarian' views, former 'better able to respond to cultural diversity' by virtue of its ability to draw many into public debate, and find compromise); and for national 'accomodationist' structures, Peleg (2007), *Democratizing Hegemonic State*, at 3 for options (local autonomy, consociationalism, power-sharing regimes, etc.).

[69] Against the dichotomy, Bosniak (2006), *Citizen and Alien*, at 7 (incapable of contending with complex interpenetration of institutions and practices across borders, disables theorists from seeing that 'global' also within national borders); and for historical variation within contemporary states, Thelen (2000), 'National and Transnational Citizenship?', at 551 ('different things to different groups at different times' and 'different things at the same time in different places', US examples).

Citizenship, domicile, and residence

The decline in the importance of national citizenship is best seen in historical perspective, and in relation to alien status. Until the nineteenth century aliens were not only precluded from participation in national public life, they were also in considerable measure excluded from enjoyment of rights of private law. In common law jurisdictions this flowed from particular restrictions or prohibitions under the common law, for example on inheriting land by intestate succession; in many civil law jurisdictions it flowed from a more general denial of the 'capacity of enjoyment' ('capacité de jouissance', 'Rechtsfähigkeit') of private law rights, principally again in matters of succession. Aliens were in some measure outlaws.[70] These specific and general restrictions on legal personality were laboriously done away with through the late eighteenth and nineteenth centuries, so that today the alien is subject only to those private law disabilities that are the object of specific enactment, and now these are usually subject to constitutional review.[71] Paradoxically, citizenship thus declined in significance through the heyday of the nation-state, as the human person became widely recognized in national laws as a subject of rights. It did acquire some greater visibility in the implementation of the rights of aliens, since many states followed the teaching of Mancini in the nineteenth century and chose to submit many questions of private law, in matters of family law and successions, to the law of a person's nationality. This was a so-called 'bilateral' rule, however, and operated in favour of both local and foreign national laws.[72]

The story of citizenship or nationality in the twentieth century, however, was one of steady decline. If the rights of human beings were 'positivized' in national laws, these same national laws often extended them beyond citizens to 'persons' in general.[73] Similar considerations led to alienage or nationality being judicially established as a 'suspect' category in US constitutional law, subject therefore to 'strict' judicial scrutiny and requiring particular justification to avoid incompatibility with the guarantee of equal protection of laws.[74] In the European Union discrimination on the basis of citizenship is formally proscribed, as a means of ensuring freedom of movement, and its interpretation extends to 'indirect'

---

[70] Baker (2002), *English Legal History*, at 467 ('aliens . . . were treated in the early common law as having virtually no enforceable rights at all', though recognizing relaxations, notably in matters of contract and in courts other than those of the common law); and for the historical French position of denial of civil rights, notably in matters of succession, though admission of rights of *ius gentium*, e.g. to contract, Pillet (1923), *Traité pratique*, at 314–15 (distinguishing *inter vivos* transactions from matters of succession, noting maxim that 'foreigners live free but die as slaves').

[71] For the laborious process in France, with full civil status accorded by the 1804 Civil Code only on condition of reciprocity, Batiffol and Lagarde (1981–3), *Droit international privé*, vol. I, at 190. Alien acquisition of land remains the object of many restrictions in contemporary states.

[72] See Ch. 13, '*Private international law*'.

[73] Bosniak (2010), 'Persons and Citizens' at 11 (citing the Canadian Charter of Rights and Freedoms and its guarantees of the fundamental freedoms of 'everyone').

[74] Tribe (1988), *American Constitutional Law*, at 1544 ('compelling justification'). The guarantees of due process and equal protection under the Fourteenth Amendment to the US Constitution are extended to 'persons' as opposed to 'citizens'.

national discrimination where the touchstone or operative criterion of the legislation is residence (affecting foreign nationals more than local ones).[75] The actual legal use of citizenship as a criterion for benefits or entitlements has correspondingly declined in most states, while more cosmopolitan notions of domicile or residence (requiring no grant or conferment by a state) have become more frequent in application.[76] US law would be decidedly 'ambivalent', and not uniformly hostile, towards the alien.[77] When local or national politics turns xenophobic, as in a 'nation-state' it inevitably must, correctives often come at other levels of government. Given toughening of welfare rules against aliens at the federal level in the USA in the 1990s, 'almost all' individual states extended benefits, while there was later restoration of many benefits at the federal level.[78] There is also a discernible movement towards granting rights of political participation, at least at local or municipal levels, to non-nationals. Even the articulation of rights and duties is not an exclusive preserve of the citizen.[79]

The decline of citizenship is most obviously evidenced by a general decline in its acquisition. In their vast majority aliens who have acquired permanent residence status in a new state do not acquire the citizenship of that state. The percentage of those who do is remarkably small, under 10 per cent in European Union countries but also not high, and declining, in other countries

---

[75] For the prohibition, Art. 18 TFEU; on indirect discrimination, *Commission v. Italian Republic*, Case C388/01 ECRI–721 (prohibiting reduced rate for local museums to be granted to local nationals and residents); see Davies (2005), 'Residence is the New Nationality', notably at 55 (criticizing judgment as 'threat to solidarity on anything less than a European scale').

[76] Jacobson (1996), *Rights Across Borders* (for decline in both western Europe and the USA); for decline in Europe, Saladin (1995), *Wozu noch Staaten?*, at 26 (populations becoming 'exchangeable'); Joppke (2010), *Citizenship and Immigration*, at 73 ('overall diminished status of social citizenship'); Schuck (2000), 'Citizenship in Federal Systems', at 196 (citizenship may now be 'anachronistic'); and in specific matters of health care ('health tourists'), Harrington (2009), 'Migration and access to health care', notably at 316 (for 'national scale' no longer wholly predominant); and even in commercial aviation (citizenship historically defining airline ownership), Havel and Sanchez (2011), 'Restoring Global Aviation's "Cosmopolitan Mentality"', notably at 3, 27 (for new 'cosmopolitan mentality' of 'open aviation area' with access by foreign carriers). For citizenship never having a primary role in distribution of state benefits in common law jurisdictions, however, given the historic primacy of notions of domicile and residence: Glenn and Desbiens (2003), 'L'appartenance au Québec', notably at 124–5, and *pace* arguments of Marshall (1950), *Citizenship and Social Class*. Citizenship would also be declining as a 'connecting factor' in private international law, in favour notably of a more modern concept of habitual residence; see Scoles *et al* (2000), *Conflict of Laws*, at 238, and for the immense literature on the subject, Kegel and Schurig (2000), *Internationales Privatrecht*, at 386.

[77] For 'ambivalence', Bosniak (2006), *Citizen and Alien*, at 37–8 (ascending scale of rights for aliens as identity with society increases), 49 (aliens full due process in criminal proceedings yet possibly denied Medicaid benefits); Smith (2009), 'Beyond Sovereignty and Uniformity', at 907 (citizenship in USA never 'a uniform status').

[78] Spiro (2008), *Citizenship*, at 89; and on the 1996 measures, Ngai (2004), *Impossible Subjects: Illegal Aliens*, at 268–9 (for US Supreme Court review of treatment of aliens); Bohman (2009), 'Cosmopolitan Republicanism and Rule of Law', notably at 72 (for rights enjoyed by citizens and aliens alike, 'call this the cosmopolitan constitution').

[79] Rodriguez (2010), 'Noncitizen voting', at 31 (in 'dozens of democracies around the world', for 'permanent residents'), 34 (four countries even granting universal suffrage to non-citizens at national level—Chile, Malawi, New Zealand, and Uruguay), 36–8 (though resistance in USA, notably through state control of voting rights).

of immigration.[80] In the USA acquisition rates increased following limitation of welfare rights of aliens in the 1990s but has declined once again. In 1970, 63.5 per cent of resident aliens in the USA acquired US citizenship; by 2000 the figure had declined to 37.4 per cent.[81] The benefits of citizenship (principally the right to vote) would not outweigh the hassle.[82]

The decline in the use and importance of citizenship has had important effects on its definition.

Accommodating citizenships

A first indication of a more accommodating concept of citizenship is found in the multiplication of expressions used to describe it, in less than precise terms. There is much discussion of 'transnational', 'global', 'world', 'post-national', 'multi-cultural', 'differential', and 'plural' citizenship, though there is also much criticism of the illusory or inexact use of these expressions.[83] Some of them are terminological attempts, in the language of citizenship, to capture notions we have already seen, such as the participatory character of membership or cosmopolitan and transnational obligations.[84] Discussion of 'denizens' is more precise in its objective, in designating those lacking formal citizenship but having associated themselves with state structures in some appropriate degree and enjoying many of the attributes of citizenship. It has historical pedigree and speaks clearly to present circumstance, also presenting the advantage of challenging 'the dichotomizing language' of membership.[85]

---

[80] Glenn and Desbiens (2003), 'L'appartenance au Québec', at 130 (noting also importance of conditions of acquisition); Sassen (1999), *Guests and Aliens*, at 118 (though increases in Germany and the Netherlands after 1990 citizenship reforms); Joppke (2010), *Citizenship and Immigration*, at 41 (0.43 per cent in Luxemburg to 7.66 per cent in Sweden).

[81] Spiro (2008), *Citizenship*, at 57 (though spikes after 1990s reforms and after terrorist attack in 2001); Joppke (2010), *Citizenship and Immigration*, at 39 (USA and Canada *c.* 80 per cent in 1950, USA now at 40 per cent though Canada at 75 per cent since more 'proactive' in matters of naturalization).

[82] Spiro (2008), *Citizenship*, at 57 (right to vote not exploited by many, estate tax benefits only affecting wealthy couples); Schuck (1989), 'Membership', at 58 ('marginal benefits' slight).

[83] For 'transnational', 'global', 'world', 'postnational', 'cosmopolitan', Bosniak (2006), *Citizen and Alien*, at 24 (citizenship 'increasingly denationalized' though 'in the sense of formal legal status remains closely bound to nation-state membership'); for 'multi-cultural', Habermas (2000), *Après l'Etat-Nation*, at 66 (based on a 'policy of recognition' of collective identities); for 'differential', Kymlicka (1989), *Liberalism, Community and Culture*, at 151 ('continuum of possibilities', advantaging aboriginal peoples); for 'plural', Ibarra Palafox (2011), 'Constitutionalism and Citizenship', at 67 ('building a plural citizenship has become a crucial project for the twenty-first century'). For criticism, Kymlicka (2003), 'New Forms of Citizenship', at 287, 293 (only real alternative to national citizenship that of international parliaments, nothing in international human rights that challenges liberal/national model of citizenship); Joppke (2010), *Citizenship and Immigration*, at 73 ('post-national' blurring meaning of citizenship); Smith (2009), 'Beyond Sovereignty and Uniformity', at 936 (no 'universalistic' citizenship possible in world of differentiated communities and identities).

[84] For participation in social movements, Bosniak (2006), *Citizen and Alien*, at 26 (labour rights activists, environmentalists, feminists, human rights workers); and for the cosmopolitan theory of transnational obligations, see Ch. 9, 'Cosmopolitan Theory'.

[85] Walker (2009), 'Denizenship and Deterritorialization', notably at 261 (for foreigner in common law acquiring some of privileges of English subject, through royal prerogative, paralleling idea of *metic* of

The most precise examples of cosmopolitan citizenship, however, are those in which citizenship is aggregated, so that it is cosmopolitan according to the dictionary meaning of the term, as having characteristics that arise from different countries.[86] The most visible example in the world of this aggregation of citizenships is now found in the European Union, where the creation of European citizenship has been by way of addition to the existing citizenships of the states of Europe.[87] The citizen of France is now also a citizen of the wider legal and political community of Europe. This is not simply a declaration of ultimate objectives or a meaningless reaffirmation that France is found in Europe. It attracts notably the right of mobility into and within the European Union, which is one of the primary characteristics of citizenship in any state.[88] This has had profound consequences for the lives of people in Europe. It has also had great importance for the denizens of Europe, those citizens of third countries who have acquired long-standing permanent residence in Europe, so that they too can exercise their denizen rights within the community.[89] Territory is not what it was.

The European developments must be situated, however, in a still broader context of cosmopolitan citizenship. There are general 'liberalizing trends', with new entitlements to citizenship granted to second- and third-generation migrants and facilitated naturalization rules (with lower residence requirements).[90] This

Greek city state), 262 (as 'in-between concept'); and see Dauvergne (2008), *Making People Illegal*, at 121 (not citizen but not 'other'); and for 'alien citizenship', Bosniak (2006), *Citizen and Alien*, at 81.

[86] See Preface, note 3.

[87] European citizenship was created by the Treaty of Maastricht in 1992; see Joppke (2010), *Citizenship and Immigration*, at 164 ('postnational citizenship in its most elaborate form', European Court of Justice transforming from derivative status into 'a free-standing source of rights'); Kostakopoulou (2007), 'European Union Citizenship', passim for its inclusive, multi-layered, and multi-cultural character and, at 624, as 'concrete citizenship beyond the Nation State', 630, as instilling a 'cosmopolitan consciousness within national citizenship' such that, at 632, the 'nation' and cosmopolitanism appear to be 'mutually reinforcing'). See also, for potential inclusiveness, Topidi (2010), *EU Law, Minorities*, notably at 115 ('ethnic minorities and EU citizenship: in search of cosmopolitan citizenship', on eliminating distinction between 'belongers' and 'non-belongers'). The USA also combines state citizenship with national citizenship, but the former is constituted by simple residence and not by ascriptive grant; also, national citizenship not dependent on state citizenship: Rosenfeld (2010), *Identity of Constitutional Subject*, at 237; though for even the federal experience as implying rejection of the exclusive, nation-state concept of citizenship, Di Fabio (1998), *Das Recht offener Staaten*, at 135 (ongoing idea of being citizen of city, province, state, etc.).

[88] For the strictly interpreted character of limits on the right of mobility and the need for any such limits to meet a test of proportionality, Kostakopoulou (2007), 'European Union Citizenship', at 639; and for the right of European citizens to receive services, including health services, in another EU country, *Luisi and Carbone* v. *Ministero del Tesoro*, Cases 286/82 and 26/83, [1984] ECR 377 (ECJ); and generally Harrington (2009), 'Migration and access to health care', at 326. Access to the benefits of EU law would now be attaching to EU citizens as such, in the absence of any cross-border activity or movement: Kochenov (2011a), 'A Real European Citizenship', at 55 (on 'intensity of interference' with rights of EU citizens, and not borders, that triggers application of EU law).

[89] Walker (2009), 'Denizenship and Deterritorialization', at 265 (net impact of changes in standing of denizens in Europe even greater than changes affecting second-country European citizens); Guiraudon (1998), 'Citizenship Rights for Non-Citizens', at 272 (for a continuum of rights attached to membership rather than a 'sharp distinction between citizen and non-citizen').

[90] Joppke (2008), 'Comparative Citizenship', at 4, though noting also at 6 and 34 more restrictive developments (tests on language, civics, etc.), though latter as limits on increasingly liberal regimes; Dauvergne (2004a), 'Making People Illegal', at 95 (denationalization also rarer).

general widening of the criteria for citizenship necessarily means more possibilities of overlapping citizenships, and perhaps the most striking development of the law of citizenship over the last century has been the slow overturning of the principle of a single and exclusive citizenship. At the beginning of the twentieth century almost all European states allowed only one nationality and it was said polemically that one could no more have two mother countries ('patries') than two mothers.[91] In Europe all but five states now allow dual citizenship and Europe is symptomatic of a world-wide phenomenon.[92] The movement attracts general approbation, even Winston Churchill having supported it as a means to reduce conflict.[93]

The rise of dual or plural citizenship is significant in two respects. It is a further indication of the thin and abstract nature of the concept, presenting the advantage (however) of being more potentially inclusive than thicker and more historically rooted forms of belonging. It is more cosmopolitan than ethnicity and may prove to be more cosmopolitan in potential than either religion or language, though this will depend in some measure on the religion and the language. Plural citizenship is also significant for the contribution it makes to the knowledge base of the citizenry. If each citizen of a state must learn to become a cosmopolitan citizen,[94] this is facilitated by multiple personal loyalties. The dual citizen becomes a source, moreover, of cosmopolitan education for others.[95]

---

[91] De Groot and Schneider (2006), 'Zuhehmende Akzeptanz von Fällen mehrfacher Staatsangehörigkeit', at 65 (citing André Weiss in 1907) and 66 (for legislative technique of loss of first nationality if second acquired); and for Franklin Roosevelt's view of dual nationality as 'a self-evident absurdity', Spiro (2008), *Citizenship*, at 61.

[92] For Europe, Joppke (2008), 'Comparative Citizenship', at 5; and for more than fifty states now permitting dual citizenship explicitly or recognizing to some extent, Faist and Gerdes (2008), 'Dual Citizenship in Age of Mobility', App. B; US Office of Personnel Management (2001), *Citizenship Laws of the World,* for country-specific listing; and see generally Hansen and Weil (2002), *Dual Nationality*; Martin and Hailbronner (2003), *Rights and Duties of Dual Nationals*; Barry (2006), 'Home and Away', at 34 (for emigration states 'reconfiguring citizenship' to increase economic benefits from migrants), 42 ('around half' of countries of world recognizing 'plural citizenship'); Spiro (2008), *Citizenship*, at 6 ('completely tolerated' under present US practice), 59 (encouraged by states of emigration), 67 (a 'core incident of globalization'); Dauvergne (2008), *Making People Illegal*, at 119, 135 (new Indian 'overseas citizenship').

[93] De Groot and Schneider (2006), 'Zuhehmende Akzeptanz von Fällen mehrfacher Staatsangehörigkeit', at 69; Spiro (2010), 'Dual Citizenship as Human Right' at 111 (facilitates naturalization and advances integration); Morris (1998), *Essay on Modern State*, at 261 (since states less authority than claimed, case for exclusive membership weakened); Green (1988), *Authority of the State*, at 218; Di Fabio (1998), *Das Recht offener Staaten*, at 134 (unity-giving idea of Volk as pre-law category no longer plausible, multiple citizenship having dissolving effect on it); Benhabib (2002), *Claims of Culture*, at 180–1 (decline of Weberian idea of unity, need to come to grips with 'the end of unitary citizenship').

[94] Holden (2000), *Global Democracy*, at 29 (a person 'capable of mediating between national traditions').

[95] On the importance of cosmopolitan education, Nussbaum (1994), 'Patriotism and Cosmopolitanism', at s. III.1 (comparing 'unexamined feeling that one's own current preferences and ways are neutral and natural', reinforced by teaching of moral salience of national boundaries), 7 (need for 'talking', respecting 'traditions and commitments').

❧ 11 ❧

Cosmopolitan Sources I: Constitutionalism

Different states adjust in different ways to the current circumstances of globalization. They have all become adaptive and there is even (exaggerated) language of
an open state.[1] The territorial and national closures attempted in recent centuries
thus are increasingly challenged by surrounding texture.[2] Cosmopolitan methods
inevitably become resurgent, particularly those that have been sustained
throughout the period of closure. The state is complicit in this process, however,
and recently its role has been described as one of integration, seen moreover as
an ongoing process.[3] There is understandable concern about the effect of a
multiplicity of sources on legal unity, and a corresponding concern with conflicts
of laws, in a broad sense. This must, however, be placed in its historical context.
It was the emergence of the contemporary state that gave rise to a notion of
conflict of laws, while the legal unity that the state sought to create did not
eliminate diversity but simply displaced it to the territorial boundary.[4] The
movement for national legal unification in Europe was one that created legal
disunity at a European level. Unity and diversity cannot therefore be seen as
binary opposites, one or the other necessarily prevailing, but must be seen rather
as correlatives.[5] There is always both unity *and* diversity, and all lies in knowing
their respective ambits. From an internal state perspective there may be unity (at
least theoretically), but diversity is then located at the periphery of the state.
From a pan-state perspective there is diversity, of multiple state laws, with unity
found within the individual states. The essential process is to determine those

---

[1] See Ch. 9, *'The adaptive state'*.

[2] MacCormick (1999), *Questioning Sovereignty*, at 9 ('[t]he coercively predominant normative orders
have been those of states, though they have rarely if ever succeeded in absolutely eliminating rival orders
of one kind or another'); and see Lawson (2001), *Closure*, at 6 (on phenomenon that 'the particular
closures we happen to have realised are often mistaken for a description of the world').

[3] Saladin (1995), *Wozu noch Staaten?*, at 189 (notably as a process particular to each state), 197 (ongoing
since accomplishment would be total and state totalitarian, integration as walking a fine line—'Wanderug
auf schmalen Grat'); and see Migdal (2001), *State in Society*, at 153 ('the ability of states to remain intact
rests in part on their relationship to these other sets of law').

[4] See Ch. 8, *'Private international law'*, notably for influence of Huber, presumption of conflicting laws in
present-day Europe.

[5] Aristotle spoke of unity and diversity as representing contrariety and relativity though not
contradiction: Aristotle (2008a), *Metaphysics*, at 1054a; and for unity and diversity as 'this antithetical yet
complementary pair', Nora (1996b), 'Introduction', at 21; and see generally Glenn (2010a),
'Accommodating Unity'. For necessary toleration of 'disuniformity' within states, Frost (2008), '(Over)
Valuing Uniformity' (on unreasonable costs of establishing judicial methods to ensure uniformity); and
for 'perfect unity' as 'synonymous with sterility and death', Thuan (2001), *Chaos and Harmony*, at 253
('Nature delights in trying as many variations as possible').

state, regional, and transnational unities, of concept and present persuasive force, that can be relied upon as law, and this requires both judgement and cosmopolitan methods.[6] Conflict can give way to conciliation.

The cosmopolitan methods that have been examined have been those of institutional cosmopolitanism, constitutionalism, and common laws, historically in that order of priority.[7] These have all been sustained over centuries though their respective importance has varied. Institutional cosmopolitanism declined in the period of construction of the contemporary state, while the importance of common laws was essential to the spread of European law and state structures in the world.[8] Today the state has become implanted, in various degrees, everywhere in the world, and constitutionalism appears as the most visible of the cosmopolitan methods. The importance, however, of the concepts of common law and institutional cosmopolitanism is renewed. Given the implanting of the state, the relative importance of these cosmopolitan methods plays out in the debate over sources of law within the contemporary state.

The twentieth century was a century of constitutional law. The number of states in the world increased greatly as did the number of written constitutions.[9] The manner and form of this spread of constitutionalism was of profound importance, moreover, for the present discussion of cosmopolitanism in the sources of constitutional law. The operative constitutional structures lent themselves unmistakably to cosmopolitan concepts of sources. These constants in the spread of constitutionalism, moreover, have generated what may today be described as a cosmopolitan turn in the sources of constitutional law.

CONSTITUTIONAL STRUCTURES AND SOURCES OF LAW

How has the spread of constitutionalism throughout the world contributed to a cosmopolitan understanding of sources? Four constants in the diffusion process are identifiable.

The first relates to the drafting of the written constitutions of the world. The multiplication of written constitutions was not a process of spontaneous, national, and autonomous developments. Most constitutions were developed in the process of emergence from imperial structures. There were therefore structural relations that preceded the written constitutions and that inevitably influenced them.[10] A recent empirical study of the 'transnational origins of constitutions', examining 188 countries over the 61 years 1946–2006 and a total of 729 constitutions, found both that constitutions do have transnational origins

---

[6] See Walker (2008), 'Beyond boundary disputes', at 373 ('[i]t is likely we will not witness the reestablishment of a new dominant order of orders but, instead, will depend on the terms of accommodation reached among these competing models and among the actors . . . who are influential in developing them').

[7] See Ch. 3, 'Persistence of Cosmopolitan Ways'.

[8] See Chs 6, 7, and 8.

[9] For the growth of written constitutions, see Ch. 4, 'Constitutions'.

[10] See Ch. 7.

and that 'the most important predictor of constitutional diffusion is whether states share a common legal origin ... constitution-makers borrow from states with whom they already share important pre-existing similarities'.[11] Thus national constitutions are based upon and infused with the concepts of the common laws derived from former imperial authority; the 'constitutional iso-morphism' noted in colonial and post-colonial times continues apace today.[12] This first structural reality of constitutionalism translates inevitably, in at least some measure, into ongoing use of the shared common law.[13]

A second constant of the diffusion process also relates to the process of drafting. Cosmopolitan populations are characterized by profound differences in belief, and a present-day document is unable to resolve such profound differences. The modern constitutions are 'disharmonic' and therefore formu-lated in 'incrementalist' fashion, through deferring controversial choices, using deliberately ambivalent and vague language, and even including contrasting texts.[14] They therefore invite resort to sources beyond themselves and cosmo-politan methods of interpretation. These are the only ways to resolve the dilemmas of convivencia.

---

[11] Goderis and Versteeg (2011), 'Transnational Origins of Constitutions', at 3 ('borrowing follows the functional logic of learning'), with lesser importance of trade, language, military alliances; and for 'striking' similarity of language across constitutions, Osiatynski (2003), 'Paradoxes of constitutional borrowing', at 244 ('no one begins writing a constitution from scratch'), 245 (though often 'minute differences behind seemingly similar solutions', Eastern European drafters 'wanted to borrow in their own way'); and for the process as one of 'cross-constitutional influence' as opposed to 'borrowing' or 'copying', Scheppele (2003), 'Aspirational and aversive constitutionalism', at 296 (a 'range of possible influences—positive and negative, direct and indirect', texts 'reverently accepted, reinvented through bricolage'); and for the process in Africa, Deng (2008), *Identity, Diversity, and Constitutionalism*, at 17 ('the constitutional principles of the colonial powers').

[12] See Ch. 6, 'Common Laws beyond Europe'; Ch. 7, *'The United States of America'*, in particular for the constitutional world derived from the English common law. For the 'remarquable extension' of French public law concepts, both constitutional and administrative, Picq (2005), *Histoire et droit des États*, at 279 (extending notably beyond former French colonies, and thus from 'Turkey to Colombia'); and for example of French public law influence in Poland, Skrzydlo (2006), 'De la reception des principes constitutionnels', at 291 ('conscious choice' of French models of Third and Fifth Republics). For the English model being 'more influential' than the American since Great Britain had more colonies, though USA 'radiated the idea of constitutionalism', Osiatynski (2003), 'Paradoxes of constitutional borrowing', at 248 (English influence particularly 'where independence came as a result of negotiations and peaceful agreement').

[13] See Ch. 6, 'Common Laws beyond Europe'; Ch. 7, passim.

[14] Jacobsohn (2003–4), 'Permeability of Constitutional Borders', at 1767 (for 'disharmonic'), 1812 (on 'contradictions that lie at the core of constitutional arrangements', 'constitutional imperfection'); Lerner (2010), 'Constitution-writing', at 70 (for 'incrementalist approach', using examples of India, Ireland, Israel), 80 ('evolutionary and not revolutionary moment' of constitution-making, reflecting divided character of the people); Lerner (2011), *Making Constitutions*, at 30 (fuller development of 'incrementalist approach'); Scarciglia (2011), *Introducción al derecho constitucional comparado*, at 142 (Afghan example, with 'contradictions' between constitution and precepts of shari'a); Ginsburg, Elkins, and Blount (2007), 'Does Constitution-Making Matter?', at 215 (drafters feeling need to signal positions to their constituents outside the process, potentially leading to more extreme positions, also grandstanding); Reed (2008), 'Foreign Precedents', at 261 (foreign experience valuable basis for reflection given 'generality of the provisions' of a constitution); Harvey and Schwartz (2012), *Rights in Divided Societies* (for compatibility of common doctrine of rights with recognition of difference); and for 'antinomies' within the EU, see Ch. 13, 'States and Regional Law'.

A third constant of the diffusion process is the structural accommodation of population differences, within the cadre of the liberal state. These measures fall short of the institutional cosmopolitanism to be examined later in this chapter, and are consistent with contemporary notions of the state as exclusive source of law. The diversity of such arrangements has already been noted, and federalism is the obvious example.[15] Yet federalism is not simply a sharing-out of legislative authority; it is cosmopolitan in recognizing the need for doing so, and in recognizing that the populations of the constituent units of the federation may have different ideas of the sources of law. Accordingly, the Nigerian federation accommodates Islamic law in twelve of its northern states, and federation in very diverse states inevitably approaches a type of institutional cosmopolitanism.[16] It also appears to be increasing in importance in the world.[17]

The fourth and final constant in the diffusion of constitutionalism in the world is judicial review. It has already been noted that some four-fifths of the states of the world have now accepted some form of judicial review (there are important variations in its structural implementation) and that this is profoundly related to the existence of minorities within states.[18] There is debate on the extent to which a judicial power to strike down legislation can be rooted in the common law tradition derived from England,[19] but in a broader sense the entire process of judicial review is rooted in general principles and concepts ('due process', 'life, liberty and security of the person', 'unreasonable search and seizure') inevitably drawn from common law sources, whatever the common law. By their large and abstract nature these principles and concepts must draw significant content from

---

[15] See Ch. 7, *'Structures'*.

[16] Ostien and Dekker (2010), 'Sharia and national law', at 575 ('Sharia implementation' by legislation in twelve states in Nigeria, notably for criminal law); and see Iwobi (2004), 'Great Sharia Controversy', notably at 121 (for islamicization in both civil and criminal law); Schachar (2001), *Multicultural Jurisdictions*, at 117 ('federal-style accommodation of territorially concentrated national minorities . . . has led to considerable internal transformations among these national minorities').

[17] See generally Tarr, Williams, and Marko (2004), *Federalism, Subnational Constitutions, and Minority Rights*. For Italy as a 'nascent federalism', Del Duca and Del Duca (2006), 'An Italian Federalism?', at 799 (and 'a decentralized, federal-type constitutional democracy'); Chevallier (2004a), *L'État post-moderne*, at 79 (Italy no longer unitary state); and for Spain as becoming, 'unwillingly, a highly decentralized federal state', Castells (2004), *The Information Age*, vol. II, at 49; and as an 'Etat des autonomies', Arbos (2005), 'Le constitutionalisme espagnol', at 82. For a general tendency in federal states for states and provinces to develop their own foreign relations ('paradiplomatie'), Paquin (2005), 'De l'importance de la paradiplomatie', at 226–7 (US states totalling 183 delegations abroad). Cf., however, for a declining percentage of federal states in the world, given the increase in states, Law and Versteeg (2012), 'Declining Influence of US Constitution', at 786 (now 12 per cent of states of world).

[18] See Ch. 7, *'Structures'*. The principal structural difference is between a common law model of review by a court of general jurisdiction, and the German and now French model of a specialized constitutional court; for the variations, Harding and Heyland (2009), *Constitutional Courts* (examining forty-seven different courts); and for an overview Doehring (2000), *Allgemeine Staatslehre*, at 196–202 (types of court, abstract review, incidental review, initiative of parties, political actors, etc.); Osiatynski (2003), 'Paradoxes of constitutional borrowing', at 247 (for German and French 'European' shape of judicial review); and for predominance of German model in post-communist constitutions, Dupré (2003), *Importing the Law*, at 27 (though Romania following French model with 'less powerful' court).

[19] Helmholz (2009), *'Bonham's Case'*, notably at 326 (for 'commonly accepted principles' at time of Coke stopping short of judicial review in the modern sense); Jenkins (2003), 'From Unwritten to Written', at 892 (for Coke's 'concept of judicial review' growing in prominence in USA).

outside themselves, as is the case for all legal standards or general clauses.[20] The search for content will inevitably be in cosmopolitan directions, since the standards are not clearly linked to particular national sources or concepts. The cosmopolitanism of the process is still more evident in jurisdictions with no local tradition of a structurally independent judiciary and where the process of judicial review is obviously an imported product.[21]

All of these factors have contributed to the current cosmopolitan turn in constitutional law and constitutional sources.

THE COSMOPOLITAN TURN IN CONSTITUTIONAL SOURCES

We have seen that current cosmopolitan theory and the historic, unfulfilled movement towards world government have generated a notion of 'international' or even 'global' constitutionalism.[22] This too has been unfulfilled, and through the twentieth century there were vigorous defences of a purely national concept of public law in general. Otto Kahn-Freund famously decried comparative reasoning in matters of public law as a 'misuse' of comparative law.[23] By the end of the twentieth century, however, comparative public law reasoning had become 'inevitable', given the circumstances dealt with in the preceding section.[24] Today the use and citation of non-national sources in public law cases is a world-wide and documented phenomenon.[25] It is practised in states as diverse as Argentina, Australia, Austria, Belgium, Brazil, Canada, Germany, Greece, Hungary (and other East European states), India, Israel, Italy, Japan, Luxemburg, Malaysia, Mexico, The Netherlands, New Zealand, Portugal, Singapore, South Africa, Spain, Switzerland, Taiwan, Turkey, the United Kingdom, the United States of America, Vietnam, and many others.[26] It is a transcontinental

---

[20] Bergel (1988), *Les standards*; and for 'rights-protecting instruments' inviting comparative reflection since resting on shared constitutional conception transcending history of any particular state, Weinrib (2002), 'Constitutional Conceptions', at 15; Di Fabio (1998), *Das Recht offener Staaten*, at 61 (human rights 'pre-state source', no source within single states).

[21] See e.g. Belaïd (1994), 'Les constitutions dans le Tiers-Monde', at 109 (for bills of rights constituting novel concept of 'l'homme valeur' or human value, often constituting a rupture with structures of local societies in Asia or Africa).

[22] See Ch. 9, 'Cosmopolitan Theory'.

[23] Kahn-Freund (1974), 'Uses and Misuses', notably at 12, 13 ('the question is . . . how closely [the foreign rule] is linked with the foreign power structure').

[24] Jackson (2010), *Constitutional Engagement*, at 15 ('given increasingly transnational environment'); and for the field having 'grown immensely' in two decades, Rosenfeld and Sajó (2012a), *Oxford Handbook*, at 1.

[25] For the phenomenon generally, Slaughter (2003), 'Global Community of Courts'; L'Heureux-Dubé (1998–9), 'Importance of Dialogue'; Drobnig and van Erp (1999), *Use of Comparative Law*; Choudhry (2006), *Migration of Constitutional Ideas*; and see Bingham (1992), '"There is a World Elsewhere"', at 527 ('not, I think, establishing a new tradition but reverting to an old and preferable one . . . an old and honourable tradition').

[26] For Argentina, Spector (2008), 'Constitutional Transplants', Rosenkrantz (2003), 'Against borrowings'; for Australia, Stone (2009), 'Comparativism in Constitutional Interpretation', Smyth (1999), 'What do Intermediate Appellate Courts Cite?', Saunders (2006), 'Use and Misuse'; for Austria and Belgium, Gelter and Siems (2013), 'Language, Legal Origins, and Culture before the Courts'; for Brazil, Rosenn (1990), 'Brazil's New Constitution', Dolinger (1990), 'Influence of American Constitutional Law'; for Canada,

phenomenon in Africa,[27] in Latin America,[28] and widespread through Commonwealth jurisdictions.[29] There is also a remarkable level of institutionalization of judicial collaboration and discussion.[30] The importance of the phenomenon should not, however, be exaggerated. National legal traditions have many resources at their disposal and citation of non-national sources is generally reserved for cases of exceptional difficulty. In the Commonwealth, by the end of the twentieth century, studies of case citation patterns indicate non-national sources constituting some 20 per cent of citations, though in the USA the practice had shrunk to less than 1 per cent in the state of California.[31] A recent study of

Glenn (1999), 'Use of Comparative Law'; for Germany, Drobnig (1999), 'Use of Foreign Law'; for Greece, Agallopoulou and Deliyanni-Dimitrakou (1999), 'L'utilisation du droit comparé'; for Hungary (and other East European states), Dupré (2003), *Importing the Law*; for East Europe generally, von Beyme (2002), 'Globalisierung, Europäsierung', Granat (2006), 'Réception de la justice constitutionnelle', at 143; for India, Smith (2006), 'Making Itself at Home—Understanding Foreign Law', at 239; for Israel, Barak (2005), 'Response to *The Judge as Comparatist*', at 200; for Italy, Sacco (1992), *Introduzione diritto comparato*, Ch. VII, s. 6 ('L'Italia paese imitatore'); for Japan, Jackson (2010), *Constitutional Engagement*, at 76, Hasebe (2003), 'Constitutional Borrowing', at 226; for Luxemburg, Elvinger (1999), 'Le recours aux tecniques de droit comparé'; for Malaysia, Salim (2009), 'Are Legal Transplants Impossible?', at 282 (for fiduciary duties of corporate directors, but describing UK and Australian case law as generally 'sacred'), Ahmad (1999), *Malaysian Legal System*, at 106, Lee (2007), 'Interpreting bills of rights'; for Mexico, Ferrer MacGregor and Sánchez Gil (2012), 'Foreign Precedents'; for The Netherlands, van Erp (1999), 'Use of Comparative Law Method'; for New Zealand, Allan, Huscroft, and Lynch (2007), 'Citation of Overseas Authority', Keith (2005), 'Unity of Common Law', at 208, Richardson (2001), 'Trends in Judgment'; for Portugal, Brito Malgarejo (2010), 'El uso de sentencias extranjeras', at 15; for Singapore, Ramraj (2002), 'Comparative Constitutional Law'; for South Africa, Davis (2003), 'Constitutional Borrowing', Lollini (2007), 'Legal argumentation based on foreign law'; for Spain, Gelter and Siems (2013), 'Language, Legal Origins, before the Courts'; for Switzerland, Hamann and Ruiz Fabri (2008), 'Transnational networks', at 499; for Taiwan, Law and Chang (2011), 'Limits of Transnational Judicial Dialogue'; for Turkey, Örücü (2008), 'Judicial navigation', at 48; for the United Kingdom, Örücü, (1999), 'Comparative Law', Reed (2008), 'Foreign Precedents'; for the United States of America see the following discussion and references in this chapter; for Vietnam, Sidel (2002), 'Analytical Models', at 44.

[27] Bryde (2001), 'Der Verfassungsstaat in Afrika', at 213 (also noting objections to practice); Bryde (2003), 'Internationalization of Constitutional Law', at 192 (Supreme Court of Zambia citing other African countries, India, European Court of Human Rights); Jackson (2010), *Constitutional Engagement*, at 78 (Malawi, Angola, Cape Verde).

[28] Dam (2006), *Law–Growth Nexus*, at 45 (Spanish and US influences, latter notably for due process, *habeas corpus*).

[29] Matson (1993), 'Common Law Abroad', notably at 779 ('in most countries an attachment to the basic tenets, if not to the detailed rules, of the common law').

[30] Canivet (2010), 'Trans-Judicial Dialogue', notably at 24 (for websites on judicial collaboration), 27 (on 'legal cosmopolitanism' of national judgments of international interest), 31 (on the development of 'judicial diplomacy', networks of judges in Europe responsible for implementing policies of judicial cooperation), 34 (judicial exchange programmes), 60 (for International Network of Judges); Lenoir (2000), 'Response of the French Constitutional Court', at 165 (emerging judicial dialogue going 'far beyond the bounds of official cooperation'); and for the judges' group in the African Network of Constitutional Jurists (ANCL), established in 2011, Fombad (2012), 'Internationalization of Constitutional Law'. For a series of reflections on the topic by high court judges of Canada, France, Great Britain, and India, with academic comments, Muller and Richards (2010), *Highest Courts and Globalisation*.

[31] For Supreme Court of India averaging 24.6 per cent of all citations 1950–2004, 20 per cent in 2004, Smith (2006), 'Making Itself at Home', at 239; for Canadian provincial high courts citing non-Canadian sources as *c.* 20 per cent of all citations, Glenn (1995), 'Common Law in Canada', at 287; though for decline in Commonwealth citing of English sources, Fausten, Nielsen, and Smyth (2001), 'A Century of Citation Practice', at 758 (13 per cent in state of Victoria in 2005). For California, Merryman (1977), 'Toward a Theory of Citations', at 400 (foreign citations exclusively to English sources). Federal US

cross-citation patterns in Europe found that foreign citations occurred in only 1 per cent of cases.[32] The nature, volume, and accessibility of sources play a role in this. No national tradition, however, is complete and external sources may play a vital role in opening new conceptual paths, or closing them.

There has, however, been a large and visible debate in the USA concerning citation by the United States Supreme Court of foreign sources in constitutional cases.[33] This too must be placed in historical context. Courts in the USA have always made use of foreign decisions, particularly those of other anglo-american jurisdictions, though this use declined during the two centuries of efforts towards national and territorial closures, just as it declined elsewhere.[34] Opposition to the citation of foreign sources in the US Supreme Court is thus both reactionary and nostalgic, though neither of these expressions is used in a pejorative manner. It reacts to the resurgence of cosmopolitan methods in the world and is nostalgic in recalling a time, largely imaginary, when national closure would preclude such use of non-indigenous sources. In both cases there is reflection of the nationalist teaching of the last two centuries, now in decline. Cosmopolitan states must accommodate the local as well as the non-local, however, so the debate reflects the particular US version of a type of cosmopolitan debate that is played out everywhere. The good news is that the US version is played out in the law reviews and not in the streets or (battle) fields. Has the debate provided any major new elements to the world-wide discussion?

US opposition to the use of foreign sources is centred on three fundamental ideas, those of sovereignty, democracy, and the primacy of the US constitution.

---

courts would have increased their citations to foreign authority from the period 1945 to 2005, but the number of citations totals only some twenty per year in recent years: Zaring (2006), 'Use of Foreign Decisions', at 313 (and may be due to increase in number of opinions). For US state courts as still more reluctant, DeLaquil (2006), 'Foreign Law in State Courts', at 701 (though European Court of Human Rights cited six times in state courts).

[32] Gelter and Siems (2013), 'Language, Legal Origins, before the Courts', at 45 (SSRN).

[33] The literature would now include some 3,000 law review articles; for an overview, Alford (2008), 'Lower Courts and Constitutional Comparativism', at 647 (articles commenting on recent decisions of the US Supreme Court using foreign materials and that contain the words 'foreign', 'international', or 'comparative'); and for the debate itself echoing nineteenth-century debates over adoption of 'civil-law-based reforms', Morag-Levine (2006), 'Judges, Legislators', at 34 ('striking similarity').

[34] For the historical process of (partial) closure in North America, Glenn (1987a) 'Persuasive Authority'; and for the 'all-encompassing practice' over time of the US Supreme Court citing non-US sources, Calabresi (2006), 'Shining City on a Hill', at 1336 (practice 'deeply rooted' in the Court's case law); Calabresi and Zimdahl (2005), 'Supreme Court and Foreign Sources', for exhaustive review of Supreme Court cases, notably at 907 ('old tradition', even increasing use of foreign sources in last sixty-five years); Seipp (2006), 'Our Law, Their Law', at 1417 (novelty of citing non-US sources 'bad history and bad law'), 1427 (late-eighteenth-century state statutes prohibiting citation of post-1776 English sources not long in force, evidence that not enforced; evidence of 'Anglophobia, not xenophobia'); Rahdert (2007), 'Comparative Constitutional Advocacy', at 571 (decline in Supreme Court foreign citations from mid-nineteenth century); Easterbrook (2006), 'Foreign Sources', at 223 (for Supreme Court cases citing foreign law 'since the nation's founding'); Farber (2007), 'The Supreme Court', at 1336 ('practice actually has a long pedigree, but few were aware of this history'); and for use of Roman and Jewish sources, reflecting the eclecticism in drafting of US Constitution, Stein (1966), 'Attraction of Civil Law'; Bryson (1984), 'Use of Roman Law'; Hoeflich (1984), 'Roman and Civil Law'; Mirow (2010), 'La tradición romanística', (with references); Maoz (1998), 'Values of Jewish and Democratic State', at 149 (Jewish sources in US Supreme Court decisions).

They are all important arguments. The sovereignty argument has been made with vigour and has inevitably received some echo from the population.[35] It affirms the constitutional impossibility of delegating law-making authority to non-national authorities, and equates the citation of foreign authority to such delegation. It is closely related to the argument based on the democratic character of the US polity. It would be 'the people' who are sovereign, echoing the language of the US founding,[36] so delegation of authority in a way incompatible with democratic control would be unconstitutional.[37] Yet the two related arguments of sovereignty and democracy have not prevailed even within the United States in relation to citation of foreign sources.[38] Sovereignty is not the argument it might have been in the sixteenth century and would not have dominated even in US constitutional history.[39] Both the sovereignty argument

---

[35] See, perhaps most vigorously, Rabkin (2004), *The Case for Sovereignty*, at 29 (incompatibility of international and national authority), 174 (constitution not allowing permanent delegation to international authorities); Rabkin (2005), *Law Without Nations?*, notably at 53–4 (citing French author Bodin), 68–9 (on lack of authority of foreign bodies), 213 (acknowledging 'small exception' in arbitration procedure of NAFTA), 232 (difficulties of world government might lead to a 'return to recognizing the appeal of sovereignty'); Delahunty and Yoo (2005), 'Against Foreign Law' (constitution not authorizing transfer of authority to outside entities). For Congressional Resolutions and popular referenda that would prohibit resort to foreign law, Ginsburg (2005), '"A Decent Respect"', at 582 (concern that resolutions 'fuel the irrational fringe'); Symeonides (2011), 'Choice of Law', at 320 (qualified as 'xenophobic hysteria'); and see Calabresi (2006), 'Shining City on a Hill', at 1337 (American 'popular culture' rejecting idea that USA has much to learn from foreign law); Ralph (2007), *Defending Society of States*, at 122 ('the popular understanding of accountability'). Popular referenda prohibiting application of particular laws, such as the shari'a, will however be contrary to the equal treatment guaranteed by the First Amendment: *Award v. Ziriax*, 670 F. 3d 1111 (10th Cir. 2012). These 'popular' reactions, however, are consistent with much of the nationalist teaching of the last two centuries and there are clear analogies with (unsuccessful) European efforts to prohibit foreign (and Roman) sources in the process of constructing contemporary states; for references, Glenn (2007c), *Common Laws*, at 46.

[36] See Ch. 5, 'Nation and State', Ch. 7, 'The United States of America'.

[37] Posner (2005), 'A Political Court', at 88, under the heading 'The Cosmopolitan Court' ('the undemocratic character of relying (or pretending to rely) on foreign decisions to shape American constitutional law'); Anderson (2005), 'Foreign Law and US Constitution', at 49 (requiring 'fidelity to the principle of democratic self-governing provenance over substantive content'); Rubenfeld (2003), 'Two World Orders', at 27 (contrasting 'international constitutionalism' with 'American, or democratic, national constitutionalism').

[38] See notably, for ongoing justification, the views of Justice Ginsburg of the Supreme Court, Ginsburg (2005), '"A Decent Respect"', notably at 580 ('foreign opinions are not authoritative; they set no binding precedent for the US judge. But they can add to the store of knowledge'); and Chief Justice Wald of the US Court of Appeals in Wald (2004), 'Use of International Law', at 439 ('[i]t's hard for me to see that the use of foreign decisional law is an up-or-down proposition'); and for the view of another federal judge that it is not the citing of foreign law that is unconstitutional, but any effort to prohibit it, Messitte (2005), 'Citing Foreign Law', at 181 ('an effort at mind-control . . . Congress seeking to intrude on judicial independence'), though for US scholarship that 'lacks an intellectual framework capable of comprehending this legitimacy', Post (2001), 'Challenge of Globalization', at 328.

[39] On the historical European origins of the idea, see Ch. 4, 'An emerging theory of the state'; and for ongoing cosmopolitan methods, see Chapters 6, 7, and 8. For the historical practice of US delegation of judicial authority to binational panels, Monaghan (2007), 'Article III and Supranational Judicial Review', notably at 842 ('sanctioned by an ancient lineage'); and more generally of 'delegation' in favour of foreign law, Rutledge (2009), 'Delegation and Conflicts (of Law)', at 218 (where sovereign calculation that 'benefits from cooperation exceed the costs'). See also Tushnet (2003), 'Transnational/Domestic Constitutional Law', at 261 ('a sovereign nation can decide that its sovereign interests are advanced overall by making agreements with other nations that limit what it can otherwise do'). On the practice of delegating sovereign power to external authority, notably in Germany ('positive sovereignty'), see Ch. 9, 'Hierarchy'.

and the democracy argument, moreover, dwindle in strength when applied to the precise question of foreign sources. If it is not undemocratic for an elected legislature to rely on foreign models, then it is not the foreign provenance of legal models that makes them undemocratic. Judges too may therefore use them, in effecting judicial review, if it can be said that this judicial function is compatible with democracy. Opinion is divided on this more fundamental issue.[40]

The third important idea raised in the USA in the debate on foreign sources has the advantage of concentrating on the actual question. It would limit the sources used in interpretation of the Constitution to those demonstrably linked to the origins of the constitution itself. Just as ordinary legislation should be interpreted in pursuing the original meaning of the text, it is said, so a constitution should remain faithful to what it originally was. This notion of 'originalism' is a powerful one.[41] It is, however, both inherently cosmopolitan itself and eventually inadequate to prevent resort to foreign authority by independent judges. The latter point is the most evident, and is demonstrated by the ongoing practice of US Supreme Court justices to cite extra-national sources.[42] Debate over the methods of interpretation is never definitively resolved and the discursive judgments of high court judges cannot be confined to a pre-ordained set of sources. The citation of sources in the US Supreme Court is remarkably eclectic and the use of foreign sources is part of a wider interpretive debate. More significantly for present purposes, however, originalism is itself cosmopolitan in character, since it refers to sources embedded in eighteenth-century legal thought and these include extra-national sources, notably those of the common law and classical and Roman legal authors. These sources, moreover, antedated notions of positive law and were and remain remarkably flexible and variable.[43] Originalism is valuable in

---

[40] Strauss (2010), *The Living Constitution*, at 47 ('what makes our system undemocratic is judicial review'); Wood (1997), 'Comment', at 59 ('we have never had a purely democratic system of government in any traditional meaning of that term'); Waldron (2012), *'Partly Laws Common to All Mankind'*, at 149 (adherence to framers' views, precedent, undemocratic, 'let us not kid ourselves'); and more generally Beatty (2004), *The Ultimate Rule of Law*, at 59 (no theory 'able to explain how giving judges the authority to stop politicians acting on the platforms that got them elected is compatible with our core ideas of democracy'). Cf. for federal judges having 'at least an attenuated democratic legitimacy', Posner (2005), 'A Political Court', at 88; or USA as 'democracy over time [that] requires that a nation's constitutional law be made and interpreted by that nation's citizens, legislators and judges', Anderson (2005), 'Foreign Law and US Constitution', at 49 (materials used in 'countermajoritarian act of judging them nonetheless have, in some fashion, even indirectly, democratic provenance and consent').

[41] For its defence Scalia (1997), 'Common Law Courts', notably at 47 ('[i]f the courts are free to write the Constitution anew, they will, by God, write it the way the majority wants . . . This, of course, is the end of the Bill of Rights'); and for US features explaining it, Greene (2009), 'Origins of Originalism', at 62–82 ('canonizing influence of time', US revolution, even 'relatively evangelical religious culture').

[42] Most recently demonstrated in *Graham* v. *Florida*, 130 SC 2011 (2010), at 2033 where Kennedy, J., speaking for the majority, stated that the Court continues 'that longstanding practice in noting the global consensus against the sentencing practice in question', citing both foreign law and the UN Convention on the Rights of the Child, not ratified by the USA. It is of course inconsequential, from a cosmopolitan perspective, whether foreign sources are cited by a majority or a minority of the judges of a court.

[43] On the diversity of sources relied on by the authors of the Constitution, see Ch. 7, *'The United States of America'*, with reference also to sources derived from Scottish enlightenment. For the diversity and variability of the common law of English derivation, and its corresponding inability to provide single, fixed rules, Myler (2006), 'Common Law Originalism', at 556 ('disparate strands' of the common law,

concentrating attention on fundamental initial ideas; it cannot in itself bear the demands of contemporary constitutional practice. Moreover, a sharp dichotomy between originalist and non-originalist methods of interpretation is now breaking down in actual practice, as originalists admit the necessity of exceptions, and non-originalists accept the importance of constitutional text.[44]

The debate on citation of foreign sources, moreover, is remarkably narrow and remarkably luxurious. It is narrow in focusing exclusively on a single, though important, court and in neglecting the wider process of engagement with foreign sources in other US courts and fora through the federalized structure of the country.[45] It is also narrow in focusing on the particular common law practice of citation, since contemporary French practice shows that a high court can be remarkably cosmopolitan in its use of foreign sources without ever citing them in its judgments.[46] The debate is luxurious for the underlying presumption that what is cited actually matters, given the underlying integrity of the process and the necessity of reasoned justification in the adjudication. In much of the world this integrity cannot be presumed, and citation of foreign sources is vital not for the outcome of particular cases but for the effort to bring about an operative

some from colonies, others from England), 557 ('flexible and susceptible to change'), 558 ('framing questions for judges but refusing to settle them definitively'), 567 (a 'disunified field'); and for the unwritten character of much of US constitutional understanding, Tribe (2008), *The Invisible Constitution*, notably at 185 (for US Supreme Court practice of foreign citations since 1814); and on the difficulty of knowing *whose* initial understanding counts, Solum (2011), 'What is Originalism?', at 17ff. (framers, ratifiers, original public understanding?); Strauss (2010), *The Living Constitution*, at 11 (original public meaning in ascendance); Kay (2009), 'Original Intention' (for public understanding).

[44] Solum (2011), 'What is Originalism?', at 34–5 (originalist exceptions in cases of vagueness, or where precedents may be adhered to); Balkin (2011), *Living Originalism*, at 21 ('framework originalism'); and for exceptions to originalism, even by its proponents, Zaring (2006), 'Use of Foreign Decisions', at 309; Fontana (2004), 'Next Generation Transnational/Domestic', at 458–9; Strauss (2010), *The Living Constitution*, notably at 12–4, 17 (on need to except constitutional developments clearly not dictated by previous understandings, ensuing notion of the 'fainthearted originalist'); DeGirolami (2010–11), 'Vanity of Dogmatizing', at 220 ('theoretically complex middle road'); and for both 'exclusivists' and 'universalists' resorting to foreign law, the former negatively and accenting difference, the latter positively and accenting similarities, Rosenfeld (2012b), 'Comparative Constitutional Analysis', at 52.

[45] See notably Resnik (2006), 'Law's Migration' (America's federalist structure serving as path for movement of international rights across borders, extending to mayors, city council, state legislature, and state judges, with significant popular engagement in reframing American norms, that which is 'foreign' domesticated by several routes) and notably at 1576 ('[t]he conceit that United States law is basically bounded is inaccurate. Rather, laws (like people) migrate').

[46] The Court of Cassation, for reasons of republican theory based ultimately on concepts of the sovereignty of legislative authority and current notions of democracy, cites only French laws in its judgments, yet for documentation of extensive research and consideration of foreign law in its work, Canivet (2004), 'Use of Comparative Law Before French Private Law Courts', notably at 193 ('deference . . . to the self-sufficiency of national law is now obsolete'); Smits (2006), 'Comparative Law and its Influence', at 522 (elaborate comparative work by Advocate-General). In matters of public law the Conseil d'Etat in 2008 created a comparative law unit in its research division; see Stirn (2012), 'De l'intérêt de faire vivre le droit comparé'; for the Conseil's citation for the first time in 2003 of a foreign (English) decision, Andenas and Fairgrieve (2004), 'Finding a Common Language', at xxxii. The practice of *not* citing influential foreign models is also subject to criticism; see Cram (2009), 'Resort to Foreign Constitutional Norms', at 129 ('the overriding problem is one of a failure to make an explicit attribution', citing Supreme Court of Canada's failure to recognize German origins of doctrine of proportionality).

constitutionalism and to overcome 'façade' or 'sham' constitutions.[47] It may constitute a type of 'compensatory constitutionalism'.[48]

Cosmopolitan constitutionalism is thus today a very visible phenomenon, as are written constitutions themselves. Both function, however, on the basis of underlying, though less visible, common laws of historical origins.

---

[47] For the façades, Vincent (1987), *Theories of the State*, at 81 (even 'prevalence'); Frison-Roche (2006), 'De l'interprétation des textes', at 59 (texts insufficient to understand 'reality' of regimes in central and eastern Europe, Baltic); Granat (2006), 'Réception de la justice constitutionnelle', at 141 (image of constitutionalism in post-communist countries 'not fully exact'); and on the need for 'importing legitimacy from the outside', James (2006), *Roman Predicament*, at 39. For the thinness of constitutionalism in much of Africa, Latin America, Asia, and the Arab world, Fombad (2007), 'Challenges to Constitutionalism', at 17 (low levels of trust in state courts); Kreijen (2000–4), *State Failure, Sovereignty*, at 263 (for state failure as threat to 'international constitutionalism'); Schor (2006), 'Constitutionalism Through the Looking Glass', notably at 5 (on need for 'attitudinal shift'); Law and Versteeg (2013), 'Sham Constitutions' (notably for judicial review, ratification of human rights not 'statistically associated' with respect for human rights); Belaïd (1994), 'Constitutions dans le Tiers-Monde', at 121 (state legal system gravely compromised by religious, traditional, or regional legal sub-systems, in Asia, Africa, Latin America, Arab world); though for constitutional progress in Africa, Prempeh (2007), 'Constitutional Revival', in spite of ongoing dangers, notably at 472 ('constitutions without constitutionalism') and 482 ('predatory state').

[48] Peters (2006), 'Compensatory Constitutionalism'.

∝ 12 ∝

Cosmopolitan Sources II: Common Laws

We have seen the historic importance of common laws, originally within Europe as a means of reconciling overarching laws with local or particular laws, then again throughout the world as European law arrived with European colonizers and lingered on as an ongoing source. In both of these cases the common law was suppletive or relational in character, yielding to local laws when they claimed imperative application and imposing no law or legal content as binding in character.[1] The common laws of the world, as suppletive or relational laws, are increasing in importance in a time of globalization. Their nature provides some explanation of why this is the case. They provided underlying justification for the state structures that emerged everywhere in the world, as the 'droit avant le droit', and continued as the primary vehicle for the cosmopolitan constitutionalism that has been examined in the preceding chapter.[2] National state laws existed as particular laws within the various common laws of the world, which all left much space for the development of national particularity. Since national legal space was in principle open, according to all the relational common laws, there was no overarching principle or rule that state law itself had to completely displace all else. In some cases it may have purported to do so, at least apparently, as the French Law of 1804 introducing the Civil Code abolished all Roman laws, ordinances, general or local customs, statutes, and regulations.[3] Yet even here this occurred only, according to the law itself, for the matters that were the object of the code, leaving open the possibility of earlier law surviving, wraith-like, outside the actual text of the code. Even revolutions do not purport to abolish *everything*.[4] So the basic principle of accommodation of particular laws is not displaced by a general principle of the exclusivity of state law. State laws too can accommodate other laws. They are inherently cosmopolitan, which is why the territorial and national closures attempted in recent centuries required such massive efforts. It is also why the efforts were eventually unsuccessful.

Common laws thus supply an ongoing source for cosmopolitan constitutionalism, but they are important in other respects as well. They are resurgent in matters of private law; they continue to exercise influence in the reconciliation with non-state laws; they are developing more intense and visible reciprocal relations amongst themselves.

---

[1] See Ch. 3, '*Common laws*', and Ch. 6.

[2] For the 'droit avant le droit', see Ch. 6, 'Common Laws within Europe'.

[3] The Loi du 30 ventôse an XII, Art. 7.

[4] See Ch. 6, 'Common Laws within Europe'.

RESURGENCE

The common laws of the world were originally concerned principally with what we today call private law. The common law, the *ius commune*, the droit commun, the derecho commún, the gemeine Recht were all concerned principally with the legal relations of individuals, though there were public law concerns lurking behind the sanctity of sources.[5] As they spread through the world from the sixteenth century they were cited in many places, though this was often seen simply as a by-product of imperialism. The phenomenon has continued in post-colonial times, however, favoured by circumstances of availability, knowledge, and language.[6] It was a countercurrent in a time of attempts at national closure; with the current cosmopolitan turn in sources it has become mainstream and a major area of transborder judicial dialogue. The French Court of Cassation is an entirely private-law court and a leading participant in comparative research and debate; the House of Lords (prior to its transformation into the UK Supreme Court) had increased the attention it paid to foreign law in private law cases, almost tripling its references to foreign sources since the mid-1990s.[7] The phenomenon is most visible in common law jurisdictions but is not limited to them. German Pandectist legal thought is widely influential in the world and is increasing in importance, as post-communist states (most notably) are attracted to German legal science, this without any colonial or imperial sense of necessity having played a role.[8]

There is resurgence, however, not simply in the application and practice of historic common laws. There is also resurgence of non-state sources of private law that approach in their importance that of the historic common laws. The obvious example is that of the *lex mercatoria* which, like many common laws, went into a phase of self-effacement or 'hibernation' during periods of national closure but which is now increasingly visible in transnational commercial practice and dispute resolution.[9] Some had already concluded that, historically, the *lex*

---

[5] See Ch. 7, 'Sources'.

[6] See, on the relations of the laws of New Zealand and England, Denning MR in *Attorney General of New Zealand* v. *Ortiz* [1982] 3 All ER 432 at 452 ('we use the same language . . . to express the same principles, to define the same concepts, and to give the same meaning').

[7] For the Court of Cassation, see Ch. 11, 'The Cosmopolitan Turn in Constitutional Sources'; and for the House of Lords, Örücü (1999), 'Comparative Law in British Courts', at 264 (foreign citations averaging *c.* twenty-five per year between 1972 and 1992, then increasing threefold in 1994 and 1995); Smits (2006), 'Comparative Law and its Influence', at 522 (for 'most spectacular' developments in England, with references to cases).

[8] For Estonian adoption of 'a pandect system' with its new Civil Code, Liin (2004), 'New Estonian Civil Code', at 125; and for Pandectist influence in Italy, Alpa (2005), *Tradition and Europeanization*, at 99 (neither French nor German law, the latter more recently influential, considered 'foreign'); and in Japan, Noda (1976), *Introduction Japanese Law*, at 41–58; Kitagawa (1970), *Rezeption und Fortbildung*; Rahn (1990), *Rechtsdenken und Rechtsauffassung*, notably at 113 (for known expression in Japan that 'that which is not German law is not law'). The Swiss Civil Code retains its influence in Turkey after the 1926 adoption of a Swiss-based Civil Code: Aslan,(2005), 'Rückfahrkarte', notably at 36 (process of transfer not completed in 1926 with codification).

[9] For 'hibernation', Hatzimihail (2008), 'Many Lives of *Lex Mercatoria*', at 186, citing Goldman, and for the self-effacement of relational common laws generally, see Ch. 3, 'Common laws'.

mercatoria had reached equal status with the common laws, that the 'mother and daughter' had become 'unfriendly sisters',[10] but the case today has become much stronger. The traditional commercial requirements of rapidity and simplicity have become more pressing in an age of compression of space and time. Markets have their own dynamic and commercial actors such as banks are now abandoning their internal organization by country in favour of organization by industrial sector.[11] The parallel growth of arbitration has also freed the dispute resolution process from state law, in some measure, so institutional space has been added to the conceptual space provided by the notion of common laws.[12]

Unlike many of the historic common laws, the *lex mercatoria* has no imperialist history. It conquered no territory, fielded no battalions. It is not an extra-territorial projection of a law drawn from a single source but is itself varied in its origins. It epitomizes 'a sensibility of legal cosmopolitanism'.[13] In its current form it is best seen not as an anational law but as a law that freely combines elements of national and non-national law.[14] There has been discussion of its 'Americanization' and unquestionably US law plays a major role in many transnational transactions, but the diffusion process inevitably overcomes any effective notion of domination, just as was the case in the diffusion of the common laws. In the Swiss context the resulting mix has been described as 'muesli'.[15]

---

[10] Cordes (2001), 'Auf der Suche nach der Rechtswirklichkeit', at 175 (varying earlier descriptions of a relationship of mother to daughter); and for the debate over a millennium, with references to the vast literature, Glenn (2007c), *Common Laws*, at 114–16; Hatzimihail (2008), 'Many Lives of *Lex Mercatoria*', at 173.

[11] Sassen (2000), 'Institutional Embeddedness', at 73; and see for 'market-driven' approximation of laws and emergence of common principles of corporate governance in Europe, Hopt (2000), 'Common Principles of Corporate Governance', notably at 114 (transnational influence of New York Stock Exchange accounting standards); and for soft law as best for a 'high-speed economy', Scheuerman (2001), 'Global Law', at 115–6 (global time and space compression resulting in exploitation of non-formal decision-making in novel ways). The breadth of the contemporary *lex mercatoria* is best captured in Dalhuisen (2010), *Transnational Comparative, Commercial, Financial and Trade Law*; and see Dalhuisen (2004), Review of H. Kronke, *Capital Markets*, at 505, for 'offshore' character of much financial activity ('[t]his market does not have a location in any particular country . . . the essence of these offerings is also truly transnational'), 507 (few conflicts cases in national stock market activity because most cases governed by the 'law of the market').

[12] For arbitration, see Chapter 13, 'States and Transnational Law'.

[13] Hatzimihail (2008), 'Many Lives of *Lex Mercatoria*', at 171 and at 179 (for never losing its 'international dimension' even during time of commercial codification); and for modern 'protagonists' (Goldman, Schmitthoff, Horn, Lando, Lowenfeld, Goode), Dalhuisen (2010), *International Commercial, Financial and Trade Law*, at 225–6.

[14] Michaels (2007), 'The True *Lex Mercatoria*', at 448 (making distinction between anational and state law 'simply irrelevant by transcending it . . . a law beyond, not without, the state'); and for inclusion in informal corporate governance codes of both texts of national law and 'recommendations and suggestions', Calliess and Zumbansen (2010), *Rough Consensus and Running Code*, at 183 and 197 (on 'vivid' debate on legal nature of these codes).

[15] Böckli (1997), 'Osmosis of Anglo-Saxon Concepts', at 26 ('aggressive kernels' mixed into a milder mass, and many exceptions); and for US concept of 'leasing' giving rise to many different laws of leasing, notably with or without an option to purchase, Gonzalez del Campo (2005), 'Neue Vertragsformen', at 49, 52 (reception only of underlying economic notion of leasing); and for French debate on 'Americanisation', the colloquium at (2001) 45 Archives de philosophie du droit, notably Cadiet (2001), 'L'hypothèse de l'américanisation' (in matters of civil procedure largely at level of 'discourse').

The *lex mercatoria* is applied more often by parties and arbitrators than by state courts. Its significance is not found, however, in formal judicial recognition but in the space that it occupies in the resolution of transnational commercial disputes. It has not been ousted by state law, and the states that have been complicit in its contemporary growth are cosmopolitan in recognizing it and its multiple sources.

RECONCILIATION

Common laws have been the major instrument for reconciling laws throughout legal history. Divergent laws are often seen as conflicting, and when they coexist on the same territory there is need for reconciliation. In providing suppletive normativity the common laws ensured both their own survival (as a valued, non-conflicting source) and that of the local or particular laws to which they provided content and legitimacy (where needed). The states of the world have inherited this capacity for accommodation and in any event have been unable to fully occupy the legal field themselves. The reconciliation function of the common laws thus continues under the umbrella of the state. This is most evident in the process of reconciling state and common laws with the law of indigenous or chthonic peoples.

It has been said that the 1990s were characterized by a 'jurisprudence of reconciliation' between written state laws and the unwritten laws of indigenous or chthonic peoples. The reconciliation was concerned with 'restoring a balance to relations' between them.[16] The phenomenon has been widespread in the world, with constitutional, legislative, or judicial recognition of indigenous or chthonic rights and law in North America, Australasia, Latin America, Africa, Europe, and Africa.[17] Where the constitution is invoked this represents, as has

---

[16] McHugh (2005), *Aboriginal Societies and Common Law*, at 439, 540; and see at 366 for a preceding 'era of recognition' in the 1970s and 1980s. For formal recognition of the notion by the Supreme Court of Canada, *Minister of National Revenue* v. *Mitchell* [2001] 1 SCR 911 at 916 ('the constitutional objective is reconciliation not mutual isolation'); and see Walters (2008), 'Jurisprudence of Reconciliation', at 179 (for reconciliation rendering aboriginal claims 'consistent with the assertion by the Crown of sovereignty over the territory'). One of the major techniques of reconciliation has been the imposition of a fiduciary duty on the crown in relation to aboriginal peoples, creating a 'middle position' between crown discretion and a constant obligation of respect for aboriginal norms: see Fox-Decent (2006), 'Crown–Native Fiduciary Relationship', at 113 (crown thus held to certain obligations but within 'present constitutional arrangements'); and more generally Fox-Decent (2011), *Sovereignty's Promise: The State as Fiduciary*, notably pp 55ff.

[17] See generally McHugh (2005), *Aboriginal Societies and Common Law*; Havemann (1999), *Indigenous People's Rights*, notably Pt. VI ('Constitutionalising Indigenous Rights?'); and more specifically, for recent important settlements in the USA, Banner (2005), *How Indians Lost their Land*, at 291 ($248 million to Cayuga in New York; 40 million acres and nearly $1 billion in Alaska). For recognition in specific countries and regions, notably in Melanesia, Brown (2005), *Reconciling Customary Law*, notably at 15 ('in theory no question of clashes between custom and received law'), 19 (reconciliation as making two apparently conflicting things compatible with one another); for Nicaragua, *The Mayagna (Sumo) Awas Tingni Community Case*, Series C No. 79 [2001] IACHR 9, notably para. 153 (Inter-American Court of Human Rights finding Inter-American Convention extends to 'communal property right'); for Brazil and Mexico, Valades (2002), 'Les derechos de los indígenas', at 16–7 (constitutionalization in both); for Andean countries, Fajardo (2004), 'Legal Pluralism', at 32, 33 (for breakdown of binomials 'nation-state'

been noted above, a form of cosmopolitan constitutionalism.[18] In North America it is even a form of cosmopolitan constitutionalism acknowledging the 'fundamental constitution', in the form of treaties between European powers and the original peoples of the continent.[19] In the USA the language of 'tribal sovereignty' is thus firmly anchored, and though there is a constant fluctuation in ongoing case law, the 'underlying story' of two sovereignties would remain 'undisturbed'.[20] In Canada the recognition of the unwritten laws of original peoples would now have moved 'beyond territoriality' though without denying it. The law of first nations people is recognized both on and off aboriginal territories, in a manner consistent with the territoriality of state law and the sovereignty of European-derived political authority.[21]

The recognition by states of the non-state law of original peoples is a cosmopolitan phenomenon, and it is matched by the recognition by original peoples of state law itself. Thus the demands for autonomy of indigenous peoples is not an attack on the sovereignty of states but complementary to it, said to enrich its structure. Accordingly, the constitution of Mexico states, in its Article 4, paragraph 2 that '[t]he indigenous peoples have the right to free determination and, as expression of this right, to autonomy as a part of the Mexican state'.[22] Correspondingly, the

---

and 'state-law'), 35 (for recognition of unwritten law extending even to criminal law); Bastos and Camus (2004), 'Multiculturalismo', at 91 (five of seven central American constitutions recognizing 'multiethnic character' of population; for South Africa, Ndima (2003), 'The African law of the 21st century', at 340 (constitutionalization in South Africa); for Norway, Svensson (2005), 'Interlegality', at 62ff. (for cases on Sami claims); for Indonesia, Burns (2004), *The Leiden Legacy*, at 249 (for adat law); for The Philippines, Santos, Jr. (2000), 'Philippine Mixed Legal System', at 35.

[18] See Ch. 7, *'France and the world'*.

[19] Tully (1995), *Strange multiplicity*, at 136 (though largely 'overwhelmed by the theory and practice of modern constitutionalism', with treaties seen as mere contracts, indigenous rights as individual ones).

[20] Resnik (1989), 'Dependent Sovereignties', at 743 and see at 672 (for indigenous peoples of USA 'holding simultaneous membership in two political entities'), 679 ('truly distinct sovereigns', never having ceded sovereignty) and 693 ('no consent of the governed' can be offered in support of authority over tribes); McHugh (2005), *Aboriginal Societies and Common Law*, at 62 ('a distinct aboriginal sovereignty survived'); Miller (2011), 'Tribal Constitutions', at 1 (more than 565 present indigenous tribal governments in USA, exercising extensive sovereign and political powers); Valencia-Weber (1994), 'Tribal Courts: Custom', for tribal courts generally and notably at 228 (tribes persist in asserting a sovereignty the basis for which lies outside the foundation of a social contract); Carpenter (2008), 'Real Property and Peoplehood', at 349 (a 'separate people' with 'government-to-government' relationship with USA); Idleman (2004), 'Multiculturalism and Tribal Sovereignty', at 607 ('irreducibly political and sovereign'); though for sovereignty of US tribes having become 'more vestigial than vital', with tribes as 'domestic dependent nations', Raustiala (2009), *Does Constitution Follow the Flag?*, at 41–2; and for recent declines in tribal jurisdiction in Federal US courts, Ford (2010), *Settler Sovereignty*, at 206 ('state over indigenous sovereignty', e.g. highways, settler-sojourners on tribal reservations). For historical origins, see Ch. 7, *'Relations and guarantees'*.

[21] See Otis (2006), 'Territorialité, personnalité', notably at 785 (logic of territoriality one of normative uniformity), 803 (bands as political communities transcending territoriality, 'deterritorialisation'); Otis (2007), 'L'autonomie personnelle', notably at 677 (autochthonous political authority breaking with territorial model inherited from colonialism, 'interpersonal law'—'droit interpersonnel'); and for recognition and application of aboriginal law of adoption in common law Canada, prevailing even over provincial legislation, *Casimel* v. *Insurance Corporation of British Columbia* (1993) 106 DLR (4th) 720 (also citing previous authority); and for the same result in Quebec, *Deer* c. *Okpik* (1980) 4 CNLR 93.

[22] González Galván (2002), *Constitución y derechos indígenas*, at 21 (also for enriching constitutional structure); and for adoption by indigenous peoples of 'western rights discourse', McHugh (2005), *Aboriginal Societies and Common Law*, at 57.

Declaration on the Rights of Indigenous Peoples adopted by the UN General Assembly in 2007 provides in its Article 46 that the required recognition of customary laws shall be without prejudice to the state structures within which such recognition takes place.[23] The organization of the societies of indigenous or chthonic peoples may be pre-state, in the large sense of preceding even those state forms that preceded the contemporary state and in being non-formal and tribal in character.[24] Tribes therefore are not interested in emulating states, though they might have no fundamental objection to living with them. This view is becoming widespread and articulate amongst indigenous peoples, as their own movements globalize with the assistance of modern means of communication.[25] The process of reconciling indigenous or chthonic law with the law of the state would be facilitated, moreover, by the variety and intensity of states in the world, the thinner or less affirmative states seeing fewer conceptual problems in recognition of non-state law.[26]

Recognition of the unwritten law of indigenous or chthonic people may take place not only with respect to land claims and specific rights, such as a right to hunt, but by way of defence to criminal charges. Indigenous law is not alone in this regard, however, and there is now a transnational debate on the legitimacy of the so-called 'cultural defence' in criminal law. One may question the use of a concept of 'culture' in relation to specific criminal defences but the expression appears now to be established in some measure in the literature. What is striking is the degree of recognition of different forms of non-state law in the application of criminal law, generally assumed to be of uniform application and of an imperative (or public order) character. In some states, non-state law may provide a defence on the merits, eliminating culpability, as in India where there appears to be rejection of any 'abstract' standard of reasonableness in applying the defence of provocation.[27] Elsewhere there is resistance to variable determinations of culpability but much more widespread acceptance of non-state law in the sentencing process.[28] Even in matters of crime, therefore, all or most states

---

[23] Accessible at <http://www.un.org/esa/socdev/unpfii/documents/DRIPS_en.pdf >; see notably, for guarantees of collective rights, the preambular paras, Arts 5 and 34, and for non-impairment of states, Art. 46; and generally Errico (2007), 'UN Declaration on Rights of Indigenous Peoples'; Allen and Xanthaki (2010), *Reflections on United Nations Declaration on the Rights of Indigenous Peoples*.

[24] See Ch. 1, 'The State Tradition through Time', for large historical and anthropological conception of the state not extending to tribal structures.

[25] Brysk (2000), *Tribal to Global Village*, at 2 ('global symbolic appeals', 'scattered triumphs' coming from 'Goliath's own arsenal: from the United Nations to the World Wide Web'), 26 (varying levels of 'internationalization' of indigenous communities, e.g. very high in Nicaragua, moderate in Ecuador, Bolivia), 97 ('Global Panindigenous Movement', World Council of Indigenous Peoples, World Rainforest Movement).

[26] Ørebech et al (2005), *Role of Customary Law*, notably at 99 (tribal, religious, and similar identities 'continue to dominate over the national identity in weak states').

[27] Shah (2005), *Legal Pluralism in Conflict*, at 78 (citing *Nanavata* v. *State*, AIR 1962 SC 605 and stating Indian position as the 'most radical').

[28] For resistance in England, Shah (2005), *Legal Pluralism in Conflict*, at 80 (plea of provocation now being rejected in so-called honour killings); Woodman (2009), 'The Culture Defence', at 33 (culture defence as 'distinct general exemption defence' unlikely in England in the absence of a determination that

retain a cosmopolitan perspective where criminal sanctions are to be applied. There are now indications that similar accommodation is taking place in private law.[29]

Common laws have relations, however, not only with particular laws; they also have reciprocal relations with one another.

RECIPROCITY

In providing suppletive normative information to particular laws the common laws of the world functioned as vast repositories of information, freely available to those in need. In particular jurisdictions the national laws of which were formed through reception of a common law there were few conceptual or linguistic obstacles to ongoing fruitful relations. From one common law to another, however, there were and remain significant differences. These do not amount to incommensurability, a notion that should be confined to its rightful place in number theory, but commensurability should not be equated with convergence or the existence of a 'western legal tradition'.[30] Translation is a difficult art and translation of law over space, societies, languages, and conceptual difference is one of the most difficult forms of translation. It does, however, occur and is increasing in frequency and importance.

The judicial dialogue that is today developing is not one that occurs exclusively within established legal traditions or common laws. The increasing use of extra-national authority by the House of Lords (now the UK Supreme Court) in England has reverted to the nineteenth-century practice of resort to continental writers and case law.[31] It also extends backwards in time to acknowledgement of Roman

---

England a multi-cultural society); and for Canada, Robert (2004), *La défense culturelle*, notably at 28 (on 'inherent' problems of 'culture'), 91 (though other defences of self-defence, constraint, necessity, provocation can encompass claims under non-state law); though in favour of defence on the merits, Anon. (1986), 'The Cultural Defense', notably at 1298 ('individualized justice') and 1300 (difficulty in conforming with 'conflicting laws'). For widespread use in the sentencing process, however, Renteln (2004), *Cultural Defense*; Berman (2002), 'Globalization of Jurisdiction', at 448–9 for lesser sentences in US law, e.g. where tribal custom of 'marriage by capture'; Robert (2004), *La défense culturelle*, notably at 98 (for codification in Canada of use of 'alternative sanctions' appropriate in circumstances); Bakalis and Edge (2009), 'Taking due account of religion', at 421 (religion as 'personal mitigating factor'), 424 (though only in 25 per cent of cases); Pendu (2008), *Le fait religieux*, at 182; Sharma (2006), 'Customary Law' (customary punishment as sentence mitigation in Micronesia); Örücü (2008), 'Judicial navigation', at 49 (reduction of sentences for honour killings in Turkey).

[29] Berryman (2007), 'Accommodating Ethnic and Cultural Factors' (in fixing damages for personal injury).

[30] Glenn (2010c), 'A Western Legal Tradition?' (ongoing distinction between civil and common law traditions rooted in institutional features, as has always been the case); and further Glenn (2001a), 'Are Legal Traditions Incommensurable?', at 135–7 (for erroneous assertions of incommensurability, e.g. fried eggs and number 9). A true instance of incommensurability is the inexpressible character of the square root of 2 in integers.

[31] For cases, Reed (2008), 'Foreign Precedents', at 265–7 (for 'only three amongst many examples'); Smits (2006), 'Comparative Law and its Influence', at 522–3 (citing Lord Bingham on England ceasing to be 'a legal island'). In the nineteenth century, the authority of Pothier was 'the highest that can be had, next to a decision of a court of justice in this country': *Cox* v. *Troy* (1822), 5 B. & All. 474, 106 ER 1264, *per* Best J.

legal authority.[32] Nor is the comparative research undertaken for the work of the French Court of Cassation limited by geography or legal tradition. In the work of international courts and tribunals there is increasing need to canvass possible sources of aid and Article 21 of the Rome Statute of the International Criminal Court provides specifically that the Court shall have resort to 'general principles of law' that can be derived from the national laws of the world.[33] Specific national laws thus become illustrative of broader tendencies or consensus. They are representative of broader forms of common law, each of which becomes supportive of other common laws in the work of both national and international legal institutions.

In providing legal support for one another, the common laws of the world provide alternative forms of normativity and each may exercise greater or lesser influence in the world depending on the quality of its content. This has become the object of a vigorous contemporary debate centred on the influence of legal origins on the efficiency of national economies. In its most radical form the argument is presented that the common law is more economically efficient than the civil law, notably but not exclusively in its French variant.[34] Others have responded that the law used is wrong,[35] that the general conclusion is wrong,[36] and that there are other and better explanations.[37] This is not a debate that will ever be resolved but it has had the most significant effect of juxtaposing in an

[32] See for example *Mark v. Mark* [2005] UKHL 42 at paras 7–9 (citing of Digest 51,1,31 by Lord Hope of Craighead on acquisition of domicile of choice in spite of illegality of presence); and generally Lee (2009), '*Confusio*'.

[33] For resort to pan-traditional sources in constructing an international law of individual criminal responsibility, Roberts (2007), 'Comparative Law for International Criminal Justice', at 339 (comparative processes at work in seven concentric circles of international criminal justice activity); del Ponte (2006), 'Investigation and Prosecution' (international criminal procedure containing elements of civil and common law traditions); Langer (2005), 'Rise of Managerial Judging', notably at 849 (on different 'structures and interpretation of meaning' in criminal adjudication process); Cassese (2008), *International Criminal Law*, at 6, 7.

[34] See notably La Porta, de Silanese, and Shleifer (2008), 'Economic Consequences of Legal Origins', notably at 285–6 ('legal rules protecting investors vary systematically among legal traditions or origins, with the laws of common law countries (originating in English law) being more protective of outside investors than the law of civil law (originating in Roman law) and particularly French civil law countries'); and the symposium on the issue at (2009) 57 AJCL (contributions of Michaels, Spamann, Fauvarque-Cosson, and Kerhuel, Milhaupt, Reitz, and Curran).

[35] See, for a French response, Association Henri Capitant (2006), *Les droits de tradition civiliste* (questioning basic postulate that source of law is causally linked to economic development; cataloguing errors of law in analysis; insisting on virtues of accessibility, flexibility, and certainty of French civil law).

[36] Dam (2006), *Law–Growth Nexus*, notably at 24 ('little merit' to thesis of common law superiority), 39 (French economic superiority over UK), 204, 226 (misleading and incomplete data); Allen, Qian, and Qian (2005), 'Law, finance, and economic growth in China' (China as major counterexample to alleged link between economic growth and particular western legal traditions; importance of Confucianism); Ohnesorge (2007), 'Developing Development Theory', notably at 277 (on Korea, Japan, Thailand, 'having a structurally Civilian legal system cannot be much of a handicap').

[37] Siems (2007), 'Legal Origins' (variations due to differences in combination of civil and common law in different states); Roe (2006), 'Legal Origin' (variations due to political and economic measures taken in contemporary states rather than historical origins); Daniels, Trebilcock, and Carson (2011), 'Legacy of Empire' (diversity of rule of law indicators in former British colonies, importance of local representatives in legislative bodies, degree of integration of court structures).

active and dialogical manner the civil and common law traditions, arguably the most visible of the common laws of the world. The lawyers of each have become more cognizant of the features of the other; it is a necessarily cosmopolitan debate. To the extent that it is rooted in institutional features of the common law it can also be seen as an instance of institutional cosmopolitanism, the last of our cosmopolitan methods in matters of sources.

⤶ 13 ⤷

Cosmopolitan Sources III: Institutional Cosmopolitanism

The world has known institutional cosmopolitanism since the time of coexistence in a same territory of the laws of church, empire, city, and crown.[1] All of these prevailed, in some measure, and collaboration and governance was the order of the day, in the absence of alternatives. Empires and cities have declined in legal importance, but the state exists today in a world filled with religions and other states.[2] Institutional cosmopolitanism necessarily continues, manifested both in relation to religion and with respect now to the international, the regional, and the transnational. The most ancient of these forms of institutional cosmopolitanism is collaboration between religious and temporal authority.

STATES AND RELIGIOUS AUTHORITY

The rise of the contemporary state has been at the expense of non-state law, but the respective roles of state and non-state law vary widely in the world. The institutional dimensions of this variety have been examined earlier in this book,[3] where it was noted that all states in the world have formal relations with religious authority, extending to various forms of establishment, and that a very large number of states acknowledge the ongoing validity of personal or religious laws. This institutional variety then plays out in the debate over contemporary sources. In the most successful and affirmative of states, the debate is formulated in terms of a constitutionally guaranteed right to religious liberty, which may involve reliance on religious law. In less successful and less affirmative states, the debate is formulated in terms of a less circumscribed and ongoing delineation of the roles of state and religious law.

---

[1] See Ch. 2.

[2] For 'religious pluralisation', Martinez-Torrón and Durham (2010b), 'Religion and Secular State', at 4 (and number of religious minorities proliferating in every country); and for transition of Muslims in the USA from 'outsiders' to a minority seeking recognition, Moore (1995), *Al-Mughtaribun*, Ch. 4. The city as a legal entity has become subject to state norms in all but those few city-states noted above in Ch. 2, 'Collaborative Cities', though the 'global city' may exercise influence beyond its formal status as a municipality.

[3] See Ch. 8, 'Churches and Religions'.

Religious liberty

The right to religious liberty is now the most widely accepted right in the constitutions of the world.[4] It is contested by some at a theoretical level, vigorously defended by others but, as a result of historical and ongoing necessity, is unavoidable.[5] It is also necessarily compatible with many of the varying levels of church establishment that have emerged.[6] Judges play the dominant role in its respect and must walk a fine and cosmopolitan line between state and religious sources of law. As judges of law they are ethically bound to neutrality towards parties, and must hear the arguments that parties present. The parties themselves will argue as they will, and the neutrality of the judge requires hearing of the arguments, though the arguments might not sharply distinguish between state and non-state sources. The neutrality of the judge is reflected at a second level, however, in the idea that the judge is one of law and not of religion. The parties' right to religious liberty, and the judge's neutrality towards religion, means that the judge's role in ensuring respect for religious liberty is a distant one. The judge must ensure respect for the religious choices of others, without impinging on those choices.[7] The essential question is that of knowing whether the choices are religious ones, and the task of answering this question is challenging. The judge must ensure respect for that which is religious but must do so without commitment to any particular view of what a religion might be.

Earlier efforts at definition of religion, notably those of the US Supreme Court in the nineteenth century, are now seen as narrow and theistic, leaving little room for protection of less conventional forms of belief.[8] There have since been

---

[4] See Ch. 7, '*Relations and guarantees*'; and, for the emergence of religious liberty from the time of royal imposition of a single religion, see Ch. 5, 'Religion'.

[5] Sager (2008), 'Moral economy of religious freedom', at 17 (privileging claims on behalf of religion is 'morally indefensible and self-defeating'), 18 (no distinction from 'other deep passions and commitments'); Eisgruber and Sager (2007), *Religious Freedom*, at 4 (denying that religion 'demands special benefits and/or necessitates special restrictions', proposing 'Equal Liberty'); Leiter (2010), 'Foundations Religious Liberty', at 940 (toleration not justification since allowing disapproval, need for 'thick' version of respect), 945 (religion however 'insulated from evidence'); but in defence, Webber (2008), 'Understanding the religion in religious freedom', notably at 32 ('special respect for individual's religious obligations'); Koppelman (2010), 'How Shall I Praise Thee?' (reducing religion to personal conscience under-inclusive, religion broader, notably giving legitimation to institutions); Finnis (2009), 'Does Free Exercise?', notably at 43, 56 (critics reduce religious liberty to personal commitment whereas religion a 'practical expression of, or response to, truths about human society'); Ahdar and Leigh (2005), *Religious Freedom*, Part I (Christian and liberal justifications, latter including civil peace, fostering civic virtue, personal autonomy).

[6] Ahdar and Leigh (2005), *Religious Freedom*, at 154 ('acknowledgement' rather than 'establishment').

[7] On the corresponding autonomy of religious authority, or religious decision-making, Martinez-Torrón and Durham (2010b), 'Religion and Secular State', at 20 (rights to select, manage, and dismiss personnel, to communicate with religious personnel and members of the faith, to establish educational and charitable organization, to own and sell property, to solicit and expend funds, to say nothing of establishing the tenets of religious belief).

[8] Choper (1995), *Securing Religious Liberty*, at 67 ('less complicated' conception of religion, now 'fractured' by 'present multireligious society') and 85 (for difficulties of 'single feature definition'); and for expansion of the concept over time, Greenawalt (2006), *Religion and the Constitution*, vol. 1, at 126 (to inclusion of Buddhism, Taoism, secular humanism, and 'ethical culture'); Freeman (1983), 'Misguided Search', at 1524 (notably for suggestion earlier definitions themselves unconstitutional).

many attempts, moving through structural or institutional definitions (that look to institutions and a body of precepts or rules)[9] to 'functional' definitions (such as Tillich's insistence on that which fulfils a role of 'ultimate concern' to people).[10] There are also methodological proposals, such as proceeding in an analogical manner from that which is already accepted as religion,[11] or looking in a Wittgensteinian manner to 'family resemblances'.[12] Given the evident difficulties, however, definitional efforts are in decline, bringing both a realization that a formal definition is unnecessary for judicial purposes, and a corresponding increase in the number of recognized religions.[13] This itself is a cosmopolitan phenomenon, taking us further and further from the crown-imposed state religions (*cuius regio, eius religio*) of the Westphalian era.[14]

Since no structured definition of religion appears possible there has been an inevitable tendency towards subjective or individualized concepts of religion. These may be in entirely individualistic or solipsistic terms, or in terms of individual interpretation of major religions.[15] Given such a potentially anarchic

---

[9] Ariens and Destro (2002), *Religious Liberty*, at 985; Landheer-Cieslak (2007), *La religion devant les juges*, at 255 ('une approche communautaire et institutionnelle'); Durham, Jr. and Sewell (2006), 'Definition of Religion', at 21; and see the minority judgment of Justice Bastarache in *Syndicat Northcrest* v. *Amselem* [2004] 2 SCR 551, 2004 SCC 47, para. 105, notably at para. 135 (religion a 'system of beliefs and practices').

[10] Tillich (1957), *Dynamics of Faith*, at 11–12; and for some movement in US courts to such functional definitions in the late twentieth century, Durham, Jr. and Sewell (2006), 'Definition of Religion', at 22.

[11] Greenawalt (2006), *Religion and the Constitution*, vol. 1, at 139 ('more flexible analogical approach').

[12] Greenawalt (2006), *Religion and the Constitution*, vol. 1, at 139.

[13] For avoidance of definitional efforts by the US Supreme Court for a half-century, Ariens and Destro (2002), *Religious Liberty*, at 985; in western democracies generally, Ahdar and Leigh (2005), *Religious Freedom*, at 112 (on danger of early exclusion of what may become a major faith); in France, Forey (2007), *État et institutions religieuses*, at 57 (neither legislative nor judicial definition); in the European Convention on Human Rights, or any other human rights treaty, Evans (2001), *Freedom of Religion*, at 51; Uitz (2007), *Freedom of Religion*, at 281; and for justification of the absence of definition, Borgeaud (2004), *Aux origines des religions*, at 9 (plural and polemical nature of what is known as religion constantly constructed and reconstructed, study necessarily transhistorical and comparative). An 'outer definition' was proposed by the Canadian Supreme Court in *Syndicat Northcrest* v. *Amselem* [2004] 2 SCR 551, 2004 SCC 47, at para. 39 ('[d]efined broadly, religion typically involves a particular and comprehensive system of faith and worship . . . also tends to involve the belief in a divine, superhuman or controlling power'). For the number of recognized religions in the USA now passing 1,000, Ariens and Destro (2002), *Religious Liberty*, at 986, and for this constituting an increasingly non-Eurocentric understanding of religion, indicating greater need for intellectual means of accommodation or conciliation, Tribe (1988), *American Constitutional Law*, at 1154; and for definitional generosity of the European Court of Human Rights, Evans (2001), *Freedom of Religion*, at 55 (including atheism). Religion thus would extend to 'any set of answers to religious questions, including the negative and sceptical answers of atheists, agnostics and secularists': Laycock (2008), 'Religious Liberty', at 174; and see similarly Hoffman and Rowe (2003), *Human Rights in the UK*, at 210.

[14] See Ch. 5, 'Religion'.

[15] Renan concluded in the nineteenth century that 'religion has become an individual matter': Renan (1991), *Qu'est-ce qu'une nation?*, at 238 (rejecting religion as basis of 'nation'); for twentieth-century judicial affirmations of the theme, Uitz (2007), *Freedom of Religion*, at 25; add *Syndicat Northcrest* v. *Amselem* [2004] 2 SCR 551, 2004 SCC 47 at para. 41 ('the right to entertain such religious beliefs as the person chooses . . . to work out for himself or herself what his or her religious obligations, if any, should be', this in the context of Jewish religion); and for its advantages, Bouchard and Taylor (2008), *Building for the Future*, at 58 (court need not become religious tribunal, avoids majority rule in religious matters, circumvents 'virtually insolvable problem' of defining religion).

drift, courts have created other techniques of limitation. These have been perhaps most visible in countries of non-establishment or 'laïcité', such as the USA and France, but the limits themselves have been subjected to cosmopolitan reaction or interpretation. In the USA a test of 'sincerity' of religious beliefs has emerged, based not on determining the truth of religious statements but rather on the genuineness of their being held.[16] Insincerity is difficult to establish, however, and in the USA attention has turned rather to a notion of 'generally applicable' state laws that exclude accommodation of sincere religious belief. This was the technique used in the now leading case of *Employment Division* v. *Smith* in which a majority of the court refused a religious exemption from a legislative prohibition of the use of peyote to an indigenous group that used it as an essential element of religious life.[17] Scalia J. stated that the conclusion followed from the fact that 'we are a cosmopolitan nation made up of people of almost every conceivable religious preference', this excluding the 'luxury' of treating general laws presumptively invalid in affecting religious beliefs.[18] What is striking about the decision and its general language is the flexibility it would still allow (no regulation of beliefs as such, no imposition of special disabilities, no preference for particular religious views) and perhaps most importantly the strong legal and political reaction it generated, both Federal and state governments enacting subsequent legislation designed to 'restore' religious freedom.[19] There can be religious exemptions to 'generally applicable' laws, and a cosmopolitan nation apparently cannot be governed in a rigorously uniform manner.

France has been less ecumenical and less individualistic in its definition of religion, and there have been efforts to distinguish true religions (the major ones)

---

[16] Durham, Jr. and Sewell (2006), 'Definition of Religion', at 50 (no obligation to protect 'pseudo-norms' or those not held); and see *US* v. *Ballard* 322 US 78 (1944) (established mail fraud by those soliciting money as 'divine messengers', once established that they had composed form-letter testimonials from non-existent persons claiming to have been healed).

[17] 494 US 872 (1990); cf. the decision of the Constitutional Court of South Africa in *Prince* v. *President of the Law Society of the Cape of Good Hope*, 2002 (2) SA 794, refusing to allow a religious exception for use by Rastafarians of cannabis and relying less on the generality of the prohibitive legislation than on a process of proportional balancing and the widespread and illegal use of cannabis, as opposed to peyote, and ensuing problems of enforcement.

[18] 494 US 872 at 888. For the decision abandoning a free exercise doctrine that had prevailed during the previous quarter-century, Greenawalt (2006), *Religion and the Constitution*, vol. I, at 77 (state having to show a 'compelling interest' in applying a law against people whose religious exercise is burdened); and similarly Ariens and Destro (2002), *Religious Liberty*, at 986 (decision to 'greatly reduce' importance of First Amendment guarantee of religious liberty); and for critique in the name of 'permeable' or partial state sovereignty, with primary burden that of justifying state law, exemptions as constitutional right, Greene (2012), *Against Obligation*, at 116, 123ff. (though only *prima facie* right).

[19] For such flexibility, Martinez-Torrón and Durham (2010b), 'Religion and Secular State', at 26; Tebbe (2011), '*Smith* in Theory and Practice', at 2056–8 (if constitutional interest other than religion present, e.g. free speech, cases of 'individual assessment'); Duncan (2008), 'Free Exercise is Dead', at 186 (on 'locating the borders' of neutrality and general applicability). For federal and state legislation reinstating the requirement of a 'compelling' state interest for burdening religious exercise, Berg (2008b), 'Introductory Essay', at 20; Martinez-Torrón and Durham (2010b), 'Religion and Secular State', at 27 (some twenty-five states enacting such legislation); Greenawalt (2006), *Religion and the Constitution*, vol. I, at 84; Carpenter (2008), 'Real Property and Peoplehood', at 336 (for constitutionality of such 'legislative accommodation'). The federal legislation was applied by the Supreme Court itself in *Gonzalez* v. *Uniao Do Vegetal* 126 SC 1211 (2006).

from 'sects', a position that has been described ironically, given French republicanism, as 'communautaire'.[20] Yet French judicial and even legislative practice inevitably reflects the profoundly cosmopolitan nature of contemporary French society.[21] In public law a heterogeneous process of accommodation lies beyond the highly visible rejection of public religious apparel which,[22] as has been seen, involves state financing of religious institutions.[23] The private law is still more nuanced and, in spite of the basic principle of 'laïcité' anchored in the French constitution, French private law judges accommodate claims based on different religious laws through a variety of devices that essentially throw a veil of secularity over what remains a religious norm. Thus they generally deal with the 'religious fact' ('le fait religieux') and make decisions based on facts, as secular judges quite rightly do.[24] Religious norms may thus be 'subsumed' or 'incorporated' under civil ones and there may be a process of 'contractualization' of religious law.[25] This case law or jurisprudence is not, of course, uniformly in favour of application of religious law in secular guise. The French Court of Cassation, for example, dismissed religious justification for the construction of a Jewish succah on an apartment balcony, stating summarily though less than evidently that 'however fundamental religious liberty might be' it could not

---

[20] Landheer-Cieslak (2007), *La religion devant les juges*, at 254 and see 334–46 and 380–405 (on judicial efforts to distinguish sects from religions). See also Forey (2007), *État et institutions religieuses*, at 180–202 (French state acting against 'dangerosité' of certain sects, delictual conduct); and Tawil (2009), *Du gallicanisme administratif*, notably at 173 (Conseil d'Etat exercising 'benevolent tolerance' to 'newly present' religions), 182 (extending recognition in spite of 'agitation politico-médiatique').

[21] For statistics on immigration see Ch. 10, 'Citizenship and Mobility'; and see Chemin (2009), 'Le nouveau visage de la France', at 10 (one of the most multi-cultural of countries, 'the America of Europe'); and for still earlier judicial reflection of population diversity, Rouland (2000), 'Le droit français multiculturel?' (notion of indivisibility of state yielding to 'multi-culturalism').

[22] Tawil (2009), *Du gallicanisme administratif*, at 175–81 (for the tension between the Conseil d'État and political authorities on the question); Malaurie (2005), 'L'État et la religion' (on decisions of Conseil d'État as 'pacifying').

[23] See Ch. 8, 'Churches and Religions'; and for diverse regimes more widely of regional languages, special status (of Corsica, for example), and overseas territories, Fenet (1989), 'Présentation générale', at 10; Lochak (1989), 'Minorities et droit public français', at 111, notably at 113 ('pragmatic' administration of differences, henceforth not only tolerated but even 'institutionalized'), 138 (marginal adjustments, limited derogations).

[24] See generally Pendu (2008), *Le fait religieux*, notably at 27–9 (on religion as sufficient 'interest' for change to Muslim name as required by Islam), 39 (for awarding damages for failure to provide a Jewish divorce or get), 49 (for Catholic resistance to divorce as possible ground for denying divorce on grounds of 'hardship'), 190–1 (limits on employer's refusal to allow religious days off work); Forey (2007), *État et institutions religieuses*, at 20, 22 (recognition of individual religious norms though not religious legal order compatible with secularity, a 'legal fact'), 211 (religious norm as 'element' in determination of solution).

[25] Landheer-Cieslak (2007), *La religion devant les juges*, at 455, 460 (submitting to religious marriage as submission to religious rules of divorce, employment at Catholic school as consent to Catholic religious rules); Forey (2007), *État et institutions religieuses*, at 140 (kosher quality of meat as question of substantive quality), 244 (time taken off work not ground for dismissal when required by religious law); and for the general phenomenon of departure from uniform rules of the Civil Code, Mestre (2002), 'Droit civil: Rapport général', at 231 (minorities obtaining 'special' civil law, contrary to civilian principle of unity); De Béchillon (1997), *Qu'est-ce qu'une règle?*, at 150 (customary male succession in French region still applied in 'absolute contradiction' with Civil Code); Glenn (1987b), 'Use of Computers' (computer recovery of case law providing evidence of case law variety).

prevail over a set of condominium by-laws.[26] Case law on religious liberty will never be uniform, however, and French decisions are now subject to the surveillance of the European Court of Human Rights, which has already rendered one decision finding the French notion of 'sects' to be incompatible with the guarantee of religious liberty in the European Convention on Human Rights.[27] The inherent cosmopolitanism of the French tribunals is thus compounded by this extra-national regard, which will be returned to in the larger context of regionalization.[28]

State and religious legal sources

The visibility of the notion of religious liberty is paradoxically an indication of the primacy of the contemporary state in many parts of the world. Religion can be downsized and converted into a subjective right, belonging to the individual, and then in considerable measure the institutional or collective force of religion disappears. The state would have prevailed over intermediate bodies and organizations; the individual would have no collective support in his or her relations with the state. This state of affairs, to the extent it exists, is an indication both of the importance of Christianity (the 'religion for leaving religion')[29] in the emergence of the contemporary state and of the institutionalization of the state as a permanent, ongoing legal personality (itself largely the product of canonical doctrine).[30] This permissiveness of the Christian religion towards secular and permanent institutions is not replicated, however, in many parts of the world. In the result, the contemporary state does not always nest in environments as welcoming as those of its original jurisdictions. Here the debate over sources of law is not confined to the precise question of religious liberty, but overflows at least potentially into all areas of law. The state is all the more cosmopolitan in this constant and ongoing process of delineating authority. The process is most evident in Islamic jurisdictions but is not exclusively confined to them.

There are some forty-four states in the world whose populations are 'predominantly Muslim'. As is to be expected, there is considerable variety amongst them. Ten are officially declared to be Islamic states; a further twelve declare simply that Islam is their official religion.[31] In these jurisdictions the place of Islamic

---

[26] Cass. Civ. 8 June 2006, Bull. III, no. 140, p. 115, *Epoux X c. Syndicat des copropriétaires les Jardins de Gobrella*; cf. the opposite conclusion of the Supreme Court of Canada in *Syndicat Northcrest v. Amselem* [2004] 2 SCR 551, 2004 SCC 47. For the same court refusing a religious exemption from a legislative requirement for a personal photo on a driver's licence, however, *Alberta v. Hutterian Brethren of Wilson Colony* 2009 SCC 37, [2009] 2 SCR 567.

[27] *Palau-Martinez c. France*, HUDOC 16 December 2003.

[28] See this chapter, 'States and Regional Law'.

[29] See Ch. 2, 'The church within', 'The church without'; and see Augenstein (2012), 'Religious pluralism and national constitutional traditions', at 267 (European Christians accepting distinction between secular public sphere and religious private sphere 'because they contributed to its creation in the first place', but national variations in implementation).

[30] See Ch. 3, 'Hierarchy'; Ch. 4, 'The state as body, crown, or corporate person'.

[31] Stahnke and Blitt (2005), 'The Religion–State Relationship', at 954, and at 955–6 (with maps, charts), 981ff. (appendix listing constitutional provisions); Baderin (2003), *International Human Rights*, at 9 (for fifty-seven members and three observer states of Organization of Islamic Conference (OIC)).

sources of law is formally guaranteed (since the Islamic religion is a legal one). A further eleven predominantly Muslim states have declared themselves to be secular; the balance, including Indonesia, have made no declaration of either secularity or Islamic fidelity.[32] In legal terms the entire group thus ranges from a 'purist' Saudi Arabia (relying on the Koran itself as constitution) to a 'secular' Turkey.[33] In all cases, however, the majority of the population will respect Islamic normativity, in varying measure. There will therefore be underlying scepticism both towards the state as an enduring and constant legal personality (Islamic teaching never having accepted the notion of a corporate fiction or legal personality)[34] and towards its fixed territorial boundaries.[35] The state is a weaker, and necessarily cosmopolitan, legal institution in these social and religious circumstances.

The debate over the possibility of an Islamic state is polarized in some measure.[36] In one direction is the affirmative, Shi'ite position, most vigorously affirmed in Iran, that the sovereignty of God entails clerical control of the state, a position the details of which are not fully established.[37] Thus Saudi Arabia, a

---

[32] Stahnke and Blitt (2005), 'The Religion–State Relationship', at 955 ('secular' states representing only 13.5 per cent of Islamic world population).

[33] Esposito (1999b), 'Contemporary Islam', at 651–2. For Saudi Arabia's 'Basic Regulation' (not 'constitution') providing in its Art. 1 that '[t]he religion [of Saudi Arabia] is Islam, its constitution is the Book of God', Vogel (2000a), *Islamic Law and Legal System*, at 3 and xiv (Islamic law the law of the land, western concepts never invading 'essential core' of Saudi law).

[34] Kuran (2005), 'Absence of Corporation in Islamic Law' (on fear of corporate loyalties, role of both partnerships and waqf as instruments of finance, charity). For further references on 'individualization' of corporations created by legislation in Islamic lands, Glenn (2010b), *Legal Traditions*, at 195; and for 'personification' of the state in European teaching, see Ch. 4, 'The state as body, crown, or corporate person'. The word 'state' historically did not exist in Islamic jurisdictions: Crone (2004a), *God's Rule*, at 3 (Muslims seeing themselves as 'governed by persons rather than institutions'), 4 (Arabic word dawla (Persia dowlat) adopted in nineteenth century for state).

[35] For territoriality as 'present' but 'hardly emphasized' in Islamic teaching, Hashmi (2003), 'Political Boundaries and Moral Communities', at 196–7 (given expansive nature of Islam, frontiers 'extremely fluid'; land of Islam (dar al-Islam) thought of not in territorial terms but as 'logical derivative of the moral ideal of the united Muslim umma'—community), 198 (even in Ottoman, Safavid, and Mughal empires travel across borders relatively unimpeded), 206 (emphasis rather on tearing boundaries down than on erecting them, common ontology of human beings); El Fadl (2003), 'The Unbounded Law of God' at 214 (hostility to ethos of blind loyalty to tribe, clan, family, or even piece of land, commitment rather to justice), 215 (challenge to legitimacy of formal borders), 226 (political boundaries threatening to transform moral communities into political entities, 'a closed, determined and parochial reality'). Art. 11 of the new Iranian Constitution provides that 'all Muslims form a single nation'.

[36] For an 'essentially impossible' consensus on an Iranian state, Harding (2002a), 'The Keris, The Crescent', at 156; and for a major contribution to the debate, on whether there is an 'Islamic constitutionalism' across many jurisdictions, Grote and Röder (2012), *Islamic Constitutionalism*.

[37] Amir-Moezzi and Jambet (2004), *Qu'est-ce que le shî'isme?*, at 219 (on Khomeini's notion of 'government of the jurist', only an Islamic government ensuring application of Islamic precepts), 220 (dominance of rationalist tradition in Shi'ite teaching); Zaman (2002), *The Ulama*, at 105 (jurists delegates of the hidden imam, not only in faith but in 'politics'), 107 (collapsing of distinction between authority of jurists and authority of state); Mallat (1993b), *Renewal of Islamic Law*, at 4 (on 'turmoil' around constitutional law in Islamic jurisdictions), 89 (Iranian constitution 'riddled with constitutional ambiguities'); and for the coexistence in Iran of clerical control with a largely French-inspired constitutional model, Hosen (2005), 'Constitutionalism and Syar'i'ah', at para. 75 (republican form of government, separation of powers, directly elected officials, concepts of legality, national sovereignty).

monarchy, would not constitute an Islamic state, in spite of the importance accorded to the shari'a.[38] In the other direction is the view, most recently and vigorously defended by Abdullahi An-Na'im, that the notion of an Islamic state is 'conceptually incoherent, historically inaccurate and practically not viable today'.[39] The state must therefore be separate from Islam, yet this separation would not involve separation of Islam from politics and there could be political adoption of Islamic principles as secular state law.[40] These positions appear to be absolutist ones and can well be formulated as conflicting claims over the *situs* of sovereignty, located either with God or with the people. One would have to choose, in spite of the difficulty of precisely locating sovereignty in the European states having given birth to the idea.[41]

There have, however, been major theoretical efforts to reconcile Islam with the contemporary state, and there has been much practice of different combinations of them. If there is no possibility of radical separation, there is one type or other of institutional cosmopolitanism. The theoretical efforts at reconciliation start necessarily from a view that neither the secular nor the Islamic represent 'totalistic' religious or political/legal goods.[42] Therefore there would always be room for various combinations of both, though the problem is one of facilitating their coexistence, guarding against a situation in which 'the one challenges and negates the other'.[43] Neither the notion of God's sovereignty nor an essentialist

---

[38] For royal authority in Saudi Arabia as 'unbridled' and 'absolute', van Eijk (2010), 'Sharia and national law', at 152, 172.

[39] An-Na'im (2008), *Islam and Secular State*, at 104 (enforcement of shari'a through institutions of state 'fundamentally inconsistent with nature of Shari'a, as religious normative system'); and An-Na'im (1998–9), 'Shari'a and Positive Legislation', at 37 (Islamic state 'conceptually impossible'); and for 'modern intellectual consensus' that Islam incompatible with idea of the state, Piscatori (1986), *Islam in World of Nation-States*, at 42, 76–7, though, at 109 (a 'dissenting intellectual line persists'), 110 (south-east Asian Muslims less negative).

[40] An-Na'im (2008), *Islam and Secular State*, at 4; and An-Na'im (2010), 'The Compatibility Dialectic', at 4 (Islamic law 'cannot be enforced as state law and remain Islamic law', need to abandon claims that Islamic law principles can be enacted into state law as a matter of religious obligation). For criticism of An-Na'im's 'binary structure' and urging of 'reflective equilibrium', Fadel (2013), 'Seeking an Islamic Reflective Equilibrium', at 1258, 1266.

[41] See Ch. 4, '*An emerging theory of the state*'; and see Mallat (1993b), *Renewal of Islamic Law*, at 70 (citing Sadr that '[o]riginal sovereignty rests only with God'); Fadel (2009), 'Islamic Politics and Secular Politics', at 106 (for notion of 'two sets of normative duties [that] cannot be reconciled'); or for formulation in terms of either a law already given through revelation, or a law still capable of creation by secular authority, Belaïd (1994), 'Constitutions dans le Tiers-Monde', at 119; Jackson (1996), *Islamic Law and State*, at xiv (state seen as 'only true repository of legal authority', Islamic legal authority 'totally outside the apparatus of the state').

[42] Elshtain (2004), 'Response', at 40 (more common case that of 'putting together belief and law and bringing them to bear on one another'); Feldman (2003a), *After Jihad*, at 11 (democracy and Islam 'need not be opposed', tentative, provisional compromises), 30 (flexibility of Islamic tradition, democracy potentially wider than western models).

[43] El Fadl (2003–4), 'Islam and Challenge Democratic Commitment', at 4 and 68 (for shari'a not as fixed set of rules but as 'symbolic construct for the Divine perfection that is unreachable by human effort . . . as understood by human beings Shari'ah is imperfect and contingent'); and see Emon (2003–4), 'On Democracy', at 78 ('between the ideals of Islam and democracy . . . lies a role for human agents . . . by which both ideals are actualized'); Kahn (2010), 'The Qur'an and the Constitution', at 189 ('mutually supportive; one does not negate the other'); Hosen (2005), 'Constitutionalism and Syar'i'ah' (shari'a

notion of the state or democracy can prevail in this process, since each lacks the necessary precision. God as a sole legislator would be a 'fatal fiction', incompatible with Islamic theology, while secularism is not capable of definition given the variety of its instantiations in the world.[44] Both western and Islamic states, moreover, know the phenomenon of law before the state, so in each case it is a question of the extent to which such law is continually operative in the functioning of the state, beyond the law it has itself created.[45] Historically, the Islamic world would thus have known both secular rulers and democratic forms of consultation (or shura).[46]

Given the divine and historical primacy of Islamic teaching, the growth of apparently secular norms was within the cadre of an authorizing and legitimating shari'a.[47] There is a clear parallel with the legitimating influence of the common laws of Europe. The notion of a 'common Islamic constitutional law' is now even

compatible with constitution either as formal source (Egypt, Iran) or as 'inspiration' for constitution (Indonesia)); and for further 'normative-juristic' writers showing Islam 'not incompatible' with democracy, Jackson (1996), *Islamic Law and State*, at xxxvi (though emphasis 'away from the historical record').

[44] El Fadl (2003–4) 'Islam and Challenge Democratic Commitment', at 16 for 'fatal fiction' (since no human has perfect access to God's will) and see also at 10 (for authoritarianism inflicted in name of religion as transgression on bounds of God), and 62 (for imprecision of secularism); and for notion of 'divine sovereignty' (al-hakimiyya) as twentieth-century construction and 'rupture' with Sunni thought, Afsaruddin (2006), 'Islamic State', at 161. On the perils of essentializing the state, Fadel (2011), 'Tragedy of Politics?', notably at 112 (criticizing Hallaq's notion of state as 'a living organism with immutable characteristics'), 118 ('binary framework that assumes the radical incommensurability of the Islamic legal order and the modern legal order'); and cf. Ch. 1, 'The State as Tradition' (for state as tradition or normative information).

[45] Feldman (2008), *Fall and Rise of Islamic State*, at 13 (on shari'a and 'inalienable rights of life, liberty and property' existing before written constitutions).

[46] For the absence of fusion of the religion and political in early Muslim centuries, Crone (2004), *God's Rule*, at 14 ('complex societies are usually much too differentiated . . . to tolerate the incorporation of all of their interests in a single structure'), 146 (fragmentation of Islamic society transferring power from caliph to amirs, kings, sultan, 'government had separated from religion'), 248–9 ('something similar to the division between state and church' though on basis of single law, the shari'a, and not multiple laws of Europe). For emergence of secular authority based on the Koran (IV.5. 'O you who believe. Obey God and those amongst you who are in charge'), Botiveau (1993), 'Contemporary Reinterpretations of Islamic Law', at 261; and for Sunni theory that caliphate must be based on contract or bay'ah between caliph and people, El Fadl (2003–4), 'Islam and Challenge of Democratic Commitment', at 22, though cf. at 30 (on fear of 'wide range of temporal non-Shari'ah based law'). For the belief of many that Islam is already democratic, notably through customary form of shura or consultation, Piscatori (1986), *Islam in World of Nation-States*, at 41; Feldman (2003a), *Beyond Jihad*, at 52–4 ('democratic readings' of Islamic tradition, caliphs appointed by group, duty of consultation or shura); al-Hibri (1992), 'Islamic Constitutionalism', at 11–13 (for bay'ah), 21 (for Koranic imperative of consultation); Afsaruddin (2006), 'Islamic State', at 160 (dynastic rule un-Islamic, ideal of 'collective decision making').

[47] Feldman (2008), *Fall and Rise of Islamic State*, at 43 ('the authority of the ruler that was recognized by the shari'a'); and for religious (and hence legal) authority resting not on high office but 'entirely on knowledge', Crone (2004b), *Medieval Islamic Political Thought*, at 128 ('truth dispersed among the believers at large . . . the caliph was no different from any other Muslim in this respect'); Belaïd (1994), 'Constitutions dans le Tiers-Monde', at 119 (secular authority having task of application, not creation of law); Lombardi (2006), *State Law as Islamic Law*, at 49 (for notion of syasa traced to fourteenth century).

being used explicitly, at least by western observers.[48] Islam-compliant temporal regulation (syasa or qanun, the latter from the Greek *kanon*) could thus be adopted; in the Ottoman empire this was said to occur initially where the shari'a was 'silent' or not extensive.[49] Thereafter there was growth, stimulated notably by the appearance of nineteenth-century European codifications, to the point of the exhaustive Ottoman codification (the Medjelle) of the 1870s.[50] It was not a success, but has been seen as the most advanced attempt in a process of 'positivization' of the shari'a. The latter would imply that the shari'a had authority only insofar as incorporated into secular law,[51] yet this is done in part to enlist the shari'a in support of secular authority.[52] There are again European parallels, notably in official redaction of customary law.[53] The attempts at positivization were widespread, though far from uniformly successful, and there is now a recognizable process of 'Islamization' or return to the shari'a (e.g. in Pakistan, Aceh).[54] It consists, however, of legislative statement of the content of Islamic law, indicating a shift in method or understanding if not in Islamic content. The 'new expression' of qanun-islami would represent an attempt to overcome the dichotomy between shari'a and legislation.[55] If the enacted content of shari'a appeared initially in secular regulatory and private-law

---

[48] Mikunda-Franco (2001), 'Verfassungsstaat in der islamischen Welt', at 170 ('gemeinislamischen Verfassungsrecht' based on Arabic, general principles of Islamic law, notion all states stand before God); Hoffman (2001), Review of Festschrift P. Häberle, at 6 for further authors; and for parallels with western common laws, Glenn (2007c), *Common Laws*, at 134–40 (both relational in ceding to local forms of custom (urf) and legislation).

[49] Karcic (2001), 'Applying the Shari'ah', at 212 (citing modern banking, maritime trade, constitutional, and administrative law); Feldman (2008), *Fall and Rise of Islamic State*, at 61 (little objection from Islamic scholars).

[50] Badie (2000), *The Imported State*, at 146 (a 'technical imperative', though its sixteen volumes a typical case of 'dysfunctional importation' and 'quickly failed'); and for replacement in many instances of shari'a courts by those of the state, Masud et al (2006), *Dispensing Justice*, at 42–3 ('to unify the judiciary').

[51] Arabi (2001), *Studies Modern Islamic Law*, at 19 (for 'positivization', posing 'burning questions'); Feldman (2008), *Fall and Rise of Islamic State*, at 64 (a 'historic reversal, even if its effects were not immediately apparent'); and see Botiveau (1993), 'Contemporary Reinterpretations of Islamic Law', at 265–6 (for 'state takeover' of shari'a, fiqh 'shaped in the mould of positive law').

[52] An-Na'im (2006), *African Constitutionalism*, at 16; and for the radical character of the process, Al-Muhairi (1996), 'Islamisation and Modernisation', at 46 (no Islamic authority giving modern state any right to make 'binding declarations of what constitutes detailed Shari'a law'); Zaman (2002), *The Ulama*, at 97 (shari'a best understood not as code in modern sense but 'ongoing discursive tradition', process rather than content).

[53] See Ch. 4, 'Customs'; and for the subsequent process of taking that law as stated and no longer relying on the earlier sources, Masud et al (2006), *Dispensing Justice*, at 42 (and traditional madrasa education no longer required).

[54] Karcic (2001), 'Applying the Shari'ah', at 215 (first in Muslim-majority countries, then Muslim-minority countries, caused by failure of modernization projects); Al-Muhairi (1996), 'Islamisation and Modernisation', at 43 (partly 'reaction against corruption and repression . . . and partly . . . desperation at the abject failure of the imported secular ideologies').

[55] Karcic (2001), 'Applying the Shari'ah', at 208 (distinction 'is fading'); and for reintroduction of Islamic criminal law as 'Islamic substantive rules in a Western garb', Peters (2005), *Crime and Punishment*, at 148 (with 'Western-type courts and Western institutions such as the state prosecutor'); or as a 'tendency to codify', Jackson (1996), *Islamic Law and State*, at xvi (though Schacht having pointed out that Islamic law incompatible with code).

instruments, there is also now a recognizable phenomenon of its incorporation into written state constitutions.[56]

In the result not only does the state exist in predominantly Islamic countries but its basic methodological concepts have been received with some success. There is, however, constant interaction with Islamic normativity, in various ways. It has been said that one should not attempt a description of an Islamic state but look rather to the Islamic *nature* of the state, as represented by a sliding scale.[57] Iran and Saudi Arabia would presently represent the most Islamic forms of the state, with clerical control of legislation in Iran and the shari'a as general and even constitutional law in Saudi Arabia.[58] Thus the state can accommodate even these major elements of Islamic normativity. Further along the sliding scale, states may also be Islamic in nature through conferring upon Islamic law a less prominent but still important role, notably in providing that it constitutes 'a' or even 'the' source of legislation. Correspondingly, a Supreme Court may be entrusted with the task of ensuring that state legislation is Islam-compliant. Egypt is the most evident example, and the Egyptian Supreme Court has now had decades of experience in reconciling Egyptian legislation with the shari'a.[59] It must decide which of the revealed texts should be seen as controlling but also have regard to 'liberal constitutional values' in reaching its conclusions. The state instruments of legislation and judicial review are thus accepted, but are sought to be infused with Islamic teaching or content.[60]

---

[56] Belaïd (1994), 'Constitutions dans le Tiers-Monde', at 104 (though Iran rather a process to 'unsettle' ('déclasser') the constitution by imposing a Proclamation of shi'ite faith upon it).

[57] Harding (2002a), 'The Keris, The Crescent', at 157 (need to locate particular examples on the scale); and for the range over space and time, Otto (2010a), *Sharia Incorporated* (incorporation of shari'a into state law in twelve Muslim countries over past and present); Brown (2001), *Constitutions in Non-Constitutional World* (Arab constitutions from nineteenth century).

[58] The Iranian constitution in Art. 2(1) states that '...the Islamic Republic is a system based on the belief...in the sovereignty of God', currently ensured through the responsibility of 'just [and] competent jurists': Mallat (1993b), *Renewal of Islamic Law*, at 71. The shari'a remains uncodified in Saudi Arabia, interpreted by the traditional doctrinal sources of the ulama, but the secular government has decreed that it is the Hanbali tradition that prevails as the law of the state and many characteristics of western law have been installed: Vogel (2000b), 'Exploring Contradictions and Traditions', at 135 (regulation of judiciary, multiple levels of appeal, formal university education for judges, etc.).

[59] Lombardi (2006), *State Law as Islamic Law*, at 124 (for 1978 Egyptian constitution providing for shari'a as 'a' source of law, becoming 'the' source in 1980, though reform 'deeply ambiguous').

[60] Lombardi (2006), *State Law as Islamic Law*, at 174 (drawing on 'wide range of competing theories of Islamic law...not adhered to any one theory...ambiguous in places'), 185 (for occasional citation of particular hadiths, though no explanation of why seen as authentic, also 'checking' against classical jurists), 188 (in absence of 'absolutely certain' Islamic texts, test of 'overarching goals of the shari'a'); Lombardi (1998), 'Islamic Law as Constitutional Law', at 89 (for non-retroactive character of 1980 constitutional change); Skovgaard-Petersen (1997), *Defining Islam for Egyptian State*, at 156 (for Muslim Brother slogan 'Islam is religion and state' though opposition to position of state mufti); Sherif (2000), 'Rule of Law in Egypt', at 4 (for Supreme Court's use of foreign and international human rights instruments); Johansen (2006), 'Constitution and Islamic Normativity', at 191 (classical norms no longer *ipso facto* binding, only if 'sufficiently flexible and rational to stand the test of functional and constitutional scrutiny'), 192 (remaining with the 'broad framework' of Islamic normativity); Bälz (2000), 'Human Rights, the Rule of Law', at 37 (influence of Islamic law, however, 'rather minimal'); Dupret (1997), 'La constitutionalité de la shari'a' (distinguishing conclusive Islamic texts from those authorizing individual reason); Baker (2003), *Islam Without Fear*, at 161 ('moderate secularism' of 'New Islamists'), 121 ('New Islamist' view of 'corrective ijtihad' for essential equality of men and women); and for the process as one of 'Islamization', Bälz (1998), '"Islamisierung" des Rechts'.

The Egyptian model is now that being attempted also in Pakistan, Afghanistan, and Iraq.[61]

The use of cosmopolitan sources is also implicit in the many jurisdictions in which Muslim populations are a majority or a large minority and in which an Islamic personal law or 'statut personnel' is guaranteed.[62] Thus Malaysia and Singapore guarantee application of shari'a for their Islamic populations in matters of family law and both the content and boundaries of these laws must be established through a combination of state and Islamic law. Here, the constitution would be sovereign, however, ensuring an Islamic personal law but not providing a fetter on legislation as in Egypt.[63] In current processes of Islamization, the enactment of Islamic rules may reach outside traditional areas of the law of family and succession and extend even to criminal law, as recently in Aceh, though again subject to overarching national or constitutional law.[64] Where a predominantly Muslim state has declared its secularity and enacted a full panoply of western-style civil, commercial, and penal codes, as in the case of Turkey, there remain possibilities of Islamic sources being called into play outside the field of religious liberty. Esin Örücü thus is able to detail judicial consideration of Islamic norms as complements to state law, in areas of compensation for death in work-related injury and injury to farm animals.[65] Islamic law can be seen

[61] For Pakistan, Zaman (2002), *The Ulama*, at 88 (Pakistan's 'repugnancy clause'), 101 (though British colonial practice more influential than Islamic texts), 189 (jurisdiction on repugnancy not in shari'a courts but high courts), Lau (2008), 'Legal Reconstruction and Islamic Law', at 226 (greatest effect in criminal law, allowing punishment to be avoided by paying compensation compatible with Islamic law of retaliation and blood money); for Afghanistan, Jones-Pauly and Nojumi (2004), 'Balancing Relations', at 825 (criteria of Islamic law though 'along with the Constitution', no law to be contrary to either), Lau (2008), 'Legal Reconstruction and Islamic Law', at 217 (judicial review for compliance with 'the Constitution', this by implication including Islamic law); for Iraq, Benard (2008), 'The Advantage to Islam', at 67, for Art. 2 of Iraq's constitution (Islam 'a' fundamental source', no law to contradict 'established provisions' of Islam); Stilt (2004), 'Islamic Law and Iraqui Legal System', at 698 (Islamic provisions 'general' and subject to interpretation).

[62] See Ch. 8, 'Churches and Religions'.

[63] Harding (2002a), 'The Keris, The Crescent', at 167 (and no provision for shari'a to be 'a' or 'the' source of legislation), 170 (each Malaysian state having own system of Islamic law and religious administration), and 173 (civil courts retaining judicial review of shari'a courts); Abdullah and Hua (2007), 'Legislating Faith in Malaysia', at 267 (case law relying on introduction of secular sovereignty by British), 288 (civil courts abdicating role of upholding fundamental liberties, however); Neoh (2008), 'Islamic State and the Common Law ' (for case of Lina Joy in Malaysia and judicial refusal to recognize her renunciation of Islam). For Singapore, Bell (2006), 'Multiculturalism in Law', at 325 (though 'much more plural under the British than it is now').

[64] Siregar (2008), 'Islamic Law in National Legal System', notably at 13 (for criminalization of sale and consumption of alcohol, gambling, illicit relations between men and women, Islamic punishment of caning); Otto (2010b), 'Sharia and national law', at 474 (penalty of stoning for adultery, governor stating will not be applied). For enactment of the Hudood ordinances in Pakistan, implementing Islamic criminal law and sanctions and reviewable only for compatibility with Islamic law, Lau (2010), 'Sharia and national law', at 418 (though rape and fornication no longer treated as hadd crimes); and re-islamization of criminal law in twelve northern states of Nigeria, Ostien and Dekker (2010), 'Sharia and national law', at 575–7.

[65] Örücü (2008), 'Judicial navigation', at 45 (women married only in religious ceremony entitled to compensation, though at lesser rate than those officially married; sexual abuse of (untouchable) cow giving rise to damages, given that local religious belief resulted in decline in value); and see Koçak (2010),

here as functioning as a 'religious fact', as in French law, and its respect seen as compatible with the secularity of the state.[66]

The state in predominantly Muslim jurisdictions is therefore a flexible institution; the state tradition is not a uniformly imperative one and its information often may yield to non-state or Islamic information. This may be the result of the normative base within which the state tradition has been received in Islamic jurisdictions. If Islamic law is the law before the state, which inevitably influences the state model that is received, it is the case that historically Islamic law has been remarkably tolerant of legal diversity. This is inevitable in a legal tradition with no central authority capable of eliminating divergent legal opinion. It has meant that adherents to different schools of Islamic thought have coexisted in the same territory and that legal techniques had to develop to accommodate this diversity.[67] From the thirteenth century there was thus a type of 'full faith and credit' concept that called for recognition of the law of other schools of law and of judgments handed down by a judge of a different school. There is talk of the schools as 'constitutional units'.[68] This internal diversity extended to those of other faiths and in the notion of the dhimmi there was effective legal autonomy granted to legal traditions other than those of Islam, and this within Islamic territories.[69] Islam would thus represent a tradition of 'political inclusion' that the tradition of the contemporary state has not been able to overcome entirely in Islamic lands.[70] Islamic normativity thus accommodates the diverse state forms that have been received, even to the point of the civil code and other forms of legislation in Iran and the considerable authority of the Saudi Arabian monarchy.[71] The view is thus defended that Islamic jurisdictions may maintain

---

'Islam and national law' at 263 (non-application of civil code in 'traditional' areas in Turkey, disputes solved with 'little or nothing to do' with state structures).

[66] For religious norms acknowledged as 'religious fact' (le 'fait religieux') in France, see this chapter, '*Religious liberty*'.

[67] For the inner diversity of Islamic states in terms of Sunni and Shi'ite populations (to say nothing of the diversity of Sunni schools), Matyssek (2008), 'Zum Problem der Trennung', at 163 (almost none ('nahezu keine') with exclusively Sunni or Shi'ite populations).

[68] Jackson (1996), *Islamic Law and State*, at xxi ('having to accommodate multiple, equally authoritative interpretations of what the law is'), 72 (madhhab becoming 'constitutional units'), 143 (subject to control of recognition by originating school); and for further intellectual and metaphorical techniques of accommodation, the doctrine of ikhtilaf or doctrinal diversity, and the hadith that such diversity is a 'sign of the bounty of God', Glenn (2010b), *Legal Traditions*, at 207 ('Of Schools and Schism'), with references.

[69] See generally Siddiqi (1969), *Non-Muslims Under Muslim Rule*, at 7 ('the award of social and judicial autonomy' citing Koran V 42–8); Cohen (1994), *Under Crescent and Cross*, Ch. 5 ('The Legal Position of Jews in Islam'); Rouland, Pierré-Caps, and Poumarède (1996), *Droit des minorities* (1996), at 65 (Arab conquest of Spain in 711 ce as liberation); and for the dhimmi, those contracting a fictional contract of dhimma or residence in return for taxes, Glenn (2010b), *Legal Traditions*, at 231 (under 'Jihad') (for non-Muslims exempt from both Islamic privileges and Islamic duties, largely equal in entire field of private law, contrasted with law of aliens in western jurisdictions).

[70] Shatzmiller (2005), 'Conclusion', in Shatzmiller (2005), *Nationalism and Minority Identities*, at 285 ('authoritarian nation-state' effecting 'complete reversal' of Islamic traditions of inclusion), 285 ('secular nationalism' excluding minorities whose identities were incompatible with state ideology).

[71] For Saudi Arabia, see earlier in this section.

constitutional guarantees that 'compare favourably with international standards'.[72]

Islamic countries are not the only examples, however, of a 'godly state'.[73] Israel, according to its Basic Laws, is a 'Jewish and democratic state' and both of these adjectives have been described as 'correct'.[74] There is here, again, law before the state and the law in question is Jewish law, itself familiar with the notion of internal diversity and even 'deviation', so that there would be room even within an all-encompassing law for development of a 'political tradition'.[75] Seeing contradiction between the Jewish religion and the state of Israel would thus be both a recent development and derived from debates between political parties whose objectives are immediate 'achievement'.[76] Neither democracy nor Judaism would be fixed in character so neither can be absolutist in opposition to the other.[77] Moreover, while the law of Israel recognizes a 'statut personnel' of religious law for both Jewish and Islamic people, Jewish law may also play a larger and suppletive role in throwing light on the values of the state of Israel, the

[72] Stahnke and Blitt (2005), 'The Religion–State Relationship', at 964 (including rights to freedom of expression, association, and assembly, rights to equality, and non-discrimination).

[73] Neusner and Sonn (1999), *Comparing Religions*, at 5 (contrasting recognition by Christianity of a 'distinction between the state and the church that Judaism and Islam never contemplated and could never have conceived').

[74] The expression first appeared in Amendment No. 9 to Basic Law. The Knesset, amending s. 7A, adopted in 1985; for 'correct', Maoz (1998), 'Values of Jewish and Democratic State', at 148 ('a democratic state which derives its values from Jewish teachings . . . presents no contradiction to democracy'); and for the view that both components must be 'approached on equal terms', Mautner (2011), *Law and Culture of Israel*, at 52 (on debate between Justices Elon and Barak).

[75] On the importance of this 'compromise', Stone (2008), 'Religion and state', at 641 (given predominance of view that Jewish law is all-encompassing). For the content of the tradition, Walzer, Lorberbaum, and Zohar (2000), *Jewish Political Tradition*; and for the emergence of 'politics' in European jurisdictions, see Ch. 2, 'The church within'. For the possibility of 'deviation' from the law, at least according to the Babylonian Talmud, Ben-Menahem (1996), 'Postscript', at 428 ('at times even views such deviation favourably'), 430 (given plurality of sources, no strict system of precedent); and for conciliation of contradictory schools of Jewish law, the references in Glenn (2010b), *Legal Traditions*, at 119 (notably on the words of the Babylonian Talmud: '[t]hese and these are [both] the words of the Living God').

[76] Schweid (1998), 'Israel as a Jewish-Democratic State', at 125 ('a very heavy price is paid for this tactical convenience'), 129 (notion of contradiction only becoming generalized in period after Yom Kippur war of 1973), 131 (contrasting 'national democracy' with 'individualistic democracy' based on 'itself alone'), 139 (dilemmas those *of* democracy, not ones that undermine democracy); and for Israel as only one of many states having a national base (with laws of return or 'kin states' favouring diaspora abroad), Menashi (2010), 'Ethnonationalism and Liberal Democracy', at 67 ('national aspect of Israeli democracy makes Israel no different from other democratic states'). For a 'polemic' against both sides of the contradictory view, though arguing for 'historical and theological priority of Judaism', social contract being formulated out of Jewish traditional resources, the law before the state, Novak (2005), *Jewish Social Contract*, at 4 (parties to social contract because of Judaism not in spite of it).

[77] Schweid (1998), 'Israel as a Jewish-Democratic State', at 126 (Judaism not 'platonic ideal' but rather 'process of cultural-historical life of Jewish nation', democracy not 'fixed constitutional formula'); Gavison (2011), 'Can Israel Be Both Jewish and Democratic?' (Jewish state may be seen as state of Jewish majority, state of Jewish nation, or theocratic state; democracy best seen in 'thin' version not necessarily implying human rights, liberalism), and also notably at 124 ('important to leave the ambiguity', democracy not 'all or nothing'), 133 (only theocratic state is incompatible with democracy); Novak (2005), *Jewish Social Contract*, notably at 4 ('Jews first need to think out a democratic theory by themselves for themselves').

state situating itself within a larger cadre.[78] Moreover, just as Islamic law traditionally saw no difficulty in recognizing distinct legal identities of non-Islamic peoples in Islamic lands, resident aliens in Jewish territories are entitled to 'benevolent protection' and the Israeli Supreme Court has nullified a prohibition of Arab acquisition of land in Israel.[79]

It is not only in 'godly' states, however, that the debate over religious and state sources of law takes place. Increasingly, within western states generally perceived as 'secular' there are institutionalized forms of recourse to religious law. These may take a number of forms. State courts have frequently had recourse to religious legal principles in purely secular cases, as a form of persuasive authority,[80] but the distinction between secular and religious cases is now blurring and in many areas of law religious norms are advanced as doing the work of state norms (there being no presumption of the exclusive character of the latter).[81] Unlike the religious liberty cases seen above, where what is at stake is the freedom to pursue a specifically religious activity in the face of general and apparently contrary state laws (building a sucah, using peyote in religious ceremonies),[82] here religious norms are advanced as the normative base for recognizably civil or private law questions. Thus, in the USA courts may enforce an Islamic mahr as the governing instrument in dissolution of a matrimonial property regime,[83] and in Canada the Supreme Court has decided that a contract between husband and wife for the husband to grant a religious divorce following civil divorce proceedings is enforceable as a civil contract.[84] There is here, as in French practice in matters of religious liberty, 'subsumption' or incorporation of religious norms under civil ones and the religious law nests in an accommodating civil law structure.[85]

Resort to religious norms by state courts is now also accompanied by an expanding recognition of the authority of religious institutions and tribunals, seen as free to make use of religious sources of law in their own work. This has occurred for centuries, of course, as Christian and Jewish tribunals have

---

[78] Friedell (2010), 'Role of Jewish Law in a Secular State', at 4; though for controversy on the question, see references in Glenn (2010b), *Legal Traditions*, at 126.

[79] Walzer, Lorberbaum, and Zohar (2000), *Jewish Political Tradition*, at 525 (citing Herzog), 545 (citing *Kaadan v. Israel Lands Administration* (2000) 54 (1) PD 258, [2000] IsrSC 54(1) 258).

[80] For use of Jewish law, by US courts for example, Bambach (2009–10), 'Enforceability of Arbitration Decisions', at 380 (notably US Supreme Court citation of Maimonides in its *Miranda* decision); Ashburn (1994), 'Appealing to Higher Authority?'.

[81] See Ch. 12, introductory remarks.

[82] See this chapter, '*Religious liberty*'.

[83] Menski (2008), 'Law, Religion and Culture', at 56 for cases 'granting the full mahr'; though for variability of results and dependence on question of economic justice between the parties, Haddad, Smith, and Moore (2006), *Muslim Women in America*, at 115 ('mixed variety of rulings'); Siddiqui (2007), 'Interpretation of Islamic Marriage Contracts', at 651–4 (enforcement in England, variable enforcement in USA, Germany); and see generally Estin (2004), 'Pluralism in American Family Law', notably at 541–2 (US judges creating 'space for traditions to flourish').

[84] *Bruker v. Marcovitz* [2007] 3 SCR 607, 2007 SCC 514.

[85] See this chapter, '*Religious liberty*'.

continued their millennia-old jurisdiction over matters defined as religious (internal church or religious matters, religious marriage) and even as consensual courts of arbitration where religious matters overlap with the secular and commercial world. Jewish Beth Din tribunals have always exercised an important commercial jurisdiction, today said to be growing in importance, and their decisions receive state judicial enforcement as arbitral awards.[86] Christian institutions have now moved beyond the traditional domains of canon and ecclesiastical law to generalized mediation and arbitration.[87] To these long-established practices is now being added the possibility of arbitration by Islamic authorities, again within the accommodating terms of state arbitration legislation and through use, where necessary, of court orders for purposes of enforcement. The practice appears widespread in both the UK and the USA and is documented in some measure, though elsewhere it is less visible.[88] In Canada it is used in all provinces, though Quebec precludes arbitration in family matters and Ontario has enacted legislation requiring 'family arbitration' to be effected according to the law of a Canadian province, this inevitably leaving a measure of party autonomy in family property matters.[89] Beyond the family there appear to be no limitations on party acceptance of religious mediators or arbitrators.

Institutional cosmopolitanism in choice of sources of law is also evident in the relations of states to international law, regional law, and transnational law.

---

[86] Grossman (2007), 'Is this Arbitration?' (also on extent of judicial review of religious questions); Bambach (2009–10), 'Enforceability Arbitration Decisions', at 393, 399 (on conditions of enforceability as form of screening for protection of constitutional rights, rights of children), 403 (as model for enforcement of Islamic forms of arbitration); Helfand (2011), 'Religious Arbitration', at 1249 (for doubling of Beth Din cases over previous eight years).

[87] For Christian arbitration in the USA, Walter (2012), 'Religious Arbitration', at 519 (Peacemaker Ministries and Institute for Christian Conciliation, with between 2,000 and 2,500 dispute resolutions each year).

[88] For the USA, Bambach (2009–10), 'Enforceability Arbitration Decisions', at 381 (for appellate decisions on Islamic arbitration); Helfand (2011), 'Religious Arbitration', at 1238 (for US courts 'routinely' enforcing religious arbitration awards though recent political opposition), 59 (for criterion of unconscionability as 'safety net'); Quraishi and Syeed-Miller (2004), 'No Altars: a survey of Islamic family law', notably at 182 (preference for Islamic dispute resolution given costs of litigation), 215 (judicial reference of case to Islamic authorities, subsequent homologation of their decision). For the UK, Hofri-Winogradow (2010), 'A Plurality of Discontent', at 105; Poulter (1999), *Ethnicity, Law and Human Rights*, at 234 ('widespread acceptance'). UK practice has developed in spite of negative public reaction to endorsement of the idea in general terms by the Archbishop of Canterbury, though a subsequent supporting declaration by Lord Justice Phillips appears to have provoked less resistance. For text of the addresses, and commentary, Ahdar and Aroney (2010), *Shari'a in the West*; and for a similar public reaction in Germany to political musing on utility of Islamic arbitration, *Die Zeit*, 9 February 2012, p. 1.

[89] Art. 2639, Civil Code of Quebec; *An Act to Amend the Arbitration Act*, L.O. 2006, ch. 1. The law followed controversy following a private proposal in 2002 for a formal Islamic 'judicial tribunal' (Darul Qada) with an extensive jurisdiction over a wide range of matters of family and succession law, described as 'Muslim Personal Law'. Opposition voiced concern over the status of women in Islamic law though this in turn was criticized as a 'product of empire': see, e.g. Razak (2008), 'Canadian Muslim Women's Responses to Faith-Based Arbitration', at 85 (Muslim women 'caught between the proverbial rock (a state likely to use their rights as a means to police Muslim populations) and a hard place (patriarchal and conservative religious forces)') and 86 ('feminism can be easily annexed to the project of empire'); and for further references, Glenn (2009b), 'Un statut personnel?'.

STATES AND INTERNATIONAL LAW

The decline of empires and the proliferation of states in the twentieth century meant the end of an international law controlled by, and limited to, a small group of western or 'civilized' states.[90] The consequences have been felt in both public international law and private international law. Arguably international law has grown in importance as a result of these developments,[91] but it is not the same international law as it was thought in the nineteenth century.

Public international law

Public international law lacks the authority of state enactment but there is nevertheless a positivist conception of it,[92] relying both on the reality of state consent to international obligations (as evidenced by international treaties and their incorporation into state law) and on the positive reality of state practice ('custom'). The sources of international law are here seen as formal or, in the case of custom, demonstrable. This concept of public international law was developed in tandem with the efforts of territorial and national closure of states and constitutes a similar form of closure of sources of law.[93] Closure of the sources of public international law facilitated not only the construction of states (they became the primary source of the law of their own relations) but the exclusion from the international realm of non-state or 'uncivilized' peoples. There would be no need for substantive engagement with sources other than the formally authorized ones. As the closure of states could not resist ambient texture, however, so the closed concept of public international law has had to accommodate a wider field of relations and a wider and more cosmopolitan concept of the sources of law.

[90] For proliferation of states, see Ch. 5, *'Fragmentation, failure, and violence'*; and for the role and decline of empire, see Ch. 8, 'Internationality and Empire'.

[91] For an increasing number of cases 'that directly implicate foreign or international law', from the perspective of justices of the US and Canadian Supreme Courts, Breyer (2003), 'Keynote Address', at 265; LaForest (1996), 'Expanding Role of the Supreme Court'; and for process of globalization making states more 'vulnerable' to external norms, Auby (2003), *Globalisation, droit, Etat*, at 27, 78 (speaking of 'perméabilisation'), 80 (multiplication of implicated vectors). States would even be becoming 'interpretive communities' (wissenschaftliche Interpretationsgemeinschaften') as opposed to 'law-producing institutions', given increased influence of international law: Möllers (2001), 'Globalisierte Jurisprudenz', at 47; and for state as 'mezzanine', Saladin (1995), *Wozu noch Staaten?*, at 237; or 'conduit', Auby (2003), *Globalisation, droit, Etat*, at 24. Some 40 per cent of Canadian federal statutes would implement international rules: De Mestral and Fox-Decent (2008), 'Rethinking the Relationship', at 578 (listing vast areas of shipping, aeronautics, broadcasting, customs, oceans, double taxation, environment, heritage, arbitration).

[92] For the 'early positivists', see Ch. 8, *'Public international law'*; and for this positivist conception as still the 'dominant jurisprudential approach' but now encountering 'so many internal critiques and internal challenges . . . that its viability is seriously in question', Kingsbury (2003), 'International Legal Order', at 272–3.

[93] For efforts at territorial and national closure, see Chapters 4 and 5. The prior *ius gentium* not only extended to both public and private law but drew in a cosmopolitan way on transnational authority; see Ch. 8, *'Public international law'*.

This is evident even with respect to the most formal of the sources of public international law, international treaties. Whether a ratified treaty forms part of the binding law of a land would depend on characterization of the state in question as 'monist' or 'dualist'. In the first case the ratified treaty would be 'directly applicable' or 'self-executing'; in the second, implementing legislation would be required. The characterization itself would be a matter of national law and the 'dualist' option would be the most hostile to extra-national law. Yet it is becoming increasingly difficult to know whether a state is monist or dualist, as courts clearly engage in context-sensitive engagement with the content and consequences of the ratified treaty.[94] Hierarchies and structures are no longer controlling. In the USA, a 'hybrid monist' state, recent particular treaties have been denied self-executing status, so that the USA *might* be 'becoming more dualist'.[95] In 'traditional dualist' jurisdictions there is a notion of 'sector monism' and a view that implementation does not require specific legislation but only sufficient existing authority to enable officials to comply.[96] The view is correspondingly expressed that both monism and dualism are exhausted as concepts and that 'a new and more comprehensive theory' is required.[97] 'Prescriptively', it is said that 'less attention should be paid to the formal sources of law, and more to the substances of the rules in question'.[98] Behind the process would be a 'blurring of international law into comparative law', a horizontal as opposed to vertical 'engagement of ideas'.[99]

Ratified but non-implemented treaties may also be treated in a more subtle fashion, now, not as either binding law or not, but as interpretive guides in the application of domestic law. This 'creeping monism' is now becoming widespread, particularly with respect to international human rights treaties that states have signed or ratified but not (yet) enacted into domestic law.[100]

---

[94] Shelton (2011), 'Introduction', at 3–4 (of twenty-five states examined rare to find one entirely monist or dualist).

[95] Dubinsky (2010), 'International Law in United States', at 461, citing *Medellin* v. *Texas*, 552 US 491 (2008) (majority finding that treaties establishing International Court of Justice not self-executing, decision of International Court of Justice not enforceable as domestic law); and see *Sanchez-Llamas* v. *Oregon*, 548 US 331 (2006) (majority of court referring to 'presumption' that international treaties do not create judicially enforceable rights).

[96] For the language of 'traditional dualist', Sloss (2009), *Role of Domestic Courts*, at 6; Wildhaber (2007), 'European Convention on Human Rights', at 217 (Anglo-Saxon and Scandinavian countries 'traditionally supported' the 'dualist approach'). For 'sufficient legislative and regulatory authority', De Mestral and Fox-Decent (2008), 'Rethinking the Relationship', at 576.

[97] Von Bogdandy (2008), 'Pluralism, direct effect', at 397 (monism a 'moribund' notion, dualism also to be 'overcome'; need for 'coupling' rather than pyramid); Wildhaber (2007), 'European Convention on Human Rights', at 219 (need for 'more realistic and more comprehensive theory'; 'reality is more complex . . . there are various shades of monism and dualism'); and for 'many states' not fitting into either category, Sloss (2009), *Role of Domestic Courts*, at 6.

[98] Peters (2009b), 'Supremacy Lost', at 197 (citing Ost and van de Kerchove (2002), *Pyramide au reseau*, on concept of network prevailing over that of pyramid), and 196 (for lack of hierarchy, a 'polyarchy or heterarchy . . . no legal rule to decide which norm should prevail . . . no supremacy').

[99] Knop (2000), 'Here and There', at 525–6; and to the same effect Breyer (2003), 'Keynote Address', at 266 ('enormous value' in any discipline of 'trying to learn from the similar experience of others').

[100] For 'creeping monism', Waters (2007), 'Judicial Trend toward Interpretive Incorporation', notably at 632 (for critique of 'all or nothing' approach, preference for that of 'narrow lens'), 689 (for table of

Thus, in the Supreme Court of Canada case of *Baker* v. *Canada*, the ratified but non-implemented UN Convention on the Rights of the Child was cited in support of a successful challenge to the expulsion of a woman who had given birth to children in Canada while unlawfully within the country.[101] Canadian legislation had to be interpreted in compliance with the international norms and the 'binding/non-binding' distinction was abandoned.[102] The process would now have become a 'transnational trend'.[103]

The treaty as formal source of international law, moreover, would have been displaced in some measure by the growth in informal international agreements. These now proliferate like mushrooms on the ground, as they say in Germany, but they represent a qualitative as well as a quantitative change.[104] Both national and international law are changed. National law must accommodate an expanded executive law-making function, over a wide area of law, and international law must be more inclusive in accepting non-diplomatic sources of international obligation. The process is part of the wider phenomenon that we have seen Anne-Marie Slaughter describe as 'transgovernmentalism' and that sees all government actors as competent to deal with their foreign counterparts on transnational problems.[105] It recalls the cosmopolitan character of state organization

'interpretive techniques' of 'gilding the lily' (where conclusion already reached on other grounds), presumption that statutes not in violation of international law, entrenching human rights by 'updating' common law, entrenching in bill of rights, etc.); and see Sloss (2009), *Role of Domestic Courts*, at 3 (importance of 'indirect' enforcement), 21 (Australia applying 'legitimate expectations' doctrine, Canada presumption of conformity); Hopkins (2011), 'New Zealand', at 437 (New Zealand refusing executive change of law but accepting ratified conventions as aid to statutory interpretation); Krisch (2010), *Beyond Constitutionalism*, at 8 (contrast with 'classical dualist stance'); Provost (2008), 'Judging in Splendid Isolation', notably at 146 (on need to acknowledge norms of 'variable normative character'), 148 (recognizing 'complex identity' of membership in 'superimposed communities').

[101] [1999] 2 SCR 817.

[102] Knop (2000), 'Here and There', notably at 515 (contrasting 'traditional model' structured by 'a set of binary choices' including the 'binding/non-binding distinction').

[103] Waters (2007), 'Judicial Trends toward Interpretive Incorporation', at 633, citing US Supreme Court decision in *Roper* v. *Simmons*, 543 US 551 (2005) (unratified UN Convention on the Rights of the Child cited in declaring unconstitutionality of US legislation subjecting minors to death penalty); and see subsequently *Graham* v. *Florida*, 130 S. Ct. 2011 (2010) (same unratified UN Convention cited in declaring unconstitutionality of US legislation subjecting minors to life imprisonment).

[104] See notably Pauwelyn, Wessel, and Wouters (2012), *Informal International Lawmaking*, notably Ch. 6, Pauwelyn, 'Is It International Law Or Not and Does It Even Matter?'); the US National Security Strategy at 41, accessible at <http://www.whitehouse.gov/sites/default/files/rss_viewer/national_security_strategy.pdf > ('strengthening bilateral and multilateral cooperation cannot be accomplished simply by working inside formal institutions and frameworks'); Dubinsky (2010), 'International Law in United States', at 459 (on increase in USA of both 'congressional-executive' international agreements and 'sole executive' international agreements, latter not requiring congressional approval), 468 (not used however, for interpretation of domestic law); Sassen (2004), 'De-Nationalized State Agendas' at 58 ('sharp increase in the work of establishing convergence', e.g. anti-trust regulators).

[105] See Ch. 9, '*The adaptive state*'; and see Dewost (2000), 'Globalization and rule of law', at 33 ('prevailing pragmatic approach' has yielded impressive results, with mutual recognition agreements, 'comity' arrangements); Turner (2007), 'Transnational Networks' (judicial, prosecutorial, and investigative networks for international crime); Ahdieh (2008), 'Foreign Affairs, International Law' (accommodating also constituent units of federation, citing at 1186 International Carbon Action Partnership of States, states, and provinces); Kingsbury (2003), 'International Legal Order', at 282 (for 'functional' and not 'categorical' view of sovereignty); Koskenniemi (2001), *Gentle Civilizer of Nations*, at 486 (as implying

prior to the general adoption of ministries of foreign affairs during the period from the sixteenth to the nineteenth centuries.[106]

The expansion of sources of public international law is evident beyond the field of treaties and agreements, notably with respect to 'custom' as a source. Blackstone stated that customary international law was part of the common law and this is consistent with the role that common laws played as foundational, though non-binding, laws of state construction.[107] Many national laws thus state that customary international law is part of national law.[108] There is opposition, however, and since common laws yield to imperative state law there is an ongoing process of delineating the respective roles of local imperative law and international suppletive law.[109] Any general conclusion on the incorporation of international law into domestic laws is therefore difficult.[110] Resistance to customary international law requires, however, principled justification. Beyond the debate on principle, there is also the question of how to determine the content of international customary law, and here as well there is a strong cosmopolitan dimension to the debate. That which is customary over many national laws can only be determined by their examination, as expressed both in doctrinal opinion (*opinio juris*) and state practice. There would even be a 'sliding scale' of their respective importance, such that an increase in the frequency and consistency of state practice could offset an absent or weak doctrinal position, and vice versa. The exact nature of the trade-off, moreover, would depend on evaluation of the *content* of the putative norm and its efficacy in achieving international goals.[111]

---

transition 'from normative practice to instrumental technique'), 488 (leading to a 'liberal agenda'); Dupuy (1999), 'Danger of Fragmentation', at 796 (on 'inherent dangers', absence of 'hierarchical relations').

[106] See Ch. 8, 'Internationality and Empire', Ch. 9, *'The adaptive state'*.

[107] Blackstone (1773), *Commentaries*, Bk IV, at 67 ('the law of the land'); and for the importance of common laws in state construction, see Ch. 6.

[108] Ginsburg, Chernykh, and Elkins (2008), 'Commitment and Diffusion', at 206 (for UK, customary international law 'directly applicable' unless overruled by subsequent statute or judicial decision, with references), 201 (incorporation part of more general trend of diffusion of constitutional sources); De Mestral and Fox-Decent (2008), 'Rethinking the Relationship', at 587 (for 2007 Canadian *Hape* decision, though experts still called on its content); Shelton (2011), 'Introduction', at 7, 14 (for constitutional adoption of international law as part of domestic law in Greece, Italy, Poland).

[109] In the USA the 'traditional view', dating from the *Paquete Habana* case in 1900, 175 US 677, favours incorporation, yet for recent opposition, echoing the general debate over foreign sources seen, see Ch. 11, 'The Cosmopolitan Turn in Constitutional Sources'; Dubinsky (2010), 'International Law in United States', at 462 (with references); and see Cleveland (2006), 'Our International Constitution', notably at 88 (for 'longstanding resort' to international law), 101–2 (response to criticism founded on 'democracy deficit'); Koh (2004), 'International Law Part of Our Law'; McGinnis (2006), 'Foreign to Our Constitution'; McGinnis and Somin (2007), 'Should International Law be Part of Our Law?', notably at 1178 (for 'raw' international law). The US debate is markedly influenced by federalist concerns and identification of customary international law as Federal, state, or otherwise; see Bellia and Clark (2009), 'Federal Common Law of Nations', notably at 7 (international customary law 'tied to the constitution's allocation of powers'); Bradley and Goldsmith (1997), 'Customary Law as Federal Common Law'.

[110] Shelton (2011), 'Introduction', at 1 (for 'growing complexity').

[111] Tasioulas (2007), 'Customary international law', at 324, 325, and 326 (for necessity of 'value judgements'); and see Kirgis (1987), 'Custom on a Sliding Scale' (need to see more or less *opinio juris* as constitutive element, as frequency and consistency of state practice rises or falls); Knop (2000), 'Here and There', at 525 (on process of abstracting from different laws in order to formulate an international legal

The international can only be determined, and evaluated, through immersion in many versions of the national.

The growth in sources of public international law is accompanied by growth in the institutions charged with their application. Over the last half-century there has been a remarkable proliferation of international judicial institutions, covering an 'almost bewildering array' of subjects, including crime, human rights, expropriation, trade, the environment, and so on.[112] This might be simply a multiplication of instances of 'internationality' and there is unquestionable room for an expansion of formal inter-state collaboration. Yet the cosmopolitan character of the expansion of institutions belies a simple growth of the international. The multiplication of institutions would thus constitute a 'fragmentation' of the subject, and while there is debate on what this might mean,[113] its cosmopolitan character is unquestionable. It is evidenced perhaps most obviously by the horizontal character of the new institutions, the 'loss of hierarchical position by institutions of the ancient regime'.[114] The horizontal character of the institutional development is accompanied, moreover, by the unquestionably cosmopolitan character of their operation, as international judges seek both procedure and substance from national legal orders to launch and maintain their international institutions.[115] There would now be a place for 'comparative international law'.[116] As well, the new institutions are more open to non-state litigants, putting into question the classic nature of international law as limited exclusively to states and opening the door to a range of non-state solutions, requiring substantive

norm); Roberts (2011), 'Comparative International Law?', at 73ff. (for citing of foreign decisions in determining content).

[112] MacKenzie *et al* (2009), *Manual on International Courts*, at ix (now also an 'international judiciary', with list of courts and tribunals); and see Romano (1999), 'Proliferation' (with 'synoptic chart' of tribunals in appendix); Alter (2006), 'Private Litigants and International Courts', at 22 (nineteen international courts created since 1990). The Project on International Courts list 125 judicial and quasi-judicial international institutions having some effect on state legal authority: see <www.pict-pcti.org/publications/synoptic_chart/synop_c4.pdf>. It is also the case that national courts have become a 'major institutional force' in protecting the international rule of law, operating in a 'mixed zone' that is neither fully national nor fully international: Nollkaemper (2011), *National Courts*, at 1, 26 (principle of sovereignty that local remedies must be exhausted making national courts 'first port of call'), and 224 ('the international quality of domesticated international law').

[113] For fragmentation, Koskenniemi and Laino (2002), 'Fragmentation of International Law?, notably at 559 ('a kaleidoscope reality'), 560 ('yet this is not new'), 561 (the 'effects of politics and not technical mistakes'); yet for such tribunals as 'clearly engaged in the same dialectic' with 'fundamentals' remaining the same, Charney (1999), 'Impact of Growth of International Courts', at 699; and as not a 'serious problem', Kingsbury (2003), 'International Legal Order', at 281 (only 'prospect' of fragmentation'); and for a bibliography on the large subject, Loughlin (2010), *Foundations of Public Law*, at 462.

[114] Koskenniemi (2005), 'Global Legal Pluralism', at 6, and see at 8 for tendency of 'European lawyers' to call for international constitutionalism, 'to organise the proliferating institutions and rationalities into firm hierarchies'; Sand (2007), 'From National Sovereignty', at 296 (for 'regime-collisions and fragmentation' as 'better solutions than attempts of creating hierarchies on the international level').

[115] For international criminal law and procedure, international human rights, see later in this section.

[116] Koskenniemi (2011), 'The Case for Comparative International Law'.

justification.[117] These latter developments, however, are part of a still-larger phenomenon affecting the nature of public international law.

The closure of the sources of public international law was effected around a basic principle that only states could be recognized as subjects of law. The world of the international was a world of states, and only states. We now know this was an unsustainable proposition. It excluded human beings in their cross-border relations, notably as potential plaintiffs having suffered injury at the hands of a state or states.[118] There is at present a slow redressing of the situation, and as the human being reappears in the *ius gentium* there is a slow growth in legal sources, which both allow this to happen and facilitate its execution. The human being can now act as a plaintiff in international cases, notably for damage inflicted by a state or states in violation of human rights. This had to occur since human rights can only be expressed in terms of the human. The emergence of international and regional courts of human rights is accompanied by a supra-national law of human rights that closely parallels, however, national determinations of rights under national instruments. It is 'neither constitutional nor international' and cosmopolitan may be the only appropriate adjective.[119] It is also the case that the human being can now be found criminally responsible in international law, and new sources both allow this to happen and determine when it should happen. An international criminal law has come into being, which might be closer to basic criminal law than classic international law. The International Criminal Court has been called an 'innovative form of cosmopolitanism' and the work of its judges in developing the law they apply is certainly cosmopolitan in character.[120]

---

[117] Romano (1999), 'Proliferation', at 710 (those institutions granting access to non-state entities 'far outnumber' those that do not); Alter (2006), 'Private Litigants and International Courts', at 24 (private party standing not necessarily as plaintiffs, also to present evidence, etc.); Glenn (2000), 'Globalization and Dispute Resolution', at 142 (for private parties in NAFTA proceedings).

[118] For criticism of the 'old regime', Allott (2002), *Health of Nations*, at 418 ('defensive concepts' of sovereignty, sovereign equality of states, non-intervention) and 419 (no concept of an international society); and for the new regime, Meron (2006), *Humanization of International Law*, notably Ch. IV ('Humanization of State Responsibility: From Bilateralism to Community Concerns'); Parlett (2011), *Individual in International Legal System*, notably at 17 (on importance of 1928 ICJ decision in *Jurisdiction of the Court of Danzig*), 370 (international system still largely 'state-centric', human beings no control over the way in which they receive rights and obligations); McCorquodale (2010), 'Individual and the International Legal System', at 289 (for individual rights) and 291 (individual responsibility).

[119] Eleftheriadis (2003), 'Cosmopolitan Law', notably at 255 ('does not make use of a strict theory of sources, procedural or otherwise'); and for inevitable local translation of universalist human rights norms, Griffin (2012), 'Human Rights Parochial?', at 162 (though 'not a different framework of basic evaluations but merely a highly constrained difference in a rational opting'); Chibundu (2012), 'Parochial Foundations', at 179 ('conceptions cannot be "universal" . . . There is nothing timeless about a concept'); Carmody (2012), 'Rights in Reverse', at 213 ('the actual product of rights discourse will vary from place to place and time to time'); and for 'over-inclusivity' in matters of gender discrimination, requiring responsiveness to local particularity, Aoláin (2010), 'Learning the Lessons: What Feminist Legal Theory Teaches', at 281. For criticism of supranational human rights as 'the sole approved discourse of resistance', Rajagopal (2003), *International Law from Below*, at 9 (main filter of developing world resistance) and 186 (still according leading role to states in realization of human rights).

[120] Kleingeld and Brown (2006), 'Cosmopolitanism' ('going much beyond Kant's conception of "cosmopolitan law"'). For the mixed or cosmopolitan character of the law, Roberts (2007), 'Comparative Law for International Criminal Justice' (comparative processes at work in seven concentric circles of international criminal justice activity); del Ponte (2006), 'Investigation and Prosecution' (international

Private actors function not only as parties to litigation, however, but also as contributors to the sources of public international law. There is now a large literature on the contribution of international non-governmental organizations (INGOs) to public international law and a developing notion of an 'inclusive' international law.[121] Prior to the adoption by the United Nations General Assembly of the Declaration on the Rights of Indigenous Peoples, a transnational network of indigenous peoples played the essential role in bringing the Declaration to fruition.[122] Thus international law would be becoming 'transcivilizational'; it is increasingly capable of normative engagement with non-state and non-western legal orders.[123] The same phenomenon is becoming evident in private international law.

Private international law

By the end of the nineteenth century private international law exhibited many of the same characteristics of 'internationality' as did public international law. States were the object of attention, and just as public international law purported to regulate their relations, so did private international law purport to allocate all private law relations to one or another of them. 'Material justice' would have disappeared in favour of 'conflicts justice', understood as the appropriate spatial distribution of legal relations to state territories.[124] The nationalization of the subject that had occurred from the end of the nineteenth century even accelerated in the late twentieth century with a widespread phenomenon of national

criminal procedure containing elements of civil and common law traditions); Langer (2005), 'Rise of Managerial Judging', notably at 849 (on different 'structures and interpretation of meaning' in criminal adjudication process); Cassese (2008), *International Criminal Law*, at 6, 7; Delmas-Marty (2006), 'Interaction National and International Criminal Law', at 9 ('hybridization'); Pradel (2001), 'Mondialisation du droit pénal' (harmonization of national criminal laws accompanied by appearance of 'supranational' criminal law).

[121] Tasioulas (2007), 'Customary international law', at 328 (listing Red Cross, Human Rights Watch, Amnesty International); McCorquodale (2004), 'An Inclusive International Legal System'; Keane (2003), *Global Civil Society*, at 5 (for some 50,000 in the world, nearly 90 per cent formed since 1970). Private actors may also function as proxies to states in achieving regulatory outcomes, at the insistence of states: see Farrell (2006), 'Regulating Information Flows', at 353 (USA looking to banks to prevent transactions between US gamblers and Antiguan gambling websites).

[122] Miranda (2010), 'Indigenous Peoples as International Lawmakers', notably at 207 (though operating 'within certain discursive and structural limitations'); Tasioulas (2007), 'Customary international law', at 328 (for 'peoples' both subjects of international law and contributors to customary international law); and see Makkonen (2000), *Concepts of 'People'*, at 33 (for need to avoid 'essentialist' understanding of 'nation'), 44 (need to 'take into account the real human cultural and biological diversity'). For a 'principle of humanity' applied to understanding indigenous or chthonic peoples, in the sense 'that we should try to interpret others as saying something true', Lear (2006), *Radical Hope*, at 4 (citing Davidson's principle of charity); and for increasing awareness of Islamic understandings of 'international' law, Allain (2011), 'Islamic Law of Nations'.

[123] For 'transcivilizational', Onuma (2010), *A Transcivilizational Perspective on International Law*; and for development of the idea of engagement, beyond states, Glenn (2011a), 'Ethic of International Law'.

[124] On the conflictual character of the process and the underlying notion of conflict, see Ch. 8, 'Private international law'.

codification of the subject.[125] The codes were composed largely of allocative rules using traditional 'connecting factors' such as domicile, nationality, the *situs* of property, or the place of a tort or wrong to territorialize abstract legal questions. Huber's comity of the seventeenth century had crystallized into fixed rules dictating the application of foreign law to cases properly localized abroad. Yet a cross-border private law case could be dealt with by private law lawyers without having any contact whatsoever with foreign law. National rules dictated the application of local or foreign law; if foreign law was applicable its content would be supplied by university institutes or experts in the designated foreign law.[126]

By the second half of the twentieth century there was increasing frustration with the process. Localization of complex, private law relations, often implicating more than two parties, appeared increasingly as an arbitrary technique.[127] The conflicts of conflict-of-laws rules, resulting from their nationalization, meant that there was never any certitude in their application, while the resulting uncertainty was compounded by the necessity in all cases of evaluating the possible application of foreign law in terms of the (imprecise) public policy of the forum. Reaction was most severe in the USA, where a series of doctrinal attacks on the rule-centred first Restatement on the Conflict of Laws led to its general abandonment and a shift towards interpretive methods. There have been many varieties of these but they generally centre on the nature of the local, material rules and the reasons for extending their application in space. Brainerd Currie thus famously stated that '[w]e would be better off without choice-of-law rules' and proposed that courts ascertain whether there is a 'legitimate basis' for the assertion of a governmental interest in the application of its policy in a transborder case.[128] Rules designed to protect a vulnerable person could thus be interpreted as following the person across a border. Currie's proposals entailed examining the policy expressed by foreign law but only 'if necessary' (where the forum state had no interest), while a local government interest always prevailed over a foreign one.[129] The method provided a normative, as opposed to

---

[125] Symeonides (2012), 'Codification and Flexibility', at 167.

[126] In many continental jurisdictions the application of the private international rules was on the judge's own intitiative (von Amts wegen, d'office) and spatial allocation had to take place even where none alleged a difference amongst the potentially applicable laws. However, the resulting presumption of conflict of laws, necessitating a laborious choice of law in all cases and highly unsuitable particularly in a common market, was avoided in common law jurisdictions through retention of the historical rule that proof of foreign law occurred only on its invocation in the written pleadings. A presumption of conflict is thereby displaced by a presumption of harmony: Glenn (1993), 'Harmonization of Law'.

[127] Juenger (1985), *General Course*, at 256 ('[l]egal relationships that straddle territorial boundaries do not sit exclusively in one geographical location or another . . . since every law has both a territorial and a personal application, the selection of one or the other type of contact is inherently arbitrary').

[128] Currie (1963), *Selected Essays on Conflict of Laws*, at 183. Currie's proposal was accepted by the New York Court of Appeals in *Babcock* v. *Jackson*, 12 NY 2d 473, 191 NE 2d 279 (1963). The same court reverted in some measure to more fixed rules in guest passenger automobile accident cases in *Neumeier* v. *Kuehner* 31 NY 2d 121, 286 NE 2d 454 (1972), though still allowing for advancing 'the relevant substantive law purposes' in a number of situations.

[129] Currie (1963), *Selected Essays on Conflict of Laws*, at 184.

geographic, reason for choice of law but was scarcely cosmopolitan in its attitude towards non-state law. An advance was provided by Baxter whose notion of 'comparative impairment' involved choice of the law whose non-application in the given case would give rise to the greatest impairment of the underlying governmental policy.[130] The judge is thus required to engage with the material policies of the laws in question and assess the normative case for application of one or the other. It is a very cosmopolitan process, most evidently appropriate for judges within a federation but also potentially beyond, once the judge is seen as other than a local enforcement officer.[131]

Elsewhere in the world there has been less enthusiasm for the abandonment of choice-of-law rules but their non-monotonic character is becoming more and more evident and judges are called upon, even within a cadre of choice-of-law rules, to engage with the substance of local and foreign material rules. In francophone jurisdictions the notion that local rules of 'immediate application' displace choice-of-law rules in particular cases has become widely known and accepted and the same notion is found in the German notion of rules of 'special connections' (Sonderanknüpfungen).[132] More significantly, the necessity of applying foreign material rules because of their own, underlying imperativity has been accepted at the European level in Rome I, the European Regulation governing choice of law in matters of contracts.[133] Even the notion of national public order has recently assumed a cosmopolitan, conciliatory function, since the French Court of Cassation decides on the recognition of Islamic talaq divorces (granted unilaterally by husbands) not in terms exclusively of equality of the sexes guaranteed by the European Convention of Human Rights but also in terms of whether the divorce has provided adequate financial resources to the divorced spouse.[134]

---

[130] Baxter (1963), 'Choice of Law and Federal System', notably at 9 ('[t]he extent to which the purpose underlying a rule will be furthered by application or impaired by non-application to cases of a particular category may be regarded as the measure of the rule's pertinence and of the state's interest in the rule's application to cases within the category. Normative resolution of real conflicts cases is possible . . . ').

[131] For use of comparative impairment by the Supreme Court of Canada in deciding private law cases involving two or more provinces, *Interprovincial Cooperatives Ltd* v. *The Queen in Right of Manitoba* (1975), 53 DLR (3d) 321, *per* Laskin, J. at 339 ('Manitoba's predominant interest in applying its own law . . . is undeniable. Neither Saskatchewan nor Ontario can put forward as strong a claim to have their provincial law apply . . . '). The notion of comparative impairment was adopted legislatively for the state courts of Louisiana: see Symeonides (1990), 'Codifying Choice of Law for Torts', at 437–8.

[132] Francescakis (1966), 'Quelques précisions sur les "lois d'application immediate"'; the concept is codified in the Quebec Civil Code in Art. 3076 ('[t]he rules contained in this Book apply subject to those rules of law in force in Québec which are applicable by reason of their particular object').

[133] Regulation EC No. 593/2008 of 17 June 2008 on the law applicable to contractual obligations, Art. 9 ('overriding mandatory provisions'); and for its application by the highest French court, Cass. comm. 16 March 2010, No. 08–21511. In Quebec the possibility has been codified in Art. 3079 of the Civil Code ('[w]here legitimate and manifestly preponderant interests so require, effect may be given to a mandatory provision of the law of another country with which the situation is closely connected').

[134] Canivet (2003), 'Convergence des systèmes juridiques', at 19–22 ('la voie du dialogue . . . la solution la plus juste dans chaque cas').

While the French talaq divorce cases assume the operation of a choice-of-law rule and then ask whether it should be set aside in the name of public order, a further process is now identifiable: allowing a particular substantive result to control the choice-of-law process itself. Here control is given, not to government interests but, for example, to the need to provide a given level of protection to vulnerable, individual human beings, such as a child, or consumer, or tort victim. The law that provides the desired protection is thus the law that should be chosen, either by the court or by the plaintiff himself or herself. This type of 'Wertungsjurisprudenz'[135] is now widespread in national codifications so once again, as with comparative impairment, we see conflicts justice acknowledging the strength of other normative claims and yielding to them in considerable measure. The solution that drives the process is one that is judged appropriate for a range over many different countries, which is of course the definition of 'cosmopolitanism' of the *Oxford English Dictionary*, used throughout here.[136]

More striking modern phenomena in private international law consist of the abandonment of the choice-of-law process in its entirety in favour of 'substantivism' in international adjudication. This substantivism looks, not to the best law in the circumstances (still compatible in some measure with a process of choice of law), but generally to the best result in the circumstances. This may yield particular international solutions for private international cases, as in the famous French nineteenth-century case of *Lizardi*, where it was decided that a local contracting party may rely on a contract signed by a person incapable under the rules of their (foreign) nationality if the local party was in a state of 'excusable ignorance' of the foreign law.[137] All will depend on the equities in the individual case, including familiarity of the parties with each other, dissimulation of the status of minor, the nature of the contract (purchasing land is different from purchasing consumer goods), and so on. Substantivism also underlies much of contemporary private international family law now, as recent, operative Hague Conventions on the protection of children place the emphasis on collaboration of national judiciaries to ensure the highest level of protection, with little regard for any choice-of-law process.[138] Further, judges in international bankruptcy cases now regularly engage in collaborative efforts to ensure equitable distribution of assets scattered over national boundaries.[139]

---

[135] Vrellis (2007), *Conflit ou coordination de valeurs*, at 192, with examples at 368ff.; and generally Symeonides (2001), 'Material Justice and Conflicts Justice'. See e.g. the Quebec Civil Code in Arts 3119 (consumer-contract choice of law cannot deprive consumer of protection accorded by consumer's place of residence), 3118 (likewise for protection by law of employee's place of work), 3119 (insurance contract governed by law of Quebec if applied for in Quebec).

[136] See Preface.

[137] Req. 16 January 1861, D. P. 1861.1.193, S. 1861.1.305; and for the importance of the decision. Glenn (1975), *Capacité en droit international privé*, at 110–18, 241–4.

[138] Silberman (2006), *Co-operative Efforts in Private International Law*, notably at 276 ('structure of formal cooperation').

[139] The process originated in the territorialist bankruptcy jurisdictions of North America, as a matter of practical necessity, but has now become generalized. It extends notably to joint protocols and

Harold Berman has asked whether the conflict of laws is becoming passé and the answer must be yes, at least in some measure, not because a 'global law' is emerging, as he suggested, but because other types of solution, as indicated above, are becoming more persuasive.[140] They are more cosmopolitan in character and more appropriate for a world of interdependent states. Is the result one of increased conflict and legal uncertainty? Professor Gaillard argues to the contrary and that international arbitration, in which arbitrators are free to apply a substantive *lex mercatoria*, has given rise to greater foreseeability of results than the choice-of-law process.[141] The USA has functioned largely without choice-of-law rules for a half century and the world has not come to an end. This is entirely compatible with the necessary absence of certainty that follows from choice-of-law rules, which represent a 'jump into the unknown' ('saut dans l'inconnu') in their references to foreign law the content of which is unknowable in advance.

The traditional fields and methods of international law are thus declining in significance in the face of more appropriate and cosmopolitan solutions. This is confirmed in examining the rise of both regional law and transnational law.

STATES AND REGIONAL LAW

Regional law has become a vigorous alternative to the traditional dichotomy between the national and the international (or global). Regional trade blocs are seen by many as alternatives to the global regulatory model of the WTO.[142] They are multiplying rapidly, in both multilateral and bilateral form.[143] One must, however, distinguish between regions; they differ, as do states. The European Union, for many and diverse reasons, has chosen a regime of pan-state institutions and considerable legal harmonization; the NAFTA countries are institutionally light, with no harmonization; MERCOSUR would be somewhere

---

teleconference proceedings: see Fletcher (2005), *Insolvency in Private International Law*, at 269 (judges using 'modern telecommunications facilities' to establish direct contact).

[140] Berman (2005), 'Is Conflict of Laws becoming Passé?'

[141] Gaillard (2008), *Aspects philosophiques de l'arbitrage*, at 90. From the perspective of this international, substantive, commercial law, the choice-of-law process developed over the nineteenth century even appears to be an 'aberration': see Dalhuisen (2000), *International Commercial, Financial and Trade Law*, at vii.

[142] Duina (2006), *Social Construction of Free Trade*, at 26 (GATT, WTO 'plagued by difficulties', Regional Trade Agreements (RTAs) as alternative 'more aggressive and deeper'), 30 (WTO with new members, new needs, talks 'increasingly complex and time-consuming', compliance rates declining); yet for RTAs as 'termites' undermining global free trade, Bhagwati (2008), *Termites in the Trading System*.

[143] For regional and priority trade agreements now numbering in the hundreds, most created since 1990, Duina (2006), *Social Construction of Free Trade*, at 3 (sixty-eight RTAs to 1994, a further hundred from 1995 to 2001); Estevadeordal and Suominen (2009), *Sovereign Remedy*, at 4 (over 200 Priority Trade Agreements registered with WTO by 2007, many more unregistered). All of these represent institutionalization of Rosecrance's notion of the 'trading state', one necessarily dependent on others for products it is incapable of producing itself: see Ch. 9, 'Hierarchy'. The 'import substitution' economy is no more.

between the two.[144] It is true that there is less legal diversity within regions than across them, but even differences in expression of formal, written, state law imply cosmopolitanism in their appreciation and resolution. European states share common constitutional traditions, but there are antinomies amongst them, and if the notion of human rights is widespread there are said to be conflicts of rights.[145] Members of NAFTA arbitration panels must work with national administrative law standards that are not their own.[146] All regions therefore imply levels of cosmopolitanism that surpass those of classic public or private international law. Europe has developed the most vertical, state-like structures, but the cosmopolitan character of contemporary Europe is unquestionable. It may even surpass the more bottom-up cosmopolitan workings of the other regions.

The construction of the European Union was facilitated by the notion of 'open' states that were able to delegate to the EU a portion of their sovereign authority.[147] The notion of national sovereignty has suffered even more in this process within Europe than it has beyond it.[148] There is corresponding opinion that the EU is best thought of in terms of constitutional law and vertical structures, and EU institutions have developed a notion of the 'direct effect' of EU norms.[149] Yet

---

[144] For the contrast between the EU and NAFTA, Glenn (2001c), 'NAFTA Experiment'; Glenn (2002), 'North America as Medieval'; and for MERCOSUR measures of harmonization, Duina (2006), *Social Construction of Free Trade*, notably at 74 ('cognitive standardization').

[145] For antinomies, Martinico (2011), 'Constitutional Complexity of the EU', at 82 (EU as 'complex' reality'); and conflicts Pérez (2009), *Conflicts of Rights in the EU*, notably at 103 (for ensuing turn to 'dialogue as a source of legitimacy', 'particular and evolving truths'); Potvin-Solis (2004), 'Le concept de dialogue', at 24 (for need to render compatible 'positions opposées ou divergentes').

[146] Glenn (2000), 'Globalization and Dispute Resolution', at 142 (in applying national administrative law standards); Glenn (2001b), 'Comparative Law and Legal Practice', at 993 ('constant search for equivalent or analogous standards', citing López-Ayllón and Fix-Fierro).

[147] See Ch. 9, 'The adaptive state'; and see von Bogdandy (1996), 'Contours of Integrated Europe', at 507 (idea of 'closed legal system, a defining characteristic of the sovereign nation-state, has been overcome'); Di Fabio (1998), *Das Recht offener Staaten*, at 74 (European states using more cooperation and consensus); Sand (2007), 'From National Sovereignty to Cooperation', at 280 ('delegated considerable and quite vital parts of their constitutional competences to the EU ... cannot be taken back without leaving the organization'), 288 (constitutions of some EU states authorize membership; others do not, but extent of cooperation impossible to read from constitutional texts); MacCormick (1993), 'Beyond the Sovereign State', at 3 (membership compatible with UK sovereignty since withdrawal possible, but 'conceded that it is not at all likely to happen').

[148] For decline elsewhere, see Ch. 9, 'Hierarchy'; and for it being within Europe 'in no way still a relevant problem ("keineswegs mehr ein relevantes problem")', Baldus (1997), 'Zur Relevanz des Souveränitätsproblems', at 382; and for similar views Birkinshaw (2003), *European Public Law*, at 551 ('vitally affected by Community membership'); Schiemann (2007), 'Europe and Loss of Sovereignty', at 475 ('no nation is sovereign'); MacCormick (1999), *Questioning Sovereignty*, at 132 ('beyond the sovereign state'), 142 ('post-sovereign' Europe).

[149] For constitutional law, though often qualified, Shaw (1999), 'Postnational constitutionalism', at 579 (from 'classic notion' of 'constitutionalization of the treaties' to 'postnational constitutionalism'); Halberstam (2009), 'Constitutional Heterarchy'; Grewe and Ruiz Fabri (1995), *Droits constitutionnels européens*, at 10 (at least question of 'droit constitutionnel européen'); Martinico (2011), 'Constitutional Complexity of the EU', at 90 (for 'multilevel constitutionalism', 'constitutional pluralism'); Neuwahl and Haack (2007), *Unresolved Issues of Constitution for Europe*. Yet for constitutional perspective being 'dream' today only of a 'minority', Cooper (2005), *Breaking of Nations*, at 37; and for opposition to the idea of constitutionality, Ziller (2011), 'Nature of European Union', at 7ff. (for 'internationalist' character of EU);

if states have yielded some measure of their previous authority they remain essential actors within the Union;[150] the more usual language represents the EU as a *sui generis* construction, characterized by 'contrapuntal law', 'heterarchy', 'cosmopolitan democracy', or 'cooperative governance'.[151] It would constitute a 'polycentric polity' or a 'plural cooperative system'.[152] Mathias Kumm has written of its 'cosmopolitan constitutionalism'.[153] In the language of this book it represents a form of institutional cosmopolitanism, accompanied necessarily by a 'shift away from binary conceptions of law'[154] and less insistence on a 'strict theory of the sources of law'.[155]

The essentially cosmopolitan character of the EU and its states is evident both in the workings of EU institutions and in their relations with member states. The judges of the European Court of Justice (ECJ) apply EU law, but the terms of the Treaty of the European Union (TEU) and the Treaty on the Functioning of the European Union (TFEU) are frequently large and abstract. As an interpretive guide the ECJ thus looks to the 'constitutional traditions common' to the member states in order to ensure that EU law is compatible with the fundamental legal rights of the law of member states.[156] As a judge at the European level one must first acquire a working knowledge of many

Maduro (2003b), 'Europe and the constitution', at 75 (conception of national constitutionalism today 'in crisis'); Mac Amlaigh (2011), 'Questioning Constitutional Pluralism', at 21 (no 'elemental agreement'); Walker (2002), 'Idea of Constitutional Pluralism', notably at 319 ('debased conceptual currency' though possible rehabilitation as constitutional pluralism'); and for the proposition of the Prime Minister of Luxembourg to abandon entirely the idea of an EU constitution, Ladeur (2004c), 'Globalization and Conversion of Democracy', at 117 (rather 'polycentric network'). The notion of 'direct effect' of EU norms was first enunciated by the ECJ in the *Van Gend en Loos* decision in 1962, reported at [1963] ECR 1, [1970] CMLR 1, though for the EU having moved from 'total' to 'optional' or 'minimum' harmonization, Majone (2000), 'International regulatory cooperation', at 133 (minimum not excluding higher local standards).

[150] For European Union states not having lost as much autonomy as usually believed, Kohler-Koch (1996), 'Transformation of Governance in the EU', at 169 (can still set own agendas, but change in manner of doing so), 178 (notably moving to 'sub-national' level); Duina (2003), 'National Legislatures in Common Markets', at 212 (on state refusal to implement EU norms). Areas of 'direct effect' of EU norms would have been carefully chosen as 'relatively non-controversial'; Rutledge (2009), '*Medellin*, Delegation and Conflicts (of Law)', at 224. The EU principle of subsidiarity, the EU acting only if objectives cannot be achieved by member states, would also protect local sovereignty in some measure: Bermann (1994), 'Taking Subsidiarity Seriously', notably at 334 (Community not to 'needlessly trample' democratic self-government, cultural diversity); Birkinshaw (2003), *European Public Law*, at 220.

[151] See respectively Maduro (2003a), 'Contrapunctual Law'; Krisch (2010), *Beyond Constitutionalism*, at 111 (heterarchy); Eriksen (2009), 'EU: Cosmopolitan Vanguard?' at 2 (cosmopolitan democracy); Zielonka (2006), *Europe as Empire*, at 72 (logic of diversity, citing Heritier); Börzel (2002), *States and Regions in EU*, at 24 (cooperative governance).

[152] Wind (2003), 'The European Union as a polycentric polity'; Ladeur (2004d), 'Methodology and European Law', at 103 ('plural cooperative system').

[153] Kumm (2010), 'How does European Law Fit', at 127 (authority of EU law 'possibly a question of degree', national courts adopting 'intermediate position'), 135 ('cosmopolitan and not statist framework').

[154] Krisch (2010), *Beyond Constitutionalism*, at 305 ('a form of gradated authority').

[155] Eleftheriadis (2003), 'Cosmopolitan Law', at 260; and see MacCormick (1993), 'Beyond the Sovereign State', at 9 ('a broader, more diffuse, view of law').

[156] Art. 6.3, TEU; and for reliance, CJCE 14 May 1974, *Nold* v. *The Commission* [1974] CMLR 338.

national laws; it is a commonplace that the ECJ is a place of comparative legal reasoning.[157] By the terms of the TFEU itself, its judges must also look to the 'general principles common to the law of the member states' to determine the civil liability of EU institutions.[158] Legal education is (slowly) accommodating the necessity of teaching more than national law in EU countries.

EU institutions also have subtle relations with the institutions of member states. It is not an obviously hierarchical, vertical relationship. This has become most evident in the so-called *Solange* jurisprudence of the German Constitutional Court, the Bundesverfassungsgerichthof (BVerfG), which is indicative in general of the relations between national high constitutional courts and the ECJ. Must a high constitutional court verify EU rules against national articulation of rights and give priority to the latter? This was the original position of the German Constitutional Court in the first of a series of decisions in 1974 (*Solange I*),[159] but since then the BVerfG has taken a more conciliatory position, stating that, while it retains an ultimate power of review, it will refrain from review as long as (*Solange II*) the EU guarantees fundamental rights in a manner essentially similar to that of national law.[160] A presumption of constitutional validity of EU law has emerged, but there is a constant tension and a constant need for evaluation of different articulations of rights.[161] Both the national and the European are presumptively valid, and the underlying reasoning would be multivalent.[162] There would be 'strategic interaction' between courts in balancing inherent 'centripetal and centrifugal' forces in EU structures.[163] It also appears unlikely that there will be a European Civil Code, so the European

---

[157] Van der Mensbrugghe (2003), *Méthode comparative en droit européen*, with references; for comparative legal reasoning as 'built into legal reasoning' in the institutions of the European Union, Maduro (2007), 'Interpreting European Law', text accompanying notes 11, 12 ('a question of determining what legal solution fits better with the EU legal order').

[158] Art. 340, TFEU. Where the principles are not common, the ECJ would nevertheless have drawn on principles of the law of member states to develop its own specific principles: Steiner, Woods, and Twigg-Flesner (2006), *EU Law*, at 289; Toriello (2000), *I principi generali del diritto communitario*, at 283 (also for the much larger theme of general principles of EU law itself).

[159] [1974] 2 CMLR 540. For which see Waibel (2010), 'Salutory Warning for EU'.

[160] See *Solange II* [1987] 3 CMLR 225.

[161] For the case law, Krisch (2010), *Beyond Constitutionalism*, at 287 ('conditional recognition... paradigmatic for interactions in pluralist orders'); Ziller (2009), '*Solange III*' at 8 (on 'European law-friendliness (Europarechtsfreundlichkeit)' of BVerfG); Martinico (2007), 'Complexity and Cultural Sources of Law' (for positions of other European national courts); Jackson (2010), *Constitutional Engagement*, at 93 (move to 'assumption' that ECJ protecting fundamental rights); Waibel (2010), 'Salutory Warning for EU', at 40 (for 'warning shot across the bow' of the ECJ); Koch (2003–4) 'Envisioning a Global Legal Culture', at 15 ('softened'); Rosenfeld (2008), 'Rethinking constitutional ordering', at 419 (ECJ going 'out of its way' to incorporate respect for rights in its jurisprudence, 'actual conflicts' thus avoided); Kumm (2005), 'Jurisprudence of Constitutional Conflict', notably at 303 (ECJ should allow national courts to set aside EU law as a matter of EU law).

[162] As to which, see Ch. 14, '*The cosmopolitan character of the new logics*'.

[163] Waibel (2010), 'Salutory Warning for EU', at 40; and for France and the position of the Conseil d'État, Potvin-Solis (1999), *L'effet des jurisprudences européennes*, notably at 726 ('la coopération juridictionelle') and organized generally around the theme of a European 'effect' both commanded by the authority of European law and conditioned by the autonomy of the Conseil d'État.

Union will continue to resemble the North American federations in their private law diversity.[164]

European cosmopolitanism is not derived only from the relations between the EU and its member states. There is also the European Court of Human Rights (ECtHR), exercising a jurisdiction beyond EU membership and now extending to some forty-seven signatories to the European Convention on Human Rights. The ECtHR has relations both with signatory states and with the ECJ and in neither case is this a hierarchical relation of command.[165] The ECtHR does not bind the ECJ by its decisions (they can be seen as international equals) but it is now becoming a 'banalisation' that the ECJ takes ECtHR decisions into account in its own work.[166] The ECtHR in its turn exercises deference in possible review of EU norms on human rights grounds, given that the EU would offer 'equivalent protection'.[167] It is a matter of influence. ECtHR relations with national high courts (and there are frequently more than one of these, as is notably the case in France) are also characterized by subtlety. In principle, ECtHR decisions are only declaratory in character and it is left to the signatory state to take remedial measures.[168] State courts may resist acceptance and implementation and, though this 'sounds highly conflictual', the actual relations between the courts would be characterized by a high level of cooperation.[169] The ECtHR, moreover, would be even more explicitly comparative in its work than the ECJ and has been the

---

[164] The recently created European Law Institute may be an instrument of informal harmonization, as is the American Law Institute in the USA: see Zimmermann (2012), 'Challenges for the European Law Institute'. For the debate on a European civil code, or even a common frame of reference, Glenn (2010b), *Legal Traditions*, at 168. The EU persists, however, in codification of choice-of-law rules at the European level, presuming underlying conflict of national rules, a relic of nineteenth-century views on the relations of private laws; see Ch. 8, '*Private international law*'.

[165] For 'parallel constitutional protection', Garlicki (2008) 'Cooperation of courts', at 511 ('multidimensionality').

[166] Cohen-Jonathan, and Flauss (2005), *Le rayonnement international*, at 269 (even 'banalisation quasi-complète'); and see also Koch (2003–4) 'Envisioning a Global Legal Culture', at 16 (ECJ 'has not found itself bound' by ECtHR decisions, but regularly refers to them).

[167] De Hert and Korenica (2012), 'The Doctrine of Equivalent Protection', notably at 881 (parallel with *Solange* jurisprudence of German Constitutional Court), 882 (doctrine only presumptive force) and 886 (inapplicable where 'manifest deficiency').

[168] Ress (2005), 'Effect of Decisions of the ECtHR', at 371 (though states must cease violation in future and effect *restitutio in integrum*), 374 ('not executable as such in domestic orders'); and for Council of Europe preoccupation with the level of domestic recognition, Council of Europe Committee of Ministers (2008), *Supervision of the execution of judgments*, notably at 11, 12 (for problem of repetitive or 'clone' cases, indicating a lack of precedental effect of decisions; Lambert-Abdelgawad (2002), *Execution of Judgments of ECtHR*, at 6 (contrasting initial proposals that Court could 'prescribe remedies'); and for the Court's impact as 'broad and pervasive in some states, and weak in others', Keller and Stone Sweet (2008), *A Europe of Rights*, at 4 (also variance across time in particular states). The Court would now be becoming more explicit in the directions it gives for *restitutio in integrum*, but there would be an ongoing need for 'embedding' it in domestic legal orders: Helfer (2008), 'Redesigning the European Court of Human Rights', at 130 (to 'bolster the remedies' provided by domestic judges and legislatures).

[169] Krisch (2010), *Beyond Constitutionalism*, at 127 ('friction has been rare'); and see for 'more and more' extensive recognition of a direct effect of ECtHR decisions, Council of Europe Committee of Ministers (2008), *Supervision of the execution of judgments*, at 11 (and so 'increasingly important role played by domestic courts').

major contributor to a widely recognized 'dialogue' between European and national judges.[170]

The relations of the ECtHR with other courts in Europe is thus an example of institutional cosmopolitanism. There is even a further dimension to this institutional cosmopolitanism, moreover, in that the Court must reconcile national laws with religious and church laws in giving effect to Article 9 of the ECHR. It replicates, at a European level, the cosmopolitan work of national courts in matters of religious liberty that has already been examined above,[171] while situating both national laws and religious norms in the broader cadre of the ECHR. In this process the Court has not created a binary logic between national law on the one hand and Article 9's protection of religious liberty on the other; rather, it has created a 'margin of appreciation' by virtue of which each state signatory to the Convention is allowed a zone of discretion in the manner in which it implements local policy and respects religious liberty.[172] This is particularly the case where there is no pan-European consensus on a particular question such that the ECHR should not be given a univocal reading. The case law of the Court does not escape criticism, either from those favouring European uniformity[173] or from those who champion individual liberties,[174] but the technique of the margin of appreciation serves the function of accommodating national differences, religious norms, and pan-European conceptions of rights.

---

[170] See notably, from a large literature, Mahoney (2004), 'Comparative Method in European Court of Human Rights'; Reed (2008), 'Foreign Precedents', at 254 (comparison 'built into legal reasoning'); Peoples (2008), 'The Use of Foreign Law', for wide range of areas of law and notably at 259 (for citations to USA, Canada, Japan, Australia), 263 (citations dictated in part by 'threat of the available'); Cohen-Jonathan and Flauss (2005), *Le rayonnement international*, at 273 (for citation of non-European jurisdictions, international criminal courts); Ambrus (2009), 'Comparative Law Method in the ECHR', at 353 (even 'excessive weight' to comparative method, question of compatibility with rule of law); Dzehtsiarou (2010), 'Comparative Law in ECHR'; and for 'dialogue' Potvin-Solis (2004), 'Le concept de dialogue', notably at 23 (appropriate for cooperation between jurisdictions, absence of hierarchy); Tomkins (2005), *Our Republican Constitution*, at 8 (for effect in Great Britain of 'simple exposure of European ideas', growth in conversations between judges); Husa (2009), ' "We the Judges" ', at 1.1 ('transnational judicial communication'); Stone Sweet (2012), 'A Cosmopolitan Legal Order' (ECtHR itself a 'cosmopolitan legal order', no formal means of coordinating rights doctrine or of resolving conflicts).

[171] See this chapter, '*Religious liberty*'.

[172] For the immense case law of the Court, even by 2002, Arai-Takahashi (2002), *Margin of Appreciation Doctrine*; and for the margin of appreciation as 'ethical de-centralisation or subsidiarity', Sweeney (2005), 'Margins of Appreciation', at 467.

[173] Letsas (2009), *A Theory of Interpretation of the ECHR*, at 6 ('answers cannot be culture specific') though see also at 12 (for particularity of Court as international and not national court); and for the related criticism of imprecision, Westerfield (2006), 'Behind the Veil', at 674 (criteria for determining breadth of margin not clear, comparing with notion of 'levels of scrutiny' in US constitutional law).

[174] Evans (2001), *Freedom of Religion*, at 102 (Court 'highly deferential to the needs of the State'), 198 ('universally hostile attitude to adherents of religions or beliefs who claim the right to opt out of comprehensive legal schemes'); Evans (2008), 'Freedom of religion and the ECHR', at 312 ('secular fundamentalism') and 291 (for Court insistence on 'manifestation' of religion and not simply belief); Langlaude (2006), 'Indoctrination, Secularism', at 944 (Court's 'own conception of secularism at an unacknowledged cost to religious freedom'), though see at 942 (Court willing to intervene to protect 'very existence' of religions); Calo (2010), 'Pluralism, Secularism', at 268 ('secular logic').

STATES AND TRANSNATIONAL LAW

Much of the law discussed in this volume can today be described as transnational in character. Common laws, shared constitutional principles, and the methods of institutional cosmopolitanism all transcend particular states.[175] Prior to the efforts at territorial and national closure, however, there was little to transcend, or at least little to transcend in the form of the contemporary state. There was simply (very) local law and law that was wider in application. The notion of transnational law emerged only with the emergence of recognizable states with defined boundaries, such that there was something to transcend, and with recognition that the state could not succeed in its ambition to be an exclusive source of law. Since there was no underlying principle of such exclusivity,[176] recognition of a concept of transnational law was inevitable. It is said to have occurred in 1956 with the publication of Philip Jessup's *Transnational Law*, though the volume concentrated essentially on international law.[177] Since the mid-twentieth century, however, the notion of transnational law has become current and has acquired a general sense of law that is non-state in origin, that transcends particular states, and that does not fall within the defined spheres of international law. Its recognition implies a contextualization of the law of the state,[178] which inevitably comes to be situate within a broader normative context. This has always been the case, but the invention of the expression transnational law means there is now a general designation for the law in question, situated in relation to the state law that has been so important over recent centuries.

Transnational law is varied in character and there is no over-arching theory or justification for it.[179] Its legitimacy is judged according to circumstance, and in relation to the possible alternatives. There appear to be three areas where modern or contemporary forms of transnational law have arisen, in addition to the historical or classic forms. These are transnational law developed by state actors and their delegates, transnational law developed by private actors, and transnational law developed by legal professionals as a means to facilitate transnational forms of practice. In all cases there is necessary coexistence with state

---

[175] Thus Professor van Caenegem speaks of the *ius commune* as 'transnational by definition', and the same can be said for all of the common laws: van Caenegem (2002), *European Law in Past and Future*, at 13; Glenn (2007c), *Common Laws*, passim. Religious laws also are obviously transnational in character.

[176] See Ch. 12, introductory paragraph.

[177] Jessup (1956), *Transnational Law*, notably at 2, 3 (where the residual character of 'transnational' rules were apparently those applicable to relations between private persons or corporations and foreign governments, relations that could not properly be described as 'international'. There was little recognition of the historical breadth of the concept or of its ongoing importance.

[178] Glenn (2003b), 'Transnational Concept of Law', at 839. For 'denationalization' of law, or at least renewed recognition of it, Pinheiro (2001), 'The "Denationalization" of Transnational Relationships', notably at 442 ('paranational levels of regulation'); and for states no longer 'ontologically privileged', Held (2009), 'Restructuring Global Governance', at 535 ('states matter, but not only and not exclusively . . . they can be judged').

[179] Glenn (2003b), 'Transnational Concept of Law', at 860 ('no uniformity . . . no unicity of its sources and no systemic form of justification').

forms of law and with other forms of transnational law, so institutional cosmopolitanism plays itself out in the choice of sources of transnational law.

First, transnational law may be developed by state actors and their delegates. This is the traditional field of public international law, but we have seen above that international law has seen its sources and methods expand.[180] Executive agreements are displacing the formality of treaties in some measure. The process of diluting traditional public international law does not end, however, with executive agreements. In particular fields state agencies may enjoy considerable independence in their status and functions, and may collaborate amongst themselves in the articulation of standards that they seek to enforce. The International Organization of Securities Commissions (IOSCO) is composed of independent securities commissions and self-regulatory organizations. It adopts principles that represent a mixture of standards and guidelines, expressed at a high level of abstraction, and the principles have been described as 'transnational', and not international, in character.[181] Their respect 'neither excludes nor demands the presence of the nation-state'.[182] The phenomenon is not limited to administrative or regulatory agencies. National judges have also collaborated in issuing standards of judicial independence.[183] Where such transnational standards are enunciated through collaborative, cosmopolitan actors they may attract adherence; there is no 'command' function in the process. Their methodological foundations require appreciation of softer concepts of law.[184] It is also the case that transnational law develops even in the absence of written articulation of standards or principles. There is thus 'domestication' of solutions to transnational problems (crime, money-laundering, banking) that have been the object of discussion in 'functionally specific international fora'.[185] If there is convergence of regulatory solutions, the transnational solutions precede the convergence.[186]

Second, there is transnational law developed by private, non-state actors. This was always the case in matters of commercial law and the resurgence of a contemporary, non-state *lex mercatoria* underscores the ongoing pertinence of historical models of transnational law, now undergoing revivification.[187] It

---

[180] See this chapter, '*Public international law*', notably for 'transgovernmentalism'.

[181] Smith (2003), 'Pluralism and Globalized Securities Regulation', at 98; see the IOSCO Objectives and Principles of Securities Regulation ('international regulatory benchmarks') at <www.iosco.org/library/pubdocs/pdf/IOSCOPD154.pdf>; and generally Jordan and Majnoni (2003), 'Regulatory Harmonization and Globalization', at 260 ('worldwide dissemination of codes and standards of best practice') and 262 ('initiatives by the non-governmental sector have often taken the lead').

[182] Smith (2003), 'Pluralism and Globalized Securities Regulation', at 104.

[183] E.g. *The Bangalore Principles of Judicial Conduct*, 2003, accessible at <www.ajs.org/ethics/pdfs/Bangalore_principles.pdf>.

[184] Calliess and Zumbansen (2010), *Rough Consensus and Running Code*, at 1.

[185] Wiener (1999), *Globalization and Harmonization*, at 98 (following 'informal discussions' of, e.g., bank regulators, law enforcement officials).

[186] For convergence of occupational health and safety regulation, Shapiro (1993), 'Globalization of Law', at 50 ('globalization of protective law').

[187] For earliest forms of the *lex mercatoria*, see Ch. 3, '*Institutional cosmopolitanism*', and for the contemporary model, see Ch. 12, 'Resurgence'. Sources are found in the Transnational Law Database, at

would be complemented by a transnational *lex sportiva*,[188] a transnational *lex electronica*,[189] and more generally by a widening field of transnational private regulation (TPR). The latter is the product of a growing number of private transnational organizations, including both businesses and non-profit NGOs, that play an increasing role in both rule-making and monitoring.[190] The TPR they develop may be developed by experts or by stakeholders and cover a wide field of activity, from accounting standards to food safety to forest stewardship.[191] Their activity may be in fields where the state has allegedly failed, their legitimacy flowing from the lack of a viable alternative,[192] or where state law is non-mandatory or tolerant of private initiatives.[193] States may participate in the process and thus choose to be (more or less) tolerant of TPR.[194] The result is what has been described by Fabrizio Cafaggi as 'institutional complementarity',[195] and by Giandomenico Majone as 'spontaneous regulatory convergence'.[196] Beck concludes that transnational cooperatives and organizations

<www.trans-lex.org>; but for criticism, De Ly (2001), '*Lex mercatoria* (New Law Merchant)', at 167, 170 (philosophical justifications 'overly ambitious, irrealistic and naïve', attacked by developing countries).

[188] Nafziger and Ross (2011), *International Sports Law*; Gardiner (2006), *Sports Law*, at 91 ('The Emergence of a *Lex Sportiva*').

[189] Delmas-Marty (2004), *Le relatif et l'universel*, at 103.

[190] Cafaggi (2011a), 'Private Regulation', at 95 (states correspondingly more often rule-takers than rule-makers); Chevallier (2004), 'L'État post-moderne', at 108 (for states now meeting *competition* of new actors); Hobe (1998), *Der offene Verfassungsstaat*, at 27 (for 'emancipation' of social actors from state); and for NGOs being 'everywhere', Cranston (2004), *The Sovereignty Revolution*, at 38 (now also including Chinese GONGOs, government-organized NGOs).

[191] For the range of subjects (banking, tax, accounting, pharmaceuticals, etc.), Hale and Held (2011), *Handbook Transnational Governance*; Cafaggi (2011b), 'New Foundations', at 34 (for different models), 33 (for accounting, food safety); Meidinger (2007), 'Beyond Westphalia' (for forest stewardship, fisheries, and marine stewardship).

[192] Cafaggi (2011b), 'New Foundations', at 26 (failure of states in matters of reforestation); Meidinger (2007), 'Beyond Westphalia', at 122 (also on reforestation); and see Post (2001), 'Challenge of Globalization', at 330 (for bootstrapping of legitimacy by virtue of 'rule of law values'); and for general inadequacy of 'microstates', Koh (1996), 'Transnational Legal Process', at 192 (non-state actors, notably banks, multinational enterprises, that 'dwarf' power of many states).

[193] Cafaggi (2011a), 'Private Regulation', at 107 (state will often 'leave space', even in case of mandatory state rules, e.g. in providing minimum standards); Cafaggi and Muir Watt (2008), *Making European Private Law*, 'Introduction', at 1 (state law encompassing mandatory and default rules). States may also exercise a certain level of control through the possibility of review by state courts, as to which Benvenisti and Downs (2011), 'National Courts Review of TPR'.

[194] Wielsch (2012), 'Global Law Toolbox', at 1082–3 (relation between contract (in mass form) and statute even 'turned upside down').

[195] Cafaggi (2011a), 'Private Regulation', at 100 (complementarity through choice of state law or TPR, but also 'different combinations between the two'); Cafaggi (2011b), 'New Foundations', at 41–8 (various forms of 'hybridization', strong public institutions needed for private regulation to operate effectively and credibly).

[196] Majone (2000), 'International Regulatory Cooperation', at 121 (also 'parametric adjustment' through unilateral harmonization, policy imitation), 123 (benefits not only of explicit coordination but of making governments aware of the consequences of their actions for other countries), 124 (process of 'mutual recognition'), 133 (shift in EU from 'total' harmonization to minimal or optional harmonization and mutual recognition).

thus become private 'as-if' states, in their relations with one another and with states.[197]

Third, there is transnational law developed by legal professionals as a means to facilitate transnational forms of practice. International arbitration is the most evident manifestation of this and there would now be an 'ordre juridique arbitral' that stands independently of state law and courts and in which arbitrators are free to arrive at solutions independent of any text of state law.[198] The argument is striking, given national prohibitions of arbitration that prevailed in the nineteenth and twentieth centuries.[199] States have become tolerant, even extremely so, of international arbitration, and the US Supreme Court has decided that even state law seen as mandatory can be left to arbitrators for enforcement, or non-enforcement as the case may be.[200] International arbitrators are assisted, moreover, as in many private international cases before courts, by law firms which themselves have become transnational in character and adept in evaluating different laws for both litigation and transactional purposes.[201] States have not vigorously opposed the arrival of foreign or transnational firms in their territory; their regulation has been largely left to the professions themselves.[202] Regions such as the EU have taken positive steps to ensure mobility of the professions between national units.[203] The legal professions have become remarkably cosmopolitan since the nineteenth century. There is a corresponding form of cosmopolitan thought.

---

[197] Beck (2005), 'Cosmopolitan State', at 152 (making 'collectively binding decisions').

[198] Gaillard (2008), *Aspects philosophiques de l'arbitrage*, notably at 64, 66–83 (justifying conclusion on positive practice of arbitrators, while acknowledging a 'natural law current' of justification as well). For possible control by state courts, while acknowledging the transnational character of general principles of international commercial arbitration, Bachand (2005), *L'intervention du juge*, at 90–3.

[199] For national prohibitions, Böckstiegel (1991), 'Commercial Arbitration', at 273 (French Court of Cassation refusing to recognize *clause compromissoire* in 1843); Vagts (1987), 'Dispute-Resolution Mechanisms', at 62–3. In Quebec, arbitration of future disputes became recognized only in the 1980s: Brierley (1985), 'Quebec Arbitration Law' (on Supreme Court of Canada's *Zodiak* decision).

[200] *Mitsubishi Motors Corp* v. *Soler Chrysler-Plymouth*, 473 US 614, 105 SC 3346.

[200] Gessner, Appelbaum, and Felstiner (2001), 'Legal Culture of Global Business Transactions', at 4 (for 'transnationalisation of the legal field', influence of US model); Glenn (1990b), 'New International Legal Professions'; Glenn (2001b), 'Comparative Law and Legal Practice', notably at 991 (for expertise of law firms in Islamic financing). States themselves may resort to non-state forms of financing, as where the German Land of Sachsen-Anhalt issued an Islamic bond as a means of financing its public buildings (bond issued by Land government, the proceeds of which from Islamic investors are received by a designated public trustee that then leases the buildings to the government, passing on the rent to the Islamic investors).

[202] On practice by foreign firms in the UK and USA, originally of foreign law but increasingly of local law, Nouel (1997), 'International Practice of Law', at 198 ('tacit agreement'); and for New York encouraging personal mobility of lawyers by treating a one-year LL.M. as equivalent to a three-year law degree for purposes of local call, Vagts (1997), 'Connecting Two Legal Systems', at 253; and for the deficit in international regulation, notably at the ethical level, Terry (2005), 'US Legal Ethics'; Greer (2000), 'Challenge of globalization', at 391 (though some signs of positive steps by national regulatory bodies).

[203] See the Lawyers' Establishment Directive 98/5, OJ L77/36 (1998) (freedom to practise home or host state law, and to use host state title after three years of practice).

Cosmopolitan Thought

Contemporary cosmopolitan theory has identified the need for cosmopolitan ways of thought, and in Chapter 9 above we have seen insistence on notions of conversation, dialogue, and mediation, complemented by the *practices* of coexistence (or convivencia). These would be essential elements of 'rooted' or 'complex' cosmopolitanism and they would be foundational in large and diverse populations.[1] For the lawyer or judge, however, faced both with parties who have exhausted their capacity for dialogue and with an intractable problem of conciliation of norms, these general counsels might not provide sufficient guidance. The law of cosmopolitan states is complex, and complex forms of reasoning are both necessary and inevitable. It appears essential, therefore, to speak of cosmopolitan forms of reasoning or cosmopolitan logics.

COSMOPOLITAN LOGICS

The role of logic in law is contested. Oliver Wendell Holmes famously declared in the USA that 'the life of the law has not been logic, but experience' and more recently Susan Haack has argued in the same sense but in a more nuanced manner that logic in law may be something, 'but not all'.[2] She argues in favour of the 'deeply socio-historical character of legal systems',[3] a proposition entirely compatible with the thesis of this book that the state is best seen as the instantiation of legal tradition, and even traditions.[4] Holmes would have been reacting, however, to nineteenth-century forms of analytical and axiomatic legal reasoning prominent in Germany (and also strongly contested within Germany).[5] Haack

---

[1] See Ch. 9, 'Cosmopolitan Theory'. Arguably, more specific counsels are those of Habermas (2003), *The Future of Human Nature*, at 109 (requirement of both sides to take on the perspective of the other); Gadamer (1988), *Truth and Method*, notably at 269 ('horizon' as field of vision, person of no horizon 'overvalues what is nearest'), 270 ('when we have discovered the standpoint and horizon of the other person, his ideas become intelligible'); MacCormick (2009), *Rhetoric and Rule of Law*, at 166 ('reasonable persons' seek 'to abstract from their own position', are aware of different ways in which things, activities, and relations can have value to people, 'all values ought to be given some attention').

[2] Holmes (1881), *Common Law*, at 1; Haack (2007), 'On Logic in Law', acknowledging at 2 that Holmes would have been unaware of new logical techniques 'just begun' by the early twentieth century. For a reply to Haack, Bulygin (2008), 'What Can One Expect from Logic?', notably arguing (at 153) that while logic cannot explain why changes in the law come about, it can clarify issues involved and their resolution, this being 'not everything, but considerably more than just something'.

[3] Haack (2007), 'On Logic in Law', at 19.

[4] See Ch. 1, introductory paragraph.

[5] Hawkins (2012), 'Life of the Law: What Holmes Meant', at 344ff. ('reacting to German legal philosophy'); Postema (2011), *Legal Philosophy*, at 64 (for axiomatic reasoning as 'direct target'), though at

states that she wishes to maintain the 'important element of truth' in Holmes's insistence that a model of axioms and corollaries is 'at best partial, and at worst misleading'.[6] Both Holmes and Haack therefore target the form of reasoning usually described as syllogistic and question its importance. Their position is representative of much opinion within the common law tradition, where common law judicial reasoning historically moved (horizontally) from case to case and not down from given and incontrovertible axioms.[7] Later in his career, however, Holmes became much less categorical and much less confident in 'intuitive understanding', leaving 'experience' as second best to 'pursuing policy explicitly'.[8] There might therefore be a place for logic in legal reasoning and all would depend on its nature and use.[9]

Holmes' formulation of the problem is of interest, moreover, not only for its assertive character but also for the terms or concepts used in its formulation. Holmes presented the question of the role of syllogistic logic in law as a dichotomy. It was a question of logic *or* experience and the dichotomous nature of the problem required a choice between the two. Holmes argued against logic in law but his argument was recognizably in a logical form, that of dichotomous, binary, or even 'classical' logic.[10] Many of his adherents have been criticized for adoption of the same form of binary reasoning.[11] This presents a much larger fish to fry than that of syllogistic or axiomatic logic. Binary logic, as it is usually designated, is pervasive in much western thinking generally and legal thought would not have escaped its grip. Holmes' anti-logic affirmation is implicit evidence of its importance, though there are cosmopolitan limits to its application.

The cosmopolitan limits of binary logic

However pervasive or implicit binary logic may have become, it is possible to trace its origins and place in the worlds of logics and law. Plato appears to have

---

44 for Holmes as 'enigma'. For savagely sarcastic criticism within Germany, von Jhering (1951), 'Heaven of Legal Concepts' (heaven filled with living juridical concepts and machines—hair-splitting machine, fiction machine, dialectic-hydraulic interpretation press, dialectic drill for getting to bottom of things, dizzying path of dialectical deduction).

[6] Haack (2007), 'On Logic in Law', at 2.

[7] Weinrib (2005), *Legal Reason*, at 13, 89 (analogy 'inherent in the law' since rules always contain 'uncertainties at the boundaries'); Postema (2002), 'Philosophy of Common Law', at 594 ('neither deductive nor inductive').

[8] Hawkins (2012), 'Life of the Law: What Holmes Meant', at 371–2 (by 1894 firmly opposing role of 'intuition').

[9] See the language of John Horty in (2011), 'Rules and Reasons', at 1 ('a form of reasoning—broadly speaking, a *logic*').

[10] The expression is not free from ambiguity. As the next section indicates, its roots lie in principles enunciated in ancient Greece, though 'classical' logic is now taken largely to mean the 'Frege-Peirce' logic developed in the late nineteenth and early twentieth centuries (though still faithful to the Greek principles discussed below); Haack (2007), 'On Logic in Law', at 11.

[11] For 'realist' views of law as either objectively certain or wholly uncertain, based on unsustainable binary distinction, Letwin (2005), *History of the Idea of Law*, at 198–9; and see Tamanaha (2010), *Beyond the Formalist–Realist Divide*, at 201 (for the 'seductive attraction of narratives constructed around polar opposites').

been the original source, in arguing as he did that 'it is not at all difficult to separate into two all of those things that come into being' and that we should 'divide all cases of knowledge in this way'.[12] Given an original binary division, moreover, the process should continue, leaving an endless chain of separation, binary division, and classification. This is probably Plato's most successful idea, though his advocacy of it is less known. It has had enormous effect in the world, in spite of its early, and crude, character.[13] In Greek it was known as *diairesis*, which became in Latin *divisio*, most evident in law in the civilian teaching of various forms of a *summa divisio* such as that between public and private law, or patrimonial and non-patrimonial rights, or contractual and extra-contractual liability.[14] Notoriously, in French law schools legal writing exercises must be divided into two parts ('le plan').[15] It is not just in the categorizations of law school instruction, however, that the binary method has been important. Beyond legal taxonomy, there are still more fundamental legal dichotomies, those of law and morality, law and ethics, law and religion, law and culture, or law and custom—all impossible to avoid in contemporary legal reasoning.[16] Beyond law, and influencing it, are a whole series of 'hierarchical dualisms', those of mind/body, nature/nurture, primitive/civilized, reason/emotion, or universalism/relativism.[17] Descartes' mind/body dualism would itself have inspired a dozen further dichotomies.[18]

---

[12] Plato, *The Statesman*, 258e, 261b; and see *The Sophist*, 219a ('expertise falls pretty much into two types'); and for this form of *divisio* dominating over the then undeveloped syllogism in the early middle ages, then being superseded in large measure by syllogistic reasoning, Errera (2007), 'The Role of Logic', at 81, 104 (and situating it in the context of a notion of genus subject to separation into a pair of contrasting species).

[13] For its 'taxonomic effectiveness' over centuries, Errera (2007), 'The Role of Logic', at 91; and for use by Aristotle, Schiebinger (2004), *Nature's Body*, at 43 (animals divided into blooded and bloodless, blooded into quadrupeds and non-quadrupeds, quadrupeds into mammals and reptiles); though for views from contemporary science, see this chapter, '*The cosmopolitan character of the new logics*'.

[14] For the distinctions in Roman law Descheemaeker (2009), 'Roman Division of Wrongs', at 4 (obligations *vel ex contractu nascitur vel ex delicto*); Talamanca (1977), 'Lo schema "genus–species"', generally for Greek influence and notably at 4 (genus–species reasoning paradigmatic example of divisory technique) and 22 (for dichotomous character); though for Roman law in spite of *divisio* being 'un tissu de contradictions', Villey (1967), 'Histoire de la logique juridique', at 74 (even basket of crabs that devour themselves).

[15] Hence the rejection of the three-part 'plan' and the expression 'thèse, anti-thèse, foutaise', with the third part dismissed as nonsense (foutaise).

[16] For the dilemma of any attempt to conflate law and ethics, and the absence of any appropriate vocabulary for doing so, Glenn (2011a), 'Ethic of International Law', at 246, 249 (dichotomy of law and ethics yielding no vocabulary adequate for their conflation); yet for reconceptualization of 'law and . . .' as 'law as . . .', and working towards 'a new framework that does not depend on a binary, or a conjunction of two distinct fields imagined as outside of each other', Fisk and Gordon (2011), '"Law As . . ."', at 524 ('imagined as the same domain').

[17] Haraway (1991), *Simians, Cyborgs, and Women*, at 163.

[18] Toulmin (1990), *Cosmopolis*, at 107–8 (e.g. mental/material, actions/phenomena, performances/happenings, thoughts/objects, voluntary/mechanical, active/passive, creative/repetitive) and 161 (arguing for restoring 'unities dichotomized' in seventeenth century); cf. Bellah (2011), *Religion in Human Evolution*, at 599 ('there is no dichotomy in my book') and criticizing at 598 even Kant for 'radical dichotomy of us and them'.

Much has been derived from this primary, given, principle of binary *divisio*. Most evidently, the so-called 'laws of thought'[19] of classical logic may be seen as following inevitably from it. Since one can draw lines through physical and intellectual worlds, the resulting products are distinct from one another and each would have an identity of its own. There is thus a 'law of identity', formalized as 'A is A'. In the eighteenth century Bishop Butler concluded that not only the physical or ontological world could be so described but also the ethical one. 'Everything is what it is, and not another thing,' he wrote, speaking of that which is good, or not.[20] 'A is A' may appear tautological, as necessarily true, but its truth is dependent on the unexpressed possibility of radical separation of A from all that is not-A. There is an underlying and justificatory principle of conceptual and physical autonomy.[21]

From the law of identity are logically drawn the two further 'laws of thought': the law of non-contradiction and the law of the excluded middle. Given A, which is radically distinct from not-A, the two cannot be affirmed at the same time, or overlap, so we cannot have A *and* not-A: Not [A and not-A], since this would be contradictory, affirming at the same time a proposition and its negation.[22] Given the law of identity and the law of non-contradiction, what we therefore must have, and which is where many current legal problems arise, is A *or* not-A, which is the law of the excluded middle.[23] There is no middle ground between contradictory positions. Why *must* we have a logical rule of A *or* not-A? It flows from the principle of radical separation or identity. Since A exists, independently of that which is not-A, the boundary of not-A begins precisely where the boundary of A ends and there can be no middle ground between them. Not-A is galactic in character and devours any possible middle ground. As recently put, you either have $3.75 to buy a latte or you do not.[24]

The binary logic of Greek philosophers was largely lost during the early middle ages. Even following its rediscovery from the twelfth century (through

---

[19] The expression is from the 1854 book of the same name by George Boole (he of Boolean algebra). Bertrand Russell is reported as praising the book but remarking that 'if his book had really contained the laws of thought, it was curious that no one should ever have thought in such a way before'; cited in Gleick (2011), *The Information*, at 167.

[20] Butler (1964), *Fifteen Sermons*, Preface, at §39. The antecedents include the pre-Socratic Parmenides, in his *On Nature*, Frag. 8.16 ('either it is, or it is not'); and Aristotle, in *Metaphysics*, VIII.17 ('a thing is itself . . . each thing is inseparable from itself').

[21] Lawson (2001), *Closure*, at 111 (the term 'A' 'already presupposes the possibility of closure . . . By avoiding the specific and referring to the possibility of closure as an "x", mathematics and logic make it look as if complete closure is possible . . . they deal with imagined closures, but the imagined closures are impossible in the context of the characteristics of closure and openness').

[22] Authorship is usually attributed to Aristotle, Plato having been 'somewhat ambivalent' on the question, and some pre-Socratics accepting that contradictions could be true: Priest (2007), 'Paraconsistency and Dialetheism', at 137 (with references and texts), concluding at 139 that Aristotle's defence of non-contradiction must 'be reckoned a failure' though 'high orthodoxy'). For Aristotle's formulation (2008a), *Metaphysics* IV.3 ('it is impossible for anything at the same time to be and not to be').

[23] For Aristotle once again (2008a), *Metaphysics*, III.2 ('everything must be either affirmed or denied').

[24] Though you may be able to make it up with the loose change left in the bowl on the counter by others.

Islamic channels), it did not achieve dominance in the thought of the times. Dualities were recognized if they existed but lines were not sharply drawn and the major effort was to establish bridging techniques and methods. There were two swords but they were collaborative ones. There were two kingdoms but choice between them was not necessary.[25] This explains much of the cosmopolitan character of the law. Osmosis prevailed over separation, though judgement, and judgments, remained possible. Binary or classical logic became highly visible once again, however, with the efforts of territorial and national closure that took place from the sixteenth and seventeenth centuries, described in Chapters 4 and 5 above. Stephen Toulmin has identified the resurgence of Platonic forms of reasoning that then occurred, and the idea that purely logical relations hold between eternal objects.[26] Bodin, now seen as the father of the concept of sovereignty, pronounced *divisio* to be the 'universal rule of the sciences' and law was unquestionably seen as a 'science juridique'.[27] He proceeded by way of 'separation and juxtaposition' and perceived the state as an 'entity', though still concerned with human legal diversity.[28] Hobbes advanced the binary cause still further, and presented the radical, binary option of amoral anarchy *or* Leviathan. As has been noted, he was a 'notorious dichotomiser' and had major, though unfulfilled, ambitions in the field of 'Logike'.[29] The ancient substratum of Greek thought was here bubbling to the surface, in the tumultuous relations of the time. Its influence became more and more apparent as notions of sovereignty and autonomous national legal systems came to dominate legal thought, at least at the explicitly theoretical level, by the twentieth century.

Most famously, Kelsen relied on binary logic in the construction of a legal system, at least in his initial formulation. A legal system would be characterized notably by its internal consistency and the laws of non-contradiction and the excluded middle both played an essential role in ensuring this consistency.[30] Codification had, as its most essential role, the elimination of diversity within

---

[25] See Chapters 2 (notably 'The Church as State') and 3; and see this chapter, the following sections.

[26] Toulmin (1958), *Uses of Argument*, at 182 (on the 'new thinkers' of the enlightenment); and see Toulmin (1990), *Cosmopolis*, at 108 (for the 'sharpness' of Descartian separations, seen 'around 1700 as having indispensable merits'); and for the 'essential duality' of modern philosophy underlying modern notions of law, Villey (1967), 'Histoire de la logique juridique', at 67 (two distinct worlds of Descartes (mind/body), Kant (being/phenomenon or existence/norm)); and for first, 'modern' attempts at classical logic by Althusius (1563–1638), Gierke (1939), *Development of Political Theory*, at 43 (though often the 'required dichotomy' only set up by resort to arbitrary antitheses) or Grotius (1583–1645), Villey (1967), 'Histoire de la logique juridique', at 68 (first major attempt at axiomatic system).

[27] Turchetti (2010), 'Jean Bodin', under s. 2 ('Bodin's methodology of History and Law', recalling also that Plato had designated the principle of *divisio* as 'divine').

[28] See Ch. 4, 'An emerging theory of the state'.

[29] See Ch. 4, 'An emerging theory of the state'.

[30] Kelsen (1989), *Pure Theory of Law*, at 206, at 206 ('the Principle of the Exclusion of Contradictions . . . To say that *a* ought to be and at the same time ought not to be is just as meaningless as to say that *a* is and at the same time that it is not'. In the case of contradictory norms, 'only one of the two can be regarded as objectively valid'). In his later writing, however, Kelsen acknowledged the possibility of conflicting norms both being valid, a contradiction that could not be solved by logic and that required the intervention of an act of will of legal authority or 'customary non-observance': Kelsen (1973), *Essays*, at 235 ('that two mutually conflicting norms should both be valid, is possible').

states, and codes themselves were elaborate efforts towards logical coherence, understood in the classical sense.[31] Inconsistent texts or sources could not persist, and choice between them was necessary. The codes had considerable success, and there have been declarations of the absence of 'antinomies' in national law in the twentieth century.[32] If the national legal system could thus be seen as coherent, from an internal perspective, at the international level it stood as an example of the law of identity. It would be indivisible, in the language of the present French constitution,[33] and hence the laws of non-contradiction and the excluded middle could find application once again. Contemporary, national, private international law is generally hostile to the application of two laws (presumed to be contradictory) and choice is necessary between the law of the forum *or* the foreign law designated by a choice-of-law rule.[34] There is no perceived space between the two.

The role of binary logic in all of this can never be precisely established, but its visibility precludes any conclusion that it has played no role. Holmes was correct to back away from his initial proposition, even from the perspective of common law jurisdictions, not immune themselves from efforts at national coherence (through national *stare decisis*) and the binary *divisio* between the national and the international. It is not the case, however, that classical or binary logic is entirely incompatible with cosmopolitan perspectives. There are cosmopolitan limits to the closures it would bring about. At the height of legal nationalism there were ongoing notions of public international law, private international law, and comparative law, though all laboured under a regime of (variously rigorous) separation of national territories and national laws.[35] As has been seen above, closures are never definitive and ongoing texture provides the stuff of newer and

---

[31] See Ch. 4, *'Codes'*; for the so-called laws of non-contradiction and excluded middle as fundamental properties of French codification; De Béchillon (1998), 'L'imaginaire d'un Code', at 182.

[32] Gavazzi (1959), *Delle antinomie*, at 106 (total inconsistencies rare in present codifications).

[33] Art. 1, Constitution of the Fifth Republic ('France shall be an indivisible, secular, democratic and social republic'). The Constitution of the Year I (1793) was even clearer: '[t]he French Republic is one and indivisible'; see van Caenegem (1995), *Historical Introduction Western Constitutional Law*, at 187.

[34] See Ch. 8, *'Private international law'*; and for challenge to the idea see Glenn (2013), *La conciliation des lois*. There are also contradictions amongst the choice-of-law rules, such as where different choice-of-law rules are used, or where the personal law of the parties (national or domiciliary) is declared applicable to the substantive conditions of marriage but there are then two (contradictory) personal laws to be applied; for this as an 'antinomy' in private international law, Perelman (1965c), 'Les antinomies', at 400 (no legislative solution given, but the solution in practice is derived from a cosmopolitan interpretation of the 'bilateral' or 'unilateral' character of whatever prohibitions are called into play); and for further apparent antinomies in private international law (notably between guarantees of equality of sexes and national or religious laws of differential treatment), Gannagé (2001), *Hiérarchie des norms*, at 81–5 (though contrasting private law notion of antinomy with 'large' notion of antinomy in public law, where antinomy seen in simple opposition of objectives of laws). As has been noted in Ch. 8, 'Private International Law', if the rules of national private international law must be enforced by the judge even in the absence of any difference between them, antinomies are omnipresent in private international legal relations.

[35] See Ch. 8, *'Public international law'* and *'Private international law'*. For the taxonomic and even nationalist character of nineteenth- and twentieth-century comparative law, Glenn (2006), 'Comparative Legal Families'. There were also the ongoing ambiguities of empire, as to which see Ch. 8, 'Internationality and Empire'.

larger forms of coherence.[36] The challenge to the exclusivist identity of the state has been seen in the chapters above dealing with cosmopolitan sources. The challenge has now become one of logic as well as of law.

The cosmopolitan character of the new logics

There has recently been a 'many valued turn' in logic, accompanied by development of 'new' logics.[37] It is a turn away from classical or binary logic and towards recognition that the world is a more complex place than that contemplated by Plato's methodology of *divisio*. It has come about because classical logic was inherently vulnerable as a general intellectual instrument. It inevitably came to be challenged, ontologically, logically, and legally.

Classical logic was inherently vulnerable since it purported to deal with pure logical relations without regard to any possible field of application. It would have been 'topic-neutral' and it was even a point of honour 'not to know what it was talking about'.[38] Only crisp concepts notationally expressed were appropriate for logical analysis. The law of the excluded middle (A or not-A) thus becomes A v ¬A. Ordinary language would suffer from irremediable vagueness and would have been banished by many from a formal language of logic.[39] The result, however, was a conundrum. The useful application of formal logic to the subtle processes of everyday reasoning, in an ordinary language, was 'very limited'[40] so logicians could be taxed with 'sheer irrelevance'.[41] Logic could not, however, be isolated somehow from other subjects and it in fact spread to other areas (such as law), in spite of the likelihood that it would make 'a hash' of these other areas.[42] The result today has been an expansion of the field and a move to develop more

---

[36] See Ch. 1, 'The State as Tradition'.

[37] Gabbay and Woods (2007), *Many Valued Turn* (Amsterdam: North Holland).

[38] For topic-neutrality, Haack (1978), *Philosophy of Logics*, at 5 (asking what it means for a formal system to be 'applicable', and how to distinguish forms of argument from content); for 'ne pas savoir de quoi elle parle', Gardiès (1967), 'Méthode logique', at 184 (reasoning entirely in terms of symbols); and as based on 'no more than formal considerations' and 'not with the actual merits of any argument or proposition', Toulmin (1958), *Uses of Argument*, at 173 (also 'severely limited class of analytic arguments') and 147 ('field-invariant terms', fitting in nicely with 'some other influential prejudices', notably mathematical elegance).

[39] Haack (1978), *Philosophy of Logics*, at 162 (citing Frege, Russell). There is debate, however, on whether vagueness is a basic circumstance of the world and of language, or results simply from our inability to know or discern the necessary boundaries of things or concepts. For this view, and 'parsimony' therefore requiring maintenance of classical logic, Sorenson (2001), *Vagueness and Contradiction*, at 11 (avoiding 'gratuitous complexity'), 15 (though acknowledging that 'less than 10 per cent of current experts' persuaded by argument for crisp boundaries); Williamson (1994), *Vagueness*; further references in Tye (2000), 'Vagueness and Reality', at 195 (notably Bertrand Russell's affirmation that '. . . there can be no such thing as vagueness'). This 'epistemic' view of vagueness has been said, however, to be inadequate to accommodate the 'genuine value of vagueness in the law' (often deliberately chosen, e.g. by legislators), since it cannot rely on 'partial definition and context sensitivity' ('more probable than not' reasoning): Soames (2012), 'Vagueness and Law', at 107.

[40] Malinowski (1993), *Many-Valued Logics*, at 99.

[41] Toulmin (1958), *Uses of Argument*, at 169.

[42] Priest (2007), 'Paraconsistency and Dialetheism', at 197–8 (logic as 'package deal').

flexible and extended forms of logical analysis, capable of capturing ordinary-language reasoning. This would be necessary to ensure that 'logic is to have teeth'.[43] It also has necessary consequences for the nature of logical reasoning. The process has been accelerated by the different challenges to classical logic.

The ontological challenge has come from the physical sciences, since much contemporary scientific learning is inconsistent with the law of identity and a process of binary division. In biology, species today are seen as 'evolving lineages' and not 'static classes' or organisms. Taxonomy is undertaken but the process has become one of deciding on alternative methods, including notably those of 'cluster analysis' (in which similar traits are brought together, though no one of them is essential) and historical classification by community of descent.[44] Quantum physics also appears to have renounced the simple identification of particles. In the language of a Nobel laureate, the underlying reality of protons 'unseats classical logic', and allows reconciliation of 'two seemingly contradictory ideas about what protons are'.[45] In the result, the physical divisions of Plato and Aristotle appear 'logically arbitrary', even the 'results of creativity and invention'. They would be limited only by the 'willingness of co-speakers to accept them'.[46] What was for Bodin the 'universal rule of the sciences'[47] appears today even to be scientifically indefensible. Moreover, if we allow objects, and sets generally, to have imprecise boundaries, 'then the two classically important principles—the laws of contradiction and excluded middle—will no longer always be true'.[48]

The logical challenge to classical logic appears today more controversial than the ontological one but the 'new' logics are said to have 'successfully challenged' classical logic.[49] They have done so in two identifiable ways. The first is to show that there are theoretical paradoxes ('this statement is false') that are incompatible with the binary division between truth and falsehood.[50] There are statements

---

[43] Hyde (2007),'Logics of Vagueness', at 296 ('restoration' of ordinary language, vagueness seen as 'less superficial'); Jacquette, 'Introduction', in Jacquette (2007a), *Philosophy of Logic*, at 4 ('need to make logic more expressively adapted to specific areas of linguistic usage inadequately served by existing classical logics'); and see Haack (1978), *Philosophy of Logics*, at 163 ('logicians must take vagueness more seriously'); Soames (2012), 'Vagueness and Law', at 95 (growing interest in vagueness in law and philosophy though separate inquiries to date); for philosophically informed enquiry in law, however, Endicott (2000), *Vagueness in Law* (vagueness a feature of law and not merely its language; rule of law not requiring, however, that content of law be determinate in all cases).

[44] Ereshefsky (2001), *Poverty of the Linnaean hierarchy*, at 3 (for evolving lineages), 15 (contrasting cluster analysis with genealogical descent), and 20 (later, empirical, Aristotle concluding that *divisio* 'splits natural groups').

[45] Wilczek (2010), *Lightness of Being: Mass, Ether and Unification of Forces*, at 43, and 54 ('we can eat our quarks and have them too').

[46] Viehweg (1994), *Topics and Law*, 57.

[47] See this chapter, 'The cosmopolitan limits of binary logic'.

[48] Klir, St. Clair, and Yuan (1997), *Fuzzy Set Theory*, at 75.

[49] Bimbó (2007), 'Relevance Logics', at 723 ('once the overpowering dominance of classical logic has been successfully challenged (and it has been) . . . ').

[50] If the statement is taken to be true it affirms its own falsehood. So if true, then false. If taken to be false, its affirmation of falsehood is false. So if false then true. For extended treatment of semantic and set theoretical paradoxes, as examples of *dialetheias* that are both true and false, Priest (2006), *In Contradiction*, Chs 1 and 2, and rejecting, at 5, 6, the 'explosion' principle (*ex contradictione quodlibet*—any conclusion

that 'face' both truth and falsehood, in spite of the principles of classical logic. This debate is complex and abstract with little evident application in things legal.[51] It does, however, strike at the universal character of so-called laws of thought. The second way in which the new logics challenge the old is through acceptance and generalization of the ontological challenge, which must then be reflected in logic. Logic now has to accept and deal with the imprecision and vagueness of language and the real world. It can no longer be 'topic-neutral' in dealing entirely with crisp concepts and sets.

Two of the new logics would thus be 'paraconsistent' in admitting the possibility of true contradictions in the world and providing means of dealing with them (beyond radical and definitive choice of one or the other). The first such new logic, and the most senior, is that of multivalent or many-valued logic. Multivalent logic appears intuitively relevant in a multi-valued world and for cosmopolitan thought. Its origins date from the early twentieth century though there would be a 'prehistory' dating from Aristotle.[52] The essential characteristic of multivalent logic is that it is 'degree-theoretic' in replacing a binary option with one that tolerates degrees, usually expressed as degrees of truth (as in the statement 'there is some truth in that').[53] Where different and contradictory laws are seen in conflict under classical logic, a multivalent logic would admit assessment of relative degrees of applicability and more nuanced means of choice, as will be seen below.[54] It might be objected that multivalent logic involves assessment of degrees of truth and that law is not expressed in terms of truth values.[55] This may or may not be the case, however, since many laws are expressed not simply in imperative form ('it is forbidden to . . .') but in declarative form ('property is . . .') and even argumentative form (as in Talmudic

---

flows from a contradiction) on grounds that not every conclusion is true and that 'inconsistency does not entail incoherence'). Similarly Beall and Restall (2006), *Logical Pluralism*, at 49 and 56 ('a situation in which A and not A is true need not be one in which B is true. A situation might well be *inconsistent* about A without involving *everything*').

[51] See, however, Perez and Teubner (2006), *Paradoxes and Inconsistencies in the Law* (accepting such paradoxes and inconsistencies, arguing that they cannot be resolved only with the tools of logic).

[52] Gottwald (2007), 'Many-Valued Logics', at 680 (citing Lukasiewicz and Post in the 1920s) and 681 ('prehistory' with Aristotle's future contingencies, notably sea battle that will or will not take place); Malinowski (2007), 'Many-valued Logic', at 14 (for future sea battle as root of many-valued logics); Haack (1978), *Philosophy of Logics*, at 204.

[53] For 'degree-theoretic', Smith (2008), *Vagueness and Degrees*, at 10 (replacing binary values with 'infinitely many degrees of truth'); and for the logic, Malinowski (1993), *Many-Valued Logics*; Gabbay and Woods (2007), *Many Valued Turn*; Priest (2001), *Introduction Non-Classical Logic*, Ch. 7 ('many-valued logic'), notably at 126 for 'truth-value gluts', where something is both true and false or in a momentary state of change. Multivalent logic is often referred to as 'n-valued' where n is the number of truth values a proposition may have. Sartor speaks of factors that are 'scalable' as opposed to binary: Sartor (2005), *Legal Reasoning*, at 182.

[54] In the remaining sections of this chapter.

[55] See e.g. Lindahl (1992), 'Conflicts in Systems', at 41 ('[i]f we deny that genuine deontic expressions have truth value, we cannot speak of inconsistency of such sentences in the technical sense of formal logic'); Kelsen (1989), *Pure Theory*, at 73 ('norms enacted by the legal authority . . . are neither true nor false, but only valid or invalid') and 205–6 ('a norm is neither true nor false', yet accepting that it may be true or false that a norm is valid or invalid, and so contradiction is possible, to be resolved through interpretation and higher-order norms).

debate).[56] More importantly, where laws are apparently in conflict, the question for an adjudicator is whether the conduct in question has violated a law, or not, and the declarative conclusion is expressed in truth values. It does not therefore appear impossible to move from an abstract notion of degrees of truth to degrees of applicability or imperativity of laws, or to degrees of fault or culpability.[57] There can be a continuum of values.[58]

The second type of paraconsistent logic is modal logic, which deals with different modes in which things may be true or false, particularly their necessity, possibility, or impossibility. The cosmopolitan dimension of modal logic is found in the idea that modes might vary according to 'possible worlds' in which they are found.[59] It would therefore be necessary to reason across 'possible worlds' in a way that might reveal itself to be cosmopolitan and conciliatory. How this might happen in law will have to be returned to.[60] One difficulty may be in the fact that modal logic is often treated as simply supplementary to classical logic, not challenging it as directly as does multivalent logic.[61]

Choice of logic is therefore possible and there is increasing recognition of this. 'Logical pluralism' would even provide a more 'charitable interpretation' of many important but difficult philosophical debates; it would do 'more justice' to them.[62] If this is the case it should follow that the choice between classical and new logics should not be formulated in classical or binary terms. It is not a choice, definitively and generally, in favour of *either* classical *or* new logics. One need not declare oneself. Choice amongst the full range of logics is an ongoing one and none is excluded by previous choices. The logics are not to be seen as 'rivals' but

---

[56] For Talmudic argumentation, Glenn (2010b), *Legal Traditions*, at 112 ('the style of the text'); for the declaratory form of the French Civil Code, see notably Art. 544 ('[l]a propriété est . . . '), and Rémy (1982), 'Éloge de l'exégèse', at 122 (Civil Code declaring the law, not creating it, therefore even descriptive and not prescriptive).

[57] See Haack (2007), 'Logic in law', at 13 ('since non-declarative sentences are not truth-valued, some analogue of validity couched in other terms than truth-preservation will be needed'); and for explicit defence of application of truth values to law (truth of validity of laws, truth in applicability), MacCormick (2009), *Rhetoric and Rule of Law*, at 63–5 ('that a certain question calls for the use of judgement and interpretation . . . is not incompatible with its being true or false'). Degrees of fault or negligence are already widely used ('faute lourde', 'gross negligence'); for greater resistance to degrees of criminal culpability, see Ch. 12, 'Reconciliation', though for degrees of homicide, see this chapter, 'The Cosmopolitan Logic of Common Laws'.

[58] Smith (2008), *Vagueness and Degrees*, at 211 ('all these ideas are captured by positing a continuum of truth values').

[59] Priest (2001), *Introduction Non-Classical Logic*, Ch. 2 ('basic modal logic' as 'possible-world semantics'); Garson (2009), 'Modal Logic', s. 6 ('possible worlds semantics').

[60] See later in this section.

[61] Haack (1978), *Philosophy of Logics*, at 222 (modal as simple extension of classical logic, multivalent logic as challenging it).

[62] Beall and Restall (2006), *Logical Pluralism*, at 30 (and comes at little or no cost); and see Priest (2007), 'Paraconsistency and Dialetheism', at 200 (determination of correct logic a 'fallible and revisable business', need for historical perspective); Jacquette (2007b), 'Relation of Informal to Symbolic Logic', at 132 ('whatever logical methods are best suited for my analytic purposes in trying to understand different types of logical problems').

as ongoing and versatile intellectual instruments.[63] Put slightly differently, multi-valent logic is necessarily inclusive of bivalent logic. That which is used will depend on that which is more adequate or appropriate.[64] This may be a conclusion that has already been reached in law, and through the legal challenge to classical logic.

The explicit legal challenge to classical logic, in its modern formulation, had begun by the mid-twentieth century. Its most visible representative was Stephen Toulmin, a non-lawyer, who criticized classical logic precisely because of its allegedly 'topic-neutral' character and its over-simplification of the subtlety of argumentation in the real world, most notably in law. He saw logic as 'generalised jurisprudence' and criticized it for its generality.[65] For Toulmin, effective arguments would be 'field-dependent' rather than 'field-invariant'[66] and the subtlety of legal argument would be represented by the range of types of legal 'utterance', such as statements of claim, evidence of identification, testimony, interpretations of legislation or discussions of its validity, claims to exemption from the application of a law, pleas in extenuation, verdicts, sentences, and so on.[67] The claim that 'Harry is a British subject' depends on a datum that Harry was born in Bermuda and a 'warrant' that a man born in Bermuda will 'generally' be a British subject, this 'on account of' the (often implicit) validity of British legislation, and 'unless' both his parents were aliens or another exception is applicable.[68] Legal argument thus entails a complex package of claims, data, warrants, their 'backing', rebuttal, and qualifiers. 'Complete logical candour' would thus require employment of 'a pattern of argument no less sophisticated than is required in the law'.[69]

Toulmin's critique of classical logic on logical grounds has been echoed by lawyers, and the criticisms have been multiplying. They exist across legal traditions. In France in 1968 Professor Husson protested against those who would force complex legal transactions into single categories.[70] Also in France,

---

[63] Against 'rivals', Beall and Restall (2006), *Logical Pluralism*, at 45, and see at 54 ('we have not abandoned classical logic'); Bimbó (2007), 'Relevance Logics', at 723 ('no single superior way to formalize what is a logically valid inference'); Malinowski (2007), 'Many-valued logic', at 70 (each 'classical' set is a special case of a fuzzy set).

[64] Da Costa, Krause, and Bueno (2007), 'Paraconsistent Logics', at 794–5; and for defence of 'juridical bivalence', at least in instances of validity/invalidity, guilt/innocence, Endicott (2000), *Vagueness in Law*, at 73 ('graded standards *might* be undesirable. Juridical bivalence radically simplifies some of the law's most difficult tasks') (emphasis added); and for absence of need for a 'universally valid' rule in determination of guilt, Priest (2007), 'Paraconsistency and Dialetheism', at 146 ('sufficient that the situation in question is such as to enable one to rule out inconsistency in that particular case'); cf. the discussion of *res judicata* later in this section.

[65] Toulmin (1958), *Uses of Argument*, at 7 ('logic (we may say) is generalized jurisprudence') and asking at 39 ('how far is a *general* logic possible?').

[66] Toulmin (1958), *Uses of Argument*, at 147 (logicians restricting notions of soundness, validity, cogency, or strength of arguments and attempting to define them in field-invariant terms).

[67] Toulmin (1958), *Uses of Argument*, at 96.

[68] Toulmin (1958), *Uses of Argument*, at 105.

[69] Toulmin (1958), *Uses of Argument*, at 89.

[70] Husson (1967), 'Les apories de la logique', at 55 (a transaction of 'location-vente' is not one either of lease or sale, but shares characteristics of both, an argument recalling the 'chattels real' multivalence of the common law).

Mireille Delmas-Marty has called for use of the full 'palette' of modern logic in 'ordering the multiplicity' of world laws,[71] and Johanna Guillaumé has found that internationality now is found in degrees.[72] In Belgium François Rigaux has written of the 'illusion' of categorization by dichotomy and of the 'perversity' of binary taxonomies,[73] while in Switzerland Andrea Büchler would have the debate on Islamic family law in Europe move 'from dichotomies to discourse'.[74] In Quebec Dominique Goubeau has described a North American abandonment of the dichotomy between 'open' and 'closed' adoptions, seeing rather 'degrees of openness' in the relations between adoptees and biological parents.[75] In the common law world Martin Krygier has criticized 'pernicious' dichotomies, which 'might just be aspects of complex phenomena which can manage to include them both'.[76] Michael Taggart has decided that contemporary administrative law in New Zealand is no longer well served by dichotomies that have prevailed in the past—appeal/review, merits/legality, process/substance, discretion/law, law/policy, fact/law—and that they should be replaced with a 'sliding scale or rainbow' of possibilities of review, from correctness review at one end of the rainbow to non-justiciability at the other.[77] Moreover, as in a rainbow, colours or internal categories 'imperceptibly blur or merge into one another'; there are no 'jolts'.[78] Joseph Singer has written of the need to create 'a middle path' based on reviving the notion of 'practical reason',[79] and in construction of a law of peace or *lex pacificatoria* Christine Bell has written of the need to straddle binary distinctions and to develop 'constructive ambiguity'.[80] Binary distinctions in the law of citizenship have been particularly criticized and Neil Walker has expressed dissatisfaction with the 'dichotomizing language of membership',

---

[71] Delmas-Marty (2004), *Le relatif et l'universel*, at 412 (on using classic binary logic for 'hard concepts' such as indefeasible rights or *ius cogens* norms, fuzzy logic where less determinacy).

[72] Guillaumé (2011), *L'affaiblissement de l'Etat-Nation*, at 276.

[73] Rigaux (1997), *La loi des juges*, at 69, 250–1.

[74] Büchler (2012), 'Islamic family law in Europe?', at 197.

[75] Goubeau (2000), '"Open adoption" au Canada', at 65 (passive or active, anonymous or not).

[76] Krygier (2004), 'False Dichotomies', at 251, and see also at 253 ('they postulate contradictions between which one *must* choose', making choice the first task and excluding other and perhaps more appropriate options, 'like refusing to choose').

[77] Taggart (2006), 'Administrative Law', at 83.

[78] Taggart (2006), 'Administrative Law', at 82, a phenomenon recently described in logical terms as 'fuzzy plurivaluationism': Smith (2008), *Vagueness and Degrees*, at 277ff. and notably at 292 (for resolution of the 'jolt' problem). This is an example of new logics tracking the vagueness of ordinary-language categories, as in 'Greece is less broke this week than last week'. This may be seen as 'higher-order vagueness', in the language of the new logics, since there is imprecision not just at the extreme ends of the rainbow (the dichotomy has become less crisp) but also everywhere else within it.

[79] Singer (2009), 'Normative Lessons', at 906 and see at 944 ('[p]ractical reason can handle incommensurable values . . . it is possible to make considered, reasoned judgments in the face of plural value'), 947 (possible to 'compare values in the context of particular cases'), 968 (reinterpretation to show that one of asserted values not actually implicated, or that 'the conflicting values are both operative but that one value should be subordinated to the other in the context of the case').

[80] Bell (2008), *On the Law of Peace*, at 166, and see 291 (law as 'holding device'), 302 (embracing what would be otherwise an excluded middle).

arguing for denizenship as an 'in-between concept, one that challenges the series of binary oppositions . . . that reflect the political imaginary of the Westphalian system of states'.[81] Linda Bosniak deliberately uses a notion of 'alien citizenship' to accommodate an 'ascending scale' of the rights of aliens who gradually augment their identification with a local society.[82] Nick Barber writes of the dichotomy of citizen or subject but prefers to think of them 'as poles on a spectrum rather than as hermetically sealed categories'.[83] Perhaps most visibly and fully, towards the end of his career Neil MacCormick decided that legal reasoning was essentially defeasible,[84] and that its forms of argumentation 'cannot be properly conceived of in simply bivalent true-or-false terms'.[85] The conclusion is based in part on the impossibility of avoiding contradiction in legal systems, so that simple deduction from axiomatic, given premises is impossible in such cases.[86] In the language of the new logics, therefore, the application of legal rules is non-monotonic in character. Given a presumptively applicable rule, there is always the possibility of 'invalidating intervention'.[87] If this is the case for general rules, legislative or precedential in origin, it appears necessary to accept it even for the *res judicata* effect of judgments. Many legal traditions do not accept *res judicata* (definitive determination of the law for the parties is not accepted) and amongst those that do there is wide variation in its breadth.[88] The common law has the widest and most vigorous notion of *res judicata* but even in common law jurisdictions it is possible to test the reach of a given decision by suing again on a varied claim. There are thousands and thousands of cases. The reach of any decision, if tested, will always require 'precisification'[89] and parties are likely to exhaust themselves before that process can be taken as complete.

---

[81] Walker (2009), 'Denizenship', at 262, 266 (binary oppositions of insider/outsider, national/international, territiorial/extraterritorial, domestic/foreign, franchised/disenfranchised); and see Ch. 10, '*Accommodating citizenships*'.

[82] Bosniak (2006), *Citizen and Alien*, at 38, 81, 89.

[83] Barber (2010), *Constitutional State*, at 48.

[84] MacCormick (2009), *Rhetoric and the Rule of Law*, at 28 ('rule statements . . . are always defeasible'), 33 (certainty in law is 'at best, qualified and defeasible certainty'), 240 (validity of legal arrangements 'presumptively sufficient').

[85] MacCormick (2009), *Rhetoric and the Rule of Law*, at 77, and see also at 54 ('strictly deductive inferences from axiomatic premises is indeed an idea at some remove from anything to be found in legal argumentation', legal deduction 'embedded in a web of other practical arguments').

[86] MacCormick (2009), *Rhetoric and the Rule of Law*, at 53–4 ('judicial decision-making includes the task of seeking to resolve contradictions as they emerge').

[87] MacCormick (2009), *Rhetoric and the Rule of Law*, at 240 (resulting in 'defeasance').

[88] For rejection in Jewish and Islamic law, Glenn (2010b), *Legal Traditions*, at 106, 109. The common law recognizes a notion of merger and bar often refused in civil law jurisdictions, and even issue estoppel from case to case. There are also motions to reconsider.

[89] See e.g. *Angel* v. *M. N. R.* [1975] 2 SCR 248, in which the Supreme Court of Canada decided that, while a transaction had been decided in a previous judgment to represent a taxable and gratuitous benefit to Mrs Angel, it was open in a subsequent proceeding to find that the transaction was also a debt for which she was liable, the transaction constituting both benefit and debt (A and not-A), and this in the precise world of tax law. Dixon J. stated at p. 256 that '[a] tax assessment in respect of a benefit or advantage received is not inconsistent with an obligation to pay for the benefit or advantage where, for example, there is no apparent intention to honour the obligation'.

The case against classical, binary logic, however, has not been made only by legal academics. It has also been made by courts in deciding cases. Thus in *In re Vivendi Universal, S.A. Securities Litigation*,[90] a large US class action case involving foreign class members, the court decided that risk of non-recognition abroad of the possible preclusive effect of the judgment should be 'evaluated along a continuum' and not in terms of a bivalent choice between recognition and non-recognition.[91] In one of the leading cases on determining jurisdiction in internet cases in the USA, *Zippo Manufacturing Company* v. *Zippo DotCom, Inc.*, the court decided that the likelihood of constitutionally permissible jurisdiction is directly proportionate to the nature and quality of commercial activity that an entity conducts over the internet, and that '[t]his sliding scale is consistent with well-developed personal jurisdiction principles'.[92] At the international level the criticism of bivalent logic has reached the International Court of Justice. In the *Kosovo* decision the Court decided that Kosovo's declaration of independence was in accordance with international law, reasoning that in the absence of an explicit prohibition of such declarations there is no need to demonstrate a permissive rule.[93] In his declaration concurring in the result, however, Judge Simma criticized the reasoning of the Court as representing 'an old, tired view of international law' and even as 'obsolete'.[94] Judge Simma would have preferred 'a more comprehensive answer, assessing both permissive and prohibitive rules of international law' that would have allowed assessment of 'the possible degrees of non-prohibition, ranging from "tolerated" to "permissible" to "desirable"'.[95] This would have allowed for 'something which breaks from the binary understanding of permission/prohibition and which allows for a range of non-prohibited options'.[96] These judicial statements in favour of non-binary logic demonstrate the possibility of its choice in judicial proceedings. Choice of logic is inherent in the deciding of cases, though the choice should not be presented as a definitive and bivalent one.[97]

Debate on the application of the new logics to law, in an explicitly logical manner, has now begun, though the debate is still in its infancy. There have been (largely isolated) attempts by lawyers to apply a new logic in a particular field of law, though these do not appear as yet, and sauf erreur, to have been taken over

---

[90] 242 FRD 76, (SDNY 2007).

[91] 242 FRD at 95.

[92] 952 F Supp 1119 at 1123–4 (WD Pa 1997), the court also noting a 'middle ground' between actively selling products in a jurisdiction through the internet and simply posting information on an available website, the middle ground being an interactive website on which information could be exchanged.

[93] 'Accordance with international law of the unilateral declaration of independence in respect of Kosovo', (22 July 2010), accessible at <http://www.icj-cij.org/docket/files/141/15987.pdf>.

[94] Declaration of Judge Simma, paras. 2 and 3, accessible at <http://www.icj-cij.org/docket/files/141/15993.pdf>, at paras 2 and 3. I am grateful to Morag Goodwin of the University of Tilburg for this reference.

[95] Declaration of Judge Simma, note 94 above, at para. 8.

[96] Declaration of Judge Simma, note 94 above, at para. 9.

[97] See the discussion of logical pluralism earlier in this section.

into legal practice.[98] They may have misjudged the receptivity of the field, or practice in the field may have misjudged the new logic. The most extended efforts to extend new logic to law have been undertaken, however, by logicians. This is consistent with the process of extending formal logic to informal types of reasoning, ensuring that logic would have 'teeth'. Accordingly, Henry Prakken has formally analysed reasoning about evidence;[99] Giovanni Sartor has done the same for adversarial reasoning generally;[100] and John Horty has advanced Neil MacCormick's case for defeasibility, as non-monotonic reasoning.[101] The most general of these efforts, and of greatest interest for the cosmopolitan state, has been that of Graham Priest, who has defended at length the application of paraconsistent logic to cases of true contradictions in law.[102] He maintains that such true contradictions exist, and that they are not dealt with, or not adequately dealt with, by such well-known devices as giving priority to a higher law, or to a law later in time, or to a more specific law.[103] In his writing to date, Priest has not argued explicitly in favour of either multivalent or modal forms of logic to resolve true contradictions in law, though both appear potentially applicable. To the extent that multivalent logic is degree-theoretic and modal logic is not, the former may provide more subtle forms of resolution than the latter.[104] Priest

---

[98] The first such example appears to have been Thorne (1980), 'Mathematics, Fuzzy Negligence', notably at 156 ('negligence is simply fuzzy' in that some cases clearly negligence, others not, and large middle ground); other efforts include Yablon (1991), 'Allocation of Burdens of Proof in Corporate Law'; Adams, Nickles, and Ressler (1994), 'Secured Credit and a Fuzzy System' (being secured or not a matter of degree, forcing judge to seek more facts, and to seek intersections of agreement); Williams (1994), 'Fraudulent Transfer Law as a Fuzzy System'; Adams and Farber (1999), 'Expert Reasoning, Fuzzy Logic, and Complex Statutes'; and for fuzzy logic in legal theory, Adams and Spaak (1995), 'Fuzzifying the Natural Law—Legal Positivist Debate'. More recently Kevin Clermont of Cornell has argued extensively for the application of fuzzy logic to questions of proof: see notably Clermont (2012), 'Death of Paradox'.

[99] Prakken (2004), 'Analysing Reasoning about Evidence', on 'defeasible argumentation', non-monotonic reasoning, even, at 36, 'quick and dirty reasoning' (subject to revision).

[100] Sartor (1993), A Simple Computational Model', also for non-monotonic; and see Sartor (2005), *Legal Reasoning*, 310ff. ('the persuasion dialogue: the structure').

[101] Horty (2011), 'Rules and Reasons' (non-monotonic presentation of precedent, rules of previous cases not strict but defeasible, with reasons as premises for rules); and for the general and ongoing debate on non-monotonicity, Beltran and Ratti (2012), *Logic of Legal Requirements: Essays on Defeasibility*, notably at 3 (for existence of 'implicit exceptions' to rules, which can never be specified *ex ante*).

[102] Priest (2006), *In Contradiction*, Ch. 13 ('Norms and the Philosophy of Law').

[103] Priest (2006), *In Contradiction*, at 187 ('to insist that . . . one or other of the laws has implicit exceptive clauses is mere whimsy'); and on these methods, see Malt (1992), 'Methods for solution of conflicts', at 203–4 (though 'common treatment . . . misleading both substantively, methodologically and formally'); Bobbio (1965), 'Critères pour résoudre antinomies', at 241 (expressed as 'chronological, hierarchical and special'); Malgaud (1965), 'Les antinomies et droit', at 12–13 (in using such priority rules, law 'univocal' and there are no antinomies, antinomies only where law 'en défaut' through inapplicability of principles of resolution).

[104] True contradictions are possible in both but it is not presently clear whether the truth values found in the different possible worlds of modal logic are expressed in binary or multivalent terms. If the latter, multivalent logic is common to both and modal logic could accommodate the degrees of imperativity (or non-monotonicity) characteristic of legal traditions in their relations with others; see Glenn (2010b), *Legal Traditions*, at 374–5 (by their complexity complex legal traditions not universalizing in character); and see Priest (2001), *Introduction Non-Classical Logic*, at 20–1 (modes in which things may be true/false in different worlds).

himself acknowledges that in the case of a true contradiction a *'practical'* problem is posed for which his notion of a dialetheism or true contradiction 'gives no help'.[105] He does oppose 'consistentising' through application of constant, priority-giving devices, arguing that this would be a 'retrograde' step since such contradictions are not uniformly dysfunctional.[106] There is a place for ongoing diversity. Where a judge must nevertheless decide a case in the face of conflicting norms,[107] Priest would have him or her simply make law, there being, even *ex hypothesi*, 'no legal grounds on which to base the decision', so that 'extra-legal (socio-political) grounds' must be used.[108]

The task for a cosmopolitan, paraconsistent logic in law would thus be to acknowledge legal contradictions, to preserve existing legal diversity, and to provide cosmopolitan and practical forms of dispute resolution for the judge of the cosmopolitan state. Law may have already discovered such cosmopolitan forms of logic.

COSMOPOLITAN LOGICS AND LEGAL DIVERSITY

Binary or classical logic is hostile to the existence of contradictions in law, either seeking to eliminate them through legal means (legal unification or application of superior, priority-giving principles) or rejecting the possibility of legal resolution of them (since an extra-legal intervention is required), or both.[109] Even a proponent of paraconsistent logic such as Graham Priest accepts the need to make new law in such a case, accepting a sharp law/non-law distinction.[110] An underlying theme of this volume, however, has been the ongoing availability of 'law before the law', most notably the common laws upon which national laws are based and that continue to provide the means of resolution for legal differences, historically between the common laws and their multiple *iura propria*. It is also the case that constitutionalism provides bridging mechanisms, of cosmopolitan origin, for the inconsistencies and outright contradictions of modern constitutions, and that institutional cosmopolitanism is a generic expression for the multiple ways in which diverse institutions can coexist.[111] It is not the case, however, that these cosmopolitan ways oblige us to 'consistentise', in the sense that all differences become subject to a massive, normative scheme of ordering and hierarchical structuring, as where national contradictions are resolved through resort to a higher law or a law later in time. These latter devices are

---

[105] Priest (2006), *In Contradiction*, at 197 (the example is of 'inconsistent moral obligations' but the 'practical problem' appears the same in law).

[106] Priest (2006), *In Contradiction*, at 202.

[107] See the formulation of Perelman (1965b), 'Avant-propos', at 5 that if incoherence is 'irremediable' in formal logic, the judge, obliged to judge, must 'reabsorb' (résorber) the antinomy.

[108] Priest (2006), *In Contradiction*, at 188.

[109] See this chapter, 'The cosmopolitan limits of binary logic', 'The cosmopolitan character of the new logics'.

[110] For Priest, see this chapter, 'The cosmopolitan character of the new logics', *in fine*.

[111] For the logic of these cosmopolitan ways see later in this chapter.

binary in character and univalent in their choice of one only of the possible norms in question. Cosmopolitan forms of legal ordering are different and employ cosmopolitan forms of logic.

They are different first of all in fully accepting the existence and even the need for recognition of contradictory norms. This is perhaps most evident in contemporary private international law where differences in national laws applicable to transnational cases are ineradicable.[112] It is also increasingly evident within national laws, since the multiplication of sources used by national judges inevitably brings into play a wider range of rules and an increased likelihood of contradiction between them.[113] Law rarely chooses to express itself in terms of a single value, Professor Husson has written, and the ensuing conflicts (the word is his) both require choice and efforts at conciliation.[114] There is increasing recognition today of the phenomenon of what is designated as conflict in law and this recognition is itself a cosmopolitan development.[115]

Cosmopolitan forms of legal ordering are also different in avoiding univalent choice between norms seen as conflicting. The logic is one that sustains diversity, avoids imposing consistency and opens up an included middle where multivalent options are available. If Gratian wrote in the twelfth century on discordant canons and sought their reconciliation, he did so with the object of unifying a *corpus* of law within a single institution.[116] Cosmopolitan logic works within a larger intellectual cadre. There is no single unity to be obtained, but conciliatory recognition of multiple unities, corresponding to the present state of the world.[117] The process is in a large sense interpretive, in the original Latin sense of being intermediate amongst values,[118] and in the sense of working with existing law. It also resorts generally to non-monotonicity, or defeasance in Neil MacCormick's language, since none of the contradictory laws can be seen as monotonic in application or constantly binding. There is room for 'play in the joints' as has been said of the relations between religion and state in US constitutional

---

[112] See Ch. 8, 'Private international law'; and for antinomies between conflict resolution rules in national laws (fundamental rights under the European Convention on Human Rights or national choice of law rules), Gannagé (2001), *Hiérarchie des normes*, at 81ff.

[113] See Chs 11–13.

[114] Husson (1967), 'Les apories de la logique', at 47 (hence incessant movement in search of precarious equilibrium); and see for 'antinomies' of the current French constitution, Turpin (1985), 'Le traitement des antinomies', notably at 91 (for use of 'constitutional principles' in the resolution of such antinomies).

[115] See, for example Gavazzi (1959), *Delle antinomie*, notably at 5 (for legal task of *conciliatio legum*), 6 (for antinomies that are only 'apparent', resolvable through a principle of 'coherence'); Vander Elst (1965), 'Antinomies', at 175 (distinguishing 'apparent, relative and absolute' antinomies); Lindahl (1992), 'Conflicts in Systems', at 39 ('distinguishing between different kinds of conflict is an important task for legal theory'), 45 ('we say that N1 conflicts with N2 if both norms are mandatory, and each of them is realizable, while they are not jointly realizable'); Besson (2005), *Morality of Conflict*, at 419 ('conflict of rights' giving rise to incompatible actions differing from 'competition of rights').

[116] See Ch. 2, 'The Church as State'.

[117] See Ch. 11, in introductory section.

[118] Martinico (2011), 'Constitutional Complexity of the EU', at 73.

law.[119] The refusal of univalent choice is also consistent with judicial neutrality in the face of contradictory, but equally legitimate, norms. Both can be maintained, and there need be no categorical rejection of an entire set of arguments of one of the parties.

In the result cosmopolitan logic and cosmopolitan forms of ordering have the compatible objectives of maintaining diversity while avoiding conflict, in law. It is thus possible to speak of contradictions or conflicts in law as being only 'apparent', and even to deny their existence altogether, while at the same time maintaining the diversity of sources of law from which the apparent contradiction or conflict derives. The conclusion, as has been noted, is not inconsistent with ongoing use of binary or classical logic, where its use is appropriate. The multivalence of the logic that prevailed throughout most of the legal history discussed in this volume yielded to bivalence in some measure during the time of national legal construction. Bivalence will continue to be operative, though it may be some time until it reaches the pre-eminence it obtained in some jurisdictions in recent centuries. In the foreseeable future it will be more obviously challenged by the logics of cosmopolitan ways.

THE COSMOPOLITAN LOGIC OF CONSTITUTIONALISM

We have seen how twentieth century legal theory often saw the state as a 'dichotomischer Fixbegriff', a dichotomous fixed idea.[120] The state would either exist or not, and all purported states would be subject to this rigorous, taxonomic process. The dichotomous nature of constitutionalism breaks down in constitutional experience, however, and this is demonstrably so with respect to the origin of states, the failure of states, and the functioning of states. The underlying logic is non-classical and the real action occurs throughout a large and included middle. There are few dichotomous 'jolts'.[121]

The origin of states

It is impossible to fix the origins of most states of the world. If the concept of the state cannot be limited to its modern form, as much informed opinion holds,[122] all modern states would have simply emerged from earlier state forms, assuming many of their benefits and burdens. The French state did not originate with the French revolution, though there was a significant change of regime in the ongoing French state.[123] State construction emerges as an incremental process,

---

[119] *Walz v. Tax Commission of the City of New York*, 397 US 664, 669 (1970), *per* Burger, C. J. ('[t]here is room for play in the joints productive of a benevolent neutrality which will permit religious exercise to exist without sponsorship and without interference').

[120] See Ch. 1, 'Degrees and Varieties of States'.

[121] On avoidance of the 'jolt' problem in passing from one taxonomic category to another, see this chapter, 'The cosmopolitan character of the new logics'.

[122] See Ch. 1, 'The State Tradition through Time'.

[123] See Ch. 7, 'Justifying the Contemporary State'.

an accumulation of normative tradition that has been tried and tested over time and found less imperfect than other pieces of normative tradition. There is, moreover, no fixed end point to the process and each state that is presently seen as existing is subject to inevitable forces of decay. There are no developed states. The logic here is cosmopolitan and multivalent, since there is ongoing appreciation, evaluation, and choice amongst earlier models and prior aggregations of normative information, all measured against present need. Much may be dismissed as old lumber, but even this process is cosmopolitan in requiring knowledge, appreciation, and judgement.[124] New forms of closure are 'constrained . . . by the historical legacy of previous closures'.[125]

The non-classical logic of state emergence has been observed explicitly in the emergence of many states of the present Commonwealth, the present independence of which is rooted, paradoxically, in an act of the Parliament of the United Kingdom. Thus, Peter Oliver maintains that these states 'have the constitutional cake and eat it too', in that constitutional continuity is affirmed at the same time as rupture with imperial norms.[126] It would thus be 'differing perspectives' that would see the Westminster parliament as having continuing sovereign authority over its former Dominions (in being able to repeal a grant of independence), while from the perspective of the ex-colonies the metropolitan authority would maintain only 'spent self-embracing powers', having bound itself by the grant of independence.[127]

The more obvious forms of rupture with prior constitutional order, such as unilateral declarations of independence or political revolutions, do not appear to escape the necessity of living with ongoing contradiction. 'Founding' instruments in the form of written constitutions may clearly mark the emergence of a new political and legal structure, which has no obvious predecessor, yet in all cases examined here the founding instrument is rooted in concepts and norms of existing law, which continue to be drawn upon in the ensuing process of interpreting the written instrument.[128] The founding instrument both founds and does not found, since it is creative of the new yet not destructive of the old. There are shifts in influence, but genuine legal rupture appears impossible to bring about over a wide range of public and private law.[129]

The creation of federations must overcome the 'fundamental point, that an individual independence of the States is utterly irreconcilable with the idea of an aggregate sovereignty', so that some 'middle ground' must be found that 'will at

---

[124] For cosmopolitan thought being conscious of its origins, and of the intellectual origins of 'presentism', Glenn (2009a), 'Cosmopolitan Legal Orders', at 33ff.

[125] Lawson (2001), *Closure*, at 6, as cited in Ch. 3, 'Persistence', in introductory section.

[126] Oliver (2005), *Constitution of Independence*, at 7 (maintaining 'constitutional continuity while achieving constitutional independence', notably for states of Australia, Canada, New Zealand).

[127] Oliver (2005), *Constitution of Independence*, at 312 (Hartian explanation of change of ultimate rule of recognition not explaining how or why this happens).

[128] For the USA, notably, see Ch. 7, '*The United States of America*', especially for resort to cosmopolitan range of earlier sources.

[129] Glenn (1990a), 'Law, Revolution and Rights'.

once support a due supremacy of the national authority, and leave in force the local authorities so far as they can be subordinately useful'.[130] Federations have been established, however, in this middle ground, and multivalence in creation then inevitably leads to multivalence in operation, as will be seen below.[131]

The failure of states

Multivalence in the origins of states is paralleled by multivalence in their failure. There are certainly criteria for the recognition of states in international law (people, territory, government)[132] but no obvious instances of formal de-recognition. States, like old soldiers, thus often, and increasingly, fade away. There are therefore degrees of state existence and the reality of some forty to sixty failed or failing states in the world today is the best evidence of the impossibility of deploying binary or classical logic to capture the situation. There is some relation to the degrees of corruption in states, now being reported by Transparency International.[133] The state is thus a 'dichotomischer Fixbegriff' only in certain circles of legal philosophy; nuance is required on the ground. Between the binary notions of an existing state and its termination there is often a long, extended period where neither is obviously true. In appreciating this we do not appear to be troubled by the difficulty of applying truth values to deontic propositions.[134] Given the circumstances of its origin there may be no difficulty in the assertion that a state should exist. What is of overriding interest is the degree of truth in the statement that such a state exists.

Explicit recognition of the logic required to understand the phenomenon of failed and failing states is not easy to find. This is in large part the result of ongoing diplomatic recognition, by other states, of states that have lost much control over their presumed territory and population. This is compatible with, and reinforced by, historical and dichotomous attitudes towards state existence. More realistic appreciations are sometimes found, however, in discussion of particular jurisdictions or legal traditions antagonistic to the state tradition. In discussing the rule of law and judicial independence in Africa, Charles Fombad counsels that we must think not of their existing or not existing, but in terms of 'more of or less of'.[135] Noel Feldman, in considering Arab constitutions, speaks of 'partial constitutionalism' in much of the world, where legal and constitutional

---

[130] Wood (1969), *Creation of American Republic*, at 473. For earlier views on the possibility of a federation, notably that of Pufendof (a 'monstrosity'), see Ch. 7, '*Structures*'.

[131] See this chapter, '*The functioning of states*'.

[132] See Ch. 1, 'Degrees and Varieties of States', notably for gradations or degrees in the recognition process.

[133] See <http://www.transparency.org>, with global corruption report, corruption perceptions index (rating countries of world in terms of perceived levels of corruption), TI Source Book by J. Pope on national integrity systems, and 2007 *Global Report on Corruption in Judicial Systems* (through both bribery and political interference).

[134] See this chapter, '*The cosmopolitan character of the new logics*'.

[135] Fombad (2007), 'Challenges to Constitutionalism', at 15.

rules 'affect' government actors 'without binding them absolutely'.[136] There would therefore be a need for students of comparative constitutional law 'to promote conceptual clarity by finding a way to talk about partial rule of law or partial constitutionalism'.[137] Similar ideas are found in recognition that 'a centralized, Western-style administration' will be dysfunctional unless means are found to connect the state with 'local, informal, internally driven political and economic processes'.[138] In all of these discussions, there is some appreciation that the complexity of the informal world necessitates more gradated or degree-theoretic understanding. It also requires understanding of the relations of different normative orders with which the state, in a particular jurisdiction, must compose.

The functioning of states

It has already been seen that many lawyers agree with proponents of the new logics that there are contradictions within state law.[139] This has been attributed in part to the process of drafting constitutions, where conflicting positions have not been reconciled and where the open nature of the process makes the granting of concessions more difficult.[140] Thus India 'contradicts itself' in guaranteeing equality and maintaining personal laws,[141] though the phenomenon of ongoing, internal contradiction cannot be limited to states with personal laws. It can be seen as inherent in federations, while Bills and Charters of Rights enumerate different rights and many have seen conflicts in such enumerations. In the USA conclusions have even been drawn that 'disorder reigns', or that the law is 'riddled with major defects and inconsistencies'.[142] Samantha Besson concludes that none of the means of avoiding conflicts has been successful, so conflicts of rights remain with us,[143] while Lorenzo Zucca affirms that 'constitutional

---

[136] Feldman (2003b), Review of N. J. Brown, *Constitutions in a nonconstitutional world*, at 390 (on 'tendency, especially prevalent in the developed West, to think of the rule of law and constitutional governance in binary terms: either you have them or you don't') and 391 ('partial conditions . . . obtain in much of the world').

[137] Feldman (2003b), Review of N. J. Brown, *Constitutions in a nonconstitutional world*, at 391.

[138] Kaplan (2008), *Fixing Fragile States*, at 9 (and 'foolish for the international community to continue propping up' state institutions incapable of self-regenerating development); also see Fukuyama (2004), *State Building*, at 84 (on some 'high-specificity activities with low transaction volume like central banking that do not permit a high degree of variance in institutional structure and approach', contrasted with 'low-specificity activities with high transaction volume like education or law', where 'input from people immersed in local conditions will be the most critical').

[139] See this chapter, 'Cosmopolitan Logics and Legal Diversity'.

[140] See Ch. 11, 'Constitutional Structures and Sources of Law'.

[141] Narain (2008), *Reclaiming the Nation*, at 6, and 154 (though question of uniform code or personal laws 'far too harsh a binary'); and see Menski (2003), *Hindu Law*, at 194 (existence of Hindu law in contemporary India not an 'either/or' question but involving 'assessment of the actual extent of more or less invisible Hindu law input in any sphere of life').

[142] For disorder, Feldman (2005), *Divided by God*, at 216; and major defects Choper (1995), *Securing Religious Liberty*, at 38.

[143] Besson (2005), *Morality of Conflict*, at 419 ('well-established fact' that rights can conflict); though see Finkelstein (2001), 'Symposium on Conflicts of Rights', at 235 (contemporary rights theorists having 'generally *assumed* that rights cannot conflict'); and see Christie (2011), *Philosopher Kings? Adjudication of Conflicting Human Rights*, notably at 37 (for rights described as 'defeasible').

dilemmas' flow from the very structure of fundamental legal rights, which overlap so as to be 'mutually incompatible'.[144]

However, constitutional dilemmas may be resolved, though their resolution requires thinking beyond the terms of the initial or apparent conflict. In England conflict between King and Parliament was resolved by settling sovereignty on King *and* Parliament, described as an example of 'both/and' logic as opposed to 'either/or logic'.[145] In Israel the existence of a 'Jewish and democratic state' is accomplished by opening up the (multiple) meanings of both adjectives to find those that are compatible with one another.[146] A dichotomy between 'vertical' and 'horizontal' application of rights guarantees (vertical against governments, horizontal against private parties) is alleviated by recognition of 'indirect' horizontal effect, so that the *conduct* of private parties is not directly subject to constitutional rights but private *laws* are subject to them.[147] The task of reconciling federal with state or provincial laws in a federation has been seen, not as a simple process of subsumption of laws under federal or state/provincial powers, but as a situation of 'competing classifications' in which many laws 'fall both ways'.[148] William Lederman thus acknowledged 'overlap and ambiguity' in the operation of the Canadian federation and formulated the idea of 'mutual exclusion, if practical, but concurrency if necessary'.[149] The Supreme Court of Canada has agreed that '[w]hen a federal statute can be properly interpreted so as not to interfere with a provincial statute, such an interpretation is to be applied in preference to another applicable construction which would bring about a conflict between the two statutes'.[150] The relations between the central legislative authority in Italy and regional legislatures have been described as a 'grey zone' in the jurisprudence of the Italian Corte costituzionale, since regional charters of rights and liberties are maintained not as potentially contradictory laws but as 'cultural statements'.[151] In the USA there are problems of reconciliation not only of federal with state laws, but of 'conflicts' on the meaning of federal law amongst circuits

---

[144] Zucca (2008), *Constitutional Dilemmas*, at 4 (application of one fundamental right implies violation of the other, citing Kelsen, though distinguishing between 'spurious' and 'genuine' conflicts).

[145] Brunner (1963), 'Vom Gottesgnadentum', at 282 ('Sowohl-als-auch' and not 'Entweder-Oder'). Today the notion of the King or Queen in Parliament is usually expressed in hyphenated form, e.g. the Queen-in-Parliament.

[146] See Ch. 13, '*State and religious legal sources*', and for the underlying multivalence of Jewish law, Ben-Menahem (1996), 'Postscript: The Judicial Process', at 427 ('having *two* conflicting, but equally binding, norms incorporated into the system').

[147] See Gardbaum (2012), 'The Place of Constitutional Law', at 180 (an 'intermediate third position', with further distinction between strong and weak forms of indirect horizontal application).

[148] Lederman (1963), 'Concurrent Operation', at 187 (citing commercial laws that are also laws relating to property and civil rights).

[149] Lederman (1963), 'Concurrent Operation', at 189 (dangerous driving offence thus both (federal) criminal offence and (provincial) traffic violation).

[150] *A. G. of Canada* v. *Law Society of B. C.* [1982] 2 SCR 307, at 356 (*per* Estey J.).

[151] Delledonne and Martinico (2009), 'Regional Charters', at 219 (with references to cases) and 220 (preparing Italy for 'the transition to a quasi-federal (or federal) State').

of the federal courts; these may go on for decades, and are lived with.[152] Where the Supreme Court is seized with a 'conflict' between state and federal law in diversity cases the Court may divide over whether such a conflict exists. A more bivalent view would see conflict and necessary priority of federal law; a more multivalent view would see compatibility and concurrent application of federal and state law. Both types of reasoning are well represented in the current Court. Choice of logic is necessary, though it need not be seen as a binary choice.[153]

Given the prevalence of enumerations of basic rights in contemporary constitutions,[154] the most visible application of multivalent logic in constitutional law is now found in the widespread and related processes of 'balancing' rights in apparent conflict (e.g. freedom of expression and the right to privacy) or 'balancing' a given right against a violative government measure. The latter process is often designated as one of 'proportionality analysis' in which the measure must satisfy a test of proportionality, designed to ensure the appropriate balance between the benefit of the measure and the harm to the right.[155] Given the

---

[152] Whitman (2008), 'No Right Answer?', at 384 (Supreme Court accepting a caseload far too small to permit it to regularize case law at the federal level); for justification of such diversity in terms of excessive cost of attempting to eliminate it, Frost (2008), '(Over)Valuing Uniformity' (questioning whether inherent value in uniformity, notably in eliminating 'moderate disuniformity' in interpretation of ambiguous federal statutes; 70 per cent of Supreme Court docket already now spent on resolving inter-circuit disagreements, many of which persist over time; litigants in any case accustomed to dealing with diversity of fifty state laws).

[153] See recently *Shady Grove Orthopedic Associates, P.A. v. Allstate Insurance,* 130 SC 1431, 176 L. Ed. 2d 311 (2010), the majority finding conflict between New York's prohibition of a type of class action and the general authorization of Federal procedural law, and applying paramount Federal law; the minority finding the two laws pursuing different objectives and thus mutually sustainable, state law being therefore applicable. Justice Stevens, however, concurring in the result but opining separately, was of the view that there might be cases in which Federal law may not 'displace a state law that is procedural in the ordinary use of the term but is so intertwined with a state right or remedy that it functions to define the scope of the state-created right': *Shady Grove* at 1452. Procedure and substance would not be mutually exclusive categories and in such cases separation would be well-nigh impossible: *Shady Grove* at 1450. He was of the view, however, that this was not such a case. Justice Ginsburg in the minority asked rhetorically in her judgment 'is this conflict really necessary?': *Shady Grove* at 1460, citing Traynor (1959), 'Is this Conflict Really Necessary?', which see at 657 (on need for 'prevention of needless conflicts engendered by mechanical rules'). For subsequent lower court decisions accepting the 'intertwined' character of state laws, Lyon (2011), '*Shady Grove*', at 1042ff. (opinion of Stevens J. 'controlling').

[154] See Ch. 7, '*Structures*'; Ch. 11, 'Constitutional Structures and Sources of Law'.

[155] Hickman (2008), 'Substance and Structure of Proportionality', notably at 699 (proportionality itself allowing 'zone of proportionality'), 703 (for 'least injurious means'), 705 (on importance of initial statement of government aim; narrow statement more likely to ensure proportionality of means taken), 715 (not 'hard-edged'); Barak (2010), 'Proportionality', at 8 ('a balancing, *writ small,* namely the need to balance between the marginal advantage to the law's goal (apart from the proportionate alternative) and the importance of preventing the limits to the right from which it derives'). On the history of 'balancing' and 'proportionality', notably in the USA and Germany, Bomhoff (2010), 'Genealogies of Balancing', notably at 116 (US focus on interests, German on methodology); Porat and Cohen-Eliya (2010), 'American Balancing and German Proportionality', at 271–7 (German proportionality rooted in administrative law, US balancing in private law, possible contemporary convergence); Aleinikoff (1987), 'Constitutional Law in Age of Balancing', at 944 (US balancing first appearing late 1930s, early 1940s, becoming dominant through 1950s and 1960s), 965 (listing many constitutional areas where balancing used, e.g. Fourth Amendment and 'unreasonable' search and seizure); Rückert (2011), 'Abwägung', notably at 914 ('enormous change' since 1900 and particularly

prevalence of 'balancing' and 'proportionality', the contemporary state would even have become 'the balancing state' and the present age would be an 'age of balancing'.[156] In its turn, proportionality would represent the 'ultimate rule of law'.[157]

In the vast debate over this subject, the essential element would be found in a shift in types of reasoning from one that accords priority to rules, categories, and subsumption, to one making more use of principles, overlapping, and accommodation. The latter process would represent 'value pluralism' in which a 'range of valid answers is possible and reasonable'[158] and there would be a 'shift away from binary conceptions of law', allowing multiple levels of 'scrutiny'.[159] Interestingly enough, the process may have begun with Oliver Wendell Holmes, who argued for a 'distinction of degree' in dealing with rights that run against one another, and for decisions that fix 'points in the line' in weighing considerations of social advantage.[160] The reasoning has become more complex and subtle since then but its basic characteristics remain constant. There is recognition of the inherent legitimacy of the rights or norms in presence, in spite of apparent conflict,[161] recognition of varying degrees of their impairment or 'optimization',[162] and recognition that the principles or norms are not definitive or binding in

since 1950, giving word counts for 'balancing' in German Federal Constitutional Court), 919 (on creating 'collision' out of 'equally legitimate' texts).

[156] Leisner (1997), *Der Abwägungsstaat*; Aleinikoff (1987), 'Constitutional Law in Age of Balancing'.

[157] Beatty (2004), *Ultimate Rule of Law*, notably at 163 ('[a] constitution without some principle to resolve cases of conflicting rights would be incoherent; it just wouldn't make sense').

[158] Zucca (2008), *Constitutional Dilemmas*, at 13 (this portraying 'more accurately the actual conditions of deliberation and decision-making in modern Western societies').

[159] Krisch (2010), *Beyond Constitutionalism*, at 305 (norms 'foreign' to one of sub-orders 'often escape the binding/non-binding dichotomy that is so characteristic of the legal system', rather acquire 'a form of gradated authority'); and see Alexy (2010b), 'Construction of Constitutional Rights' (contrasting 'rule construction' using subsumption or classification with 'principles construction' that sees balancing as 'inevitable and unavoidable'); Cook (2001), 'Fuzzy Logic and Judicial Decision Making', at 73 (for balancing as 'quintessentially a fuzzy decisional method', listing of 'fuzzy' tests of US constitutional law such as intermediate scrutiny, chilling effect, compelling state interests, least restrictive means); Aleinikoff (1987), 'Constitutional Law in Age of Balancing', at 949 (on 'non-balancing past' in which US Supreme Court used 'categorical reasoning' of 'differences in kind, not degree', allowing, e.g., states to exercise police power but regulate commerce), 968 (on more categorical 'degrees of scrutiny' of impugned legislation yielding to 'sliding scale balancing approach'); Adams and Farber (1999), 'Beyond the Formalism Debate', at 1313 ('balancing' often attacked as arbitrary but 'in principle reducible to understandable (though non-binary) rules'); Turpin (1985), 'Le traitement des antinomies', at 90 (for conciliation of 'antinomic rights' that renders useless any serious attempt at ' "hierarchization" of norms').

[160] For the diverse references to Holmes, Porat and Cohen-Eliya (2010), 'American Balancing and German Proportionality', at 278.

[161] Alexy (2010a), *Theory of Constitutional Rights*, at 50 (on one of two principles being 'outweighed' but 'this means neither that the outweighed principle is invalid nor that it has to have an exception built into it . . . the outweighed principle may itself outweigh the other principle in certain circumstances . . . principles have different weights in different cases').

[162] Alexy (2010b), 'Construction of Constitutional Rights', at 28 ('weight formula' in terms of light, moderate, and serious impairment); Alexy (2010a), *Theory of Constitutional Rights*, at 47 (for principles as 'optimization requirements' that can be satisfied to varying degrees).

application, but defeasible or non-monotonic.[163] There is criticism of the reasoning, by those who see it as protecting too little, or too much, of the rights in question, or as being irremediably vague.[164] The metaphor of 'balancing' or 'weighing' is in itself unhelpful, but it is pointed out that the metaphor overshadows a more precise process of 'giving reasons'[165] and that 'specification' of particular solutions can take place for specific reasons in the process of conciliation of norms.[166] Whatever its faults, the process of 'balancing' appears to be here to stay, given the multiplication of norms and sources in the world. It is inherently cosmopolitan in its ability to bridge multiple and apparently conflicting sources, state or non-state in origin. It is also consistent with notions of judicial impartiality. The United States Supreme Court has thus received considerable praise for its ability to sustain 'what had seemed to be a vanishing middle ground' in appreciating rights of due process and measures of national security.[167]

THE COSMOPOLITAN LOGIC OF COMMON LAWS

Constitutionalism has acquired a national veneer in recent centuries and it is necessary to probe beneath the veneer to discover cosmopolitan origins and ongoing cosmopolitan logic in the operation of states.[168] The same process has occurred with the notion of common law and over the last three centuries the Roman understanding—of a law common to a territory and binding throughout

---

[163] Alexy (2010b), 'The Construction of Constitutional Rights', at 21 ('merely a *prima facie* requirement'); Alexy (2010a), *Theory of Constitutional Rights*, at 57 (requiring realization 'to the greatest extent possible'); and for defeasance or non-monotonicity as a necessary characteristic of multivalent logic, see this chapter, '*The cosmopolitan character of the new logics*'.

[164] For US insistence on 'absolute' character of rights, notably those of First Amendment, Tsakyrakis (2009), 'Proportionality: an assault on human rights?', at 468; Aleinikoff (1987), 'Constitutional Law in Age of Balancing', at 944 (balancing first attacked for 'illiberal' results in free speech cases, now recognized as leading to 'liberal as well as conservative' results), 1003 (balancing and non-balancing approaches existing 'side-by-side' in many areas of constitutional law); Bomhoff (2010), 'Genealogies of Balancing', at 135 (criticism of Forsthoff in Germany as not a 'legal method'); Schauer (2010), 'Balancing, Subsumption, and Role of Text', at 35, (citing Scalia J. that balancing equivalent to determining 'whether a particular line is longer than a particular rock is heavy', the latter statement suggesting incommensurability not only of values themselves but of their means of measurement, this latter being obviously incorrect—since length and weight are comparable as means of measurement, largely in terms of what they measure, though it makes no sense to attempt to apply them comparatively to objects), 38 (little about balancing to suggest that one or other side of the balance ought necessarily to prevail); Porat and Cohen-Eliya (2010), 'American Balancing and German Proportionality', at 285 (balancing now associated in USA not only with dilution of rights but with protection of rights, as is proportionality).

[165] Alexy (2010a), *Theory of Constitutional Rights*, at 53 (a principle of greater weight than another when 'sufficient reasons for supposing it to have precedence').

[166] Moreso (2012), 'Ways of Solving Conflicts', at 39. The process is comparable to judicial decision-making in application of general norms of legal professional ethics; as to which see Glenn (1990c), 'Professional Structures'.

[167] Witt (2007), 'Anglo-American Empire', at 794.

[168] See Ch. 7, 'Justifying the Contemporary State'; Ch. 11, 'The Cosmopolitan Turn in Constitutional Sources'; this chapter, 'The Cosmopolitan Logic of Constitutionalism'.

it—has once again become visible in both civilian and common law jurisdictions.[169] Common law would thus be synonymous with general law or ordinary law (in both cases national, state, or provincial in origin).[170] Yet the primary sense of common law—that of a law that is relational or supplemental in character and that must be designated as common in order to distinguish it from particular laws—has remained operative throughout the period of national or jurisdictional closures. It has even received greater visibility outside Europe than within Europe, as an essential element in the expansion of European laws throughout the world. While there were English, French, Spanish, Dutch, and German common laws, of transnational dimensions, they all functioned and continue to function as relational laws and all yielded and yield in principle to local laws.[171] They were essential elements in the diversity of empires, and are essential in the ongoing diversity of post-colonial states.

The underlying logic of common laws, in this primary sense of the term, is unmistakably cosmopolitan or multivalent in character. There is first of all recognition of multiple, legitimate, legal orders and therefore of the ongoing necessity of legal diversity. European and aboriginal populations are 'now acknowledging the permanence of the other's presence'[172] and mutual recognition on the ground has long characterized colonial–local relations.[173] The common laws that legitimate state constitutions leave space for both state law and non-state law, so common laws also exist in ongoing relations with personal laws or 'statuts personnels'.[174] In the world of states a common law once received does not suffer a radical and total loss of influence on the independence of the receiving state and there is even a process of mutual, ongoing influence.[175] The

---

[169] In Quebec, according to the Preliminary Provision of the 1994 Civil Code, the Code itself would establish the common law of Quebec; though for a broader interpretation of the Provision, relying on the text doing so 'expressly or by implication', Glenn (2005), 'La Disposition préliminaire'. In the USA the view that each state has its own common law has been widespread through the history of the country: Horwitz (1992), *Transformation of American Law*, citing, at 20, the 1798 essay of J. Root, 'On the Common Law of Connecticut'.

[170] See e.g. Art. 1725 of the Quebec Civil Code, the French version speaking of the 'droit commun de propriété' and the English version of 'ordinary law of ownership'.

[171] See Ch. 6.

[172] McHugh (2005), *Aboriginal Societies and the Common Law*, at 538 (need for reconciliation 'as least contestatively' as possible); and for a 'large middle ground' between 'contract and conquest', Banner (2005), *How Indians Lost Their Land*, at 3 ('no sharp distinction between voluntariness and involuntariness. The difference . . . is one of degree, not kind').

[173] McHugh (2005), *Aboriginal Societies and the Common Law*, at 539 ('reconciliation could not be possible without recognition'); Tully (1995), *Strange Multiplicity*, at 119 ('the initial reason Crown negotiators recognized the Aboriginal peoples as nations is that they did not redescribe the Aboriginal peoples in the forms of recognition constructed by the armchair European theorists'); see Lamer C. J. in *R. v. Van der Peet* [1996] 2 SCR 507, at para. 50 ('[t]rue reconciliation will, equally, place weight on each'); see Svensson (2005), 'Interlegality', at 74 ('it is the respect for Sami legal perceptions . . . which has meaning'); and for 'fuzzy' relations between socialist legislation in Vietnam and upland villages in northern Vietnam, with different parties holding different claims to the same resources, Phuc (2007), 'Fuzzy Property Relations'.

[174] See Ch. 12, introductory section; and for personal laws, see Ch. 8, 'Churches and Religions'.

[175] See Ch. 6, 'Common Laws beyond Europe'. Thus, in principle reception of the common law is unaffected by any purported 'cut-off date' and would continue as a matter of ongoing persuasive authority. See e.g. the

process of mutual recognition, moreover, is not an exclusively colonial phenomenon, and the influence of Pandectist German thought in the world is an example of recognition of normative force based simply on persuasion and voluntary choice.[176] In all these cases there is no possibility of creating consistency, no overarching, imperative legal order capable of setting down fixed rules of hierarchical ordering. The ongoing diversity is deeply rooted and ongoing.

In the ongoing relations of different legal orders the inherently multivalent logic implies recognition and acknowledgement not only of difference but of contradiction. As has been seen, this in itself is a cosmopolitan perspective;[177] and mutual recognition implies that contradictory laws are both valid. A and [not-A] is even a frequent phenomenon amongst the laws of the world, in a given territory. Ownership of land is individual in European traditions; it is collective for many (if not most) peoples of unwritten law. Both may remain operative within national territory.[178] There is well-known divergence in the case law of jurisdictions historically attached to the English common law, reflected in the citation patterns of Commonwealth legal treatises (the transnational 'but see').[179] Recovery of pure economic loss, for example, receives contradictory solutions through contemporary common law jurisdictions, though there remains a shared dialogical tradition.[180] The contrary, transnational, authority must still be cited. The ongoing transnational influence of French law, which corresponds fully to a notion of a French 'droit commun' in the primary sense of a relational and supplemental common law, is even tolerant of different and contradictory civil codes within it.[181] There is even second-order contradiction, at a more abstract level of logic, which is accepted. Thus European and Christian thought is 'quite dualistic—given to sharp dichotomies', though aboriginal ideas see opposite tendencies as potentially 'contained within a single deity or saint...mutually constituting'.[182] Both perspectives are implicit in the recent UN Declaration of the Rights of Indigenous Peoples, which remarkably provides that contemporary states recognize the collective rights of indigenous peoples, and this without impairing the territorial integrity or political unity of the same states.[183] The

South Australia case of *State Government Insurance Commission (SA)* v. *Trigwell* (1979) 142 CLR 617 at 625, *per* Gibbs J. ('[i]t is the common law rules as expounded from time to time that are to be applied').

[176] Glenn (2007c), *Common Laws*, at 79 ('Pandectist common law, in the world').

[177] See this chapter, 'Cosmopolitan Logic and Legal Diversity'.

[178] For increasing recognition of collective forms of land-holding, Glenn (2010b), *Legal Traditions*, at 89–90, with references.

[179] Glenn (1995), 'Common Law in Canada', at 284; and recall Bilder (2004), *Transatlantic Constitution*, at 89, cited in Ch. 6, 'Common Laws beyond Europe', for relations between North American colonies and England as 'not so binary'.

[180] For 'striking contrast' between law of England and laws of Australia, New Zealand, Canada in matters of liability for damage caused to defective products, Feldthusen (2008), *Economic Negligence*, at 183.

[181] Glenn (2007c), *Common Laws*, at 72–3 (notably on influence of French Civil Code, and its case law or jurisprudence, in other codified jurisdictions).

[182] Taylor (1996), *Magistrates of the Sacred*, at 50.

[183] See Ch. 12, 'Reconciliation'; and for commensurability of indigenous rights and state structures, Glenn (2011b), 'Three Ironies' at 171, notably at 179 (for the multivalent character of the Declaration).

recognized legitimacy of contradictory laws requires means for resolution of contradiction between common and particular laws. Unlike the hierarchical, bright-line rules that exist within states for contradictory provisions of state law (the later in time or the hierarchically superior prevails), resolution of tension between common and particular laws is brought about by general principles that preserve existing contradictions but that allow for casuistic decision-making in an included middle. The relations are not hierarchical and structured, but transversal and indeterminate. Historically, common laws thus yield to imperative particular laws, but the imperativity of local laws is always a matter of interpretation, of precise texts in precise circumstances. This was the classic method for determining the application, or not, of the *ius commune* in continental Europe. It relied notably on presumptions of application.[184] In the reception of English common law the question asked was about the 'suitability' of its application, in the face of local need and local texts.[185]

In the relations of common laws and particular laws the need for interpretation in effecting a choice between them is indicative of a further feature of cosmopolitan legal logic. The contradictory laws in question each have the potential to yield. Each is non-monotonic, or defeasible in the language of Neil MacCormick.[186] The actual extent of defeasibility can never be fixed in advance since all will depend on circumstance, while defeasibility in one circumstance says little or nothing about defeasibility in other circumstances. The contradictory texts remain in force and there is no process of making them consistent; bias in favour of one or the other of them can be revealed only over time. The judge takes both as given in the ongoing debate. In present circumstances, where the historic (and imperial) justifications for application or non-application have lost much of their grip, much will depend today on the perceived adequacy of national or local law, given a visible alternative in a common law. The debate has not therefore changed greatly since imperial times. 'Suitability' of common law has become adequacy of local law, but the underlying notion of local priority and distant aid (or supplement) remains operative. Neither the local nor the common can purport to monotonicity.

THE LOGIC OF INSTITUTIONAL COSMOPOLITANISM

The essential feature of institutional cosmopolitanism is the coexistence of institutions, often on the same territory. Their mutual recognition dispels any notion of a single *locus* of sovereign authority and ensures the legitimacy of both. This phenomenon of legitimate coexistence has been seen to extend to relations of the state with churches and religions and to relations of the state with other states,

---

[184] For restrictive application of 'odious' or prejudicial local legislation, Vogenauer (2001), *Die Auslegung von Gesetzen*, at 448–9; Zimmermann (1997), '*Statuta sunt stricte interpretanda?*', at 315; Lange (1997), *Römisches Recht im Mittelalter*, at 106.

[185] For the vast common law sources on the question, Dupont (2001), *The Common Law Abroad*.

[186] See this chapter, '*The cosmopolitan character of the new logics*'.

regional authorities, and transnational private authorities.[187] Their coexistence necessarily implies a multitude of values, and multivalent logic.

Cooperation has been seen as the most dominant form of church–state relations in Europe, derived from the 'multitude of common tasks' that link state and religious authority.[188] There even exists in the world a more general model of such cooperation and coexistence.[189] Yet conflict may easily be perceived in the relations of the state with churches and religions, whether derived from claims to religious liberty, the operation of religious personal laws, or the efforts to create a religious state. It is said that there is 'conflict' between 'legal secularism' and 'values evangelicanism' in the USA,[190] yet both are rooted in the First Amendment to the US Constitution with its non-establishment clause and its guarantee of freedom of religion. Both are thus affirmed and the division 'cannot be healed by the victory of either side'.[191] The binary division thus serves to mark the boundaries of the necessary middle ground and in this middle ground there would be no 'uniform answer', with much depending on the particular claim involved and 'discrete issues'.[192] In France a similar dichotomy between secular state law and religious norms is mediated by the 'religious fact' (le 'fait religieux'), a factual characterization of religiosity that brings many of its norms within the jurisdiction of secular courts.[193] In predominantly Muslim states the vesting of sovereignty in either God or the people is avoided by seeing neither option as 'totalistic', with the result that secular norms exist within the cadre of shari'a (which may or may not have been codified). Nor is it a question of having an Islamic state or not, but rather of states being Islamic in varying *degrees*.[194] Gordon Woodman has pointed out that many apparent conflicts between state and religious law may be matters not of outright conflict but of degree, as where religious law simply recommends or disapproves of types of conduct (as opposed to requiring or prohibiting it), and that this notion of degrees of culpability also exists in state law.[195] Here the law is 'degree-theoretic'.[196] Even in cases of

---

[187] See Ch. 13.

[188] Doe (2011), *Law and Religion in Europe*, at 2, 29, and see at 3 (for necessary creation of 'structures of dialogue').

[189] See Ch. 13, '*State and religious legal sources*'.

[190] Feldman (2005), *Divided by God*, at 235.

[191] Feldman (2005), *Divided by God*, at 236 (and need for reconciliation through 'simultaneously respecting' both religious liberty and institutional separation).

[192] Greenawalt (2006), *Religion and the Constitution*, at 1 (ideas of free exercise and non-establishment 'are not reducible to any single value; a number of values count') and see at 201 (for general terms of legal standards that require courts to 'evaluate burdens' on religious exercise and strength of governmental interests); and for similar 'weighing' of religious freedom and governmental interests in Japan, notably since withdrawal of the prohibition of Christianity in 1872 and establishment of religious freedom in 1875, Takahata (2007), 'Religious Accomodation in Japan', at 742, 733.

[193] See Ch.13, '*Religious liberty*'.

[194] See Ch.13, '*State and religious legal sources*'.

[195] Woodman (2008), 'Possibilities of Co-Existence', at 30 (citing degrees of homicide); and for degrees of civil fault or negligence, see this chapter, '*The cosmopolitan character of the new logics*'.

[196] For the notion as a characteristic of multivalence, see this chapter, '*The cosmopolitan character of the new logics*'.

clear incompatibility of texts it is not always necessary that one supersede the other. Woodman observes that it is feasible for 'two conflicting norms to coexist for very long periods, each being observed, and being disobeyed, to a certain extent'.[197] Joseph Raz has also observed that we do not know even how to calculate the degree to which a law is obeyed.[198] Incompatible texts may thus drift on and there is space between them for much individual choice.

The relations of states to one another are marked by cosmopolitan logic, in varying degrees. During the attempts at territorial and national closure binary logic was the order of the day, though its limits were evident in the necessary emergence of the disciplines of public and private international law and comparative law. These in their turn were constructed as much as possible along binary lines.[199] Today public international law has seen the return of the human person as a subject of rights, a phenomenon that requires normative appreciation of national law in the context of international human rights law.[200] Neither can be dismissed peremptorily; both are seen as presumptively applicable, in spite of contradiction. There is already discussion of the 'degree of bindingness' of both international and national norms,[201] and of the application in international law of both a principle of proportionality[202] and a 'margin of appreciation' of national law.[203] We have seen that customary international law could also be established according to a 'sliding scale'.[204] In private international law the binary process of deciding either according to the law of the forum or the law designated by a national choice-of-law rule is being openly subverted by various forms of 'substantivism' by virtue of which national laws are subject to appreciation in terms of established (though often

---

[197] Woodman (2008), 'Possibilities of Co-Existence', at 30 (hence the saying that laws 'observed more in the breach than in the observance').

[198] Raz (1980a), *Concept of a Legal System*, at 203 (asking how to calculate effect of multiple violations of speeding laws, or number of opportunities to obey the law); and see Raz (1980b), *Authority of Law*, at 42 ('[e]fficacy is the least controversial of these conditions. Oddly enough it is also the least studied and least understood. Perhaps there is not much which legal philosophy can contribute in this respect').

[199] See this chapter, '*The cosmopolitan limits of binary logic*'. Even comparative law was conceptualized as aiming at taxonomic classification of legal systems, though the project failed entirely: Glenn (2006), 'Comparative Legal Families', at 437 (citing the 'legal families trap').

[200] For this process of 'humanization', see Ch. 13, '*Public international law*'.

[201] Provost (2008), 'Judging in Splendid Isolation', at 148 (and 'the spectrum of bindingness'); McCrudden (2000), 'A Common Law of Human Rights?', notably at 512 (for national law less binding in field of human rights, gradations in strength of authorities); Ghai (2000), 'Human Rights as Framework', at 1139 ('simple polarities such as universalism/particularism, secular/religious, or tradition/modernity do not explain the complexity; a large measure of flexibility is necessary . . . ').

[202] Franck (2010), 'Proportionality in International Law', notably at 242 (on 'gradual narrowing of the range of indeterminacy inherent in the term proportionality'). For the notion in constitutional law, see this chapter, 'The Cosmopolitan Logic of Constitutionalism'.

[203] Shany (2006), 'Toward a General Margin of Appreciation', at 913 (particularly where application of international norms 'inherently or inevitably uncertain', as with norms expressed as standards, discretionary norms, and result-oriented norms); and for multivalent origins of the margin of appreciation in the law of the European Union, see this section.

[204] See Ch. 13, '*Public international law*'.

informal) criteria of material justice, or mutually interpreted to determine their appropriate application in space. Geographically dictated univalence is declining in importance.[205]

States have relations not only with churches, religions, and other states, but increasingly with regional organizations. The greater the role the regional organization is called upon to play, the greater the potential for apparent conflict with the states that are members of the organization. This has become a major subject of debate within Europe and the European Union; it is less visible within the lighter structures of NAFTA, MERCOSUR, or ASEAN.[206] Contemporary Europe has been described as functioning according to a 'logic of diversity' that entails both 'vague, innocuous-looking framework legislation' and 'political regulatory competition'.[207] A logic of diversity is accompanied necessarily by a 'shift away from binary conceptions of law'.[208] European law has therefore been described by Miguel Maduro as 'contrapunctual' and this would entail 'integrating the claims of validity of both national and EU constitutional law'.[209] This 'both and' logic (A and not-A) is thus inherent in institutional cosmopolitanism. It 'allows the different legal orders to adjust to the claims of the others and so prevents conflict between these claims'.[210] Nicholas Barber has stated explicitly that the law of non-contradiction is inapplicable in EU institutional relations, where one encounters 'inconsistent' rules of recognition and there is no higher constitutional body to resolve the dispute through adjudication or legislation.[211] 'Consistentising' the contradictions is therefore impossible, and the institutions must look beyond the contradictions to sustain their mutual relations. The best example is in the *Solange* jurisprudence, by virtue of which the German Constitutional Court acts on a presumption of the validity of EU legislation in German constitutional law, while reserving its ultimate power of appreciation.[212] The laws in question are non-monotonic, subject to intervening invalidation. Both sides may claim victory; neither side must admit defeat, and 'inconsistent laws need

---

[205] See Ch. 13, '*Private international law*'.

[206] For differences in structure, see Ch. 13, 'States and Regional Law'.

[207] Zielonka (2006), *Europe as Empire*, at 72 (and for increased diversity not yielding decision-making paralysis).

[208] Krisch (2010), *Beyond Constitutionalism*, at 305 ('a form of gradated authority').

[209] Maduro (2003a), 'Contrapunctual Law', at 524.

[210] Maduro (2003a), 'Contrapunctual Law', at 525.

[211] Barber (2006), 'Legal Pluralism and the EU', notably at 327 ('this inconsistency is sustainable if each side shows institutional restraint') and see at 309–10 (hope of establishing a system of deontic logic independent of particular systems of moral philosophy is too ambitious and 'the principle of non-contradiction need not be present in every plausible normative order').

[212] See Ch. 13, 'States and Regional Law'; and see Barber (2006), 'Legal Pluralism and the EU', at 323 on the *Solange* cases ('what makes these rival claims to adjudicative supremacy [of the ECJ and the German Constitutional Court] inconsistent is their assertion of finality ...') and 327 ('this inconsistency is sustainable if each side shows institutional restraint ... the simple certainties of sovereignty appear increasingly implausible').

not demand inconsistent action'.[213] Institutional cosmopolitanism requires adjustment of competing claims.[214]

The best-known instance of paraconsistent and multivalent logic in Europe is of course the margin of appreciation of national laws developed by the European Court of Human Rights.[215] By virtue of this margin or zone of discretion the Court refuses to construct a univocal or univalent interpretation of the European Convention on Human Rights, and this in order to allow multiple and varied state interpretations of it. Neither national sovereignty nor a single European standard necessarily prevails. The notion is closely linked to the 'institutional competence' of the ECtHR and is therefore an essential element of European institutional cosmopolitanism.[216] A continuum or range of alternatives is opened up, which may be seen as more or less compatible with European objectives.[217] The doctrine is similar to the variable levels of scrutiny developed by the United States Supreme Court.[218] In determining the breadth of the margin of appreciation in particular cases the Court relies on the presence or absence of a European consensus on the reading of a right. Where there is a Europe-wide consensus, the margin is narrow and the national law will be scrutinized closely. In the absence of such a European consensus, the margin is wide and there is an initial presumption in favour of the defendant state.[219]

Finally, there is a cosmopolitan and multivalent logic in the relations between states and private legal regulators. To the extent that states stand back and leave large fields of human activity to private regulation, now perhaps most visibly through transnational private regulation (TPR), there is a process of mutual recognition, mutual restraint, and collaboration.[220] The 'institutional complementarity' that results is one that relies necessarily on a 'both and' form of logic. Potential conflict is avoided through the mutual restraint; diversity or its potential is maintained throughout.

---

[213] Barber (2006), 'Legal Pluralism and the EU', at 328 ('the constitutional dilemma can remain unresolved').

[214] Maduro (2003a), 'Contrapunctual Law', at 527 (on 'coherent legal order in a context of competing determinations of the law'); Barber (2006), 'Legal Pluralism and the EU', at 316 ('possible to have inconsistent legal rules without forcing people or institutions to act unlawfully or, necessarily, compelling them to choose between the rules . . . there are sometimes political reasons for embracing inconsistent rules').

[215] See Ch. 13, 'States and Regional Law'.

[216] For 'institutional competence', Letsas (2006), 'Two Concepts of Margin of Appreciation', at 721 (also a 'structural concept' of margin of appreciation, though criticizing absence of European uniformity).

[217] The same concept has been used at least on one occasion by the European Court of Justice in *Dynamic Medien Vertriebs* v. *Avides Media* [2008] Case C–244/06, [2008] ECR I–505, para. 44, and its extension to the ECJ is urged in Gerards (2011), 'Pluralism, Deference and Margin of Appreciation'.

[218] See this chapter, '*The functioning of states*'.

[219] O'Donnell (1982), 'Margin of Appreciation Doctrine', at 475. The margin once established, the principle of proportionality then comes into play to determine whether the national measure involves no more than is necessary to achieves its objective.

[220] See Ch. 13, 'States and Transnational Law'.

⤳ 15 ⤳

Concluding Remarks

The closure of the contemporary state now appears as a thing of the past, if indeed it ever existed. This should not be seen as a failure (though there are failing individual states) but as a simple decline in the influence of important and ongoing ideas. Closure is inherently problematic, and remains constantly vulnerable to surrounding texture and the challenge of new and different forms of closure.

Our thinking of the contemporary state can therefore be facilitated by awareness of its cosmopolitan character. In each case the state is an instantiation of normative tradition, more precisely of normative traditions. States are therefore cosmopolitan in their origins. There is nothing binding in this and each state has been largely free to construct its own particular identity and institutions. Originality is found in detail and combination, but no state has been free from the influence of diverse strands of the state tradition. The information of the past, moreover, teaches both normativity and contingency. It is non-monotonic in character and its present reception always depends on present circumstance and present appreciation. This has been seen in the historical importance of notions of common law, constitutionalism, and institutional cosmopolitanism.

The cosmopolitan character of the contemporary state also explains much of its present operation. The state creates law but state law cannot replace, and often does not purport to replace, legal traditions that precede, justify, and continue to surround the law of the state. Nor can state law displace in their entirety legal traditions that are less compatible with state law. In all cases, however, we are dealing with legal information and, while individual pieces of information may be incompatible with one another, this form of contradiction does not necessarily yield conflict. The French philosophers Deleuze and Guattari once wrote that 'no one has ever died of contradictions' and the statement is an affirmation of the human capacity to overcome contradictions and to avoid human conflict.[1] Cosmopolitan legal thought may therefore seek to provide consistency and legal certainty where possible, but may also be paraconsistent in character where necessary. The new paraconsistent logics appear to be an important ally in this process.

---

[1] Deleuze, G. and Guattari, F. (2004), *Anti-Oedipus*, at 166 ('jamais personne n'est mort de contradictions').

Bibliography of References

Abdullah, N. and C. Hua (2007), 'Legislating Faith in Malaysia', Singapore Journal of Legal Studies 264.

Ackerman, B. (1997), 'The Rise of World Constitutionalism', 83 Virginia Law Review 771.

Acton, J. (1948), *Essays on Freedom and Power* (Boston: Beacon Press).

Adams, E. and D. Farber (1999), 'Beyond the Formalism Debate: Expert Reasoning, Fuzzy Logic, and Complex Statutes', 52 Vanderbilt Law Review 1243.

Adams, E., S. Nickles, and T. Ressler (1994), 'Wedding Carlson and Schwartz: Understanding Secured Credit and a Fuzzy System', 80 Virginia Law Review 2233.

Adams, E. and T. Spaak (1995), 'Fuzzifying the Natural Law—Legal Positivist Debate', 43 Buffalo Law Review 85.

Adamson, R. (2005), 'Law, Sovereignty, and Transnationalism: Delivering Social Goods Using a Functional Approach to Borders', in Nicol and Townsend Gault (2005), *Holding the line: Borders in a global world* (Vancouver: UBC. Press) at 59.

Afsaruddin, A. (2006), 'The "Islamic State": Genealogy, Facts and Myths', 48 Journal of Church and State 153.

Agallopoulou, P. and C. Deliyanni-Dimitrakou (1999), 'L'utilisation du droit comparé par les tribunaux helléniques', in Drobnig and van Erp (1999), *Use of Comparative Law*, at 149.

Agamben, G. (2000), *Means without End[:] Notes on Politics*, trans. V. Binetti and C. Casarino, (Minneapolis: University of Minnesota Press).

Ahdar, R. and I. Leigh (2005), *Religious Freedom in the Liberal State* (Oxford: Oxford University Press).

Ahdar, R. and N. Aroney (2010), *Shari'a in the West* (Oxford: Oxford University Press).

Ahdieh, R. (2008), 'Foreign Affairs, International Law, and the New Federalism: Lessons from Coordination', 73 Missouri Law Review 1185.

Ahmad, S. (1999), *Malaysian Legal System* (Singapore: Butterworths).

Aleinikoff, A. (1987), 'Constitutional Law in the Age of Balancing', 96 Yale Law Journal 943.

Alexy, R. (2010a), *A Theory of Constitutional Rights*, trans. J. Rivers (Oxford: Oxford University Press).

Alexy, R. (2010b), 'The Construction of Constitutional Rights', 4(1) Law & Ethics of Human Rights Article 2.

Alford, R. (2008), 'Lower Courts and Constitutional Comparativism', 77 Fordham Law Review 647.

al-Hibri, A. (1992), 'Islamic Constitutionalism and the Concept of Democracy', 24 Case Western Reserve Journal of International Law 1.

Allain, J. (2011), 'Acculturation through the Middle Ages: The Islamic Law of Nations and its place in the History of International Law', in A. Orakhelashvili (ed.) (2011), *Research Handbook on the Theory and History of International Law* (Cheltenham: Edward Elgar), at 394.

Allan, J., G. Huscroft, and N. Lynch (2007), 'The Citation of Overseas Authority in Rights Litigation in New Zealand: How Much Bark? How Much Bite?', 11 Otago Law Review 1.

Allard, J. and A. Garapon (2005), *Les juges dans la mondialisation: la nouvelle révolution du droit* (Paris: Seuil).

Allen, C. K. (1861), 'Introduction', in Maine (1861), Ancient Law.

Allen, F., J. Qian, and M. Qian (2005), 'Law, Finance, and Economic Growth in China', 77 Journal of Financial Economics 57.

Allen, S. and A. Xanthaki (eds) (2010), *Reflections on the United Nations Declaration on the Rights of Indigenous Peoples and International Law* (Oxford: Hart).

Allen, S. and A. Xanthaki (2011), *Reflections on the UN Declaration on the Rights of Indigenous Peoples* (Oxford: Hart Publishing).

Allison, J. (1996), *A Continental Distinction in the Common Law* (Oxford: Oxford University Press).

Allott, P. (2001), *Eunomia. New Order for a New World* (Oxford: Oxford University Press).

Allott, P. (2002), *The Health of Nations[:] Society and Law beyond the State* (Cambridge: Cambridge University Press).

Al-Muhairi, B. (1996), 'Islamisation and Modernisation within the UAE Penal Law: The Shari'a in the Modern Era', 11 Arab Law Quarterly 34.

Alpa, G. (2005), *Tradition and Europeanization in Italian Law* (London: British Institute of International and Comparative Law).

Alter, K. (2006), 'Private Litigants and the New International Courts', 39 Comparative Political Studies 22.

Alvarez, J. (2005), *International Organizations as Law-Makers* (New York: Oxford University Press).

Aman, A., Jr. (1998), 'The Globalizing State: A Future-Oriented Perspective on the Public/Private Distinction, Federalism, and Democracy', 31 Vanderbilt Journal of Transnational Law 769.

Amar, A. (2012), *America's Unwritten Constitution: The Precedents and Principles We Live By* (New York: Basic Books).

Ambrus, M. (2009), 'Comparative Law Method in the Jurisprudence of the European Court of Human Rights in the Light of the Rule of Law', 2 Erasmus Law Review 353.

Amin, S. (1985), *Middle East Legal Systems* (Glasgow: Royston).

Amir-Moezzi, M. and C. Jambet (2004), *Qu'est-ce que le shî'isme?* (Paris: Fayard).

Anagnostou, D. and E. Psychogiopoulou (eds) (2010), *The European Court of Human Rights and the Rights of Marginalised Individuals and Minorities in National Context* (Leiden: Martinus Nijhoff).

Anaya, S. (2004), *Indigenous Peoples in International Law*, 2nd edn (Oxford: Oxford University Press).

Andenas, M. and D. Fairgrieve (2004), 'Introduction: Finding a Common Language for Open Legal Systems', in Canivet, Andenas, and Fairgrieve, *Comparative Law Before the Courts*, at xxvii.

Anderheiden, M., S. Huster, and S. Kirste (eds) (2001), *Globalisierung als Problem von Gerechtigkeit und Steuerungsfähigkeit des Rechts* (Stuttgart: Franz Steiner).

Anderson, B. (1983), *Imagined Communities: Reflections on the Origin and Spread of Nationalism* (New York: Verso).

Anderson, K. (2005), 'Foreign Law and the US Constitution', 131 Policy Review 33.

Angelo, T. (1999), 'Culture Protection, Language and Law', in Jayme (1999), *Langue et Droit*, at 271.

Anghie, A. (2004), *Imperialism, Sovereignty and the Making of International Law* (Cambridge: Cambridge University Press).

An-Na'im, A. (1998–9), 'Shari'a and Positive Legislation: is an Islamic State Possible or Viable?', 5 Yearbook of Islamic & Middle Eastern Law 29.

An-Na'im, A. (2006), *African Constitutionalism and the Role of Islam* (Philadelphia: University of Pennsylvania Press).

An-Na'im, A. (2008), *Islam and the Secular State[:] Negotiasting the Future of Shari'a* (Cambridge, MA: Harvard University Press).

An-Na'im, A. (2010), 'The Compatibility Dialectic: Mediating the Legitimate Coexistence of Islamic Law and State Law', 73 MLR 1.

Anon. (1986), 'The Cultural Defense in the Criminal Law', 99 Harvard Law Review 1293.

Anthony, G., J-B. Auby, J. Morison, and T. Zwart (eds) (2011), *Values in Global Administrative Law* (Oxford: Hart).

Aoláin, F. (2010), 'Learning the Lessons: What Feminist Legal Theory Teaches International Human Rights Law and Practice', in M. Fineman (ed.) (2010) *Transcending the Boundaries of Law: Generations of Feminism and Legal Theory* (New York: Routledge), at 281.

Aoun, M. (ed.) (2009), *Les statuts personnels en droit comparé* (Leuven: Peeters).

Appiah, K. (2005), *The Ethics of Identity* (Princeton, NJ: Princeton University Press).

Appiah, K. (2006), *Cosmopolitanism[:] Ethics in a World of Strangers* (New York: W. W. Norton & Company).

Arabi, O. (2001), *Studies in Modern Islamic Law and Jurisprudence* (The Hague: Kluwer).

Arai-Takahashi, Y. (2002), *The Margin of Appreciation Doctrine and the Principle of Proportionality in the Jurisprudence of the ECHR* (Antwerp: Intersentia).

Arbos, X. (2005), 'Le constitutionalisme espagnol et le fédéralisme', in Noreau and Woehrling (2005), *Appartenances, institutions et cioyenneté*, at 81.

Archibugi, D. (2008), *The Global Commonwealth of Citizens: Toward Cosmopolitan Democracy* (Princeton, NJ: Princeton University Press).

Archibugi, D., S. Benhabib, and M. Croce (2010), 'Towards a Converging Cosmopolitan Project', published on openDemocracy, accessible at <http://www.danielarchibugi.org/downloads/papers/cosmopolitanoproject.pdf.>

Ariens, M. and R. Destro (2002), *Religious Liberty in a Pluralistic Society*, 2nd edn (Durham, NC: Carolina Academic Press).

Aristotle (2008a), *The Metaphysics*, trans. J. H. McMahon (New York: Cosimo).

Aristotle (2008b), *Politics*, trans. B. Jowett and H. W. C. Davis (New York: Cosimo).

Armitage, D. (2002), *The Ideological Origins of the British Empire* (Cambridge: Cambridge University Press).

Armitage, D. (2007), *The Declaration of Independence[:] A Global History* (Cambridge, MA: Harvard University Press).

Asch, R. (1997), *The Thirty Years War: The Holy Roman Empire and Europe, 1618–48* (New York: St. Martin's Press).

Ashburn, D. (1994), 'Appealing to a Higher Authority? Jewish Law in American Judicial Opinions', 71 University of Detroit Mercy Law Review 295.

Aslan, M. (2005), 'Rückfahrkarte', 7 Rechtsgeschichte 33.

Assies, W., G. Van der Haar, and A. Hoekema (2000), *The Challenge of Diversity* (Amsterdam: Thela Thesis).

Assimakopoulou, K. (1986), 'Comparative Law in the History of Greek Law', 39 Revue hellénique de droit international 323.

Association Henri Capitant (2002), *Les minorities* (Mexico: Instituto de Investigaciones Jurídicas).

Association Henri Capitant (2006), *Les droits de tradition civiliste en question* (Paris: Société de législation comparé).

Auby, J-B. (2003), *La globalisation, le droit et l'Etat* (Paris: Montchrestien).

Augenstein, D. (2012), 'Religious Pluralism and National Constitutional Traditions in Europe', in Zucca and Ungureanu (2012), *Law, State and Religion*, at 261.

Austin, J. (1832), *The Province of Jurisprudence Determined* (London: John Murray).

Avineri, S. (1972), *Hegel's Theory of the Modern State* (Cambridge: Cambridge University Press).

Bachand, F. (2005), *L'intervention du juge canadien avant et durant l'arbitrage commercial international* (Paris: LGDJ).

Baderin, M. (2003), *International Human Rights and Islamic Law* (Oxford: Oxford University Press).

Badie, B. (2000), *The Imported State[:] The Westernization of the Political Order*, trans. C. Royal (Stanford, CA: Stanford University Press).

Bagehot, W. (1958), *The English Constitution* (London: Oxford University Press).

Bailyn, B. (1967), *The Ideological Origins of the American Revolution* (Cambridge, MA: Belknap Press of Harvard University Press).

Bakalis, C. and P. Edge (2009), 'Taking Due Account of Religion in Sentencing', 29 LS 421.

Baker, J. H. (1998), 'The Three Languages of the Common Law' (1998),) 43 McGill Law Journal 5.

Baker, J. H. (2002), *An Introduction to English Legal History*, 4th edn (London: Butterworths).

Baker, R. (2003), *Islam Without Fear[:] Egypt and the New Islamists* (Cambridge, MA: Harvard University Press).

Balaguer-Callejon, F. (2001), 'Der Verfassungsstaat in ibero-amerikanischen Kontext', in Morlok (2001), *Die Welt des Verfassungsstaates* (Baden-Baden: Nomos), at 189.

Baldus, M. (1997), 'Zur Relevanz des Souveränitätsproblems für die Wissenschaft vom öffentlichen Recht', 36 Der Staat 381.

Balkin, J. (2011), *Living Originalism* (Cambridge, MA: Harvard University Press).

Ball, T., J. Farr, and R. Hansen (eds) (1989), *Political Innovation and Conceptual Change* (Cambridge: Cambridge University Press).

Bälz, K. (1998), 'Die "Islamisierung" des Rechts in Ägypten und Libyen: Islamische Rechtsetzung im Nationalstaat', Rabels Zeitschrift fur Auslandisches und Internationales Privatrecht, 437.

Bälz, K. (2000), 'Human Rights, the Rule of Law and the Construction of Tradition: The Egyptian Supreme Administrative Court and Female Circumcision', in Cotran and Yamani (2000), *Rule of Law in Middle East*, at 35.

Bambach, L. (2009–10), 'The Enforceability of Arbitration Decisions made by Muslim Religious Tribunals: Examining the Beth Din Precedent', 25 Journal of Law and Religion 379.

Banner, S. (2005), *How the Indians Lost Their Land* (Cambridge, MA: Harvard University Press).

Barak, A. (2005), 'Response to *The Judge as Comparatist*: Comparison in Public Law', 80 Tulane Law Review 195.

Barak, A. (2010), 'Proportionality and Principled Balancing', 4(1) Law & Ethics of Human Rights, Article 1.

Barber, N. (2006), 'Legal Pluralism and the European Union', 12 European Law Journal 306.

Barber, N. (2010), *The Constitutional State* (Oxford: Oxford University Press).

Barker, E. (1957), 'Introduction', in Gierke (1957), *Natural Law and the Theory of Society*, trans. E. Barker (Boston: Beacon Press).

Barker, G. (2006), *The Agricultural Revolution in Prehistory* (Oxford: Oxford University Press).

Barry, K. (2006), 'Home and Away: The Construction of Citizenship in an Emigration Context' (2006),) 81 NYU Law Review 11.

Bart, W. (2008), *On Cultural Rights: The Equality of Nations and the Minority Legal Tradition* (Leiden: Martinus Nijhoff).

Bartelson, J. (1995), *A Genealogy of Sovereignty* (Cambridge: Cambridge University Press).

Bartelson, J. (2001), *The Critique of the State* (Cambridge: Cambridge University Press).

Bartlett, R. (1993), *The Making of Europe[:] Conquest, Colonization and Cultural Change 930–1350* (London: Penguin).

Bassett, W. (1978), 'Canon Law and the Common Law', 29 Hastings Law Journal 1383

Bastos, S. and M. Camus (2004), 'Multiculturalismo y pueblos indígenas: reflexiones a partir del caso de Guatemala', 1 Revista centroamericana de ciencias sociales 87.

Bates, R. (2008), *When Things Fell Apart[:] State Failure in Late-Century Africa* (Cambridge: Cambridge University Press).

Batiffol, H. and P. Lagarde (1981–3), *Droit international privé*, vol. I (1981), vol. II (1983), (Paris: LGDJ).

Baxter, W. (1963), 'Choice of Law and the Federal System', 16 Stanford Law Review 1.

Baylis, J. and S. Smith (eds) (2001), *The Globalization of World Politics[:] An introduction to international relations*, 2nd edn (Oxford: Oxford University Press).

Bayly, C. A. (2004), *The Birth of the Modern World 1780–1914[:] Global Connections and Comparisons* (Oxford: Blackwell).

Beall, J. C. and G. Restall (2006), *Logical Pluralism* (Oxford: Clarendon Press).

Beatty, D. (2004), *The Ultimate Rule of Law* (Oxford: Oxford University Press).

Beaulac, S. (2000), 'The Westphalian Legal Orthodoxy—Myth or Reality?', 2 Journal of the History of International Law 148.

Beaupré, R. M. (1986), *Interprétation de la législation bilingue* (Montreal: Wilson & Lafleur).

Beauthier, R. (2007), *Droit et genèse de L'État*, 3rd edn (Brussels: Editions de l'Université de Bruxelles).

Beck, U. (2005), 'The Cosmopolitan State: Redefining Power in the Global Age', 18 Internationall Journal of Politics, Culture and Society 143.

Beck, U. and C. Lau, (2004), *Entgrenzung und Entscheidung: Was ist neu an der Theorie reflexiver Modernisierung?* (Frankfurt: Suhrkamp).

Bederman, D. (2008a), *The Classical Foundations of the American Constitution[:] Prevailing Wisdom* (Cambridge: Cambridge University Press).

Bederman, D. (2008b), 'The Classical Constitution: Roman Republican Origins of the *Habeas* Suspension Clause', 17 Southern California Interdisciplinary Law Journal 405.

Beiner, R. (ed.) (1995), *Theorizing Citizenship* (Albany: State University of New York Press).

Beitz, C. (2000), 'Rawls's Law of Peoples', 110 Ethics 669.

Belaïd, S. (1994), 'Les constitutions dans le Tiers-Monde', in Troper and Jaume (1994), *1789*, at 100.

Bell, C. (2008), *On the Law of Peace* (Oxford: Oxford University Press).

Bell, D. (2003), 'The Making and Unmaking of Boundaries: A Contemporary Confucian Perspective', in Buchanan and Moore (2003), *States, Nations, and Borders*, at 57.

Bell, D. A. (2001), *The Cult of the Nation in France[:] Inventing Nationalism 1680–1800* (Cambridge, MA: Harvard University Press).

Bell, G. (2006), 'Multiculturalism in Law is Legal Pluralism: Lessons from Indonesia, Singapore and Canada', Singapore Journal of Legal Studies 315.

Bellah, R. (2011), *Religion in Human Evolution: From the Paleolithic to the Axial Age* (Cambridge, MA: Belknap Press).

Bellamy, R. (2004), 'Introduction: The Making of Modern Citizenship', in Bellamy, Castiglione, and Santoro (2004), *Lineages of European Citizenship*, at 1.

Bellamy, R., D. Castiglione, and E. Santoro (eds) (2004), *Lineages of European Citizenship[:] Rights, Belonging and Participation in Eleven Nation-States* (New York: Palgrave Macmillan).

Bellia, A. and B. Clark (2009), 'The Federal Common Law of Nations', 109 Columbia Law Review 1.

Beltran, J. and G. Ratti (eds) (2012), *The Logic of Legal Requirements: Essays on Defeasibility* (Oxford: Oxford University Press).

Benard, A. (2008), 'The Advantage to Islam of Mosque–State Separation: What the American Founders Can Teach', 147 Policy Review 65.

Bender, T. (2006a), *A Nation Among Nations[:] America's Place in World History* (New York: Hill and Wang).

Bender, T. (2006b), 'No Borders: Beyond the Nation-State', *Chronicle of Higher Education*, 7 April (2006), at B6.

Bendix, R. (1978), *Kings or People[:] Power and the Mandate to Rule* (Berkeley: University of California Press).

Beneke, C. (2006), *Beyond Toleration: The Religious Origins of American Pluralism* (New York: Oxford University Press).

Benhabib, S. (2002), *The Claims of Culture* (Princeton, NJ: Princeton University Press).

Benhabib, S. (2004), *The Rights of Others[:] Aliens, Residents, and Citizens* (Cambridge: Cambridge University Press).

Benhabib, S. (2006), *Another Cosmopolitanism*, R. Post (ed.) (New York: Oxford University Press).

Ben-Menahem, H. (1996), 'Postscript: The Judicial Process and the Nature of Jewish Law', in Hecht *et al* (eds), *Introduction to History and Sources of Jewish Law*, at 421.

Bentham, J. (1970), *An Introduction to the Principles of Morals and Legislation* (1789), ed. J. Burns and H. L. A. Hart (Cambridge: Cambridge University Press).

Benton, L. (2010), *A Search for Sovereignty: Law and Geography in European Empires, 1400–1900,* (New York: Cambridge University Press).

Benton, L. and B. Straumann (2010), 'Acquiring Empire by Law: From Roman Doctrine to Early Modern European Practices' (2010) 28 Law & History Review 1.

Benvenisti, E. and G. Downs (2011), 'National Courts Review of Transnational Private Regulation', accessible at <http://ssrn.com/abstract=1742452>.

Benyekhlef, K. (2008), *Une possible histoire de la norme[:] Les normativités émergentes de la mondialisation* (Montreal: Thémis).

Berg, T. (ed.) (2008a), *The First Amendment[:] The Free Exercise of Religion Clause* (Amherst, NY: Prometheus Books).

Berg, T. (2008b), 'Introductory Essay', in Berg (2008a), *The First Amendment*, at 17.

Bergel, J-L. (1988) (ed.), *Les standards dans les divers systèmes juridiques*, 13 Revue de la recherche juridique 805.

Berger, S. and C. Lorenz (eds) (2010), *Nationalizing the Past: Historians as Nation Builders in Modern Europe* (New York: Palgrave Macmillan).

Bering, R. (2000), 'Legal Information and the Search for Cognitive Authority', 88 California Law Review 1675.

Berman, H. (1983), *Law and Revolution: The Formation of the Western Legal Tradition* (Cambridge, MA: Harvard University Press).

Berman, H. (1995), 'World Law', 18 Fordham International Law Journal 1617.

Berman, H. (2003), *Law and Revolution, II[:] The Impact of the Protestant Reformation on the Western Legal Tradition* (Cambridge, MA: Harvard University Press).

Berman, H. (2005), 'Is Conflict of Laws becoming Passé? An Historical Response', in H-E. Rasmussen-Bonne, R. Freer, and W. Lüke, *Balancing of Interests, Liber Amicorum Peter Hay* (Frankfurt: Recht und Wirtschaft) at 43.

Berman, P. (2002), 'The Globalization of Jurisdiction', 151 University of Pennsylvania Law Review 311.

Bermann, G. (1994), 'Taking Subsidiarity Seriously: Federalism in the European Community and the United States', 94 Columbia Law Review 331.

Bermann, G., M. Herdegen, and P. Lindseth (eds) (2000), *Transatlantic Regulatory Co-operation* (New York: Oxford University Press).

Berryman, J. (2007), 'Accommodating Ethnic and Cultural Factors in Damages for Personal Injury', 40 University of British Columbia Law Review 1.

Bertelli, S. (2001), *The King's Body*, trans. R. B. Litchfield (University Park: Pennsylvania State University Press).

Besson, S. (2005), *The Morality of Conflict[:] Reasonable Disagreement and the Law* (Oxford: Hart).

von Beyme, K. (2002), 'Globalisierung, Europäisierung, nationalstaatliche Integration und Regionalisierung', in H. Münkler, M. Llanque, and C. K. Stepina (eds) (2002), *Der demokratische Nationalstaat in den Zeiten der Globalisierung, Festschrift Iring Fetscher* (Berlin: Akademie Verlag), at 101.

Bhagwati, J. (2008), *Termites in the Trading System: How Preferential Agreements Undermine Free Trade* (New York: Oxford University Press).

Biggs, M. (1999), 'Putting the State on the Map: Cartography, Territory and European State Formation', 41 Comparative Studies in Society & History 374.

Bilder, M. (2004), *The Transatlantic Constitution[:] Colonial Legal Culture and the Empire* (Cambridge MA: Harvard University Press).

Bilder, M. (2009), 'Colonial Constitutionalism and Constitutional Law', in A. Brophy and D. Hamilton (eds) (2009), *Transformations in American Legal History: Essays in Honor of Morton J. Horwitz* (Cambridge, MA: Harvard University Press), at 28.

Billias, G. (2009), *American Constitutionalism Heard Round the World, 1776–1989: A Global Perspective* (New York: New York University Press).

Bimbó, K. (2007), 'Relevance Logics', in Jacquette (2007), *Philosophy of Logic*, at 723.

Bingham, T. (1992), ' "There is a World Elsewhere": The Changing Perspectives of English Law', 41 ICLQ 513.

Birkinshaw, P. (2003), *European Public Law* (London: Butterworths LexisNexis).

Black, J. (1997), *Maps and Politics* (London: Reaktion Books).

Black, J. (2004), *Kings, Nobles and Commoners: States and Societies in Early Modern Europe, a Revisionist History* (London: IB Tauris).

Blackman, J. (2010), 'Original Citizenship', 159 University of Pennsylvania Law Review 95.

Blackstone, W. (1773), *Commentaries on the Laws of England* (Dublin: J. Exshaw).

Blake, G., C. Sien, C. Grundy-Warr, M. Pratt, and C. Schofield (eds) (1997), *International Boundaries and Environmental Security* (The Hague: Kluwer International).

Bloxham, D. (2009), *The Final Solution[:] A Genocide* (Oxford: Oxford University Press).

Blumenthal, U-R. (1988), *The Investiture Controversy[:] Church and Monarchy from the Ninth to the Twelfth Century* (Philadelphia: University of Pennsylvania Press).

Bobbio, N. (1965), 'Des critères pour résoudre les antinomies', in Perelman (1965a), *Les antinomies en droit*, at 237.

Bobbitt, P. (2002), *The Shield of Achilles[:] War, Peace and the Course of History* (London: Allen Lane).

Böckenförde, E-W. (1991), *Recht, Staat, Freiheit* (Frankfurt: Suhrkamp).

Böckli, P. (1997), 'Osmosis of Anglo-Saxon Concepts in Swiss Business Law', in N. P. Vogt, *The International Practice of Law[:]* Liber Amicorum *for Thomas Bär and Robert Karrer* (The Hague: Kluwer), at 9.

Böckstiegel, S. (1991), 'Commercial Arbitration—Practice and Prospects', in Hague Academy of International Law (D. Bardonnet ed.), *The Peaceful Settlement of International Disputes in Europe: Future Prospects* (Dordrecht: Martinus Nijhoff), at 269.

Bodin J. (1986), *Les six livres de la République* (Paris: Fayard).

von Bogdandy, A. (1996), 'The Contours of Integrated Europe: The Origin, Status and Prospects of European Integration', in V. Gessner, A Hoeland, and C. Varga (eds) (1996), *European Legal Cultures* (Aldershot: Dartmouth) at 506.

von Bogdandy, A. (2008), 'Pluralism, direct effect, and the ultimate say: On the relationship between international and domestic constitutional law', 6 International Journal of Constitutional Law 397.

Boggs, S. W. (1940), *Boundaries[:] A Study of Boundary Functions and Problems* (New York: Columbia University Press).

Bohman, J. (2009), 'Cosmopolitan Republicanism and the Rule of Law', in S. Besson and M. Luis (eds), *Legal Republicanism* (Oxford: Oxford University Press, (2009)) at 60.

Bohman, J. and M. Lutz-Bachman (eds) (1997), *Perpetual Peace: Essays on Kant's Cosmopolitan Ideal* (Cambridge, MA: MIT Press).

Bomhoff, J. (2010), 'Genealogies of Balancing as Discourse', 4(1), Law & Ethics of Human Rights, Article 6.

Bonventre, V. (2006), 'Aristotle, Cicero and Cardozo: A Perspective on External Law', 69 Albany Law Review 645.

Borda, A. (2009), 'Constitutional Law in the Commonwealth: A brief comparative analysis', Journal of the Commonwealth Lawyers' Association 37.

Boreham, K. (2008), 'International Law as an Influence on the Development of the Common Law: *Evans v. State of New South Wales*', 19 Public Law Review 271.

Borgeaud, Ph. (2004), *Aux origines de l'histoire des religions* (Paris: Éditions du Seuil).

Börzel, T. (2002), *States and Regions in the European Union[:] Institutional Adaptation in Germany and Spain* (Cambridge: Cambridge University Press).

Bosniak, L. (2000), 'Citizenship Denationalized', 7 Indiana Journal of Global Legal Studies 447.

Bosniak, L. (2006), *The Citizen and the Alien[:] Dilemmas of Contemporary Membership* (Princeton, NJ: Princeton University Press).

Bosniak, L. (2010), 'Persons and Citizens in Constitutional Thought', 8 International Journal of Constitutional Law 9.

Bossuat, A. (1971), 'The Maxim "The King is Emperor in his Kingdom": Its Use in the Fifteenth Century before the *Parlement* of Paris', in Lewis (1971), *The Recovery of France*, at 185.

Botiveau, B. (1993), 'Contemporary Reinterpretations of Islamic Law: The Case of Egypt', in Mallat (1993a), Islam and Public Law, at 261.

Bouchard, G. and C. Taylor (2008), *Building for the Future: A Time for Reconciliation (Abridged Report)* (Quebec: Gouvernement du Québec).

Bowden, B. (2005), 'The Colonial Origins of International Law. European Expansion and the Classical Standards of Civilization', 7 Journal of the History of International Law 1.

Bowyer, G. (1854), *Commentaries on Universal Public Law* (London: Stevens & Norton).

Boyarin, J. (1992), *Storm from Paradise[:] The Politics of Jewish Memory* (Minneapolis: University of Minnesota Press).

Boyarin, J. (ed.) (1994a), *Remapping Memory[:] The Politics of TimeSpace* (Minneapolis: University of Minneapolis Press).

Boyarin, J. (1994b), 'Space, Time and the Politics of Memory', in Boyarin (1994a), *Remapping Memory*, at 1.

Boyle, J. (1987), 'Thomas Hobbes and the Invented Tradition of Positivism: Reflections on Language, Power, and Essentialism', 135 University of Pennsylvania Law Review 383.

Bracken, P. (1995), 'The Military Crisis of the Nation State: will Asia be different from Europe', in Dunn (1995), *Contemporary Crisis of the Nation State?*, at 97.

Bradley, C. and J. Goldsmith (1997), 'Customary Law as Federal Common Law', 110 Harvard Law Review 815.

Bragg, M. (2003), *The Adventure of English* (London: Hodder and Stoughton).

Brague, R. (2005), *La Loi de Dieu* (Paris: Gallimard).

Brandom, R. (1994), *Making it Explicit[:] Reasoning, Representing and Discursive Commitment* (Cambridge MA: Harvard University Press).

Breen, M. (2011), 'Law, Society and the State in Early Modern France', 83 Journal of Modern History 346.

Breyer, S. (2003), 'Keynote Address', 97 ASIL Proceedings 214.

Brierly, J. (1963), *The Law of Nations[:] An Introduction to the International Law of Peace*, 6th edn by H. Waldock (Oxford: Clarendon Press).

Brierley, J. (1985), 'Quebec Arbitration Law: A New Era Begins' (1985) 40 Arbitration Journal 31.

Brissaud, J. (1915), *A History of French Public Law*, trans. J. W. Garner (London: John Murray).

Brito Malgarejo, R. (2010), 'El uso de sentencias extranjeras en los Tribunales Constitucionales', (2010) 2 InDret (online; available at <http://www.indret.com/en/>).

Brock, G. (2009), *Global Justice[:] A Cosmopolitan Account* (Oxford: Oxford University Press).

Brock, G. and H. Brighouse (eds) (2005), *The Political Philosophy of Cosmopolitanism* (Cambridge: Cambridge University Press).

Brouwer, B. (ed.) (1992), *Coherence and Conflict in Law* (Deventer: Kluwer, (1992)).

Brown, E. G. (1964), *British Statutes in American Law 1776–1836* (Ann Arbor: University of Michigan Press).

Brown, K. (2005), *Reconciling Customary Law and Received Law in Melanesia: the Post-Independence Experience in Solomon Islands and Vanuatu* (Darwin: Charles Darwin University Press).

Brown, N. (2001), *Constitutions in a Non-Constitutional World: Arab Basic Laws and the Prospects for Accountable Government* (Albany, NY: SUNY Press).

Brown, P. (2003), *The Rise of Western Christendom*, 2nd edn (Oxford: Blackwell).

Brubaker, R. (ed.) (1989), *Immigration and the Politics of Citizenship in Europe and North America* (Latham, MD: University Press of America).

Brubaker, R. (1992), *Citizenship and Nationhood in France and Germany* (Cambridge, MA: Harvard University Press).

Brunner, O. (1963), 'Vom Gottesgnadentum zum monarchischen Princip: Der Weg der europäischen Monarchie seit dem hohen Mittelalter', in Mayer (1963), *Das Königtum*, at 279.

Brunot, F. (ed.) (1927–43), *Histoire de la langue française* (13 vols) (Paris: Armand Colin.

Brütsch, C. and D. Lehmkuhl (eds) (2007), *Law and Legalization in Transnational Relations* (New York: Routledge).

Bryde, B-O. (2001), 'Der Verfassungsstaat in Afrika', in Morlok (2001), *Die Welt des Verfassungsstaates*, at 203.

Bryde, B-O. (2003), 'The Internationalization of Constitutional Law', in T. Gross (ed.) (2003), *Legal Scholarship in International and Comparative Law* (Frankfurt: Peter Lang), at 191.

Brysk, A. (2000), *From Tribal Village to Global Village[:] Indian Rights and International Relations in Latin America* (Stanford, CA: Stanford University Press).

Bryson, W. (1984), 'The Use of Roman Law in Virginia Courts', 28 American Journal of Legal History 135.

Buchanan, A. (2000), 'Rawls's Law of Peoples: Rules for a Vanished Westphalian World', 110 Ethics 697.

Buchanan, A. (2003), 'The Making and Unmaking of Boundaries: What Liberalism Has to Say', in Buchanan and Moore (2003), *States, Nations, and Borders*, at 231.

Buchanan, A. and M. Moore (2003), *States, Nations, and Borders[:] The Ethics of Making Boundaries* (Cambridge: Cambridge University Press).

Büchler, A. (2012), 'Islamic Family Law in Europe: from Dichotomies to Discourse', 8 International Journal of Law in Context 196.

Bulygin, E. (2008), 'What Can One Expect from Logic in the Law? (Not Everything but More than Something: A Reply to Susan Haack)', 21 Ratio Juris 150.

Burbank, J. and F. Cooper (2010), *Empires in World History* (Princeton, NJ: Princeton University Press).

Burns, J. H. (1988), *The Cambridge History of Medieval Political Thought c. 350–c. 1450* (Cambridge: Cambridge University Press).

Burns, J. H. (1991), *The Cambridge History of Political Thought 1450–1700* (Cambridge: Cambridge University Press).

Burns, P. (2004), *The Leiden Legacy[:] Concepts of Law in Indonesia* (Leiden: KITLV Press).

Burns, R. I. (ed.) (2000), *Las Siete Partidas*, trans. S. P. Scott (Philadelphia: University of Pennsylvania Press).

von Busse, G. (1928), *Die Lehre vom Staat als Organismus* (Berlin: Junker und Dunnhaupt).

Butler, J. (1964), *Fifteen Sermons Preached at the Rolls Chapel* (London: G. Bell).

Büttner, H. (1963), 'Aus den Anfängen des abendländischen Staatsgedankens', in Mayer (1963), *Das Königtum*, at 143.

Cabrera, L. (2004), *Political Theory of Global Justice[:] A Cosmopolitan Case for the World State* (London: Routledge).

Cadiet, L. (2001), 'L'hypothèse de l'américansation de la justice française[:] Mythe et réalité', 45 Archives de philosophie du droit 89.

Cafaggi, F. (2011a), 'Private Regulation in European Private Law', in A. Hartkamp, M. Hesselink, E. Hondiua, C. Mak, and C. E. du Perron (2011), *Towards a European Civil Code,* 4th edn (The Hague: Kluwer International), at 91.

Cafaggi, F. (2011b), 'New Foundations of Transnational Private Regulation', 38 Journal of Law & Society 20.

Cafaggi, F. and H. Muir Watt (eds) (2008), *Making European Private Law* (Cheltenham: Edward Elgar, (2008).

Cairns, J. and P. du Plessis (eds) (2010), *The Creation of the Ius Commune* (Edinburgh: Edinburgh University Press).

Calabresi, S. (2006), '"A Shining City on a Hill": American Exceptionalism and the Supreme Court's Practice of Relying on Foreign Law', 86 Boston University Law Review 1335.

Calabresi, S. and S. Zimdahl (2005), 'The Supreme Court and Foreign Sources of Law: Two Hundred Years of Practice and the Juvenile Death Penalty Decision', 47 William & Mary Law Review 743.

Calasso, F. (1970), *Introduzione al diritto commune* (Milano: Giuffrè).

Calliess, G. and P. Zumbansen (2010), *Rough Consensus and Running Code: A Theory of Transnational Private Law* (Oxford: Hart).

Calo, Z. R. (2010), 'Pluralism, Secularism and the European Court of Human Rights', 26 Journal of Law and Religion 261.

Cane, P., C. Evans, and Z. Robinson (eds) (2008), *Law and Religion in Theoretical and Historical Context* (Cambridge: Cambridge University Press).

Caney, S. (2006), *Justice Beyond Borders: A Global Political Theory* (Oxford: Oxford University Press).

Caney, S. (2007), 'Cosmopolitanism, Democracy and Distributive Justice', in D. Weinstock (ed.) (2007), *Global Justice, Global Institutions* (Calgary: University of Calgary Press), at 29.

Canivet, G. (2003), 'La convergence des systèmes juridiques du point de vue du droit privé français', [2003] Revue internationale de droit comparé 7.

Canivet, G. (2004), 'The Use of Comparative Law Before the French Private Law Courts', in Canivet, Andenas, and Fairgrieve (2004), *Comparative Law Before the Courts*, at 181.

Canivet, G. (2010), 'Trans-Judicial Dialogue in a Global World', in Muller and Richards (2010), *Highest Courts and Globalisation*, at 21.

Canivet, G., M. Andenas, and D. Fairgrieve (eds) (2004), *Comparative Law Before the Courts* (London, British Institute of International and Comparative Law).

Canning, J. (1988a), 'Introduction: politics, institutions and ideas', in Burns (1988), *Cambridge History of Medieval Political Thought c. 350–c. 1450*, at 341.

Canning, J. (1988b), 'Law, Sovereignty and Corporation Theory, 1300–1450', in Burns (1988), *Cambridge History of Medieval Political Thought c. 350–c. 1450*, at 454.

Caparros, E. (2000), 'Le droit religieux et son application par les juridictions civiles et religieuses. Coexistence, interrelations, influences réciproques', in Caparros and Christians (2000), *Religion in Comparative Law*, at 1.

Caparros, E. and L-L. Christians (2000), *Religion in Comparative Law at the Dawn of the 21st Century* (Brussels: Bruylant).

Caportorti (1977), 'Study on the Rights of Persons belonging to Ethnic, Religious and Linguistic Minorities' (UN).

Carbonnier, J. (1982), '*Usus hodiernus pandectarum*', in R. Graveson *et al* (eds), *Festschrift für Imre Zajtay* (Tübingen: JCB Mohr) at 107.

Carbonnier, J. (2001), 'The French Civil Code', in Nora (2001), *Rethinking France*, at 335.

Carens, J. (1995), 'Aliens and Citizens: The Case for Open Borders', in Kymlicka (1995), *Rights of Minority Cultures*, at 331.

Carens, J. (2000), *Culture, Citizenship and Community[:] A Contextual Exploration of Justice as Evenhandedness* (Oxford: Oxford University Press).

Carey Miller, D. (1997), 'Scottish Celebration of European Legal Tradition', in Carey Miller and Zimmermann (1997), *Civilian Tradition*, at 19.

Carey Miller, D. and R. Zimmermann (1997), *The Civilian Tradition and Scots Law* (Berlin: Duncker & Humblot).

Carmody, C. (2012), 'Rights in Reverse: International Human Rights as Obligations', in Sellers (2012), *Parochialism, Cosmopolitanism*, at 212.

Carpenter, K. (2008), 'Real Property and Peoplehood', 27 Stanford Environmental Law Journal 313.

Carré de Malberg, R. (1920), *Contribution à la théorie générale de l'État* (Paris: Sirey).

Cassese, A. (2008), *International Criminal Law*, 2nd edn (Oxford, Oxford Univ Press).

Castellino, J. and E. Domíngo Redondo (2006), *Minority Rights in Asia* (Oxford: Oxford University Press).

Castellino, J. and D. Keane (2009), *Minority Rights in the Pacific Region* (Oxford: Oxford University Press).

Castells, M. (2000–2004), *The Information Age*, 2nd edn, vol. I, *The Rise of the Network Society* (2000), vol. II, *The Power of Identity* (2004), vol. III, *End of Millennium* (2000) (Oxford: Blackwell).

Chanda, N. (2007), *Bound Together* (New Haven, CT: Yale University Press).

Charney, J. (1999), 'The Impact on the International Legal System of the Growth of International Courts and Tribunals', 31 Journal of International Law & Politics 697.

Chemin, A. (2009), 'Le nouveau visage de la France, terre d'immigration', *Le Monde hebdomadaire*, 12 December (2009), at 10.

Cheneval, F. (2005), *La cité des peuples[:] Mémoires de cosmopolitismes* (Paris: Editions du cerf).

Chevalier, B. (1971), 'The Policy of Louis XI towards the *Bonnes Villes*: The Case of Tours', in Lewis (1971), *The Recovery of France*, at 265.

Chevallier, J. (ed.) (1999), *L'État* (Paris: Dalloz).

Chevallier, J. (2004a), *L'État post-moderne*, 2nd edn (Paris: LGDJ).

Chevallier, J. (2004b), 'L'État post-moderne: retour sur une hypothèse', 39 Droits 107.

Chibundu, M. (2012), 'The Parochial Foundations of Cosmopolitan Rights', in Sellers (2012), *Parochialism, Cosmopolitanism*, at 172.

Choper, J. (1995), *Securing Religious Liberty[:] Principles for Interpretation of the Religion Clauses* (Chicago: University of Chicago Press).

Choudhry, S. (2006), *The Migration of Constitutional Ideas* (Cambridge: Cambridge University Press).

Choudhry, S. (2008), *Constitutional Design for Divided Societes: Integration or Accommodation?* (Oxford: Oxford University Press).

Christenson, G. (2012), '"Liberty in the Exercise of Religion" in the Peace of Westphalia', 21 Transnational Law & Contemporary Problems (forthcoming), accessible at <http://ssrn.com/abstract=2152628>.

Christie, G. (2011), *Philosopher Kings? The Adjudication of Conflicting Human Rights and Social Values* (New York: Oxford University Press).

Church, W. (1969), *Constitutional Thought in Sixteenth-Century France* (New York: Octagon Books).

Cipolla, C. (1976), *Before the Industrial Revolution[:] European Society and Economy, 1000–1700* (London: Methuen).

Claessen, H. and P. Skalnik (eds) (1978), *The Early State* (The Hague: Mouton).

Clanchy, M. (1993), *From Memory to Written Record*, 2nd edn (Oxford: Blackwell).

Clark, D. (2011), 'Comparative Law in Colonial British North America', 59 AJCL 673.

Clermont, K. (2012), 'Death of Paradox: The Killer Logic Beneath the Standards of Proof' (forthcoming) 88 Notre Dame Law Review.

Cleveland, S. (2006), 'Our International Constitution', 31 Yale Law Journal 1.

Clough, S. and C. Cole (1952), *Economic History of Europe*, 3rd edn (Boston: D. C. Heath).

Cohen, D. (2006), *Globalization and Its Enemies*, trans. J. Baker (Cambridge, MA: MIT Press).

Cohen, M. (1994), *Under Crescent and Cross: The Jews in the Middle Ages* (Princeton, NJ: Princeton University Press).

Cohen-Eliya, M. and I. Porat (2010), 'American Balancing and German Proportionality: The historical origins', 8 International Journal of Constitutional Law 263.

Cohen-Jonathan, G. and J-F. Flauss (eds) (2005), *Le rayonnement international de la jurisprudence de la Cour européenne des droits de l'homme* (Brussels: Bruylant).

Cohn, H. (ed.) (1972), *Government in Reformation Europe 1520–1560* (New York: Harper and Row).

Coleman, J. (2007), 'Beyond the Separability Thesis: Moral Semantics and the Methodology of Jurisprudence', 27 OJLS 581.

Colley, L. (1992), *Britons: Forging the Nation, 1707–1837* (New Haven, CT: Yale University Press).

Commission on Global Governance (1995), *Our Global Neighbourhood* (Oxford: Oxford University Press).

Condorcet, M. J. (1785), 'Essai sur l'application de l'analyse à la probabilité des decisions rendues à la pluralité des voix' (Paris: Imprimerie nationale), online at Bibliothèque nationale de France <http://gallica.bnf.fr/ark:/12148/bpt6k417181>.

Condren, C. (2002), '*Natura naturans*: Natural Law and the Sovereign in the Writings of Thomas Hobbes', in Hunter and Saunders (2002), *Natural Law and Civil Sovereignty*, at 61.

Congar, Y. (1963), *Tradition and Traditions* (London: Burns & Oates).

Connor, W. (1994), *Ethnonationalism[:] The Quest for Understanding* (Princeton, NJ: Princeton University Press).

Cook, B. (2001), 'Fuzzy Logic and Judicial Decision Making', 85 Judicature 70.

Cooper, R. (2005), *The Breaking of Nations[:] Order and Chaos in the Twenty-First Century* (Toronto: McClelland & Steward).

Cordes, A. (2001), 'Auf der Suche nach der Rechtswirklichkeit der mittelalterlichen *Lex mercatoria*', 118 Zeitschrift der Savigny-Stiftung für rechtsgeschichte germanistische Abteilung 168.

Cormack, B. (2007), *A Power to do Justice: Jurisdiction, English Literature, and the Rise of Common law, 1509–1625* (Chicago: University of Chicago Press).

Cornford, T. (2008), *Towards a Public Law of Tort* (Aldershot: Ashgate).

Cotran, E. and M. Yamani (eds) (2000), *The Rule of Law in the Middle East and the Islamic World* (London: IB Tauris).

Council of Europe (1995), Explanatory Report to the Framework Convention for the Protection of National Minorities, accessible at <http://conventions.coe.int/Treaty/EN/Reports/Html/157.htm>.

Council of Europe (2012), *Human Rights of Roma and Travellers in Europe* (Strasbourg: Council of Europe).

Council of Europe Committee of Ministers (2008), 'Supervision of the execution of judgments of the European Court of Human Rights', 1st annual report (Strasbourg: Council of Europe).

Courchene, T. and D. Savoie (eds) (2003), *The Art of the State: Governance in a World Without Frontiers* (Montreal: Institute for Research on Public Policy).

Coutu, M. *et al* (1999), *Droits fondamentaux et citoyenneté: Une citoyenneté fragmentée, limitée, illusoire?* (Montreal: Thémis).

Cover, R. (1982), 'The Origins of Judicial Activism in the Protection of Minorities', 91 Yale Law Journal 1287.

Coyle, S. (2002), 'Hart, Raz and the Concept of a Legal System', 21 Law & Philosophy 275.

Cram, I. (2009), 'Resort to Foreign Constitutional Norms in Domestic Human Rights Jurisprudence with Reference to Terrorism Cases', 68 CLJ 118.

Cranston, A. (2004), *The Sovereignty Revolution* (Stanford, CA: Stanford Law and Politics).

Crawford, J. (2007), *The Creation of States in International Law* (Cambridge: Cambridge University Press).

Crone, P. (2004a), *God's Rule[:] Government and Islam* (New York: Columbia University Press).

Crone, P. (2004b), *Medieval Islamic Political Thought* (Edinburgh: Edinburgh University Press).

Cruz Barney, S. (1999), *Historia del derecho en México* (Mexico: Oxford University Press).

Currie, B. (1959), 'Notes on Methods and Objectives in the Conflict of Laws', 2 Duke Law Journal 171.

Currie, B. (1963), *Selected Essays on the Conflict of Laws* (Durham, NC: Duke University Press).

Da Costa, N., D. Krause, and O. Bueno (2007), 'Paraconsistent Logics and Paraconsistency', in Jacquette (2007), *Philosophy of Logic*, at 791.

Dahrendorf, R. (1994), 'Die Zukunft des Nationalstaates', 48 *Merkur* 751.

Dale, W. (1993), 'The Making and Remaking of Commonwealth Constitutions', 42 ICLQ 67.

Dalhuisen, J. (2000), *Dalhuisen on International, Commercial, Financial and Trade Law*, (Oxford: Hart).

Dalhuisen, J. (2004), Review of H. Kronke, *Capital Markets and the Conflict of Laws*, 52 AJCL 504.

Dalhuisen, J. (2010), *Dalhuisen on Transnational Comparative, Commercial, Financial and Trade Law*, 4th edn (Oxford: Hart).

Dam, K. (2006), *The Law–Growth Nexus* (Washington: Brookings Institution).

Daniels, R., M. Trebilcock, and L. Carson (2011), 'The Legacy of Empire: The Common Law Inheritance and Commitments to Legality in Former British Colonies', 59 AJCL 111.

Dauvergne, C. (ed.) (2003), *Jurisprudence for an Interconnected Globe* (Aldershot: Ashgate).

Dauvergne, C. (2004a), 'Making People Illegal', in P. Fitzpatrick and P. Tuitt (2004), *Critical Beings: Law, Nation and the Global Subject* (Aldershot: Ashgate), at 83.

Dauvergne, C. (2004b), 'Sovereignty, Migration and the Rule of Law in Global Times', 67 MLR 588.

Dauvergne, C. (2008), *Making People Illegal[:] What Globalization Means for Migration and Law* (Cambridge: Cambridge University Press).

Davies, G. (2005), '"Any Place I Hang My Hat?" or: Residence is the New Nationality', 11 European Law Journal 43.

Davies, N. (2011), *Vanished Kingdoms: The History of Half-Forgotten Europe* (London: Allen Lane).

Davis, D. (2003), 'Constitutional Borrowing: The Influence of Legal Culture and Local History in the Reconstitution of Comparative Influences: The South African Experience', 1 International Journal of Constitutional Law 181.

De Béchillon, D. (1997), *Qu'est-ce qu'une règle de Droit?* (Paris: Editions Odile Jacob).

De Béchillon, D. (1998), 'L'imaginaire d'un Code', 27 Droits 173.

De Bonth, M. (2002), 'Sovereignty Revisited', in Schrauwen (2002), *Flexibility in Constitutions*, at 97.

DeGirolami, M. (2010–11), 'The Vanity of Dogmatizing', 27 Constitutional Commentary 201.

De Groot, G-R. (1999), 'Language and Law', in Jayme (1999), *Langue et Droit*, at 333.

De Groot, G-R. and H. Schneider (2006), 'Die zuhehmende Akzeptanz von Fällen mehrfacher Staatsangehörigkeit in West-Europa', in H. Menkhaus and F. Sato (eds) (2006), *Japanischer Brückenbauer zum deutschen Rechtskreis* (Berlin: Duncker & Humblot), at 65.

De Hert, P. and F. Korenica (2012), 'The Doctrine of Equivalent Protection: Its Life and Legitimacy Before and After the European Union's Accession to the European Convention on Human Rights', 13 German Law Journal 874.

Delacroix, S. (2006), *Legal Norms and Normativity[:] An Essay in Genealogy* (Oxford: Hart Publishing).

Delahunty, R. and J. Yoo (2005), 'Against Foreign Law', 29 Harvard Journal of Law & Public Policy 291.

DeLaquil, M. (2006), 'Foreign Law and Opinion in State Courts', 69 Albany Law Review 697.

Del Duca, L. and P. Del Duca (2006), 'An Italian Federalism?—The State, its Institutions and National Culture as Rule of Law Guarantor', 54 AJCL 799.

Deleuze, G. and F. Guattari (2004), *Anti-Oedipus*, trans. R. Hurley, M. Seem, and H. Lane (London: Continuum).

del Ponte, C. (2006), 'Investigation and Prosecution of Large-Scale Crimes at the International Level: The Experience of the ICTY', 4 Journal of International Criminal Law 539.

Delledonne, G. and G. Martinico (2009), 'Handle with Care! The Regional Charters and Italian Constitutionalism's "Grey Zone"', 5 European Constitutional Law Review 218.

Delmas-Marty, M. (2004), *Le relatif et l'universel[:] Les forces imaginantes du droit* (Paris: Seuil).

Delmas-Marty, M. (2006), 'Interaction between National and International Criminal Law in the Preliminary Phase of Trial at the ICC', 4 Journal of International Criminal Law 2.

De Ly, F. (2001), '*Lex mercatoria* (New Law Merchant): Globalisation and International Self-Regulation', in R. P. Abbelbaum, W. L. F. Felstiner, and V. Gessner (2001), *Rules and Networks[:] The Legal Culture of Global Business Transactions* (Oxford: Hart), at 159.

De Mestral, A. and E. Fox-Decent (2008), 'Rethinking the Relationship between International and Domestic Law', 53 McGill Law Journal 573.

Deng, F. (2008), *Identity, Diversity, and Constitutionalism in Africa* (Washington: United States Institute of Peace Press).

Descheemaeker, E. (2009), 'The Roman Division of Wrongs', 5 Roman Legal Tradition 1.

De Senarclens, P. (2009), *Les frontières dans tous leurs états: Les relations internationales au défi de la mondialisation* (Brussels, Bruylant).

Dewost, J-L. (2000), 'Globalization and the Rule of Law', in Bermann, Herdegen, and Lindseth (2000), *Transatlantic Regulatory Cooperation*, at 29.

Dictionnaire de l'Académie françoise (1762), 4th edn (Paris: Brunet).

Dictionnaire de l'Académie françoise (1798), 5th edn (Paris: Smits).

Di Fabio, U. (1998), *Das Recht offener Staaten[:] Grundlinien einer Staats- und Rechtstheorie* (Tübingen: Mohr Siebeck).

Diogenes Laertius (2005), *Lives of Eminent Philosophers*, trans. R. Hicks, vol. II (Cambridge, MA: Harvard University Press).

Djoli, J. (2005), 'Le constitutionalisme africain: entre l'officiel et le réel . . . et les mythes. État de lieux', in C. Kuyu (ed.) (2005), *A la recherche du droit africain du XXIe siècle* (Paris: Connaissance et Savoirs) at 182.

Doe, N. (2011), *Law and Religion in Europe: A Comparative Introduction* (Oxford: Oxford University Press).

Doehring, K. (2000), *Allgemeine Staatslehre[:] Eine systematische Darstellung*, 2nd edn (Heidelberg: C. F. Müller).

Dolinger, J. (1990), 'The Influence of American Constitutional Law on the Brazilian Legal System', 38 AJCL 803.

Domingo, R. (2010), *The New Global Law* (Cambridge: Cambridge University Press).

Donahue, C. (1974), 'Roman Canon Law in the Medieval English Church: *Stubbs v Maitland* Re-examined after 75 Years in the Light of Some Records from the Church Courts', (1974) 72 Michigan Law Review 647.

Doumanis, N. (2013), *Before the Nation* (Oxford: Oxford University Press).

Dowdall, H. (1923), 'The Word "State"', 153 LQR 98.

Dreisbach, D. (2002), *Thomas Jefferson and the Wall of Separation between Church and State* (New York: New York University Press).

Drobnig, U. (1999), 'The Use of Foreign Law by German Courts', in Drobnig and van Erp (1999), *Use of Comparative Law*, at 127.

Drobnig, U. and S. van Erp (1999), *The Use of Comparative Law by Courts* (The Hague: Kluwer).

Dubinsky, P. (2010), 'International Law in the Legal System of the United States', 58 AJCL (Supp.) 455.

Dufour, A. (1991), 'Pufendorf', in Burns (1991), *Cambridge History of Political Thought 1450–1700*, at 561.

Duguit, L. (1923), *Traité de droit constitutionnel*, 2nd edn, vol. II, *La théorie générale de l'État* (Paris: Boccard).

Duina, F. (2003), 'National Legislatures in Common Markets: Autonomy in the European Union and Mercosur', in Paul, Ikenberry, and Hall (2003), *The Nation-State in Question*, at 183.

Duina, F. (2006), *The Social Construction of Free Trade* (Princeton, NJ: Princeton University Press).

Duncan, R. (2008), 'Free Exercise is Dead, Long Live Free Exercise!', in Berg (2008), *The First Amendment*, at 183.

Dunn, J. (ed.) (1995), *Contemporary Crisis of the Nation State?* (Oxford: Blackwell).

Dunoff, J. and J. Trachtman (eds) (2009), *Ruling the World: Constitutionalism, International Law and Global Governance* (Cambridge: Cambridge University Press).

Du Plessis, M. (1999), 'Report on Language and Law', in Jayme (1999), *Langue et Droit*, at 37.

Dupont, J. (2001), *The Common Law Abroad[:] Constitutional and Legal Legacy of the British Empire* (Littleton, CO: Fred B. Rothman).

Dupré, C. (2003), *Importing the Law in Post-Communist Transitions[:] The Hungarian Constitutional Court and the Right to Human Dignity* (Oxford: Hart).

Dupret, B. (1997), 'A propos de la constitutionalité de la shari'a', 4 Islamic Law & Society 91.

Dupuy, P-M. (1995), *Droit international public*, 3rd edn (Paris: Dalloz).

Dupuy, P-M. (1999), 'The Danger of Fragmentation or Unification of the International Legal System and the International Court of Justice', 31 Journal of International Law & Politics 791.

Durham Jr., C. and E. Sewell (2006), 'Definition of Religion', in Serritella (2006), *Religious Organizations in the United States*, at 21.

Duxbury, N. (2008), 'Kelsen's Endgame', 67 CLJ 51.

Dyson, H. F. (1980), *The State Tradition in Western Europe: A Study of an Ideal and Institution* (Oxford: Martin Robertson).

Dyzenhaus, D. (ed.) (2004), *The Unity of Public Law* (Oxford: Hart Publishing).

Dzehtsiarou, K. (2010), 'Comparative Law in the Reasoning of the ECHR', 10 University College Dublin Law Review 109.

Easterbrook, F. (2006), 'Foreign Sources and the American Constitution', 30 Harvard Journal of Law and Public Policy 223.

Eberhard, C. (2006), *Le droit au miroir des cultures* (Paris: LGDJ).

Eisenstadt, S. (2003), *Comparative Civilizations and Multiple Modernities* (Leiden: Brill).

Eisgruber, C. and L. Sager (2007), *Religious Freedom and the Constitution* (Cambridge, MA: Harvard University Press).

Eleftheriadis, P. (2003), 'Cosmopolitan Law', 9 European Law Journal 241.

El Fadl, K. A. (2003), 'The Unbounded Law of God and Territorial Boundaries', in Buchanan and Moore (2003), *States, Nations, and Borders*, at 214.

El Fadl, K. A. (2003–4), 'Islam and the Challenge of Democratic Commitment', 27 Fordham International Law Journal 4.

Elliott, J. (2006), *Empires of the Atlantic World: Britain and Spain in America 1492–1830* (New Haven, CT: Yale University Press).

Ellul, J. (1955), *Histoire des institutions*, vol. 1, *Institutions grecques, romaines, byzantines, francques* (Paris: PUF).

Ellul, J. (1956), *Histoire des institutions*, vol. 2, *Institutions françaises* (Paris: PUF).

Elshtain, J. (2004), 'Response', in D. Farrow (2004), *Recognizing Religion in a Secular Society* (Montreal: McGill-Queen's University Press), at 35.

Elton, G. (1953), *The Tudor Revolution in Government[:] Administrative Changes in the Reign of Henry VIII* (Cambridge: Cambridge University Press).

Elton, G. (1963), *Reformation Europe, 1517–1559* (New York: Harper & Row).

Elvinger, M. (1999), 'Le recours, par les juridictions luxembourgeoises, aux techniqes de droit comparé dans l'interprétation et l'application du droit luxembourgeois', in Drobnig and van Erp (1999), *Use of Comparative Law*, at 231.

Emon, A. (2003–4), 'On Democracy as a Shari'a Moral Presumption: Response to Khaled Abou El Fadl', 27 Fordham International Law Journal 72.

Endicott, T. (2000), *Vagueness in Law* (Oxford: Oxford University Press).

Eppler, E. (2005), *Auslaufmodell Staat* (Frankfurt: Suhrkamp).

Ereshefsky, M. (2001), *The Poverty of the Linnaean Hierarchy: a Philosophical Study of Biological Taxonomy* (Cambridge: Cambridge University Press).

Eriksen, E. (2009), 'The EU: A Cosmopolitan Vanguard?', 9 Global Jurist Advances, Article 6 (available online at <http://www.degruyter.com/view/j/gj.2009.9.1/gj.2009.9.1.1304/gj.2009.9.1.1304.xml?format=INT>).

Errera, A. (2007), 'The Role of Logic in the Legal Science of the Glossators and Commentators. Distinction, Dialectical Syllogism, and Apodictic Syllogism: An Investigation into the Epistemological Roots of Legal Science in the Late Middle Ages', in A. Padovani and P. Stein (eds) (2007), *The Jurists' Philosophy of Law from Rome to the Seventeenth Century*, vol. 7 of E. Pattaro (ed.) (2007), *A Treatise of Legal Philosophy and General Jurisprudence* (Dordrecht: Springer), at 79.

Errico, S. (2007), 'The UN Declaration on the Rights of Indigenous Peoples is Adopted: An Overview', 7 Human Rights Law Review 756.

Ertman, T. (1997), *Birth of the Leviathan[:] Building States and Regimes in Medieval and Early Modern Europe* (Cambridge: Cambridge University Press).

Esposito, J. (ed.) (1999a), *The Oxford History of Islam* (Oxford: Oxford University Press).

Esposito, J. (1999b), 'Contemporary Islam: Reformation or Revolution?', in Esposito (1999), *Oxford History of Islam*, at 643.

Estevadeordal, E. and K. Suominen (2009), *The Sovereign Remedy: Trade Agreements in a Globalizing World* (Oxford: Oxford University Press).

Estin, A. (2004), 'Embracing Tradition: Pluralism in American Family Law', 63 Maryland Law Review 540.

Evans, C. (2001), *Freedom of Religion under the European Convention on Human Rights* (Oxford: Oxford University Press).

Evans, M. (2008), 'Freedom of religion and the European Convention on Human Rights: approaches, trends and tension', in Cane, Evans, and Robinson (2008), *Law and Religion*, at 291.

Evans, P., D. Rueschemeyer, and T. Skocpol (1985), *Bringing the State Back In* (Cambridge: Cambridge University Press).

Evans, R. (2009), *Cosmopolitan Islanders: British Historians and the European Continent* (Cambridge: Cambridge University Press).

Ewig, E. (1963), 'Zum christlichen Königsgedanken im Frühmittelalter', in Mayer (1963), *Das Königtum*, at 7.

Fadel, M. (2009), 'Islamic Politics and Secular Politics: Can They Co-Exist?' (2009) 25 Journal of Law and Religion 101.

Fadel, M. (2011), 'A Tragedy of Politics or an Apolitical Tragedy?', 131 Journal of the American Oriental Society 109.

Fadel, M. (2013), 'Seeking an Islamic Reflective Equilibrium: A Response to Abdallahi A. An-Na'im's Complementary, Not Competing, Claims of Law and Religion: An Islamic Perspective', 39 Pepperdine Law Review 1257.

Fairgrieve, D. (ed.) (2007), *The Influence of the French Civil Code on the Common Law and Beyond* (London: BIICL).

Faist, T. and J. Gerdes (2008), 'Dual Citizenship in an Age of Mobility' (Washington: Migration Policy Institute), Appendix B, accessible at <http://www.migrationpolicy.org/transatlantic/docs/faist-final.pdf>.

Fajardo, R. (2004), 'Legal Pluralism, Indigenous Law and the Special Jurisdiction in the Andean Countries', 10 Beyond Law 32.

Farber, D. (2007), 'The Supreme Court, the Law of Nations, and Citation of Foreign Law: The Lessons of History', 95 California Law Review 1335.

Farrell, H. (2006), 'Regulating Information Flows: States, Private Actors, and E-Commerce', 9 Annual Review of Political Science 353.

Fausten, D., I. Nielsen, and R. Smyth (2001), 'A Century of Citation Practice on the Supreme Court of Victoria', 31 Melbourne University Law Review 733.

Fearon, J. (2003), 'Ethnic and Cultural Diversity by Country', 8 Journal of Economic Growth 195.

Feldman, N. (2003a), *After Jihad: America and the Struggle for Islamic Democracy* (New York: Farrar, Straus, and Giroux).

Feldman, N. (2003b), Review of N. J. Brown, *Constitutions in a nonconstitutional world: Arab basic laws and the prospects for accountable government* (Albany, NY: SUNY Press, (2002), 1 Journal of International Constitutional Law 390.

Feldman, N. (2005), *Divided by God[:] America's Church–State Problem—and What We Should do About It* (New York: Farrar, Straus, and Giroux).

Feldman, N. (2007), 'Cosmopolitan Law?', 116 Yale Law Journal 1022.

Feldman, N. (2008), *The Fall and Rise of the Islamic State* (Princeton, NJ: Princeton University Press).

Feldthusen, B. (2008), *Economic Negligence: The Recovery of Pure Economic Loss*, 5th edn (Toronto: Thomson Carswell).

Fenet, A. (1989), 'Présentation générale', in Fenet and Soulier (1989), *Les minorités et leurs droits*, at 9.

Fenet, A. and G. Soulier (eds) (1989), *Les minorités et leurs droits depuis 1789* (Paris: L'Harmattan).

Ferling, J. (2003), *A Leap in the Dark[:] The Struggle to Create the American Republic* (New York: Oxford University Press).

Ferrer MacGregor, E. and R. Sánchez Gil (2012), 'Foreign Precedents in Mexican Constitutional Adjudication', 4 Mexican Law Review 293.

Fessha, Y. (2010), *Ethnic Diversity and Federalism* (Farnham: Ashgate).

Fichtenau, H. (1964), *The Carolingian Empire[:] The Age of Charlemagne* (New York: Harper & Row).

Field, C. (2008), 'A Shilling for Queen Elizabeth: The Era of State Regulation of Church Attendance in England, 1552–1969', 50 Journal of Church and State 213.

Fieldhouse, D. (1973), *Economics and Empire* (Ithaca, NY: Cornell University Press).

Figgis, F. (1931), *Political Thought from Gerson to Grotius, 1414–1625*, 2nd edn (Cambridge: Cambridge University Press).

Filhol, R. (1972), 'The Codification of Customary Law in France in the Fifteenth and Sixteenth Centuries', in Cohn (1972), *Government in Restoration Europe*, at 265.

Fine, R. (2007), *Cosmopolitanism* (London: Routledge).

Finkelstein, C. (2001), 'Introduction to the symposium on Conflicts of Rights', 7 Legal Theory 235.

Finnis, J. (1980), *Natural Law and Natural Rights* (Oxford: Clarendon Press).

Finnis, J. (2009), 'Does Free Exercise of Religion Deserve Constitutional Mention?', 54 American Journal of Jurisprudence 41.

Fisch, J. (2004), 'Power or Weakness? On the Causes of the Worldwide Expansion of European International Law', 6 Journal of the History of International Law 21.

Fisk, C. and R. Gordon (2011), '"Law As . . .": Theory and Method in Legal History', 1 UC Irvine Law Review 519.

Fletcher, I. (2005), *Insolvency in Private International Law* (Oxford: Oxford University Press).

Foblets, M-C. and A. D. Renteln (2009), *Multicultural Jurisprudence: Comparative Perspectives on the Cultural Defense* (Oxford: Hart).

Follesdahl, A. (2007), 'Why International Human Rights Judicial Review might be Democratically Legitimate', in P. Wahlgren (ed.) (2007), *Constitutional Law*, 52 Scandinavian Studies in Law 103.

Fombad, C. (2007), 'Challenges to Constitutionalism and Constitutional Rights in Africa and the Enabling Role of Political Parties: Lessons and Perspectives from Southern Africa', 55 AJCL 1.

Fombad, C. (2012), 'Internationalization of Constitutional Law and Constitutionalism in Africa', 60 AJCL 439.

Fontana, D. (2004), 'The Next Generation of Transnational/Domestic Constitutional Law Scholarship: A Reply to Professor Tushnet', 38 Loyola of Los Angeles Law Review 445.

Ford, L. (2010), *Settler Sovereignty[:] Jurisdiction and Indigenous People in America and Australia, 1788–1836* (Cambridge, MA: Harvard University Press).

Forey, E. (2007), *État et institutions religieuses* (Strasbourg: Presses universitaires de Strasbourg).

Forsyth, M. (1981), *Unions of States: The Theory and Practice of Confederation* (Leicester: Leicester University Press).

Foucault, M. (1979), *Discipline and Punish*, trans. A. Sheridan (New York: Vintage Books).

Fox-Decent, E. (2006), 'Fashioning Legal Authority from Power: The Crown–Native Fiduciary Relationship', 4 New Zealand Journal of Public and International Law 91.

Fox-Decent, E. (2011), *Sovereignty's Promise: The State as Fiduciary* (Oxford: Oxford University Press).

Francescakis, Ph. (1966), 'Quelques précisions sur les "lois d'application immediate" et leurs rapports avec les règles de conflits de lois', [1966] Revue critique de droit international privé 1.

Franck, T. (2010), 'Proportionality in International Law', 4(2) Law & Ethics of Human Rights 230.

Franklin, J. (1963), *Jean Bodin and the Sixteenth-Century Revolution in the Methodology of Law and History* (New York/London: Columbia University Press).

Franklin, J. (1991), 'Sovereignty and the Mixed Constitution: Bodin and his critics', in Burns (1991), *Cambridge History of Political Thought 1450–1700*, at 298.

Freeman, G., III (1983), 'The Misguided Search for the Constitutional Definition of "Religion"', 71 Georgetown Law Journal 1519.

Fresco, M. and P. van Tongeren (1991), *Perspectives on Minorities[:] Philosophical Reflections on the Identity and the Rights of Cultural Minorities* (Tilburg: Tilburg University Press).

Friedell, S. (2010), 'The Role of Jewish Law in a Secular State', accessible at <http://ssrn.com/abstract=1646963> (forthcoming, Jewish Law Association Studies).

Friedman, L. (1996), 'Borders: On the Emerging Sociology of Transnational Law', 32 Stanford Journal of International Law 65.

Friedrich, C. J. (1939), 'The Deification of The State', 1 *Review of Politics* 18.

Friedrich, M. (1997), *Geschichte der deutschen Staatsrechtswissenschaft* (Berlin: Duncker & Humblot).

Friedrichs, C. (1995), *The Early Modern City 1450–1750* (London: Longman).

Friedrichs, C. (2000), *Urban Politics in Early Modern Europe* (London: Routledge).

Frison-Roche, F. (2006), 'De l'interprétation des textes en droit constitutionnel comparé: l'exemple de l'Europe post-communiste', in P. Gélard (ed.) (2006), *L'État et le droit d'est en ouest* (Paris: Société de legislation comparée), at 35.

Frost, A. (2008), '(Over)Valuing Uniformity', 94 Virginia Law Review 1567.

Frost, M. (2009), *Global Ethics* (New York: Routledge).

Fukuyama, F. (2004), *State Building* (Ithaca, NY: Cornell University Press).

Füsser, K. (1996), 'Farewell to "Legal Positivism": The Separation Thesis Unravelling', in R. George (1996), *Autonomy of Law[:] Essays on Legal Positivism* (Oxford: Clarendon) at 119.

Gabbay, D. and J. Woods (eds) (2007), *The Many Valued and Nonmonotonic Turn in Logic* (Amsterdam: North Holland).

Gadamer, H-G. (1988), *Truth and Method* (New York: Crossroad).

Gaillard, E. (2008), *Aspects philosophiques du droit de l'arbitrage international* (Leiden: Martinus Nijhoff).

Gambaro, A. (2002), 'The Structure of Legal Systems' in *Italian National Reports to the XVIth International Congress of Comparative Law, Brisbane (2002)*, (Milan: Giuffrè), at 41.

Gammeltoft-Hansen, T. (2011), *Access to Asylum: International Refugee Law and the Globalisation of Migration Control* (Cambridge: Cambridge University Press).

Gannagé, L. (2001), *La hiérarchie des normes et les méthodes du droit international privé[:] Etude de droit international privé de la famille* (Paris: LGDJ).

Ganshof, F. (1968), *Frankish Institutions under Charlemagne*, trans. B and M. Lyon, (Providence, RI: Brown University Press).

Garcia, F. (2005), 'Globalization and the Theory of International Law', 11 International Legal Theory 9.

Gardbaum, S. (2008–9), 'The Myth and the Reality of American Constitutional Exceptionalism', 107 Michigan Law Review 391.

Gardbaum, S. (2012), 'The Place of Constitutional Law in the Legal System', in Rosenfeld and Sajó (2012a), *Oxford Handbook of Comparative Constitutional Law*, at 169.

Gardiès, J-L. (1967), 'Méthode logique et method phénoménologique, en face du Droit', in Villey *et al* (1967), *La logique juridique*, at 183.

Gardiner, S. (2006), *Sports Law*, 3rd edn (London: Cavendish).

Gardner, J. (ed.) (1997), *Citizenship[:] The White Paper* (London: Institute for Citizenship Studies & British Institute of International and Comparative Law).

Gardner, J. (2011), 'Can There Be a Written Constitution?', in L. Green and B. Leiter (2011), *Oxford Studies in Philosophy of Law*, vol. I (Oxford: Oxford University Press), at 162.

Garlicki, L. (2008), 'Cooperation of courts: The role of supranational jurisdictions in Europe', 6 International Journal of Constitutional Law 508.

Garnett, G. (2006), *Marsilius of Padua and 'the Truth of History'*, (Oxford: Oxford University Press).

Garson, J. (2009), 'Modal Logic', in E. Zalta (ed.) (2009), *The Stanford Encyclopedia of Philosophy*, accessible at <http://plato.stanford.edu/entries/logic-modal/>.

Gauchet, M. (1985), *Le désenchantement du monde, une histoire politique de la religion* (Paris: Gallimard).

Gaudemet, J. (1997), *Les naissances du droit* (Paris: Montchrestien).

Gaurier, D. (2005), *Histoire du droit international* (Rennes: Presses universitaires de Rennes).

Gavazzi, G. (1959), *Delle antinomie* (Turin: G. Giappichelli).

Gavison, R. (2011), 'Can Israel Be Both Jewish and Democratic?', 21 Jewish Law Association Studies 115.

Geary, P. (2002), *The Myth of Nations[:] The Medieval Origins of Europe* (Princeton, NJ: Princeton University Press).

Gelber, H. (1997), *Sovereignty Through Independence* (The Hague: Kluwer).

Gellner, E. (1983), *Nations and Nationalism* (Ithaca. NY: Cornell University Press).

Gelter, M. and M. Siems (2013), 'Language, Legal Origins, and Culture before the Courts: Cross-Citations between Supreme Courts in Europe', accessible at <http://papers.ssrn.com/sol3/papers.cfm?abstract_id=1719183>, forthcoming in 21 Supreme Court Economic Review.

Gémar, J-C. and N. Kasirer (2005), *Jurilinguistique/tics: Between Law and Language* (Brussels/Montreal: Bruylant/Thémis).

Genschel, P. (2005), 'Globalization and the Transformation of the Tax State', in Leibfried and Zürn (2005), *Transformations of the State?*, at 53.

George, R. (1996), *The Autonomy of Law[:] Essays on Legal Positivism* (Oxford: Clarendon Press).

Gerards, J. (2011), 'Pluralism, Deference and the Margin of Appreciation Doctrine', 17 European Law Journal 80.

Gessner, V., R. Appelbaum, and W. Felstiner (2001), 'Introduction: The Legal Culture of Global Business Transactions', in R. P. Abbelbaum, W. L. F. Felstiner, and V. Gessner (2001), *Rules and Networks[:] The Legal Culture of Global Business Transactions* (Oxford: Hart) at 1.

Gessner, V. and A. Budak (1998), *Emerging Legal Certainty: Empirical Studies in the Globalization of Law* (Aldershot: Ashgate).

Geuss, R. (2008), *Philosophy and Real Politics* (Princeton, NJ: Princeton University Press).

Gewirth, A. (1980), 'Introduction', in Marsilius (1980), *Defensor Pacis*, trans. A. Gewirth (Toronto: University of Toronto Press).

Ghai, Y. (2000), 'Universalism and Relativism: Human Rights as a Framework for Negotiating Interethnic Claims', 21 Cardozo Law Review 1095.

Ghani, A. and C. Lockhart (2008), *Fixing Failed States[:] A Framework for Rebuilding a Fractured World* (Oxford: Oxford University Press).

Ghéhenno, J-M. (1995), *The End of the Nation-State*, trans. V. Elliott (Minneapolis: University of Minnesota Press).

Ghosh, B. (2003a), *Managing Migration: Time for a new International Regime?* (Oxford: Oxford University Press).

Ghosh, B. (2003b), 'Towards a New International Regime for Orderly Movements of People', in Ghosh (2003a), *Managing Migration*, at 25.

Gibert, R. (1968), *Historia general del derecho español* (Granada: F. Roman).

Gierke, O. (1939), *The Development of Political Theory*, trans. B. Freyd (New York: W. W. Norton).

Gierke, O. (1951), *Political Theories of the Middle Age*, trans. F. W. Maitland (Cambridge: Cambridge University Press).

Gierke, O. (1957), *Natural Law and the Theory of Society*, trans. E. Barker (Boston: Beacon Press).

Gilby, T. (1953), *Between Community and Society[:] A Philosophy and Theology of the State* (London: Longmans, Green).

Gilby, T. (1958), *Principality and Polity[:] Aquinas and the Rise of State Theory in the West* (London: Longmans, Green).

Gillespie, M. (2008), *The Theological Origins of Modernity* (Chicago: University of Chicago Press).

Gilmore, M. (1941), *Argument from Roman Law in Political Thought 1200–1600* (New York: Russell & Russell).

Ginsburg, R. (2005), '"A Decent Respect to the Opinions of [Human]kind": The Value of a Comparative Perspective in Constitutional Adjudication', 64 CLJ 575.

Ginsburg, T. (2008), 'The Global Spread of Judicial Review', in K. Whittington, R. Kelemen, and G. Caldeira (eds), *The Oxford Handbook of Law and Politics* (Oxford: Oxford University Press), at 81.

Ginsburg, T., S. Chernykh, and Z. Elkins (2008), 'Commitment and Diffusion: How and Why National Constitutions Incorporate International Law', [2008] University of Illinois Law Review 206.

Ginsburg, T., Z. Elkins, and J. Blount (2007), 'Does the Process of Constitution-Making Matter?', 5 Annual Review of Law and Social Science 201.

Ginsburg, T., J. Melton, and Z. Elkins (2009), *The Endurance of National Constitutions* (Cambridge: Cambridge University Press).

Girard, P. and J. Phillips (2011), 'Rethinking "the Nation" in National Legal History: A Canadian Perspective', 29 Law & History Review 607.

Given, J. (1990), *State and Society in Medieval Europe[:] Gwynedd and Languedoc under Outside Rule* (Ithaca, NY: Cornell University Press).

Gleick, J. (2011), *The Information: A History, A Theory, A Flood* (New York: Vintage).

Glenn, H. P. (1975), *La capacité de la personne en droit international privé français et anglais* (Paris: Dalloz).

Glenn, H. P. (1987a), 'Persuasive Authority', 32 McGill Law Journal 261.

Glenn, H. P. (1987b), 'The Use of Computers: Quantitative Case Law Analysis in the Civil and Common Law', 36 ICLQ 360.

Glenn, H. P. (1990a), 'Law, Revolution and Rights', in Archives for Philosophy of Law and Social Philosophy, Beiheft No. 41, Revolution and Human Rights at 9.

Glenn, H. P. (1990b), 'Private International Law and the New International Legal Professions', in *Mélanges von Overbeck* (Fribourg: Presses de l'Université de Fribourg), at 31.

Glenn, H. P. (1990c), 'Professional Structures and Professional Ethics', 35 McGill Law Journal 424.

Glenn, H. P. (1992), *Strangers at the Gate: Refugees, Illegal Entrants and Procedural Justice* (Cowansville, Quebec: Yvon Blais).

Glenn, H. P. (1993), 'Harmonization of Law, Foreign Law and Private International Law', 1 European Review of Private Law 47.

Glenn, H. P. (1995), 'The Common Law in Canada', 74 Canadian Bar Review 261.

Glenn, H. P. (1997a), 'The Capture, Reconstruction and Marginalization of "Custom"', 45 AJCL 613.

Glenn, H. P. (1997b), 'The Historical Origins of the Trust', in A. Rabello (ed.) (1997), Aequitas *and Equity: Equity in Civil Law and Mixed Jurisdictions* (Jerusalem: Sacher Institute), at 749.

Glenn, H. P. (1998), 'The Grounding of Codification', 31 UC Davis Law Review 765.

Glenn, H. P. (1999), 'The Use of Comparative Law by Canadian Common Law Courts', in Drobnig and van Erp (1999), *Use of Comparative Law*, at 59.

Glenn, H. P. (2000), 'Globalization and Dispute Resolution', 19 Civil Justice Quarterly 136.

Glenn, H. P. (2001a), 'Are Legal Traditions Incommensurable?', 49 AJCL 133.

Glenn, H. P. (2001b), 'Comparative Law and Legal Practice: On Removing the Borders', 75 Tulane Law Review 977.

Glenn, H. P. (2001c), 'Conflicting Laws in a Common Market? The NAFTA Experiment', 76 Chicago-Kent Law Review 1789.

Glenn, H. P. (2002), 'North America as a Medieval Legal Construction', 2(1) Global Jurist Article 1 (available online at <http://www.bepress.com>).

Glenn, H. P. (2003a), 'The Nationalist Heritage', in R. Munday and P. Legrand (eds) (2003), *Comparative Legal Studies: Traditions and Transitions* (Cambridge: Cambridge University Press) at 76.

Glenn, H. P. (2003b), 'A Transnational Concept of Law', in P. Cane and M. Tushnet (eds) (2003), *The Oxford Handbook of Legal Studies* (Oxford: Oxford University Press) at 839.

Glenn, H. P. (2004), 'Conclusions générales: La codification à la française, une petite histoire d'une grande tradition', in R. Beauthier and I. Rorive (eds), *Le Code Napoléon, un ancêtre vénéré? Mélanges offerts à Jacques Vanderlinden* (Brussels: Bruylant) at 529.

Glenn, H. P. (2005), 'La Disposition préliminaire du Code civil du Québec, le droit commun et les principes généraux du droit', 444446 Cahiers de Droit 339.

Glenn, H. P. (2006), 'Comparative Legal Families and Comparative Legal Traditions', in Reimann and Zimmermann (2006), *Oxford Handbook of Comparative Law*, at 421.

Glenn, H. P. (2007a), 'Continuity and Discontinuity of Aboriginal Entitlement', 7 Oxford University Commonwealth Law Journal 23.

Glenn, H. P. (2007b), 'The National Legal Tradition', in K. Boele-Woelki and S. van Erp (2007), *General Reports of the XVIIth Congress of the International Academy of Comparative Law* (Brussels/Utrecht: Bruylant/Eleven International), reproduced in (2007) 11(3) Electronic Journal of Comparative Law (available online at <http://www.ejcl.org>).

Glenn, H. P. (2007c), *On Common Laws* (Oxford: Oxford University Press).

Glenn, H. P. (2008), 'A Concept of Legal Tradition', 34 Queen's Law Journal 427.

Glenn, H. P. (2009a), 'Cosmopolitan Legal Orders', in A. Halpin and V. Roeben, *Theorising the Global Legal Order* (Oxford: Hart), at 25.

Glenn, H. P. (2009b), 'Un statut personnel qui n'ôse pas dire son nom?', in Aoun (2009), *Les statuts personnels*, at 265.

Glenn, H. P. (2010a), 'Accommodating Unity', in Muller and Richards (2010), *Highest Courts and Globalisation*, at 85.

Glenn, H. P. (2010b), *Legal Traditions of the World*, 4th edn (Oxford: Oxford University Press).

Glenn, H. P. (2010c), 'A Western Legal Tradition?' (2010) Supreme Court Law Review 601–19; reproduced in J. Walker and O. Chase (eds), *Common Law, Civil Law and the Future of Categories* (Markham, Ontario: LexisNexis) at 601–19.

Glenn, H. P. (2011a), 'The Ethic of International Law', in D. Childress, III (ed.) (2011), *Ethics in International Law* (Cambridge: Cambridge University Press), at 246.

Glenn, H. P. (2011b), 'The Three Ironies of the UN Declaration on the Rights of Indigenous Peoples', in Allen and Xanthaki (2011), *Reflections on UN Declaration*, at 171.

Glenn, H. P. (2012), 'On the Origins of Peoples and of Laws', in B. Melkevik (ed.), *Standing Tall: Hommages à Csaba Vargas* (Budapest: Pázmány Press), at 167.

Glenn, H. P. (2013, forthcoming), *La conciliation des lois*, General Course of Private International Law, Hague Academy of International Law, Recueil des cours.

Glenn, H. P. and D. Desbiens (2003), 'L'appartenance au Québec: citoyenneté, domicile et residence dans la masse legislative québécoise', 48 McGill Law Journal 117.

Goderis, B. and M. Versteeg (2011), 'The Transnational Origins of Constitutions: An Empirical Investigation', accessible at <http://papers.ssrn.com/sol3/papers.cfm?abstract_id=1865724>.

Godfrey, S. and F. Unger (eds) (2004), *The Shifting Foundations of Modern Nation-States: Realignments of Belonging* (Toronto: University of Toronto Press).

Goldie, M. (1991), 'The reception of Hobbes', in Burns (1991), *Cambridge History of Political Thought 1450–1700*, at 589.

Goldie, M. (2006), 'The English system of liberty', in Goldie and Wokler (2006), *Cambridge History of Eighteenth-Century Political Thought*, at 40.

Goldie, M. and R. Wokler (eds) (2006), *The Cambridge History of Eighteenth-Century Political Thought* (Cambridge: Cambridge University Press).

Goldman, D. (2007), *Globalisation and the Western Legal Tradition: Recurring Patterns of Law and Authority* (Cambridge: Cambridge University Press).

Golove D. and D. Hulsebosch (2010), 'A Civilized Nation: The Early American Constitution, the Law of Nations, and the Pursuit of International Recognition', 85 NYU Law Review 932.

Gong, G. (1984), *The Standard of 'Civilization' in International Society* (Oxford: Oxford University Press).

Gonzalez del Campo, F. (2005), 'Neue Vertragsformen als Rechtstransfer?', 7 Rechtsgeschichte 46.

González Galván, J. (2002), *Constitución y derechos indígenas* (Mexico: UNAM).

Gotlieb, A. (2006), *The Washington Diaries 1981–1989,* (Toronto: McClelland & Stewart).

Gottwald, S. (2007), 'Many-Valued Logics', in Jacquette (2007), *Philosophy of Logic,* at 675.

Goubeau, D. (2000), ' "Open adoption" au Canada', in A. Fine and C. Neirinck (2000), *Parents de sang: Parents adoptifs* (Paris: LGDJ), at 63.

Gough, J. (1955), *Fundamental Laws in English Constitutional History* (Oxford: Clarendon Press).

Gouron, A. (1993), *Droit et coutume en France aux XIIe et XIIIe siècles* (Aldershot: Variorum).

Goyard-Fabre, S. (1975), *Le droit et la loi dans la philosophie de Thomas Hobbes* (Paris: Librairie C. Klincksieck).

Granat, M. (2006), 'La réception de la justice constitutionnelle dans les pays d'Europe Centrale et Orientale', in P. Gélard (ed.) (2006), *L'État et le droit d'est en ouest* (Paris: Société de legislation comparée), at 141.

Grandon, J. B. (2000), *Historia del derecho indiano del descubrimiento colombino a la codificación,* vol. I, *Ius Commune—Ius Proprium en las Indias occidentales* (Rome: Il Cigno Galileo Galilei).

Gratian (1993), *The Treatise of Laws,* trans. A. Thompson, with *The Ordinary Gloss,* trans. J. Gordley (Washington: Catholic University of America Press).

Graves, M. (2001), *The Parliaments of Early Modern Europe* (London: Longman).

Great Law of Peace of the Longhouse People: Iroquois League of Six Nations (1977) (Rooseveltown, NY: Akwesasne Notes, Mohawk Nation, 5th printing).

Green, L. (1988), *The Authority of the State* (Oxford: Clarendon Press).

Greenawalt, K. (2006), *Religion and the Constitution*, vol. I, *Free Exercise and Fairness* (Princeton, NJ: Princeton University Press).

Greenawalt, K. (2009), *Religion and the Constitution*, vol. II, *Establishment and Fairness* (Princeton, NJ: Princeton University Press).

Greene, A. (2012), *Against Obligation: The Multiple Sources of Authority in a Liberal Democracy* (Cambridge, MA: Harvard University Press).

Greene, J. (2009), 'On the Origins of Originalism', 88 Texas Law Review 1.

Greer, B., Jr. (2000), 'The challenge of globalization' [2000] Business Law International 388.

Grewe, C. and H. Ruiz Fabri (1995), *Droits constitutionnels européens* (Paris: PUF).

Griffin, J. (2012), 'Are Human Rights Parochial', in Sellers (2012), *Parochialism, Cosmopolitanism*, at 149.

Griffiths, A. L. (ed.) (2002), *Handbook of Federal Countries* (Montreal/Kingston: McGill-Queen's University Press).

Grossi, P. (1998), *Assolutismo giuridico e diritto privato* (Milan: Giuffrè).

Grossman, M. (2007), 'Is this Arbitration? Religious Tribunals, Judicial Review, and Due Process', 107 Columbia Law Review 169.

Grote, R. and T. Röder (eds) (2012), *Constitutionalism in Islamic Countries* (New York: Oxford University Press).

Guenée, B. (2001), 'From Feudal Boundaries to Political Boundaries', in Nora (2001) *Rethinking France*, at 81.

Guibernau, M. (2003–4), 'Nations Without States: Political Communities in the Global Age', 25 Michigan Journal of International Law 1251.

Guichonnet, P. and C. Raffestin (1974), *Géographie des frontières* (Paris: PUF).

Guillaumé, J. (2011), *L'affaiblissement de l'Etat-Nation et le droit international privé* (Paris: LGDJ).

Guiraudon, V. (1998), 'Citizenship Rights for Non-Citizens: France, Germany and the Netherlands', in Joppke (1998), *Challenge to the Nation-State*, at 272.

Gulzad, Z. (1994), *External Influences and the Development of the Afghan State in the Nineteenth Century* (New York: Peter Lang).

Gurr, T. (1993), *Minorities at Risk: A Global View of Ethnopolitical Conflicts* (Washington, DC: United States Institute of Peace Press).

Gustavsson, S. and L. Lewin (eds) (1996), *The Future of the Nation State[:] Essays on Cultural Pluralism and Political Integration* (London/Stockholm: Routledge/Nerenius & Santérus).

Guterman, S. (1972), *From Personal to Territorial Law* (Metuchen, NJ: The Scarecrow Press).

Guth, D. (2004), 'Law', in R. Tittler and N. Jones (eds) (2004), *A Companion to Tudor Britain* (Oxford: Blackwell), 77.

Gutmann, A. (ed.) (1997), *A Matter of Interpretation* (Princeton, NJ: Princeton University Press).

Gutzwiller, M. (1929), *Le développement historique du droit international privé*, 29 IV Recueil des Cours 287.

Haack, S. (1978), *Philosophy of Logics* (Cambridge: Cambridge University Press).

Haack, S. (2007), 'On Logic in the Law: "Something, but not All"', 20 Ratio Juris 1.

Haakonssen, K. (2006), 'German natural law', in Goldie and Wokler (2006), *Cambridge History of Eighteenth-Century Political Thought*, at 251.

Haas, P. (1992), 'Epistemic Communities and International Policy Coordination', 46 *International Organization* 1.

Häberle, P. (1992), *Rechtsvergleichung im Kraftfeld des Verfassungsstaates: Methoden und Inhalte, Kleinstaaten und Entwicklungsländer* (Berlin: Duncker & Humblot).

Habermas, J. (1998), *The Inclusion of the Other* (Cambridge, MA: MIT Press).

Habermas, J. (2000), *Après l'Etat-Nation* (Paris: Fayard).

Habermas, J. (2001), *The Postnational Constellation* (Cambridge, MA: MIT Press).

Habermas, J. (2003), *The Future of Human Nature* (Cambridge: Polity Press).

Haddad, Y., J. Smith, and K. Moore (2006), *Muslim Women in America* (New York: Oxford University Press).

Häfelin, U. (1959), *Die Rechtspersönlichkeit des Staates* (Tübingen: Mohr-Siebeck).

Hahm, C. and S. Kim (2010), 'To Make "We the People": Constitutional Founding in Postwar Japan and South Korea', 8 International Journal of Constitutional Law 800.

Halberstam, D. (2009), 'Constitutional Heterarchy: The Centrality of Conflict in the European Union and the United States', in Dunoff and Trachtman (2009), *Ruling the World*, at 337.

Hale, T. and D. Held (2011), *Handbook of Transnational Governance: Institutions and Innovations* (Cambridge: Polity Press).

Hallaq, W. (2003), '"Muslim Rage" and Islamic Law', 54 Hastings Law Journal 1705.

Halliday, P. (2010), *Habeas Corpus[:] From England to Empire* (Cambridge, MA: Harvard University Press).

Hallis, F. (1930), *Corporate Personality[:] A Study in Jurisprudence* (Oxford: Oxford University Press).

Halpérin, J–L. (2000), 'L'approche historique et la problematique du Jus Commune', [2000] Revue Internationale de Droit Comparé 717.

Halpérin, J–L. (2004), *Histoire des droits en Europe de 1750 à nos jours* (Paris: Flammarion).

Halphen, L. (1949), *Charlemagne et l'empire carolingien* (Paris: Editions Albin Michel).

Hamann, A. and H. Ruiz Fabri (2008), 'Transnational networks and constitutionalism', 6 International Journal of Constitutional Law 481.

Hamburger, P. (2002), *The Separation of Church and State* (Cambridge, MA: Harvard University Press).

Hamburger, P. (2008), *Law and Judicial Duty* (Cambridge, MA: Harvard University Press).

Handl, G. and J. Zekoll (eds) (2012), *Beyond Territoriality: Transnational Legal Authority in an Age of Globalization* (Leiden: Martinus Nijhoff).

Hansen, R. and P. Weil (eds) (2002), *Dual Nationality: Social Rights and Federal Citizenship in the US and Europe* (New York: Berghahn).

Haraway, D. (1991), *Simians, Cyborgs, and Women: The Reinvention of Nature* (New York: Routledge).

Harding, A. (2002a), 'The *Keris*, The Crescent and the Blind Goddess: The State, Islam and the Constitution in Malaysia', 6 Singapore Journal of International & Comparative Law 154.

Harding, A. (2002b), *Medieval Law and the Foundations of the State* (Oxford: Oxford University Press).

Harding A. and P. Heyland (2009), *Constitutional Courts: A Comparative Study* (London: Wildy, Simmonds, & Hill).

Hardt, M. and A. Negri (2000), *Empire* (Cambridge, MA: Harvard University Press).

Hardy, J., Jr. (1967), *Judicial Politics in the Old Regime[:] The* Parlement *of Paris during the Regency* (Baton Rouge: Louisiana State University Press).

Harrington, J. (2009), 'Migration and Access to Health Care in English Medical Law: a Rhetorical Critique', 4 International Journal of Law in Context 315.

Harris, H. (1927), 'The Greek Origins of the Idea of Cosmopolitanism', 38 International Journal of Ethics 1.

Harris, J. (2004), 'Nationality, Rights and Virtue: Some Approaches to Citizenship in Great Britain', in Bellamy, Castiglione, and Santoro (2004), *Lineages of European Citizenship*, at 73.

Harvey, C. and A. Schwartz (eds) (2012), *Rights in Divided Societies* (Oxford: Hart).

Hasebe, B. (2003), 'Constitutional Borrowing and Political Theory', 1 International Journal of Constitutional Law 224.

Hashmi, S. (2003), 'Political Boundaries and Moral Communities: Islamic Perspectives', in Buchanan and Moore (2003), *States, Nations, and Borders*, at 181.

Hathaway, J. (2005), *The Rights of Refugees under International Law* (Cambridge: Cambridge University Press).

Hattenhauer, H. (1994), *Europäisches Rechtsgeschichte*, 2nd edn (Heidelberg: C. F. Muller).

Hatzimihail, N. (2008), 'The Many Lives—and Faces—of *Lex Mercatoria*: History as Genealogy in International Business Law', 71 Law & Contemporary Problems 169.

Havel, B. and G. Sanchez (2011), 'Restoring Global Aviation's "Cosmopolitan Mentality"', 29 Boston University International Law Journal 1.

Havemann, P. (ed.) (1999), *Indigenous People's Rights in Australia, Canada and New Zealand* (Auckland/Oxford: Oxford University Press).

Hawkins, B. (2012), 'The Life of the Law: What Holmes Meant', 33 Whittier Law Review 323.

Hay, C., M. Lister, and D. Marsh (eds) (2006), *The State: Theories and Issues* (New York: Palgrave Macmillan).

Hayden, P. (2005), *Cosmopolitan Global Politics* (Aldershot: Ashgate).

Headley, J. (2008), *The Europeanization of the World[:] On the Origins of Human Rights and Democracy* (Princeton, NJ: Princeton University Press).

Hecht, N., B. Jackson, S. Passamaneck, D. Piatelli, and A. Rabello (eds) (1996), *An Introduction to the History and Sources of Jewish Law* (Oxford: Clarendon Press).

Hegel, G. (2008), *Philosophy of Right* (New York: Cosmos).

Held, D. (1995), *Democracy and the Global Order* (Stanford, CA: Stanford University Press).

Held, D. (2005), 'Principles of Cosmopolitan Order', in Brock and Brighouse (2005), *Political Philosophy of Cosmopolitanism*, at 10.

Held, D. (2009), 'Restructuring Global Governance: Cosmopolitanism, Democracy and the Global Order', 37 *Millennium* 535.

Held, D. (2010), *Cosmopolitanism: Ideas and Realities* (Cambridge: Polity Press).

Held, D., A. McGrew, D. Goldblatt, and J. Perraton (1999), *Global Transformations [:] Politics, Economics and Culture* (Stanford, CA: Stanford University Press).

Helfand, M. (2008), 'When Religious Practices become Legal Obligations: Extending the Foreign Compulsion Defence', 23 Journal of Law and Religion 535.

Helfand, M. (2011), 'Religious Arbitration and the New Multiculturalism: Negotiating Conflicting Legal Orders', 86 NYU Law Review 1231.

Helfer, L. (2008), 'Redesigning the European Court of Human Rights: Embeddedness as a Deep Structural Principle of the European Human Rights Regime', 19 European Journal of International Law 126.

Helmholz, R. (1991), 'Conflicts between Religious and Secular Law: Common Themes in the English Experience, 1250–1640', 12 Cardozo Law Review 707.

Helmholz, R. (1992), 'Use of the Civil law in Post-Revolutionary Jurisprudence', 66 Tulane Law Review 1649.

Helmholz, R. (2009), '*Bonham's Case*, Judicial Review, and the Law of Nature', 1 Journal of Legal Analysis 325.

Henke, W. (1988), *Recht und Staat[:] Grundlagen der Jurisprudenz* (Tübingen: Mohr-Siebeck).

Herbert, U. (2001), *Geschichte der Ausländerpolitik in Deutschland* (Munich: C. H. Beck).

Herbst, J. (2000), *States and Power in Africa* (Princeton, NJ: Princeton University Press).

Herder, J. (1991), *Briefe zu Beförderung der Humanität* (Frankfurt: Deutscher Klassiker Verlag).

Herringa, A. and P. Kiiver (2007), *Constitutions Compared* (Antwerp: Intersentia).

Hertz, F. (1962), *The Development of the German Public Mind[:] A Social History of German Political Sentiments Aspirations and Ideas* (London: George Allen & Unwin).

Herzog, R. (1988), *Staaten der Frühzeit* (Munich: C. H. Beck).

Hickman, T. (2008), 'The Substance and Structure of Proportionality', [2008] Public Law 693.

Hicks, D. (1991), *Border writing: the multidimensional text* (Minneapolis: University of Minnesota Press).

Higuchi, Y. (2006), *Constitution[:] Idée universelle expressions diversifiées* (Paris: Société de législation comparée).

Himmelfarb, G. (2004), *The New History and the Old[:] Critical Essays and Reappraisals* (Cambridge, MA: Harvard University Press).

Hite, J. and D. Ward (1990), *Readings, Cases, Materials in Canon Law* (Collegeville, PA: The Liturgical Press).

Hobbes, T. (1958), *Leviathan[:] Parts One and Two*, Introduction by H. Schneider (New York: The Liberal Arts Press).

Hobe, S. (1998), *Der offene Verfassungsstaat zwischen Souveränität und Interdependenz* (Berlin: Duncker & Humblot).

Hobsbawm, E. J. (1990), *Nations and Nationalism since 1780[:] Programme, Myth, Reality* (Cambridge: Cambridge University Press).

Hobson, J. (2004), *The Eastern Origins of Western Civilisation* (Cambridge: Cambridge University Press).

Hoeflich, M. (1984), 'Roman and Civil Law in American Legal Education and Research Prior to 1930: A Preliminary Survey', [1984] University of Illinois Law Review 719.

Hoerder, D. (2012), 'Migrations and Belongings', in Rosenberg (2012), *A World Connecting 1870–1940*, at 435.

Höffe, O. (2006), *Kant's Cosmopolitan Theory of Law and Peace*, trans. A. Newton (Cambridge: Cambridge University Press).

Hoffman, D. and J. Rowe (2003), *Human Rights in the UK[:] A General Introduction to the Human Rights Act 1998* (Harlow: Pearson Longman).

Hoffman, F. (2001), Review of Festschrift P. Häberle, *Die Welt des Verfassungsstaates* (Baden-Baden: Nomos), (2003) 4 German Law Journal 1, accessible at <http://www.germanlawjournal.com>.

Hoffmann, M. (1985), *Martin Luther and the Modern Mind* (New York: Edwin Mellen Press).

Hofmann, H. (1999), 'Von *Der Staatssoziologie* zu einter Soziologie der Verfassung?' [1999] Juristen Zeitung 1065.

Hofri-Winogradow, A. (2010), 'A Plurality of Discontent: Legal Pluralism, Religious Adjudication and the State', 26 Journal of Law and Religion 57.

Holden, B. (2000), *Global Democracy[:] Key Debates* (London/New York: Routledge).

Hollinger, D. (2003), 'Not Universalists, Not Pluralists: The New Cosmopolitans Find Their Own Way', in Vertovec and Cohen (2003), *Conceiving Cosmopolitanism*, at 227.

Holmes, O. W., Jr. (1881), *The Common Law* (Boston, MA: Little, Brown).

Hont, I. (1995), 'The Permanent Crisis of a Divided Mankind: "Contemporary Crisis of the Nation State" in Historical Perspective', in Dunn (1995), *Contemporary Crisis of Nation State*, at 166.

Hopkins, W. J. (2011), 'New Zealand', in D. Shelton (ed.), *International Law and Domestic Legal Systems: Incorporation, Transformation, and Persuasion* (Oxford: Oxford University Press), at 429.

Hopt, K. (2000), 'Common Principles of Corporate Governance in Europe?', in B. Markesinis (ed.) (2000), *The Coming Together of the Common Law and the Civil Law* (Oxford: Hart), at 105.

Horowitz, D. (1985), *Ethnic Groups in Conflict* (Berkeley: University of California Press).

Horowitz, D. (2009), 'The *Federalist* Abroad in the World', in I. Shapiro (ed.), *The Federalist Papers* (New Haven, CT: Yale University Press), at 502.

Horowitz, R. (2004), 'International Law and State Transformation in China, Siam, and the Ottoman Empire during the Nineteenth Century', 15 Journal of World History 445.

Horsman, M. and A. Marshall (1994), *After the Nation-State[:] Citizens, Tribalism and the New World Disorder* (London: HarperCollins).

Horty, J. (2011), 'Rules and Reasons in the Theory of Precedent', 17 Legal Theory 1.

Horwitz, M. (1992), *The Transformation of American Law, 1780–1860* (New York: Oxford University Press).

Horwitz, M. (2007), 'The Many Uses of Federalism', 55 Drake Law Review 953–66.

Horwitz, M. (2009), 'Constitutional Transplants', 10(2) Theoretical Inquiry in Law, Art. 9.

Hosen, N. (2005), 'Constitutionalism and Syar'i'ah', 11 Murdoch University Electronic Journal of Law, accessible at <http://www.murdoch.edu.au/elaw/issues/viini/hoseniii_text.html>.

Hulsebosch, D. (2005), *Constituting Empire[:] New York and the Transformation of Constitutionalism in the Atlantic World, 1664–1830* (Chapel Hill: University of North Carolina Press).

Hunter, V. and J. Edmondson (eds) (2000), *Law and Social Status in Classical Athens* (Oxford: Oxford University Press).

Hunter, I. and D. Saunders (eds) (2002), *Natural Law and Civil Sovereignty[:] Moral Right and State Authority in Early Modern Political Thought* (New York: Palgrave).

Husa, J. (2009), '"We the Judges . . . .": Discovering Constitutional *Ius Commune Europaeum*', accessible at <http://ssrn.com/abstract=1334607>.

Husson, L. (1967), 'Les apories de la logique juridique', in Villey *et al* (1967), *La logique juridique*, 29.

Huyler, J. (1995), *Locke in America: The Moral Philosophy of the Founding Era* (Lawrence: University of Kansas Press).

Hyde, D. (2007), 'Logics of Vagueness', in Gabbay and Woods (2007), *Many Valued Turn*, at 285.

Ibarra Palafox, F. (2011), 'Constitutionalism and Citizenship: Facing the Multicultural Challenge', 4 Mexican Law Review 59.

Idleman, S. (2004), 'Multiculturalism and the Future of Tribal Sovereignty', 35 Columbia Human Rights Law Review 589.

Ikenberry, G. J. (2003), 'What States Can Do Now', in Paul, Ikenberry, and Hall (2003), *The Nation-State in Question*, at 350.

Ivison (2002), 'Property, Territory and Sovereignty: Justifying Political Boundaries', in Hunter and Saunders (2002), *Natural Law and Civil Sovereignty*, at 219.

Iwobi, A. (2004), 'Tiptoeing through a Constitutional Minefield: The Great Sharia Controversy in Nigeria', 48 Journal of African Law III.

Jackson, R. (1987), 'Quasi-states, dual regimes, and neoclassical theory: international jurisprudence and the Third World', 41 International Organization 519.

Jackson, R. (1990), *Quasi-States: Sovereignty, International Relations and the Third World* (Cambridge: Cambridge University Press).

Jackson, S. (1996), *Islamic Law and the State* (Leiden: E. J. Brill).

Jackson, V. (2010), *Constitutional Engagement in a Transnational Era* (New York: Oxford University Press).

Jackson, V. and M. Tushnet (eds) (2002), *Defining the Field of Comparative Constitutional Law* (Westport, CT: Praeger).

Jacob, R. (1994), 'Doctrine et culture nationale. La naissance de la littérature juridique en langue populaire en France et en Allemagne', [1994] Droits 5.

Jacob, R. (1995), 'Le jugement de Dieu et la formation de la fonction de juger dans l'histoire européenne', 39 Archives de philosophie du droit 87.

Jacob, R. (ed.) (1996), *Le juge et le jugement dans les traditions juridiques européennes* (Paris: LGDJ).

Jacobsohn, G. (2003), *The Wheel of Law[:] India's Secularism in Comparative Constitutional Context* (Princeton, NJ/Oxford: Princeton University Press).

Jacobsohn, G. (2003–4), 'The Permeability of Constitutional Borders', 82 Texas Law Review 1763.

Jacobson, D. (1996), *Rights Across Borders: Immigration and the Decline of Citizenship* (Baltimore: Johns Hopkins University Press).

Jacquette, D. (ed.) (2007a), *Philosophy of Logic* (Amsterdam: Elsevier).

Jacquette, D. (2007b), 'On the Relation on Informal to Symbolic Logic', in Jacquette (2007), *Philosophy of Logic*, at 131.

James, H. (2006), *The Roman Predicament[:] How the Rules of International Order Create the Politics of Empire* (Princeton, NJ: Princeton University Press).

Jansen, N. (2010), *The Making of Legal Authority: Non-legislative Codifications in Historical and Comparative Perspective* (Oxford: Oxford University Press).

Jansen, N. (2013), 'Legal Pluralism in Europe—National Laws, European Legislation, and Non-Legislative Codifications', in L. Niglia (2013), *Legal Pluralism* (Oxford: Hart), at 109.

Jasanoff, M. (2006), *Edge of Empire[:] Lives, Culture, and Conquest in the East, 1750–1850* (New York: Alfred A. Knopf).

Jasanoff, M. (2011), *Liberty's Exiles: American Loyalists in the Revolutionary World* (New York: Alfred A. Knopf).

Jayme, E. (ed.) (1999), *Langue et Droit* (Brussels: Bruylant).

Jellinek, G. (1922), *Allgemeine Staatslehre* (Berlin: Julius Springer).

Jenkins, D. (2003), 'From Unwritten to Written: Transformation in the British Common-Law Constitution', 36 Vanderbilt Journal of Transnational Law 863.

Jennings, I. (1956), *The Approach to Self-Government* (Cambridge: Cambridge University Press).

Jennings, I. (1959), *The Law and the Constitution*, 5th edn (London: University of London Press).

Jennings, J. (1996), 'From "Imperial State" to "L'Etat de Droit": Benjamin Constant, Blandine Kriegel and the Reform of the French Constitution', 44 Political Studies 488.

Jessup, P. (1956), *Transnational Law* (New Haven, CT: Yale University Press).

von Jhering, R. (1951), 'In the Heaven of Legal Concepts', in M. Cohen and F. Cohen (eds) (1951), *Readings in Jurisprudence and Legal Philosophy* (New York: Prentice Hall), at 678.

Joerges, C., I-J. Sand, and G. Teubner (eds) (2004), *Constitutionalism and Transnational Governance* (Oxford: Hart).

Joffe, R. (2007), 'Schneller, besser, reicher . . .', *Die Zeit*, 31 May 2007, at 3.

Johansen, B. (2006), 'The Constitution and the Principles of Islamic Normativity against the rules of *Fiqh*. A Judgment of the Supreme Constitutional Court of Egypt', in M. Masud, R. Peters, and D. Powers (eds) (2006), *Dispensing Justice in Islam* (Leiden: Brill) at 169.

Johnson, C. (1990), *Aristotle's Theory of the State* (London: Macmillan).

Johnston, D. (1997), 'The General Influence of Roman Institutions of State and Public Law', in D. L. Carey Miller and R. Zimmermann (eds), *The Civilian Tradition and Scots Law* (Berlin: Duncker & Humblot) at 87.

Jones, C. (2006), 'Cosmopolitanism', in D. Borchert (ed.), *Encyclopedia of Philosophy*, 2nd edn, vol. II (Detroit: Macmillan) at 567.

Jones, J. W. (1977), *The Law and Legal Theory of the Greeks* (Aalen, Netherlands: Scientia).

Jones, S. (1973), 'Boundary Concepts in the Setting of Place and Time', in H. J. de Blij (1973), *Systematic Political Geography,* 2nd edn (New York: John Wiley & Sons) at 167.

Jones, W. (1970), 'Relations of the Two Jurisdictions: Conflict and Cooperation in England during the Thirteenth and Fourteenth Centuries', 7 *Studies in Medieval & Renaissance History* (OS) 77.

Jones-Pauly, C. and N. Nojumi (2004), 'Balancing Relations between Society and State: Legal Steps Toward National Reconciliation and Reconstruction of Afghanistan', 52 AJCL 825.

Joppke, C. (ed.) (1998), *Challenge to the Nation-State: Immigration in Western Europe and the United States* (Oxford: Oxford University Press).

Joppke, C. (2008), 'Comparative Citizenship: A Restrictive Turn in Europe?', 2(1) Law & Ethics of Human Rights, Article 6.

Joppke, C. (2010), *Citizenship and Immigration* (Cambridge: Polity Press).

Jordan, C. and G. Majnoni (2003), 'Regulatory Harmonization and the Globalization of Finance', in J. Hanson, G. Majnoni, and P. Honohan (eds), *Globalization and national financial systems* (Washington: The World Bank/ Oxford University Press), at 259.

Jordan, D. (2001), 'Introduction', in Nora (2001), *Rethinking France.*

Juenger, F. (1985), *General Course on Private International Law,* 193 Receuil des Cours 119.

Juenger, F. (1993), *Choice of Law and Multistate Justice* (Dordrecht: Martinus Nijhoff).

Juss, S. (2007), 'The Slow Death of Citizenship Rights', 18 King's Law Journal 95.

Jutras, D. (2000), 'Énoncer l'indicible: le droit entre langues et traditions', [2000] Revue internationale de droit comparé, 781.

Kahn, L. (2010), 'The Qur'an and the Constitution', 85 Tulane Law Review 161.

Kahn-Freund, O. (1974), 'On Uses and Misuses of Comparative Law', 37 MLR 1.

Kaiser, R. (1993), *Das Römische Erbe und das Merowinger-Reich* (Munich: R. Oldenbourg Verlag).

Kammen, M. (1988), *Sovereignty and Liberty: Constitutional Discourse in American Culture* (Madison: University of Wisconsin Press).

Kant, I. (1974), *On the old saw: that may be right in theory but it won't work in practice,* trans. E. Ashton (orig.: 1793) (Philadelphia: University of Pennsylvania Press).

Kant, I. (1996), *Metaphysics of Morals,* trans. M. Gregor (Cambridge: Cambridge University Press).

Kant, I. (2005), *Perpetual Peace* (New York: Cosimo).

Kantorowicz, E. (1957), *The King's Two Bodies[:] A Study in Mediaeval Political Theology* (Princeton, NJ: Princeton University Press).

Kaplan, A. (2002), *The Anarchy of Empire in the Making of US Culture* (Cambridge, MA: Harvard University Press).

Kaplan, S. (2008), *Fixing Fragile States[:] A New Paradigm for Development* (Westport, CT: Praeger).

Karcic, F. (2001), 'Applying the Shari'ah in Modern Societies: Main Developments and Issues', 40 Islamic Studies 207.

Karst, K. L. and K. Rosenn (1975), *Law and Development in Latin America[:] A Casebook* (Berkeley: University of California Press).

Kaser, M. (1967), *Römische Rechtsgeschichte,* 2nd edn (Göttingen: Vandenhoeck & Ruprecht).

Kasirer, N. (2006), 'L'outre-langue du droit', in L. Castonguay and N. Kasirer (eds) (2006), *Études offertes à Jacques Vanderlinden* (Cowansville, Quebec/ Brussels: Bruylant/Yvon Blais) at 329.

Kaviraj, S. (1995), 'Crisis of the Nation-state in India', in Dunn (1995), *Contemporary Crisis of the Nation State?,* at 115.

Kay, R. (2009), 'Original Intention and Public Meaning in Constitutional Interpretation', 103 Northwestern University Law Review 703.

Kay, R. (2011), 'Constituent Authority', 59 AJCL 715.

Kayaoğlu, T. (2010), *Legal Imperialism: Sovereignty and Extraterritoriality in Japan, the Ottoman Empire, and China* (Cambridge: Cambridge University Press).

Keane, J. (2003), *Global Civil Society* (Cambridge: Cambridge University Press).

Kegel, G. and K. Schurig (2000), *Internationales Privatrecht*, 8th edn (Munich: C. H. Beck).

Keith, K. (2005), 'The Unity of the Common Law and the Ending of Appeals to the Privy Council', 54 ICLQ 197.

Keller, H. and A. Stone Sweet (2008), *A Europe of Rights—The Impact of the ECHR on National Legal Systems* (New York: Oxford University Press).

Kelsen, H. (1973), *Essays in Legal and Moral Philosophy*, selected by O. Weinberger, trans. P. Heath (Dordrecht: D. Reidel).

Kelsen, H. (1989), *Pure Theory of Law*, trans. M. Knight (Gloucester, MA: Peter Smith).

Keohane, N. (1980), *Philosophy and the State in France[:] The Renaissance to the Enlightenment* (Princeton, NJ: Princeton University Press).

Keohane, R. and J. Nye (1989), *Power and interdependence*, 2nd edn (Glenview, IL: Scott, Forseman).

Kern, F. (1985), *Kingship and Law in the Middle Ages* (Westport, CT: Greenwood Press).

Kim, K. (2000), *Aliens in Medieval Law[:] The Origins of Modern Citizenship* (Cambridge: Cambridge University Press).

Kincaid, J. and G. A. Tarr (eds) (2005), *Constitutional Origins, Structure, and Change in Federal Countries* (Montreal/Kingston: McGill-Queen's University Press).

King, P. (1988), 'The barbarian kingdoms', in Burns (1988), *Cambridge History of Medieval Political Thought c.350–c.1450*, at 123.

Kingsbury, B. (2003), 'The International Legal Order', in Reimann and Zimmermann (2006), *Oxford Handbook of Comparative Law*, at 271.

Kingsbury, B. and B. Straumann (2011), *The Roman Foundations of the Law of Nations* (New York: Oxford University Press).

Kirgis, F. (1987), 'Custom on a Sliding Scale', 81 American Journal of International Law 146.

Kitagawa, Z. (1970), *Rezeption und Fortbildung des europäischen Zivilrechts in Japan* (Frankfurt: A. Metzner).

Kleingeld, P. (1999), 'Six Varieties of Cosmopolitanism in Late Eighteenth-Century Germany', 60 Journal of Historical Ideas 505.

Kleingeld, P. (2004), 'Approaching Perpetual Peace: Kant's Defence of a League of States and his Ideal of a World Federation', 12 European Journal of Philosophy 304.

Kleingeld, P. (2012), *Kant and Cosmopolitanism: The Philosophical Ideal of World Citizenship* (Cambridge: Cambridge University Press).

Kleingeld, P. and E. Brown (2006), 'Cosmopolitanism', in E. Zalta (ed.) (2006), *The Stanford Encyclopedia of Philosophy*, accessible at <http://plato.stanford .edu/search/searcher.py?query=Cosmopolitanism&prepend=title%3A>.

Klerman, D. (2009), 'The Emergence of English Commercial Law: Analysis Inspired by the Ottoman Experience', 71 Journal of Economic Behavior and Organization 638.

Klir, G., U. St. Clair, and B. Yuan (1997), *Fuzzy Set Theory: Foundations and Applications* (Upper Saddle River, NJ: Prentice Hall).

Kneebone, S. (2009), *Refugees, Asylum Seekers and the Rule of Law* (Cambridge: Cambridge University Press).

Knop, K. (2000), 'Here and There: International Law in Domestic Courts', 32 NYU Journal of International Law & Politics 501.

Koçak, M. (2010), 'Islam and national law in Turkey', in Otto (2010a), *Sharia Incorporated*, at 231.

Koch, C., Jr. (2003–4), 'Envisioning a Global Legal Culture', 25 Michigan Journal of International Law 1.

Kochenov, D. (2011a), 'A Real European Citizenship; A New Jurisdiction Test; A Novel Chapter in the Development of the Union in Europe', 18 Columbia Journal of European Law 55.

Kochenov, D. (2011b), 'EU Citizenship, Naturalisations, and Mythical Cultural Exceptionalism in Europe Today', 3 *Perspectives on Federalism* E106 (available online at <http://www.on-federalism.eu/index.php/-dimitry-kochenov/77 -essay/101-eu-citizenship-naturalisations-and-mythical-cultura-l-exceptionalism -in-europe-today>).

Koh, H. (1996), 'Transnational Legal Process', 75 Nebraska Law Review 181.

Koh, H. (2004), 'International Law as Part of Our Law', 98 AJIL 43.

Kohler-Koch, B. (1996), 'The Strength of Weakness: The Transformation of Governance in the EU', in Gustavsson and Lewin (1996), *The Future of the Nation State*, at 169.

Kohli, A. (2004), *State-Directed Development[:] Political Power and Industrialization in the Global Periphery* (Cambridge: Cambridge University Press).

Koopmans, T. (2003), *Courts and Political Institutions[:] A Comparative View* (Cambridge: Cambridge University Press).

Koppelman, A. (2010), 'How Shall I Praise Thee? Brian Leiter on Respect or Religion', 47 San Diego Law Review 961.

Koselleck, R. (2002), *The Practice of Conceptual History*, trans. T. Presner (Stanford, CA: Stanford University Press).

Koskenniemi, M. (2001), *The Gentle Civilizer of Nations* (Cambridge: Cambridge University Press).

Koskenniemi, M. (2005), 'Global Legal Pluralism: Multiple Regimes and Multiple Modes of Thought', accessible at <http://www.helsinki.fi/eci/Publications/ Koskenniemi/MKPluralism-Harvard-05d[1].pdf>.

Koskenniemi, M. (2011), 'The Case for Comparative International Law' [2011] Finnish Yearbook of International Law 3.

Koskenniemi, M. and P. Laino (2002), 'Fragmentation of International Law? Postmodern Anxieties', 15 Leiden Journal of International Law 553.

Kostakopoulou, D. (2007), 'European Union Citizenship: Writing the Future', 13 European Law Journal 623.

Kramnick, I. and R. Moore (1997), *The Godless Constitution: The Case Against Religious Correctness* (New York: W. W. Norton).

Krasner, S. (1999), *Sovereignty[:] Organized Hypocrisy* (Princeton, NJ: Princeton University Press).

Kratochwil, F. (1986), 'Of Systems, Boundaries, and Territoriality: An Inquiry into the Formation of the State System', 39 *World Politics* 27.

Krawietz, W. (1993), 'Recht ohne Staat? Spielregeln des Rechts und Rechtssystem in normen- und systemtheoretischer Perspective', 24 *Rechtstheorie* 81.

Kreijen, G. (2000–4), *State Failure, Sovereignty and Effectiveness[:] Legal Lessons from the Decolonization of Sub-Saharan Africa* (Leiden: Martinus Nijhoff).

Kriegel, B. (1995), *The State and the Rule of Law*, trans. M. A. LePain and J. C. Cohen (Princeton, NJ: Princeton University Press).

Kriegel, B. (1998), *Philosophie de la République* (Paris: Plon).

Kriegel, B. (2002), 'The Rule of the State and Natural Law', in Hunter and Saunders (2002), *Natural Law and Civil Sovereignty*, at 13.

Krieger, L. (1957), *The German Idea of Freedom: History of a Political Tradition* (Boston, MA: Beacon Press).

Krisch, N. (2010), *Beyond Constitutionalism: The Pluralist Structure of Postnational Law* (Oxford: Oxford University Press).

Krüger, H. (1966), *Allgemeine Staatslehre*, 2nd edn (Stuttgart: Kohlhammer).

Krygier, M. (2004), 'False Dichotomies, True Perplexities, and the Rule of Law', in A. Sajó (ed.) (2004), *Human Rights with Modesty: The Problem of Universalism* (Leiden: Martinus Nijhoff), at 251.

Kumm, M. (2005), 'The Jurisprudence of Constitutional Conflict: Constitutional Supremacy in Europe before and after the Constitutional Treaty', 11 European Law Journal 262.

Kumm, M. (2009), 'The Cosmopolitan Turn in Constitutionalism: On the Relationship between Constitutionalism in and beyond the State', in Dunoff and Trachtman (2009), *Ruling the World?*, at 258.

Kumm, M. (2010), 'How does European Law Fit into the World of Public Law? Costa, Kadi and Three Conceptions of Public Law', in J. Neyer and A. Wiener (eds) (2010), *Political Theory of the EU* (Oxford: Oxford University Press), at 111.

Kunkel, W. (1973), *An Introduction to Roman Legal and Constitutional History*, 2nd edn, trans. J. Kelly (Oxford: Clarendon Press).

Kuran, T. (2005), 'The Absence of the Corporation in Islamic Law: Origins and Persistence', 53 AJCL 785.

Kuriki, H. (2001), 'Der Verfassungsstaat in den ostasiatischen Traditionen', in Morlok (2001), *Die Welt des Verfassungsstaates*, at 175.

Kymlicka, W. (1989), *Liberalism, Community and Culture* (Oxford: Clarendon Press).

Kymlicka, W. (ed.) (1995), *The Rights of Minority Cultures* (Oxford: Oxford University Press).

Kymlicka, W. (1995), *Multicultural Citizenship: A Liberal Theory of Minority Rights* (Oxford: Clarendon Press).

Kymlicka, W. (1996), 'Social Unity in a Liberal State', 13 *Social Philosophy & Policy* 105.

Kymlicka, W. (2003), 'New Forms of Citizenship', in Courchene and Savoie (2003), *The Art of the State: Governance in a World Without Frontiers*, at 265.

Kymlicka, W. (2007), *Multicultural Odysseys* (Oxford: Oxford University Press).

Kymlicka, W. and B. Bashir (eds) (2008), *The Politics of Reconciliation in Multicultural Societies* (Oxford: Oxford University Press).

Kymlicka, W. and W. Norman (1995), 'Return of the Citizen: A Survey of Recent Work on Citizenship Theory', in Beiner (1995), *Theorizing Citizenship*, at 283.

Kymlicka, W. and W. Norman (eds) (2000a), *Citizenship in Diverse Societies* (Oxford: Oxford University Press).

Kymlicka, W. and W. Norman (2000b), 'Citizenship in Culturally Diverse Societies: Issues, Contexts, Concepts', in Kymlicka and Norman (2000), *Citizenship Diverse Socieities*, at 1.

Kysar, D. (2010), *Regulating from Nowhere: Environmental Law and the Search for Objectivity* (New Haven, CT: Yale University Press).

Laborde, C. (2004), 'Republican Citizenship and the Crisis of Integration in France', in Bellamy, Castiglione, and Santoro (2004), *Lineages of European Citizenship*, at 46.

LaCroix, A. (2010), *The Ideological Origins of American Federalism* (Cambridge, MA: Harvard University Press).

Ladeur, K-H. (ed.) (2004a), *Public Governance in the Age of Globalization* (Aldershot: Ashgate).

Ladeur, K-H. (2004b), 'Globalization and Public Governance—A Contradiction?', in Ladeur (2004a), *Public Governance*, at 1.

Ladeur, K-H. (2004c), 'Globalization and the Conversion of Democracy to Polycentric Networks: Can Democracy Survive the End of the Nation State?', in Ladeur (2004a), *Public Governance*, at 89.

Ladeur, K-H. (2004d), 'Methodology and European Law: Can Methodology Change so as to Cope with the Mulitiplication of the Law', in M. van Hoecke (ed.) (2004), *Epistemologie and Methodology of Comparative Law* (Oxford: Hart), at 91.

LaForest, J. (1996), 'The Expanding Role of the Supreme Court of Canada in International Law Issues', 34 Canadian Yearbook of International Law 89.

Laitin, D. (2007), *Nations, States, and Violence* (Oxford: Oxford University Press).

Lalinde Abadia, J. (1983), *Derecho histórico español*, 3rd edn (Barcelona: Editorial Ariel).

Lambert-Abdelgawad, E. (2002), *The Execution of Judgments of the European Court of Human Rights* (Strasbourg: Council of Europe Publishing).

Landes, D. (1999), *The Wealth and Poverty of Nations* (London: Abacus).

Landheer-Cieslak, C. (2007), *La religion devant les juges français et québécois de droit civil* (Cowansville, Quebec: Yvon Blais).

Lange, H. (1997), *Römisches Recht im Mittelalter*, vol. I, *Die Glossatoren* (Munich: C. H. Beck).

Langer, M. (2005), 'The Rise of Managerial Judging in International Criminal Law', 53 AJCL 835.

Langlaude, S. (2006), 'Indoctrination, Secularism, Religious Liberty and the ECHR', 55 ICLQ 929.

Lanni, A. and A. Vermeule (2012), 'Constitutional Design in the Ancient World', 64 Stanford Law Review 907.

Laporta, F. (2005), 'Globalization and the Rule of Law: Some Westphalian Doubts', vol. III, *Democracy and Fundamentalism*, A. Aarnio (ed.), The Tampere Club ePublications, (accessible online at <http://www.tampereclub.org/e-publications/vol3_laporta.pdf>).

La Porta, R., de Silanese, F., and A. Shleifer (2008), 'The Economic Consequences of Legal Origins', 46 Journal of Economic Literature 285.

Lau, M. (2008), 'Legal Reconstruction and Islamic Law in Afghanistan', in P. Bearman, W. Heinrichs, and B. Weiss (eds) (2008), *The Law Applied[:] Contextualizing the Islamic Shari'a* (London: IB Tauris), at 216.

Lau, M. (2010), 'Sharia and national law in Pakistan', in Otto (2010a), *Sharia Incorporated*, at 373.

Law, D. and W-C. Chang (2011), 'The Limits of Transnational Judicial Dialogue', 86 Washington Law Review 523.

Law, D. and M. Versteeg (2012), 'The Declining Influence of the United States Constitution', 87 NYU Law Review 762.

Law, D. and M. Versteeg (2013), 'Sham Constitutions', forthcoming 101 California Law Review, accessible at <http://papers.ssrn.com/sol3/papers.cfm?abstract_id=1989979>.

Lawson, H. (2001), *Closure: a Story of Everything* (New York: Routledge).

Laycock, D. (2008), 'Religious Liberty as Liberty', in Berg (2008), *The First Amendment*, at 172.

Lear, J. (2006), *Radical Hope[:] Ethics in the Face of Cultural Devastation* (Cambridge, MA: Harvard University Press).

Lederman, W. R. (1963), 'The Concurrent Operation of Federal and Provincial Laws in Canada', 9 McGill Law Journal 185.

Lee, J. (2009), '*Confusio*: Reference to Roman Law in the House of Lords and the Development of English Private Law', 5 Roman Legal Tradition 24.

Lee, J. T. (2007), 'Interpreting Bills of Rights: The Value of a Comparative Approach', 5 International Journal of Constitutional Law 122.

Lee, J-A. and C-Y. Liu (2012), 'Forbidden City Enclosed by Great Firewall: The Law and Power of Internet Filtering in China', 13 Minnesota Journal of Law, Science & Technology 125.

Leersen J. (2006), *National Thought in Europe[:] A Cultural History* (Amsterdam: Amsterdam University Press).

Leibfried, S. and M. Zürn (2005), *Transformations of the State?* (Cambridge: Cambridge University Press).

Leisner, W. (1997), *Der Abwägungsstaat: Verhältnismässigkeit als Gerechtigkeit?* (Berlin: Duncker & Humblot).

Leiter, B. (2010), 'Foundations of Religious Liberty', 47 San Diego Law Review 935.

Lemaire, A. (1907), *Les lois fondamentales de la monarchie française d'après les théoriciens de l'ancien régime* (Paris: Fontemoing).

Lenoir, N. (2000), 'The Response of the French Constitutional Court to the Growing Importance of International Law', in B. Markesinis (ed.) (2000), *The Coming together of the Common Law and the Civil Law* (Oxford: Hart), at 163.

Lepointe, G. (1965), *Histoire du droit public français*, 2nd edn (Paris: PUF).

Lerner, H. (2010), 'Constitution-writing in Deeply Divided Societies: the Incrementalist Approach', 16 *Nations & Nationalism* 68.

Lerner, H. (2011), *Making Constitutions in Deeply-Divided Societies* (Cambridge: Cambridge University Press).

Lessaffer, R. (2011), 'Roman Law and the Early Historiography of International Law: Ward, Wheaton, Hosack and Walker', in T. Marauhn and H. Steiger (eds) (2011), *Universality and Continuity in International Law* (The Hague: Eleven Publishing), at 149.

Letsas, G. (2006), 'Two Concepts of the Margin of Appreciation', 26 OJLS 705.

Letsas, G. (2009), *A Theory of Interpretation of the European Convention on Human Rights* (Oxford: Oxford University Press).

Letwin, S. (2005), *On the History of the Idea of Law*, ed. N. Reynolds (Cambridge: Cambridge University Press).

Lewis, P. (1968), *Later Medieval France* (London: Macmillan).

Lewis, P. (ed.) (1971), *The Recovery of France in the Fifteenth Century*, trans. G. F. Martin (London: Macmillan).

L'Heureux-Dubé, C. (1998–9), 'The Importance of Dialogue: The International Impact of the Rehnquist Court', 34 Tulsa Law Review 15.

Lichère, F., L. Potvin-Solis, and A. Raynouard (eds) (2004), *Le dialogue entre les juges européens et nationaux: incantation ou réalité?* (Brussels: Bruylant).

Lieberman, D. (2006), 'The Mixed Constitution and the Common Law', in Goldie and Wokler (2006), *Cambridge History of Eighteenth-Century Political Thought*, at 317.

Liégeois, J-P. (2012), *The Council of Europe and Roma: 40 Years of Action* (Strasbourg: Council of Europe).

Liin, U. (2004), 'The New Estonian Civil Code: How We Got to Where We Are', in Swiss Institute of Comparative Law, *Imperialism and Chauvinism in the Law* (Zurich: Schulthess), at 121.

Likhovski, A. (2006), *Law and Identity in Mandate Palestine* (Chapel Hill: University of North Carolina Press).

Lindahl, H. (2007), 'Constituent Power and Reflexive Identity: Towards an Ontology of Collective Selfhood', in Loughlin and Walker (2007), *Paradox of Constitutionalism*, at 9.

Lindahl, H. (2010), 'A-Legality: Postnationalism and the Question of Legal Boundaries', 73 MLR 30.

Lindahl, H. (2011), 'Recognition as Domination: Constitutionalism, Reciprocity and the Problem of Singularity', in Walker, Tierney, and Shaw (2011), *Europe's Constitutional Mosaic*, at 205.

Lindahl, L. (1992), 'Conflicts in Systems of Legal Norms: a Logical Point of View', in Brouwer (1992), *Coherence and Conflict in Law*, at 39.

Lintott, A. (1999), *The Constitution of the Roman Republic* (Oxford: Clarendon Press).

Lloyd, H. (1983), *The State, France and the Sixteenth Century* (London: George Allen & Unwin).

Lloyd, H. (1991), 'Constitutionalism', in Burns (1991), *Cambridge History of Political Thought 1450–1700*, at 254.

Lobban, M. (2007), *A History of the Philosophy of Law in the Common Law World, 1600–1900*, vol. 8, in E. Pattaro (ed.) (2007), *A Treatise of Legal Philosophy and General Jurisprudence* (Dordrecht: Springer).

Lochak, D. (1989), 'Les minorities et le droit public français: du refus des différences à la gestion des différences', in Fenet and Soulier (1989), *Les minorités et leurs droits*, at 111.

Locke, J. (1933), *Two Treatises of Government*, ed. M. Goldie (London: J. M. Dent).

Locke, J. (1983), *A Letter Concerning Toleration*, ed. J. Tully (Indianapolis: Hackett).

Lollini, A. (2007), 'Legal Argumentation based on Foreign Law [:] An example from case law of the South African Constitutional Court', 3 Utrecht Law Review 60.

Lombardi, C. (1998), 'Islamic Law as a Source of Constitutional Law in Egypt: The Constitutionalization of the Sharia in a Modern Arab State', 37 Columbia Journal of Transnational Law 81.

Lombardi, C. (2006), *State Law as Islamic Law in Modern Egypt[:] The Incorporation of the Shari'a into Egyptian Constitutional Law* (Leiden: Brill).

Lorenzen, E. (1947), 'Huber's *De Conflictu Legum*', in E. Lorenzen, *Selected Essays on the Conflict of Laws* (New Haven, CT: Yale University Press), at 136.

Loughlin, M. (2010), *Foundations of Public Law* (Oxford: Oxford University Press).

Loughlin, M. and N. Walker (eds) (2007), *The Paradox of Constitutionalism* (Oxford: Oxford University Press).

Lück, H. (1999), *Über den Sachsenspiegel[:] Entstehung, Inhalt und Wirkung des Rechtsbuches* (Halle an der Saale: Verlag Janos Stekovics).

Lupoi, M. (2000), *The Origins of the European Legal Order*, trans. A. Belton (Cambridge: Cambridge University Press).

Luscombe, D. (1988), 'Introduction: the Formation of Political Thought in the West', in Burns (1988), *Cambridge History of Medieval Political Thought c.350–c.1450*, at 157.

Luther, M. (1989), 'On the Councils and the Church' (1539), in T. Lull (ed.), *Martin Luther's Basic Theological Writings* (Minneapolis, MN: Fortress Press).

Lutz-Bachmann, M. (1997), 'Kant's Idea of Peace and the Philosophical Conception of a World Republic', in Bohman and Lutz-Bachman (1997), *Perpetual Peace*, at 59.

Lyon, M. (2011), '*Shady Grove*, the Rules Enabling Act, and the Application of State Summary Judgment Standards in Federal Diversity Cases', 85 St John's Law Review 1011.

Mac Amlaigh, C. (2011), 'Questioning Constitutional Pluralism', accessible at <http://papers.ssrn.com/sol3/papers.cfm?abstract_id=1905053>.

MacCormick, N. (1993), 'Beyond the Sovereign State', 56 MLR 1.

MacCormick, N. (1999), *Questioning Sovereignty[:] Law, State and Nation in the European Community* (Oxford: Oxford University Press).

MacCormick, N. (2007), *Institutions of Law[:] An Essay in Legal Theory* (Oxford: Oxford University Press).

MacCormick, N. (2009), *Rhetoric and the Rule of Law: A Theory of Legal Reasoning* (Oxford: Oxford University Press).

MacCulloch, D. (2009), *Christianity: The First Three Thousand Years* (London: Penguin).

MacDowell, D. M. (1978), *The Law in Classical Athens* (Ithaca, NY: Cornell University Press).

MacKenzie, R., C. Romano, Y. Shany, and P. Sands (2009), *Manual on International Courts and Tribunals* (Oxford: Oxford University Press).

Macklem, P. (2008), 'Indigenous Recognition in International Law: Theoretical Observations', 39 Michigan Journal of International Law 177.

Maddicott, J. (2010), *The Origins of the English Parliament* (Oxford: Oxford University Press).

Maduro, M. (2003a), 'Contrapunctual Law: Europe's Constitutional Pluralism in Action', in Walker (2003), *Sovereignty in Transition*, at 501.

Maduro, M. (2003b), 'Europe and the constitution: what if this is as good as it gets?', in Weiler and Wind (2003), *European Constitutionalism beyond the State*, at 74.

Maduro, M. (2007), 'Interpreting European Law: Judicial Adjudication in Context of Constitutional Pluralism' (2007) 2 European Journal of Legal Studies, available online at <http://www.ejls.eu/2/25UK.htm>.

Magnette, P. (2005), *Citizenship: the History of an Idea*, trans. K. Long (Essex: ECPR Press).

Mahmood, T. (1995), *Statutes of Personal Law in Islamic Countries*, 2nd edn (New Delhi: India and Islam Research Council).

Mahoney, P. (2004), 'The Comparative Method in Judgments of the European Court of Human Rights: Reference Back to National Law', in Canivet, Andenas, and Fairgrieve (2004), *Comparative Law Before Courts*, at 135.

Maine, H. S. (1861), *Ancient Law* (London: Oxford University Press, 1931 reprint).

Majone, G. (2000), 'International Regulatory Cooperation: a neo-institutionalist approach', in Bermann, Herdegen, and Lindseth (2000), *Transatlantic Regulatory Cooperation*, at 119.

Major, J. (1960), *Representative Institutions in Renaissance France 1421–1559* (Madison: University of Wisconsin Press).

Major, J. (1971), 'The French Renaissance Monarchy as seen through the Estates General', in Cohn (1972), *Government in Reformation Europe*, at 43.

Makkonen, T. (2000), *Identity, Difference and Otherness[:] The Concepts of 'People', 'Indigenous People' and 'Minority' in International law* (Helsinki: University of Helsinki).

Malaurie, Ph. (2005), 'L'État et la religion', Répertoire du notariat, Defrénois (2005) (no. 7) 572.

Malcolm, N. (1991), 'Hobbes and Spinoza', in Burns (1991), *Cambridge History of Political Thought 1450–1700*, at 530.

Malcolm, N. (2000), *Aspects of Hobbes* (Oxford: Clarendon Press).

Malgaud, W. (1965), 'Les antinomies en droit; à propos de l'étude de G. Gavazzi', in Perelman (1965a), *Les antinomies*, at 7.

Malinowski, G. (1993), *Many-Valued Logics* (Oxford: Clarendon Press).

Malinowski, G. (2007), 'Many-valued Logic', in Gabbay and Woods (2007), *Many Valued Turn*, at 13.

Mallat, C. (1993a), *Islam and Public Law* (London: Graham and Trotman).

Mallat, C. (1993b), *The Renewal of Islamic Law[:] Muhammad Baqer as-Sadr, Najaf and the Shi'i International* (Cambridge: Cambridge University Press).

Malt, G-F. (1992), 'Methods for the Solution of Conflicts between Rules in a System of Positive Law', in Brouwer (1992), *Coherence and Conflict*, at 201.

Manguel, A. (2006), *The Library at Night* (Toronto: Alfred A. Knopf).

Mann, C. C. (2005), *1491/Ancient Americans* (New York/London: Knopf/Granta).

Mann, M. (1986), *The sources of social power*, vol. II, *The rise of classes and nation-states, 1760–1914* (Cambridge: Cambridge University Press).

Maoz, A. (1998), 'The Values of a Jewish and Democratic State', in N. Rakover (1998), *Jerusalem City of Law and Justice* (Jerusalem: Library of Jewish Law), at 147.

Mapel, D. and T. Nardin (eds) (1998), *International Society: Diverse Ethical Perspectives* (Princeton, NJ: Princeton University Press).

Margadant S. G. F. (1994), *Introducción a la historia del derecho mexicano*, 9th edn (Mexico: Editorial Esfinge).

Maritain, J. (1951), *Man and the State* (Chicago: University of Chicago Press).

Marshall, M. and B. Cole (2009), *Global Report 2009: Conflict, Governance and State Fragility* (Severn: Center for Systemic Peace), accessible at <http://www.humansecuritygateway.com>.

Marshall, P. J. (2012), *Remaking the British Atlantic* (Oxford: Oxford University Press).

Marshall, T. H. (1950), *Citizenship and Social Class* (Cambridge: Cambridge University Press).

Marsilius (1980), *Defensor Pacis*, trans. and intro. A. Gewirth (Toronto: University of Toronto Press).

Martin, D. and K. Hailbronner (2003), *Rights and Duties of Dual Nationals: Evolution and Prospects* (The Hague: Kluwer).

Martinez-Torrón, J. and C. Durham (eds) (2010a), *Religion and the Secular State/La religion et l'Etat laïque* (Provo, UT: Brigham Young University).

Martinez-Torrón, J. and C. Durham (2010b), 'Religion and the Secular State', in Martinez-Torrón and Durham (2010), *Religion and the Secular State*, at 1.

Martinico, G. (2007), 'Complexity and Cultural Sources of Law in the EU Context: From the Multilevel Constitutionalism to the Constitutional *Synallagma*', 8 German Law Journal 205.

Martinico, G. (2011), 'Born to Be Together: The Constitutional Complexity of the EU', 16 Review of Constitutional Studies 63.

Maskens, A. (2005), 'Résilience des ideologies mono-identaires: le cas de la Belgique', in Noreau and Woehrling (2005), *Appartenances, institutions et citoyenneté*, at 13.

Mason, A. (2004), 'The Common Law in Final Courts of Appeal Outside Britain', 78 Australian Law Journal 183.

Masud, M., R. Peters, and D. Powers (2006), *Dispensing Justice in Islam* (Leiden: Brill).

Matson, J. (1993), 'The Common Law Abroad: English and Indigenous Laws in the British Commonwealth', 42 ICLQ 754.

Matyssek, U. (2008), 'Zum Problem der Trennung von Religion und Politik im Islam', in Muckel (2008), *Islam im öffentlichen Recht*, at 158.

Mautner, M. (2011), *Law and the Culture of Israel* (Oxford: Oxford University Press).

Mayer, P. (2007), 'Le phénomène de la coordination des ordres juridiques étatiques en droit privé', 327 Receuil des cours 9.

Mayer, T. (ed.) (1963), *Das Königtum: seine geistigen und rechtlichen Grundlagen*, vol. III (Lindau: Jan Thorbecke Verlag).

Mazower, M. (2009), *No Enchanted Palace: The End of Empire and the Ideological Origins of the United Nations* (Princeton, NJ: Princeton University Press).

McCorquodale, R. (2004), 'An Inclusive International Legal System', 17 Leiden Journal of International Law 477.

McCorquodale, R. (2010), 'The Individual and the International Legal System', in M. Evans (ed.) (2010), *International Law*, 3rd edn (Oxford: Oxford University Press), at 284.

McCrudden, C. (2000), 'A Common Law of Human Rights? Transnational Judicial Conversations on Constitutional Rights', 20 OJLS 499.

McGinnis, J. (2006), 'Foreign to Our Constitution', 100 Northwestern University Law Review 303.

McGinnis, J. and I. Somin (2007), 'Should International Law be Part of Our Law?', 59 Stanford Law Review 1175.

McHugh, P. (2005), *Aboriginal Societies and the Common Law* (Oxford: Oxford University Press).

McLean, I. and F. Hewitt (trans. and eds) (1994), *Condorcet: Foundations of Social Choice and Political Theory* (Aldershot: Edward Elgar).

McLean, J. (2012), *Searching for the State in British Legal Thought* (Cambridge: Cambridge University Press).

McNeill, W. (1986), *Polyethnicity and National Unity in World History* (Toronto: University of Toronto Press).

McPherson, B. (2007), *The Reception of English Law Abroad* (Brisbane: Supreme Court of Queensland Library).

Mehdi, R., H. Petersen, E. Sand, and G. Woodman (eds) (2008), *Law and Religion in Multicultural Societies* (Copenhagen: DJØF).

Meichtry, S., 'Vatican Lashes Out at China over Bishop's Appointment', *Wall Street Journal*, 24 November 2010.

Meidinger, E. (2007), 'Beyond Westphalia: Competitive Legalization in Emerging Transnational Regulatory Systems', in Brütsch and Lehmkuhl (2007), *Law and Legalization in Transnational Relations*, at 121.

Menashi, S. (2010), 'Ethnonationalism and Liberal Democracy', 32 University of Pennsylvania International Law Review 57.

Menski, W. (2003), *Hindu Law* (New Delhi: Oxford University Press).

Menski, W. (2008), 'Law, Religion and Culture in Multicultural Britain', in Mehdi *et al* (2008), *Law and Religion in Multicultural Societies*, at 43.

Meron, T. (2006), *The Humanization of International Law* (Leiden: Martinus Nijhoff).

Merryman, J. (1977), 'Toward a Theory of Citations: An Empirical Study of the Citation Practice of the California Supreme Court in 1950, 1960, and 1970', 50 California Law Review 381.

Messitte, P. (2005), 'Citing Foreign Law in US Courts: Is our Sovereignty Really at Stake?', 35 Baltimore Law Review 171.

Mestre, J. (2002), 'Droit civil: Rapport général', in Association Henri Capitant (2002), *Les minorities*, at 223.

Mettam, R. (ed.) (1977), *Government and Society in Louis XIV's France* (London: Macmillan).

Meyer, E. (1907), *Geschichte des Altertumes*, vol. I, *Erste Hälfte* (Stuttgart: J. G. Cotta).

Meyer, E. (2004), *Legitimacy and Law in the Roman World[:]* Tabulae *in Roman Belief and Practice* (Cambridge: Cambridge University Press).

Michaels, R. (2005), 'Welche Globalisierung für das Recht? Welches Recht für die Globalisierung?', 69 Rabels Zeitschrift fur Auslandisches und Internationales Privatrecht 525.

Michaels, R. (2007), 'The True *Lex Mercatoria*: Law Beyond the State', 14 Indiana Journal of Global Legal Studies 447.

Migdal, J. (1988), *Strong Societies and Weak States* (Princeton, NJ: Princeton University Press).

Migdal, J. S. (2001), *State in Society[:] Studying How States and Societies Transform and Constitute One Another* (Cambridge: Cambridge University Press).

Mikunda-Franco, E. (2001), 'Der Verfassungsstaat in der islamischen Welt', in Morlok (2001), *Die Welt des Verfassungsstaates*, at 151.

Mill. J. S. (1862), *Considerations on Representative Government* (New York: Harper and Bros.).

Miller, D. (1998), 'The Limits of Cosmopolitan Justice', in Mapel and Nardin (1998), *International Society*, at 164.

Miller, D. (2000), *Citizenship and National Identity* (Cambridge: Polity Press).

Miller, M. (2003), 'Migration in Post-Cold War Relations', in Ghosh (2003a), *Managing Migration*, at 42.

Miller, N. (2008), 'The Dawn of the Age of Toleration: Samuel Pufendorf and the Road not Taken', 50 Journal of Church and State 255.

Miller, R. (2011), 'Tribal Constitutions and Native Sovereignty', accessible online at <http://papers.ssrn.com/sol3/papers.cfm?abstract_id=1802890>.

Mills, A. (2006), 'The Private History of International Law', 55 ICLQ 1.

Miranda, L. (2010), 'Indigenous Peoples as International Lawmakers', 32 University of Pennsylvania Journal of International Law 203.

Mirow, M. (2004), *Latin American Law* (Austin: University of Texas Press).

Mirow, M. (2010), 'La tradición romanística en los Estados Unidos con una nota sobre el estado de la Florida', 32 *Revista de Estudios Históricos* 383.

Mirow, M. (2013), 'Pre-Constitutional Law and Constitutions: Spanish Colonial Law and the Constitution of Cádiz', 12 Washington University Global Studies Law Review; accessible online at <http://ssrn.com/abtract=2056384>.

Mitteis, H. (1975), *The State of the Middle Ages*, trans. H. Orton (Amsterdam: North-Holland).

Molfessis, N. (1999), 'La Langue et le Droit', in Jayme (1999), *Langue et Droit*, at 177.

Möllers, C. (2000), *Staat als Argument* (Munich: C. H. Beck).

Möllers, C. (2001), 'Globalisierte Jurisprudenz: Einflüsse relativierter Nationalstaatlichkeit auf das Konzept des Rechts und die Funktion seiner Theorie', in Anderheiden, Huster, and Kirste (2001), *Globalisierung als Problem*, at 41.

Monaghan, H. P. (2007), 'Article III and Supranational Judicial Review', 107 Columbia Law Review 833.

Monahan, A. (1994), *From Personal Duties towards Personal Rights[:] Late Medieval and Early Modern Political Thought, 1300–1600* (Montreal/Kingston: McGill-Queens University Press).

Montesquieu (1989), *The Spirit of the Laws*, trans. A. Cohler, B. Miller, and H. Stone (Cambridge: Cambridge University Press).

Moore, K. (1995), *Al-Mughtaribun[:] American Law and the Transformation of Muslim Life in the United States* (Albany: State University of New York Press).

Moore, M. (2001), *The Ethics of Nationalism* (Oxford: Oxford University Press).

Moote, A. (1971), *The Revolt of the Judges[:] The* Parlement *of Paris and the Fronde 1643–1652* (Princeton, NJ: Princeton University Press).

Morag-Levine, N. (2006), 'Judges, Legislators, and Europe's Law: Common-law Constitutionalism and Foreign Precedents', 65 Maryland Law Review 32.

Morand, Ch-A. (ed.) (2001), *Le droit saisi par la mondialisation* (Bruxelles: Bruylant).

Moreso, J. (2012), 'Ways of Solving Conflicts of Constitutional Rights: Proportionalism and Specificationism', 25 Ratio Juris 31.

Morgan, E. (1988), *Inventing the People[:] The Rise of Popular Sovereignty in England and America* (New York: W. W. Norton).

Morlok, M. (ed.) (2001), *Die Welt des Verfassungsstaates* (Baden-Baden: Nomos).

Morris, C. (1998), *An Essay on the Modern State* (Cambridge: Cambridge University Press).

Morris, L. (2010), *Asylum, Welfare and the Cosmopolitan Ideal* (Abingdon: Routledge).

Muckel, S. (ed.) (2008), *Der Islam im öffentlichen Recht des säkularen Verfassungsstaates* (Berlin: Duncker & Humblot).

Muldoon, J. (1999), *Empire and Order[:] The Concept of Empire, 800–1800* (London: Macmillan).

Muller, S. and S. Richards (2010), *Highest Courts and Globalisation* (The Hague: Hague Academic Press).

Munters, Q. (1975), 'Some Remarks on the Opening Up of Rural Social Systems', 15 *Sociologica Ruralis* 34.

Munz, P. (1960), *The Origin of the Carolingian Empire* (Leicester: Leicester University Press).

Murkens, J. (2007), 'The Future of *Staatsrecht*: Dominance, Demise or Demystification', 70 MLR 731.

Muthu, S. (2003), *Enlightenment Against Empire* (Princeton, NJ: Princeton University Press).

Muthu, S. (2006), 'Justice and Foreigners: Kant's Cosmopolitan Right', in S. Byrd and J. Hruschka (2006), *Kant and Law* (Aldershot: Ashgate), at 449.

Myler, B. (2006), 'Towards a Common Law Originalism', 59 Stanford Law Review 551.

Nafziger, J. and S. Ross (2011), *Handbook on International Sports Law* (Northampton, MA: Edward Elgar).

Narain, V. (2008), *Reclaiming the Nation* (Toronto: University of Toronto Press).

Navot, S. (1999), 'Language Rights in Israel', in Jayme (1999), *Langue et Droit*, at 199.

Ndima, D. (2003), 'The African Law of the 21st Century in South Africa', 36 Comparative and International Law Journal of Southern Africa 325.

Nederman, C. (1995), *Community and Consent* (Lanham, MD: Rownan and Littlefield).

Nelson, B. (2006), *The Making of the Modern State[:] A Theoretical Evolution* (New York: Palgrave MacMillan).

Nelson, E. (2010), *The Hebrew Republic[:] Jewish Sources and the Transformation of European Political Thought* (Cambridge, MA: Harvard University Press).

Nelson, J. (1986), *Politics and Ritual in Early Medieval Europe* (London: Hambledon Press).

Nelson, J. (1988), 'Kingship and empire', in Burns (1988), *Cambridge History of Medieval Political Thought c.350–c.1450*, at 211.

Nelson, J. (1996), *The Frankish World 750–900* (London: Hambledon Press).

Neoh, J. (2008), 'Islamic State and the Common Law in Malaysia: A Case Study of Lina Joy', 8(2) Global Jurist Advances, Article 4.

Neusner, J. and T. Sonn (1999), *Comparing Religions Through Law: Judaism and Islam* (London: Routledge).

Neuwahl N. and S. Haack (eds) (2007), *Unresolved Issues of the Constitution for Europe: Rethinking the Crisis* (Montreal: Thémis).

Ngai, M. (2004), *Impossible Subjects: Illegal Aliens and the Making of Modern America* (Princeton, NJ: Princeton University Press).

Nicholas, D. (1997),*The Growth of the Medieval City[:] From Late Antiquity to the Early Fourteenth Century* (London: Longman).

Nicholas, D. (1999), *The Transformation of Europe 1300–1600* (London: Arnold).

Nicholas, D. (2003), *Urban Europe, 1100–1700* (New York: Palgrave Macmillan).

Nicol H. and I. Townsend Gault (2005), *Holding the line: Borders in a global world* (Vancouver: UBC. Press).

Nietzsche, F. (1969), *Thus Spoke Zarathustra[:] A Book for Everyone and No One*, trans. R. J. Lollingdale (London: Penguin).

Niglia, L. (ed.) (2013), *Pluralism and European Private Law* (Oxford: Hart).

Noda, Y. (1976), *Introduction to Japanese Law*, trans. A. Angelo (Tokyo: Tokyo University Press).

Nollkaemper, A. (2011), *National Courts and the International Rule of Law* (Oxford: Oxford University Press).

Noonan, J. (1993), 'God Does Not Take Bribes', in Noonan and Winston (1993), *Responsible Judge*, at 3.

Noonan, J. and K. Winston (1993), *The Responsible Judge* (Westport, CT: Praeger).

Nora, P. (ed.) (1996a), *Realms of Memory[:] Rethinking the French Past*, vol. 1, *Conflicts and Divisions* (New York: Columbia University Press).

Nora, P. (1996b), 'Introduction to Volume I; *Conflicts and Divisions*', in Nora (1996a), *Realms of Memory*, at 21.

Nora, P. (2001), *Rethinking France: Les Lieux de Mémoire*, trans. M. Trouille (Chicago: University of Chicago Press).

Nordman, D. (1982),'Problématique historique: des frontières de L'Europe aux frontières du Maghreb (19e siècle)', in *Frontières[:] Problèmes de frontières dans le tiers monde* (Paris: L'Harmattan).

Noreau, P. and J. Woehrling (2005), *Appartenances, institutions et citoyenneté* (Montreal: Wilson & Lafleur).

North, D., J. Wallis, and B. Weingast (2009), *Violence and Social Orders: A Conceptual Framework for Interpreting Recorded Human History* (New York: Cambridge University Press).

Nouel, P. (1997), 'The International Practice of Law', in N. P. Vogt (ed.) (1997), *The International Practice of Law* (The Hague: Kluwer), at 183.

Novak, D. (2005), *The Jewish Social Contract* (Princeton, NJ: Princeton University Press).

Nussbaum, A. (1947), *A Concise History of the Law of Nations* (New York: Macmillan).

Nussbaum, M. (1994), 'Patriotism and Cosmopolitanism', *Boston Review*, reprinted in Nussbaum, M. (1996), *For Love of Country* (Boston, MA: Beacon Press), at 3.

Oakeshott, M. (2006), *Lectures in the History of Political Thought* (ed. T. Nardin and L. O'Sullivan) (Exeter: Imprint Academic).

Oakley, F. (2003), *The Conciliarist Tradition: Constitutionalism in the Catholic Church 1300–1870* (Oxford: Oxford University Press).

Oakley, F. (2005), *Natural Law, Laws of Nature, Natural Rights[:] Continuity and Discontinuity in the History of Ideas* (New York: Continuum).

O'Brien, P. (2006), 'Historiographical Traditions and Modern Imperatives for the Restoration of Global History', (2006) 1 Journal of Global History 3.

O'Donnell, T. A. (1982), 'The Margin of Appreciation Doctrine: Standards of Jurisprudence of the European Court of Human Rights', 4 Human Rights Quarterly 474.

O'Donovan, O. (2003), 'Christianity and Territorial Right', in Buchanan and Moore (2003), *States, Nations, and Borders*, at 127.

Ohmae, K. (1995), *The End of the Nation State* (New York: The Free Press).

Ohnesorge, J. (2007), 'Developing Development Theory: Law & Development Orthodoxies and the Northeast Asian Experience', 28 University of Pennsylvania Journal of International Economic Law 219.

Oliver, P. (2005), *The Constitution of Independence* (Oxford: Oxford University Press).

O'Neill, O. (2000), *Bounds of Justice* (Cambridge: Cambridge University Press).

Ong, W. (1982), *Orality and Literacy: The Technologizing of the Word* (London: Methuen).

Ong, W. (2002), *Orality and Literacy: TheTechnologizing of the Word*, 2nd edn (London: Methuen).

Onuma, Y. (2000), 'When was the Law of International Society Born?—An Inquiry of the History of International Law from an Intercivilizational Perspective', 2 Journal of the History of International Law 1.

Onuma, Y. (2010), *A Transcivilizational Perspective on International Law* (The Hague: Hague Academy of International Law).

Opello, W., Jr. and S. Rosow (2004), *The Nation-State and Global Order[:] A Historical Introduction to Contemporary Politics* (Boulder, CO/London: Lynne Rienner).

Ørebech, P., F. Bosselman, J. Bjarup, D. Callies, M. Chanock, and H. Petersen (2005), *The Role of Customary Law in Sustainable Development* (Cambridge: Cambridge University Press).

Örücü, E. (1999), 'Comparative Law in British Courts', in Drobnig and van Erp (1999), *Use of Comparative Law*, at 253.

Örücü, E. (2008), 'Judicial Navigation as Official Law meets Culture in Turkey', 4 International Journal of Law in Context 35.

Örücü, E. and D. Nelken (eds) (2007), *Comparative Law: A Handbook* (Oxford: Hart).

Osiatynski, W. (2003), 'Paradoxes of Constitutional Borrowing', 1 International Journal of Constitutional Law 244.

Oskal, N. (1999), 'The Moral Foundation for the Disqualification of Aboriginal People's Proprietary Rights to Land and Political Sovereignty', in Svensson (1999), *On Customary Law*, at 99.

Ost, F. and M. Van de Kerchove (2002), *De la pyramide au réseau?* (Brussels: Publications des Facultés universitaires Saint-Louis).

Osterhammel, J. and N. Petersson (2005), *Globalization[:] a short history*, trans. D. Geyer (Princeton, NJ: Princeton University Press).

Ostien, P. and A. Dekker (2010), 'Sharia and national law in Nigeria', in Otto (2010a), *Sharia Incorporated*, at 553.

Ostler, N. (2005), *Empires of the World[:] A Language History of the World* (London: HarperCollins).

Ostrom, E. (1990), *Governing the Commons* (Cambridge: Cambridge University Press).

Otis, G. (2006), 'Territorialité, personnalité et gouvernance autochtone', 47 Cahiers de Droit 781.

Otis, G. (2007), 'L'autonomie personnelle au coeur des droits ancestraux: *sub qua lege vivis?*', 52 McGill Law Journal 657.

Otto, J. (ed.) (2010a), *Sharia Incorporated: A Comparative Overview of the Legal Systems of Twelve Muslim Countries in Past and Present* (Leiden: Leiden University Press).

Otto, J. (2010b), 'Sharia and national law in Indonesia', in Otto (2010a), *Sharia Incorporated*, at 433.

Owensby, B. P. (2008), *Empire of Law and Indian Justice in Colonial Mexico* (Stanford, CA: Stanford University Press).

Padovani, A. (2007), 'The Metaphysical Thought of Late Medieval Jurisprudence', in E. Pattaro (ed.), *A Treatise of Legal Philosophy and General Jurisprudence*, vol. 7 (Dordrecht: Springer), at 31.

Pagden, A. (1995), *Lords of All the World* (New Haven, CT: Yale University Press).

Pagden, A. (2003), 'The Christian Tradition', in Buchanan and Moore (2003), *States, Nations and Borders*, at 103.

Palermo, F. and N. Sabanadze (2011), *National Minorities in Inter-State Relations* (Leiden: Martinus Nijhoff).

Palmer, M. (2006), 'Using Constitutional Realism to Identify the Complete Constitution: Lessons from an Unwritten Constitution', 54 AJCL 587.

Paquette, G. (2011), 'The Brazilian origins of the 1826 Portuguese Constitution', 41 *European History Quarterly* 444.

Paquin, S. (2005), 'De l'importance internationale de la paradiplomatie', in Noreau and Woehrling (2005), *Appartenances, institutions et cioyenneté*, at 219.

Parker, K. (2011), 'Law "In" and "As" History: The Common Law in the American Polity, 1790–1900', 1 UC Irvine Law Review 587.

Parlett, K. (2011), *The Individual in the International Legal System: Continuity and Change in International* Law (Cambridge: Cambridge University Press).

Parsons, T. (2010), *The Rule of Empires* (Oxford: Oxford University Press).

Paul, J. (2008), 'The Transformation of International Comity', 71 Law & Contemporary Problems 19.

Paul, T., G. Ikenberry, and J. Hall (eds) (2003), *The Nation-State in Question* (Princeton, NJ: Princeton University Press).

Pauwelyn, J., R. Wessel, and J. Wouters (eds) (2012), *Informal International Lawmaking* (Oxford: Oxford University Press).

Pawlish, H. (1985), *Sir John Davies and the Conquest of Ireland[:] A Study in Legal Imperialism* (Cambridge: Cambridge University Press).

Peirce, C. (1958), *Selected Writings (Values in a Universe of Chance)* (New York: Dover).

Peleg, I. (2007), *Democratizing the Hegemonic State[:] Political Transformation in the Age of Identity* (Cambridge: Cambridge University Press).

Pendu, M. (2008), *Le fait religieux en droit privé* (Paris: Defrénois).

Pennington, K. (1988), 'Law, Legislative Authority and Theories of Government, 1150–1300', in Burns (1988), *Cambridge History of Medieval Political Thought c.350–c.1450*, at 424.

Peoples, L. (2008), 'The Use of Foreign Law by the Advocates General of the Court of Justice of the European Communities', 35 Syracuse Journal of International Law and Commerce 218.

Perdue, P. (2005), *China Marches West[:] The Qing Conquest of Central Eurasia* (Cambridge, MA: Harvard University Press).

Perelman, Ch. (ed.) (1965a), *Les antinomies en droit* (Brussels: Bruylant).

Perelman, Ch. (1965b), 'Avant-propos', in Perelman (1965a), *Les antinomies*, at 5.

Perelman, Ch. (1965c), 'Les antinomies en droit: Essai de synthèse', in Perelman (1965a), *Les antinomies*, at 392.

Pérez, A. (2009), *Conflicts of Rights in the European Union* (Oxford: Oxford University Press).

Perez, O. and G. Teubner (eds) (2006), *Paradoxes and Inconsistencies in Law* (Oxford: Hart).

Perju, V. (2010), 'Cosmopolitanism and Constitutional Self-government', 8 International Journal of Constitutional Law 326.

Petermann, Ch. (2001), 'Kant, précurseur de la mondialisation du droit', in Morand (2001), *Le droit saisi*, at 171.

Peters, A. (2006), 'Compensatory Constitutionalism: The Function and Potential of Fundamental International Norms and Structures', 19 Leiden Journal of International Law 580.

Peters, A. (2009a), 'The Merits of Global Constitutionalism', 16 Indiana Journal of Global Legal Studies 397.

Peters, A. (2009b), 'Supremacy Lost: International Law Meets Domestic Constitutional Law', 3 Vienna Online Journal of International Constitutional Law 170.

Peters, R. (2005), *Crime and Punishment in Islamic Law* (Cambridge: Cambridge University Press).

Petot, P. (1961), 'Le droit commun en France selon les coutumiers', (1961) Revue historique de droit français et étranger 413.

Pew Forum on Religion and Public Life (2009), 'Global Restrictions on Religion', accessible online at <http://www.pewforum.org/government/global-restrictions-on-religion.aspx>.

Pfander, J. and D. Birk (2011), 'Article III and the Scottish Judiciary', 124 Harvard Law Review 1613.

Philpott, D. (2000), 'The Religious Roots of Modern International Relations', 52 *World Politics* 206.

Phuc, X. (2007), 'Fuzzy Property Relations in the Vietnamese Uplands: Ethnography of Forest Access and Control', 55 Journal of Legal Pluralism & Unofficial Law 73.

Picq, J. (1995a), *Il faut aimer l'État* (Paris: Flammarion).

Picq, J. (1995b), *L'État en France[:] Servir une nation ouverte sur le monde (Rapport au Premier ministre)* (Paris: La Documentation Française).

Picq, J. (2005), *Histoire et droit des États* (Paris: Presses de Sciences Po).

Pihlajamäki, H. (2003), 'La heterogeneidad del *Ius Commune*: Observaciones comparativas sobre la relación entre el derecho europeo y el derecho indiano', in XIII Congreso del Instituto internactional de historia del derecho indiano, L. E. González Vale (ed.) *Actas y Estudios* (San Juan: Asamblea Legislativa de Puerto Rico), at 57.

Pillet, A. (1923), *Traité pratique de droit international privé*, vol. 1 (Paris: Sirey).

Pinheiro, H. (2001), 'The "Denationalization" of Transnational Relationships—Regulation of Transnational Relationships by Public International Law, European Community Law and Transnational Law', in J. Basedow *et al* (eds) (2001), *Aufbruch nach Europea* (Tübingen: Mohr-Siebeck), at 429.

Pinker, S. (2011), *The Better Angels of our Nature: Why Violence has Declined* (New York: Viking).

Piscatori, J. (1986), *Islam in a World of Nation-States* (Cambridge: Cambridge University Press).

Pison, G. (2010), 'The Number and Proportion of Immigrants in the Population: international comparisons', 472 *Population and Societies* (INED) 1.

Plasseraud, Y. (1989), 'Les revendications des minorités autochtones de France métropolitaine deux siècles après 1789', in Fenet and Soulier (1989), *Les minorités*, at 205.

Plato, *The Sophist*, many editions.

Plato, *The Statesman*, many editions.

Pocock, J. G. A. (1987), *The Ancient Constitution and the Feudal Law—A Study of English Historical Thought in the Seventeenth Century[:] A Reissue with a Retrospect* (Cambridge, Cambridge University Press).

Pocock, J. G. A. (1995), 'The Ideal of Citizenship Since Classical Times', in Beiner (1995), *Theorizing Citizenship*, at 29.

Pocock, J. G. A. (2003), *The Machiavellian Moment[:] Florentine Political Thought and the Atlantic Republican Tradition* (Princeton, NJ: Princeton University Press).

Pogge, T. (1994), 'An Egalitarian Law of Peoples', 23 *Philosophy & Public Affairs* 195.

Pogge, T. (2006), 'Kant's Theory of Justice', in S. Byrd and J. Hruschka (2006), *Kant and Law* (Aldershot: Ashgate), at 41.

Poggi, G. (1978), *The Development of the Modern State[:] A Sociological Introduction* (Stanford, CA: Stanford University Press).

Poggi, G. (1990), *The State[:] Its Nature, Development and Prospects* (Cambridge: Polity Press).

Popper, K. (1963), (1966), *The Open Society and its Enemies*, 5th edn, vol. I, *The Spell of Plato*, vol. II, *The High Tide of Prophecy: Hegel, Marx, and the Aftermath* (Princeton, NJ: Princeton University Press).

Porat, I. and M. Cohen-Eliya (2010), 'American Balancing and German Proportionality: The Historical Origins', 8 International Journal of Constitutional Law 263.

Posner, R. (2005), 'Foreword: A Political Court', 119 Harvard Law Review 31.

Post, G. (1964), *Studies in Medieval Legal Thought[:] Public Law and the State, 1100–1322* (Princeton, NJ: Princeton University Press).

Post, R. (2001), 'The Challenge of Globalization to American Public Law Scholarship', (2001) 2 Theoretical Inquiries in Law 323.

Postema, G. (2002), 'Philosophy of the Common Law', in J. Coleman and S. Shapiro (eds), *The Oxford Handbook of Jurisprudence and Philosophy of Law* (Oxford: Oxford University Press), at 588.

Postema, G. (2011), *Legal Philosophy in the Twentieth Century: The Common Law World*, vol. II of E. Pattaro (ed.), *A Treatise of Legal Philosophy and General Jurisprudence* (Springer: Dordrecht).

Potvin-Solis, L. (1999), *L'effet des jurisprudences européennes sur la jurisprudence du Conseil d'État français* (Paris: LGDJ).

Potvin-Solis, L. (2004), 'Le concept de dialogue entre les juges en Europe', in Lichère *et al* (2004), *Le dialogue entre les juges*, at 19.

Poulter, S. (1999), *Ethnicity, Law and Human Rights[:] The English Experience* (Oxford: Oxford University Press).

Pradel, J. (2001), 'La mondialisation du droit pénal: enjeux et perspectives', 35 Revue Juridique Themis 241.

Prakken, H. (2004), 'Analysing Reasoning about Evidence with Formal Models of Argumentation', 3 Law, Probability and Risk 33.

Preece, J. (1998), *National Minorities and the European Nation-States System* (Oxford: Clarendon Press).

Prempeh, H. (2007), 'Africa's "constitutional revival": False start of new dawn?', 5 International Journal of Constitutional Law 469.

Preuss, U. (2004), 'Citizenship and the German Nation', in Bellamy, Castiglione, and Santoro (2004), *Lineages of European Citizenship*, at 22.

Priest, G. (2001), *An Introduction to Non-Classical Logic* (Cambridge: Cambridge University Press).

Priest, G. (2006), *In Contradiction[:] A Study of the Transconsistent* (Oxford: Clarendon Press).

Priest, G. (2007), 'Paraconsistency and Dialetheism', in Gabbay and Woods (2007), *Many Valued Turn*, at 129.

Prodi, P. (2003), *Eine Geschichte der Gerechtigkeit[:] vom Recht Gottes zum modernen Rechtstaat*, trans. A Seemannn (Munich: C. H. Beck).

Provost, R. (2008), 'Judging in Splendid Isolation', 56 AJCL 125.

Puett, M. (2006), 'Innovation as Ritualization: The Fractured Cosmology of Early China', 28 Cardozo Law Review 23.

Pufendorf, S. (2007), *The Present State of Germany*, trans. E. Bohun (Indianapolis: Liberty Fund).

Pufendorf, S. (2005), *On the Law of Nature and Nations*, trans. B Kennett (Clark, NJ: Lawbook Exchange).

Quraishi, A. and N. Syeed-Miller (2004), 'No Altars: a survey of Islamic family law in the United States', in Welchman (2004), *Women's Rights & Islamic Family Law*, at 177.

Rabkin, J. (2004), *The Case for Sovereignty* (Washington, DC: The AEI Press).

Rabkin, J. (2005), *Law Without Nations? Why Constitutional Government Requires Sovereign States* (Princeton, NJ: Princeton University Press).

Radin, M. (1932), 'The Endless Problem of Corporate Personality', 32 Columbia Law Review 643.

Rae, H. (2002), *State Identities and the Homogenisation of Peoples* (Cambridge: Cambridge University Press).

Rahdert, M. (2007), 'Comparative Constitutional Advocacy', 56 American University Law Review 553.

Rahn, G. (1990), *Rechtsdenken und Rechtsauffassung in Japan* (Munich: C. H. Beck).

Raič, D. (2002), *Statehood and the Law of Self-Determination* (The Hague: Kluwer).

Rajagopal, B. (2003), *International Law from Below[:] Developments, Social Movements, and Third World Resistance* (Cambridge: Cambridge University Press).

Ralph, J. (2007), *Defending the Society of States[:] Why America Opposes the International Criminal Court and its Vision of World Society* (Oxford: Oxford University Press).

Ramraj, V. (2002), 'Comparative Constitutional Law in Singapore', 6 Singapore Journal of International & Comparative Law 302.

Ranger, T. and O. Vaughan (1993), *Legitimacy and the State in Twentieth-Century Africa* (New York: Palgrave).

Ratner, S. (2011), 'Between Minimum and Optimum World Public Order: An Ethical Path for the Future', in M. Arsanjani *et al* (eds) (2011), *Looking to the Future: Essays on International Law in Honor of W. Michael Reisman* (Leiden, Brill), at 195.

Raustiala, K. (2009), *Does the Constitution Follow the Flag? The Evolution of Territoriality in American Law* (Oxford: Oxford University Press).

Rawls, J. (1971), *A Theory of Justice* (Cambridge, MA: Belknap Press of Harvard University Press).

Rawls, J. (1993), *Political Liberalism* (New York: Columbia University Press).

Rawls, J. (1999), *The Law of Peoples* (Cambridge, MA: Harvard University Press).

Raz, J. (1980a), *The Concept of a Legal Stystem*, 2nd edn (Oxford: Clarendon Press).

Raz, J. (1980b), *The Authority of Law* (Oxford: Clarendon Press).

Razak, S. (2008), 'Between a Rock and a Hard Place: Canadian Muslim Women's Responses to Faith-Based Arbitration', in Mehdi *et al* (2008), *Law and Religion*, at 83.

Reed, R. (2008), 'Foreign Precedents and Judicial Reasoning: The American Debate and British Practice', 124 LQR 253.

Reimann, M. (1989), 'The Historical School Against Codification: Savigny, Carter and the Defeat of the New York Civil Code', 37 AJCL 95.

Reimann, M. and R. Zimmermann (eds) (2006), *The Oxford Handbook of Comparative Law* (Oxford: Oxford University Press).

Rémy, P. (1982), 'Éloge de l'exégèse', 7 Revue de la recherche juridique 254, reproduced in (1985) 1 Droits 115.

Renan, E. (1991), *Qu'est-ce qu'une nation?* (Paris: Pierre Bordas).

Renteln, A. D. (2004), *The Cultural Defense* (New York: Oxford University Press).

Resnik, J. (1989), 'Dependent Sovereignties: Indian Tribes, States, and the Federal Courts', 56 University of Chicago Law Review 671.

Resnik, J. (2006), 'Law's Migration: American Exceptionalism, Silent Dialogues, and Federalism's Multiple Ports of Entry', 115 Yale Law Journal 1564.

Ress, G. (2005), 'The Effect of Decisions and Judgments of the European Court of Human Rights in the Domestic Legal Order', 40 Texas International Law Journal 359.

Richardson, I. (2001), 'Trends in Judgment Writing in the New Zealand Court of Appeal', in R. Bigwood (ed.) (2001), *Legal Method in New Zealand* (Wellington: Butterworths), at 261.

Riché, P. (1993), *The Carolingians[:] A Family who Forged Europe*, trans. M. Allen (Philadelphia: University of Pennsylvania Press).

Ricoeur, P. (2004), *Memory, History, Forgetting*, trans. K. Blamey and D. Pellauer (Chicago: University of Chicago Press).

Riesenberg, P. (1970), *Inalienability of Sovereignty in Medieval Political Thought* (New York: AMS Press).

Rigaux, F. (1997), *La loi des juges* (Paris: Editions Odile Jacob).

Riker, W. (1957), 'Dutch and American Federalism', 18 *Journal of Historical Ideas* 495.

Risse, M. (2012), *On Global Justice* (Princeton, NJ: Princeton University Press).

Robert, M-P. (2004), *La défense culturelle: un moyen de défense non souhaitable en droit pénal canadien* (Cowansville, Quebec: Yvon Blais).

Roberts, A. (2011), 'Comparative International Law? The Role of National Courts in Creating and Enforcing International Law', 60 ICLQ 57.

Roberts, J. M. (1997), *A History of Europe* (New York: Allen Lane).

Roberts, P. (2007), 'Comparative Law for International Criminal Justice', in Örücü and Nelken (2007), *Comparative Law*, at 339.

Robertson, C. (2010), *The Passport in America: The History of a Document* (New York: Oxford University Press).

Robinson, I. (1988), 'Church and papacy', in Burns (1988), *Cambridge History of Medieval Political Thought c. 350–c. 1450*, at 252.

Rodriguez, C. (2010), 'Noncitizen Voting and the Extraconstitutional Construction of the Polity', 8 International Journal of Constitutional Law 30.

Roe, M. (2006), 'Legal Origin and Modern Stock Markets', 120 Harvard Law Review 460.

Román, E. (2010), *Citizenship and its Exclusions* (New York: New York University Press).

Romano, C. (1999), 'The Proliferation of International Judicial Bodies: The Pieces of the Puzzle', 31 Journal of International Law & Politics 708.

Rörig, F. (1967), *The Medieval Town* (London: B. T. Batsford).

Rosecrance, R. (1986), *The Rise of the Trading State* (New York: Basic Books).

Rosecrance, R. (1999), *The Rise of the Virtual State[:] Wealth and Power in the Coming Century* (New York: Basic Books).

Rosenberg, E. (ed.) (2012), *A World Connecting 1870–1945* (Cambridge, MA: Belknap Press of Harvard University Press).

Rosenfeld, M. (2008), 'Rethinking Constitutional Ordering in an era of Legal and Ideological Pluralism', 6 International Journal of Constitutional Law 415.

Rosenfeld, M. (2010), *The Identity of the Constitutional Subject* (New York: Routledge).

Rosenfeld, M. and A. Sajó (eds) (2012a), *The Oxford Handbook of Comparative Constitutional Law* (Oxford: Oxford University Press).

Rosenfeld, M. (2012b), 'Comparative Constitutional Analysis in United States Adjudication and Scholarship', in Rosenfeld and Sajó (2012a), *Oxford Handbook of Comparative Constitutional Law*, at 38.

Rosenkrantz, C. (2003), 'Against Borrowings and other Nonauthoritative Uses of Foreign Law', 1 International Journal of Constitutional Law 270.

Rosenn, K. (1990), 'Brazil's New Constitution: An Exercise in Transient Constitutionalism for a Transitional Society', 38 AJCL 773.

Ross, R. (2008), 'Legal Communications and Imperial Governance: British North America and Spanish America Compared', in C. L. Tomlins and M. Grossberg (eds), *Cambridge History of Law in America*, vol. I, *Early America, 1580–1815* (Cambridge: Cambridge University Press), at 104.

Rouland, N. (2000), 'Le droit français devient-il multiculturel?' 46 Droit et Société 519.

Rouland, N., S. Pierré-Caps, and J. Poumarède (1996), *Droit des minorities et des peuples autochtones* (Paris: PUF).

Rousseau, J-J. (1948), *Émile*, trans. B. Foxley (London: J. M. Dent).

Rousseau, J-J. (2003), *On the Social Contract*, trans. G. D. H. Cole (1762) Mineola, NY: (Dover).

Rowen, H. (1980), *The King's State[:] Proprietary Dynasticism in Early Modern France* (New Brunswick, NJ: Rutgers University Press).

Rubenfeld, J. (2000–3), 'The Two World Orders', 27 Wilson Quarterly 22.

Rubin, A. (1997), *Ethics and Authority in International Law* (Cambridge: Cambridge University Press).

Rückert, J. (2011), 'Abwägung—die juristische Karriere eines unjuristischen Begriffs oder: Normenstrenge und Abwägung im Funktionswandel', [2011] Juristen Zeitung 913.

Ruston, R. (2004), *Human Rights and the Image of God* (London: SCM Press).

Rutledge, P. (2009), '*Medellin*, Delegation and Conflicts (of Law)', 17 George Mason Law Review 191.

Ryan, M. (2010), 'Succession to Fiefs: A *Ius Commune Feudorum?*', in Cairns and du Plessis (2010), *Creation of the* Ius Commune, at 143.

Rynhold, D. (2005), *Two Models of Jewish Philosophy* (Oxford: Oxford University Press).

Sacco, R. (1992), *Introduzione al diritto comparato*, 5th edn (Turin: Utet).

Sacco, R. (1999), 'Langue et Droit', in Jayme (1999), *Langue et Droit*, at 223.

Sacco, R., M. Guadagni, R. Aluffi Beck-Peccoz, and L. Castellani (1995), *Il diritto africano* (Turin, UTET).

Safrin, S. (2008), 'The Un-Exceptionalism of US Exceptionalism', 41 Vanderbilt Journal of Transnational Law 1307.

Sager, L. (2008), 'The Moral Economy of Religious Freedom', in Cane, Evans, and Robinson (2008), *Law and Religion*, at 16.

Sahlins, P. (2004), *Unnaturally French: Foreign Citizens in the Old Regime and After* (Ithaca, NY: Cornell University Press).

Saladin, P. (1995), *Wozu noch Staaten?* (Bern/Munich/Vienna: Stämpfli/ C. H. Beck/Manzsche).

Salim, M. (2009), 'Are Legal Transplants Impossible?' (2009) 4 Journal of Comparative Law 182.

Sand, I-J. (2007), 'From National Sovereignty to International and Global Cooperation: The Changing Context and Challenges of Constitutional Law in a Global Society', in P. Wahlgren (ed.) (2007), *Constitutional Law[:] Constitutions*, 52 Scandinavian Studies in Law 273.

Santos, S., Jr. (2000), 'Philippine Mixed Legal System', 2 Australian Journal of Asian Law 34.

Šarčević, S. (1997), *New Approach to Legal Translation* (The Hague: Kluwer).

Sarooshie, D. (2005), *International Organizations and their Exercise of Sovereign Powers* (Oxford: Oxford University Press).

Sartor, G. (1993), 'A Simple Computational Model for Nonmonotonic and Adversarial Legal Reasoning', in *Proceedings of the Fourth International Conference on Artificial Intelligence and the Law* (New York: ACM) at 192.

Sartor, G. (2005), *Legal Reasoning: A Cognitive Approach to the Law*, vol. 7 of E. Pattaro (ed.), *A Treatise of Legal Philosophy and General Jurisprudence* (Dordrecht: Springer).

Sasken, S. (2001), *The Global City: New York, London, Tokyo* (Princeton, NJ: Princeton University Press).

Sassen, S. (1999), *Guests and Aliens* (New York: The New Press).

Sassen, S. (2000), 'The locational and institutional embeddedness of the global economy', in Bermann, Herdegen, and Lindseth (2000), *Transatlantic Regulatory Cooperation*, at 47.

Sassen, S. (2004), 'De-Nationalized State Agendas and Privatized Norm-Making', in Ladeur (2004a), *Public Governance*, at 51.

Saunders, C. (2006), 'The Use and Misuse of Comparative Constitutional Law', 13 Indiana Journal of Global Legal Studies 37.

Saviano, R. (2011), 'Ist Italien überhaupt eine Nation?', *Die Zeit* 10 March 2011, at 12.

von Savigny, F. (1831), *Of the Vocation of Our Age for Legislation and Jurisprudence*, trans. A. Hayward (London: Littlewood).

von Savigny, F. (1840), *System des heutigen römischen Rechts*, vol. I (Berlin: Deit).

von Savigny, F. C. (1869), *Private International Law: A Treatise on the Conflict of Laws and the Limits of their Operation in Respect of Place and Time*, trans. W. Guthrie (Edinburgh: T. & T. Clark).

Sawyer, P. H. and I. N. Wood (eds) (1977), *Early Medieval Kingship* (Leeds: School of History, University of Leeds).

The Saxon Mirror[:] A Sachsenspiegel of the Fourteen Century (1999), trans. M. Dobozy (Philadelphia: University of Pennsylvania Press).

Scalia, A. (1997), 'Common-Law Courts in a Civil-Law System: The Role of United States Federal Courts in Interpreting the Constitution and Laws', in Gutmann (1997), *Matter of Interpretation*, at 3.

Scarciglia, R. (2011), *Introducción al derecho constitucional comparado* (Madrid: Dykinson).

Schachar, A. (2001), *Multicultural Jurisdictions[:] Cultural Differences and Women's Rights* (Cambridge: Cambridge University Press).

Schauer, F. (2010), 'Balancing, Subsumption, and the Constraining Role of Legal Text', 4(1) Law & Ethics of Human Rights 34.

Scheppele, K. (2003), 'Aspirational and Aversive Constitutionalism: The Case for Studying Cross-constitutional Influence through Negative Models', 1 International Journal of Constitutional Law 296.

Scheppele, K. (2008), 'A Constitution between Past and Future', 49 William and Mary Law Review 1377.

Scheuerman, W. (2001), 'Global Law in Our High Speed Economy', in R. P. Abbelbaum, W. L. F. Felstiner, and V. Gessner (2001), *Rules and Networks[:] The Legal Culture of Global Business Transactions* (Oxford: Hart), at 103.

Scheuner, U. (1956), 'Begriff und Entwicklung des Rechtsstaats', in H. Dombois and E. Wilkens (1956), *Macht und Recht* (Berlin: Lutherisches Verlagshaus), at 76.

Schiebinger, L. (2004), *Nature's Body* (Piscataway, NJ: Rutgers University Press).

Schiemann, K. (2007), 'Europe and the Loss of Sovereignty', 56 ICLQ 475.

Schirmer, D. (2004), 'Closing the Nation: Nationalism and Statism in Nineteenth- and Twentieth-Century Germany', in Godfrey and Unger (2004), *Shifting Foundations of Modern Nation-States*, at 35.

Schmidhauser, J. (1997), 'The European Origins of Legal Imperialism and Its Legacy in Legal Education in Former Colonial Regimes', 18 International Political Science Review 337.

Schmitt, C. (1928), *Verfassungslehre* (Munich/Leipzig: Duncker & Humblot).

Schmitt, C. (1976), *The Concept of the Political*, trans. G. Schwab (New Brunswick, NJ: Rutgers University Press).

Schmitter, P. (1996), 'If the Nation-State were to Wither Away in Europe, What Might Replace It?', in Gustavsson and Lewin (1996), *Future of the Nation State*, at 211.

Scholte, J. (2001), 'The Globalization of World Politics', in Baylis and Smith (2001), *The Globalization of World Politics* (2001), at 13.

Schor, M. (2006), 'Constitutionalism Through the Looking Glass of Latin America', 41 Texas International Law Journal 1.

Schrauwen, A. (2002), *Flexibility in Constitutions: Forms of Closer Cooperation in Federal and Non-federal Settings* (Groningen: Europa Law).

Schroth, P. (1999), 'Language and Law', in Jayme (1999), *Langue et Droit*, at 153.

Schuck, P. (1989), 'Membership in the Liberal Polity: The Devaluation of American Citizenship', in Brubaker (1989), *Immigration and Politics of Citizenship*, at 51.

Schuck, P. (2000), 'Citizenship in Federal Systems', 48 AJCL 195.

Schulze, H. (1996), *States, Nations and Nationalism[:] From the Middle Ages to the Present*, trans. W. E Yuill (Oxford: Blackwell).

Schweid, E. (1998), 'Israel as a Jewish-Democratic State: Historical and Theoretical Aspects', in N. Rakover (1998), *Jerusalem City of Law and Justice* (Jerusalem: Library of Jewish Law), at 125.

Scoles, E., P. Hay, P. Borchers, and S. Symeonides (2000), *Conflict of Laws*, 3rd edn (St. Paul, MN: West).

Scott, J. (1998), *Seeing Like a State[:] How Certain Schemes to Improve the Human Condition Have Failed* (New Haven, CT: Yale University Press).

Scott, T. (2012), *The City-State in Europe, 1000–1600: Hinterland, Territory, Region* (Oxford: Oxford University Press).

Sealey, R. (1987), *The Athenian Republic[:] Democracy or the Rule of Law?* (University Park, PA/London: Pennsylvania State University Press).

Searle, J. (1995), *The Construction of Social Reality* (New York: Free Press).

Seipp, D. (2006), 'Our Law, Their Law, History and the Citation of Foreign Law', 86 Boston University Law Review 1417.

Sellers, M. (2009a), 'The Influence of Marcus Tullius Cicero on Modern Law and Politics', in L. Gamberale (ed.), *Cicerone e il diritto nella storia d'Europa: Ciceroniana XIII* (Conference Proceedings: Rome), at 244, accessible online at <http://ssrn.com/abstract=1354102>.

Sellers, M. (2009b), 'Revolution, French', in A. Grafton, G. Most, and S. Settis (eds) (2010), *The Classical Tradition* (Cambridge: Cambridge University Press), at 822.

Sellers, M. (ed.) (2012), *Parochialism, Cosmopolitanism, and the Foundations of International Law* (New York: Cambridge University Press).

Sen, A. (1999), *Reason before Identity* (The Romanes Lecture for 1998) (Oxford: Oxford University Press).

Sen, A. (2000), *Development as Freedom* (New York: Anchor).

Sen, A. (2007), *Identity and Violence[:] The Illusion of Destiny* (New York: W. W. Norton).

Sen, A. (2009), *The Idea of Justice* (Cambridge, MA: Belknap Press of Harvard University Press).

Serritella, J. (2006), *Religious Organizations in the United States[:] A Study of Identity, Liberty and the Law* (Durham, NC: Carolina Academic Press).

Shah, P. (2005), *Legal Pluralism in Conflict[:] Coping with Cultural Diversity in Law* (London: Glasshouse).

Shany, Y. (2006), 'Toward a General Margin of Appreciation Doctrine in International Law?', 16 European Journal of International Law 907.

Shapiro, I. and L. Brilmayer (eds) (1999), *Global Justice* (New York: New York University Press).

Shapiro, M. (1993), 'The Globalization of Law', 1 Global Legal Studies Journal 37.

Sharma, A. (2006), 'Customary Law and Received Law in the Federated States of Micronesia', 10 Journal of South Pacific Law (available online at <http://www.paclii.org/journals/fJSPL/vol10/7.shtml>).

Shatzmiller, M. (ed.) (2005), *Nationalism and Minority Identities in Islamic Societies* (Montreal/Kingston: McGill-Queen's University Press).

Shaw, J. (1999), 'Postnational Constitutionalism in the European Union', 6 Journal of European Public Policy 579.

Shaw, M. (2008), *International Law*, 6th edn (Cambridge: Cambridge University Press).

Shelton, D. (2011), 'Introduction', in D. Shelton (ed.), *International Law and Domestic Legal Systems: Incorporation, Transformation, and Persuasion* (Oxford: Oxford University Press), at 1.

Shennan, J. (1974), *The Origins of the Modern European State 1450–1725* (London: Hutchinson & Co.).

Sherif, A. (2000), 'The Rule of Law in Egypt from a Judicial Perspective: A Digest of the Landmark Decisions of the Supreme Constitutional Court', in Cotran and Yamani (2000), *Rule of Law in the Middle East*, at 1.

Siddiqi, A. (1969), *Non-Muslims Under Muslim Rule and Muslims Under Non-Muslim Rule* (Karachi: Jamiyatul Falah Publication).

Siddiqui, T. (2007), 'Interpretation of Islamic Marriage Contracts by American Courts', 41 Family Law Quarterly 639.

Sidel, M. (2002), 'Analytical Models for Understanding Constitutions and Constitutional Dialogue in Socialist Transitional States: Re-interpreting Constitutional Dialogue in Vietnam', 6 Singapore Journal of International & Comparative Law 42.

Siegmund, S. (2006), *The Medici State and the Ghetto of Florence[:] The Construction of an Early Modern Jewish Community* (Stanford, CA: Stanford University Press).

Siems, M. (2007), 'Legal Origins: Reconciling Law & Finance and Comparative Law?', 52 McGill Law Journal 55.

Silberman, L. (2006), *Cooperative Efforts in Private International Law on Behalf of Children*, 323 Recueil des Cours 261.

Simons, P. (2003), 'The Emergence of the Idea of the Individualized State in the International Legal System', 5 Journal of the History of International Law 293.

Simpson, A. W. B. (2001), *Human Rights and the End of Empire: Britain and the Genesis of the European Convention* (Oxford: Oxford University Press).

Singer, J. (2009), 'Normative Lessons for Lawyers', 56 UCLA Law Review 899.

Singh, K. (2005), *Questioning Globalization* (London: Zed Books).

Siregar, H. (2008), 'Islamic Law in a National Legal Sysem: A Study on the Implementation of Shari'ah in Aceh, Indonesia', 3(1) Asian Journal of Comparative Law, Article 4, accessible online at <http://www.degruyter.com/view/j/asjcl.2008.3.1/asjcl.2008.3.1.1056/asjcl.2008.3.1.1056.xml?format=INT>.

Sirico, L., Jr. (2006), 'The Federalist and the Lessons of Rome', 75 Mississippi Law Journal 431.

Skinner, Q. (1978), *The Foundations of Modern Political Thought*, vol. 2, *The Age of Reformation* (Cambridge: Cambridge University Press).

Skinner, Q. (1989), 'The State' in Ball, Farr, and Hansen (1989), *Political Innovation*, at 90.

Skinner, Q. (2000), *Machiavelli* (Oxford: Oxford University Press).

Skinner, Q. (2002), *Visions of Politics*, vol. 2, *Renaissance Virtues* (Cambridge: Cambridge University Press).

Skovgaard-Petersen, J. (1997), *Defining Islam for the Egyptian State[:] Muftis and Fatwas of the Dār al-Iftā* (Leiden: Brill, (1997)).

Skrzydlo, W. (2006), 'Le problem de la receptions des principes constitutionnels', in P. Gélard (ed.) (2006), *L'État et le droit d'est en ouest* (Paris: Société de legislation comparée), at 291.

Slaughter, A-M. (2003), 'A Global Community of Courts', 44 Harvard International Law Journal 191.

Slaughter, A-M. (2004), *A New World Order* (Princeton, NJ: Princeton University Press).

Slauter, E. (2009), *The State as a Work of Art[:] The Cultural Origins of the Constitution* (Chicago: University of Chicago Press).

Sloss, D. (2009), *The Role of Domestic Courts in Treaty Enforcement* (Cambridge: Cambridge University Press).

Smith, A. (2007), 'Nation and Covenant [:] The Contribution of Ancient Israel to Modern Nationalism', 151 *Proceedings of the British Academy* 213.

Smith, A. M. (2006), 'Making Itself at Home—Understanding Foreign Law in Domestic Jurisprudence: The Indian Case', 24 Berkeley Journal of International Law 218.

Smith, D. Kingsbury (2003), 'Networks, Norms and the Nation State: Thoughts on Pluralism and Globalized Securities Regulation', in Dauvergne (2003), *Jurisprudence for an Interconnected Globe*, at 93.

Smith, N. (2008), *Vagueness and Degrees of Truth* (Oxford: Oxford University Press).

Smith, R. (1997), *Civic Ideals[:] Conflicting Visions of Citizenship in US History* (New Haven, CT: Yale University Press).

Smith, R. (2009), 'Beyond Sovereignty and Uniformity: The Challenges for Equal Citizenship in the Twenty-First Century', 122 Harvard Law Review 907.

Smits, J. (2006), 'Comparative Law and its Influence on National Legal Systems', in Reimann and Zimmermann (2006), *Oxford Handbook of Comparative Law*, at 513.

Smyth, R. (1999), 'What do Intermediate Appellate Courts Cite? A Quantitative Study of the Citation Practice of Australian State Supreme Courts', 21 Adelaide Law Review 51.

Soames, S. (2012), 'Vagueness and the Law', in A. Marmor (ed.), *The Routledge Companion to the Philosophy of Law* (New York: Routledge), at 95.

Solum, L. (2011), 'What is Originalism? The Evolution of Constitutional Originalist Theory', in G. Huscroft and B. Miller (eds) (2011), *The Challenge of Originalism: Theories of Constitutional Interpretation* (Cambridge: Cambridge University Press), at 12.

Somek, A. (2009), 'Transnational Constitutional Law: The Normative Question', 3 Journal of International Constitutional Law 144.

Sorenson, R. (2001), *Vagueness and Contradiction* (Oxford: Clarendon Press).

Sørensen, G. (2004), *The Transformation of the State[:] Beyond the Myth of Retreat* (London: Palgrave Macmillan).

Sørensen, G. (2006), 'The Transformation of the State', in Hay, Lister, and Marsh (2006), *The State: Theories and Issues*, at 190.

Spector, H. (2008), 'Constitutional Transplants and the Mutation Effect', 83 Chicago-Kent Law Review 129.

Spellman, W. M. (1998), *European Political Thought: 1600–1700* (New York: St. Martin's Press).

Spiro, P. (2008), *Citizenship[:] American Identity After Globalization* (Oxford: Oxford University Press).

Spiro, P. (2010), 'Dual Citizenship as Human Right', 8 International Journal of Constitutional Law 111.

Springborg, P. (1976), '*Leviathan*, the Christian Commonwealth Incorporated', 24 *Political Studies* 171.

Spruyt, H. (1994), *The Sovereign State and its Competitors[:] An Analysis of System Change* (Princeton. NJ: Princeton University Press).

Stahnke, T. and R. Blitt (2005), 'The Religion–State Relationship and the Right to Freedom of Religion or Belief: A Comparative Textual Analysis of the Constitutions of Predominantly Muslim Countries', 36 Georgetown Journal of International Law 947.

Stankiewicz, W. (1976), 'Sovereignty as Political Theory', 24 *Political Studies* 141.

Starck, C. (2005), 'Allgemeine Staatslehre in Zeiten der europaischen Union', in K. Dicke (ed.), *Weltinnenrecht[:]* Liber amicorum *Jost Delbrück* (Berlin: Duncker & Humblot), at 711.

Stasavage, D. (2010), 'When Distance Mattered: Geographic Scale and the Development of European Representative Assemblies', 104 American Political Science Review 625.

Stein, P. (1966), 'The Attraction of the Civil Law in Post-Revolutionary America', 52 Virginia Law Review 403.

Stein, P. (1999), *Roman Law in European History* (Cambridge: Cambridge University Press).

Steiner, G. (2001), *Grammars of Creation* (New Haven, CT: Yale University Press).

Steiner, J., L. Woods, and C. Twigg-Flesner (2006), *EU Law* (Oxford: Oxford University Press).

Stern, P. J. (2011), *The Company-State* (Oxford: Oxford University Press).

Stilt, K. (2004), 'Islamic Law and the Making and Remaking of the Iraqi Legal System', (2004) 36 George Washington International Law Review 695.

Stirn (2012), 'De l'intérêt de faire vivre le droit comparé', (2012) Juris Classeur Periodique 1025.

Stock, B. (1990), *Listening for the Text: On the Uses of the Past* (Baltimore, MD: John Hopkins University Press).

Stojanovic, N. (2011), 'When is a Country Multinational? Problems with Statistical and Subjective Approaches', 24 Ratio Juris 267.

Stolleis, M. (ed.) (1987), *Staatsdenker im 17. Und 18. Jahrhundert*, 2nd edn (Frankfurt: Alfred Metzner Verlag).

Stolleis, M. (1990), *Staat und Staatsräson in der frühen Neuzeit* (Frankfurt: Suhrkamp).

Stolleis, M. (2001), *Public Law in Germany 1800–1914* (New York: Berghahn).

Stone, A. (2009), 'Comparativism in Constitutional Interpretation', [2009] New Zealand Law Review 45.

Stone, S. (2008), 'Religion and State: Models of separation from within Jewish law', 6 International Journal of Constitutional Law 630.

Stone Sweet, A. (2012), 'A Cosmopolitan Legal Order: Constitutional Pluralism and Rights Adjudication in Europe', 1 Journal of Global Constitutionalism 53.

Story, J. (1994), *Commentaries on the Constitution of the United States*, vol. 1, 5th edn (Buffalo, NY: W. S. Hein).

Strassler, R. (ed.) (2007), *The Landmark Herodotus[:] The Histories*, trans. A. Purvis (New York: Pantheon).

Strauss, D. (1996), 'Common Law Constitutional Interpretation', 63 University of Chicago Law Review 877.

Strauss, D. (2010), *The Living Constitution* (New York: Oxford University Press).

Strauss, G. (1986), *Law, Resistance and the State: the Opposition to Roman Law in Reformation Germany* (Princeton, NJ: Princeton University Press).

Strayer, J. (1970), *On the Medieval Origins of the Modern State* (Princeton, NJ: Princeton University Press).

Sueur, Ph. (2007), *Histoire du droit public français,* 4th edn, vol. I, *La constitution monarchique*, vol. II, *Affirmation et crise de l'Etat sous l'Ancien Régime* (Paris: PUF).

Svensson, T. (ed.) (1999), *On Customary Law and the Saami Rights Process in Norway* (Tromsø: University of Tromsø).

Svensson, T. (2005), 'Interlegality, A Process for Strengthening Indigenous Peoples' Autonomy: The Case of the Sámi in Norway', 51 Journal of Legal Pluralism and Unofficial Law 51.

Sweeney, J. (2005), 'Margins of Appreciation: Cultural Relativity and the European Court of Human Rights in the Post-Cold War Era', 54 ICLQ 459.

Swiss Institute of Comparative Law (2004), *Imperialism and Chauvinism in the Law* (Zurich: Schulthess).

Sylvest, C. (2004), 'International Law in Nineteenth-Century Britain', 75 British Yearbook of International Law 9.

Symeonides, S. (1990), 'Problems and Dilemmas in Codifying Choice of Law for Torts: The Louisiana Experience in Comparative Perspective', 38 AJCL 431.

Symeonides, S. (2001), 'Material Justice and Conflicts Justice in Choice of Law', in P. Borders and J. Zekoll (eds) (2001), *International Conflict of Laws for the Third Millennium: Essays in Honor of Friedrich K. Juenger* (Ardsley, NY: Transnational Publishers), at 125.

Symeonides, S. (2011), 'Choice of Law in the American Courts in 2010', 59 AJCL 303.

Symeonides, S. (2012), 'Codification and Flexibility in Private International Law', in K. Brown and D. Snyder (eds) (2012), *General Reports of the XVIIIth Congress of the International Academy of Comparative Law* (Dordrecht: Springer), at 167.

Taggart, M. (2006), 'Administrative Law' [2006] New Zealand Law Reports 75.

Takahata, E. (2007), 'Religious Accomodation in Japan' [2007] Brigham Young University Law Review 729.

Talamanca, M. (1977), 'Lo schema "genus–species" nelle sistematiche dei giuristi romani', in Accademia Nazionale dei Lincei, *La filosofia greca e il diritto romano*, vol. 2 (Rome: Accademia nazionale dei Lincei), at 1.

Tamanaha, B. (2010), *Beyond the Formalist–Realist Divide* (Princeton, NJ: Princeton University Press).

Tan, K-C. (2004), *Justice without Borders* (Cambridge: Cambridge University Press).

Tarr, G. A. (2005), 'Introduction: Constitutional Origins, Structure and Change', in Kincaid and Tarr (2005), *Constitutional Origins*, at 8.

Tarr, G. A., R. Williams, and J. Marko (2004), *Federalism, Subnational Constitutions, and Minority Rights* (Westport, CT: Praeger).

Tasioulas, J. (2007), 'Customary International Law and the Quest for Global Justice', in A. Perreau-Saussine and J. Murphy (2007), *The Nature of Customary Law* (Cambridge: Cambridge University Press) at 324.

Tawil, E. (2009), *Du gallicanisme administratif à la liberté religieuse* (Aix-en-Provence: Presses University d'Aix-Marseille).

Taylor, C. (1975), *Hegel* (Cambridge: Cambridge University Press).

Taylor, C. (1979), *Hegel and Modern Society* (Cambridge: Cambridge University Press).

Taylor, C. (1994), *Multiculturalism: The Politics of Recognition* (Princeton, NJ: Princeton University Press).

Taylor, C. (2007), *A Secular Age* (Cambridge, MA: Harvard University Press).

Taylor, W. (1996), *Magistrates of the Sacred: Priests and Parishioners in Eighteenth-Century Mexico* (Stanford, CA: Stanford University Press).

Tebbe, N. (2011), '*Smith* in Theory and Practice', 32 Cardozo Law Review 2055.

Teló, M. (2005), *L'État et l'Europe[:] Histoire des idées politiques et des institutions européennes*, trans. J. Vogel (Brussels: Éditions Labor).

Terrill, R. (2003), *The New Chinese Empire* (New York: Basic Books).

Terry, L. (2005), 'US Legal Ethics: The Coming of Age of Global and Comparative Perspectives', 4 Global Studies Law Review 463.

Teubner, G. (2004), 'Societal Constitutionalism: Alternatives to State-centred Constitutional Theory?', in Joerges, Sand, and Teubner (2004), *Constitutionalism and Transnational Governance*, at 3.

Theissen, F. and H-M. Napel (2009), 'Taking Pluralism Seriously: The US and the EU as Multicultural Democracies', in B. Labuschagne and R. Sonnenschmidt (eds) (2009), *Religion, Politics and Law. Philosophical Reflections on the Sources of Normative Order in Society* (Leiden: Brill), at 365.

Thelen, D. (2000), 'How Natural are National and Transnational Citizenship? A Historical Perspective', 7 Indiana Journal of Global Legal Studies 549.

Thornberry, P. (1991), *International Law and the Rights of Minorities* (Oxford: Clarendon Press).

Thorne, J., III (1980), 'Mathematics, Fuzzy Negligence, and the Logic of *Res Ipsa Loquitur*', 75 Northwestern University Law Review 147.

Thorne, S. (1985), 'Sovereignty and the Conflict of Laws', in S. Thorne (1985), *Essays in English Legal History* (London: Hambledon Press), at 171.

Thuan, T. (2001), *Chaos and Harmony* (Oxford: Oxford University Press).

Tierney, B. (1982), *Religion, law and the growth of constitutional thought 1150–1650* (Cambridge: Cambridge University Press).

Tierney, B. (1988), 'Villey, Ockham and the Origin of Individual Rights', in Witte and Alexander (1988), *Weightier Matters*, at 1.

Tierney, B. (1997), *The Idea of Natural Rights: Studies on Natural Rights, Natural Law and Church Law* (Atlanta, GA: Scholars Press).

Tierney, S. (2004), *Constitutional Law and National Pluralism* (Oxford: Oxford University Press).

Tierney, S. (2005), 'Reframing Sovereignty? Sub-State National Societies and Contemporary Challenges to the Nation-State', 54 ICLQ 161.

Tillich, P. (1957), *Dynamics of Faith* (London: Allen & Unwin).

Tilly, C. (1994a), 'Entanglements of European Cities and States', in Tilly and Blockmans (1994), *Cities and the Rise of States in Europe*, at 1.

Tilly, C. (1994b), 'Afterword: Political Memories in Space and Time', in Boyarin (1994a), *Remapping Memory*, at 241.

Tilly, C. and W. Blockmans (1994), *Cities and the Rise of States in Europe*, AD 1000 to 1800 (Boulder, CO: Westview Press).

Tinnevelt, R. (2012), 'Federal world government: The road to peace and justice?', 47 Cooperation and Conflict 220.

Tomaselli, S. (2006), 'The spirit of nations', in Goldie and Wokler (2006), *Cambridge History of Eighteenth-Century Political Thought*, at 9.

Tomkins, A. (2005), *Our Republican Constitution* (Oxford: Hart).

Tomlins, C. (2010), *Freedom Bound: Law, Labor, and Civic Identity in Colonizing English America, 1580–1865* (New York: Cambridge University Press).

Topidi, K. (2010), *EU Law, Minorities and Enlargement* (Antwerp: Intersentia).

Toriello, F. (2000), *I principi generali del diritto communitario: Il ruolo della comparazione* (Milan: Giuffrè).

Torpey, J. (2000), *The Invention of Passports* (Cambridge: Cambridge University Press).

Toulmin, S. (1958), *The Uses of Argument* (Cambridge: Cambridge University Press).

Toulmin, S. (1990), *Cosmopolis* (Chicago: University of Chicago Press).

Tourard, H. (2000), *L'internationalisation des constitutions internationales* (Paris: LGDJ).

Townsend-Gault, I. (1997), 'Regional Maritime Cooperation Post-UNCLOS/ UNCED: Do Boundaries Matter Anymore?', in Blake *et al* (1997), *International Boundaries*, at 3.

Trakman, L. (1983), *The Law Merchant: The Evolution of Commercial Law* (Littleton, CO.: Fred B. Rothman).

Traynor, R. (1959), 'Is this Conflict Really Necessary?', 37 Texas Law Review 657.

Tribe, L. (1988), *American Constitutional Law*, 2nd edn (Mineola, NY: Foundation Press).

Tribe, L. (2008), *The Invisible Constitution* (Oxford: Oxford University Press).

Trigger, B. (2003), *Understanding Early Civilizations[:] A Comparative Study* (Cambridge: Cambridge University Press).

Troper, M. and L. Jaume (1994), *1789 et l'invention de la constitution* (Paris: LGDJ).

Tsagourias, N. (ed.) (2007), *Transnational Constitutionalism* (Cambridge: Cambridge University Press).

Tsakyrakis, S. (2009), 'Proportionality: An assault on human rights?', 7 International Journal of Constitutional Law 468.

Tuck, R. (1991), 'Grotius and Selden', in Burns (1991), *Cambridge History of Political Thought 1450–1700*, at 499.

Tuck, R. (2003), 'The Making and Unmaking of Boundaries from the Natural Law Perspective', in Buchanan and Moore (2003), *States, Nations, and Borders*, at 143.

Tully, J. (1995), *Strange Multiplicity[:] Constitutionalism in an Age of Diversity* (Cambridge: Cambridge University Press).

Turchetti, M. (2010), 'Jean Bodin', in E. Zalta (ed.) (2010), *The Stanford Encyclopedia of Philosophy*, accessible online at <http://plato.stanford.edu/entries/bodin>.

Turner, J. (2007), 'Transnational Networks and International Criminal Justice', 105 Michigan Law Review 985.

Turpin, D. (1985), 'Le traitement des antinomies des droits de l'homme par le Conseil constitutionnel', [1985] Droits 85.

Tushnet, M. (2003), 'Transnational/Domestic Constitutional Law', 37 Loyola of Los Angeles Law Review 239.

Tusk, M. (2003), 'No Citation Rules as a Prior Restraint on Attorney Speech', 103 Columbia Law Review 1202.

Twining, W. (2000), *Globalisation and Legal Theory* (London: Butterworths).

Twining, W. (2003), 'The Province of Jurisprudence Re-examined', in Dauvergne (2003), *Jurisprudence for an Interconnected Globe*, at 13.

Twining, W. (2007), 'General Jurisprudence', 15 University of Miami International & Comparative Law Review 1.

Twining, W. (2009), *General Jurisprudence: Understanding Law from a Global Perspective* (Cambridge: Cambridge University Press).

Tye, M. (2000), 'Vagueness and Reality', 28 Philosophical Topics 195.

Uitz, R. (2007), *Freedom of Religion in European Constitutional and International Case Law* (Strasbourg: Council of Europe Publishing).

Ullmann, W. (1961), *Principles of Goverment and Politics in the Middle Ages* (London: Methuen).

Ullmann, W. (1969), *The Carolingian Renaissance and the Idea of Kingship* (London: Methuen).

Ullmann, W. (1976), *Law and Politics in the Middle Ages[:] An Introduction to the Sources of Medieval Political Ideas* (Cambridge: Cambridge University Press).

Ullmann, W. (1988), *Law and Jurisdiction in the Middle Ages*, ed. by George Garnett (London: Variorum Reprints).

Unger, F. (2004), 'Are We Dreaming? Exceptional Myths and Myths of Exceptionalism in the United States', in Godfrey and Unger (2004), *Shifting Foundations of Modern Nation-States*, at 82.

United Nations Development Program (2004), *Human Development Report 2004[:] Cultural Liberty in Today's World* (New York: UNDP).

US Department of State (2010), *International Religious Freedom Report, 2010*, accessible online at <http://www.state.gov/j/drl/rls/irf/2010/>.

US Office of Personnel Management, Investigations Service (2001), *Citizenship Laws of the World*, accessible online at <http://www.opm.gov/extra/investigate/IS-01.pdf>.

Vagts, D. (1987), 'Dispute-Resolution Mechanisms in International Business', in Hague Academy of International Law, 203 Recueil des cours 9.

Vagts, D. (1997), 'Bär and Karrer: Connecting Two Legal Systems', in N. Vogt, *The International Practice of Law[:] Liber Amicorum for Thomas Bär and Robert Karrer* (The Hague: Kluwer), at 247.

Valades, D. (2002), 'Los derechos de los indígenas y la renovación constitucional en México', in González Galván (2002), *Constitución y derechos indígenas*, at 13.

Valencia-Weber, G. (1994), 'Tribal Courts: Custom and Innovative Law', 24 New Mexico Law Review 225.

Van Caenegem, R. (1988), 'Government, Law and Society', in Burns (1988), *Cambridge History of Medieval Political Thought c.350–c.1450*, at 174.

Van Caenegem, R. (1995), *An Historical Introduction to Western Constitutional Law* (Cambridge: Cambridge University Press).

Van Caenegem, R. (2002), *European Law in the Past and the Future: Unity and Diversity over Two Millennia* (Cambridge: Cambridge University Press).

van Creveld, M. (1999), *The Rise and Decline of the State* (Cambridge: Cambridge University Press).

Van den Berg, P. (2007), *The Politics of European Codification: A History of the Unification of Law in France, Prussia, the Austrian Monarchy and the Netherlands* (Groningen: Europa Law Publishing).

Van der Mensbrugghe, F. (ed.) (2003), *L'utilisation de la méthode comparative en droit européen* (Namur: Presses universitaires de Namur).

Van Eijk, E. (2010), 'Sharia and national law in Saudi Arabia', in Otto (2010a), *Sharia Incorporated*, at 139.

Van Erp, S. (1999), 'The Use of the Comparative Law Method by the Judiciary', in Drobnig and van Erp (1999), *Use of Comparative Law*, at 235.

Van Gelderen, M. (1992), *The Political Thought of the Dutch Revolt 1555–1590* (Cambridge: Cambridge University Press).

Van Hooft, S. (2007), 'Cosmopolitanism as Virtue', 3 *Journal of Global Ethics* 303.

Vander Elst, R. (1965), 'Les antinomies en droit international privé', in Perelman (1965a), *Les antinomies*, at 138.

Vanderlinden, J. (1967), *Le concept de code en Europe occidentale du XIIIe siècle au XIXe siècle* (Brussels: Institut de sociologie).

Vanderlinden, J. (1999), 'Langue et Droit', in Jayme (1999), *Langue et Droit*, at 65.

Verlinden, C. (1954), *Précédents médiévaux de la colonie en Amérique* (Mexico: Editorial Fournier).

Vertovec, S. and Cohen, R. (2003), *Conceiving Cosmopolitanism[:] Theory, Context, and Practice* (Oxford: Oxford University Press).

Viau, P. (1999), 'Quelques considérations sur la langue, le droit, le bilinguisme et le bijuridisme au Canada', in Jayme (1999), *Langue et Droit*, at 141.

Viehweg, T. (1994), *Topics and Law*, trans. W. Cole Durham, Jr. (Frankfurt: Peter Lang).

Villey, M. (1967), 'Histoire de la logique juridique', in Villey *et al* (1967) *La logique juridique*, at 65.

Villey, M. (1983), *Le droit et les droits de l'homme* (Paris: PUF).

Villey, M. *et al* (1967), *La logique juridique*, 15 Annales de la Faculté de droit et des sciences économiques de Toulouse.

Vincent, A. (1987), *Theories of the State* (Oxford: Basil Blackwell).

Vives, J. (1972), 'The Administrative Structure of the State in the Sixteenth and Seventeenth Centuries', in Cohn (1972), *Government in Reformation Europe*, at 58.

Vogel, F. (2000a), *Islamic Law and Legal System[:] Studies of Saudi Arabia* (Leiden: Brill).

Vogel, F. (2000b), 'Exploring Contradictions and Traditions', in Cotran and Yamani (2000), *Rule of Law in Middle East*, at 128.

Vogenauer, S. (2001), *Die Auslegung von Gesetzen in England und auf dem Kontinent* (Tübingen: Mohr-Siebeck).

Vosskuhle, A. (2004), 'Die Renaissance der "Allgemeinen Staatslehre" im Zeitalter der Europäisierung und Internationalisierung', 44 Juristischen Schulung 2.

Vrellis, S. (2007), *Conflit ou coordination de valeurs en droit international privé*, 328 Recueil des Cours 175.

Wachspress, M. (2009), 'Rethinking Sovereignty with Reference to History and Anthropology', 5 International Journal of Law in Context 315.

Wahl, R. (2003), 'Der offene Staat und seine Rechtsgrundlagen', 43 Juristischen Schulung 1145.

Waibel, M. (2010), 'A Good Day and Salutory Warning for the European Union', (2010) 69 CLJ 38.

Wald, P. (2004), 'The Use of International Law in Judicial Decisions', 27 Harvard Journal of Law & Public Policy 431.

Waldron, J. (2006), 'Cosmopolitan Norms', in Benhabib (2006), *Another Cosmopolitanism*, at 83.

Waldron, J. (2012), *'Partly Laws Common to All Mankind': Foreign Laws in American Courts* (New Haven, CT: Yale University Press).

Walker, N. (2002), 'The Idea of Constitutional Pluralism', 65 MLR 317.

Walker, N. (ed.) (2003), *Sovereignty in Transition* (Oxford: Hart).

Walker, N. (ed.) (2006), *Relocating Sovereignty* (Aldershot/Dartmouth: Ashgate).

Walker, N. (2008), 'Beyond Boundary Disputes and Basic Grids: Mapping the global disorder of normative orders', 6 International Journal of Constitutional Law 373.

Walker, N. (2009), 'Denizenship and the Deterritorialization in the EU', in H. Lindahl (ed.), *A Right to Inclusion and Exclusion?* (Oxford: Hart Publishing), at 261.

Walker, N., S. Tierney, and J. Shaw (eds) (2011), *Europe's Constitutional Mosaic* (Oxford: Hart).

Wallace, E. G. (2009–10), 'Justifying Religious Freedom: The Western Tradition', 114 Penn State Law Review 485.

Wallace-Hadrill, J. (1971), *Early Germanic Kingship in England and on the Continent* (Oxford: Clarendon Press).

Walter, N. (2012), 'Religious Arbitration in the United States and Canada', 52 Santa Clara Law Review 501.

Walters, M. (2004), 'The Common Law Constitution and Legal Cosmopolitanism', in Dyzenhaus (2004), *The Unity of Public Law*, at 431.

Walters, M. (2008), 'The Jurisprudence of Reconciliation: Aboriginal Rights in Canada', in Kymlicka and Bashir (2008), *Politics of Reconciliation in Multicultural Societies*, at 165.

Walzer, M., M. Lorberbaum, and N. Zohar (eds) (2000), *The Jewish Political Tradition* (New Haven, CT: Yale University Press).

Ward, L. (2008), 'Locke on Toleration and Inclusion', 21 Ratio Juris 518.

Waters, M. (2007), 'Creeping Monism: The Judicial Trend toward Interpretive Incorporation of Human Rights Treaties', 107 Columbia Law Review 628.

Watson, A. (1974), *Legal Transplants* (Edinburgh: Scottish Academic Press).

Watson, A. (1992), *Joseph Story and the Comity of Errors* (Athens, GA: University of Georgia Press).

Webber, J. (2008), 'Understanding the Religion in Freedom of Religion', in Cane, Evans, and Robinson (2008), *Law and Religion*, at 26.

Weber, E. (1976), *Peasants into Frenchmen* (Stanford, CA: Stanford University Press).

Webster, T. (2011), 'Insular Minorities: International Law's Challenge to Japan's Ethnic Homogeneity,' 36 North Carolina Journal of International Law & Commercial Regulation 101.

Weil, P. (2008), *How to Be French: Nationality in the Making since 1789*, trans. C. Porter (Durham, NC: Duke University Press).

Weiler, J. and M. Wind (eds) (2003), *European Constitutionalism beyond the State* (Cambridge: Cambridge University Press).

Weinrib, Ll. (2005), *Legal Reason: The Use of Analogy in Legal Argument* (Cambridge: Cambridge University Press).

Weinrib, Lo. (2002), 'Constitutional Conceptions and Constitutional Comparativism', in Jackson and Tushnet (2002), *Defining the Field of Comparative Constitutional Law*, at 3.

Weiss, G. (2000), 'The Enchantment of Codification in the Common-Law World', 25 Yale Journal of International Law 435.

Weiss, L. (1998), *The Myth of the Powerless State* (Ithaca, NY: Cornell University Press).

Welchman, L. (ed.) (2004), *Women's Rights & Islamic Family Law* (London: Zed).

Wells, C. (1995), *Law and Citizenship in Early Modern France* (Baltimore, MD: Johns Hopkins University Press).

Wesel, U. (2001), *Geschichte des Rechts*, 2nd edn (Munich: C. H. Beck).

Wesel, U. (2006), *Geschichte des Rechts[:] von den Frühformen bis zum Vertrag von Maastricht*, 3rd edn (Munich: C. H. Beck).

Westerfield, J. (2006), 'Behind the Veil: An American Legal Perspective on the European Headscarf Debate', 54 AJCL 637.

Weston, C. (1991), 'England: Ancient Constitution and Common Law', in Burns (1991), *Cambridge History of Political Thought 1450–1700*, at 374.

Wheatley, S. (2005), *Democracy, Minorities and International Law* (Cambridge: Cambridge University Press).

White, G. (2004), *Nation, State and Territory[:] Origins, Evolutions and Relationships*, vol. 1 (Lanham, MD: Rowman & Littlefield).

Whitman, J. (2003), 'Long Live the Hatred of Roman Law!', [2003] Rechtsgeschichte 40.

Whitman, J. (2008), 'No Right Answer?', in J. Jackson, M. Langer, and P. Tillers (eds) (2008), *Crime, Procedure and Evidence in a Comparative and International Context[:] Essays in Honour of Professor Mirjan Damaska* (Oxford: Hart), at 371.

Whitman, J. (2011), 'Separating Church and State: The Atlantic Divide', in R. Gordon and M. Horwitz (eds) (2011), *Law, Society and History* (Cambridge: Cambridge University Press), at 233.

Whitman, W. (1881), *Leaves of Grass: Preface to the Original Edition, 1855* (London: Trübner).

Whittaker, C. R. (2004), *Rome and its Frontiers: The Dynamics of Empire* (London: Routledge).

Wickham, C. (2003), *Courts and Conflict in Twelfth-Century Tuscany* (Oxford: Oxford University Press).

Wickham, C. (2005), *Framing the Early Middle Ages[:] Europe and the Mediterranean 400–800* (Oxford: Oxford University Press).

Wieacker, F. (1995), *A History of Private Law in Europe: with Particular Reference to Germany*, trans. T. Weir (Oxford: Clarendon Press).

Wielsch, D. (2012), 'Global Law's Toolbox: Private Regulation by Standards', 60 AJCL 1075.

Wiener, J. (1999), *Globalization and the Harmonization of Law* (London/New York: Pinter).

Wijffels, A. (2005), 'Qu'est-ce que le *ius commune*?', in A. Wijffels (ed.) (2005), *Le Code civil entre* ius commune *et droit privé européen* (Brussels: Bruylant), at 643.

Wilczek, F. (2010), *The Lightness of Being: Mass, Ether and the Unification of Forces* (New York: Basic Books).

Wildhaber, L. (2007), 'The European Convention on Human Rights and International Law', 56 ICLQ 217.

Wilf, S. (2011), 'Law/Text/Past', 1 UC Irvine Law Review 543.

Wilkinson, J. (1991), *Arabia's Frontiers; The Story of Britain's Boundary Drawing in the Desert* (London: IB Tauris).

Williams, J. (1994), 'The Fallacies of Contemporary Fraudulent Transfer Models as Applied to Intercorporate Guaranties: Fraudulent Transfer Law as a Fuzzy System', 15 Cardozo Law Review 1403.

Williamson, T. (1994), *Vagueness* (London: Routledge).

Wilson, P. (2004), *From Reich to Revolution: German History, 1558–1806* (London: Palgrave Macmillan).

Wind, M. (2003), 'The European Union as a polycentric polity: returning to a neo-medieval Europe?', in Weiler and Wind (2003), *European Constitutionalism beyond the State*, at 103.

Wink, A. (1986), *Land and Sovereignty in India[:] Agrarian Society and Politics under the Eighteenth-century Maratha Svarajya* (Cambridge: Cambridge University Press).

Witt, J. F. (2007), 'Anglo-American Empire and the Crisis of the Legal Frame (Will the Real British Empire Please Stand Up?)', 120 Harvard Law Review 754.

Witte, J., Jr. (2002), *Law and Protestantism[:] The Legal Teachings of the Lutheran Reformation* (Cambridge: Cambridge University Press).

Witte, J., Jr. (2006), 'Facts and Fictions about the History of Separation of Church and State', 48 Journal of Church and State 15.

Witte, J., Jr. and F. Alexander (1988), *The Weightier Matters of the Law: Essays on Law and Religion* (Atlanta, GA: Scholars Press).

Woehrling, J. (1999), 'Les droits et libertés dans la construction de la citoyenneté, au Canada et au Québec', in M. Coutu *et al* (1999), *Droits fondamentaux et citoyenneté* (Montreal: Thémis) at 269.

Wokler, R. (2006), 'Ideology and the Origins of Social Science', in Goldie and Wokler (2006), *Cambridge History of Eighteenth-Century Political Thought*, at 688.

Wood, G. (1969), *The Creation of the American Republic, 1776–1787* (Williamsburg, VA: University of North Carolina Press).

Wood, G. (1997), 'Comment', in Gutmann (1997), *Matter of Interpretation*, at 49.

Wood, G. (2006), 'The American Revolution', in Goldie and Wokler (2006), *Cambridge History of Eighteenth-Century Political Thought* (Cambridge: Cambridge University Press), at 601.

Wood, G. S. (2009), *Empire of Liberty: A History of the Early Republic, 1789–1815* (New York: Oxford University Press).

Wood, I. (1977), 'Kings, Kingdoms and Consent', in Sawyer and Wood (1977), *Early Medieval Kingship*, at 6.

Woodbine, G. (1943), 'The Language of English Law', 18 *Speculum* 395.

Woodman, G. (2008), 'The Possibilities of Co-Existence of Religious Laws with Other Laws', in Mehdi *et al* (2008), *Law and Religion*, at 23.

Woodman, G. (2009), 'The Culture Defence in English Common Law: The Potential for Development', in Foblets and Renteln (2009), *Multicultural Jurisprudence*, at 7.

Woolfson, J. (1998), *Padua and the Tudors: English Students in Italy 1485–1603* (Toronto: University of Toronto Press).

World Bank (1997), *World Development Report 1997[:] The State in a Changing World* (Oxford: Oxford University Press).

World Bank (2011), *World Development Report 2011[:], Conflict, Security and Development* (Washington, DC: World Bank).

Wormald, P. (1977), '*Lex Scripta* and *Verbum Regis*: Legislation and Germanic Kingship, from Euric to Cnut', in Sawyer and Wood (1977), *Early Medieval Kingship*, at 105.

Wormald, P. (1999), *The Making of English Law: King Alfred to the Twelfth Century*, vol. I, *Legislation and its Limits* (Oxford: Blackwell).

Wormald, P. (2005), 'Kings and Kingship', in P. Fouracre (ed.), *The New Cambridge Medieval History* (Cambridge: Cambridge University Press), at 571.

Wormald, P. (2006), *Lawyers and the State: the Varieties of Legal History* (London: Selden Society).

Wren, J. (2006), 'The Common Law of England in Virginia 1776 to 1830', in W. H. Bryson and S. Danchy (2006), *Ratio Decidendi* (Berlin: Duncker & Humblot) at 151.

Yablon, C. (1991), 'On the Allocation of Burdens of Proof in Corporate Law: An Essay on Fairness and Fuzzy Sets', 13 Cardozo Law Review 497.

Yack, B. (2003), 'Nationalism, Popular Sovereignty, and the Liberal Democratic State', in Paul, Ikenberry, and Hall (2003), *The Nation-State in Question*, at 29.

Yack, B. (2006), 'Popular Sovereignty and Nationalism', in Walker (2006), *Relocating Sovereignty*, at 205.

Yeatman, A. (2004), 'The Idea of the Constitutional State and Global Society', 8 Law Text Culture 83.

Yildiz, I. (2007), 'Minority Rights in Turkey', [2007] Brigham Young University Law Review 791.

Yntema, H. (1953), 'The Historic Bases of Private International Law', 2 AJCL 297.

Young, E. (2007), 'The Constitution Outside the Constitution', 117 Yale Law Journal 408.

Yuker, J. (2011), *The Idea of World Government* (New York: Routledge).

Zaman, M. (2002), *The Ulama in Contemporary Islam* (Princeton, NJ/Oxford: Princeton University Press).

Zaring, D. (2006), 'The Use of Foreign Decisions by Federal Courts: An Empirical Analysis', 3 Journal of Empirical Legal Studies 297.

Zeefeld, W. (1969), *Foundations of Tudor Policy* (London: Methuen & Co).

Zheng, Y. (2008), *Technological Empowerment: The Internet, State, and Society in China* (Stanford, CA: Stanford University Press).

Zielonka, J. (2006), *Europe as Empire[:] The Nature of the Enlarged European Union* (Oxford: Oxford University Press).

Ziller, J. (2009), '*Solange III* (or the Bundesverfassungsgericht's Europefriendlyness): On the decision of the German Federal Constitutional Court over the ratification of the Treaty of Lisbon', English trans. from 2009, 5 Rivista Italiana di Diritto Pubblico Comunitario 973, accessible online at <http://ssrn.com/abstract=1474698>.

Ziller, J. (2011), 'The Nature of European Union Law', in J. Beneyto, B. Becerril, and J. Maillo (eds) (2011), *Tratado de derecho de la Union Europea*, T. IV (Madrid: Aranzadi), accessible online at <http://ssrn.com/abstract=1919481>.

Zimmermann, R. (1995), 'Codification: History and Present Signification of an Idea', 3 European Review of Private Law 95.

Zimmermann, R. (1997), '*Statuta sunt stricte interpretanda?* Statutes and the Common Law: A Continental Perspective', 56 CLJ 315.

Zimmermann, R. (2012), 'Challenges for the European Law Institute', 16 Edinburgh Law Review 5.

Zoller, E. (2006), '*Laïcité* in the United States or The Separation of Church and State in a Pluralist Society', 13 Indiana Journal of Global Legal Studies 561.

Zolo, D. (1997), *Cosmopolis: Prospects for World Government* (Cambridge: Polity Press).

Zucca, L. (2008), *Constitutional Dilemmas: Conflicts of Fundamental Rights in Europe and the USA* (Oxford: Oxford University Press).

Zucca, L. and C. Ungureanu (eds) (2012), *Law, State and Religion in the New Europe: Debates and Dilemmas* (Cambridge: Cambridge University Press).

Zürn, M. and S. Leibfried (2005), 'Reconfiguring the National Constellation', in Leibfried and Zürn (2005), *Transformations of the State?*, at 1.

Index